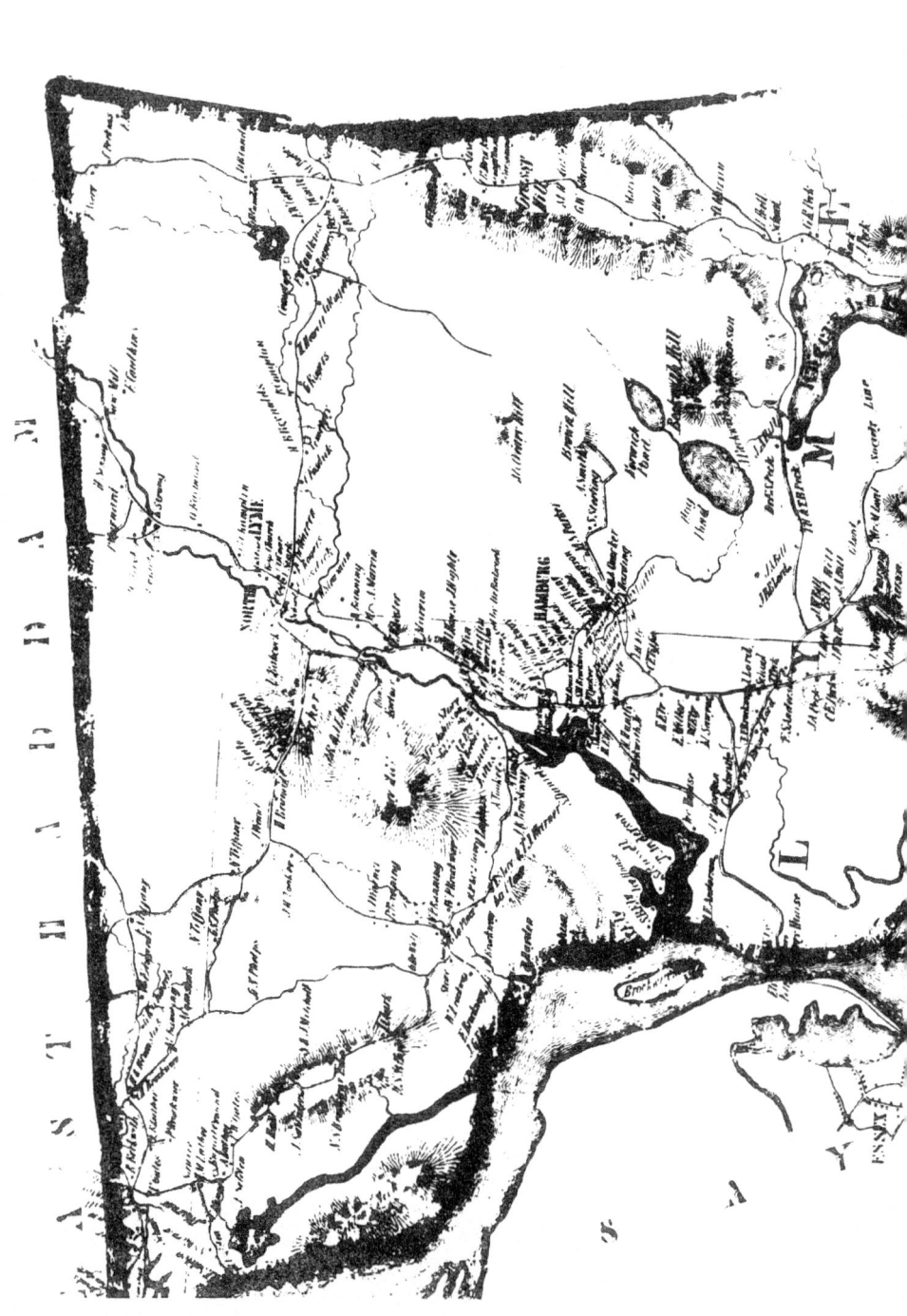

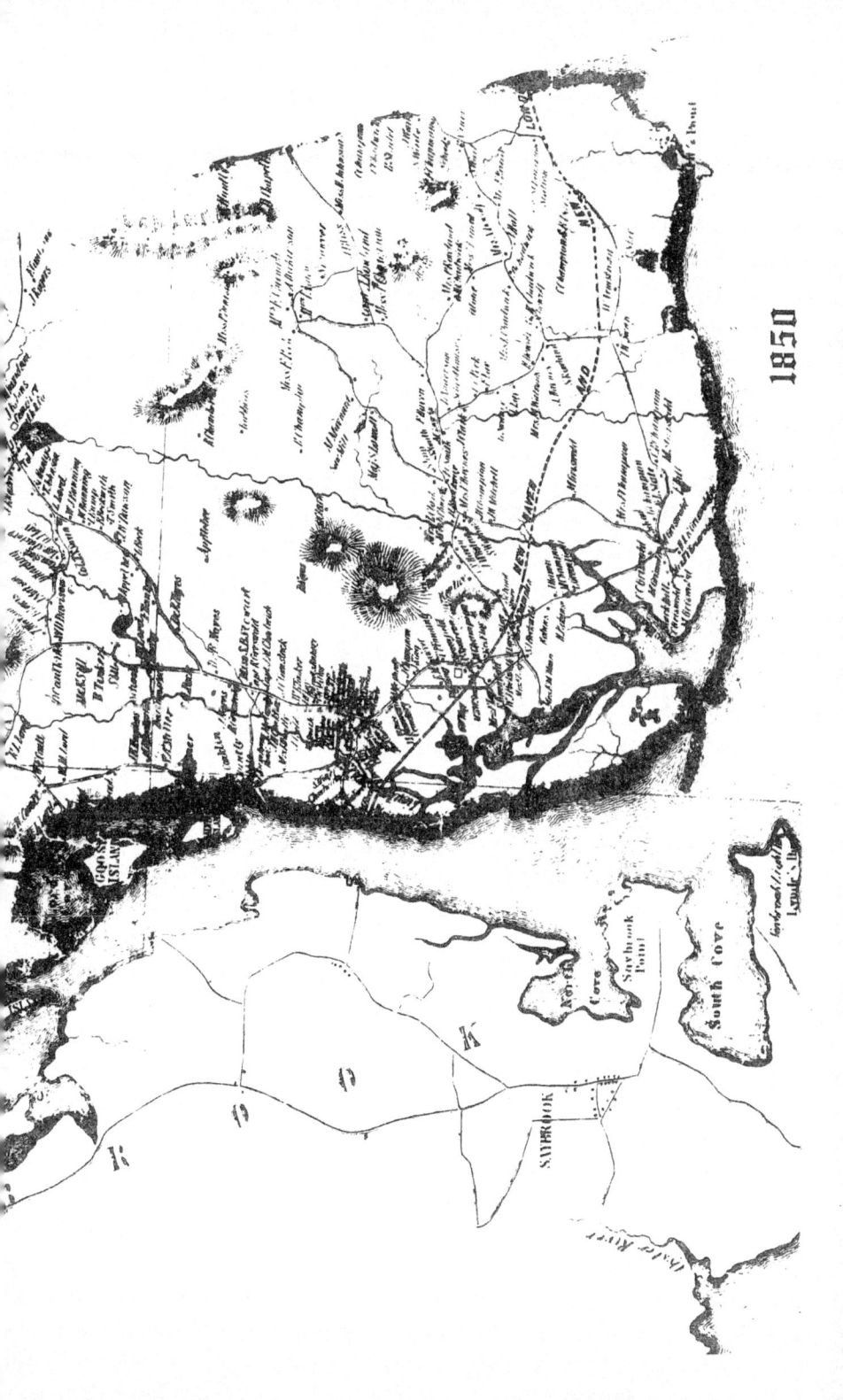

Vital Records of Lyme, Connecticut to the End of the Year 1850

Literally Transcribed under
the Direction
of
Verne M. Hall
and
Elizebeth B. Plimpton

Originally Published by
The American Revolution Bicentennial Commission
of
Lyme, Connecticut
1976

HERITAGE BOOKS
2012

HERITAGE BOOKS
AN IMPRINT OF HERITAGE BOOKS, INC.

Books, CDs, and more—Worldwide

For our listing of thousands of titles see our website at
www.HeritageBooks.com

Published 2012 by
HERITAGE BOOKS, INC.
Publishing Division
100 Railroad Ave. #104
Westminster, Maryland 21157

Copyright © 1976 Elizebeth B. Plimpton

Library of Congress Catalog Card Number: 76-46849

Verne M. Hall and Elizebeth B. Plimpton
COMMITTEE ON THE LYME VITAL RECORDS

Jenny Stark	Jean Bartman
Iva Hawthorne	Maureen Brevoort
Erma Hall	Elizabeth Putnam
Agnes Brodeur	Verne Hall

Elizebeth Plimpton

All rights reserved. No part of this book may be reproduced or transmitted in any form or by any means, electronic or mechanical, including photocopying, recording or by any information storage and retrieval system without written permission from the author, except for the inclusion of brief quotations in a review.

International Standard Book Numbers
Paperbound: 978-1-55613-316-9
Clothbound: 978-0-7884-9457-4

This volume is dedicated
to the Town Clerks of Lyme
Past and Present
Custodians of our ancient records

CONTENTS

Introduction	vii
"Loving Parting"	viii
First Settlers of Lyme	ix
Vital Records of Lyme, Volume I	1
Volume II	108
Volume III	164
Volume IV	198
Vital Records Extracted from the Land Records	217
Vital Records extracted from the Church Records	272
Membership	274
Baptisms	283
Marriages	288
Deaths	293
Extracts from the Selectmen's Book of Bills 1796-1809	299
Lyme men - Lexington Alarm Lyme Vetrans of Colonial Wars Through Civil War buried in Lyme	301
Addenda	311
Index of Persons	312
Index of Church Records	395

INTRODUCTION

"Lyme has reason to be very proud of its records dating from 1665 and among the oldest and most complete in the State. Because of their antiquity, covering as they do not only our entire history as a town, but also the early days of Old Lyme, much of East Lyme and about half of Salem, their value is priceless . . .

"Our Vita Records are as old as those for the land and are of great interest to those in search of genealogical data."

These were the words of the late Judge William Marvin, Custodian of these records for fifty-three years.

It seems appropriate, in this Bicentennial Year, that we should share these records and that we should retire our ancient volumes.

Copy was made in long-hand from the original records and then the copy was proof-read against the original record by a team of two people. The typescript was made from the copy and compared with the long-hand copy and again revised. Final revision on the proof-sheets was made in the same manner. Throughout the years additional information has been written in the original records and in the Arnold Index. We have included this information in square brackets. Also, torn page edges have left blanks in information. Whenever possible, we have supplied the information from our Arnold Index in square brackets.

It should be remembered that town clerks were often lax in recording vital statistics: exact birth dates were sometimes omitted, a person's name frequently varied in spelling within the same entry. We have made a true copy of the original records including the varient spelling. However, to avoid additional charges for superior lettering, words such as Dan^{ll} will appear as Danll, Sam^{ll} as Samll, s^{d} as sd etc.

Our thanks to:

Miss Jennie Stark who spent hours on the long and arduous task of extracting vital records from the Land Records.

Joan Meyers, Julia Smith and Barbara Sisk for their cooperation and for making the Town Hall a pleasant and cheerful place to work.

Susan H. Ely for the idea in the first place and her encouragement and advice throughout the project.

The committee who gave generously of their time, our deepest appreciation, for without them this project would never have become reality.

Mr. Horace S. Rockwood, Sr., Chairman of the Lyme Bicentennial Commission, and Miss Bess A. Rockwood for their enthusiasm and attention to the many minute details involved in publishing this volume.

Susan B. Tiffany, typist, for her patience in transcribing difficult copy.

This book is sponsored by the Lyme Bicentennial Commission with the generous support of the Town of Lyme.

       Verne M. Hall
       Elizebeth B. Plimpton

November, 1976
Lyme, Conn.

"THE LOVING PARTING"
ARTICLES OF AGREEMENT BETWIXT

Wharas thar hath been several propositions betwixt the inhabitants of the east side of the River and the inhabitants of the west side of the River of the towne of Saybrook toward a Loveing Parting:

The inhabitants on the east side of the River desiring to be a plantation by them selfe do declare that they have a competency of Lands to entertain thirty familyes.

They declare that they will pay all areres of rates past and all rates dew by the first of May next ensuing that belong unto the town and ministry to be brought in unto the townsmen in the town plots, to wit: Richard rayment and Abraham Post now in place.

At the request of those on the east side of the River to abate them thar proportion belonging to the ministry from the first of May to the later end of January next ensuing, the town do consent thar unto; and in case they have not a minister settled amongst them, they are to pay Rates as for the future to the minister on the west side as formerly until a minister be settled amongst them.

In reference to the lands of Hamanask, they on the east side of the River doe fully and freely resine up all thar rights, rirells, [Titles] and slames [Claims] to all and every parcel of the land to the inhabitants of the west side, engaging them selfs to afford what help they have amongst them for the recovery of those lands they being raisonably considered for their pains.

That the Indians at Nehanick have the land agreed upon by the covenants made betwixt eh inhabitants of Saybrook and them.

The above said articles being agreed upon by the Committees chosen of both sides of the River, the inhabitants of the east side have Liberty to be a plantation to them selfs. In witness whereof, the committee chosen on both sides have set their hands:

<table>
<tr><td>For the West Side
John Westall
William Pratt
Robert Lay
William Parker
Zackeriah Sanford</td><td>For the East Side
Matthew Griswold
William Waller
Renold Marvin
John Lay
Richard Smith
John Comstock</td></tr>
</table>

FIRST SETTLERS OF LYME

Matthew Beckwith
John Borden
Thomas Bradford
William Briggs
Wolston Brockway
Henry Champion
John Comstock
Balthazar DeWolfe
Thomas Dunk
George Duren
Richard Ely
Matthew Griswold
Joseph Hand
John Huntley
John Lay
John Lay, Jr.
Thomas Lee
Hugh Lees
William Lord
Lt. Renold Marvin
William Measure
The Rev. Moses Noyes
Joseph Peck
Robert Perigo
Henry Peterson
John Robbins
Richard Smith
John Tinker
John Tillotson
Ens. William Waller
Capt. Abraham Watrous
Ens. Isaac Watrous

Note: There is no recorded list of first settlers of Lyme but the above names appear in the Lyme Land Records. There were, without doubt, others living on the East Side at the time of Loving Parting.

VITAL RECORDS OF LYME, CONNETICUT

1st Book of Marriages
Lyme Book of Record of The Birthes Deathes
and Marriages of the Inhabitants of y Town
of Lyme: May ye 26th 1743 to 1790

F John Harrisons marriage entered wrong
Masey Resncik Higgins birth not entered right
John Hazen marriage entered wrong --

William?

Napolean Bonaparte
born on the 15 of August 1770
Recorded May 27th 1811
David F. Sill Town

Lyme

[p 1] Capt. John Lee's Marriage and Birthes
Saybrook october ye-7th 1741: This may certifye that Capt. John Lee of Lyme was Married to Mrs. Abigail Tullsy of Say-Brook this Evening by me _____ William Hart
Eunice Lee the Daughter of John and Abigail Lee was born January ye 14th: 1742/3 _____
Andrew Lee Son of Capt- John and Abigail Lee was born ye 7th Day of May AD 1745 June 5 1745
Capt John Lee died ye 26th day of August _____ A.D. 1745
Horace L. Sill

Zeruiah Watsrouse was Born September ye 22nd Day A.D. 1715 _____ Richard Mathers etc.
Richard Mather and Deborah Ely boath of Lyme Was Married together May ye 18th: 1742
Mehetabel Mather Daughter of Richard and Deborah Mather was born ye 7th Day of March   A.D. 1742/3
Samuel Mather -- Son of Richard and Deborah Mather was born ye 22nd Day of February Anno Dom: _____ 1744/5
William Mather Son of Richard and Deborah Mather was born ye 15th Day of September A.D. 1746
The above said William Mather died the 27th day of said September A.D. 1746
William Mather Son of Richard and Deborah Mather was born the 21st Day of November 174--
Elias Mather Son of Richard and Deborah Mather was born (in the town of East Haddam in Hartford County) the 10th Day of February: 1750
Deborah Mather Daughter of Richard and Deborah Mather was born October ye - 3rd - A.D. 1752
Ezra Mather Son of Richard and Deborah Mather was born February 25th; 1755 and Departed this Life June 7th 1755
Ezra Mather Son of Richard and Deborah Mather was born April 27: 1756
Stephen Mather Son of Richd and Deborah Mather was born the fifth Day of September: 1758
Ezra Mather Son of Richard and Deborah Mather Died the 10th Day of November A.D. 1758

[p 2] George Hall and Eunice Gates were married together on ye - 17th-Day of October A.D.: 1738
Elisha Hall was born ye-7th of April: 1740

LYME, CONNECTICUT, VITAL RECORDS

Samuel Hall was born ye-27th Day of August 1742
Daniel Hall was born the 13th Day of October --AD: 1744
Rufus Hall Son of George and Eunice Hall was born ye 20th Day of July --AD 1747
Rufus Hall Son of George and Eunice Hall Died ye - 16th - Day of January -- A.D. 1748/9
Rufus Hall (ye second) Son of George and Eunice Hall born ye -14th of May AD 1749
Phebe Hall Daughter of George and Eunice Hall born November 21 - A.D. 1753

[p.4] In Windsor on ye 10th Day of November. Anno: Domo 1743
Capt. Matthew Griswold of Lyme and Mrs. Ursula Wolcott of Windsor were Joyned in Marriage --- by me -- Roger Wolcott Dept- Govr -- Certified -- Novemr - 11th--- 1743
Ursula Griswold Daughtor of Capt ___ Matthew and Ursula Griswold was born ye 18th of November A.D. 1744 ---- and died february ye 14th-- A.D: 1744/5____
Hannah Griswold Daughter of Capt Matthew Griswold and Ursulah his Wife was born the 22nd Day of May A.D: 1746____
Marianna Griswold Daughter of Capt. Matthew Griswold and Ursula his Wife was born the 17th Day of April A.D: 1750 ____
John Griswold son of Capt Matthew Griswold and Ursul his Wife was born February ye 20th 1752
Ursula Griswold Daughter of Capt Matthew Griswold and Ursula his Wife was born April 13th 1754
Hannah Griswold Daughter of Matthew Griswold Esqr and Ursula his Wife Died December 15th of 55____
Matthew Griswold son of Matthew Griswold Esqr and Ursula his Wife was born April 17 1760
Roger Griswold son of Matthew Griswold Esqr and Ursula his Wife was born May 21st of 62

Uriah Roland etc.
I ye Subscriber having Receivd Lawfull Certificate of ye bains of Matrimony between Uriah Roland and Lydia Lee boath of Lyme and at thear Desire ye Said Persons were Joyned Together in Wedlock and Pronounced Man and Wife according to ye Laws of God and this Government October ye 13th Day A.D: 1737 attest____ Recorded December 29th 1737____ Jonathan Parsons - Pastr ____
William Roland was born ye 5th Day of December: A.D: 1738
Lydia Roland was born ye 13th of December ____ AD: 1740
Lydia Roland Died December ye 28th ____ 1741
Ye second Lydia Roland was born January ye 20th 1742/3
Pheby Roland their Daughter was born the 24th Day of January ____ A.D: 1744/5

[p.5] Daniel Rathbone
Daniel Rathbone of Lyme and Thankfull Higgains of Haddam were Married together on ye 19th Day of March: A.D. 1741____
William Rathbone thire Son was born January ye first: ____ A.D. 1741/2
Sarah Rathbone their Daughter was born the 8th of March: A.D: 1743/4
Disdamy Rathbone Daughter of Daniel and Thankfull Rathbone was born August 30th: 1748
Mary Rathbone Daughter of Daniel and Thankfull Rathbone was born January 27th: 1750/51

These may Certifie that Elezar Mather of Lyme was Married to Anna Waterouse of Lyme on Novemr - 5th ____: A.D: 1741 By me Jonath Parsons ____ Lyme January the 21st: 1743/4____
Samuel Son of Elezar Mather and Anna his Wife was born the Tenth Day of February Anno: Domini ____ 1742/3
Fredrick Mather Son of Elezar Mather and Anna Mather was born ye 10th Day of April: A.D. 1745
Fredrick Mather Son of Elezar Mather and Anna Mather Decesd ye 6th Day of May: A.D: 1745

Fredrick Mather Son of Elezar Mather and Anna Mather was born ye 1st Day of June: A.D. 1746
Augustas Mather Son of Elezar and Anna Mather was born June ye 24th A.D. 1748
Nabby Mather Daughter of Elezar and Anna Mather was born July 30th: A.D 1751
Eleazer Mather Son of Eleazer and Anna Mather was born June 22nd (Newstile) A.D. 1753
Elisha Mather Son of Elezar and Anna Mather was born March: 18th A.D. 1755

John Lewis Junior was born ey - 30th Day of June _____ AD 1728

Edward Haven was married to Patience Beebe Dec. 7th Ad _____ 1768
George Son of said Edward and Patience was born the 27th Day of August AD 1769
David Son of said Eward and Patience was born the 4th Day of June AD 1771
Lydia Daughter of sd Edward and Patience was born the 22d Day of Novr AD 1772
Edward Son of said Edward and Patience was born The 29 Day of Oct AD 1774
Daniel Son of the said Edward and Patience was born the 26 Day of Augt AD 1776
Reuben Son of said Edward and Patience was born the 14 Day of Augt AD 1778
Anner Daughter of said Edward and Patience was born the 4 Day of July AD 1780
Sarah Daughter of sd Edward and Patience was born the 30 Day of Dec AD 1784

[p. 6] Walston Brockway of Lyme was Married to Anna Brooks of New London the 30th Day of September in the year: AD _____ 1736
Brigget Brockway their Daughter was born ey 25th Day of December: 1737
Sarah Brockway their Daughter was born ey 29 Day of August: AD: 1739
William and Wolston their sons was born ey - 9th Day of March: AD: 1741/2
Anna Brockway their Daughter was born ey - 14th - Day of March: AD: 1743/4

Samuel Gustin Jr was Married to Mary Tommas the fifth Day of January: 1740/41
Their Son Samel Gustin was born ey - 12-Day of September: AD 1741
John Gustin their Son was born ey - 12th Day of February: AD: 1743/4 _
Elisha Gustin son of Samuel and Mary Gustin Jun. was born ye 19th Day of April: AD: 1747
Josiah Gustin Son of Samuel and Mary Gustin June - was born ye 21st Day of January: AD: 1748/9
Mary Gustin Daughter of Samuel and Mary and Jun was born July 23rd AD -- 1751
Thomas Gustin Son of Samue Jun and Mary Gustin was born the 3rd Day of May AD 1757
Joshua Gustin son of Samuel Gustin Junr and Mary his wife was born 28th August 1756
Anna Gustin Daughter of Samll Gustin Jun and Mary his wife was born 15th June 1760
Hannah Gustin Daughter of Samuel Gustin Jun and Mary his wife was born July 21st 1764
Samll Gustin Gun: son of Samuel Gustin and Mary his wife Died June 30th 1763

[p. 7] Richard Person was married to Mary Ann Ely the 9th of May: 1743
Elisebeth Person their Daughter was born ey - 29th - Day of March: 1743/4
Pheby Person Daughter of Richd and Mary-Ann Person was born ye 14th - of December: 1745
Sarah Person Daughter of Richard and Mary Anna Person was born ye - 1r Day of December: 1747
Richard Person Son of Richard and Mary Ann Person was born ye - 25th - of March: 1749
Mehetable Person Daughter of Richard and Mary Ann Person was born February 15th 1752
Mary Person Daughter of Richard and Mary Ann Person born February 28th - Day: 1754
Peter Person Son of Richard and Mary Ann Person was born the 23rd - Day of October: 1756
William Ely Person Son of Richd and Mary Anna Person was born November 4th AD: 1758
Richd Person Son of Richd and Mary Ann Persen Died April 28th 1762
Anna Person Daughter of Richd and Mary Ann Person was Born March the 24th AD 1764

New London March: 12th: 1744: These May Certify that Andrew Waterouse of Lyme and Dinah Westcot of New London were joined in Marriage December 22nd 1743: by me Eliphalet Adams

Bettey Waterouse Daughter of Andrew and Dinah Waterouse was born - 17th day of September - Anno Dom: 1744
Naomi Waterouse Daughter of Andrew and Dinah Waterouse was born on - 9th day of October A.D. - 174-
Temperance Watrous Daughter of Andrew and Dinah Watrous was born March 31st -- A.D: 1749
Anna Watrous Daughter of Andrew and Dinah Watrous was born February 23rd A.D. 1751 and Died August the 2nd - A.D. - 1752
Edward Allen Watrous Son of Andrew and Dinah Watrous was born (at the Town of Milford) the 11th Day of September: A.D. - 1753 --
Rebeckah Watrous Daughter of Andrew and Dinah Watrous was born the 31st Day of August: A.D: 1756 --
Mary Ann Watrous Daughter of Andrew and Dinah Watrous was born October 12th 175-

These are to certifie whom-so-ever it may concearn that Mr. Allen McKnight and Mrs. Esther Comstock boath of Lyme were Lawfully married together - the 5th Day of November A.D. 1772: by me Stephen Johnson - Pastor of the first Church in sd Lyme Dated in sd Lyme this 4th Day of May A.D. 1780
John McKnight Son of Allen and Esther McKnight was born 24th of May 1774

[p. 8] Patience Vaugn was born ye Fifth Day of December: --- A.D. 1722
Jabez Huntley son of Moses and Rachel Huntley was born ye 21st Day of September: A.D. -- 1721
These may certify that Jabez Huntley was Married to Patience Vaun both of Lyme. March ye 27th A.D. 1746: by me George Beckwith: _____ Lyme December ye 5th 1746
Edward Ransom was born in Lyme in February 3rd A.D.: 1745 _____
Anna Tooker was born December the 28th Day A.D: 1754 _____
These may Signifie and Certifie that Edward Ransom was on the 25th Day of November 1773 Married to Ann Tooker both of Lyme by me - George Beckwith - Pastor
Elizabeth Ransom Daughter of Edward and Ann Ransom was born March 9th 1775
Polly Daughter of the said Edward and Anne was born 4th Day of Jany 1777
Hannah Daughter of the said Edward and Anna was born July 10th 1781
Isaac, Son of the said Edward and Anna was born on the 29th Day of March 1784
Amharst C. Son of the said Edward and Anna was born on the 24th Day of Feby 1789
  (Amharst appeared Septr 1810 and requested to have the letter C. added to his name)
Abijah Beckwith of Lyme and Susanah Leet of Guilford were Married together the 11th Day of August _____ A.D.: 1742
Rhoda Beckwith their Daughter was born the Second Day of June - A.D: 1743
Asa Beckwith son of Abijah and Susanah Beckwith was born ye 20th of February 1744/5 Recorded Novemr 11th 1744

Lyme in the Colony of Connecticut on the 3rd Day of June: 1766 Joseph Wait & Luranah Chadwick boath of Lyme were married to Each other by me - Matthew Griswold Assistant -
The above written is a True Copy Extracted from my office Book of Records Examined for -- Matthew Griswold late one of the Assistants
Certified for Matthew Griswold late Assistant as aforesaid --
Charlottey Wait Daughter of Joseph and Lurany Wait was born March 10th 1767
Luranah Wait Daughter of Joseph and Luranah Wait was born November 22nd 1769
Luranah Wait Wife of sd Joseph Wait Departed this life ye 30th of Decemr: 1769
Joseph Wait was Married to Mrs. Bettey Manwarring of New London August 26th 1770
Joseph Wait Son of Joseph and Bettey Wait was Born December 20th - A.D.: 1772
Hannah Wait Daughter of Joseph and Bettey Wait was Born February: 25th - A.D: 1774
Bettey Wait Daughter of Joseph and Bettey Wait was Born October 14th - A.D: 1780
Fanney Wait Daughter of Joseph and Bettey Wait was Born February 10th A.D: 1785
Sarah Wait Daughter of Joseph and Bettey Wait was Born January 14th - 1788
Betty Wait wife of the said Joseph died on the day of   A.D. 17

Joseph Wait was Married to Wd Hannah Peck on the 19th day of October A.D. 1790
Diodate Son of said Joseph and Hannah was born on the 30th of April A.D. 1795

[p. 9] Capt Elisha Sheldon was Married to Elizabeth Ely Daughter of Mr Samuel Ely Deceased the Seventh Day of October A.D. 1735
Their Daughter Mary Sheldon was born the 6th Day of June -----A.D. 1737
Mary Sheldon died the 28th Day of August ----- A.D: 1737
Lous Sheldon was born the 24th Day of June ---- A.D: 1738
Elisha Sheldon their Son was born the 6th Day of March ----A.D. 1739/40
Mary Sheldon their Daughter was born the 19th Day of January A.D: 1741/42
Thomas Sheldon their Son was born the 13th Day of October ---A.D: 1743
Thomas Sheldon Died the 5th Day of November: A.D. 1743
Thomas Sheldon Son of Capt Elisha Sheldon was born the 5th day of August A.D 1745
Samuel Sheldon son of Capt Elisha and Elizabeth Sheldon was born ye 9th Day of March A.D. 1746/7
Samuel Sheldon son of Capt Elisha and Elizabeth Sheldon died the 20th Day of December: 1747
Samuel Sheldon son of Capt Elisha and Elizabeth Sheldon was born Septemr: 26th Day 1750
Recorded the 5th Day of Novemr 1744 Dr John Lay 3rd Clerk

Joseph Lay was Married to Marcy Deming Daugher of Mr David Deming the 5th Day of February _____ A.D. 1734/5
Their first Daughter was born the 14th Day of November - A.D. 1735
and their said Daughter died the 28th Day of said November - A.D: 1735
Marcy Lay their Daughter was born the 31st Day of January: A.D. 1736/7
Recorded November 24: 1744 pr John Lay 3rd Clerk
Bridgeham Lay their Son was born the 31st Day of May -- A.D. 1739
Joseph Lay their Son was born the 10th Day of September -- A.D: 1741
Samuel Lay son of Joseph and Marcy Lay was born ye 19th Day of March A.D: 1746
Ruben Lay son of Joseph and Marcy Lay was born ye 25th Day of September A.D: 1751
Edward Lay son of Joseph and March Lay was born the 2nd Day of June - A.D: 176-

[p. 10] Simeon DeWolf of Lyme was Married to Parnall Kirtland of Saybrook the 23rd - day of July _____ A.D. 1741
Bettey DeWolf Daughter was born the 19th Day of June ---- A.D: 1742
Benjamin DeWolf their Son was born the 15th Day of October ---- A.D. 1744

Richard Wait was Married to Elisabeth Marvin the 8th day of Novr A.D: 1733
Phebe Daughter of the said Richard and Elisabeth was born the 31st day Sept A.D. 1734
Lois Daughter of said Richard and Elisabeth was born the 3rd day Decr 1735
Richard Son of said Richard and Elisabeth was born the 28th day Novr - 1739
Elisabeth Daughter of said Richard and Elisabeth was born the 12th day August 1741
Sarah Wait Daughter of said Richard and Elisabeth was born the 25th day Feby 1745
Marvin Son of said Richard and Elisabeth was born the 16th day Decr 1746
John Son of said Richard and Elisabeth was born the 21st day Jany 1749
Daniel Son of said Richard and Elisabeth was born the 2d day Feby 1751
Elisabeth Wife of the said Richard Wait departed this Life 27 May 1755
Richard Wait Esq was married to Miss Rebecca Higgins the 13 day Jany 1757
Remmick Son of the said Richard and Rebecca was born the 10th day April 1758
Ezra Son of the said Richard & Rebecca was born the 31st day May 1763
Rebecca wife of the said Richard Wait died on the 17th day of May 1785
Rebecca wife of said Richard was born May 3 1724 daughter of Capt. Joseph Higgins and Mercy Remick his wife
Taken from 2d book Page 239

Capt. Daniel Starling was Married to Mary Ely the Relict of Mr. Richard Ely of Lyme Deceased the 6th Day of June: -- A.D. 1699

Their Daughter Elisabeth Starling was born the: 18th Day of April: A.D: 1700
Daniel Starling their Son was the 28th Day of October ---- A.D: 1702
John Starling their Son was born the 28th Day of October -- A.D 1704
Joseph Starling was born the 30th Day of June -- A.D: 1707
Abigail Starling their Daughter was born the 9th September A.D: 1709
Mary Starling the Wife of Sd Capt. Daniel Starling departed this Life the 16th Day of October -- A.D: 1744
Entered December ye 27th: 1744 pr John Lay 3rd Reg-

Capt. Daniel Starling was Married to ye Widdow Mary Beckwith - the 16th Day of May: --- A.D: 1745
Capt. Daniel Starling Died ye 30th Day of June ------ A.D: 1747

Richard Smith Senr Departed this Life ye 24th Day of June 1745
Entered this 7th Day of July 1745 pr John Lay 3rd Clerk
Roger Alger Juniors
Roger Alger Juniors and Elisabeth Greenfield were married together the 28th Day of December AD: 1741
Hannah Alger was born ye 5th Day of January AD: 1742/3
Elijah Alger their son was born ye 28th day of November: A.D. 1744
Elizabeth Alger Daughter of Roger Alger Junr and Elizabeth his wife was born November the 30th - A.D: 1752
Greenfield Alger Son of Roger Alger Junr and Elizabeth his Wife was born the 18th Day of May A.D: 1755

Mr Joseph Tucker & Mrs. Lucy Emerson both of Lyme was Legally Join'd in Marriage on the 26th Day of January A.D 1789

Sanford Saunders Son of Simeon Sanders and Hannah his wife was born on the 2nd day of February _____ A.D. 1778

[p. 3] Lyme January 27th 1736/7 John Lay ye 3rd and Hannah Lee boath of Lyme were Joyn'd together in the Holy State of Marriage accordin to the Law and Custom of this Government ----- By me Jonathan Parsons Pastr _____
John Lay ye son of John Lay ye 3rd - and Hannah his Wife was born the 29th Day of December - A.D: - 1737
Hannah Lay was born ye 18th of February: 1739/40
Lydia Lay was born ye 19th Day of April A.D: 1742 _____ 1742
Peter Lay born ye 6th Day of March _____ A.D. 1743/4
Lee Lay son of John Lay ye - 3rd - and Hannah his Wife was born ye first Day of January A.D. 1745/6
Chorine Lay Daughter of John Lay 3rd and Hannah his wife was born June 15th A.D. 1748
Richard Lay Son of John Lay 3rd and Hannah his Wife was born September ye 11th A.D. 1750
Abigail Lay Daughter of John Lay 3rd and Hannah his Wife was born April ye 7th A.D 1753
Sarah Lay Daughter of John Lay 3rd and Hannah his Wife was born March 16th 1755
Bettey Lay Daughter of John Lay 3rd and Hannah his Wife was born 10th Day of August 1757
Jean Lay Daughter of John Lay 3rd and Hannah his Wife was born August 6th 1759
Silas Lay and Luce Lay Son and Daugher of John Lay 3rd and Hannah his Wife was born April 13th 1762: being twins
Silas Lay above named died Sept 27th 1762
Mrs. Hannah Lay Wife of John Lay 3rd above said Died the 3rd Day of August 1784
John Lay Esqr. above said Died _____ 3rd Day April 1792

Benjamin Marvin and Deborah Mather were married together on ye 11th Day of November Anno Dom _____ 1742
Their Son Benjamin Marvin was born ye 7th Day of November Anno Dom. 1743

Mehitabel Marvin Daughter of Benja and Deborah Marvin was born ye 4th of October 1745
Azubah Marvin Daughter of Benjamin and Deborah Marvin was born December 23rd AD 1748
Mr. Benjamin Marvin Died January 21st 1775

[p.11] Benjamin Hide and Abigail Lee were Married together the fifth Day of May: A.D: 1740
Amelia Hide was born on thursday the: 11th day of December ----A.D. 1740
Amelia Hide Died on Wednesday the 6th Day of January------A.D. 1741/-
Amelia Hide ye 2nd was born the 11th day of October: (on Tuesday) -- A.D: 1742
Alaexander Hide was born on Monday the 6th day of August --- A.D: 1744

John Phelps and Dorothy Rathbun were married together on ye 10th of Nov. 1737
Charles Phelps son of John Phelps was born ye 22d of January 1738/9 (Taken from Vol 7)

Thomas Griswold was married to Susannah Lynde of SayBrook the 17th Day of December: ---------A.D. 1741
Pheby Griswold their Daughter was born the 18th Day of August: A.D: 174[3]
Lucy Griswold Daughter of Thomas and Susannah Griswold was born October 7th 1745
Lous Griswold Daughter of Thomas & Susannah Griswold was born Septemr first 1747
Sarah Griswold Daughter of Thomas & Susannah Griswold was born August 26th 1749
Lovice Griswold Daughter of Thomas & Susannah Griswold was born July 25th 1751
Anna Griswold Daughter of Thomas & Susannah Griswold was born March 31st 175[3]
Anna died on the   day of --------- 176[2]
Susannah Wife of Mr. Thomas Griswold died the   day Novr 1768
Mr. Thomas Griswold departed this life on the   day of August 1770

[p. 12] Jonathan Deming was born the 29th Day of February ----- A.D: 1743/4
Elisabeth Deming Daughter of David and Mehetabel Deming was born ye first of October 174[8]
Downing [Pownall] Deming Son of David and Mehetable Deming was born September 30th 1749
Henry Deming Son of David and Mehetabel Deming was born March 2nd 1752
Julius Deming Son of David and Mehetabel Deming was born April 16th 1755
Asa Deming Son of David and Mehetable Deming was born June 14th A.D: 1758

The Revnd Mr. David Deming Departed this Life ye 10th Day of February 1745/6
Jonathan Deming Departed this Life ye 6th Day of March: A.D: 1738

Robert Mentor was Married to Abigail Bennet Daughter of Mr. John Bennet the 11th day of September ----- A.D. 1729
Mary Mentor their Daughter was born the 29th day of June: A.D: 1730
Abigail Mentor was born the 26th Day of February ---- A.D: 1733
Robert Mentor was born the 17th Day of December ----- A.D: 1735
Jane Mentor was born the 10the Day of January ------ A.D: 1737
Ruben Mentor was born the 5th Day of January ------ A.D: 1739
Patience Mentor was born the 19th Day of April ------ A.D: 1741
Anna Mentor was born the 4th Day of June ----- A.D: 1743
  Gabrel Mentor Son of Robert and Abigail Mentor was born ye 18th Day of September: 1745
  Elijah Bennet Mentor Son of Robert and Abigail Mentor was born ye 29th of March -- A.D: 1746/7
  Ruth Mentor Daughter of Robert and Abigail Mentor was born ye 15th Day of March: A.D: 1748/9
Jane Mentor Daughter of Robert Mentor and Abigail his Wife died 20th January: 1750/51
Felix Mentor son of Robert and Abigail Mentor was born the 17th Day July 1751

8   LYME, CONNECTICUT, VITAL RECORDS

Mr. David Deming jr. was Married to Mrs. Mehetibeel Champion --- the 18th Day of December ------ A.D: 1740
Prudence Deming was born the 18th Day of May --- A.D: 1741

[p.13]   Mr. James Ely was Married to Mrs. Dorcase Andrews the 6th Day of April 1742
Elisabeth Ely their Daughter was born the 14th Day of December: A.D: 174[-]
James Ely their Son was born the 9th Day of February --- A.D: 174[-] [2]
Ruhama Ely Daughter of James Ely and Dorcase Ely was born February ye 5th (174[5]
Jacob Ely Son of James and Dorcase Ely was born ye 19th Day of January A.D: 174[-] [7/8]
Dorcase Ely Daughter of James and Dorcas Ely was born January 15th: 1749/50
Tahatha Ely Daughter of James and Dorcas Ely was born January the 18th A.D: 175[-] [1] and Died January the 25th: 1752
Aaron Ely Son of James and Dorcas Ely was born the second Day of August: 175[-] [3]
Andrew Ely Son of James and Dorcas Ely was born January 5th A.D: 1756
John Ely Son of James and Dorcas Ely was born the 28th Day of February: A.D: 1758
Gad Ely Son of James and Dorcas Ely was born May 24th day -- A.D: 1762
James Ely Seignor Died May the 12th --- A.D: 1766 [Dorcas Ely d. Jan. 25, 1752]
Aaron Ely was killed at King's Bridge in the Revolutionary War Jany or Feby A.D: 1777

Jonathan Smith was Married Jean Lewis the 10th Day of December 1741
Sarah Smith their Daughter was born the 6th Day of October -- A.D. 174[2]
Esther Smith Daughter of Jonathan & Jean Smith was born the 14th Day of February A.D: 174[4]
Peter Smith son of Jonathan & Jean Smith was born the 26th of December A.D. 174[6]
Luce Smith Daughter of Jonathan and Jean Smith was born March ye 3rd A.D: 174 [8]

James Blague was Married to Abigail Renolds on the 4th Day of November: 1743
Jeremiah Blage Son of James & Abigail Blague was born July 30th: A.D. 174 [4]
James and Jonathan Blagues Sons of James and Abigail Blague was born September 6th ---- 1746
Joshua Blague Son of James & Abigail Blague was born April 21st A.D. 174 -
Esther Blague Daughter of James & Abigail Blague was born Septemr 16th A.D. 175 [0]
John Blague Son of James & Abigail Blague was born March 16th A.D. 175 [3]

[p. 14]   Duran Wade was married to Phebe Ransom the 3rd Day of January AD 1741/2
Anna Wade their Daughter was born the 27th Day of January AD 1742/3
Pheby Wade their Daughter was born the 18th Day of March 1744/5
Thomas Wade son of Duran and Phebe Wade was born ye first Day of April AD 1747
John Wade son of Duran and Phebe Wade was born ye 9th Day of June AD 1749

William Robins Junior was Married to Esther Huntly the 20th Day of May: A.D: 1741
Pheby Robins their Daughter was born the 27th Day of May A.D: 1742
Esther Robins their Daughter was born the 5th Day of March A.D. 1743/4
William Robins Son of William and Esther Robins was born ye 10th Day of September 1745
Jemima Robins Daughter of William and Esther Robins was born ye 3rd day of April: A.D. 1747
Birnhal Robins son of William and Esther Robins was born 20th Day of April 1754
Lydia Robins Daughter of William and Esther Robins was born 18th Day of October 1756
Ruben Robins son of William and Esther Robins was born the 10th Day of March 1759

This may Signifie and certifye that I the Subscriber Married Mr. Richard Ely Selden to Mrs. Desier Coult October the 2nd A.D. 178 [2]
Juliana Selden Daughter of Richard Ely and Desier Selden was born July 29th 1784
Asanath Selden Daughter of Richd Ely and Desire Selden was born December the 28th 1785

[p. 15]   Mr. Josiah Smith was Married Mrs. Rhoda ---- the 8th Day of October: A.D: ----
Joseph Smith their Son was born the 18th Day of September A.D 17 --

Josiah Smith their Son was born the 14th Day of May A.D: 172 --
Joseph Smith their Son Departed this Life the 29th Day of December: A.D: 1728
Rhoda Smith their Daughter was born the Second Day of March A.D: 1729
Lydia Smith their Daughter was born the 31st Day of March A.D. 1731
Lucrecia Smith their Daughter was born the 9th Day of Novemr: A.D. 1734
Pheby Smith their Daughter was born the 18th Day of October: A.D: 1737
Lube [Azubah Zube] Smith their Daughter was born the 8th Day of November: A.D: 1739
William Smith their Son was born the 23rd day of July: A.D. 1745

John Huntly Junior was Married to Hannah Person of Gilford the 22nd Day of
    July: A.D. 1741
Hannah Huntly their Daughter was born the 21st Day of June A.D: 1742
Zeletoes Huntly their Son was born the 28th Day of March: A.D. 174[4]
Zephaniah Huntly son of John and Hannah Huntly was born ye 3rd Day of
    February A.D. 1745/6
Jehiel Huntly son of John and Hannah Huntly was born February ye 7th: A.D: 1748/9

These lines may Certifye that Dan Gallit and Grace Gates were Lawfully married March:
    5th A.D. 1788: Certifyed by   Abel Palmer Pastor of 2nd Baptist Church
    in Colchester

Dan Marvin Son of said Dan & Grace was born the 21st Day of February 179 [-]

Esther Scovil Daughter of John and Sarah was born ye 24th Day of November: A.D. 1743

[p. 16]   Noah Miller was Married to Mary Waller ye 9th of July - A.D: 1733
William Miller their Son was born January the 27th - A.D. 1734
Diadaymea their Daughter was born the 12th Day of September: 1736
William Miller their Son died the 19th day of March: - A.D: 1737/8
Mary Miller their Daughter was born the 14th Day of December - A.D: 1738
Hannah Miller their Daughter was born the 5th Day of November: A.D. 1741
Entered 26 August 1743
Billey Miller was born the 27th Day of January --- A.D: 1743/4
Noah Miller Son of Noah and Mary Miller was born October ye 5th Day: A.D: 1746
Elisha Miller Son of Noah and Mary Miller was born September ye 14th Day -- A.D. 1748
Elisabeth Miller Daughter of Noah and Mary Miller was born Septemr 22nd 1750
Elias Miller Son of Noah and Mary Miller was born the 24th Day Septemr 1752
Lous Miller Daughter of Noah and Mary Miller was born May 4th A.D: 1757

Jabez Waterouse was Married to Sarah [Richards] his Wife the 30th Day of
    December -- A.D: 1713
Zerviah Waterouse their Daughter was born the 22nd Day of September -- A.D: 1715
Jabez Waterouse their Son was born the 20th Day of January -- A.D: 1718
Jerusha Waterouse their Daughter was born the 15th Day of August: A.D: 1720
Sarah and Ruth Wateroses were born the 7th Day of February - A.D: 1723
John Waterouse their Son was born the 17th Day of February - A.D: 1726

Stephen Champion was Married to Deborah Leech of New London the 28th Day of
    September: 1726
Ruben Champion Son of Stephen and Deborah Champion was born the 4th Day of
    September: 1727
Deborah Champion Daughter of Stephen and Deborah Champion was born the
    19th Day of June: A.D: 1732
entered this 9th Day of July: 1745 pr John Lay 3rd Town Clerke
Sarah Daughter of Sarah Armstrong was born February 12th A.D. 1769

[p. 17]   Jonathan Alger and Irene Way were Married together the 9th Day of April:
    A.D: 1740
Elisabeth Alger was born the first Day of January -- A.D: 1740/1
Elisabeth Alger Died ye 7th of March -- A.D: 1740/1

10 LYME, CONNECTICUT, VITAL RECORDS

Elisha Alger was born the 5th Day of April -- A.D: 1742
Elisha Alger dyed the 12th Day of April -- A.D: 1742
George Alger was born the 24th Day of February -- A.D. 1742/3
Sarah and Lydia Alger were born the 13th Day of January: A.D. 1744/5
Irene the above said wife of Said Alger Departed this Life the 26th Day of February: A.D. 1744/5
Johathan Alger was married to Lydia Hudson ye 12th Day of December - A.D: 1745
Nathaniel Alger Son of Jonathan and Lydia Alger was born the 2nd Day of August - A.D: 1746
Elisha Alger Son of Jonathan and Lydia Alger was born the 2nd Day of August -- A.D. 1746
William Alger Son of Jonathan and Lydia Alger was born September ye 4th -- A.D: 1748
Jonathan Alger Son of Jonathan and Lydia Alger was born October ye 6th Day - A.D: 1750
Irene Alger Daughter of Jona & Lydia Alger was born 16th Day of October -- A.D: 1752
Joseph Agr Son of Jonahan and Lydia Alger was born March 22nd -- A.D: 1755
Dan Alger Son of Jonahan and Lydia Alger was born March ye 11th A.D: 1758
Susannah Alger Daughter of Jona & Lydia Alger was born March ye 12th -- A.D: 1761
Ruth Alger Daughter of Jona & Lydia Alger was born September 4th -- A.D: 1763
Susannah Alger above Named Departed this Life March 13th -- A.D: 1764
Ruth Alger above Named Departed this Life April 20th   A.D. 1764
Sarah Alger above Named Died the 16th Day of March -- A.D: 1765
Sarah Alger Daughter of Jona and Lydia Alger was born April ye 9th -- A.D: 1765

Richard Brockway the 3rd of Lyme was Married to Hannah Randal of Colchester the 14th Day of May A.D: 1740
Lous Brockway their Daughter was born the 15th Day of March -- A.D: 1741
Elisabeth Brockway daughter of Richd and hanah Brockway was born ye 13th of March -- 1744/5
Hettey Brockway Daughter of Richard and Hannah Brockway was born ye 3rd of Decemr -- 1746
Lous Brockway Daughter of Richd & Hannah Brockway Died 15th July: 1756
Enos Brockway Son of Richard and Hannah Brockway was born April 25th -- A.D: 1759

May ye 26th 1754: then Eber Lewis of Lyme was Lawfully Married to Jemima Huntly: by me -- Stephen Gorton Elder --
Lydia Lewis Daughter of Eber and Jemima Lewis was born October ye 28th A.D. 1770

[p. 18]   Josiah Dewolf Junior was Married to Martha Ely the 13th Day of September A.D: 1739
William Dewolf was born the 13th Day of June -- A.D: 1740
Anna Dewolf was born the 11th Day of April -- A.D: 1742
Daniel Dewolf was born the 7th Day of November -- A.D: 1743
Azuba Dewolf Daughter of Josiah and Martha Dewolf was born the 11th of April - A.D: 1745
Martha Dewolf Daughter of Josiah and Martha Dewolf was born the 24th of January - A.D: 1746/7
Hannah Dewolf Daughter of Josiah and Martha Dewolf was born the 20th Day of June 1749
Samuel Dewolf Son of Josiah and Martha Dewolf was born the 24th Day of December - 1750
Esther Dewolf Daughter of Josiah and Martha Dewolf was born the 25th Day of January A.D: 1753
Hannah Dewolf Daughter of Josiah and Martha Dewolf Died the 23rd of September -- A.D: 1753

Samuel Bennet was Married to Hannah Wade the 3rd Day of August - A.D: 1732
their Son Zadock Bennet was born the 13th Day of August - A.D: 1733

Nathan Bennet their Son was born the 23rd Day of December - A.D: 1734
Mary Bennet their Daughter was born the 6th Day of September - A.D: 1736
Hannah Bennet their Daughter was born the 13th of October - A.D: 1738
Jean Bennet their Daughter was born the 10th Day of October - A.D: 1740
Eunice Bennet their Daughter was born the 14th Day of February - A.D: 1743
Bettey Bennet their Daughter was born the 11th Day of May -- A.D: 1744
Lydia Bennet Daughter of Samll & Hannah Bennet was born Novemr 6th - A.D: 1746
Jean Bennet Daughter of Samll & Hannah Bennet Died Novemr 5th -- 1746
Jean Bennet Daughter of Samll & Hannah Bennet was born March 17th A.D: 1749
Elijah Bennet Son of Samll & Hannah Bennet was born Novemr ye 3rd - 1753
Nathan Bennet Son of Samll & Hannah Bennet Died October 13th - A.D: 1757
Ye 2nd Jane Bennet Daughter of Saml & Hannah Bennet Died August 16th - A.D: 1759

[p. 19]   Nathaniel Peck was Married to Lucy Mather the 24th Day of May A.D: 1744
Joseph Peck their son was born the 4th Day of February - A.D: 1744/5

Isaac Hall was Married to Sarah Gates the 3rd Day of June - A.D: 1742
Abel Hall their Son was born the 5th Day of October -- A.D: 1743
Ezra Hall their Son was born the 17th Day of February -- A.D: 1744/5
Hepsabe Hall Daughter Isaac and Sarah Hall was born ye 11th Day of December - 1746
Jacob Hall Son of Isaac and Sarah Hall was born ye 13th Day of August - A.D: 1748
Josiah Hall Son of Isaac and Sarah Hall was born March 9th - A.D: 1750 and Died
    March ye 4th 1751
Sarah Hall Daughter of Isaac and Sarah Hall was born November 30th - 1752 and Died
    August ye 2nd A.D: 1753
Mary Hall Daughter of Isaac and Sarah Hall was born October 22: 1754 and Died October
    the first 1760
Eunice Hall Daughter of Isaac & Sarah Hall was born March 2nd 1758
Abigial Hall Daughter of Isaac & Sarah Hall was born June 12th A.D: 1761
Mr. Isaa Hall Departed this Life the 26th Day of July -- A.D: 1778
Mrs. Sarah Hall the relect of Mr. Isaac Hall Departed this life on the 27th Day of
    January: 1786 in the 68th year of her age.

[p. 20]   Elisha Tubbs was Married to Anna Miller the 31st Day of July -- A.D: 1738
John Miller Tubbs their Son was born the 5th Day of May -- A.D: 1739
Amos Tubbs their Son was born the 8th Day of October -- A.D: 1741
Ahimaz Tubbs their Son was born the 13th Day of January -- A.D: 1743/4

John Mach was Married to Mehetable Smith ye 20th Day of February A.D: 1740/1

These may Certifie whomever it may Consearn that Greenfield Alger and Lucy Wade both
    of Lyme were lawfully Married together the 26th Day of March -- A.D: 1778 by me
    Stephen Johnson, Pastor of First Church in sd Lyme.
Elisabeth Alger Daughter of Greenfield & Lucy Alger was born Septemr 19th -- 1779
Roger Alger Son of Greenfield & Lucy Alger was born February 6th 1782
Elijah Alger Son of Greenfield & Lucy Alger was Born February: 19th 1784
Lucy Alger Wife of sd Greenfield Alger Departed this Life September: 13th - 1784
Greenfield Alger and Mehetable Hayes were Married to Each other on the Evening of the
    9th of October 1785 by Ezra Nelden Just of Peace
Richard Hayes Son of sd Greenfield & Mehitable was born 28th March - A.D: 1793
Patience Daughter of sd Greenfield & Mehitable was born 25 of Jany - A.D: 1795
William Greenfield Son of said Greenfield & Mehitable was born 19th of Decr - A.D: 1796
Mehitable wife of said Roger* died on the 16th day of November 1811
[should be wife of Greenfield]
Joseph Chadwick Son of Jonathan and Luce Chadwick was born December ye 29 -: 1730
Luce Chadwick Daughter of Jonathan & Luce Chadwick was born April ye 24th Day: 1738
David Blague Son of Jeremiah & Annah Blague was born the 4th June: 1769

[p. 21] Samll Ely was Married to Hannah Mash his now wife ye 20th Day of May: A.D: 1739
Samuel Ely their Son was born ye 6th Day of November: A.D: 1740
Elijah Ely their Son was born ye 8th Day of May: A.D: 1743
Hannah Ely their Daughter was born ye 26th Day of May - A.D: 1745

John Starling of Lyme was Married to Abigail Pratt of Colchester in Novemr - in the year - A.D: 1727
Elisabeth their Daughter was born ye 15th Day of July: - A.D 1729
Abigail Starling their Daughter was born the 25th Day of January: A.D: 1730/1
Abigail ye Wife of sd Jn Starling Departed this Life ye 10th Day of May: in ye Year - A.D: 1731
John Starling was Married to Jane Ransom ye 30th Day of December in ye year: Anno Dom 1731
John Starling their Son was born ye 10th Day of December Anno Dom: 1732
Abigail Starling Died in April: in the year: Anno Dom: 1734
Nathan Starling was Born ye 12th Day of December: A.D: 1736
Stephen Starling Son of John and Jane Starling was Born ye 3rd Day of August: 1739
Daniel Starling their Son was born ye -- in June in the Year A.D: 1740
Abigail Starling their Daughter was born ye 12th Day of May: 1742
Jacob Starling their Son was Born ye 3rd Day of March: A.D: 1744
Jane Starling Daughter of John and Jane Starling was born ye 23rd Day of April 1746
Simon Starling son of John and Jane Starling was born ye 25th Day of July A.D: 1749
Esther Starling Daughter of John and Jane Starling was born July ye 4th 1751
Lucia Starling Daughter of John and Jane Starling was born ye 13th Day of March 1753
Miriam Starlin Daughter of John and Jane Starling was born May the 8th A.D: 1755
Mary Starlin Daughter of John and Jane Starlin was born September ye 18th A.D: 1757

[p. 22] Thomas Hall of Lyme was Married to Sarah Clark of Colchester ye 30th Day of November Anno Domini 1743
John Hall Son of Thomas and Sarah Hall was born ye 20th of March 1744/5
Nathan Hall Son of Thomas and Sarah Hall was born ye 11th Day of December A.D 1746
Minderwell Hall Daughter of Thomas and Sarah Hall was born ye July 15th A.D: 1748
Thomas Hall Son of Thomas and Sarah Hall was born ye the 9th Day of September 1750

Jonathan Beebee was Married to Hannah Lewis the 12th Day of March: 1731/2
Ira Beebee Son of Jonathan and Hannah Beebee was born ye 20th Day of July: A.D: 1735
Zeruiah Beebee Daughter of Jonathan and Hannah Beebee was born ye 4th Day of February: 1737/8
Zere Beebe Son of Jonathan and Hannah Beebee was born ye 2nd Day of July: A.D: 1740
Borden Beebee Son of Jonathan and Hannah Beebee was born ye 3rd Day of August: A.D: 1742

These Certifie that Mr. Joseph Peck and wife Sarah Miller boath of Lyme were Lawfully married together the 21st Day of December A.D: 1780 by me Stephen Johnson Pastor of First Church in said Lyme
Pheby Peck Daughter of Joseph and Sarah Peck was born July 26th 1781 and Died in the seventh week of her age.
Ezra Miller Peck Son of Joseph and Sarah Peck was born July 4th -- 1784
Joseph Son of Joseph and Sarah Peck was born July 23rd A.D: 1790
William Son of Joseph and Sarah Peck was born October 16th A.D: 1792 and Died September 3 1794
Fanny Daughter of Joseph and Sarah Peck was born April 6th A.D: 1795

Abijah Bishop Son of Abraham and Patience Bishop was born 25th of June: 1780 Recorded by order of Selectmen this 10th Day of November: 1786 by John Lay 2nd
Mary Bishop Daughter of said Abm etc was born December 21st A.D: 1777

This is according to her Mother's acct of her Age
Elisha Son of said Abraham etc was born October 2nd Day 1783

Capt. Samuel Selden Died ye last day of February: A.D: 1745

[p. 23] New London May the 16th: 1745 Then Daniel Huntly of Lyme and Susannah Beckwith of New London were married together by me George Griswold as witness my hand George Griswold pastor of 2nd Church in Lyme

Susannah Huntly Daughter of Daniel and Susannah Huntly was born ye 16th Day of April: 1746

Daniel Huntly Son of Daniel and Susannah Huntly was born ye October ye 13th Day -A.D 1748

Isaac Huntly Son of Daniel and Susannah Huntly was born Decemr ye 24th Day -A.D: 1753

Isaac Huntly Son of Daniel and Susannah Huntly Died the 19th Day of September A.D. 1754

Isaac Huntly Son of Daniel and Susannah Huntly was born the 14th Day of June - 1755

Hannah Huntly Daughter of Daniel and Susannah Huntly was born the 8th Day of August: 1758

Jason Son of said Daniel and Susannah Huntly was born the 4th Day of May 1761

William Waterouse of Lyme was Married to Sarah Bartlet of Haddam the 9th day of November - A.D 1744

Samll Waterouse Son of William and Sarah Waterouse was born the 5th Day of September: 1745

John Crocker Son of John (Crocker Deceasd) and Rhoda Crocker was born Septemr 22nd 1747

Lucia Lord Daughter of Samuel and Katharine Lord was born ye 1st Day of August 1751
Sarah Lord Daughter of Samuel and Katharine Lord was born July first Day: 1753
Theophilus Lord Son of Samuel and Katharine Lord was born September 16th: 1756

[p. 24] Recorded 28th October 1745

Lyme October 23: 1745 these may Certifye the Town Clerk of Lyme and all others whom it may Concern, that Stephen Lee Junr and Mehetabel Marvin the 3rd both of Lyme were Joyned together in Marriage on the 25th Day of September Anno Domini: 1744 by me Jonathan Parsons, Pastr of 1st Church of Lyme.

John Lee Son of Stephen and Mehetabel Lee was born the 10th Day of July: Anno Domini: - 1745

John Lee Son of Stephen and Mehetabel Lee Died ye 26th Day of Septemr: 1745

Elias Lee Son of Stephen and Mehetabel Lee was born ye 25th Day of Septemr A.D: 1747

Abraham Bishop was Married to Hannah Champion the 26th Day of October: Anno Domini: 1743

John Bishop Son of Abraham & Hannah Bishop was born ye 5th Day of October: A.D. 1745

Abraham Bishop Son of Abraham & Hannah Bishop was born ye 30th Day of June: 1747

Hannah Bishop Wife of Abraham Bishop died ye 13th Day of July A.D 1747

The Evening following the 23rd Day of Decemr A.D: 1747: Abraham Bishop and Sarah Gladding were Married by me Abraham Knott Pastor of ye Second Church of Christ in Saybrook

Hannah Bishop Daughter of Abraham and Sarah Bishop was born July 26th A.D: 1749
Isaac Bishop Son of Abraham and Sarah Bishop was born May ye 26th - 1751
Mary Bishop Daughter of Abraham and Sarah Bishop was born July 26th - A.D: 1753
Enos Bishop Son of Abraham and Sarah Bishop was born August 7th A.D: 1755
Abraham Bishop Son of Abraham and Hannah Bishop Died February 15th - 1754

LYME, CONNECTICUT, VITAL RECORDS

Gershom Bardner was Married to Susannah Smith ye 17th Day of December Anno Domini 1741

[p. 25] Samuel Seldon of Lyme in the County of New London was Married to Elisabeth Ely of said Lyme the 23rd Day of May Anno Domini: 1745
Elisabeth Seldon Daughter of Samuel and Elisabeth Selden was born ye 16th Day of April 1747
Samuel Selden Son of Samuel and Elisabeth Selden was born November the first Day 1748
Esther Selden Daughter of Samuel and Elisabeth Selden was born June 22nd Day A.D. 1750 and Died June ye 8th: A.D: 1751
Elijah Selden Son of Samll and Elisabeth Selden was born February 21st A.D: 1752
Deborah Selden Daughter of Samll and Elisabeth Selden was born December 29th N.S: 1753
Charles Selden Son of Samll and Elisabeth Selden was born November 23rd A.D: 1755
Jemima Selden Daughter of Samll and Elisabeth Selden was born September 3rd 1757
Richard Ely Selden Son of Samll and Elisabeth Selden was born May 25th A.D: 1759
Mary Selden Daughter of Samll and Elisabeth Selden was born April 22nd A.D: 1761
George Selden Son of Samll and Elisabeth Selden was born February 27th A.D: 1763
Joseph Dudley Selden Son of Samll and Elisabeth Selden was born Decemr ye 30th A.D: 1764
Dorothy Selden Daughter of Samll and Elisabeth Selden was born Decemr 26th A.D: 1766
Roger Selden Son of Samll and Elisabeth Selden was born April 16th A.D: 1769
Col. Samuel Selden departed this life on the 11th day of October A.D: 1776 after Languishing in Prison about one month being taken the 17th Day of Sept 1776 and carried into New York and there kept close Prisoner untill he expired.

Amos Lay of Lyme was Married to Mary Griswold of Norwich ye 24th Day - October: Anno Domini 1745
Eunice Lay Daughter of Amos and Mary Lay was born ye 23rd Day of February: A.D. 1746/7 and Died April ye 4th Day A.D: - 1747

This may Certify that I married John Murdock Lee to Anne Beckwith February 3rd 1788 pr Jason Lee Elder

[p. 26] Decemr 26 1745
John Ageet was Married to Abigail Graves ye 18th Day of January A.D 1738/9
Sarah Aget daughter of John and Abigail Aget was born ye 20th day of December A.D: 1739
Ebenezar Aget Son of John and Abigail Agget was born ye 18th Day April A.D: 1742
Ebenezar Ageet Son of John and Abigail Aget died ye 12th Day of May A.D: 1744
Molley Aget daughter of John and Abigail Ageet was born ye 22nd of January A.D: 1744/5
Ebenezar Agget son of John and Abigail Agget was born ye 7th of June 1747
New London County sd Lyme January 27 1788: these may Certifye that Mr. James Chadwick and Mrs. Anne Kent was Lawfully Joyned in the marriage Covenant Covenant by Ezra Selden Jst Peace
Fanny Daughter of the said James and Anna was born Decr 19th A.D: 1788
Brooks Son of the said James and Anna was born the 23rd day of January 1792
Clarissa their daughter was born on the 20th day of October 1793
Anna their daughter was born on the 24th day of Novr 1795
Hannah their daughter was born on the 28 day of February 1799
Gurdon their son was born the 30th day of January 1802

Decemr 26 1749
John Wood was Married to Lydia Mack ye 8th Day of February: A.D: 1737
Simeon Wood Son of John and Lydia Wood was born ye first Day of January 1738/9
Rachel Wood Daughter of John and Lydia Wood was born ye 4th Day of January A.D: 1740/41

Rachell Wood Daughter of John and Lydia Wood died in ye 3rd week of her
  age A.D: 1740/41
Lydia Wood Daughter of John and Lydia Wood was born ye 4th Day of
  March: A.D: 1741/42
William Wood Son of John and Lydia Wood was born ye 25th Day of March: A.D: 1743

June the last Day A.D: 1767: then I married Mathew Rogers of Lyme to his now Wife
  Lous Mack Attest Samll Ely Justice of the Peace
Abijah Rogers Son of Matthew and Lous Rogers was Born October 27th A.D: 1768
Matthew Rogers Son of Matthew and Lous Rogers was Born March 26th A.D: 1770
Lous Rogers Daughter of Matthew and Lous Rogers was Born June ye 22nd A.D: 1772
Huldah Rogers Daughter of Matthew and Lous Rogers was Born March 11th A.D: 1775
Eunice Rogers Daughter of Matthew and Lous Rogers was Born Decemr 16th A.D: 1776
Jonathan Mack Rogers son of Matthew and Lous Rogers was Born June 22nd A.D: 1778
Rhoda Daughter of said Matthew and Lous Rogers was born the 3rd day of Octr 1781
Lois Wife of the said Mathew Departed this life on the 20th Day of December 1782
Mathew Rogers was married to Wido Esther Ramon on the 20th Day of Feby 1783
Elijah the Son of the said Mathew and Esther was born the 16th Day of Sept 1786
Elisha Son of the said Mathew & Esther was born on the 16th Day of May 1789

[p. 27]   December 26 1745
Nicodemus Miller was Married to Patience Bates February ye 21st: A.D: -- 1736/7
Joanna Miller Daughter of Nicodemus and Patience Miller was born ye 13th of July:
  A.D: 1737
Patience ye said Wife of Nicodemus Miller died ye 21st Day of August - A.D: 1738
Nicodemus Miller was Married to Pheby Huntly ye 13th Day of September: A.D: 1740
Samuel Miller Son of Nicodemus and Pheby Miller was born ye 21st of June: A.D: 1742
Esther Miller daughter of Nicodemus and Phebe Miller was born ye first of July: A.D. 1744
Pathania Miller daughter of Nicodemus and Phebe Miller was born ye 16th day of
  July: A.D: 1746
Phebe Miller Daughter of Nicodemus and Phebe Miller was born January ye 10th
  A.D: 1748/9
Beththuel Miller son of Nicodemus and Phebe Miller was born Septemr 19th A.D: 1751

These are to Certify that Mr. Daniel Hall & Mrs. Mehetabel Peck boath of Lyme were
  Lawfully Married together the 13th Day of August .A.D. 1767 Lyme: Stephen Johnson
  Pastor of the First Church in sd Lyme

John Mather was Married to Marcy Higgins ye 13th Day of June: A.D: 1745
John Mather Son of John and Marcy Mather was born the 4th Day of April: A.D: 1746
Simon Mather Son of John and Marcy Mather was born ye 31st Day of October: 1747 and
  Died ye 25th Day of November A.D: 1747
Rebeckah Mather Daughter of John and Marcy Mather was born December ye 2nd
  A.D. 1748
Marcy Mather Daughter of John and Marcy Mather was born the 11th Day of
  December: 1750
Jerusha Mather Daughter of John & Marcy Mather was born March the 6th Day:
  A.D: 1753
Hannah Mather Daughter of John & Marcy Mather was born December ye 25th:
  A.D: 1754
Joseph Mather Son of John & Marcy Mather was born January 28th A.D: 1757
Stephen Mather Son of John & Marcy Mather was born February 9th A.D: 1759
Jerusha Mather Daughter of John & Marcy Mather Died March the 3rd A.D: 1760
Selvanus Mather Son of John & Mercy Mather was born January ye 17th: A.D: 1761
Jerusha Mather Daughter of John & Mercy Mather was born February 25th A.D: 1763
Dan Mather Son of John & Mercy Mather was born March 24th A.D: 1765
Jemima Mather Daughter of John & Mercy Mather was born January 22nd 1767

LYME, CONNECTICUT, VITAL RECORDS

Mehetabel Mather Daughter of John & Mary Mather was born May 5th A.D: 1769
Mrs. Marcy Mather Wife of the above said John Mather Departed this life on the 20th of October: 1782
Mr. John Mather was Married to wido Ruth Robins on the 25th of Feby 1785
Mrs. Ruth Mather Wife of said John Mather died on the 14th June 1800

[p. 28] Samuel Clark was Married to Hannah Champion ye first Day of May - A.D: 1733
Pheby Clark Daughter of Samll and Hannah Clark was born ye 13th day of November: A.D: 1744
Dan Clark Son of Samll Clark and Hannah his wife was born ye 13th day of October: A.D: 1736
Champion Clark Son of Samuel and Hannah Clark was born ye 7th day of March: A.D: 1739
Elijah Clark Son of Samuel and Hannah Clark was born ye 12th day of September: A.D: 1741
Samuel Clark Son of Samll and Hannah Clark was born ye 22 day of September: A.D: 1744

These may Signified and Certifie that Mr. Jacob Hall was on the 3rd Day of December: 1778: Married to Mrs. Hannah Clark both of Lyme - by me George Beckwith Pastor
Sarah Hall Daughter of Jacob and Hannah Hall was born September 17th A.D: 1779
Amasa Hall Son of Jacob and Hannah Hall was born July 3rd A.D: 1781
Martha Hall Daughter of Jacob and Hannah Hall was born March 27th A.D: 1783

Ezra Smith Son of Phebe Chadwick was born the 18th Day of May A.D: 1787
Sally Clark daughter of the said Phebe was born 13 day of June A.D: 1791
Susannah Clark daughter of the sd Phebe was born the 6 day of March 1793
Fanny Clark daughter of the sd Phebe was born the 24 day of May 1795
George Daor son of the sd Phebe was born the 26 day of November 1799
Levi Selden Darthwick son of the sd Phebe was born the 7 day of September 1804

Samll Chadwick was Married to Mary Adset ye 12th Day of May A.D: 1744
Bettey Chadwick daughter of Samll Chadwick and Mary Chadwick was born ye 10th of March: 1744/5
Samuel Chadwick died September the 20th day A.D. 1789
Mary Chadwick died June the 13th day A.D - 1790

These may Certifie that Mr. Samuel Coult of Lyme was Married to Mrs. Salley Fowler of Lebanon: in the year: 1778: the 15th Day of October - Richard Lord in the presence of us witness   - John Coult junr
Martin Coult Son of Samuel & Salley Coult was Born July 3rd A.D: 1779
Samuel Coult Son of Samuel & Salley Coult was Born September 22nd 1780
Dijah Coult Son of Samuel & Salley Coult was Born May 8th A.D 1782

[p. 29] Elisha Miller was Married to Elisabeth Lay ye 25th Day of February A.D: 1739/40

These Certifie whome it may Concern that Adriel Ely of Lyme was Married to Sarah Stow of Saybrook in November 14th 1780 by me Pastor of the first Church of Saybrook William Hart
Horace Ely Son of Adriel and Sarah Ely was born August 22nd A.D: 1781

James Chadwick was Married to Martha Chadwick ye 22nd Day of June A.D: 1743
Silas Chadwick Son of James Chadwick and Martha his wife was born the 31st day of January: 1743/4
Allen Chadwick Son of James and Martha Chadwick was born April the first: 1748
Dan Chadwick Son of James and Martha Chadwick was born ye 21st Day of October: 1753
Elisabeth Chadwick Daughter of James and Martha Chadwick was born September 10th 1757

These may Signifie & Certifie that Mr. Elisha Ely was on the first Day of August A.D: 1773: Married to Mrs. Anna Ely by me - George Beckwith Pastor

Elisha Olcot Ely Son of Elisha & Anna Ely was Born Septemr 15th: A.D: 1775
Marsylvia Ely Daughter of Elisha & Anna Ely was Born July 16th A.D: 1777
Eliah Ely Son of Elisha & Anna Ely was Born August ye 23rd A.D: 1779
Mary Ann Daughter of the said Elisha & Anna Ely was born 4th July A.D: 1783
Margret & Deby their daughters was born on the 1st Day of Jany 1786

[p. 30]   These may Certifye that May: 17th: 1743 Nathan Marvin and Lydia Lewis both of Lyme was Married together by me -- George Griswold Pastr of ye 2nd Church in Lyme.
Samuel Marvin Son of Nathan and Lydia Marvin was born ye 14th of February: A.D. 1743/4
Henry Marvin Son of Nathan and Lydia Marvin was born ye 21st day of December: 1745
Martin Marvin Son of Nathan and Lydia Marvin was born May the 6th 1750
Lebbeus Marvin Son of Nathan and Lydia Marvin was born February 10th 1752
Nathan Marvin Son of Nathan and Lydia Marvin was born February ye 9th 1754
Henry Marvin Son of Nathan and Lydia Marvin Died March 15th 1755
Mr. Nathan Marvin above named Departed this life March 15th A.D: 1755

John Moor Junr was Married to Temperance Avery April 2d 1772
Mary their Daughter was born on the 17th Day of May A.D: 1773
Elisha their Son was born on the 21st Day of May A.D: 1775
Avery their Son was born on the 4th Day of February A.D: 1777
Richard their Son was born on the 20th Day of October A.D: 1778
Russell their Son was born on the 9th Day of January A.D: 1781
Lucy their Daughter was born on the 6th Day of October A.D: 1783
Eunice their Daughter was born on the 29th Day of September: 1786
Abigail their Daughter was born on the 29th Day of Septemb 1788
John son of the said John and Temperance was born October 14th Day: A.D: 1790
Abel son of the said John & Temperance was born on the 12th August 1796
William son of the said John & Temberance was born the 15th September 1801

George Wade Junior of Lyme was Married to Hannah Lester of New London the 15th Day of April - A.D: 1742
Elisabeth Wade Daughter of George and Anna Wade was born the 14th of July A.D: 1743
Martin Wade Son of George and Anna Wade was born the 22nd Day of March A.D: 1745

Lyme March ye 14th 1776: Ruben Huntly Son of Wido Mary Huntly was Married to Lovice Huntly Daughter of Amos Huntly pr --- Willm Noyes Just Peace
Micarl Huntly Son of Ruben & Lovice Huntly was born October 27th: A.D: 1777
Richard Huntly Son of Ruben & Lovice Huntly was born March 18th: A.D: 1780
Giles Son of the said Ruben & Lovice was born on the 19th day of Novr A.D: 1781
Taber Son of the said Reuben & Lovice was born on the 27th day of Novr A.D: 1787
Polly Alcy Daughter of the said Reuben & Lovice was born on the 14th of Novr A.D: 1791
Ursula Daughter of the said Reuben & Lovice was born on the 19th of Novr 1797
July Ann Daughter of the said Reuben & Lovice was born on the 9 of Octr 1806

[p. 31]   Joseph Rogers and Diadamy Beckwith were Joyned together in Marriage - ye 15th Day of March: 1743/4
Matthew Rogers Son of Joseph and Diadamy Rogers was born ye 28th of May: A.D: 1746
Joseph Rogers Son of Joseph and Diadamy Rogers was born ye 25th Day of June: A.D: 1749 and Died in November A.D: 1749
Jonathan Rogers Son of Joseph and Diadamy Rogers was born March: 19th A.D. 1751
Lovice Rogers Daughter of Joseph and Diadamy Rogers was born March 15th 1757
Rhoda Rogers Daughter of Joseph and Diadamy Rogers was born April 18th 1758
Diadama Rogers Daughter of Joseph and Diadamy Rogers was born 24th of January 1761
Bettey Rogers Daughter of Joseph and Diadamy Rogers was born June 6th A.D. 1764
Joseph Rogers Son of Joseph and Diadamy Rogers was born February 28 A.D. 1768
Joseph Rogers Died in the Continentall Service the 14th Day of July: A.D 1779

LYME, CONNECTICUT, VITAL RECORDS

Ezra Lee was Married Rebecka Southworth ye 9th Day of October: A.D: 1740
Molle Lee Daughter of Ezra and Rebecka Lee was born ye 19th Day of August: 1741
Nabbe Lee Daughter of Ezra and Rebecka Lee was born ye 28th Day of April: A.D: 1743
Becca Lee Daughter of Ezra and Rebecka Lee was born ye 10th Day of March: A.D: 1745

John Fox Son of John and Mary Fox was born in Lyme ye 16th Day July: 1748
Arnold Fox Son of John and Mary Fox was born ye 29th Day of April: 1750 and Died the 26th Day of April - A.D: 1751
Arnold Fox Son of John and Mary Fox was born ye 8th Day of May A.D: 1752
Danll Fox Son of John and Mary Fox was born the 13th Day of June A.D: 1754

Lucenda Champlin Daughter of Nathan and Sarah Champlin was born April 13th 1767
John Champlin Son of Nathan and Sarah Champlin was born June 9th 1769
Sarah Champlin Daughter of Nathan and Sarah Champlin was born February 24th 1772

[p. 32] Samuel Marvin was Married to Mary Wege ye 2nd Day of April - A.D: 1740
Sarah Marvin daughter of Samuel and Mary Marvin was born ye 27th Day of Jany 1740/1
Martha Marvin daughter of Samuel and Mary Marvin was born ye 2nd Day of May: 1743-

The above said Samll Marvin Died the 18th Day of April: 1786

Elisha Miller Junr and Lydia Beckwith Junr boath of Lyme in New London county were Lawfully Married to Each other on the 24th Day of May: A.D: 1773: by
George Dorr Just- Pace
Ammasa Miller Son of Elisha and Lydia Miller was born January 25th 1774
Ezra Miller Son of Elisha and Lydia Miller was born December 7th 1775
Jeremiah Miller Son of Elisha and Lydia Miller was born January 29th 1778
Elisha Miller Son of Elisha and Lydia Miller was born March 10th 1780
Charles Pinkney
Joseph Miller Son of Elisha and Lydia Miller was born February 24th 1782
Mrs. Elisha Miller above said Died 4th of August A.D: 1782 --
The above named Joseph Miller, appeared and for several reasons request to have his name entered Charles Pinkney instead of Joseph & now request he be known by the name of Charles P. Miller 26th Feby 1803. David F. Sill Reg.

William Ely Junr was Married to Elisabeth Perkins ye 2nd Day of November: A.D: 1737
William Ely Son of William and Elisabeth Ely was born ye 6th Day of October A.D: 1738 and is deseast _____
William Ely 2nd Son of William and Elisabeth Ely was born ye 12th Day of October A.D: 1739
Elisabeth Ely Daughter of William and Elisabeth Ely was born ye first Day of June A.D: 1741 and is deceased
Abraham Ely Son of William and Elisabeth Ely was born ye last day of March: A.D: 1743
2nd Elisabeth Ely Daughter of William and Elisabeth Ely was born ye 20th of December: 1745

These may Signifie and Certifie that Mr. Joseph Burnham was on the 5th Day of June: 1777 Married to Mrs. Miriam Coult Boath of Lyme ----by George Beckwith Pastor

Joseph Burnham Son of Joseph and Miriam Burnham was born 27th Feby: 1779
Joseph Burnham Son of Joseph and Miriam Burnham Died ye 27th of April 1780
Joseph Burnham Son of Joseph and Miriam Burnham was born ye 15th Day of November 1780
Samuel Gardner Burnham Son of Joseph and Miriam Burnham was born January first 1783
Samuel Gardner Burnham Son of Joseph and Miriam Burnham Died Novemr 29th 1783
Polly Burnham Daughter of Joseph and Miriam Burnham was born Febry 2d 1785
Bettey Burnham Daughter of Joseph and Miriam Burnham was born July 31st 1787
Miriam Coult, Daughter of said Joseph and Miriam Burnham was born Jany 28th 1790

Rebecca Daughter of the said Joseph and Miriam Burnham was born
Mrs. Miriam Burnham Wife of the said Joseph died on the 12 day of August 1797

[p. 33] These may Certifye that James Tillitson was Married unto Elisabeth Davis in Lyme on ye 4th Day of February A.D. 1741/2 -- pr George Beckwith Minister
Eunice Tillitson Daughter of James and Elisabeth Tillitson was born ye 12th Day of June ; 1743
Jonathan Tillitson Son of James and Elisabeth Tillitson was born ye 6th Day of April A.D: 1746
Eunice Tillitson Daughter of James and Elisabeth Tillitson Died ye 5th Day of June A.D: 1748
Elisabeth Tillitson Daughter of James and Elisabeth Tillitson was born July the 2nd A.D: 1748
Abigail Tillitson Daughter of James and Elisabeth Tillitson was born February ye 15th A.D: 1751
Eunice Tillitson Daughter of James and Elisabeth Tillitson was born March 28th: A.D: 1753
Jemima Tillitson Daughter of James and Elisabeth Tillitson was born November 3rd: A.D: 1757
James Tillitson Son of James and Elisabeth Tillitson was born April ye 14th A.D: 1760
Danll Tillitson Son of James and Elisabeth Tillitson was born May the 5th: A.D: 1765
Salome Tillitson Daughter of James and Elisabeth Tillitson was born Novemr 6th 1767

Dan Mather and Hannah Gibs was Joined in marriage on the 28 Sept 1788

Daniel Peck was Married to Abigail Lord ye 8th Day of November: 1744 ---
Ahijah Peck Son of Danll and Abigail Peck was born ye 15th Day of Septemr A.D: 1745
Azubah Peck Daughter of Danll and Abigail Peck was born October ye 29th: A.D -- 1747
Daniel Peck above said died the first Day of March: A.D: 1750/51 --
Daniel Peck son of the above sd Daniel and Abigail Peck was born ye 7th Day of July: 1751

East Haddam May 10th. 1765. these may Certifye whome it may Conserern that Thomas Harvey of Lyme and Grace Willey of East Haddam were Joyned in Marriage: July: 18th: 1763 pr Grindal Rawson Clerk ---
Asahel Harvey son of Thomas & Grace Harvey was born June the 3rd Day A.D 1764
Elisa Harvey Daughter of Thomas and Grace Harvey was born January 13th: A.D: 1766

Silvinus Mather and Carolina Chadwick was Legally Joyned in Marriage on the 12th day of May A.D: 1785
Eunice Daughter of the said Silvinus & Carolina was born 18th of Octr: 1786
Jaminah Daughter of the said Silvinus & Carolina was born 2d March 1788
Fanny Daughter of the said Silvinus & Carolina was born 20th day June 1790
Charles Son of the said Silvinus & Carolina was born the 19th day of Augt 1792

[p. 34] Colchester July ye 7th: Anno Dom: 1746 These may Certifye that Mr. Renold Marvin of Lyme and Mrs. Mary Kellogg of Colchester were Married ye Day above said Certified by me Nathaniel Foot Justice-Peace
Ann and Eve Daughters of Deacn Renold and Mary Marvin was born ye 30th Day of Septemr Anno Domin: 1748
Ann Died ye 9th of January A.D: 1748/9
Cloe a negeo Woman Servant of Deacon Renold Marvin Died ye 10th of January A.D: 1748/9
Esther Marvin Daughter of Reynold and Mary Marvin was born February 14th A.D. 1755
Judith Marvin Daughter of Reynold and Mary Marvin was born April 16th A.D: 1757
Mary Marvin Widow & Relic of Decn Reynold Marvin died on the 9th day of March A.D. 1812 aged Ninety seven years.

James Perkins Jr Son of James and Margret Pirkins was born ye first day of February: 1734/5
Lucy Pirkins Daughter of James and Margret Pirkins was born the 27th Day of December: A.D: 1736
Elisabeth Pirkins Daughter of James and Margreet Pirkins was born ye 14th Day of October A.D: 1737
Stephen Pirkins Son of James and Margreet Pirkins was born ye 6th Day of August: A.D: 1739
John Pirkin Son of James and Margreet Pirkins was born ye first Day of December: A.D: 1741
Abijah Pirkins Son of Jame and Margreet Pirkins was born ye 2nd day of October: A.D: 1743
Margret Pirkins Daughter of Jame and Margret Pirkins was born ye 5th day of June: A.D: 1745
Sarah Pirkins Daughter of James and Margret Pirkins was born September the first: A.D: 1747
Isaac Pirkins Son of James and Margret Perkins was born June ye 14th A.D: 1749
Hannah Pirkins Daughter of James and Margret was born August 7th AD 1751 and Died March 9th 1752 - - - - - 1752
Hannah Pirkins Daughter of James and Margret Pirkins was born March 21st 1753
Seth Pirkins Son of James and Margaret Perkins was Born September 18th AD 1754
Lydia Pirkins Daughter of James and Margret Perkins was born August 26th AD 1756
James Pirkins Son of James & Margret Pirkins Died November 19th AD 1760
Stephen Pirkins Son of James & Margret Pirkins Died November ye 13th AD 1760
Ruth Pirkins Daughter of James and Margaret Pirkins was born July 10th: AD 1760 James Perkins died Sept. 7th 1789, Age 83 years
Margaret wife of James Perkins died Nov. 30, 178? age 69
Taken from headstone inscriptions by William Marvin, Town Clerk

[p. 35] Silas Peck and Elizabeth Calkins were Married together the 3rd day of November AD 1746

These may Certifye that Jabez Huntley was Married to Patience Vaun both of Lyme March the 27th AD 1746 by me George Beckwith Lyme December 5th - - AD 1746 the above was Recorded before [page 8]

April 30th: 1728: Ebenezer Mack and Hannah Huntly both of Lyme were Joyned together in a Marriage State by me George Griswold Pastr of ye 2nd Church in Lyme
Phebe Mack Daughter of Ebenezer & Hannah Mack was born January ye 20th Day: 1728/9
Deborah Mack Daughter of Ebenezer and Hannah Mack was born September ye 16 Day: 1730
Solomon Mack Son of Ebenezer and Hannah Mack was born September ye 15 Day: 1732
Hannah Mack Daughter of Ebenezer and Hannah Mack was born October 15th Day: 1734
Samuel Mack Son of Ebenezer and Hannah Mack was born November ye 15th Day: 1736
Hepzibah Mack Daughter of Ebenezer and Hannah Mack was born May ye 7th Day: 1740
Stephen Mack Son of Ebenezer and Hannah Mack was born June ye 15th Day: 1742
Elisha Mack Son of Ebenezer and Hannah Mack was born July ye 16th Day: 1745
Azuba Mack Daughter of Ebenezer & Hannah Mack was born 28th of November: 1748

These are to Certifie that Mr. Samuel Ingraham Junr and Miss Abigail Clark boath of Lyme were Lawfully Married together the 26th Day of November AD: 1772: by me Stephen Johnson Pastor of the First Church in ye Lyme

[p. 36] John Anderson was Married unto Elisabeth Minor Daughter of Mr Joseph Minor the 12th Day February Anno of Domini 1740/41
Elizabeth Anderson Daughter of John and Elisabeth Anderson was born ye 15 Day of January AD 1741/2

Daniel Anderson son of John and Elisabeth Anderson was born ye 14th Day of August AD 1743
Hannah Anderson Daughter of John and Elisabeth Anderson was born ye 12th Day of February AD 1746
Lydia Anderson Daughter of John and Elisabeth Anderson was born Septmr 13 AD 1748
Daniel Anderson Son of John and Elisabeth Anderson Died ye 2nd Day of August 1750
John Anderson Son of John and Elisabeth Anderson was born December 3rd 1751
Eunice Anderson Daughter of John and Elisabeth Anderson was born January 3rd 1756
Theody Anderson Daughter of John and Elisabeth Anderson was born March 23rd 1759

John Beckwith Ship Rite was Married Sarah Anderson ye 7th Day of July: 1724
Margret Beckwith Daughter of John and Sarah Beckwith was born ye 5th Day of March 1726
Sarah Beckwith Daughter of John and Sarah Beckwith was born ye 12th Day of July 1728
Samuel Beckwith Son of John and Sarah Beckwith was born ye 18th Day of August 1730
Anderson Beckwith Son of John and Sarah Beckwith was born ye 28th Day of September 1732
Loraine Beckwith Daughter of John & Sarah Beckwith was born ye 12th Day of July 1735
Hannah Beckwith Daughter of John & Sarah Beckwith was born ye 1st day of May 1738
Hannah Beckwith Daughter of John & Sarah Beckwith died ye last day of August 1742 Entered April ye 14th 1747

These are to Certifie whomesoever it may Concern that the Reverend Mr. Sylvanus Griswold of Springfield & Mrs. Elisabeth Marvin of Lyme were Lawfully Married together 17th Day of Novemr: A.D: 1763 by me Stephen Johnson Pastor of the first Church in sd Lyme -- Dated in sd Lyme - 7th Septemr A.D: 1772

Thomas Graves Son of Mark and Elisabeth Graves was born ye 7th Day of August: 1732 and was born at Marbelhead Neck
Esther Graves Daughter of Mark and Elisabeth Graves was born ye 20th Day of Decemr: 1734
Liverance Graves Daughter of Marke and Elisabeth Graves was born ye 14th Day of February: 1736/7
These two last born at Lyme: Recorded the 8th Day of October: 1750 Pr John Lay 3rd Regr

[p.37] John Marvin was Married to Sarah Brooker of Say-Brook ye 10th Day of February 1746/7
Hepzibah Marvin Daughter of John & Sarah Marvin was born Novemr - 7th: 1747
Sarah Marvin Daughter of John and Sarah Marvin was born ye 27th Day of June: 1749
Giles Marvin Son of John and Sarah Marvin was born ye 23rd Day of Decemr: 1751
Lous Marvin Daughter of John & Sarah Marvin was born May 12th: Day A.D: 1754
Esther Marvin Daughter of John & Sarah Marvin was born September 12th A.D: 1756
John Marvin Son of John and Sarah Marvin was born May the 6th A.D: 1759 and Died the 14th Day of June 1759
Esther Marvin Daughter of John and Sarah Marvin Deceased November 22nd 1759
Lydia Marvin Daughter of John & Sarah Marvin was born ye 4th Day of December 1760
John Marvin Son of John & Sarah Marvin was born ye 15th Day of December 1763
Molley Marvin Daughter of John & Sarah Marvin was born ye March 2nd Day A.D: 1766
Adonijah Marvin Son of John & Sarah Marvin was born at Guilsom in the Town of Surrey in the Province of New Hampshire/ April 16th D 1769

These may Certifye that Nehemiah Marvin of Lyme in New London County was Married to Hester Lord Jr. of ye Same Lyme on January ye 9th Day: 1746 by me George Beckwith Minister of ye Gospel
Phebe Marvin Daughter of Nehemiah and Hester Marvin was born ye 15th Day of October: A.D: 1746
Anna Marvin Daughter of Nehemiah and Hester Marvin was born Decemr 29th - 1748

These Certifie that Mr. Lemuel Lee [pencil] of Lyme on the 28th Day of Septemr: 1783 was Joyned in Marriage with Mrs. Sarah Starlin of Lyme by Ezra Selden Just Paec Lyme December 10th 1783
Lemuel Lee and Sarah Lee had a child Born August 2nd 1784: and Died the same Day.
Martin Lee Son of Lemuel and Sarah Lee was Born May ye: 10th: 1786
Calvin Church Lee Son of Lemuel and Sarah Lee was Born March 4th: 1788
Betsey Starling, Daughter of said Lemuel & Sarah was born Augt 19th A.D: 1790
James Son of the said Lemuel & Sarah was born on the 13 May 1792
Lemuel Son of the said Lemuel & Sarah was born the 27 Novr 1794
Samuel Stirling their son was born on the 5 day of Sepr - 1797
George Dudley their son was born on the 1 day of Sepr - 1798
Sally Marvin their daughter was born on the 3 day of Novr 1803

Elisha Avery Son of Nathaniel and Rachel Avery was born ye 16th Day of November: 1726 Recorded the 30th Day of Novemr - 1754 - Pr John Lay 3rd Reg

[p. 38] Elisha Lee of Lyme in the County of New London was married to Hepzibah Lee of sd Lyme the 25th Day of February: A.D: 1735/6
Phebe Lee daughter of Elisha and Hepzibah Lee was born the 19th Day of December: A.D: 1736
Cate Lee Daughter of Elisha and Hepzibah Lee was born the 10th day of April: A.D: 1739 and died ye 11th Day of October: --- A.D: 1740
Elisha Lee Son of Elisha and Hepzibah Lee was born ye 3rd Day of March: A.D: 1740/41
Seth Lee Son of Elisha and Hepzibah Lee was born ye 25th Day of July: A.D: 1743
Cate Lee Daughter of Elisha and Hepzibah Lee was born ye 8th Day of September: A.D: 1745
Elisha Lee above named Dyed ye 16th Day of April A.D: 1747

Zachariah Sill of Lyme was Married to Prudence Comstock of New London on the 15th Day of February: A.D: 1781: Certified by Evidence --
John Comstock Sill Son of Zachariah and Prudence Sill was born March 18th 1782

Chester in Saybrook August ye 20th: A.D: 1747
These lines may Certifye anyone Concerned that Samuel Ames and his Wife were married together ye 16th of December: A.D: 1746 by me Jared Harrison --

Rachel Rasson Daughter of James and Anna Rasson was born the 10th Day of Novemr - 1748

Franna Higgins Daughter of Benjamin & Jane Higgins was born October 25th

This may Certifie that Solem Covenant of Marriage was Entered into between Rowland Rogers and Elisabeth Champion April 8th - A.D. 1783 as witness my hand - Janson Lee Eldr
Jemima Rogers Daughter of Rowland and Elisabeth Rogers was Born April 3rd 1785
Franna Rogers Daughter of Rowland & Elisabeth Rogers was Born Octobr: 30: 1787
Elisha Son of said Rowland & Elisabeth was born January the 24th day A.D -- 1790
Joshua Rogers Son of the said Rowland & Elisabeth was born on the 1st day of May -- A.D: 1793
Daniel Rogers Son of the said Rowland & Elizabeth was born on the 13th day of Novr 1795
Eliza daughter of this said Rowland & Elizabeth was born on the 10th day of Decr 1799
Rowland & Rebecca being twins was born on the 25th day of May A.D: 1803
Elisha son of said Rowland & Eliza died on the 4th day of June A.D: 1805
Lydia Daughter of said Rowland & Elizabeth was born 27th June 1806
Rebecca Rogers daughter of said Rowland & Elizabeth died February 15th 1838

[p. 39] Samuel Waller of Lyme was Married to Rebecca Thomas ye 20th Day of December: 1744
Zeruiah Waller Daughter of Samuel and Rebecca Waller was born ye 10th Day of August A.D. 1745

Elisabeth Waller Daughter of Samel and Rebecca Waller was born ye 10th Day of May - A.D: 1746

Samel Waller Died ye 2nd Day of Decemr - 1748 -

Mary Waller Daughter of Samuel Waller Deceasd and Rebeckah Waller was born ye 19th Day of June A.D. 1749

Susannah Wood Daughter of David Wood Junr and Mary his wife was born February 15th 1756 -

Silas Wood Son of David Wood Junr & Mary his wife was born January 15th - A.D: 1758

Hannah Wood Daughter of David Wood Junr and Mary his wife was born March 12th: 1760:

Entered July 8th 1761 by John Lay 3d Regr

Simeon Alger of Lyme in the County of New London was Married to Mary Hodge of Glastenbery ye 26th Day of June -- A.D: 1746

Ashbell Alger Son of Simeon and Mary Alger was born ye 18th Day of May: A.D: 1747

Stoton Alger Son of Simeon and Mary Alger was born ye 8th Day of March: A.D: 1749/50

Eunice Alger Daughter of Simeon and Mary Alger was born the 16th Day of February: 1752

These are to Certifie that Mr. Benjamin Higgins and Miss Jane Peck boath of Lyme were Lawfully Married together the 20th Day of November A.D: 1777 by me Dated in Lyme aforesaid 17 May A.D: 1780 Stephen Johnson Pastor of the first Church in said Lyme

Franna Higgins Daughter of Benjamin and Jane Higgins was born October 25th A.D. 1778

Enoch Higgins Son of Benjamin & Jane Higgins was born August 26 1780

Patience the Daughter of Temperance Watrous of Lyme (now Deceasd) was born July the 13th: 1740

Entered by John Lay 3rd Regr

[p. 40] John Terril Junior was Married, Zillah Smith the 31st Day July -- AD 1746

Joseph Terrill Son of John and Zillah Terril was born ye 4th Day of June AD 1747

John Terrill Son of John and Zillah Terril was born the 21st Day of February AD 1749 and died the 15th Day of June: 1740

Susanna Terrill Daughter of John and Zillah Terrill was born April 29th Day AD 1751

Gardner Terrill Son of John and Zillah Terrill was born the 18th Day of February 1754

Zilla Terrill Daughter of John and Zillah Terrill was born June 4th AD 1759

Elisabeth Terrill Daughter of John and Zillah Terrill was born Septmr 4 1756

These are to Certifie that Mr. Thomas Marvin and Miss Sarah Lay, boath of Lyme, were Lawfully Married together, the 23rd Day of May AD 1784 by me -- Stephen Johnson Pastor of the first Church in sd Lyme

Dated in Lyme 11th of August 1784: Recorded 11th of August 1784 by John Lay 2nd Clerk _____

Lucy Marvin Daughter of Thomas & Sarah Marvin was born the 11th of February 1785 and died the first Day of July: AD 1785

Thomas Marvin Son of Thomas and Sarah Marvin was born July 7th AD - 1787

Abigal Daughter of said Thomas & Sarah was born

Stephen Beckwith was Married to Jerusha Watrouse the 16th Day of December AD 1742

Cyrus Beckwith Son of Stephen & Jerusha Beckwith was born ye 18th Day of October AD 1743

Jerusha Beckwith wife to Stephen Beckwith died ye 16th Day of May AD 1746

Stephen Beckwith was Married to Hannah Nuton ye 27th Day of May 1747

These are to Certifye, whomsoever it may Conserone that Mr. Zachariah Marvin Junr & Mrs. Anna Lee both of Lyme were Lawfully Married together the 23rd Day of July AD 1761: by me Stephen Johnson Pastor of the first Church in sd Lyme. Dated in Lyme 13th August AD 1776: _____

Eunice Marvin Daughter of Zachary & Ana Marvin was born May 22nd AD 1766

Lee Marvin Son of Zachariah & Ana Marvin was born September 16th AD 1768

LYME, CONNECTICUT, VITAL RECORDS

Zachariah Marvin Son of Zachariah & Ana Marvin was born June 5th AD 1771
Lucinda Marvin Daughter of Zachariah & Ana Marvin was born Septemr 23rd AD 1773
Ane Marvin Wife of sd Zachh Marvin Junr Died March the first Day: AD 1777
Lee Marvin Son of Zachh Marvin Junr and Ana his wife Died ye 21st Day of April 1777

[p. 41]   Hue Grilley was Married to Temprance Roland ye 8th Day of March AD 1726/7
Elisabeth Grilley Daughter of Hue and Temprance Grilley was born ye 5th Day of April 1728
ye above sd Elizabeth died sometime in the Month of October AD 1728
Jehaly Grilley Son of Hue and Temprance Grilley was born ye 8th Day of February AD 1728/9
John Grilley Son of Hue and Temprance Grilley was born ye 19th Day of June AD 1732
Elisabeth Grilley Daughter of Hue and Temprance Grilley was born ye 30th Day of June AD 1736
Henry Grilley Son of Hue and Temprance Grilley was born ye 19th December AD 1738
Lousia Grilley Daughter of Hue and Temprance Grilley was born ye first Day of September 1746

Lyme March ye: 23rd: 1768: These may Certify that Mr. Abner Griffing was married to Mrs. Sally Champlin ye 4 Day of July 1765 --- Lyme --- Benjamin Lee Justice of the Peace
Deborah Griffing Daughter of Abner and Sally Griffing was born April 8th: A.D: 1766
Christopher Griffing Son of Abner and Sally Griffing was Born August 31st: A.D: 1767
John Griffing Son of Abner and Salley Griffing was born April 22nd - A.D: 1770
Abner Griffing Son of Abner and Salley Griffing was Born January 22d - A.D: 1773
Salley Griffing Daughter of Abner & Salley Griffing was born August ye 7th A.D: 1775
Fanny Daughter of the said Abner & Sally was born November 22d A.D: 1786

Edward Lay Jr.was Married to Martha Center ye 24th Day of February A.D: 1742/3
Jane Lay Daughter of Edward and Martha Lay was born ye 5th Day of December: A.D: 1743
Elisha Lay son of Edward and Martha Lay was born ye 5th Day of November: 1746 and Died ye 3rd Day of Decemr_____ A.D: 1746
Jane Lay Daughter of Edward and Martha Lay Died the 14th Day of March: A.D: 1758

February 9th 1783: then Mr. David Mack of said Lyme was Married to Mrs. Sarah Rogers of Lyme aforesaid by me -- Daniel Miner Pastor of the strict Congregational Church
Recorded ye 26th of February: 1783: by John Lay 2nd Regr.
David Mack Son of David & Sarah Mack was born the 2nd Day of Novemr: 1784

[p.42]   Entered February 6th 1747/8
John B ning Junr was Married to Margaret DeWolf July ye 15th Day: A.D: 1734
John Banning Son of John Banning Junr & Margaret his wife was born ye 8th of April: 1735
Benjamin Banning Son of John Banning Junr & Margaret his wife was born ye 1st of Janr: 1740
Rureany Banning Daughter of John Banning Junr & Margaret his wife was born ye 20th of May: 1742
Margaret Banning wife of sd John Banning Junr Died ye March ye 31st: 1744

Recorded ye 6th Day of February 1747/8
John Banning Junr was Married to ye Widow Jemima Peck ye 22nd Day of May in ye year: A.D: 1744
Ebenezer Banning Son of John Banning Junr & Jemima his wife was born ye sixth Day of February A.D. 1745
William Banning Son of John Banning Junr & Jemima his wife was born ye 5th Day of November in ye year -- A.D: 1747
Joseph Banning Son of John Banning Junr & Jemima his wife was born ye 6th Day of August: 1748

Margaret Banning Daughter of John Banning Junr and Jemima his wife was born ye 6th Day of August: A.D: 1750
Sarah Banning Daughter of John Banning Junr and Jemima his wife was born April 20th: Day A.D: 1753
Elizabeth Peck Daughter of William & Jemima Peck was born ye 10th Day of December: 1736
Larumy Peck Daughter of William and Jemima Peck was born ye 12th Day of July: A.D: 1738
William Peck Son of William and Jemima Peck was born ye 11th Day of February A.D: 1740
The above Recorded Pr order of John Banning Junr the 6th Day of February: A.D: 1747/8 pr John Lay ye 3rd Regr
William Peck (son of William Peck Deceasd) died ye 20th Day of April: A.D: 1749
Isaac Bumpas Departed this Life the 19th Day of December: 1761

[p. 43] Richard Ely Junr was Married to Phebe Hubbard his Second Wife ye 26th Day of October: 1732
Richard Ely Son of Richard Ely Junr was born September ye 30th 1733
Seth Ely was born December the 11th 1734
Elihu Ely was born November the 18th 1736
Elihu Ely Died ye 7th Day of December 1736
Elihu Ely ye 2nd was born November ye 15th 1737
Josiah Ely was born July ye 20th 1739
Robert Ely was born June ye 26th 1741
Phebe Ely Daughter of Richd Ely Junr and Phebe his wife was born May ye 16th 1743
Hepzibah Ely Daughter of Richd Ely Junr & Phebe his wife was born June ye 6th 1745
David Ely Son of Richd Ely Junr and Phebe his wife was born 7th Day of July: A.D: 1749

Lyme October 18th A.D. 1781: then Mr. Samuel Peck of sd Lyme was Married to Mrs. Lucretia Ingraham widow of Francis Ingraham of Lyme aforesaid by me Daniel Miner Pastor of the Strict Conl: Church

Freelove Bump was born the 30th day of September --- A.D - 1772

William Harrison was Married to Experience Wood May ye 23rd Day: 1746 [sic prob. 1735-6]
William Harrison's first childe was born February ye 15th: 1737 and Died April ye 22nd Day: 1738: aged one year and three months
William Harrison Son of William and Experience Harrison was born September 22nd: 1739
Elihu Harrison Son of William and Experience Harrison was born January ye 24th: 1742
Dorothy Harrison Daughter of William and Experience Harrison was born May ye 23rd: 1746
Experience, wife to William Harrison Died ye 6th Day of June: A.D: 1749

Daniel Stephenson was Married to Jerusha Mather on the 18th Day of July A.D. 1790
Daniel their Son was born on the 14th Day of April -- A.D. 1791 and died on the 4th day of November 1792
Daniel Son of said Daniel and Jerusha was born the 12th day of May A.D. 1794

[p. 44] Enoch Lord was Married to Hepsibah Marvin ye 31st Day of March: A.D: 1748
Richard Lord Son of Enoch and Hepsibah Lord was born the 15th Day of Septemr: 1752
Ann Lord Daughter of Enoch & Hepsibah Lord was born ye 4th Day of Decemr - 1754
Joseph Lord Son of Enoch and Hephzibah Lord was Born June the 3rd: A.D: 1757
Enoch Lord Son of Enoch and Hephzibah Lord was born July 28th Day A.D -- 1760
William Lord Son of Enoch & Hepzibah Lord was born July 16th Day A.D -- 1762
Jean Lord Daughter of Enoch and Hepzibah Lord was born August 13th: 1764
Lynde Lord Son of Enoch and Hepzibah Lord was born July 17th 1767
Hephzibah Lord Daughter of Enoch and Hephzibah Lord was born June 30th: 1770

Richard Lord Esqr Departed this life on the 26th Day of August 1776 aged 86: years

Thomas Giddings Junr of Lyme was Married unto Mary Coult of the same Town of Lyme the first Day of May A.D: 1746 by me -- George Beckwith Minister in sd Lyme
David Giddings Son of Thomas and Mary Giddings was born ye 18th Day of June A.D: 1747
Dan Giddings Son of Thomas Giddings Junr and Mary his wife was born August 4th: 1749
Lydia Clark Daughter of Eleaser and Joanna Clark was born August 30th -- 1756
Alice Rogers Wido & Relic of Jona Rogers departed this life Jany 7th A.D 1790
Elizabeth Davis Daughter of Wm Davis and Esther his wife was born June 11th 1754

[p. 45] Joseph Tubbs was Married to Lucia Robins ye 14th Day of January A.D: 1735/6 --
Hepsibah Tubb Daughter of Joseph & Lucia Tubbs was born March 11th: A.D: 1737/8
Abisha Tubbs Son of Joseph & Lucia Tubbs was born June 16th A.D: 1740
Dan Tubbs Son of Joseph and Lucia Tubbs was born June ye 1st Day: 1743
Zephariah Tubbs Son of Joseph and Lucia Tubbs was born January ye 6th: A.D: 1745/6
Frederick Tubbs Son of Joseph and Lucia Tubbs was born July ye 4th Day: A.D: 1748
Dan Tubbs Son of Joseph and Lucia Tubbs Deceased August 22nd: A.D --: 1748
Zephaniah Tubbs Son of Joseph and Lucia Tubbs was born Septemr ye 3rd Day A.D: 1748
Lucia Tubs Daughter of Joseph and Lucia Tubbs was born ye 16th of April: A.D- 1750
Ann Tubbs Daughter of Joseph and Luce Tubbs was born October 9th A.D- 1752
Lydia Tubbs Daughter of Joseph & Luc Tubbs was born June 28th A.D -- 1756
Lucy Tubbs Daughter of Joseph and Lucy Tubbs was born December 31st: A.D - 1762

Joshua Champion Junr was Married to Elishabah Beckwith ye 17th Day of October: 1742
Lydia Champion Daughter of Joshua Champion Junr and Elishabah his wife was born ye 3rd Day of August: 1745
Joshua Champion Son of Joshua Champion Junr and Elishabah his wife was born ye 3rd Day of February: 1746/7

Daniel Daniels Junr and Sarah Wait were Married to Each other on on the 28th Day of November: 1782   Certified Pr me Richard Wait Junr Justice of ye Peace
Bill Daniels Son of Daniel and Sarah Daniels was born October 6th Day -- 1783
Joseph Daniels Son of Daniel and Sarah Daniels was born May 27th: 1786

[p. 46] John Harvey ye 2nd was Married to Elisabeth Rathbone ye 19th Day of October: A.D: 1747--
Pheby Harvey Daughter of John and Elisabeth Harvey was born ye 28th Day of October A.D: 1748 --
Thomas Harvey Son of John and Elisabeth Harvey was born April ye 20th: 1740
Elisabeth Harvey Daughter of John and Elisabeth Harvey was born September ye 20th: 1741
John Harvey Son of John and Elisabeth Harvey was born August ye 28th - A.D: 1743
Anna Harvey Daughter of John and Elisabeth Harvey was born August ye 28th: 1743
Berthenie Harvey Daughter of John and Elisabeth Harvey was born ye 6th June A.D: 1745
Elisha Harvey Son of John and Elisabeth Harvey was born ye 11th of February: 1746/7
These four last Children was born in East Haddam --

Lyme October ye 6th: 1746 Nathan Huntly and Luce Smith both of Lyme were Married togeth: Pr me George Griswold Pastr of ye 2nd Church in Lyme
Azuba Huntly Daughter of Nathan & Luce Huntly was born June ye 28th: A.D: 1747
Azubah Huntly Daughter of Nathan and Luce Huntly Deceasd ye 31st Octor: 1748
Rufus Huntly Son of Nathan and Luce Huntly was born ye 4th Day of June: 1749
Isaiah Huntly Son of Nathan and Luce Huntly was born Novemr 24th A.D - 1751
Nathan Huntly Son of Nathan and Luce Huntly was born August ye 9th - A.D. 1754
Russel Huntly Son of Nathan and Luce Huntly was born June 26th: A.D - 1758
Elisha Huntly Son of Nathan & Luce Huntly was born December: 15th 1760
Lewmon Huntly Son of Nathan and Luce Huntly was born May ye 15th -

These may Certifye that Gideon Watrous and Tabitha Wait was Married March 29th Day 1778   Pr Richard Wait Justice of ye Peace

Jared Watrous Son of Gideon & Tabitha Watrous was born Decemr ye 21st: 1778
Gideon Watrous Son of Gideon & Tabitha Watrous was Born Decemr: 15th A.D: 1780
Samuel Watrous Son of Gideon & Tabitha Watrous was born March first Day: 1783
Fanne Watrous Daughter of Gideon & Tabitha Watrous was born May 21st - 1786

[p. 48 No page 47] Thomas Clark was Married to Rebeckah Watrouse of Lyme the 25th Day of November Anno Que Domini - 1730
Issac Clark Son of Thomas and Rebeckah Clark was born March 31st - 1731
Watrouse Clark Son of Thomas and Rebeckah Clark was born February ye 16th 1733
Nun Clark Son of Thomas and Rebeckah Clark was born ye 3rd of July- 1736
Thomas Clark Son of Thomas and Rebeckah Clark was born April ye 9th - 1740
Lot Clark Son of Thomas and Rebeckah Clark was born January ye 4th 1746
Rebeckah Clark Daughter of Thomas and Rebeckah Clark was born March ye 31st: 1748

These are to Certifie that Mr. John Parsons & Mrs. Joanna Mather boath of Lyme were Lawfully Married together the 25th Day of February A.D: 1779 by me - Stephen Johnson Pastor of First Church in Lyme Dated Decemr 1st 1780
Lous Parsons Daughter of John & Joanna Parsons was Born November 25th: 1779
Abigail Parsons Daughter of John & Joanna Parsons was born August 28th: 1782
Deborah Parsons Daughter of John & Joanna Parsons was born August 25th A.D: 1784
Abigail Parsons Daughter of John & Joanna Parsons Died October 29th A.D: 1784
Mrs. Joanna Parsons Wife of John Parsons above said Departed this life January the 31st Day 1786

This may Certifie that John Parsons and Lois Wait were Married to Each other on the first Day of October: 1786: by me Richd Wait Junr Justice of Peace
Joanne Parsons Daughter of John and Lous Parsons was Born July 31st: 1787
Abigail Daughter of John & Lois Parsons was Born the 12th Day of Octr 1788
Phebe their Daughter was born on Thursday the 15th Day of April AD 1790
William their Son was born on Sunday the 30th day of July A.D. 1791

Benajah Huntly's Children's births Recorded
Nehemiah Huntly Son of Benajah; and Esther Huntly was born October ye 2nd: 1743 sd Nehemah was born in ye Town Called South Hole on Long Island in ye Province of New York
Richard Harris Huntly Son of Benajah and Esther Huntly was born ye 2nd of Decemr: 1745
Benajah Huntly Son of Benajah and Esther Huntly was born January 6th A.D: 1747/8
These two last children born in Lyme ---

Mrs. Sarah Griswold Departed this Life the 29th Day of December: 1759
Anna: Daughter of Anna Brockway was born April 17th 1767
Samel Saunders So Called: Son of Sibbel Fox was born Decemr 16th A.D. 1767
Hannah Daughter of Samuel & Phebe Saunders was born the 28th day of February 1792
Nathan Son of the said Samuel & Phebe was born on the 5th day of Feby 1794
Asa Son of the said Samuel & Phebe was born on the 31st day of March AD 1796
Phebe Daughter of the said Samuel & Phebe was born on the 27th March AD 1798
Albert Son of the said Samuel & Phebe was born on the 10th day of June A.D 1800
William Son of the sd Samuel & Phebe was born on the 14 day of October -- 1801
Christopher Palmer Son of the said Samuel & Phebe was born the 9th day of February - 1804
Samuel Son of the said Samuel & Phebe was born the 10th day of May 1806
Phebe the daughter of the said Samuel & Phebe was born 23: March 1809

[p. 49] Mr. Stephen Johnson of Newark in East New Jersey: and Mrs. Elisabeth Diodate of New Haven were Joyned in Marriage to Each other July 26th Anno Domini 1744 by the Revnd Mr. Joseph Noyes Minister in New Haven
A True Copy of Record: Test Samel Bishop Junr Town Clerk in sd New Haven
Diodate the Son of Mr. Stephen Johnson and Mrs. Elisabeth Johnson was born July 29th: 1745

A True Copy Taken of from New Haven's Reocrd - Pr me Samll Bishop Junr - Town Clerk
Sarah Johnson Daughter of the Revernd Mr. Stephen & Mrs. Elisabeth Johnson was Born ye 29th Day of January: Anno que Domini: 1747/8
Elisabeth Johnson Daughter of the Revend Mr. Stephen & Mrs. Elisabeth Johnson was born ye 22nd Day of November: Anno que Domini: 1750
Stephen Johnson Son of the Revnd Mr. Stephen & Mrs. Elisabeth Johnson was born the 22nd Day of February A.D: 1753
Catherine Johnson Daughter of the Revd Mr. Stephen & Mrs. Elisabeth Johnson was born the 6th Day of April: 1755
William Johnson Son of the Reverend Mr. Stephen and Mrs. Elisabeth Johnson was born the 29th Day of June: AD: 1757
Mrs. Elisabeth Johnson wife of the sd Reverend Mr. Stephen Johnson Died May 2nd A.D: 1761
These are to Certifie Whomsoever it may Concern that the Reverend Mr. Stephen Johnson of Lyme and Mrs. Mary Blague of Saybrook were Lawfully Married together on the first Day of December: A.D: 1762 by me - George Beckwith Pastor of the 3rd Church Lyme. Dated in Lyme 15th March: 1764
Mary Johnson Daughter of Revernd Mr. Stephen Johnson and Mary his wife was born August 9th A.D. 1768
Nathll Johnson Son of Revernd Mr. Stephen and Mrs. Mary Johnson was born August 5th A.D 1770 and Died March 4th 1771
Mrs. Mary Johnson Wife of the Reverd Mr. Stephen Johnson Died the 10th Day of December: AD 1772
William Johnson Son of the Reverend Mr. Stephen Johnson and Mrs. Elisabeth Johnson Died January 28th A.D: 1779

November ye 12th Anno Dom: 1734: then were Married together Mr. John Lord of Lyme and Mrs. Hannah Rogers Daughter of Lieut. Joseph Rogers and of Mrs. Sarah Rogers his wife of Milford: Married, Certified and attested January ye 18th 1734/5
Anna Lord Daughter of John and Hannah Lord was born April 4th: 1736
Sarah Lord Daughter of John and Hannah Lord was born January 19th A.D: 1738
John Lord Son of John and Hannah Lord was born May the 19th: A.D 1740
Luce Lord Daughter of John and Hannah Lord was Born April 24th 1749

[page 50]   This is to Certifie that Henry Roland of Lyme Married with Irene Palmer of Stoneingtown ye 27th Day of March: 1735 Pr Joseph Fish Pastr of a Church - North Stonington Octr: 14th: 1735
Henry Roland Son of Henry and Irene Roland was born ye 15th Day of October AD: 1742
Irene Roland Daughter of Henry & Irene Roland was born June ye 5th AD: 1745
Elisabeth Roland Daughter of Henry and Irene Roland was born July ye 30th AD: 1747

These Certifie that the Subscribeing authority married Silas Wood and Elisabeth Rogers of Lyme to Each other August ye 10th 1786 Test Seth Ely Justice of Peace
Benjamin Wood Son of Silas and Elisabeth Wood 20th of August: 1787 was born
William Son of said Silas & Elisabeth was born the 16th day of July AD 1789
Russel Son of said Silas & Elisabeth born May 6th AD 1791
Polly Daughter of said Silas & Elisabeth born the 8th day June 1793
Betsey Daughter of said Silas & Elisabeth born July 6th AD 1796
Fanny Daughter of said Silas & Elisabeth born January 17th AD 1798
Elisabeth Wife of said Silas Died January 17th AD 1798

Edward Champlin was Married to Elisabeth Latham ye 9th Day of Decemr: 1742
Bettey Champlin Daughter of Edward and Elisabeth Champlin was born Septemr 28th: 1743
Sally Champlin Daughter of Edward and Elisabeth Champlin was born July ye 12th AD 1745
Molley Champlin Daughter of Edward and Elisabeth Champlin was born March ye 14th: 1747

John Champlin Son of Edward and Elisabeth Champlin was born April ye first: A.D: 1749
Edward Champlin Son of Edward & Elisabeth Champlin was Born May ye 3rd AD 1751
Seabuary Champlin Son of Edward & Elisabeth Champlin was Born Decemr: 4th 1753
Nabbey Champlin Daughter of Edward & Elisabeth Champlin was Born May ye 3rd 1757
Caleb Champlin Son of Edward and Elisabeth Champlin was Born Febry: 20th: 1759
Rebeckah Champlin Daughter of Edward & Elisabeth Champlin was born March: 2nd: 1761
Fanny Champlin Daughter of Edward & Elisabeth Champlin was Born July 17th: 1763
Lucretia Champlin Daughter of Edward & Elisabeth Champlin was Born April 11th 1766
John Champlin Son of Edward & Elisabeth Champlin Died July 7th 1751
John Champlin Son of Edward & Elisabeth Champlin was Born Septemr 28th AD: 1768

Thomas Munsill and Anne Tillitson both of Lyme was Lawfully Joynd togather in Marraige Covenant on the 15th day of May AD 1788
William Son of the said Thomas & Anna was born 5th of November 1788
Thomas Son of the said Thomas & Anna was born 29th day of Septr AD 1790

[page 51] These may Certifye whomesoever it may Concern that Jeremiah Brown and Lydia Smith both Inhabitants of Lyme were married on the 3rd Day of April in -- Anno Domini: 1749: Lyme October 6th 1749: Test Stephen Johnson Pastor of the First Church in Sd: Lyme
Abigail Brown Daughter of Jeremiah and Lydia Brown was born ye 2nd Day of July: 1751
Elisabeth Brown Daughter of Jeremiah & Lydia Brown was born 27th Day of Jany: 1754
Bridgham Brown Son of Jeremiah and Lydia Brown was born 20th Day of January 1758
Lydia Brown Daughter of Jeremiah & Lydia Brown was Born October 23rd AD 1760
William Brown Son of Jeremiah & Lydia Brown was Born June 7th AD - 1763
James Sheffield Brown Son of Jeremiah & Lydia Brown was Born March 18th 1766

These may Certifie whomesoever it may Concern that Mr. Moses Noyes and Mrs. Hannah Selden both of Lyme were married ye 2nd Day of June 1748 - Pr me Stephen Johnson - Lyme January 2nd: 1749/50
Esther Noyes Daughter of Moses and Hannah Noyes was born the 16th Day of May AD: 1749
Calvin Noyes Son of Moses and Hannah Noyes was born the 19th Day of November: A.D: 1751
Moses Noyes Son of Moses and Hannah Noyes was born the 9th Day of December: A.D: 1753
Hannah Noyes Daughter of Moses & Hannah Noyes was born the 17th Day of February A.D: 1756
Anna Noyes Daughter of Moses & Hannah Noyes was born March 27th Day - A.D 1758 and Departed this Life January the first 1761
Mary Noyes Daughter of Moses and Hannah Noyes was born January ye 22nd A.D 1760 and Departed this Life June the 15th 1761
Mindwell Noyes Daughter of Moses & Hannah Noyes was born April 4th AD: 1762
Elisabeth Noyes Daughter of Moses & Hannah Noyes was born September 3rd 1765
Eunice Noyes Daughter of Moses & Hannah Noyes was born August 16th: AD 1767

Daniel Rogers of Lyme was legally Joined in Marriage with Sarah Fox of East Haddam on the 17th Day of December 1789
Daniel Son of the said Daniel & Sarah was born the 20th day of May 1793
Sarah daughter of the sd Daniel & Sarah was born the 6 day of May 1797

[page 52] These may Certifie whomesoever it may Concern that Phinehas Watrouse and Rhode Smith both of Lyme were Married March ye 3rd: 1747/8 Pr me Stephen Johnson Pastor - Lyme 3rd of January: 1749/50
Patience Watrouse Daughter of Phinehas and Rhode Watrouse was born January ye 25th Day: 1748/9
Lucretia Watrous Daughter of Phinehas and Rhoda Watrous was born 21st Day of August 1752

Gershom Watrous Son of Phinehas and Rhoda Watrous was born the 28th of November: AD 1754
Phineas Watrous Son of Phineas and Rhode Watrous was born July 28th Day AD 1758
Rhoda Watrous Daughter of Phineas and Rhode Watrous was born July 23rd Day AD 1763
Azubah Watrous Daughter of Phineas & Rhode Watrous was born July 18th Day AD 1766
Smith Watrous Son of Phinehas and Rhoda Watrous was born December 16th AD 1768
Azubah Watrous Daughter of Phinehas & Rhoda Watrous Died January 12th AD 1769
Andrew Watrous Son of Phinehas and Rhoda Watrous was born Septemr 4th AD 1771

August 13th 1747 Abner Lee and Elisabeth Lee both of Lyme were married together by me - George Griswold Pastor of the Second Church in Lyme
Ezra Lee Son of Abner and Elisabeth Lee was born January 21st: 1748/9
Lucinda Lee Daughter of Abner and Elisabeth Lee was born January 16th 1752
Lydia Lee Daughter of Abner and Elisabeth Lee was born the first Day of August: 1754
Lydia Lee Daughter of Abner and Elisabeth Lee Died the 15th of March A.D: 1755
Dan Lee Son of Abner and Elisabeth Lee was born the 6th Day of February A.D: 1757
John Lee Son of Abner & Elisabeth Lee was born ye 6th Day of April A.D. 1759
John Lee Son of Abner and Elisabeth Lee Died ye 26th Day of April: A.D - 1760
Abner Lee Son of Abner and Elisabeth Lee was born May 20th A.D - 1763
John Allen Lee Son of Abner and Elisabeth Lee was born 26th Day of May 1765
Clarisea Lee Daughter of Abner and Elisabeth Lee was born January 27th 1769 and Died June 13th 1770
Elisabeth Lee Wife of sd Abner Lee Died Novembr 2nd A.D 1781
Lyme March 5th A.D: 1782: then Capt. Abner Lee of Lyme was married to Mrs. Lucretia Jewit of Lyme aforesaid by me - Daniel Miner Pastor of strict Congregational Church
Elisabeth Lee Daughter of Abner and Lucretia Lee was born January first A.D: 1783

[page 53]   Feby 26th 1749/50
Amos Huntly and Phebe Mack -- married May ye 21st: 1749 - Pr Benjamin Lee Justice of the Peace
Martin Huntly Son of Amos and Phebe Huntly was born ye 27th Day of September: 1750
Huldah Huntly Daughter of Amos & Phebe Huntly was born ye first Day of August: 1752 and Eight weeks and two Days after she was born she Died -
Phebe Huntly Daughter of Amos and Phebe Huntly was born September ye 10th 1754
Dan Huntly Son of Amos and Phebe Huntly was born November ye 25th - 1756
Lovice Huntly Daughter of Amos and Phebe Huntly was born February ye 11th: 1759
Azubah Huntly Daughter of Amos & Phebe Huntly was born May 22nd - AD 1764
Amos Huntly Son of Amos and Phebe Huntly was born March: ye: 17th AD: 1764
Reu Huntly Son of Amos & Phebe Huntly was born October 28th AD: 1766
Lucy Huntly Daughter of Amos and Phebe Huntly was born July 7th AD 1769
Molley Huntly Daughter of Amos & Phebe Huntly was born Decemr 6th: AD: 1775
Molley their Daughter departed this Life on the 21st Day of February 1792
Amos Huntly the Elder died on the 1st day of September AD 1804

William Tubbs was married to Rebeckah Daniels ye 23rd Day of October 1729
Clement Tubbs Son of Willm & Rebeckah Tubbs was born ye 22 Day of June: 1733
Lemuel Tubbs Son of Willm and Rebeckah Tubbs was born October ye 8th Day 1734
Israel Tubbs Son of William and Rebeckah Tubbs was born August ye first Day: 1737
William Tubbs Son of William and Rebeckah Tubbs was born May ye first Day: 1740
Lydia Tubbs Daughter of William and Rebeckah Tubbs was born April ye 15th Day: 1742
Rebeckah Tubbs Daughter of Willm and Rebeckah Tubbs was born March ye 31st Day: 1744
Jonathan Tubbs Son of William and Rebeckah Tubbs was born September ye 8th Day: 1746
Judith Tubbs was born ye 13th Day of April: 1748

Martin Huntly and Mehetabel Sill Both of Lyme were Married to Each other on the 26th Day of August A.D: 1773 as certified by Evidence --
Charlotte Huntly Daughter of Martin & Mehetabel Huntly was born January 9th 1775
Jemima Huntly Daughter of Martin & Mehetabel Huntly was born January first: 1777
Jamima Daughter of the said Martin Mehetbl died on the 12 of July 1777
Sill Son of the said Martin & Mehetbl was born on the 17 day of Decr 1779
Gurdon Son of the said Martin & Mehitble was born on the 3d day of June 1782
Erastus Son of the said Martin & Mehitable was born on the 5th day of Augt 1785
Mehelable Wife of the said martin died on the 12 day of January - 1786
Martin Huntly was Married to Phebe Mack on the 3 day of September 1787
Martin Huntly Son of the sd Martin & Phebe was born on the 27th Jany 1789
Selden Son of the said Martin & Phebe was born on the 13th March AD 1791
Mehetable Daughter of the sd Martin & Phebe was born on the 17th Feby AD 1793
Clarry Daughter of the sd Martin & Phebe was born on the 5 September 1795
Elisha Son of the said Martin & Phebe was born on the 27 June AD 1797
Polly Daughter of the sd Martin & Phebe was born on the 4th April AD 1798
Erastus son of the sd Martin & Mehetable died in the West Indies in the winter in the year 1801

[page 54]   Amos Tinker Junr was married to Hannah Minor ye 7th Day of January AD: 1741/2
Joseph Tinker Son of Amos and Hannah Tinker was born January ye 24th 1742/3
Jane Tinker Daughter of Amos and Hannah Tinker was born January 18th Day 1744/5
Azubah Tinker Daughter of Amos and Hannah Tinker was born September ye 6th 1746
Silas Tinker Son of Amos and Hannah Tinker was born ye 25th Day of Novemr: 1748

Daniel Ayers was Married to Betsey Smith Jany 6th AD 1780

James Smith Junr was Joyned in Marriage with Mary Hayes ye 30th Day of Novemr A.D: 1748 -
Parnal Smith Daughter of James Smith and Mary his wife was born Septemr 26: 1749

Abselom Beckwith of Lyme was married to Lydia Haynes of New London the 27th Day of August AD 1767 by Benjamin Lee Justice of Peace as appears by said Lees Book of Record

Capt. Elisha Marvin died on the 31st day of December in the year 1801

Phebe daughter of Martin & Phebe Huntly was born on the 2nd of Novr 1802
Erastus Calvin their son was born on the 19th day of April 1805

[page 55]   Noah Beebe was married to Edey Waller the 2nd Day of May: AD: 1750
Lydia Beebe Daughter of Noah and Edey Beebe was born ye 17th Day of May: 1751
Eunice Beebe Daughter of Noah & Edey Beebe was born ye 7th Day of February: 1753
Azariah Beebe Son of Noah and Edey Beebe was born ye 20th Day of January: 1755
Edey Beebe Daughter of Noah & Edey Beebe was born ye 8th Day of January 1758
Noah Beebe Son of Noah & Edey Beebe was born the 4th Day of March: A.D 1761
Molley Beebe Daughter of Noah & Edey Beebe was born September the 24th: A.D 1764

These may certify that Mr. Manasah Leach was on the 3d day of March A.D 1774 Married to Irena Ely Both of Lyme by me. George Beckwith
Richard Son of the said Manassah & Irena was born the 25th day of Decr AD 1774
Lydia Daughter of the said Manassah & Irena was born the 22nd of October AD 1776
Elisha Son of the said Manassah & Irena was born the 6th of June AD 1779
Polly Daughter of the said Manassah & Irena was born the 7th day of May AD 1781
Elijah Son of the said Manassah & Irena was born the 1st day of May AD 1784
Irena Daughter of the said Manassah & Irena was born the 16th of March AD 1787
Deborah Daughter of the said Manassah & Irena was born the 22 of March AD 1789
Enoch Son of the said Manassah & Irena was born the 20 of January AD 1794

This may certify that Capt. Manassah Leech & Mrs. Chianna Keeny were Joined together in marriage August 21st 1823 by me - Thomas W. Strickland Just of Peace

John Giddings was married to Susannah Tozer ye 27th Day of Septemr - 1739
John Giddings Son of John and Susannah Giddings was born Septemr ye 9th 1740
Lous Giddings Daughter of John & Susannah Giddings was born July 28th: A.D: 1743

Lyme November 24th 1764 these may Certifye whomsoever it may Concern that Benjamin Hudson Junr and Bridget Brockway both of Lyme were Lawfully married togeth the 29th day of December A.D. 1761 Pr me Stephen Johnson Pastor of the first Church in sd Lyme.
Samll Hudson Son of Benjamin and Bridget Hudson was Born April 18th: A.D: 1762
Brooks Hudson Son of Benjamin and Bridget Hudson was Born January 15th 1764

Rachel Starlin Daughter of Daniel and Demiss Starlin was born Decemr: 29: 1764
Daniel Starlin Son of Danll & Demis Starlin was born April 27th AD 1768
James Starlin Son of Danll & Demiss Starlin was Born May 17th A.D: 1770
Mary Starlin daughter of Danll & Demis Starlin was Born Novemr 3rd: 1772
The children above mentioned were all of them Born in the Town of East Haddam
Sarah Starlin Daughter of Danll & Demis Starlin was born Novemr 4th A.D. 1774 in the Town of Lyme

[page 56] Joseph Huntly of Lyme in New London County was married to Eunice Welch ye 24th Day of October A.D: 1741
Susannah Huntly Daughter of Joseph and Eunice Huntly was born ye 18th of Decemr: 1742
Hannah Huntly Daughter of Joseph & Eunice Huntly was born February ye 23rd A.D: 1744/5
Joseph Huntly Son of Joseph and Eunice Huntly was born January ye 13th A.D: 1746/7
Eunice Huntly Daughter of Joseph & Eunice Huntly was born February ye 14th: A.D: 1749/50
Martha Huntly Daughter of Joseph & Eunice Huntly was born March 10th 1752
Abigail Huntly Daughter of Joseph & Eunice Huntly was born December 8 1753
David Huntly Son of Joseph and Eunice Huntly was born May 8th 1756

Mr. Chapman Warner was married to Miss Sarah Comstock 27th Decr 1787
Elisabeth Warner Daughter of said Chapman and Sarah born 26 Octr 1788

Joseph Wade was married to Esther Chadwick June ye 2nd Day: A.D: 1748
Loas Wade Daughter of Josephn and Esther Wade was born ye 16th Day of March: A.D: 1749
Jerusha Wade Daughter of Joseph & Esther Wade was born ye 18th Day of October: A.D: 1750

Mr. David Howell was Married to Mrs. Rheuami Sill the 30th day of Octr A.D. 1783
Mr. David Howell died the 16th day of November A.D. 1785

These are to Certifie that Latham Smith and Lous Miller both of Lyme were Lawfully Married togeth the 3rd Day of March: A.D: 1776 - by me Stephen Johnson Pastor of the first Church in Lyme
Lee Smith Son of Latham & Lous Smith was born January 6th A.D: 1778
Elisha Smith Son of Latham & Lous Smith was born February 6th A.D. 1780
Catee Smith Daughter of Latham & Lous Smith was born June 15th A.D. 1782

[page 57] Septemr ye 5th Day: 1733: Job Giddings was Married to Sarah Rathbone
Dorcas Giddings Daughter of Job and Sarah Giddings was born January the 6th A.D: 1735
William Giddings Son of Job & Sarah Giddings was born March ye 24th A.D: 1737
George Giddings Son of Job and Sarah Giddings was born Decemr ye 27th A.D: 1739
Sarah Giddings Daughter of Job & Sarah Giddings was born Septemr ye 30th: 1742
Job Giddings Son of Job & Sarah Giddings was born August ye 16th A.D: 1744
Anna Giddings Daughter of Job & Sarah Giddings was born July ye 25th A.D: 1746

Zebulon Giddings Son of Job & Sarah Giddings was born March ye 13th A.D: 1748
Job Giddings Died ye 25th Day of May: in ye year AD: 1748

William Biggs son of William Biggs and Mary his wife was born ye 17 Day of Septemr 1747

Jonathan Huntly Son of David and Mary Huntly was born the 9th Day of March: 1728
Lyme February the 19th: 1757: These may Certifie all whome it may Concern that Jonathan Huntly was Married to Sarah Stephens Smith on the 22nd Day of August 1754: by me Benjamin Lee Justice of Peace
Martin Huntly Son of Jonathan and Sarah Stephens Huntly was born May 9th: 1755 and Departed this Life: the 13th Day of January 1756
Marcy Huntly Daughter of Jonathan and Sarah Stephens Huntly was born 17th December: 1756
Jonathan Huntly Son of Jonathan and Sarah Stephens Huntly was born the 4th December: 1758
Zadack Huntly Son of Jonathan and Sarah Stephens Huntly was born the 8th: February: 1761
Abel Huntly Son of Jonathan and Sarah Stephens Huntly was born June 9th A.D. 1763
Elijah Huntly Son of Jonathan & Sarah Stephens Huntly was born August: 11th 1765
Naomy Huntly Daughter of Jonathan & Sarah Stephens Huntly was born August 30th 1767
Lydia Huntly Daughter of Jonathan & Sarah Stephens Huntly was born Septemr 4th 1769
Eliphalet Huntly Son of Jonathan & Sarah Stephens Huntly was born Septemr: 7th: 1771
Matthew Huntly Son of Jonathan & Sarah Stephens Huntly was born Decemr: 13: 1773

John Wilden Son of Jonas and Eunice Wilden was born the 25th Day of January: 1740 Recorded the 11th: Day of May: 1761 Pr order: Pr John Lay 2nd Clerk

[page 58] Simeon Beebe was Married to Anna Tervil ye first Day of August A.D: 1750
Elisha Beebe Son of Simeon and Anna Beebe was born ye 3rd Day of February A.D: 1750/1
Lyme July - 1754: then I married Joseph Bennet to Sarah Calkins Attests: Daniel Ely
Mary the Daughter of Joseph and Sarah Bennet was born Novemr: 25th: 1755

These are to Certifye whomesoever it may Concern that Mr. Martin Tucker and Mrs. Mary Peck both of Lyme were Lawfully married together 2nd of Novemr AD 1769 by me Stephen Johnson Pastor of the first Church in sd Lyme- Dated in Lyme 5th Jany: A.D. 1773
Lebbeus Peck Tinker Son of Martin & Mary Tinker was born August 20th AD 1770
Phebe Tinker Daughter of Martin & Mary Tinker was born July 21st AD 1772

Bridge Hampton July 30th: A.D 1751 These may certifye all whome it may Concern, that the Subscriber on Novemr ye first A.D 1748 Lawfully Joyned John Lewis of Lyme and Martha Cooper of this Parrish in Marriage James Brown Witness Present John Cooper Junr
Martha Lewis Daughter of John Lewis Junr and Martha his wife was born ye 14th Day of March A.D: 1749/50
John Lewis Junr Died ye 24th Day of August A.D: 1750
The Above Recorded ye 9th Day of August: 1751 Pr John Lay 3rd Clerk

Silas Beckwith Son of Jona & Sarah Beckwith was born Decemr 28th: 1751
David Beckwith Son of Jonathan & Sarah Beckwith was born February: 16th 1754
Jonathan Beckwith Son of Jona & Sarah Beckwith was born July 5th 1757
Lydia Beckwith Daughter of Jona & Sarah Beckwith was born February 27th 1759
Sarah Beckwith Daughter of Jona & Sarah Beckwith was born October 25th 1762

Mr. Joseph Peck and Mrs. Patience Hayes boath of Lyme in New London County were Lawfully Married to Each other on the 2nd Day of October: 1783: by Samll Ely Esqr as appears by the Evidence of Jasper P. Sears: and William Baker etc.

34 LYME, CONNECTICUT, VITAL RECORDS

[page 59] Capt John Coult Died the 2nd Day of January A.D 1750/51
John Coult Son of Benjamin Coult was Married to Mary Lord Daughter of Thomas Lord ye 16th Day of July: Anno Dom 1747
John Coult Son of John and Mary Coult was born ye 23rd of October A.D. 1743
Esther Coult Daughter of John and Mary Coult was born ye 22nd July: AD 1751
John Coult Son of John and Mary Could Died the 16th Day of February A.D: 1754
John Coult Son of John and Mary Coult was born the 7th Day of July A.D 1754
Miriam Coult Daughter of John & Mary Coult was born the firste Day of November A.D: 1756
Amherst Coult Son of John and Mary Coult was born the 27th Day of July A.D. 1759
Mary Coult Wife of sd John Coult Departed this Life ye 9th Day of August AD 1759
October: 28th 1759 John Coult of Lyme in New London County was Married to Mary Gardner of sd Lyme Pr me Richd Lord Justice of the Peace
Andrew Gardner Coult so of John & Mary Coult was Born November the 6th: A.D 1760
Benjamin Coult Son of John and Mary Coult was born October 26th: A.D: 1762
Mary Coult Wife of the above John Coult Died October 15th A.D: 1767

These are to Certifye whomesoever it may Concern that Mr. John Coult & Mrs. Abigail Matson both of Lyme were Lawfully Married together the 11th Day of May A.D 1773 Pr me Stephen Johnson Pastor of the first Church in sd Lyme Dated in Lyme 17th March A.D: 1774
William Coult Son of John & Abigail Coult was Born July 10th AD 1776
Mr. John Coult of sd Lyme Departed this Life on the 27th of May: 1784

Ezra Selden of Lyme was Married to Elisabeth Rogers of Norwich the 6th Day of May: A.D: 1754 [1751]
Ezra Selden Son of Ezra and Elisabeth Selden was born ye 23rd Day of March A.D: 1752
Theophilas Rogers Selden Son of Ezra and Elisabeth Selden was born Decemr 27th: 1753 and Died May 9th 1755
Gurdon Selden Son of Ezra and Elisabeth Selden born August 27th 1756: and Died June 27th 1759
Elisabeth Selden Daughter of Ezra & Elisabeth Selden was born Septemr: 14: 1758
Abigail Selden Daughter of Ezra & Elisabeth Selden was born March: 30th: 1761
Calven Selden Son of Ezra and Elisabeth Selden was born March ye 14 1763
Samll Rogers Selden Son of Ezra and Elisabeth Selden was born April ye 9th 1765
Elisabeth Selden the Wife of the above said Ezra Selden Died June ye 20th: 1767
Lyme Decemr 29th 1768: then Ezra Selden of Lyme was Lawfully Joyned in Marriage to Ame Ely of Lyme by me George Beckwith Minister of the 3rd Church of Christ in Lyme
Erastas Selden Son of Ezra & Ame Selden was born October 23rd A.D. 1769
Ame Selden Daughter of Ezra & Ame Selden was Born November the 29th A.D 1770
Lucretia Selden Daughter of Ezra & Ame Selden was Born June ye 24th A.D 1772
Lucretia died on the 25th day of February in the year 1776
Elisha Son of the said Ezra & Ame was born on the 31st day of July 1774 and Died on the 12th day of December 1775
Rebeckah daughter of the sd Ezra & Ame born 23d Feby & died 26th Feby 1776
Ame Wife of the said Ezra died on the 26th day of February 1776
Ezra Selden was Joined in Marriage to Hannah Merriam [Marvin] 13th April 1780

[page 60] These may Certifie Whomesoever it may Concern that Josiah Smith Junr and Abigail Tinker both of Lyme were married on the 16th Day of April: A.D: 1750 Pr me Stephen Johnson Pastor of the 1st Church in sd Lyme   Lyme August 6: 1751 --
Josiah Smith Son of Josiah Smith Junr and Abigail his wife was born 16th Day of January: A.D: 1750/51 and Died ye 10th Day of June: 1751
Abigail Smith Wife of Josiah Smith Junr. Died May ye 14th: A.D: 1751
Josiah Smith Junr: above sd was Married to Ama Tinker his second Wife the 20th Day of April A.D. 1755
Josiah Smith Son of Josiah and Ama Smith was born the 7th Day of May A.D. 1756
Elisabeth Smith Daughter of Josiah and Ama Smith was born September 17th A.D. 1757

Rhoda Smith Daughter of Josiah and Ama Smith was born February ye 18th A.D. 1759
Joseph Smith Son of Josiah & Ama Smith was born the 18th Day of October A.D: 1760
Seth Smith Son of Josiah & Ama Smith was born July 30th Day A.D. 1762
Rufus Smith Son of Josiah and Ama Smith was born the 27th Day of June A.D. 1764
John Cook Smith Son of Josiah and Ama Smith was born the 24th of May A.D. 1766
Azubah Smith Daughter of Josiah and Ama Smith was Born April 2nd Day A.D. 1768
Rufus Smith died July 15th A.D. 1770
Tinker Smith Son of Josiah and Ama Smith was born June 27th A.D. 1771
Ama Smith Daughter of Josiah & Ama Smith was Born December 19th A.D. 1773
Ambross Smith Son of Josiah & Ama Smith was Born ye 5th Day of March A.D: 1776
Tinker Smith Son of Josiah and Ama Smith Died the 11th of October A.D: 1783
Ambross Son of the said Josiah & Ame died on the   day of   17
Rhoda Daughter of the said Josiah and Ame died on the 1st day of April 1794

Andrew Sill was Married to Phebe Mather Daughter of Lieut Joseph Marther ye 19th Day of June A.D. 1744
Andrew Sill Son of Andrew and Phebe Sill was born ye 9th Day of April: A.D: 1745
Samuel Sill Son of Andrew and Phebe Sill was born ye 8th Day of February A.D: 1747
their son was born was born the 10th of Novemr 1748: and died the same Day
Uriah Sill Son of Andrew and Phebe Sill was born ye 17th Day of April A.D: 1750

These Certifie that Mr. Dan Lee and Miss Lurania Champlin boath of Lyme were Lawfully Married together the 25th Day of November A.D 1779 by me Stephen Johnson Pastor of the first Church of Christ Lyme Dated 5th of April: 1783
Silas Champlin Lee Son of Dan & Lurania Lee was born ye 9th of August A.D: 1780 and Died June ye 16th A.D 1781
Lurina Daughter of Dan and Lurania Lee was born ye 2nd Day of July: A.D. 1782
Lurina Lee Wife of Dan Lee above said Departed this Life May: 14th 1783

This Certifys that Mr. Dan Lee and Mrs. Nabbey Champlin boath of Lyme were Married February 29th: 1784 by me Andrew Griswold Justice of Peace

[page 61]   Robert Otis was Married to Margaret Sabins the 8th Day of August: 1737
Stephen Otis Son of Robert and Margaret Otis was born at the Town of Barrington the 14th Day of May: A.D: 1738
Robert Otis Son of Robert and Margaret Otis was born in the town of Lyme the 18th Day of March A.D: 1740
Richard Otis Son of Robert and Margaret Otis was born June ye 23: A.D: 1745
Anna Otis Daughter of Robert & Margaret Otis was born September ye 25th A.D: 1748
Robert Son of Robert & Lydia Otis was born on the 10th day of May A.D: 1764

These are to Certifie that Mr. Willaim Champlin & Miss Polley Mather boath of Lyme were Married together the 13th Day of January A.D: 1780 by me Stephen Johnson Pastor of the first Church in sd Lyme Dated in Lyme 5th April 1783
Lucy Champlin Daughter of William & Polley Champlin was Born February first: 1783
Lodowick Macketton Son of the said William & Polley was born the 6th day of Jany A.D 1787
Lurane Daughter of the said William & Polley was born on the 29th day of May A.D. 1792
Richard Mather Son of the said William & Polley was born on the 23rd day of May A.D. 1795

John Goold Son of James and Elisabeth Goold was born ye 4th of June: A.D: 1751
Luca Goold Daughter of James and Elisabeth Goold was born August ye 6th A.D: 1753
Marcy Goold Daughter of James and Elisabeth Goold was born July 14th Day: A.D: 1755
David Goold Son of James and Elisabeth Goold was born March: 16th: A.D: 1757
Walter Goold Son of James and Elisabeth Goold was born January 25th A.D. 1759
Elisabeth Goold Daughter of James and Elisabeth Goold was born January first 1761

Noah Smith Son of Thomas Smith 3rd & Lydia Smith was born September 2nd 1785

[page 62]   Joseph Giddings was Married to Unice Androus ye 24th Day of October: 1737
James Giddings Son of Joseph and Unice Giddings was Born July ye 24th Day A.D: 1738
Jonathan Giddings Son of Joseph Giddings and Unice his wife was born ye 18th of   : 1740
Solomon Giddings Son of Joseph and Unice Giddings was born May ye 31st: A.D.: 1743
Mary Giddings Daughter of Joseph and Unice Giddings was born January ye 27th: A.D: 1745
Hannah Giddings Daughter of Joseph and Unice Giddings was born November ye 4th 1746
Lydia Giddings Daughter of Joseph and Unice Giddings was born August ye 2nd: 1747
Benjamin Giddings was born (son of Joseph and Unice Giddings) May ye 20th A.D: 1750

These are to Certifie that Mr. Silas Champlin & Miss Bettey Lay Boath of Lyme were Lawfully Married together the 18th Day of October A.D: 1781: by me - Stephen Johnson Pastor of the first Church in sd Lyme Dated in Lyme April 7th 1783
William Champlin Son of Silas and Bettey Champlin was Born March 9th 1782
Harvey Lay Champlin Son of Silas & Bettey Champlin was Born July 16th: 1786
Abigail Daughter of Silas and Betsy Champlain Born April 11th A.D: 1793

Shadreck, Mesheck, and Abednego: Cooley's: Sons of Matthew and Jemima Cooley were born ye 26th Day of October A.D. 1750: Abednego Cooley Son of Matthew and Jemima Cooley Died ye 8th Day of January AD: 1750/51
Mesheck Cooley Son of Matthew and Jemima Cooley Died January: ye 14th A.D: 1750/51
Shadreck Cooley Son of Matthew and Jemima Cooley Died January ye 26th A.D: 1751
Eunice Cooley Daughter of Matthew and Jemima Cooley was born ye 2nd Day of January A.D: 1752
Paul Cooley Son of Matthew and Jemima Cooley was born July 26th A.D: 1755
Jemima Cooley Daughter of Matthew and Jemima Cooley was born Novemr 25th 1757
Mr. Rich Peck and Elisabeth Mather boath of Lyme in New London County were Lawfully Married to Each other by the Reverend Mr. Stephen Johnson of Sd Lyme on The 13th Day of March: 1783 as Certified by Evidence.
Nathll Peck Son of Richd and Elisabeth Peck was Born January 24th 1784
Richard Peck Son of Richd & Elisabeth Peck was Born February 5th 1786

[page 63]   These is to Inform all whome it may Consearn that John Sill of Lyme and Phebe Fithin of Bridghampton were married the 22nd Day of December 1731 - by me Ebenezer White, Minister of Bridghampton
David Fithin Sill Son of John and Phebe Sill was born April ye 24th Day A.D 1733
Joseph Sill Son of John & Phebe Sill was born ye 21st Day of February: A.D. 1735
Phebe Sill Daughter of John and Phebe Sill was born ye 19th Day of March AD 1737
Mary Sill was born (Daughter of John and Phebe Sill) June ye 16th A.D: 1739
Anna Sill Daughter of John and Phebe Sill was born May the 14th A.D 1742
John Sill son of John and Phebe Sill was born April the 16th A.D 1744
Sarah Sill Daughter of John and Phebe Sill was born August ye 8th A.D: 1746
Silas Sill Son of John and Phebe Sill was born November ye 17th Day: A.D: 1749
Phebe Sill, Wife of the sd John Sill Died May ye 23rd A.D 1751
John Sill of Lyme was married to Hepsibah Lee, the 9th Day of April A.D 1752
Enoch Sill Son of John and Hepsibah Sill was born March 15th A.D 1753
Richard Sill Son of John and Hepsibah Sill was Born July 15th Day: 1755
Enoch died on the   day of August A.D 1777
Hepzibah Wife of said John Sill died on the   Day of March 1783
Richard died at Ablany on the 4th day of June A.D: 1790
John Sill was Married to Lucy Peck on the 22d day of September A.D. 1783
John Sill deceased on the 17th day of Oct. 1796 in the 87 year of his age

These may Signifie and Certifie that Mr. Daniel DeWolf of Lyme was on the 19th Day of June A.D: 1751 then Married to Mrs. Azuba Lee of the Same Town by me the Subscriber - George Beckwith -

Elias DeWolf Son of Daniel and Azubah Dewolf was born May ye 18th: 1752
Mr. Daniel DeWolf was Removed by Death October ye 10th Day: 1752
These are to Certifie that Mr. Josiah Smith Junr and Parthena Roland both of Lyme were lawfully Married together the 17th Day of February A.D: 1779 Dated in Lyme this 25th Day of August: 1779
Eunice Smith Daughter of Josiah & Parthena Smith was Born April 5th 1780
Esther Smith Daughter of Josiah & Parthena Smith was Born 29th Demr 1781
Abigail Smith Daughter of Josiah & Parthena Smith was Born January 22nd 1784
Rhodey Smith Daughter of Josiah & Parthena Smith was Born 27th October: 1787
Tinker Son of said Josiah & Parthena Smith was born the 15th Day of June 1790

[page 64] New London June 1st 1751
These may Certifie those whome it may Consearn that Richard Smith of Lyme and Abigail Miner of New London were Joyned in Marriage by me August 1st 1745: as Witness my hand Eliphalet Adams
Anna Smith Daughter of Richard and Abigail Smith was born February first: 1746/7
Bettey Smith Daughter of Richard & Abigail Smith was born ye 7th Day of October: 1748
Richard Smith Son of Richard and Abigail Smith was born November ye 25th 1750
Abigail Smith Daughter of Richd and Abigail Smith was born Decemr 23rd 1752
Lydia Smith Daughter of Richd and Abigail Smith was born Novemr 20th 1754
Abigail Smith wife of the aforesaid Richd Smith Died August 10th 1755

These may Certifie that Mr. Richard Smith of Lyme on the 8th Day of of January: 1756; was Joyned in Marriage with Mrs. Grace Moore of New London as Appears by the Records of Benjamin Lee Esqr of sd Lyme
Deceasd who was then in full life and a Justice of the Peace
Amos Smith Son of Richd and Grace Smith was Born October 2nd Day: 1756
Abigail Smith Daughter of Richd and Abigail sd Smith's first wife Died August 21st 1757
Grace Smith Daughter of Richd & Grace Smith was Born Novemr: 16th: 1758
Asa Smith Son of Richd and Grace Smith was Born Septemr ye 6th 1762
Abigail Smith Daughter of Richd & Grace Smith was Born May 22nd Day: 1765
Russell Smith Son of Richard and Grace Smith was Born May 24th 1767
Luce Smith Daughter of Richd and Grace Smith was born February 16th: 1770
Clemment Smith Son of Ricd & Grace Smith was born January 30th 1773
Olive Smith Daughter of Richd & Grace Smith was born February 2nd 1776

Molley Daniels Daughter of John & Huldah Daniels was born May 31st: 1746
John Daniels Son of John and Huldah Daniels was born July ye 9th Day: 1748
Molley Daniels Daughter of John & Huldah Daniels Died the 30th of October: 1749
Phebe Daniels Daughter of John and Huldah Daniels was born July 27th Day 1750
Molley Daniels Daughter of John & Huldah Daniels was born November ye 4th: 1752
Nabbe Daniels Daughter of John & Huldah Daniels was born 30th Day of June AD: 1755

The Marriage of Mr. Elijah Peck and Hephzibah his Wife together with the Births of their Children are Recorded in the 6th Book of Lyme Records folio 161 and the Deaths of sd Elijah and Mehephzibah & their Children are as followeth --
Elijah Peck Junr Son of Elijah & Hepzibah Peck Died March 31st: A.D. 1766
Hephzibah Peck Wife of Elijah Peck Died October 9th A.D 1770
Mr. Elijah Peck of Lyme Died August the 6th A.D. 1771
Peter Peck Son of Elijah and Hephzebah Peck Died August the 6th A.D 1771
William Peck Son of Elijah and Hephzibah Died July the 13th A.D 1771
Luther Peck Son of Elijah & Hephzibah Died August 27th A.D. 1771

Elijah Greenfield Alger Son of Elijah & Agnice Alger was born March 27th A.D: 1766

[page 65] Stephen Smith of Lyme in the County of New London was Married to Lucia Lay of sd Lyme the 11th Day of May A.D: 1749
Seth Smith Son of Stephen and Lucia Smith was born ye 14th Day of January: 1753

Beckah Smith Daughter of Stephen and Lucia Smith was born February 9th 1755
Clerina [Clarrisa] Smith Daughter of Stephen and Lucia Smith was born May the 5th: A.D: 1757

Mr. Moses Warren Junr was Married to Miss Mehitable Raymond Daughter of Mr. Edwd Raymond of New London Jany 18th A.D. 1784
Sally Warren Daughter of the said Moses & Mehitable Born Decr 11th A.D 1784
Edward Raymond Warren Son of said Moses & Mehitable born 13th June 1787
Joshua son of the said Moses & Mehitable was born on the 24th of Octr 1789
Maria Daughter of the sd Moses & Mehitable was born on the 31 of Jany 1792
Hetty Daughter of the sd Moses & Mehitable was born on the 14th Day of May 1794
Moses [Harris] Son of sd Moses & Mehitable was born June 6th 1796
Lois Daughter of the sd Moses & Mehitable was born 28th August 1800
Robert Son of the sd Moses & Mehitable was born 24th April 1803
Eliza daughter of the sd Moses & Mehitable was born 24 August 1803
Mahitable Warren Wife Moses Warren Esqr died May 9th 1813
Caleb R. Warren Son of the said Moses & Mehitable - died June 19th 1823
Robert Son of the said Moses & Mehitable died Feby 25th 1828

James Greenfield Son of Archibald Stam [Starr] and Sarah Greenfield was born ye 7th Day of January A.D: 1752
Sarah Greenfield Daughter of Archibald Starr and Sarah Greenfield was born the 29th Day of April: 1754
Richard Greenfield Son of Archibald Starr Greenfield and Sarah his wife was born ye first Day of November A.D. 1756
Mary Greenfield Daughter of Archibald Starr Greenfiel and Sarah his wife was born the 29th Day of Septemr: 1759
Archibald Greenfield Son of Archibald Starr Greenfield and Sarah his wife was born the 17th Day of June A.D: 1762
John Greenfield Son of Starr and Sarah Greenfield was born Novemr: 6 1765
Hannah Greenfield Daughter of Starr and Sarah Greenfield was born Decemr: 2nd 1769
Mrs. Hannah Roland Relect of Mr. Richd: Roland/Died the 24th Day of Novemr: A.D 1773
Richd Greenfield above said Departed this life 25th Day of May 1781

[page 66] Capt Thomas Anderson of Lyme was Married to Mrs. Margret Reed of the same Town on the 5th Day of June Anno Domini: 1748 - Pr me George Beckwith Minister
Thomas Anderson Son of Capt Thomas and Margret Anderson was born February 18: A.D: 1749
Margret Anderson Daughter of Capt Thomas & Margret Anderson was born Septemr 6th A.D: 1750
Mary Anderson Daughter of Capt. Thomas & Margret Anderson was born August 31st - : 1752
Robert Anderson Son of Capt. Thomas and Margret Anderson was Born January 12th A.D: 1755
John Anderson Son of Capt. Thomas and Margret Anderson was Born May 23rd Day A.D: 1757
Nehemiah Rice of Lyme was Married to Abigail Gustin of the Same Town March the 14th A.D: 1739 by me George Beckwith
Samuel Rice Son of Nehemiah and Abigail Rice was born May the 13th: 1740
Reoel Rice Son of Nehemiah and Abigail Rice was born February ye 7th: 1742
Jonathan Rice Son of Nehemiah & Abigail Rice was born January 18th: 1745
Elisha Rice Son of Nehemiah and Abigail Rice was born January 20th 1748
Lydia Rice Daughter of Nehemiah & Abigail Rice was born March: 13th 1751

These are to Certifie whomesoever it may conscearn that Mr. John Anderson Junr: and
 Miss Lydia Clark boath of Lyme were Lawfully Married together the 25th Day of
 May A.D 1775   Pr me Stephen Johnson Pastor of the first in sd Lyme
Dated in Lyme first March: 1780

[page 67]   Consider Tiffany of Lyme in the County of New London was married to Mary
 Davis of New London aforesaid the 23rd Day of January: A.D: 1753
Timothy Tiffany Son of Consider and Mary Tiffany was born November ye 24th Day: 1752
Titus Tiffany Son of Consider & Mary Tiffany was born ye 9th Day of May A.D: 1754

East Haddam April 15th 1783 Watrous Beckwith & Mary Braynard were Joyned together
 in the Marriage Covenant on the 12th Day of March: 1782 A true Copy of Record
 Test -- Test Elijah Parsons, Pastor the first Chh in E. Haddam
Mary Brainard Beckwith Daughter of Watrous & Mary Beckwith was born March:
 3rd - A.D 1783
Mary Beckwith Wife of sd Watrous Beckwith Departed this life April 3rd 1783
This may Certify that I Married Mr. Watrous Beckwith to Mrs. Ruth Robins February 25th
 A.D 1784 by Jason Lee Elder
John Beckwith Son of said Watrous & Ruth Beckwith was born 2d Decr 1785 and Died
 February 27th A.D. 1786
John Beckwith Son of said Watrous & Ruth Beckwith was born July 27th A.D. 1788
Eliza daughter of the sd Watrous & Ruth Beckwith was born on the 15th day of Sept 1789
Miranda daughter of the said Watrous was born on the 17 day of Octr 1791
Watrous son of the said Watrous and Ruth was born on the 10th Jany 1797
Watrous the son was drowned in the mill floom on the 27th day of April 1801

Joseph Robins of Lyme in the County of New London was Married unto Mary Lay
 Daughter of Edward Lay of sd Lyme the first Day of June A.D: 1726
Elisha Robins son of Joseph and Mary Robins was born ye 25th Day of Decemr: 1727
Eunice Robins Daughter of Joseph & Mary Robins was born October ye first Day: 1730
Elisabeth Robins Daughter of Joseph & Mary Robins was born March ye 14th Day: 1733
Ezra Robins son of Joseph & Mary Robins was born the 24th Day of March: 1736
Elijah Robins son of Joseph and Mary Robins was born the 4th Day of March: 1741

Joseph Minor Junr Died the 23rd Day of February A.D: 1756

[page 68]   David Huntly was Married Mary Tinker the 27th Day of October A.D: 1742
Elihue Huntly son of David and Mary Huntly was born ye 30th Day of August A.D: 1743
Mehetabel Huntly Daughter of David & Mary Huntly was born Septemr ye 22nd Day: 1745
David Huntly above sd Died the 31st Day of August: A.D 1775 [See L.R. Vol. 2 p. 295]
These Certifie that Mr. Elijah Ely & Mrs. Catharine Lee: boath of Lyme were Lawfully
 Married together the 14th Day of February A.D: 1765 by me -
 Stephen Johnson, Pastor of the First Church of Christ in sd Lyme
Phebe Ely Daughter of Elijah & Catharine Ely was Born ye 10th Day of May A.D: 1766
Elihjah Ely Son of Elijah & Catharine Ely was born the 10th Day of April: A.D: 1769
Samll Ely Son of Elijah & Catharine Ely was Born the 26th Day of April: A.D: 1771
Cate Ely Daughter of Elijah & Catharine Ely was Born May 5th A.D: 1774
Hannah Ely Daughter of Elijah & Catharine Ely was born ye 12th Day of May: A.D. 1776
Hephzibah Ely Daughter of Elijah & Catharine Ely was born 22nd Day of July: 1780

John Huntly Son of Joseph Huntly of Lyme was Married to Lous [Loas] Beckwith
 Daughter of Matthew Beckwith Junr of sd Lyme the 13th Day of Decemr: 1747
Vashty Huntly Daughter of John and Lous Huntly was born the 13th Day of September
 A.D 1748
Elisheba Huntly Daughter of John and Lous Huntly was born 24th of August: 1751
William Huntly Son of John and Lous Huntly was born February 15th A.D 1756
Curtiss Huntly Son of John and Lous Huntly was born September the 20th Day: 1758
Sabra Huntly Daughter of John & Lous Huntly was born September the first Day: 1761

LYME, CONNECTICUT, VITAL RECORDS

These may Signified & Certifie that Mr. William Buttler was on November 1770 Married to Mrs. Sarah Lord boath of Lyme by me George Beckwith Pastor

[page 69] Lyme August the 21st: 1750 James Huntly and Lucretia Smith both of Lyme were Married together by me: George Griswold Pastor of the 2nd Church in Lyme
Phinehas Huntly Son of James and Lucretia Huntly was born ye 14th: January: 1754
Renold Huntly Son of James and Lucretia Huntly was born 30th Day of March 1756
Enoch Huntly Son of James & Lucretia Huntly was born 31st Day of October: 1758
Rena Huntly Daughter of James & Lucretia Huntly was born March 9th A.D: 1761
Ira Huntly Son of James & Lucretia Huntly was born June 3rd Day A.D 1764
Marvin Huntly Son of James and Lucretia Huntly was born Novemr 11th A.D 1766
Ama [Amy] Huntly Daughter of James & Lucretia Huntly was born January 2nd 1769
James Huntly Son of James & Lucretia Huntly was Born May 17th A.D: 1771
Seth Huntly Son of James & Lucretia Huntly was Born July 8th A.D: 1773
Elkanah Huntly Son of James & Lucretia Huntly was born Septemr 19th 1775
Silas Huntly Son of James and Lucretia Huntly was Born August 3d 1777
Lucretia Huntly Daughter of James & Lucretia Huntly was Born August 18th: 1781
Enoch Huntly Son of James and Lucretia Huntly Died June first: 1786
Seth Huntly Son of James and Lucretia Huntly Died September 9th 1787
Reynold Huntly son of James and Lucretia Huntly died at Manlius Center N.Y. Sept. 9, 1839 age 83 (From tomb stone inscription)
Capt. James Huntly died Feb. 25, 1816 (From tomb stone inscription at Old Stone Church Yard, East Lyme)

Lyme May 10th: 1750: Then Jesse Beckwith and Jerusha Robins both of Lyme were Married together by me George Griswold Pastor of the 2nd Church in Lyme
Jesse Beckwith Son of Jesse and Jerusha Beckwith was born April 14th A.D:1753
Azubah Beckwith Daughter of Jesse and Jerusha Beckwith was born November the 9th A.D: 1754
Phebe Wife of Jesse Beckwith departed this life on the 7th day of Jany 1796
Jesse Beckwith departed this life on the 19th day of April A.D: 1796

These are to Certifye whomsoever it may Consearn that Ebenezer Rogers and Elisabeth Mather both of Lyme were Lawfully married together November 18th A.D: 1756
Dated in Lyme 30th January: AD 1775 by me Stephen Johnson Pastor of the first Church in sd Lyme
Richard Rogers Son of Ebenezer and Elisabeth Rogers was born March y 22nd A.D 1757
Hannah Rogers Daughter of Ebenezer and Elisabeth Rogers was born Decemr - 11th: A.D 1758
Gideon Robers Son of Ebenezer and Elisabeth Rogers was born January: 14th A.D 1761
Bettey Rogers Daughter of Ebenezer and Elisabeth Rogers was Born June ye 18th A.D 1765
Elisabeth the Wife of said Ebenezer Rogers Departed this life January the first Day A.D: 1769
Mr. Ebenezer Rogers and Elisabeth Hyde was Legally Joined in Marriage August 13th A.D 1793

[page 70] Decemb the 20th: 1753 then Danll Beckwith the 3rd was Lawfully Married to Jerusha Grant: by me Stephen Gorton Elder
Jerusha Beckwith Wife of Danll Beckwith 3rd Died the 29th Day of August: 1757
This may Certifie that on the 30th Day of December A.D 1757: I married Danll Beckwith the 3rd of Lyme to his now Wife Sarah - Test Samuel Ely Justice of the Peace
Rice Beckwith Son of Danll Beckwith 3rd and Sarah his Wife was born the 20th Day of November A.D. 1758

Mr. Elisha Ayer of Lyme was Married to Mrs. Abigail Lee of sd Lyme on the 23rd Day of June A.D: 1776
Bettey Ayer Daughter of Elisha & Abigail Ayer was born June 21st: 1779

Lucy daughter of the said Elisha & Abigail was born 26th Feby - 1787
Fanny daughter of the said Elishs & Abigail was born 14th August 1789

William Tillitson of Lyme was Married to Susanna Chapman March 7th 1754
George Tillitson Son of William and Susanna Tillitson was born November ye 14 - 1754
Azubah Tillitson Daughter of William & Susannah Tillitson was born March 18th - 1756
Bela Tillitson Son of William & Susannah Tillitson was born March 13th 1762
Ame Tillitson Daughter of Wm & Susannah Tillitson was born March 24th 1758
Morehouse Tillitson Son of Wm & Susannah Tillitson was born Septemr 5th 1763
Isaac Tillitson Son of Wm & Susannah Tillitson was born May 26th 1765
Richard Tillitson Son of Wm & Susannah Tillitson was born Decemr 14th A.D 1766
Damarious Tillitson Daughter of Wm & Susannah Tillitson was Born Novemr 21st 1768
Anna Tillitson Daughter of Wm & Susannah Tillitson was Born August 11th 1770
Richard Tillitson Son of William and Susannah Tillitson Died the 10th of Decemr 1767
Susa Tillitson Daughter of Willm and Susannah Tillitson was born May 27th A.D. 1773
Lina Tillitson Daughter of Wm and Susannah Tillitson was Born January 26th 1775
Susanna Tillitson Wife of William Tillitson Departed this life on the 4th Day of Septemr 1786

[page 71] John Hazen Junr and Deborah Peck were Married together on the 10th Day of March A.D. 1754
John Hazen ye 3rd Son of John and Deborah Hazen was born the 10th Day of February A.D. 1737/8
Marcy Hazen was born the 29th Day of March 1740
Deborah Hazen Daughter of John and Deborah Hazen was born February 22nd 1743
Nathaniel Hazen Son of John and Deborah Hazen was born in the Jersey March the 17th Day 1745
Eunice Hazen Daughter of John & Deborah Hazen was born at Colchester May the 22nd Day 1747
Joseph Hazen Son of John and Deborah Hazen was born at Colchester September 28th Day 1749
Lydia Hazen Daughter of John & Deborah Hazen was born December 22nd Day 1751
Samuel Hazen Son of John and Deborah Hazen was born June the 4th 1754

May 11th 1766: then I married Stephen Starlin of Lyme to his now Wife Elisabeth Tucker Test. Samll Ely Justice Peace
Stephen Starlin Son of Stephen and Elisabeth Starlin was born March 22nd A.D. 1767
Marshfield Starlin Son of Stephen & Elisabeth Starlin was Born March 13th A.D 1769
Isaac Starlin Son of Stephen and Elisabeth Starlin was Born February 1st A.D. 1772 and Died the 10th Day of February: A.D 1772
Esther Starlin Daughter of Stephen & Elisabeth Starlin was Born Septemr 16th A.D: 1773
Elisabeth Anna Starlin Daughter of Stephen & Elisabeth Starlin was Born May 3rd A.D 1777
Stephen Starlin above named Died the first Day of March: A.D. 1777

These may Signifie that Ezekiel Rogers of Lyme was on the 15th Day of August 1753 Married to Phebe Bramble - by me George Beckwith Pastor
Sarah Rogers Daughter of Ezekiel and Phebe Rogers was born September ye 2nd 1754
Lydia Rogers Daughter of Ezekiel and Phebe Rogers was born October 23rd A.D. 1756
Ezekiel Rogers Son of Ezekiel and Phebe Rogers was born 25th Day of January: A.D 1758
Phebe Rogers Daughter of Ezekiel and Phebe Rogers was born October 30th 1759
Daniel Rogers Son of Ezekiel and Phebe Rogers was born June 6th 1761 and Died the 8th Day of November: 1762
Daniel Rogers Son of Ezekiel and Phebe Rogers was born October first: 1763
Leammy [Leoramy] Rogers Daughter of Ezekiel & Phebe Rogers was Born 9th Day of Septemr 1765

John Rogers Son of Ezekiel & Phebe Rogers was born July ye 23rd Day 1767
David Rogers Son of Ezekiel & Phebe Rogers was born March 25th Day 1769
David Rogers Died the 14th of January: 1770
Caleb Rogers Son of Ezekiel & Phebe Rogers was Born January ye 17th 1771
Caleb Rogers Died in March the 27th Day 1771
Joshua Rogers Died April 4th 1771
William Rogers Son of Ezekiel & Phebe Rogers was Born February 9th 1773
William Rogers Died October the 15th 1775
David Rogers Son of Ezekiel and Phebe Rogers was born November 6th 1774
Mary Rogers Daughter of Ezekiel & Phebe Rogers was born July ye 2nd 1777
Ezekiel Rogers Senior above mentioned departed this Life on the 7th of January A.D 1789

[page 72]   Moses Dudley was born July 29th 1714
Anna Bushnell Daughter of Ephraim Bushnell of Saybrook was born the 24th Day of October 1720 as Pr Records of Saybrook Libn, 2nd folio 149 Attested Pr John Tully Town Clerk

Moses Dudley was Married to Anna Bushnell December the 22nd 1743
Their Son Moses was born 30th 1745
their son William was born October the 12th 1747
Extracted from Saybrook Records Lib,n 2nd folio: 461: Attest Pr John Tully Town Clerk
Anna Dudley Daughter of Moses & Anna Dudley was born July 26th Day A.D: 1750
Rebeckah Dudley Daughter of Moses and Anna Dudley was born February 18th 1753
Bushnell Dudley Son of Moses and Anna Dudley was born July 19th A.D 1755
John Dudley Son of Moses and Anna Dudley was born January 29th A.D 1758

These Certifie that Mr. Nathan Avery & Mrs. Aliss Pearson both of Lyme in New London County were Lawfully Married to Each other on the 9th Day of April: A.D: 1776 by me John Lay 2nd Just. Peace
Pearson Peck Son of Nathan & Alis Avery was born April 23rd: 1779

These may Certifie that Nathan Smith of Lyme was Married to Elisabeth Starling of the Same Town: on the 7th Day of April: Anno: Dom: 1748 - by me George Beckwith Minister of the Gospel
Abigail Smith Daughter of Nathan & Elisabeth Smith was born April ye 24th 1749
Elisabeth Smith Daughter of Nathan & Elisabeth Smith was born February ye 22nd A.D - 1751
Esther Smith Daughter of Nathan & Elisabeth Smith was born April ye 10th A.D - 1753

Gasper Dowzcik was Married to Patience Brockway July 13th A.D 1760
Katharine Dowzcik Daughter of Gasper & Patience Dowzick was born Novemr 7th 1760 Fryday
Marke Dowzick Son of Gasper and Patience Dowzick was born Septemr: 13: 1761: on Sunday and Died October 3rd: 1761
Elenor Dowzick Daughter of Gasper & Patience Dowzick was Born Novemr 15th: 1762: on Monday
Anne Dowzick Daughter of Gasper and Patience Dowzick was Born Septemr: 10th 1765: on Tuesday
David Dowzick Son of Gasper and Patience Dowzick was Born June 18th: 1768: on Saturday
Peter Dowzick Son of Gasper and Patience Dowzick was Born April ye 21st A.D: 1771

[page 73]   Benjamin Mather of Lyme was Married to Irena Person of the Same Town on the 16th Day of August A.D: 1753 Pr me George Beckwith -
Irena Mather Daughter of Benja and Irena Mather was born July 8th A.D 1754
Gibbins Mather Son of Benja and Irena Mather was born May the 11th 1756
Anna Mather Daughter of Benja & Irena Mather was born March ye 12th A.D. 1758
Gibbins Mather Son of sd Ben and Irena Mather died July ye 10th A.D: 1759

Gibben Mather Son of Benja and Irena Mather was born June 22nd A.D. 1760
Irena Mather Wife of sd Benjamin Mathr Died 22nd Day of August A.D 1761

Lyme 6th January 1764: These may Certifie whomesoever it may Consearn that Mr. Benjamin Mather of Lyme and Mrs. Abigail Worthington of Colchester were Lawfully Married together: the 14th Day of March: A.D: 1763 by me Stephen Johnson Pastor of the first Church in sd Lyme
Bettey Worthington Mather Daughter of Benja & Abigail Mather was born December 17th: 1763
Nabbe Mather Daughter of Benjamin and Abigail Mather was born April: 16th 1765
Mr. William Higgins was married to Miss Fanny Bayley 24th Feby 1780
Gordon Bayley Higgins Son to said William & Fanny was Born 23d March 1781
Polley Higgins Daughter to said William and Fanny Born 30th March 1784
Mrs. Fanny Higgins died March 6th 1785 --

Lucy Latimer daughter of Nathan Latimer married Daniel Dodge of Colchester Dec. 2nd 1779 and died Apr. 7th 1832

Nathan Latimore and Jean Lee both of New London were Joyned in Marriage the 6th Day of May 1753
Hallam Latimore Son of Nathan and Jean Latimore was Born September 3rd: 1754
Nathan Latimer Son of Nathan and Jean Latimer was born July 24th 1756
Luce Latimer Daughter of Nathan and Jean Latimer was born ye 3rd Day of December 1758
Stephen Latimer Son of Nathan & Jean Latimer was born January ye 18th 1761
Abigail Latimer Daughter of Nathan and Jean Latimer was born April ye 13th 1763
Jean Latimer Daughter of Nathan & Jean Latimer was born December ye 17th: 1764
Samll Latimer Son of Nathan and Jean Latimer was Born June the 16 - A.D 1767
Anne Latimer Daughter of Nathan & Jean Latimer was Born July the 10th A.D 1769
Edward Latimer Son of Nathan and Jean Latimer was Born July the 10th A.D 1771
Lydia Latimer Daughter of Nathan and Jean Latimer was born July 5th A.D: 1773

Seth Lee and Betsy Smith was Joyn'd in Marriage Feby 19th A.D. 1769
Hepzibah, Daughter said Seth & Betsy was born Feby 10th A.D. 1772
Seth, Son of said Seth & Betsy was born Sept. 6th A.D. 1777
Betsy, Daughter of Seth & Betsy was born Sept 26th A.D 1779
Nabby, their Daughter was born August 6 day A.D - 1781
Richard, their Son was born October the 16th day A.D - 1783
Polly, their Daughter was born Sept 21st day A.D. 1786
Cate, their Daughter was born September 30th day A.D 1788
Cate died on the 2d day of June 1789
Anne daughter of the said Seth & Betsey was born the 2d day of May 1792

[page 74] Benjamin Hudson was married to Hannah Terrile the 20th Day of January A.D: 1749
Danll Hudson Son of Benjamin and Hannah Hudson was born the first Day of April A.D 1750 and Died the first Day of October 1751
Stephen Hudson son of Benjamin and Hannah Hudson was born the 22nd Day of March: A.D: 1752
Mabel Hudson Daughter of Benja and Hannah Hudson was born the 11th Day of January: A.D: 1754
Elisabeth Hudson Daughter of Benjamin & Hannah Hudson was born 26th Day of July A.D - 1756
Hannah Hudson Daughter of Benjamin & Hannah Hudson was born ye 30th Day of November: 1759

These Certifie that Mr. Joseph Noyes and Mrs. Jane Lord boath of Lyme were Lawfully Married together the 26th Day of July A.D 1784 by me - Stephen Johnson Pastor of ye first Church in Lyme

Eunice Noyes Daughter of Joseph & Jane Noyes was born the 21st Day of March: A.D: 1785
Richard Noyes Son of Joseph & Jane Noyes was Born the 12th Day of March: 1787
Eunice Noyes Daughter of said Joseph & Jane died the 28th day of February 1789
Enoch Son of the Said Joseph & Jane was born the 27th day of August 1789
Eunice Daughter of the said Joseph & Jane was born the 20th of November A.D. 1791

Entered June the 14th: 1755   Pr. J. Lay 3rd Clerk
Lyme 9th: June 1755 These May Certifie whome it may Consearn, that Mr. Josiah Burnham and Mrs. Thankfull Higgins both of Lyme were Lawfully Married November the 1st: 1753   Pr Stephen Johnson: Pastor of the First Church in Lyme
Joseph Burnham Son of Josiah and Thankfull Burnham was born the 3rd Day of March: 1755
James Burnham Son of Josiah and Thankfull Burnham was born February the 8th Day: 1757
Samuel Burnham Son of Josiah and Thankfull Burnham was born August: 14th: 1758
James Burnham Died the 3rd Day of October: A.D. 1758
Samuel Burnham Died ye 10th Day of February A.D. 1759
James Burnham Son of Josiah & Thankfull Burnham was born January 30th: A.D 1760
Samll Burnham Son of Josiah & Thankfull Burnham was Born May 11th A.D: 1762
Jemima Burnham Daughter of Josiah & Thankfull Burnham was Born March 11th A.D: 1764
John Burnham Son of Josiah & Thankfull Burnham was Born October 29th: 1765
Betsey Burnham Daughter of Josiah & Thankfull Burnham was Born March 14th: 1767
Marcy Burnham Daughter of Josiah & Thankfull Burnham was Born July 18th: 1769
Rebeckah Burnham Daughter of Josiah & Thankfull Burnham was Born June 18th: 1771
Josiah Burnham Son of Josiah & Thankfull Burnham was Born July 28th - 1773

[page 75]   Joseph Lord of Lyme was Married to Sarah Wade of sd Lyme the 11th Day of May: 1749
Ruben Lord Son of Joseph and Sarah Lord was born the 27th Day of June: A.D - 1750
Sarah Lord Daughter of Joseph and Sarah Lord was born the 18th Day of May A.D - 1752
William Lord Son of Joseph and Sarah Lord was born the 22nd Day of April: A.D - 1754

Lawrance Johnson was Married to Grace Harris 20 day of May 1784
Lawrance Johnson Son of the said Lawrance & Grace was born 23th Novr 1786
Ira Johnson Son of the said Lawrance & Grace was born 25 Aprl 1789
Persa Johnson Son of the said Lawrence & Grace was born 28 March 1792
Timothy their Son was born on the 4th day of September - AD - 1793
Lydia their Daughter was born on the 5th day of September - A.D - 1795
Grace their Daughter was born on the 29th day of April 1801
Phebe daughter of the sd Lawarance & Grace was born the 4th day of June 1804

Mr. Joshua Rogers of Lyme was married to Miss Experience Lamphier of Stoning Town the 14th Day of February AD 1732
Eunice Rogers Daughter of Joshua and Experience Rogers was born the 29th of December 1733
Josiah Rogers son of Joshua and Experience Rogers was born the 24th Day of January 1739
Joshua Rogers son of Joshua and Experience Rogers was born the 5th Day of March 1746
Mary Robers Daughter of Joshua and Experience Rogers was born March ye 30th 1749
Lois Rogers Daughter of Joshua and Experience Rogers was born January 31st 1752
Experience Rogers wife of sd Joshua Rogers Died August the 11th 1752
Mr. Joshua Rogers was married to Lydia Minor the 29th Day of January 1753
Jemima Rogers Daughter of Joshua and Lydia Rogers was born March 14th 1755
Roland Rogers Son of Joshua and Lydia Rogers was born 9th Novembr 1756
Joshua Rogers Departed this life December 28th 1756
Jemima Rogers Daughter of Joshua and Lydia Rogers died July 26th 1776

Fredrick Mather and Elizabeth Perkins Boath of Lyme in New London County were married to Each other on the 16 of October AD 1765
Anna Mather Daughter of Fredrick & Elizabeth Mather was born August 24th 1766
Elizabeth Mather Daughter of Fredk & Elizabeth Mather was born Decembr 23rd 1769
Mercy Tillotson daughter of Simeon Tillotson was born 26 Augt 1787

[page 76]   This may certify whomesoever it may conscearn that Mr. Henry Champion Junr and Mrs. Sarah Peck both of Lyme were married together December the 19th 1751   Pr me Stephen Johnson Pastor of the first Church in sd Lyme
Henry Champion son of Henry and Sarah Champion was born August the 19th Day 1752
Jude Champion Daughter of Henry and Sarah Champion was born April the 29th Day AD 1755
Elisha Champion son of Henry and Sarah Champion was born the 7th Day of March AD 1758

Capt. Henry Champion Departed this Life on the 16th Day of May AD 1792 aged 63

Simeon Tillitson of Lyme in New London County was married to Martha Welch of Ashford on the 9th Day of January AD 1755
Simeon Tilletson son of Simeon and Martha Tilletson was born the 10th Day of Decembr 1755
Temperance Tilletson Daughter of Simeon and Martha Tilletson was born 4th of April 1758
Mary Tilletson Daughter of Simeon and Martha Tilletson was born January 9th AD 1762
Daniel Tilletson son of Simeon and Martha Tilletson was born 29th of July AD 1764
Thomas Tilletson son of Simeon and Martha Tilletson was born April 4th AD 1767
Elijah Tilletson son of Simeon and Martha Tilletson was born June 9th AD 1770
Eleazer son of the said Simeon & Martha was born on the 9th Day of June AD 1773
Lucy Daughter of the said Simeon & Martha was born January 22d AD 1776
Lois Daughter of said Simeon & Martha was born the 27th Day of March 1779

Lyme August 3rd 1785: These are to certify that Mr. Abraham Avery and Miss Elizabeth Noyes was married February the 6th 1785 by me   Daniel Miner Pastor of Congrega Church
Moses Avery Son of Abraham & Elizabeth Avery was born February 12th 1786
Moses died the eighth day of August AD 1788
Elizabeth daughter of the said Abm & Elizabeth was born February 19th day AD 1788
Mary daughter of the said Abm & Elizabeth was born Feby 19th day AD 1790
Abraham Son of the said Abraham & Elizabeth was born on the 1st day of March 1792
John Son of the said Abraham & Elizabeth was born on the 25th day of March 1794
Hannah Daughter of the said Abraham & Elizabeth was born 25th Decr AD 1795
Thomas Son of the said Abraham & Elizabeth was born on the 2d day of Jany 1798
Enoch son of the said Abm & Elizabeth was born on the 13 Octr 1802
Samuel son of the said Abm & Elizabeth was born on the 4 January 1805

[page 77]   Levi Tillitson and Mary Davis both of Lyme in the County of New London were Joyned in marriage on the 16th Day of August 1748
Eleazer Tillitson son of Levi and Mary Tillitson was born the 15th Day of October 1749
Deborah Tillitson Daughter of Levi and Mary Tillitson was born January the 4th Day 1751
David Tillitson son of Levi and Mary Tillitson was born the 28th Day of January 1753
Levi Tillitson son of Levi and Mary Tillitson was born October 25th AD 1754
Phebe Tillitson Daughter of Levi and Mary Tillitson was born January ye 29th 1757
Rhoda Tillitson Daughter of Levi and Mary Tillitson was born March ye 5th 1759
Rane Tillitson Daughter of Levi and Mary Tillitson was born December 30th 1761
Delight Tillitson Daughter of Levi and Mary Tillitson was born November 28th 1764
Isaiah Tillitson son of Levi and Mary Tillitson was born August 3rd 1767
Ezra Tillitson son of Levi and Mary Tillitson was born March 14th 1770

These may certify all persons conscearnd that Guy Chadwick of Lyme was married to Eunice Beckwith of sd Lyme August the first 1754 Pr me Benjamin Lee Justice of the Peace

Azubah Chadwick Daughter of Guy and Eunice Chadwick was born July 26th AD 1755

Esther Chadwick Daughter of Guy and Eunice Chadwick was born December 14th AD 1756

Elizabeth Chadwick Daughter of Guy and Eunice Chadwick was born April first 1759

Jerusha Chadwick Daughter of Guy and Eunice Chadwick was born July 14th 1763

Cardina Chadwick Daughter of Guy & Eunice Chadwick was born Octbr 13th 1765

Guy Chadwick son of Guy and Eunice Chadwick was born March 19th 1772

Colchester N. London County October 14 1785: Then Mr. John Coult of Lyme and Miss Susannah Bulkley of Colchester were Lawfully Joyned in marriage before me John Watrous Justt Paec

John Breed

Israel Bulkley

Charles Bulkley Coult son of John & Sussannah Coult was born August 11th 1786

[page 78] These may Certifie whomesoever it may Concear that Mr. Jabez Dewolf and Mrs. Eunice Calkins both of Lyme were married the 15th Day of November: 1753 Lyme 27th Septemr AD: 1754 Pr me Stephen Johnson Pastor

Achsah DeWolf Daughter of Jabez and Eunice DeWolf was born on Wednesday the 21st Day of August: 1754: and was Baptized September 29th: 1754 by the Revd Mr. Stephen Johnson

John Dewolf son of Jabez and and Eunice DeWolf was born the 3rd Day of September: 1757

Eunice DeWolf Daughter of Jabez and Eunice DeWolf was born August 29th A.D: 1760

Eunice DeWolf wife of sd Jabez Dewolf Departed this Life January ye 14th A.D 1761

John Dewolf son of Jabez Dewolf Departed this Life the 10th Day of February: A.D 1761

Achsah Dewolf Daughter of Jabez Dewolf Died Septemr 5th A.D: 1776

Stephen Tinker and Lovina Wade boath of Lyme were Lawfully married to Each other on the 11th Day of July: 1786: by the Revered Mr. Stephen Johnson as was Certified by liveing Evidence --

Harriss Tinker Son of Stephen and Lovina Tinker was born August 11th - 1787 and Died February ye 9th 1788

Arribilla daughter of said Stephen & Lovina born Jany 22d day AD 1789

Edward Church and Mary Clemments were married together on ye 3rd Day of March A.D. 1742/3

Lous Church Daughter of Edward and Mary Church was born ye 15th Day of March: 1743/4

Susannah Church Daughter of Edward and Mary Church was born ye 18th Day of March: AD 1745/6

Ezra Church Son of Edward and Mary Church was born February the 11th Day A.D: 1748

Josiah Church Son of Edward & Mary Church was born June the first Day: A.D 1750

Athena Church Daughter of Edward and Mary Church was born May 21st A.D: 1752

Mary Church Daughter of Edward and Mary Church was born April 10th A.D: 1754

These are to Certifie whomesoever it may Conscern that Mr. Amos Smith and Mrs. Lucinda Miller boath of Lyme were Lawfully Married together - March 12th A.D: 1778: Pr me Stephen Johnson Pastor of the First Church in sd Lyme. Dated in Lyme this 5th Day of May A.D: 1779

Ezra Smith Son of Amos & Lucinda Smith was born 24th of October AD: 1778

Amos Smith Son of Amos & Lucinda Smith was born 6th of August: A.D. 1785

[page 79] Thomas Lee of Lyme was Married to Elisabeth Gilbert of sd Lyme on the 6th Day of April A.D: 1756
Elisabeth Lee Daughter of Thomas and Elisabeth Lee was born January first: A.D. 1757
Elisabeth Lee wife of Thomas Lee above said Died the 10th Day of January: 1757
Thomas Lee of Lyme was Married to Mehetabel Peck of sd Lyme the 14th Day of July A.D 1757

Martin Lee of Lyme and Sabra Miner of sd Lyme were Lawfully Married to Each other on the 23rd Day of December A.D. 1771 as appears by the Record of Benjamin Lee Esqr Late of sd Lyme Deceasd
Christopher Lee Son of Martin and Sabra Lee was born October ye 23rd 1772
Sabra Lee Daughter of Martin & Sabra Lee was born Septemr 29th: 1774
Lucretia Lee Daughter of Martin & Sabre Lee was Born March: 7th 1777

This is to Certifie all Persons to whome it may Conscearn that Elisha Merrow and Mary Munsall made their appearance the 20th of October 1751 and was Joyned together in marriage: I being the mouth in that Relation - Joshua Rogers Elder
Elisha Merrow Son of Elisha and Mary Merrow was born June 21st A.D: 1753
John Merrow Son of Elisha and Mary Merrow was born July 21st Day A.D: 1755
Nathan Merrow Son of Elisha and Mary Merrow was born March March 4th Day: A.D: 1758
Molley Merrow Daughter of Elisha & Mary Merrow was born June ye 9th A.D - 1760
Elisabeth Merrow Daughter of Elisha & Mary Merrow was born September 2nd A.D 1762
Annar Merrow Daughter of Elisha Merrow & Mary his wife was born Novemr 17th: 1764
Abigail Merrow Daughter of Elisha & Mary Merrow was born February 14th 1768
Sarah Merrow Daughter of Elisha & Mary Merrow was born March: 3rd 1770
Cate Merrow Daughter of Elisha & Mary Merrow was Born Novemr 28th: 1773

These may Certifie that Mr. Nathaniel Smith of Lyme and Miss Lucinda Armsby of Norwich are Lawfully Married November 1st 1784 John Nott Clerk
Ruth Smith Daughter of Nathll & Lucinda Smith was Born June 4th A.D: 1785
Hibbard Son of said Nathaniel & Lucinda born Sept 13th A.D. 1787
Sarah Daughter of the said Nathll & Lucinda was born on the 14th day of August 1790
Sarah Daughter of the said Nathll & Lucinda deceas'd the 13th day of Septr 1793
Nabby Daughter of the said Nathll & Lucinda was born on the 24th day of March A.D. 1793
Ichabod Son of the said Nathaniel & Lucinda was born on the 10th day of Jany A.D. 1796
Lucinda daughter of the said Nathll & Lucinda was born on the 17th day of October A.D. 1798
Nathaniel son of the said Nathll & Lucinda was born on the 13th day of February 1801
Henry Bela son of the sd Nathaniel & Lucinda was born the 13 of Decr 1803
Nancy daughter of the sd Nathll & Lucinda was born the 22d Octr 1806

[page 80] These may Certifie whomesoever it may Consearn that Mr. Jeremiah Menoir [Minor] and Mrs. Elisabeth Marvin both of Lyme were Married November the 28th A.D: 1749 Pr me Stephen Johnson Dated in Lyme 23rd Novemr A.D. 1754

Jason Smith Son of Elijah & Elisabeth Smith was Born April 7th: A.D: 1760
Lyme May 23rd A.D: 1782 then Mr. Jason Smith of sd Lyme was Married to Mrs. Nabby Harison of Lyme aforesaid by me Danll Miner Pastor of the Select Congregation of sd Lyme
Elisha Smith son of Jason & Nabby Smith was Born September 21st A.D 1782 and Died the 21st Day of January A.D: 1783

Lyme June 19th: 1755 Nathan Robins and Phebe Beckwith both of Lyme were Married together by me George Griswold Minister of the Gospel
Rufus Robins son of Nathan and Phebe Robins was born the first Day of June: A.D: 1756
Silas Robins son of Nathan and Phebe Robins was born the 20th Day of September: 1757

Nathan Robins son of Nathan and Phebe Robins was born December 12th 1760
Phebe Robins Daughter of Nathan & Phebe Robins was born December 12th A.D: 1760 the above sd Nathan and Phebe being twins.
Lydia Robins Daughter of Nathan & Phebe Robins was born June 27th A.D: 1766
Nathan Robins son of Nathan & Phebe Robins Died May 12th A.D: 1767
Zenos Robins son of Nathan & Phebe Robins was Born June 17th A.D: 1768
Lucretia Robins Daughter of Nathan & Phebe Robins was born July 20th A.D 1770
Rufus Robins Son of Nathan and Phebe Robins died August: A.D: 1781

[page 81] Lyme October 22nd 1755: Elisha Minor and Ruth Robins both of Lyme were Married together by me - George Griswold Minister of the Gospel
Zenas Minor son of Elisha and Ruth Minor was born December 19th A.D 1756

Henry Boon & Rebecca Smith was Joyn'd in Marriage the 1 day of Novr A.D 1775
Betsy Daughter of the said Henry & Rebecca was born on the 13th day of March 1776
Keturah Daughter of the said Henry & Rebecca was born on the 3d day of May A.D 1778
Jerusha Daughter of the sd Henry & Rebecca was born on the 15th day of June 1780
Henry Son of the said Henry & Rebecca was born on the 19th day of August 1782
William Son of the said Henry & Rebecca was born on the 1st day of August 1784
Charlotte Daughter of the sd Henry & Rebecca was born on the 7th day of October 1786
Zurviah Daughter of the sd Henry & Rebecca was born on the 14th day of Novr 1788
Ichabod Smith Son of the said Henry & Rebecca was born on the 2d day of Jany 1791
Sally Daughter of the said Henry & Rebecca was born on the 11th October 1793
Hezekiah Smith Son of the sd Henry & Rebecca was born on the 4 day of March 1796

These may Certifie whomesoever it may Conscearn that Mr. Elijah Hill and Miss Mary Huntly both of Lyme were married together on the 16th Day of October AD 1750 Pr me Stephen Johnson Pastor of the first Church in sd Lyme
Elijah Hill son of Elijah and Mary Hill was born June ye 28th Day AD 1751
Jemima Hill Daughter of Elijah & Mary Hill was born June the 2nd Day AD 1753
Bettey Hill Daughter of Elijah & Mary Hill was born October ye 29th AD 1755

John Robins and Esther Beckwith both of Lyme in New London were Lawfully Married to Each other on the 15h Day of February AD 1753
Edward Robins son of John and Esther Robins was born January 20th AD 1754
Ruth Robins Daughter of John & Esther Robins was born 26th
Bettey Robins Daughter of John & Esther Robins was born April 28th AD 1762

[page 82] David Peck was married to Abigail Southworth the 16th day of June 1743
Abigail Peck Daughter of David and Abigail Peck was born September first 1744
Samuel Giles Peck son of David and Abigail Peck was born October 25th AD 1746
Ezra Peck son of David and Abigail Peck was born January ye 11th Day AD 1748
David Peck son of David and Abigail Peck was born April ye 24th AD 1750 and Died the 11th Day of May AD 1750
David Peck son of David and Abigail Peck was born June 28th AD 1751
William Peck son of David and Abigail Peck was born January 6th AD 1754
Joseph Peck son of David and Abigail Peck was born June 10th AD 1756
Hananiah Peck son of David and Abigail Peck was born November 14th 1758
Mishail Peck son of David and Abigail Peck was born June 6th AD 1761
Azariah Peck son of David and Abigail Peck was born February 9th AD 1764
Daniel Peck son of David and Abigail Peck was born 28th October 1766
Elizabeth Peck Daughter of David and Abigail Peck was born first of May 1770

Hezekiah Smith of Lyme in the County of New London was married to Sarah Chadwick of sd Lyme in September AD 1732
Ichabode Smith son of Hezekiah and Sarah Smith was born June ye 10th AD 1733
Phinehas Smith son of Hezekiah and Sarah Smith was born February the first AD 1735
Stephen Smith son of Hezekiah and Sarah Smith was born March the 30th AD 1737

Nathaniel Smith son of Hezekiah and Sarah Smith was born October ye 8th AD 1739
Elias Smith son of Hezekiah and Sarah Smith was born September 10th AD 1742
Rane Smith Daughter of Hezekiah and Sarah Smith was born August 21st AD 1745
Elishaba Smith Daughter of Hezekiah and Sarah Smith was born February 15th AD 1747
Lydia Smith Daughter of Hezekiah and Sarah Smith was born Septemr ye first AD 1750
Loas Smith Daughter of Hezekiah and Sarah Smith was born August 25th AD 1753

Temme Beckwith Daughter of Willm and Luce Beckwith was born the 22nd Day of May AD 1754

[page 83]   Ezra Ely of Lyme was on the 8th Day of August 1751 married to Sarah Starling of the same town   Pr George Beckwith
Sarah Ely Daughter of Ezra and Sarah Ely was born April ye 20th 1753
Esther Ely Daughter of Ezra and Sarah Ely was born April ye 19th 1755
Zebulon Ely son of Ezra and Sarah Ely was born February ye 6th AD 1759
Sarah Ely sd Ezra Elys Wife Died June 14th 1759
Ezra Ely of Lyme was Married to Anna Starlin of Lyme August ye 21st 1760
Daniel Starlin Ely son of Ezra and Anna Ely was born October ye 15th AD 1761 and Died March 22nd 1786
Anna Ely Daughter of Ezra and Anna Ely was born September 15th 1764
Benjamin Ely son of Ezra and Anna Ely was born July ye 18th 1767
Israel Ely son of Ezra and Anna Ely was born June ye 12th 1770

Lyme 11th: February: AD 1754: These are to Certifye whomsoever it may Conscearn that Mr. Joseph Sill Sill 2nd and Mrs. Ruth Matson both of Lyme were lawfully married together on the 31st Day of December AD 1747 Pr me Stephen Johnson Pastor of the first Church in Lyme
Giles Sill son of Joseph Sill Junr and Ruth his wife was born November 21st 1748
Nathaniel Sill son of Joseph Sill Junr and Ruth his wife was born May ye 19th AD 1750
Ruhama Sill Daughter of Joseph Sill Junr & Ruth his wife was born April ye 5th 1752
Lucia Sill Daughter of Joseph Sill Junr & Ruth his wife was born May ye 14th AD 1754
Ruth Sill Daughter of Joseph Sill Junr & Ruth his wife was born March ye 14th 1756
Nathll Sill above said Died August 10th 1765
Willm Sill son of Joseph and Ruth Sill was born Decembr ye 6th AD 1760
Ruth Sill Wife of the above said Joseph Sill Junr Died August 12th 1762

These Certifye whomsoever it may Conscear that Mr. Joseph Sill and Mrs. Azubah Dewolf both of Lyme were lawfully married together the 23rd of April AD 1765 Pr me Stephen Johnson Pastor of the first Church in Lyme   Dated in Lyme 23rd Day of March AD 1774
Azubah Sill Daughter of Joseph and Azubah Sill was Born June 10th 1766
Joseph Lee Sill son of Joseph and Azubah Sill was born June 9th AD 1768
Phebe Sill Daughter of Joseph and Azubah Sill was born June 4th 1770
Mrs. Azubah Sill wife of sd Joseph Sill Died January 17th 1771
Mr. Joseph Sill departed this life on the 20th day of Jany AD 1782

[page 84]   Simon Dewolf of Lyme in the County of New London was married to Lucia Calkins of sd Lyme on the 31st Day of January AD 1745
Sarah Dewolf Daughter of Simon and Lucia Dewolf was born January 9th 1746
Elisha Dewolf son of Simon and Lucia Dewolf was born February the 16th 1748
Phebe Dewolf Daughter of Simon and Lucia Dewolf was born November the 5th 1750
Simon Dewolf son of Simon and Lucia Dewolf was born January 21st 1756
Simon Dewolf Died the 10th Day of February 1750: in the 37th year of his age

Abner Huntly and Lucretia Rowland were married to Each other on the 26th Day of June: AD: 1768
Mary Huntly Daughter of Abner and Lucretia Huntly was born April 29th 1769
Abner Huntly son of Abner and Lucretia Huntly was born August 4th 1773

William Huntly son of Abner & Lucretia Huntly was born January 22nd 1778
Seth Huntly son of Abner & Lucretia Huntly was born June 29th 1780

Ezra Brockway Brockway was born May 24th AD 1732
Ezra Brockway of Lyme in the County of New London was married to Dorcas Giddings of sd Lyme November 14th Day AD 1754
Bridget Brockway Daughter of Ezra and Dorcas Brockway was born the 26th Day of September: AD 1755

These Certified that in Lyme in the State of Connecticut on the 8th: Day of February: 1768 John Cooley [now?] Dewolf and Lydia Anderson boath of Lyme were lawfully married to each other by me Matthew Griswold then an Asistant for sd State: Certified the 18th: Day of July: 1778   Pr Matthew Griswold D: Governor
Sela Cooley Daughter of John & Lydia Cooley was born June 25th: 1768: on Saturday
Mehetabel Cooley Daughter of John & Lydia Cooley was born November 3rd: 1769 on Thursday
Matthew Cooley Son of John and Lydia Cooley was born June 8th 1771: on Saturday
Theada Cooley Daughter of John & Lydia Cooley was born Decembr 31st 1772: on Thursday
John Cooley Died on the 4th Day of July: 1774
John Cooley Son of John & Lydia Cooley was born October: ye 23rd 1774

[page 85]   Lyme 21st February AD 1757
These may Certifie whomesoever it may Conscearn that Mr. Marshfield Parsons and Mrs Loas Wait both of Lyme were married on the 9th day of October: AD 1755: Pr me Sephen Johnson: Pastor of the first Church of Christ in Lyme
John Parsons Son of Marshfield and Loas Parsons was born March 9th Day: AD 1757
William Parsons Son of Marshfield and Loas Parsons was born 27th Day of June AD 1759
William Parsons Son of Marshfield and Loas Parsons Died August 14th: AD 1761
Loas Parsons Wife of Mr. Marshfield Parsons Died 6th July: AD 1764
These are to Certify whomsoever it may Conscearn that Mr. Marshfield Parsons and Mrs. Abigail Marvin both of Lyme were Lawfully Married together the 20th of November: AD: 1766 Pr me Stephen Johnson Pastor of the first Church in sd Lyme
Dated in Lyme 2nd Decembr AD 1766
Mrs. Abigail Parsons Wife of [Cole] Marshfield Departed this life on the 22nd Day of August AD 1782
This 15th of January: 1783 was married Cole Marshfield Parsons of Lyme to Miss Abigail Waterman of Norwich: Pr Joseph Strong V D in Norwich April first: 1783
Mrs. Abigail Parsons Wife of the sd Marshfield died March 14th 1793
This Certifies that Col Marshfield Parsons & Mrs. Phebe Griffin both of Lyme was was married together Octr 10th AD 1793 By David Higgins V.D.M.
Marshfield Parsons died January 13th AD 1813 in the 80 year of his age

Jedediah Brockway of Lyme in New London County was married to Sarah Fox of New London in sd County the 3rd Day of October AD 1743
Jonah Brockway son of Jedediah & Sarah Brockway was born January 16th: 1744
Gedeon Brockway son of Jedediah and Sarah Brockway was born September 14th: 1746 Died the 12th Day of December 1749
Rachel Brockway Daughter of Jedediah & Sarah Brockway was born August 17th 1748 and Died the 13th Day of December 1749
Rachel Brockway Daughter of Jedediah and Sarah Brockway was born Novembr 5th 1750
Naomy Brockway Daughter of Jedediah and Sarah Brockway was born May 5th 1753
Lydia Brockway Daughter of Jedediah and Sarah Brockway was born April 20th 1755
Lucey Brockway Daughter of Jedediah and Sarah Brockway was born March 5th 1757
Gedeon Brockway son of Jedediah and Sarah Brockway was born the 6th Day of April 1759

Lyme Novembr: 20th AD 1777: then I married Elias Miner of Lyme to his now wife Esther Noyes Test -- Samuel Ely Justice of the Peace
Joseph Miner Son of Elias & Esther Miner was Born October 4th AD: 1778
Benjamin Miner Son of Elias & Esther Miner was Born August 16th AD: 1780
Selden Miner Son of Elias & Esther Miner was Born April 26th AD: 1783
Esther Miner Daughter of Elias & Esther Miner was Born 21st Decembr 1785
Esther Miner the wife of sd Elias Miner Departed this life January 6th: 1786
These Certifies that Elias Miner of Lyme and Sarah Ely of Haddam on the date hereof was Entered into a marriage Covenant to Each other before Israel Spenser Justice Peace East Haddam 28 of August 1786
Sarah Daughter of the said Elias & Sarah was born the 12th day of November 1789
Lydia Daughter of the said Elias & Sarah was born the 17th day of September 1791
Isaac Son of the said Elias & Sarah was born the 11th day of February 1793
Joseph Minor son of Elias and Esther Minor died May 5th AD 1796

[page 86] July 23rd: 1755: then the Subscriber Joyned together in marraiage Joseph Brown of Lyme and Anna Beckwith of New London I say Pr Stephen Gorton Elder
Joseph Brown son of Joseph and Anna Brown was born May the 22nd Day AD: 1756
Ruth Brown and Anna Brown Daughter of Joseph and Anna Brown was born July 28th: 1758
Aaron Brown son of Joseph and Anna Brown was born the 7th Day of February: 1761

Reynold Peck & Deborah Beckwith was joyned in marriage 8th March 1764
Anna their Daughter was born the 24th Day of January 1765
Hannah Daughter of the said Reynold & Deborah born 13th of April 1767
John Sean Peck Son of sd Reynold & Deborah was born 13th of May 1769
Bettee their Daughter was born on the 26 day of December 1771
Thomas Son of the sd Reynold and Deborah was born 23d May 1774
Watrous son of the said Reynold and Deborah was born 14th April 1777
George their son was born on the 26th Day of March AD 1780
Abner their son was born on the 15th Day of October AD 1782
Sally their Daughter was born on the 27th Day of August 1786

Lyme 4th March 1757: These may Certifie whomesoever it may Conscearn that Mr. Timothy Tiffany and Miss Elizabeth Lord both of Lyme was married together the 20th Day of December: 1753 Pr me Stephen Johnson Pastor of the first Church of Christ in Lyme
Nabe Lord Tiffany Daughter of Timothy and Elizabeth Tiffany was born the 26th Day of September: AD 1754

These may signifie and Certifye that Mr. Joseph Marvin 2nd was on the the 16th Day of October AD: 1783: Married to Miss Phebe Starlin both of Lyme by me   George Beckwith Clerk
Fanny Marvin Daughter of Joseph Marvin 2nd and Phebe his wife was born the 7th Day of October: 1784
Phebe Marvin Daughter of Joseph Marvin 2nd and Phebe his wife was born the 7th Day of June: 1785
William Marvin Son of Joseph and Phebe Marvin was Born May 12th 1788
Jamima Daughter of the said Joseph & Phebe was born the 28th Day of March 1791
Joseph Son of the said Joseph & Phebe was born the 8th Day of February 1793
Clarrissa Daughter of the said Joseph & Phebe was born on the 5th May AD 1795

[page 87] These may certifie whomsoever it may Concearn that Mr. Ebenezer Staples and Charity Lenard both of Lyme were Married together the 30th Day of January A.D. 1755 Pr me Stephen Johnson, Pastor of the first Church in sd Lyme
Asa Staples son of Ebenezer and Charity Staples was born Septemr 8th Day A.D. 1755
Parthene Staples Daughter of Ebenezer and Charity Staples was born December 25 1757
Lucy Staples Daughter of Ebenezer & Charity Staples was born July the 17th A.D. 1759

To John Lay 2nd Esqr: Sr. these may Certifie that Enoch Smith of Lyme and Eunice Comstock of New London County was Lawfully Married togeth by me this 18th Day of March: 1777: Joshua Morse Minister of the Gospel in New London North Parish - Joshua Morse -

Oliver Comstock Smith Son of Enoch & Eunice Smith was born June 2nd 1782

Thomas Sill of Lyme in the County of New London was married to Jemima Dudley in May A.D: 1742

Jemima Sill Daughter of Thomas and Jemima Sill was Born March 30th A.D: 1743

Samuel Sill Son of Thomas and Jemima Sill was born April the 4th Day - A.D: 1745

Thomas Sill Son of Thomas & Jemima Sill was born March: the 16th Day: A.D: 1747

Isaac Sill Son of Thomas and Jemima Sill was born April 20th Day - A.D. 1749

Mica Sill Son of Thomas and Jemima Sill was Born December ye 25th Day A.D: 1751

Mehetable Sill Daughter of Thomas and Jemima Sill was Born May ye 4th A.D: 1754

Lyme March ye 11th: 1788: then was Married Jedediah Edgerton of of Norwich and Esther Wallis of sd Lyme, by me Daniel Miner Pastor of Strict Congrll Church of sd Lyme

Lucey Edgerton Daughter of Jedediah and Esther Edgerton was Born April 11th: 1788

Polly Edgerton was born on the 12th day of Novr 1789

Daniel Edgerton was born the 29th day of Novr 1791

Isac Woodworth Died the 4th Day of December A.D. 1758

[page 88]   Jasper Griffing Junr was Married to Eunice Rogers both of Lyme in the County of New London on the 9th Day of May A.D: 1751

Joshua Griffing Son of Jasper Griffing Junr and Eunice his wife was born February 25th A.D: 1752

Jasper Griffing Son of Jasper Griffing Junr & Eunice his Wife was born February ye 28th A.D: 1754

Joseph Griffing Son of Jasper Griffing Junr and Eunice his Wife was born February ye 3rd A.D: 1756

David Griffing Son of Jasper Griffing Junr and Eunice his Wife was born April 24th 1758

Nathan Griffing Son of Jasper Griffing Junr & Eunice his wife was born August 13th 1760

The births of the children of Ezra Lee and Sarah his wife who removed to Granville, N.Y. 1787 From the Bible Record

Shubal born Aug. 14, 1770

Betsey born July 5, 1772

[page 88]   Jedediah born Aug. 18, 1774

Anson born Oct. 28, 1776

Stephen born Oct. 21, 1778

Dauther and Son born Feb. 18, 1780   died Feb. 20, 1780

Luna and Aruna born Dec. 25, 1781

David born April 2, 1784

Marshall born Sept. 17. 1786

Lyme 20th January A.D: 1758 These may Certifie whomesoever it may Conscearn that Levi Bartholomew of Saybrook and Hannah Mack of Lyme were Lawfully Married together the 11th Day October: A.D: 1757 Pr me Stephen Johnson Pastor of the first Church in Lyme

Colchester April 17th: 1761 these may Certifie that I married Nun Clark of Lyme to Anna Jones of Colchester on the 20th Day of April Anno Dom: 1758 - Nathel Foot Justice Peace

Watrous Clark Son of Nun and Anna Clark was born March the 8th: AD - 1760

Hope Clark was Born September the 28th A.D: 1760

These may Signifie and Certifie that Eleazer Mather Junr: was on May 29th Anno: 1775: Married unto Irene Starlin, both of Lyme by me George Beckwith Pastor
Eleazer Mather Junr - Son of Eleazer Mather 2nd & Irene his wife was born Decemr: 30th 1775
Watrous Mather Son of Eleazer and Irene Mather was born the 11th: Day of March: 1778

[page 89] John Hudson of Lyme was Married to Jane Fox of East Haddam 24th of March: 1747
John Hudson Son of John and Jane Hudson was born ye 9th day of September: 1749
Rhoda Hudson Daughter of John & Jane Hudson was born the 12th of November 1751
Lovicey Hudson Daughter of John & Jane Hudson was born April the first: 1754
Jane Hudson Daughter of John & Jane Hudson was born April 19th 1756
Lucy Hudson Daughter of John & Jane Hudson was born April 3rd 1758
Lous Hudson Daughter of John & Jane Hudson was born July ye 8th 1760

These may Certifie whomsoever it may Conscearn that Mr. William Roland & Mrs. Eunice Tinker both of Lyme were Lawfully Married together on the first Day of August: A.D: 1764 Pr me Stephen Johnson Pastor of the first Church in sd Lyme Dated in Lyme 19th January A.D. 1769

Elijah Beckwith and Sarah Miller was Married the 22d day of Augt. 1784
Joseph Son of said Elijah & Sally was born on the 10th day of January 1785
Lydia Daughter of said Elijah & Sally was born the 7th Day of Decembr 1787
Joanna Daughter of said Elijah & Sally was born the 20th of Febry. 1790
Ebenezer Morgan was Married to Sally Miller Septr 29th A.D. 1793

[page 90] George Griswold Junr and Elisabeth Lee both of Lyme were Married together - February 7th 1758 by me George Griswold Pastor of the 2nd Church in Lyme
Matthew Griswold Son of George Griswold Junr and Elisabeth his Wife was born January 10th 1759
Matthew Griswold Son of George Griswold Junr and Elisabeth his wife Died the 10th of February: 1759
Hannah Lyde Griswold Daughter of George and Elisabeth Griswold was born April 16th - A.D - 1760
Elisabeth Griswold Daughter of George and Elisabeth Griswold was born February 18th 1762
Candice Griswold Daughter of George and Elisabeth Griswold was born April 4th - A.D 1764
Eunice Griswold Daughter of George and Elisabeth Griswold was born March 31st A.D 1766
Matthew Griswold Son of George and Elisabeth Griswold was born June 7th A.D. 1768
Jean Griswold Daughter of George & Elisabeth Griswold was born Novemr 20th 1770
Nathel Lynde Griswold Son of George & Elisabeth Griswold was born January 19th 1773
Ursula Griswold Daughter of George & Elisabeth Griswold was born January 20th 1775
George Griswold Son of George & Elisabeth Griswold was born March 6th A.D - 1777
Thomas Griswold Son of George & Elisabeth Griswold was Born March 21st - A.D: 1779
Elisabeth Wife of the said George died on the 5th day of October AD 1797

Jonathan Reed was Married to Abigail Comstock both of Lyme the 15th Day of April A.D - 1756
Jonathan Reed Son of Jonathan and Abigail was born December 21st AD: 1757
Jonathan Reed Son of Jonathan and Abigail departed this Life ye 8th Day of April: 1759
John Ames was Joined in Marriage to Dorrilly Wood on the 21 day of February A.D. 1783
Dorrilly Wife of Jno Ames departed this life 10th Septr 1785
Eunice Daughter of the said Jno & Dorrilly was born 10th May 1778
Bradish Son of the said Jno & Dorrilly was born 19th Novr 1783
John Ames was married to Keturah Huntly 8th Jany 1786
John Noyes Son of the said Jno & Katurah was born 15 May 1787

Huldah Sawyer Daughter of Jesse and Sarah Sawyer was born February 22nd A.D: 1759
Barabas Tuthil of Lyme Died on the 7th Day of March A.D: 1773
Abia Tuthill Relect of Barnabas Tuthill Died Septemr first A.D. 1776
Samuel Mather Son of Azariah Mather and Hannah Mather was Born April 9th 1769 in the Town of Lyme
[page 91]   Nathan Woodwoth and Deborah Mack both of Lyme was Married on the 23rd Day of June A.D 1756
Ruel Woodwoth Son of Nathan and Deborah Woodwoth was born April ye 28th A.D: 1757
Huldah Woodwoth Daughter of Nathan and Deborah Woodwoth was born May first: 1759
Lucy Woodwoth Daughter of Nathan & Deborah Woodwoth was born May 27th - 1761
Asenthy Woodwoth Daughter of Nathan & Deborah Woodwoth was born June first 1764
Nathan Woodwoth Son of Nathan & Deborah Woodwoth was born April 18th 1766
Welthy Woodwoth Daughter of Nathan & Deborah Woodwoth was Born March 13th 1768
Isaac Woodwoth Son of Nathan & Deborah Woodwoth was Born December 20th 1771
The above named Nathan Woodwoth Died the 7th Day of November: A.D. 1771
Nathan Woodwoth son of Nathan & Deborah Woodworth died May 23d 1834

These may Signifie and Certifie that Samuel Starlin of Lyme was on the 2nd Day December AD. 1756: Married to Elisabeth Perkins of the same Town of Lyme by me George Beckwith Pastor
Irene Starlin Daughter of Samuel and Elisabeth Starlin was born october the 17th A.D. 1758
Sarah Starlin Daughter of Samuel & Elisabeth Starlin was born December 30th A.D. 1761
Lena Starlin Daughter of Samll & Elisabeth Starlin was born May 21st A.D 1764
Samll Starlin Son of Samuel & Elisabeth Starlin was born Septemr first: 1766
Lizze Starlin Daughter of Samll & Elisabeth Starlin was born Novemr 3rd 1768
James Starlin Son of Samll & Elisabeth Starlin was born December 25th 1770
Ruth Perkins Starlin Daughter of Samll & Elisabeth Starlin was born Septemr 27th 1773
Lucy Starlin Daughter of Samll & Elisabeth Starlin was born Decemr 9th 1775
Elisabeth Starlin Wife of the above said Samll Starlin Died March 18th 1777

I hereby Certifie whome it May Conscearn that Mr. Samll Starlin of Lyme & Mrs. Annah Dudley of Saybrook were Joyned in Marriage February 2nd 1779: by me William Hart Pastor of first Church in Saybrook
Lord Starlin Son of Samll & Annah Starlin was born April 3rd 1780
Hannah Starlin Daughter of Samll & Annah Starlin was Born Septemr 8th 1782
Annah Wif of the said Samuel Departed this life on the [12th] day of [April] A.D 179[4]
Mr. Samuel Starling was Married to Mrs. Lucretia Champin on the 12 March AD 1795

[page 92]   These may Certifie whomesoever it may Conscearn that Mr. Adonijah Marvin and Diadama Miller both of Lyme were Lawfully Married together the 20th Day of August A.D. 1755   Pr me Stephen Johnson Pastor of the first Church in sd Lyme Dated in Lyme 12th February: 1759
Elisabeth Marvin Daughter of Adonijah and Diadama Marvin was born the 30th Day of June: 1756
Diadama Marvin Daughter of Adonijah & Diadama Marvin was Born the first Day of April A.D. 1758
Adonijah Marvin above named Died the 20th Day of April A.D. 1758

These are to Certifie that Mr. Zenos Huntly and Mrs. Elisabeth Peck boath of Lyme were Lawfully Married together the 15th Day of February: A.D. 1784: by me - Stephen Johnson Pastor of the first Church in said Lyme
Caulkins Huntly Son of Zenos and Elisabeth Huntly was born the 15th of February 1785
Dan Huntly Son of Zenos & Elisabeth Huntly was born February 27th A.D 1787

Solomon Mack of Lyme in New London County was Married to Lydia Gates of East Haddam the Daughter of Danll Gates of sd East Haddam in Hartford County on the 4th Day of January A.D. 1759

These Certifie that Mr. Elisha Miller ye 3rd and Mrs. Hannah Champion boath of Lyme were Lawfully Married to Each other on the 23rd Day of July: 1772 by me - John Lay 2nd Just Peace

Sussannah Miller Daughter of Elisha Miller 3rd & Hannah his Wife was born March: 13th: 1773

Elisabeth Miller Daughter of Elisha Miller and Hannah his Wife was born August 10th: 1775

Duncan Mcintosh Son of Duncan & Rachel Mcintosh was born March: 4th: A.D. 1757
Guy Mcintosh Son of Duncan and Rachel Mcintosh was born May 2nd A.D. 1758
Jemima Mcintosh Daughter of Duncan & Rachel Mcintosh was born October 3rd A.D 1759
Timothy Mcintosh Son of Duncan and Rachel Mcintosh was born January 27th 1761
Laughlon Mcintosh Son of Duncan & Rachel Mcintosh was born August 7th 1762
Rhoda Mcintosh Daughter of Duncan & Rachel Mcintosh was born January 3rd 1764
Joseph Mcintosh Son of Duncan and Rachel Mcintosh was born August 18th 1766
Rachel Mcintosh Daughter of Duncan & Rachel Mcintosh was born June first: 1767

[page 93] These may Certifie that George Lewis of Lyme was on February the 17th 1757 Marryed to Mary Reed of the Same Town - by me - George Beckwith Pastor of the 3rd Church in sd town.

George Reed Lewis Son of George and Mary Lewis was Born July ye 25th A.D 1757
John Lewis Son of George & Mary Lewis was Born December 25th A.D 1758
Mary Lewis Daughter of George & Mary Lewis was born February 15th 1761
William Lewis Son of George and Mary Lewis was born May 19th 1763
Benjamin Lewis Son of George & Mary Lewis was born October 16th 1765
Eber Lewis Son of George and Mary Lewis was born 29th of Novemr 1767
Benjamin Lewis Son of George and Mary Lewis Died the 8th Day of February: 1770

These Certifies that I Married Dan Peck to Lovina Huntly April 19th 1786 - Jason Lee
Lemuel Son of the said Dan and Lovina was born Octr 29th - 1787 & died June 17th A.D. 1788
Silas Son of the said Dan and Lovina was born the 8th day of May A.D 1789
Edward Chapman Son of the said Dan and Lovina was born October 10th A.D. 1790
Ansel Son of the said Dan and Lovina was born the 23d Day of Septr A.D 1792
Polly daughter of the said Dan and Lovina was born the 15th June A.D. 1801

These may Certifie that Broadstreet Emmerson of Lyme was on January 4th 1758 married to the Widow Jemima Sill of the same Town by me George Beckwith Minister of the Gospel

Broadstreet Emmerson Son of Broadstreet and Jemima Emmerson was born 14th March: 1759
The above sd Broadstreet Emmerson Since his Birth was Recorded hath been Baptized and is name is now Joseph: Born on sd 14th of March: 1759
Broadstreet Emmerson Son of Broadstreet and Jemima Emmerson was born October 21st 1761
Dudley Emmerson Son of Broadstreet and Jemima Emmerson was born February 3rd: 1765
Septemr 12th 1770
Hannah Fox Daughter of Amos and Deborah Fox was born January 12th: 1755
Elisha Fox Son of Amos and Deborah Fox was born October 28th 1757'
Marcy Fox Daughter of Amos and Deborah Fox was born Septemr 6th 1760
Amos Fox Son of Amos and Deborah Fox was born June 26 1762
Timothy Fox Son of Amos & Deborah Fox was born August 28th 1764
Benjamin Fox Son of Amos & Deborah Fox was born Septemr: 16th 1766

56 LYME, CONNECTICUT, VITAL RECORDS

Benjamin Phelps Son of John Clemment Phelps was Born March 6th 1775
John Phelps Son of John Clemment Phelps was Born December 5th 1777

[page 94] Mr. Joseph Jewit of Lyme in New London County was Married unto Lucretia Rogers of Norwich in the County aforesaid on the 18th Day of May: A.D 1758
Luce Jewit Daughter of Joseph and Lucretia Jewit was Born ye 12th Day of May A.D: 1759
Mary Jewit Daughter of Joseph and Lucretia Lewit was born ye 12th Day of March: A.D 1761
Joseph Jewit Son of Joseph and Lucretia Jewit was born June ye 7th 1763
Zabdiel Rogers Jewett Son of Joseph and Lucretia Jewit was born April 20th A.D 1765
Lucretia Jewit Daughter of Joseph & Lucretia Jewit was born April 24th A.D. 1767
Elisabeth and Deborah Jewits Daughters of Joseph and Lucretia Jewit were born August 27th A.D 1769
Joshua Jewit Son of Joseph & Lucretia Jewit was born August 14th A.D 1771
Josiah Jewit Son of Joseph & Lucretia Jewit was born Decemr: 29th: A.D: 1773
George Washington Jewit Son of Joseph & Lucretia Jewit was Born March 10th A.D: 1776
Elisabeth Jewitt aforesaid Died March 12th 1775
Capt. Joseph Jewit abovesaid Died in New York August ye 31st A.D: 1776

These may Certifie that Mr. Samuel Beckwith of Lyme was Lawfully Married to Mrs. Sarah Dickins of New Shoram March the 13th 1755: by John Littlefield Dept Warden: the above is Recorded in New Shoram Records December ye 26th 1759 pr Samuel Rathbone T. Clerk --
and the within Samuel and Sarah had a Daughter born January the 27th 1756 Named Wats: The above is a true copy of Record Duly Examined by Samll Rathbone T. Clerk
Anderson Beckwith Son of Samuel and Sarah Beckwith was born in Lyme 7th February 1758

Capt. Nathan Jewit Died February 10th: 1762

Lyme 25th June: 1761 These may Certifie whomsoever it may Conscearn that Mr. John Alger & Mrs. Luce Dewolf both of Lyme were Lawfully Married the 15th Day of January A.D. 1761 Pr me Stephen Johnson Pastor of the first Church in sd Lyme
John Alger above said Died the 21st Day of January: 1769

[page 95] May 4th - 1750 Roland Rogers of New London and Lucretia Rogers of Lyme Were Married together by me George Griswold Pastor of the Second Church in Lyme
Moses Rogers Son of Roland & Lucretia Rogers was born the 2nd Day of May: 1751
Roland Rogers Son of Roland & Lucretia Rogers was born the 28th Day of February: 1754
Deborah Rogers Daughter of Roland & Lucretia Rogers was born January 25th A.D. 1756
John Rogers Son of Roland and Lucretia Rogers was born January ye first A.D: 1760

Lyme the 13th of May: 1775: These may Certifie that Nathaniel Dickerson now of Lyme was married to Anne Munsell of Lyme the first Day of September 1773 Pr me Benjamin Lee Justice Peace

Samll Dickerson Son of Nathll and Anne Dickerson was born August 30th 1774
Anne Dickerson Wife of sd Nathll Dickerson Died 17th of January: 1775

Joseph Hayes was Legally Join'd in marriage to Lucy Ely July 29th A.D. 1773
Joseph Son of the said Joseph & Lucy was born on the 30th day of July A.D. 1774
Ely Son of the said Joseph & Lucy was born on the 10th day of April A.D. 1776

Saybrook in New London County ye 11th Day of March A.D. 1756: then I the Subscriber Married Mr. Joseph Coult to his now Wife Desire [Pratt] Certified Pr Samuel Ely Justice of the Peace
Josaiah Coult Son of Joseph and Desire Coult was born September ye 5th: A.D: 1757
Deborah Coult Daughter of Joseph & Desire Coult was born October ye 27th A.D: 1759

Judah Coult Son of Joseph and Desire Coult was born the first Day of July A.D: 1761
Desire Coult Daughter of Joseph and Desire Coult was born April 11th A.D. 1763
Asenath Coult Daughter of Joseph & Desire Coult was born October 19th A.D 1764
Joseph Coult Son of Joseph & Desire Coult was born April 18th A.D. 1766
Samuel Coult Son of Joseph & Desire Coult was born June 23rd A.D. 1771
Jabez Coult Son of Joseph and Desire Coult was born January 19th A.D. 1773

Lyme May 6th 1778: then Joseph Armisted was Lawfully Joyned in Marriage with Miriam Wright by Ezra Selden Justice Peace   Certified by Ezra Selden
Willm Armisted Son of Joseph & Miriam Armisted was born January : 31: 1779
James Benson Armisted Son of Joseph & Miriam Armisted was born January 16th 1781
Betsey Armisted Daughter of Joseph & Miriam Armisted was born March 9th: 1783
Thomas Benson Son of Joseph and Miriam Armisted was born 10th Septr 1785
Henry Yeadon Son of Joseph and Miriam Armisted was born the 10th of Septemr 1785
Nicolas Armisted Son of Joseph and Miriam Armisted was born Nover 18: 1787
Joseph Son of Joseph & Miriam Armisted was born on the 29th day of May 1793
George Washington Son of Jos & Miriam was born on the lt day of May 1795

[page 96]   William Brockway 2nd and Hannah Clark was Married on the 19th Day of April: A.D. 1744
Thomas Brockway Son of William and Hannah Brockway was born January 20th A.D. 1745
Carolina Brockway Daughter of William & Hannah Brockway was born May 18th A.D. 1748
Mary Brockway Daughter of William & Hannah Brockway was born October 8th 1750
Hannah Brockway Daughter of William & Hannah Brockway was born December 28th A.D. 1752
Abner Brockway Son of William & Hannah Brockway was born December 28th A.D. 1754
Temme Brockway Daughter of William & Hannah Brockway was born November 17th A.D. 1757

Mr. Abner Shipman was Legally Joyned in Marriage to Miss Margary Avery Octr 20th 1779
William Son of the said Abner & Margary was born the 19th day of May A.D. 1780
Christopher Son of the said Abner & Margary was born the 18th day of June A.D. 1781
Hallam Son of the said Abner & Margary was born the 19th day of Septr A.D. 1782
Elijah Son of the said Abner & Margary was born the 22nd day of April A.D. 1785
Betsy Daughter of said Abner & Margary was born the 20th day of Sepr A.D. 1786
Elisha son of the said Abner & Margary was born the 6th day of April A.D. 1788
Abner son of the said Abner & Margary was born the 20th day of March 1790
Nathaniel son of the sd Abner & Margary was born the 21st day of March 1791
Josiah son of the said Abner & Margary was born the 7th of April 1793
Berwell son of the said Abner & Margary was born the 20th of October 1794
Sanford son of the said Abner & Margary was born the 22nd of Decr 1796
Parthena daughter of the said Abner & Margary was born the 6th of Septr 1798
Charles Son of the said Abner and Margary was born the 6th day of June 1802

Abner Shipman born Jany 12th: 1759 Margary Avery born Jany 11th A.D. 1757' Margery Avery Lyme November ye 10th 1760

In Lyme in the Colony of Connecticut on the first Day of August: 1765 Josiah Ely and Phebe Denison both of Lyme were Married to Each other by me the Subscriber who was then one of the Assistants of this Colony Certifyed this 10th Day of April 1770 · Pr. me Mattw Griswold D. Governor
Josiah Griswold Ely Son of Josiah and Phebe Ely was born August 26th A.D. 1766
Enoch Ely Son of Josiah and Phebe Ely was born February 10th A.D. 1769
Phebe Ely Daughter of Josiah and Phebe Ely was born January 5th A.D. 1771
David Ely Son of Josiah and Phebe Ely was Born January 13th Day A.D. 1774

Capt. Silvester Mather and Mrs. Betsey Wait was Joyn'd in Marriage on the 22nd day of May A.D. 1788

Anna Ely Daughter of Daniel Ely, was born May 16th A.D. 1760

Philip Toocker was Married to Anna Ely on the 2d day of December A.D. 1779

[page 97] Lyme October 10th: 1760 - These may Certifye all persons that Sylvanus Lord of sd Lyme was married to Huldah Brockway of aforesaid Lyme Eleventh Day of May A.D: 1758   Pr me Richard Lord Justice of the Peace
Elisabeth Lord Daughter of Sylvanus and Huldah Lord was born June ye 3rd A.D. 1759 and Died July 17th 1759
Elisabeth Lord Daughter of Sylvanus and Huldah Lord was born August 13th A.D. 1760
Sylvanus Lord Son of Sylvanus and Huldah Lord was born August 27th A.D. 1762
Sylvanus Lord Died November 29th A.D: 1762

Colchester June 15th 1746: Thomas Smith Jn and Lydia Foot were Married Pr Ephraim Little Clerk
Lydia Smith Daughter of Thomas and Lydia his Wife was born August 18th 1747
Esther Smith Daughter of Thomas & Lydia Smith was born April the 30th 1749
Rachel Smith Daughter of Thomas & Lydia Smith was born March 6th 1752
Zeruiah Smith Daughter of Thomas & Lydia Smith was Born May 16th 1754
Stephen Smith Son of Thomas and Lydia Smith was born April 4th 1756
Thomas Smith Son of Thomas and Lydia Smith was Born May 7th 1758
Ithamer Smith Son of Thomas and Lydia Smith was Born Septemr 4th 1760
Ephraim Smith Son of Thomas & Lydia Smith was Born Septemr 4th 1762
Sarah Smith Daughter of Thomas & Lydia Smith was Born Septemr 28th 1764
Dudley Smith Son of Thomas and Lydia Smith was Born May 28th 1767
Rhoda Smith Daughter of Thomas & Lydia Smith was Born June 15th 1770
Recorded the 9th of Septemr 1777: by John Lay 2nd Regr

Lyme Second February: 1758: These may Certifye all whome it may Conscearn that Mr. Abner Lord and Mrs. Temperance Coult both of Lyme were Lawfully married together the 3rd Day of February: A.D. 1757 pr me Stephen Johnson Pastor of the First Church in sd Lyme.
Thomas Lord Son of Abner and Temperance Lord was born December 29th A.D. 1757
Abner Lord Son of Abner and Temperance Lord was born August 24th A.D. 1760
Mary Lord Daughter of Abner and Temperance Lord was born May 27th 1764

Having Pleased the Almighty Creator, in the Dispensation of his Providence upon the 12th Day of November A.D. 1790 to summon by Death the Spirit of Capt. Abner Lord in to the world of spirits in the 58th Year of his Age.

These may Certifie that Mr. Samll Gilbert of Lyme &Mrs. Mary Dodge of Colchester was legally Joyned in Marriage on the 12th Day of June A.D. 1769 before me John Watrous Just Pace
Lydia Gilbert Daughter of Samll & Mary Gilbert was born July 25th 1770
Irene Gilbert Daughter of Samll & Mary Gilbert was born April 14th 1772
Hannah Gilbert Daughter of Samll & Mary Gilbert was born March 6th 1774
Eunice Gilbert Daughter of Samll & Mary Gilbert was born Septemr 22nd 1776
Anna Gilbert Daughter of Samll & Mary Gilbert was born Novemr 4th 1778
Fanney Gilbert Daughter of Samll & Mary Gilbert was born January 26th 1781

[page 98]   These may Certifye that Ezra Robins of Lyme and Elisabeth Anderson of sd Lyme Daughter of John Anderson of sd Lyme were Joyned together in Marriage July 17th 1760 by me John Griswold Justice of the Peace
Joseph Robins Son of Ezra and Elisabeth Robins was born December ye 4th A.D. 1761
Jean Lay Robins Daughter of Ezra nad Elisabeth Robins was Born Novemr 29: A.D. 1763

Daniel Robins Son of Ezra and Elisabeth Robins was born September 30th: 1765
Theody Robins Daughter of Ezra and Elisabeth Robins was born March 3rd: 1769 and Died the 28th: Day of June A.D. 1770
Ezra Robins Son of Ezra nad Elisabeth Robins was born September 27th A.D. 1772
Ezra Son of said Ezra & Elisabeth died the 8th day of Decr A.D. 1774
Phebe Daughter of said Ezra & Elisabeth was born the 29th day of June A.D. 1775
Lucy Daughter of said Ezra & Elisabeth was born the 7th day of Sept A.D. 1777
Ezra Son of said Ezra and Elisabeth was born the 10th day of Sept A.D. 1780
Colchester February 26th 1765: These may Certifie that Mr. Cullick Ely & Sarah Foot were Married January 5th 1758 Pr Ephraim Little Clerk
David Ely Son of Cullick & Sarah Ely was born April 18th A.D - 1759
Cullick Ely Son of Cullick & Sarah Ely was born ye 19th of May: A.D. 1763
Eleazer Ely Son of Cullick & Sarah Ely was born ye 13th of January: A.D: 1765
Eunice Ely Daughter of Cullick & Sarah Ely was born Jany 15th Day: A.D. 1766
Sarah Ely Daughter of Cullick & Sarah Ely was Born June ye 29th A.D: 1769
Russel Ely Son of Cullick & Sarah Ely was Born ye 8th of February A.D. 1771
Charles Ely Son of Cullick & Sarah Ely was born Septemr 14th Day A.D. 1772
Joseph Ely Son of Cullick & Sarah Ely was born ye 9th of June A.D: 1775

[page 99] Lyme March 10th 1757: Mr. Stephen Adset and Mrs. Luce Chadwick both of Lyme in New London County was Lawfully married together by me John Lay 3rd Just. Pace
Joseph Adset Son of Stephen and Luce Adset was born December 23rd A.D. 1757
Deborah Adset Daughter of Stephen & Luce Adset was born April ye 9th A.D. 1760
Sarah Adset Daughter of Stephen & Luce Adset was born February ye 3rd A.D. 1762

These may Signifie and Certifie that on the 22nd Day of March 1767 Thomas Rubey was Married to Phebe Bennet Sawyer by me George Beckwith Minister in Lyme
Christopher Rubey Son of Thomas & Phebe Bennet Rubey was born January 15th A.D 1768
Rhoda Rubey Daughter of Thomas & Phebe Bennet Rubey was Born March 19th A.D. 1769
Thomas Rubey Son of Thomas & Phebe Bennet Rubey was born April 11th A.D. 1773

Capt. Timothy Mather of Lyme in New London County was Married to Elisabeth Matson of sd Lyme the 29th Day of October: A.D. 1761
Elisabeth Mather Daughter of Timothy and Elisabeth Mather was born April 9th 1764
Capt. Timothy Mather died March 11th 1810
Mrs. Elisabeth Mather died Jany 7th 1813

Hebron November 7th 1764 These Certifye that Elihu Marvin of Lyme and Anne Beach of Hebron were Each to other Lawfully Joyned in Marriage on the 16th Day of December: 1762 Pr Benjamin Pomeroy Clerk
Anna Marvin Daughter of Elihu and Anna Marvin was born the 15th Day of May 1765
Abigail Marvin Daughter of Elihu and Anna Marvin was born August 15th 1767
Mary Mary Daughter of Elihu and Anna Marvin was born (at Hebron) on the first Day of February A.D. 1770
Elihu Marvin Son of Elihu and Anna Marvin was born Decemr 13th 1771
Mary Marvin above said Departed this life May 12th A.D. 1774

Lyme October 28th 1787: Mr. Joseph King Junr of Southold on Long Island and Mrs. Jane Lay of sd Lyme Daughter of Esqr Lay were Joyned in Marriage by William Noyes Just Pace a true copy of Record pr William Noyes Just Pace Lyme July 26th 1788
John Lay King Son of Joseph and Jane King was Born in Lyme August 20th 1788
Jonathan Son of said Joseph & Jane King was born on the 9th day of March A.D. 1790
Fanny Daughter of said Joseph and Jean was born on the 27th day of February 1792

LYME, CONNECTICUT, VITAL RECORDS

[page 100] Asael Roland of Lyme in New London County was Married to Anna Walker of Middletown in Hartford County on the 15th Day of July: A.D. 1760

Mr. Asael Roland and Mrs. Mary Champen widow was married February 16th Day 1778 by Richd Wait Justice of Peace
Jesse Roland Son of Asael and Mary Roland was born November 18th A.D. 1778

Mr. Robert Otis was Married to Miss Polly Smith on the 10th day of Janaury 1788
Lydia Daughter of the said Robert & Polly was born on the 25th day of July 1789
Anna Daughter of the said Robert & Polly was born on the 14th day of August A.D. 1791
Israel Son of the said Robert and Polly was born on the 4th day of August A.D. 1793
Polley Daughter of the said Robert & Polly was born on the 10th day of October A.D. 1795
Richard Son of the said Robert & Polly was born on the 6th day of September A.D. 1798
Thoadola daughter of the said Robt & Polly was born 10 Jany 1801
Sally daughter of the sd Robt & Polly was born 10 May 1803

These may Certifye that Samuel Holden Parsons was Lawfully Married to Mehetable Mather on the 10th Day of September: 1761 Pr me John Griswold Justice of ye Peace
William Parsons Son of Samuel Holden and Mehetable Parsons was born July ye 5th A.D. 1762
Luce Parsons Daughter of Samll Holden and Mehetable Parsons was born Novemr 8th 1764
Thomas Parsons Son of Samll Holden Parsons and his wife Mehetable was Born Decemr 12th 1767
Enoch Parsons Son of Samll Holden and Mehetable Parsons was born Novemr 5th 1769
Mehetable Parsons Daughter of Samll and Mehetable Parsons was born Decemr 24th A.D. 1772
Entered in the Second Book, with all the peticular births, deaths, etc.

These are to Certifie that Mr. William Mather & Mrs. Rhoda Marvin boath of Lyme were Lawfully married together the first Day of May A.D. 1768 Pr me Stephen Johnson Pastor of the first Church in said Lyme
Lucy Mather Daughter of William & Rhoda Mather was Born August 18th 1768
Mary Mather Daughter of William & Rhoda Mather was Born December 17th 1769
Ezra Mather Son of William and Rhoda Mather was Born February 4th 1772
Eunice Mather Daughter of William & Rhoda Mather was Born Decemr 20th 1773
Abigail Mather Daughter of William & Rhoda Mather was Born Decemr 6th 1775

Bettey Sill Daughter of Giles & Lucy Sill was Born July 10th A.D. 1774
Nathaniel Sill Son of Giles & Lucy Sill was born August 6th A.D. 1776
Enoch Sill Son of Giles & Lucy Sill was born May 3rd A.D. 1778
Jurdan Goold Sill Son of Giles and Lucy Sill was Born February 9th 1780

[page 101] February 22nd: 1759 then I married John Munsele Junr of Lyme to his now wife Sila Huntly: Test Samuel Ely Justice of the Peace ·
William Munsele Son of John Munsele Junr and Sila his wife was born February 14th 1760
Sila Munsele Daughter of John Munsele Junr & Sila his wife was born September 17th 1761
Sila Munsele Wife of John Munsele Junr Died October ye first 1761

Lyme December 24th 1761 then I married John Munsele Junr to his now Wife Elisabeth McCrary Test. Samuel Ely Justice of the Peace
Sila Munsell Daughter of John Munsel Junr and Sila his wife Died January 15th A.D. 1762
John Munsel Son of John Munsell Junr and Elisabeth his wife was born October 14th 1762
Sila Munsell Daughter of John Munsell Junr and Elisabeth his wife was born August 26th 1765
Thomas Munsell Son of John Munsell Junr & Elisabeth his wife was Born July 19th 1767
Bettey Munsell Daughter of John Munsell Junr & Elisabeth his wife was Born May 23rd 1769

Joseph Munsell Son of John Munsell Junr & Elisabeth his wife was Born February 8th 1771
Lucinda Munsell Daughter of John & Elisabeth Munsell was Born August 11th 1774
Bettey Munsell Daughter of John & Elisabeth Munsell was Born Septemr 5th 1775
Polley Munsell Daughter of John & Elisabeth Munsell was Born Septemr 13th 1781
Bettey Munsell Daughter of John & Elisabeth Munsell Died January 19th 1774
Willm Munsell Son of John and Elisabeth Munsell Died June 3rd 1776
Betey wife of the said John Munsell departed this Life on the 15th day of Jany 1802
John Munsell was married to Lydia Huntly on the 9th day of September 1802

These may Certifie all whome it may Conscearn that Thomas Merrit of Lyme was married to Ame Avery of Lyme: January in the year: 1759 Pr me Benjamin Lee Justice Peace
Amos Merrit Son of Thomas & Ame Merrit was born February the 18th 1760
Ame Merrit Wife of Thomas Merrit Died February 27th A.D. 1760

These may Certifye whomesoever it may Conscearn that Jonathan Rogers and Lydia Watrous both of Lyme were Lawfully Married together the 13th day of December A.D. 1759 Pr me Stephen Johnson Pastor of the first Church in Lyme Dated in Lyme this 13th Day of February A.D: 1762
Lydia Rogers Daughter of Jonathan & Lydia Rogers was born March 5th A.D. 1761
Lavina Rogers Daughter of Jonathan & Lydia Rogers was born January 20th A.D: 1763
William Wanton Rogers Son of Jonathan & Lydia Rogers was born June first 1766
Sarah Rogers Daughter of Jonathan & Lydia Rogers was born April 10th 1767
Nabba Rogers Daughter of Jonathan & Lydia Rogers was born April 11th 1769
Molley Rogers Daughter of Jonathan & Lydia Rogers was born April 27th 1771
Daniel Rogers Son of Jonathan & Lydia Rogers was Born February 21st: A:D: 1773
Jemima Rogers Daughter of Jonathan & Lydia Rogers was Born August 6th A.D: 1775

[page 102] November 4: 1747 Matthew Dorr of Lyme and Elisabeth Palmer formerly of Stoningtown were married together by me: George Griswold Pastor of 2nd Church in Lyme
Phebe Dorr Daughter of Matthew and Elisabeth Dorr was Born August first: 1748
Edward Dorr Son of Matthew and Elisabeth Dorr was born May 28th A.D. 1752
Helena Dorr Daughter of Matthew and Elisabeth Dorr was born July 16th A.D 1754
Matthew Dorr Son of Matthew and Elisabeth Dorr was born March 28th A.D. 1756
Samuel Griswold Dorr Son of Matthew & Elisabeth Dorr was born Septemr 15th A.D. 1758
Jonathan Dorr Son of Matthew and Elisabeth Dorr was born December 25th A.D: 1759
Joseph Dorr Son of Matthew and Elisabeth Dorr was born July 15th A.D. 1761

These may Certifye that on the 3rd Day of January: A.D 1763 I married William Starlin of Lyme to his now Wife Jemima Sill: Test Samuel Ely Justice of the Peace
Phebe Starlin Daughter of William and Jemima Starlin was born October ye 15th A.D. 1763
Elisha Starlin Son of Willm and Jemima Starlin was born November 5th A.D. 1765
William Starlin Son of Wm & Jemima Starlin was born May ye 16th A.D. 1768
Thomas Sill Starlin Son of Wm & Jemima Starlin was born April 10th A.D. 1770
Jemima Starlin Daughter of Wm & Jemima Starlin was Born July 3rd A.D. 1772
Dudley Starlin Son of Wm and Jemima Starlin was born April 11th A.D. 1774 and Died Septemr 18th A.D. 1775
Dudley Starlin Son of Willm & Jemima Starlin was Born April 24th A.D. 1776
Erastus Starlin Son of Willm & Jemima Starlin was Born March 8th A.D. 1778
Clarrissa Starlin Daughter of Wm & Jemima Starlin was born Feburary 18th 1780
Ansell Starlin Son of Willm & Jemima Starling was born February 3rd 1782
Meeah Son of the said William and Jemima was Born November 5th A.D. 1784
Joseph Son of the said William & Jemimah was born November 25th A.D. 1786

Lyme February the first: 1762: These are to Certifye all whome it may Consearn that Mr. John Lay the 4th and Mrs. Anna Sill both of Lyme were Lawfully Married together the 28th Day of February A.D. 1760 Pr me Stephen Johnson Pastor of the first Church in Lyme

Daniel Lay Son of John Lay 4th and Anna his wife was born March the 16th 1761 and Died October the 13th 1761

Filkin Lay Son of John and Anna Lay was born 28th Day of August A.D. 1762 and Died Septemr Septemr 27th 1763

John Lay Son of John and Anna Lay was born Novemr 23rd A.D. 1764

Hannah Lay Daughter of John & Anna Lay was born June 6th A.D. 1767

David Lay Son of John and Anna Lay was Born April 28th A.D. 1769

Molley Lay Daughter of John and Anna Lay was born April 7th Day A.D. 1772

Abner Lay Son of John & Anna Lay was born June 25th A.D. 1774

Lucinda Lay Daughter of Jno & Anna Lay born May 4th A.D. 1777

[page 103] Mr. Seth Ely and Mrs. Lydia Renold was Married the 31st Day of March A.D. 1762 Certifyed pr Hezekiah Huntington Assistant

John Ely Son of Seth Ely and Lydia his wife was born June the 14th A.D. 1763

Seth Ely Son of Seth and Lydia Ely was born March the 11th A.D. 1765

Lydia Ely Daughter of Seth & Lydia Ely was born Septemr 12th A.D. 1766

Abigail Ely Daughter of Seth & Lydia Ely was born September 26th A.D. 1768

Deborah Ely Daughter of Seth & Lydia Ely was Born Septemr 23rd: 1770 and Died and Died ye 29th of Septemr 1770

Richard Ely Son of Seth & Lydia Ely was born August 24th A.D. 1771 & Died Septemr ye 10th 1771

Richard Ely Son of Seth and Lydia Ely was born ye 3rd Day of May 1774 and Died the 11th Day of January 1775

Ebenezer Ely Son of Seth and Lydia Ely was Born July 30th A.D. 1776

Phebe Ely Daughter of Seth & Lydia Ely was Born March the 28: 1779

Deborah Ely Daughter of Seth & Lydia Ely was Born Decemr 19th 1781

Lyme 23rd December: A.D 1762: These may Certifye whomesoever it may Conscearn that Mr. Samuel Griswold and Mrs. Mary Marvin both of Lyme were Lawfully Married together the 13th Day of April A.D. 1762: Pr me Stephen Johnson Pastor of the first Church in sd Lyme

Sylvanus Griswold Son of Samll and Mary Griswold was born May 21st A.D. 1763

George Griswold Son of Samll & Mary Griswold was born July 13th A.D: 1766

Mrs. Mary Griswold Wife of Mr. Samuel Griswold Departed this Life 15th April: 1788

Zechariah Sill Junr was Married to Sussannah Roland Novemr 8th: 1747

Betty Sill Daughter of Zechh & Sussannah Sill was born August 10th 1748

Sussannah Sill Daughter of Zechh and Sussannah Sill was born January 30th 1750

Clarissa Sill Daughter of Zechh and Sussannah Sill was born April 28th 1752

Richard Sill Son of Zechh and Sussannah Sill was Born Novemr 19th 1754

Zechariah Sill Son of Zechh & Sussannah Sill was born May the 19th 1758

[page 104] [[in Wethersfield September 10th 1760

These may Certifye whome it Conscearns that Christian Higgins and Dorothy Williams were Married to Each other June 3rd: 1751 by me Daniel Russell

William Higgins Son of Christian & Dorothy Higgins was born June 29th old stile A.D 1751

Benjamin Higgins Son of Christian & Dorothy Higgins was born May 9th New Stile: A.D. 1753

Christopher Higgins Son of Christian & Dorothy Higgins was born March 4th A.D. 1755 and Died January the first: 1756

Christopher Higgins Son of Christian & Dorothy Higgins was born June 23rd A.D: 1757

Joseph Higgins Son of Christian & Dorothy Higgins was born December 2nd A.D. 1759

Seth Higgins & Enoch Higgins Sons of Christian and Dorothy Higgins being twins was born the 11th Day of September: A.D: 1762
Jamima Higgins & Dolly Higgins Daughters of Capt Christian and Mrs. Dorothy Higgins, twins was born June 11th A.D. 1764

These may Certifye any Person or Persons whome it may Consearn that Zadock Smith and Mary Goold was Lawfully Married in Southold on Long Island on the 20th Day of August A.D 1763 by me Benin Brown Justice

Clark Trueman
Jonathan Trueman   Recorded the 23rd Day of August: 1763
Garshom Brown   Pr John Lay 2nd Regr

Frances Smith Son of Zadock and Mary Smith was Born January 9th A.D. 1765
Mary Smith Daughter of Zadock and Mary Smith was Born February 13th A.D. 1767
James Smith Son of Zadock and Mary Smith Died January 29th A.D. 1767
Bettey Smith Daughter of Zadock and Mary Smith was born June 22nd A.D. 1769
Margaret Smith Daughter of Zadock & Mary Smith was born March 11th A.D. 1770
Jean Smith Daughter of Zadock and Mary Smith was born May 13th A.D. 1773
William Smith Son of Zadock & Mary Smith was Born Septemr A.D: 1778
Zadock Smith Son of Zadock and Mary Smith was Born Septemr 14th 1780
Fanney Smith Daughter of Zadock & Mary Smith was born July 30th: 1784

These are to Certifye that John Sears and Judith Peck boath of Lyme were Lawfully Married together the 24th Day of January: 1760 by me Stephen Johnson Pastor of the first Church in sd Lyme

Richard Sears Son of John and Judith Sears was Born August 28th A.D. 1761
Jasper Peck Sears Son of John & Judith Sears was Born July 7th A.D: 1763
Bettey Sears Daughter of John & Judith Sears was Born Novemr 22nd 1765
John Sears above named Departed this Life on the 28th of December: 1766

[page 105]   Lyme 11th February: 1764
These are to Certifye whomesoever it may Conscearn that Mr. Jabez Sill and Mrs. Elisabeth Noyes both of Lyme were Lawfully Married together on ye 28th Day of December A.D. 1749 Pr me Stephen Johnson Pastor of the first Church in sd Lyme

Elisabeth Sill Daughter of Jabez and Elisabeth Sill was Born October 22nd A.D: 1750
Mary Sill Daughter of Jabez and Elisabeth Sill was born July 11th Day A.D: 1752
Naomi Sill Daighter of Jabez & Elisabeth Sill was born November 28th Day A.D. 1754
Esther Sill Daughter of Jabez & Elisabeth Sill was born December 21st Day A.D. 1756
Shadrach Sill Son of Jabez & Elisabeth Sill was born August 12th Day A.D. 1758
Elisha Noyes Sill Son of Jabez & Elisabeth Sill was born January 15th Day A.D 1761
Jabez Sill Son of Jabez and Elisabeth Sill was born March ye 6th Day A.D. 1763
Moses Sill Son of Jabez & Elisabeth Sill was born January 9th Day - A.D. 1765
Amassa Sill Son of Jabez and Elisabeth Sill was born February 24th A.D. 1767

These are to Certifye whomesoever it may Conscearn that Mr. William Lay & Mrs. Phebe Sill both of Lyme were Lawfully Married together on the 15th Day of December A.D. 1757 by me   Dated in Lyme 1st March: 1764 Stephen Johnson Pastor of the first Church in sd Lyme

Elisabeth Lay Daughter of William and Phebe Lay was born June 16th A.d. 1759
Polley Lay Daughter of William and Phebe Lay was born August 15th A.D 1761
Ezra Lay Son of William and Phebe Lay was born September 19th A.D. 1763
Sarah Daughter of said William & Phebe was born the 2d Day of March A.D. 1766
William Son of said William & Phebe was born the first Day of May A.D. 1768
Hubbell Son of said William & Phebe was born the 23d Day of May 1770
Phebe Daughter of the said Willm & Phebe was born the 5th day of Jany 1773
Jerusha Daughter of the said William & Phebe was born the 10th Day of May 1775
Martha Jaen their Daughter was born on the 27th Day of October 1777
Wm Lay died May 5th 1816   Phebe Lay Wife of Wm Lay died Oct 12th 1802

64   LYME, CONNECTICUT, VITAL RECORDS

Richard Sill and Eunice Lee boath of Lyme were married to Each other on the 14th Day of Novemr 1776 by Benjamin Lee Esqr as appears by the Record of sd Ben Lee Deceasd
Elisha Sill Son of Richard & Eunice Sill was Born the 23rd Day of January: 1778
Mr. Gideon Rogers & Miss Lucy Ackley of Chatham were Lawfully Joyned in Marriage on the 27th Day of November A.D. 1788 as appears by a Certificate from the Revd Mr. Samuel Parsons   Test David F. Sill Town Clerk
Silvester son of the said Gideon & Lucy was born August 25th day A.D. 1789
James Ackley Son of the said Gideon & Lucy was born the 16th Day of August A.D 1792
John Sill Son of the said Gideon and Lucy was born on the 15th day of April A.D. 1796
Seth Son of the said Gideon and Lucy was born on the 24th day of September A.D. 1799
Selden Son of the sd Gideon & Lucy was born 10 day of Novr 1801

[page 106]   February 20th 1745/6 then Benjamin Robins of Lyme and Hannah Bradford living in Lyme were married together by me   George Griswold Pastor of ye 2nd Church in Lyme
Sarah Robins Daughter of Benjamin & Hannah Robins was born November ye 4th 1746
David Robins Son of Benjamin and Hannah Robins was Born March ye 11th A.D. 1748
Benjamin Robins Son of Benjamin and Hannah Robins was Born May ye 25th Day A.D. 1749
Bradford Robins Son of Benjamin & Hannah Robins was Born January the 17th Day 1751
John Robins Son of Benjamin & Hannah Robins was Born August 13th Day A.D. 1752
Joshua Robins Son of Benjamin and Hannah Robins was Born February ye 11th A.D. 1754
Hannah Robins Daughter of Benjamin & Hannah Robins was Born March 7th Day A.D 1757
Evens Robins Son of Benjamin and Hannah Robins was Born December 13th A.D. 1758
Elijah Robins Son of Benjamin and Hannah Robins was Born August 12th A.D. 1760
Alden Robins Son of Benjamin & Hannah Robins was Born July 29th A.D: 1762 and Died January 15th A.D. 1763

These may Certifye that on November 22nd A.D. 1759 Richard Ransom was Married to Mary Starlin of the same Town by me George Beckwith Pastor of a church in sd Town
Sarah Ransom Daughter of Richard and and Mary Ransom was Born November 14th: 1760
Lynes Ransom Son of Richard and Mary Ransom was born May ye 8th A.D. 1762
Lous Ransom Daughter of Richard & Mary Ransom was born 16th of February A.D. 1765
Richard Ransom Son of Richard & Mary Ransom was born 2nd Day of December: 1766
Mary Ransom Daughter of Richard & Mary Ransom was born ye 3rd Day of February 1769
John Ransom Son of Richard & Mary Ransom was born ye 26th Day of July A.D: 1770
Elisha Ransom Son of Richard & Mary Ransom was born July 27th A.D. 1772
Hannah Ransom Daughter of Richard & Mary Ransom was born June 27th A.D. 1774 and Died the 9th of July: 1774
Patience Ransom Daughter of Richard & Mary Ransom was born October 20th: 1775 and Died the 10th of March: A.D: 1776
Lucy Ransom Daughter of Richard & Mary Ransom was born September 13th: 1778
Daniel Ransom Son of Richard & Mary Ransom was born January 21st: A.D. 1781

These may Certifye that on the Second Day of February A.D. 1762 Joseph Starlin of Lyme was Married to Lydia Ransom of the same Town by me George Beckwith Pastor of the 3rd Church in sd Town
Seth Starlin Son of Joseph & Lydia Starlin was born March 18th 1763
Hannah Starlin Daughtr of Joseph & Lydia Starlin was born September: 21st September 1764
Sarah Starlin Daughter of Joseph & Lydia Starlin was born August 23rd A.D. 1766
Joseph Starlin Son of Joseph & Lydia Starlin was born the 28th of Novemr 1770
Lydia Starlin Daughter of Joseph and Lydia Starlin was Born the 6th of Novemr 1773

Elijah Starlin Son of Joseph and Lydia Starlin was Born November 24th A.D: 1775
Joseph Sterling removed to Woodstock Vt. probably 1781

[page 107]   Allen Beckwith Son of Benjamin and Patience Beckwith was born March 3rd:
1736 These Certifye that Allen Beckwith of Lyme was Married to Esther Marvin of sd
Lyme on the 26th Day of November A.D: 1755 by me John Lay 2nd Just Pace
Certified this 7th Day of May A.D. 1764
Luranah Beckwith Daughter of Allen and Esther Beckwith was born April 15th A.D. 1756
Esther Beckwith Daughter of Allen & Esther Beckwith was Born September 28th 1758
Mehetable Beckwith Daughter of Allen & Esther Beckwith was born March 29th 1761
Patience Beckwith Daughter of Allen & Esther Beckwith was Born February 17th 1764

John Lay the 3d & Rhoda Watrous was Joyned in Marraige 28th Feby 1788
Asa Son of said John and Rhoda was born the 11th day of Septr 1789
Anna Daughter of said John and Rhoda was born the 14th day of July A.D. 1791
Andrew Son of the said John & Rhoa was born the 2d day of March 1795
Charles Son of the said John & Rhoda was born the 2d day of June A.D.1797
Jenet daughter of the sd John & Rhoda was born the 11th day of August 1807

Alexander Bushnell and Cloe Wait both of Lyme in New London County was Lawfully
Married together on the 12th Day of February A.D. 1761 by me John Lay 2nd Justice
of the Peace
Thomas Bushnell Son of Alexander and Cloe Bushnel was born January: 12th 1762
Daniel Bushnell Son of Alexander & Cloe Bushnell was born December 18th: 1763

These Certifie that Stephen Smith Junr and Lydia Alger both of Lyme were Lawfully
Married to Each other on the 22nd Day of November: 1764 by me John Lay 2nd
Just Pace
The above sd Lydia sd Wife of sd Stephen Smith Junr Died 27th February: 1766

These may Signifie and Certifie that Stephen Smith 2nd of Lyme was on the 12th Day of
January: 1768: Married to Irene Ransom of the Same Town by me George Beckwith
Pastor of a Church in sd Town
Alias Smith Son of Stephen & Irene Smith was Born June ye 17th A.D. 1769
Uriah Smith Son of Stephen & Irene Smith was Born February 4th 1771
Richard Ransom Smith Son of Stephen and Irene Smith was born October 5th 1773
Lydia Smith Daughter of Stephen and Irene Smith was Born May 6th A.D. 1776

Sophia Tinker Daughter of Esther Beckwith was born the 20th day of Feby A.D. 1787
[page 108]   December 23rd A.D. 1760: Then I married Capt Zebulon Butler to his now
Wife Anna Lord Test. Samuel Ely Justice of the Peace
Lord Buttler Son of Zebulon and Anna Buttler was born December ye 11th A.D. 1767
Zebulon Buttler Son of Zebulon & Anna Buttler was Born Novemr 12th A.D. 1767
Hannah Buttler Daughter of Zeb & Anna Butler was born February 28th A.D. 1770

Nathaniel Roland and Hannah Rogers was Joynd in Marriage 4th Novr 1784
Sally their daughter was born on the third day of March A.D. 1786
Sally Roland died on the 3d day of June A.D. 1784 [?]
Silvester Roland the Son of said Nathll and Hannah born 14th May 1787
Fanney Daughter of said Nathll and Hannah was born 8th Novr A.D. 1789

Abel Beckwith and Luce Dewolf (widow and Relect of Mr. Simon Dewolf Late of sd Lyme
Deceasd) both of sd Lyme were Lawfully married to Each other on the 23rd Day of
March: A.D. 1759 by me John Lay 3rd Justice of the Peace
Martin Beckwith Son of Abel and Luce Beckwith was born May 4th 1759
Hannah Beckwith Daughter of Abel & Lue Beckwith was born December 4th A.D. 1760

Ezra Roland & Sarah Rogers was Legally Joynd in Marriage
Sally their daughter was born on the 15th day of October A.D. 1787
Sally the wife of said Ezra died

Ezra Roland and Lucy Champin was Joynd in marriage March 25th 1788
Martha daughter of the said Ezra and Lucy born the 7th day of Jany A.D. 1789
Mary Munsell Daughter of James & Esther Munsel was born June 10th 1763
These Certifie that Mr. William Noyes Junr of Lyme was Married to Mrs. Sarah Banks of Newark, New Jersey on the Second Day of October A.D. 1785 by the Reverand Mr. Stephen Johnson as appears from his Record
Abigail Leveritt Noyes Daughter Willm & Sarah Noyes was Born 17th Day of August 1786
James Noyes Son of Willm and Sarah Noyes was Born ye 25th of Novemr and Died the 29th of sd Novemr 1787
Catharine Daughter of the said William and Sarah was born 17th February 1789
William Son of the said William & Sarah was born on the 9th day May A.D. 1792
Catharine their daughter died on the 12th day of September 1806

[page 109] These Certifye that Mr. Elihu Wade of Lyme in New London County was Married to Mrs. Azubah Smith of sd Lyme on the 16th Day of September 1760 by me John Lay 2nd Just Pace
Son of Elihu and Azubah Wade was born February 11th 1762 and Died March first A.D. 1762
George Wade Son of Elihu and Azubah Wade was born March the 4th A.D. 1763
Joseph Wade Son of Elihu and Azubah Wade was born December the 14th A.D. 1765 and Died the 4th Day of January A.D. 1766
Dan Wade Son of Elihu & Azubah Wade Was born May 28th A.D. 1767
Carolina Wade Daughter of Elihu and Azubah Wade was Born Septemr 3d 1769
Azubah Wade Daughter of Elihu & Azubah Wade was Born March 5th 1773

Lucy Wife of Martin Wade died the 24th day of December A.D. 1796
Martin Wade was Married to Jan Miller on the 8th day of Decr A.D. 1797

These may Certifye whomsoever it may Conscearn that Capt Joseph Mather and Mrs. Joanna Matson both of Lyme were Lawfully Married together on the 7th Day of December 1756 Pr me Stephen Johnson Pastor of the first Church in said Lyme Dated in Lyme 10th of April A.D. 1765
Joanna Mather Daughter of Joseph & Joanna Mather was Born October 13th 1757
Nathaniel Mather Son of Joseph & Joanna Mather was born May ye 30th 1759
Thomas Mather Son of Joseph & Joanna Mather was born August 15th 1762
Moses Mather Son of Joseph & Joanna Mather was born July ye 14th 1764
Joseph Mather son of Joseph & Joanna Mather was born July ye 4th A.D. 1766
Capt. Joseph Mather died Feby the 5th A.D. 1789
Joanna Mather wife of the said Joseph died the 29th day of May 1804 aged 76

Martin Wade and Lucy Mack boath of Lyme in New London County were Lawfully Married to Each other on the 30th Day of January 1769 by Small Ely Justice of the Peace
George Wade Son of Martin and Lucy Wade was Born October 13th 1770
Thomas Wade Son of Martin & Lucy Wade was Born August 17th 1772
Anna Wade Daughter of Martin & Lucy Wade was born Septemr 6th 1774
Elisabeth Wade Daughter of Martin and Lucy Wade was born October 6th 1777
Lydia Wade Daughter of Martin & Lucy Wade was born November 4th 1779
William Wade Son of Martin and Lucy Wade was born Septemr 22nd 1781
Lucy Wade Daughter of Martin and Lucy Wade was born January 10th 1784
Elether Wade Daughter of Martin & Lucy Wade was born April 13th 1786
Lucey Wade Daughter of Martin & Lucy Wade Died the 8th of July 1785
Lucy Daughter of the said Martin & Lucy was born 28th of June A.D. 1789
Martin their Son born 24th Sept 1791 Joseph their Son born the 24 Sept twin 1791
Thomas their Son died on the day of . . . . 1792 Martin died 6 April 1792

Mrs. Sarah Mather (Widdow and Relect of Capt Timothy Mather Late of Lyme Deceasd) Departed this life August 16th 1756 in the 73rd year of her age.

[page 110]   Lyme August 20th 1764: These may Certifye that Ezra Selden and Elisabeth Rogers were Married according to Law: on May 6th 1751 pr me Benja Throop Clerk New London County Ss Lyme March 2nd A.D. 1780 then Mr. Joseph Gillet was Married to Mrs. Mary Miner boath of said Lyme Pr me Eleazer Mather Just Pace
Daniel Gillet Son of Joseph and Mary Gillet was born 20th Day of February A.D. 1782
Phebe Gillet Daughter of Joseph & Mary Gillet was born 16th October: 1784
Martin Gillet Son of Joseph and Mary Gillet was Born December ye 31st Day: 1787
Mihilable Daughter of the said Joseph and Mary was born the 7th day Novr 1789
Joseph Son of the said Joseph and Mary was born on the 5th day of April 1794
John Minor Son of the said Joseph & Mary was born the 14th day of May A.D. 1797
Noah Hallack Son of the said Joseph & Mary was born the 29th day of January 1800
Benjamin Frankling their son was born on the 24th day of September 1803

These may Certifye whomsoever it may Concearn that Mr. Uriah Hyde and Mahetabel Marvin both of Lyme were Lawfully married together the 9th of October A.D: 1764 Pr me Stephen Johnson Pastor of the first Church in sd Lyme Dated in Lyme 3rd September 1765
Marvin Hyde Son of Uriah & Mahetable Hyde was born July 7th A.D. 1765
Lous Hyde Daughter of Uriah & Mahetable Hyde was born Septemr 11th A.D. 1767
John Hyde Son of Uriah and Mahetable Hyde was born Decemr 21st A.D. 1769
Lowen Wait and Zeruiah Calkins both of Lyme in New London County were Lawfully Married together on the 3rd Day of November: 1761 by me John Lay 2nd Just Pace
Sarah Wait Daughter of Lowen and Zeruiah Wait was born March 24th 1763
Esther Wait Daughter of Lowen and Zeruiah Wait was born May ye 22nd 1765
Thomas Wait Son of Lowen and Zeruiah Wait was born February 20th A.D. 1768
Stephen Wait Son of Lowen and Zeruiah Wait was born April 11th A.D. 1770
Elisabeth Wait Daughter of Lowen and Zeruiah Wait was born April 4th 1772
Martin Wait Son of Lowen and Zeruiah Wait was born February 15th 1775
Phebe Wait Daughter of Lowen and Zeruiah Wait was born December 23rd 1778

[page 111]   John McCurdy and Anne Lord was married together on the 16th Day of January AD 1752
Lynde McCurdy Son of John & Anne McCurdy was born April ye 4th AD 1755
Elisabeth McCurdy Daughter of John & Anne McCurdy was born July 13th AD 1757
Anne McCurdy Daughter of John and Anne McCurdy was born March 14th AD 1760
Sarah McCurdy Daughter of John and Anne McCurdy was born August 25th AD 1762
Jannet McCurdy Daughter of John & Anne McCurdy was born January 19th AD 1765
John Son of the said John and Anne was born on the 2d Day of March
Richard Son of the said John and Anne was born on the 2nd Day of March AD 1769

Jordan Negro Servant of John McCurdy was born 4th April 1757
Ezelphie Servant maid of John McCurdy was born October fifth 1759
Clo was born April 18th 1761
Ceaser was born 17th of November 1762
Shambaes was born April 19th 1764

Jana Negro Servant to Mr. John Lord was born 15th May AD 1781
Curredon Negro Servant to do born 22d Ocbr AD 1783
Freedorn Negro Servant to do born 18th March AD 1789
Sharp Freeman Servt to Col. Abner Lord born the first day of Novr AD 1790
Guy Son of Peter Gould a free Negro was born the 29th day of July AD 1780
Joseph Son of said Peter was born on the 4th day of July AD 1784
Ansell born the 1st Monday of Octr 1792)
Prince born the 1st Jany 1797   )   Servants to Jasper Peck

These signifye and Certifye that Mr. William Buttler was on November 1770: to Mrs. Sarah Lord boath of Lyme by me George Beckwith Pastor

Biner Negro, Daughter of Nancy Servant of Willm Noyes was born on the 15th day of March AD 1793 as appears by certificate from Wm Noyes Esq attested Recorded David F. Sill Regr

Jack Howard son of Janny servant of Samuel Mather Junr was born 12 Jany 1795

[page 112] Colchester in Hartford County January the 15th AD 1761: then Mr. Nathaniel Matson Junr of Lyme and Mrs. Dinah Newton of Colchester were legally Joyned in Marraige before me -- John Watrous Jusc: Paec:

Susannah Matson Daughter of Nathll Matson Junr and Dinah his wife was born: December the 10th AD 1761
Abigail Matson Daughter of Nathll Matson Junr and Dinah his wife was born on the 16th Day of January AD 1764
Nathll Matson Son of Nathll Matson Junr and Dinah his wife was born on the 13th Day of September 1765
Dinah Daughter of the said Nathaniel & Dinah was born 1st day of Octr 1767
Dinah Daughter as above departed this life on the 6th day of April 1770
Israel Son of the said Nathaniel and Dinah was born the 6th of April 1770
Lois Daughter of the said Nathaniel and Dinah was born the 30th of April 1772
Joanna Daughter of the said Nathll & Dinah was born 25th of Jany 1777
Dinah Wife of the said Nathaniel departed this life on the 21st Decr 1781
Nathaniel Matson Departed this Life on the 27th day of August 1787
Abigail Matson Departed this Life on the 27 day of January 1813

John Lord Junr of Lyme was married to Sarah Way of New London the first day of July AD 1764
Richard Lord son of John Lord Junr and Sarah his wife was born January 14th 1765
Thomas Lord son of John Lord Junr and Sarah his wife was born February 2nd AD 1767
Lucy Lord Daughter of John Lord Junr and Sarah his wife was born November 8th AD 1768
Sarah Lord Daughter of John Lord Junr and Sarah his wife was born October 14th AD 1770
John Lord Son of John Lord Junr and Sarah his wife was born April 30th AD 1773
Hannah Lord Daughter of John & Sarah Lord wife was born February 11th: AD 1778
Andrew Lord son of John & Sarah Lord was born March 8th AD 1780

August 28: 1760: Then I married Willm McCrary to his now wife Elisabeth Samuel Ely Jus of the Peace
Samuel McCrary son of Wm and Elisabeth McCrary was born January 10th 1761
Wm and Elisabeth McCrarys two sons being twins were born Septemr 30th 1762 and one of them died the same Day and the other Died October first 1762
Aggness McCrary Daughter of Wm and Elisabeth McCrary was born Novembr 10th 1763
William McCrary son of Wm and Elisabeth McCrary was born February 8th 1766
Russell McCrary son of Wm and Elisabeth McCrary was born April 27th 1768
John McCrary son of Willm and Elisabeth McCrary was born August 9th 1770
Elisabeth McCrary Daughter of Willm and Elisabeth McCrary was born Septemr 7th 1772
Chapman McCrary son of Willm & Elisabeth McCrary was born June 23rd 1775
Elijah McCrary son of Willm & Elisabeth McCrary was born August 15th 1778
Susa McCrary Daughter of Willm & Elisabeth McCrary was born February 20th 1780

[page 113] These may Certifye that Peter Tubbs of Lyme was married to Abigail Moore of New London on or about the first of September in the year: 1757 Pr me Benjamin Lee Justice Peace
John Tubbs son of Peter and Abigail Tubbs was born Novembr 9th 1759

Mary Tubbs Daughter of Peter and Abigail Tubbs was born Septemr 15 1761
Abigail Tubbs Daughter of Peter and Abigail Tubbs was born July 10th 1764

Jasper Peck Junr was married to Phebe Dorr the last day of February: 1765
Palmer Peck son of Jasper & Phebe Peck was Born Decemr 18th Day AD 1765
Clark Peck son of Jasper & Phebe Peck was Born January 7th AD 1767
Palmer Peck above said son of Jasper & Phebe Peck Died May 5th AD 1768
Palmer Peck son of Jasper & Phebe Peck was born March 27th AD 1768
Jasper Peck son of Jasper Peck Junr & Phebe his wife was born August 5th 1769
Dudley Peck son of Jasper Peck Junr & Phebe his wife was born November 30th 1770
Oliver Peck son of Jasper Peck Junr & Phebe his wife was born July 20th AD 1774
Phebe Peck Daughter of Jasper Peck Junr & Phebe his wife was born August 28 1778
Elisabeth Peck Daughter of Jasper & Phebe Peck was born October 21st 1780
Matthew son of the said Jasper & Phebe was born on the 4th day of June AD 1783
Richard Sears son of the said Jasper & Phebe was born on the 22nd day of September 1784
Ame Daughter of the said Jasper & Phebe was born on the 20th day of December 1788
Dudley Son of the said Jasper & Phebe died on the 26 day of July AD 1785

David Carpender Smith and Zeruiah Sawyer boath of Lyme in New London County were married together on the 17th Day of Decemr 1772 as Certified by Evidence
Stephen Sawyer Smith son of David Carpender & Zeruiah Smiths was born Decemr 14th 1775
Zeruiah Smith Daughter of David Carpender & Zeruiah Smith was born August 25th 1778
Henry Smith son of David Carpender & Zeruiah Smith was born August 17th 1781
Jessee Smith son of David Carpender & Zeruiah Smith was born March 21st 1784
Eunice Smith Daughter of David Carpender & Zeruiah Smith was born 7th of July 1786
David Son of the said David C. & Zeruiah was born on th 2d day of October AD 1790

Isaac Freeman Son of Jordan & Nancy Freeman was born 17th May 1812

[page 114]   Harris Coult and Elisabeth Turner both of Lyme were married together on the 7th Day of April 1757
Elisha Coult Son of Harris and Elisabeth Coult was born February 26th Day AD 1758
Arnold Coult Son of Harris and Elisabeth Coult was born September 10th AD 1760
Lucretia Coult Daughter of Harris and Elisabeth Coult was born April the 19th Day 1762
Elisabeth Coult Daughter of Harris and Elisabeth Coult was born March 5th Day 1764
Harris Coult Son of Harris and Elisabeth Coult was born January 29th AD 1766
Ama Coult Daughter of Harris and Elisabeth Coult was born October 19th AD 1767 and Died August the 5th 1768
Peter Coult Son of Harris and Elisabeth Coult was born October 31st AD 1769
Ama Coult Daughter of Harris and Elisabeth Coult was born December 1st AD 1771
Temperance Coult Daughter of Harris and Elisabeth Coult was born Decemr 31st 1773
Mary Coult Daughter of Harris and Elisabeth Coult was born August 13th 1776
Salley Coult Daughter of Harris and Elisabeth Coult was born October 29th 1778
Temperance Daughter of said Harris & Elisabeth died March -- 1791

Joseph Smith Junr was married to Mary Matson February 26th 1761
Abigail Smith Daughter of Joseph and Mary Smith was born December 20th AD 1761
Joseph Smith Son of Joseph and Mary Smith was born October 17th AD 1765

John Gilbert was married to Molley Rogers Cooley the 25th of August 1764
John Cooley Gilbert son of John and Molley Rogers Gilbert was born September 2nd 1765
Molley Rogers Gilbert Daughter of John and Molley Gilbert was born August 15th AD 1767
Molley Rogers Gilbert Wife of the above said John Gilbert Died August 27th: 1767

This certifies that to the best of my knowledge that my Negro Boy called Jordan was born the 18th day of November AD 1787 Willm Noyes Lyme Decr 21st 1789 Personally

Appeared William Noyes Esq and made Oath to the above Certificate Before Ezra Selden Justice of Peace Recorded this 21st day of Decr AD 1789 By David F. Sill Register

My Negro boy Harry was born December 3d AD 1790 Lyme July 23d AD 1791 Personally appeared William Noyes the above Subscriber and Testified on Oath that the above Certificate is true according to the best of his knowledge. Before Seth Ely Justice of Peace Recorded Septr 8th AD 1791 Pr David F. Sill Register

[page 115] These are to Certifye whomesoever it may Consern that Mr. Peter Lay and Mrs. Hepzibah Peck of Lyme were Lawfully married together June 13th 1765 by me Stephen Johnson Pastor of the first Church in said Lyme Dated Lyme 28th June AD 1766

Calee Lay Daughter of Peter & Hepzibah Lay was born May 26th AD 1766
Phebe Lay Daughter of Peter & Hepzibah Lay was born October first 1768
Jean Lay Daughter of Peter & Hepzibah Lay was born October 25th 1770
Nabbey Lay Daughter of Peter & Hepzibah Lay was born March 6th 1773
Gibbon Lay Son of Peter & Hepzibah Lay was born June 2nd AD 1775
Hepzibah Lay Daughter of Peter & Hepzibah Lay was born March 28th 1777
Peck Lay Son of Peter & Hepzibah Lay was born Septembr 15th AD 1779 and died ye 19th Day of September AD: 1780
Polley Lay Daughter of Peter & Hepzibah Lay was born August: 11th Day 1781
Fanney Lay Daughter of Peter & Hepzibah Lay was born February 21st 1784
Peter Lay above said died May 12th 1802 aged 58 years

John Johnson Junr was married to Anna Brooks on the 26th Day of December AD 1759
Elisabeth Johnson Daughter of John and Anna Johnson was born the 30th of July 1760
Catharine Johnson Daughter of John & Anna Johnson was born June 16th AD 1762
Reynolds Johnson Son of John & Anna Johnson was born June ye 6th AD 1764
Anna Johnson Daughter of John & Anna Johnson was born July 15th AD 1766 and died the 20th Day of August: AD 1766
John Johnson son of John and Anna Johnson was born Septemr 16th 1768
Daniel Johnson son of John and Anna Johnson was born March 27th AD 1771
William Johnson Son of John & Anna Johnson was born June ye 5th AD 1773
John Johnson Son of John & Anna Johnson Died June ye 20th AD 1774
William Johnson Son of John & Anna Johnson Died September 25th AD 1777
William Johnson Son of John & Anna Johnson was born June 9th AD 1778
Fanny Johnson Daughter of John & Anna Johnson was born May 9: 1782

These may Signifie & Certifye that Jedediah Peck of Lyme was on the fifth 5th Day of November 1772 married to Tabitha Ely of the Same Town by me George Beckwith Pastor

Hephzibah Peck Daughter of Jedediah and Tabitha Peck was born January: 29th 1774
Polley Peck Daughter of Jedediah and Tabitha Peck was born Novemr 6th 1775
Elijah Peck Son of Jedediah and Tabitha Peck was born 29th of August: 1780 and Died the 20th of Septemr AD 1780
Elijah Peck Son of Jedediah & Tabitha Peck was born October first: 1781
Peter Peck Son of Jedediah and Tabitha Peck was born Novemr 12th AD 1783
Ama Peck Daughter of Jedediah and Tabitha Peck was born May 27th 1786
Jedediah Peck Son of Jedediah & Tabitha Peck was born May 19th Anno Domini 1788

[page 116] 1758: June 8th: Then I married Jonathan Gilbert of Lyme Son of John Gilbert Deceasd to Sarah Rogers of New London Daughter to John Rogers of New London Lately Deceasd A true Copy of Record Test Pygan Adams Jus : Pace

Elisabeth Gilbert Daughter of Jonathan and Sarah Gilbert was born November 5th: 1759
Desire Gilbert Daughter of Jonathan & Sarah Gilbert was born February ye 26th 1762
Sarah Gilbert Daughter of Jonathan & Sarah Gilbert was born January ye 6th AD 1764
Jonathan Gilbert son of Jonathan & Sarah Gilbert was born June the 18th AD 1766

Sarah Gilbert Wife of sd Jonathan Gilbert Departed this Life June 18th AD 1766 New London Decemr 18 1771: this certifies that Mr. Jonathan Gilbert of Lyme and Mrs. Lous Baker of New London were married March 26th 1767 by me David Jewet Pastor
Lous Gilbert Daughter of Jonathan & Lous Gilbert was born January 8th AD 1768
Mary Gilbert Daughter of Jona and Lous Gilbert was born August 15th 1769
Marcy Gilbert Daughter of Jona & Lous Gilbert was born October ye 29th AD 1778
Mr. John Denison Junr and Mrs. Mary Sears both of Lyme in New London County were Lawfully married to each other on the 9th Day of August: 1764 by me John Lay 2nd Jusce Paec
John Sears Denison Son of John and Mary Denison was born July 28th AD 1765
Samll Denison Son of John & Mary Denison was born July 6th Day AD 1767
Elisabeth Denison Daughter of John & Mary Denison was born April 16th AD 1769
Robert Denison Son of John & Mary Denison was born April 13th AD 1771
Anna Denison Daughter of John & Mary Denison was born April 12th AD 1773
Phebe Denison Daughter of John & Mary Denison was born November 29th AD 1775
George Washington Denison Son of John & Mary Denison was born in the town of Groton in the State of Connecticut August 4th: 1778
Oliver Denison Son of John & Mary Denison was Born in Middletown in the State of Connecticut March 12th 1782: and Died ye 4th of May AD 1782
Mary Denison Wife of sd John Denison Died April 6th AD: 1782

These may Signifye & Certifye that William Harrison of Lyme was on the 29th of December: AD: 1762 married to Hepzibah Tiffany of the same town Pr me Geo: Beckwith Pastor of a Church in Lyme
Elisha Harrison Daughter of Wm & Hepzibah Harrison was born Decemr 31st AD 1763
Polley Harrison Daughter of Wm & Hepzibah Harrison was born April 13th 1767
Line Harrison Daughter of Wm & Hepzibah Harrison was born December 22nd 1769
Bulah Harrison Daughter of Sm & Hepzibah Harrison was born Novemr 18th 1772
Richd Montgomery Harrison Son of Wm & Hepzibah Harrison was born March 31st 1776
William Harrison Son of Wm & Hepzibah Harrison was born April 20th 1779

Mr. Abner Peck was married to Miss Carolina Reed Novr 30th day AD 1786
Nathaniel Son of Abner & Carrolina was born Sepr 28th AD 1788

[page 117] Jacob Starlin and Edey Tucker both of Lyme in New London County were Lawfully married to each other on the 14th Day of October AD 1765 by me John Lay 2nd Jusc Pace
Hepzibah Starlin Daughter of Jacob and Edey Starlin was born February 19th 1767
Elisabeth Marvin Starlin Daughter of Jacob & Edey Starlin was born July 4th 1769
Edey Starlin Daughter of Jacob & Edey Starlin was born August ye 19th AD 1771
Abigail Starlin Daughter of Jacob & Edey Starlin was born August ye 30th AD 1773 and Departed this Life the 24th day of August AD 1775
Abigail Starlin Daughter of Jacob & Edey Starlin was born December 16th AD 1775
Edey Starlin Daughter of Jacob & Edey Starlin Departed this Life March 16th AD 1777
Abigail Starlin Daughter of Jacob & Edey Starlin Died March 27th AD 1777
Deborah Starlin Daughter of Jacob & Edey Starlin was born October ye 3rd AD 1778
Allias Starlin Daughter of Jacob & Edey Starlin was born Septemr ye 10th AD 1782

These may Certifye whomsoever it may Consern that Mr. Danll Lord and Mrs. Elisabeth Lord both of Lyme were Lawfully married together the 12th Day of April AD 1764: Pr me Stephen Johnson Pastor the first Church in sd Lyme Dated in Lyme 22nd May: AD 1767
Barnabas Lord son of Danll and Elisabeth Lord was born 12th of December 1764
Danll Lord son of Danll and Elisabeth Lord was born August 9th AD 1766
Reynolds Lord son of Danll and Elisabeth Lord was born Septemr 4th AD 1768
Silas Lord son of Danll and Elisabeth Lord was born February 7th AD 1771

72 LYME, CONNECTICUT, VITAL RECORDS

Abigail Lord Daughter of Danll and Elisabeth Lord was born Novemr 14 1773
Esther Lord Daughter of Danll and Elisabeth Lord was born December 4th 1776
Lemuel Tubbs and Elisabeth Scovel both of Lyme were married together on the 17th Day of November AD 1756: by the Reverend Mr. George Griswold
Israel Tubbs son of Lemuel and Elisabeth Tubbs was born October ye 9th 1757
Isaac Tubbs son of Lemuel & Elisabeth Tubbs was born April the 2nd AD 1760
Elisabeth Tubbs Daughter of Lemuel & Elisabeth Tubbs was born March 23rd AD 1762
Lydia Tubbs Daughter of Lemuel & Elisabeth Tubbs was born February 16th AD 1764
Leane Tubbs Son of Lemuel & Elisabeth Tubbs was born May the 6th AD 1766

Mr. Daniel Chadwick Died February 22nd AD 1771
Catherine [Shailer] Chadwick Relect of ye above said Daniel Chadwick Died July 8th 1771

[page 118] These may certifye whomsoever it may Conscearn that Jonathn Brockway and Phebe Smith both of Lyme were Lawfully Married together the 20th of October A.D. 1757: by me - Stephen Johnson Pastor of the first Church in sd Lyme - Dated in Lyme 18th June 1767
Asa Brockway Son of Jonathan & Phebe Brockway was born April 23rd A.D: 1758
Martin Brockway Son of Jona & Phebe Brockway was born April 26th: 1760 and Died November 30th 1760
Martin Brockway Son of Jonathan & Phebe Brockway was born December 3rd 1761
Susannah Brockway Daughter of Jona & Phebe Brockway was born March 18th 1764
Jonathan Brockway Son of Jonathan & Phebe Brockway was born February 25th 1766
Jesse Brockway Son of Jonathan & Phebe Brockway was Born April 24th A.D. 1768
Phebe Brockway Daughter of Jonathan & Phebe Brockway was Born April 29th 1770
Rufus Brockway Son of Jonathan and Phebe Brockway was Born 14th of August: 1772

These may Certifye that Vinten Beckwith of Lyme was Married to Mary Ayers of Lyme the 9th Day of October 1766: by me Benja Lee Justice of the Peace
Sarah Beckwith Daughter Vinten and Mary Beckwith was born Septemr 9th A.D. 1768
Mary Beckwith Daughters of Vinten & Mary Beckwith was Born March 21st AD 1773
Phebe Beckwith Daughter of Vinten & Mary Beckwith was Born February 28th 1780
Vinten Beckwith above said Died the 17th Day of August: 1785

These are to Certifye that Ensign Danll Chadwick and Mrs. Hannah Anderson both of Lyme were Lawfully Married together the 19th Day of January: A.D: 1763 Pr me Stephen Johnson Pastor of the first Church in sd Lyme Dated in Lyme 11th April: 1777
Ezra Chadwick Son of Danll & Hannah Chadwick was born the 2nd Day of June: 1763
Hepzibah Chadwick Daughter of Danll & Hannah Chadwick was Born May ye 18th A.D: 1766
Danll Chadwick Son of Danll & Hannah Chadwick was Born October ye 7th A.D. 1768
Anna Chadwick Daughter of Daniel & Hannah Chadwick was Born June 9th A.D. 1771
Laurana Chadwick Daughter of Danll & Hannah Chadwick was born August 17th A.D. 1774 and Died Septembr ye 24th A.D. 1776

Matthew Rowland was born on the 8th day of June in the year 1772

[page 119] These may Signifye and Certifye that on the 28th Day of March 1754: Ammi Ely was Married to Martha Peck both of Lyme by me - George Beckwith Pastor
Faunne [Fanne] Ely Daughter of Ammi & Martha Ely was Born March first: 1755 and Died the same first of March 1755
Gabriel Ely Son of Ammi & Martha Ely was Born April 5th 1756
Gurdon Ely Son of Ammi & Martha Ely was born April 30th 1760
Martha Ely Daughter of Ammi & Martha Ely was born October first: 1763
Leusenda Hannah Ely Daughter of Ammi & Martha Ely was born June 19th A.D. 1765
Fanne Ely Daughter of Ammi & Martha Ely was born June 15th A.D. 1768 and Died the 30th Day of October A.D. 1768

Zelophehad Ely Son of Ammi and Martha Ely was born November 25th 1769
Fanne Ely Daughter of Ammi and Martha Ely was born May 29th 1773
Horation Gates Ely Son of Ammi & Martha Ely was born October 30th 1777
Martha Person widdow and Relect of Mr. Peter Person Late of sd Lyme Deceased Died the 27th Day of January A.D. 1770
Duran [Doran] Huntly Son of Benjamin & Beththiah Hunlly was born August the 4th A.D. 1764
Lovina Huntly Daughter of Benjamin & Beththiah Huntly was born June the 5th A.D. 1766
Elisha Chadwick Son of Nathaniel & Betty Chadwick Born July 10th A.D. 1781
Susannah Daughter of Nathll & Betty Chadwick was born January 24th A.D. 1783
This is to Certifye that on the 20th Instant Mr. Lynde McCurdy of Lyme in the state of Connecticut Merchant was Joyned in Marriage with Mrs. Ursula Griswold of sd Lyme - East Windsor November 22nd 1777 - Test. Joseph Terry Minister of the Gospel
Ursula McCurdy Daughter of Lynde and Ursula McCurdy was born August 20th 1778

[page 120] These may Certifye whomsoever it may Conscearn that William Miller and Irena Brockway both of Lyme were Lawfully Married together 26th Day of August A.D. 1766   Pr me - Stephen Johnson Pastor of the first Church in sd Lyme   Dated Lyme 16th Decemr 1767
Elias Miller Son of William and Irena Miller was born July 8th A.D. 1767
Mary Miller Daughter of William & Irena Miller was born February 23rd A.D. 1769
William Miller Son of Wm & Irene Miller was Born April 8th Day A.D 1771
Asa Miller Son of Wm & Irene Miller was born July 8th Day A.D. 1773
Welthy Miller Daughter of William and Irene Miller was born 14th Day of April A.D. 1776
These may Certifye whomsoever it may Conscearn that Noah Miller Junr and Welthy Brockway both of Lyme were Lawfully Married together the 3rd Day of March 1767   Pr me - Stephen Johnson Pastor of the first Church in sd Lyme   Dated in 16th Decemr 1767
Lyme June ye 24th 1768: these may Certifye that Samll Brooks of Lyme was Married to Rhoda Beckwith of sd Lyme the 17th Day of March 1763   Pr me Benja Lee Justice of Peace
Rhoda Brooks Daughter of Samll and Rhoda Brooks was born April 13th A.D. 1764
Molley Brooks Daughter of Samll & Rhoda Brooks was born January 12th A.D. 1766
Phebe Brooks Daughter of Samll and Rhoda Brooks was born January 8th A.D. 1768
Fanne Brooks Daughter of Samll and Rhoda Brooks wrs born Septemr 28th A.D. 1771
Samll Brooks Son of Samll and Rhoda Brooks was born February ye 24th A.D. 1774
[page 121] These may Certifye that Daniel Miner of Lyme was married to Ama Smith of sd Lyme the 21st Day of October 1761 by me Benjamin Lee - Lyme June ye 5th 1767
Mary Miner Daughter of Danll and Ama Miner was born August 18th 1762
Abigail Miner Daughter of Danll & Ama Miner was born Decemr 2nd 1764
Mehetabel Miner Daughter of Danll & Ama Miner was born August 2nd 1766
Ama Miner Daughter of Daniel & Ama Miner was born Septemr 26 1768
Dorcas Miner Daughter of Daniel & Ama Miner was born February 25th 1771
John Mack Miner Son of Danll & Ama Miner was born Decemr 28th 1772
Daniel Miner Son of Danel and Ama Miner was born March 8th 1775
Elisabeth Miner Daughter of Danll & Ama Miner was Born February 26 1778

Lyme November ye 10th 1760   These may Certifye all whome it may Conscearn that Solomon Gee Junr of Lyme was Married to Martha Bingham the 24th Day of Decemr 1758 by me Benjamin Lee
Lewmon Gee Son of Solomon and Martha Gee was born Novemr 14th 1757
Molley Gee Daughter of Solomon & Martha Gee was born January 24th 1762
Abner Gee Son of Solomon and Martha Gee was born February 15 1765

These may Certifye whomsoever it may Conscearn that Mr. Edward Dewolf & Mrs. Hannah Huntly both of Lyme were Lawfully Married together the 5th Day of October 1762 pr me Stephen Johnson Pastor of the first Church in sd Lyme Dated 16th November: 1767
Daniel Dewolf Son of Edward and Hannah Dewolf was born October 14th AD 1763 on fryday about 2 of the clock in in the morning.
Edward Dewolf Son of Edward and Hannah Dewolf was born February 14th A.D. 1765 on Thursday about noone
Benjamin Dewolf Son of Edward and Hannah Dewolf was born August 29th A.D. 1766 on Fryday about Six of the clock in the morning
Sylvanus Dewolf Son of Edward and Hannah Dewolf was born March 2nd A.D. 1768 on Wednesday about one of the clock in the morning and sd Sylvanus Died March ye 14th 1768 about Eleven of the clock before noone
Ephriam & Manaset [Manasseh] Wolfe Sons of the sd Edward & Hannah was born 11th Feby 1772

[page 122]   Jasper Griffing was Married to Mary Reed the 7th of January A.D. 1725
Jasper Griffing Son of Jasper & Mary Griffing was born October the 3rd A.D. 1725 and Died December the 10th AD 1725
Jasper Griffing Son of Jasper & Mary Griffing was born ye 10th Day of Decemr A.D. 1726
Mary Griffing Daughter of Jasper & Mary Griffing was born the 22nd Day of Novemr 1728
Ruth Griffing Daughter of Jasper & Mary Griffing was born 29th Day of October A.D. 1730
John Griffing Son of Jasper & Mary Griffing was born January 10th A.D. 1733
Deborah Griffing Daughter of Jasper & Mary Griffing was born February 7th A.D. 1735
John Griffing Son of Jasper & Mary Griffing Died April the 10th Day A.D. 1737
John Griffing Son of Jasper & Mary Griffing was born May 16th A.D 1737
Ruth Griffing Daughter of Jasper & Mary Griffing Died August 19th 1738
Mary Griffing Daughter of Jasper & Mary Griffing Died Septemr 2nd A.D. 1738
Deborah Griffing Daughter of Jasper & Mary Griffing Died Septemr 19th A.D.1738
Abner Griffing Son of Jasper & Mary Griffing was born March 29th 1741

These may Certifye whomsoever it may Conscearn that Mr. James Ely and Mrs. Catherine Hayes both of Lyme were Lawfully Married together the 30th Day of June A.D. 1768   Pr me Stephen Johnson Pastor of the first Church in sd Lyme Dated in Lyme 11th Decemr 1768
Richd Hayes Ely Son of James and Catharine Ely was born March 28th A.D. 1769
James Ely Son of James and Catharine Ely was Born February 26th A.D. 1771
Carried into the other Book

Mr. Elisha Wade was Married to Mrs. Mary Jones of Saybrook April 11th A.D. 1765
Sally Wade Daughter of said Elisha & Mary was born March 1st A.D. 1768
Lovina Wade Daughter of said Elisha & Mary was born May 30th A.D. 1770
Polly Waid Daughter of said Elisha & Mary was born August 4th A.D. 1772
Fanny Waid Daughter of said Elisha & Mary was born July 27th A.D. 1780
Fanny Waid died Sept 27th A.D. 1782 aged two years and two months

[page 123]   Lyme in the Colony of Connecticut on the first Day of May: 1764 Richard Wait Junr and Lucia Griswold both of Lyme were married to Each other by me Mathw Griswold Assistant   Certifyed Per me Mathew Griswold Assistant
Thomas Griswold Wait Son of Richd and Lucia Wait was born 14th February: 1765
Lois Wait Daughter of Richd and Lucia Wait was born August first AD: 1766
Elizabeth Wait Daughter of Richd and Lucia Wait was born March 30th AD: 1768
Lynde Wait son of Lieut Richd & Lucia Wait was born Novemr 16th AD 1769
Richd Wait son of Lieut. Richd & Lucia Wait was born June 18th AD 1771
Lucy Wait Daughter of Lt. Richd & Lucia Wait was born June 17th AD 1773
Sussannah Wait Daughter of Richd & Lucy Wait was born April 29th 1775
James Wait Son of Richd & Lucy Wait was born March 10th 1777

Richard Wait had three Sons Born the 5th of December 1778 -- and Died the same Day that they were born
David Wait Son of Richd and Lucy Wait was born ye 12th of February: 1780
Phebe Wait Daughter of Richd & Lucy Wait was born 20th of January 1782
They had a son Born the 8th of October 1783: Died the same Day
Phebe Wait Daughter of Richard & Lucy Wait Died 16th of September 1786
Daniel Wait Son of Richd and Lucy Wait was Born 10th of January: 1786
Phebe Wait Daughter of Richd & Lucy Wait was Born January 19th 1788
Lucy wife of the said Richard diseased on the 25th day of November AD 1795
Richd Wait Esq was joined in marraige to Mrs. Mary Wood on the 27th day of April 1801

These may Certifye whomsoever it may Consern that Mr. Benjamin Marvin Junr & Mrs. Phebe Roland both of Lyme were Lawfully Married together the 29th Day of October: AD 1767: pr me Stephen Johnson Pastor of the first Church in sd Lyme
Abigail Marvin Daughter of Benja & Phebe Marvin was born August 29: 1768
Uriah Marvin son of Benja & Phebe Marvin was born August 8th 1770
John Marvin son of Benjamin Marvin Junr & Phebe his wife was born June 8th 1772
William Marvin son of Benja Marvin Junr & Phebe his wife was born April 5th 1775
Abigail Marvin Daughter of Benja & Pheby Marvin Died December 5th 1776
Nabbe Marvin Daughter of Benjamin and Phebey Marvin was born March 27th 1777
Phebe Marvin Daughter of Benjamin & Phebey Marvin was born May 18th 1779
Lucy Marvin Daughter of Benjamin & Phebey Marvin was born May 2nd 1781 and She Died on the 16th Day of August 1781
Lucy Marvin Daughter of Benjamin & Phebe Marvin was Born July 21st AD 1782
Alexander Marvin son of Benjamin & Phebe Marvin was Born January 31st 1785

Lawrance [Lawrrance] Johnson married to Lydia Comstock 23rd Day

[page 124] Ezra Miller Son of Robert and Martha Miller was born March 10th 1737
Joseph Miller Son of Robert & Martha Miller was born March 13th 1740
Eunice Miller Daughter of Robert & Martha Miller was born January 30th 1743
George Miller son of Robert & Martha Miller was born April 18th 1747
Hephzibah Miller Daughter of Robert & Martha Miller was born Febry 1st 1749
Martha Miller Daughter of Robert & Martha Miller was born April 23rd 1751
Lucinda Miller Daughter of Robert & Martha Miller was born January 3rd 1758
Joseph Miller Died October 20th AD 1759
Joseph Miller Son of Robert & Martha Miller was born May ye 24th 1760
Hephzibah Miller Died August 6th AD 1763
Recorded the 27th of Septemr 1768: by John Lay 2nd Clerk
Lieut. Robert Miller died Jan 21 1790 (Taken from gravestone by William Marvin Town Clerk)

Lyme Decemr the 7th 1768: These may Certifye that Samll Huntly Junr of Lyme was married to Susannah Huntly of Lyme the 7th of October 1767 Pr me Benjamin Lee Justice Pace
Lemuel Huntly son of Samll and Susannah Huntly was born Augst 8th 1768

New London March 3rd 1779: This to whome it Concerneth Certifies that Jesse Beckwith Junr of Chesterfield and Esther Smith of New London North Parrish were married March 24th 1777: by me David Jewitt Pastor
Betsa Beckwith Daughter Jesse Beckwith Junr & Esther his wife was born April 2nd: 1778
Ezra son of said Jesse & Esther was born on the 5th day of May AD 1779
Elijah son of said Jesse & Esther was born on the 27th day February oD 1781
Silveness Son of said Jesse & Esther was born on the 13th day of Feby AD 1783
Nathaniel Son of said Jesse & Esther was born on the 8th day of May AD 1785
Nathan Smith Son of said Jesse & Esther was born on the 6th of November 1787
Jesse son of said Jesse & Esther was born on the 9th day of April 1790

LYME, CONNECTICUT, VITAL RECORDS

Isreal son of said Jesse & Esther was born on the 11th day of May 1794

[page 125] These may Certifye whomsoever it may Consern that Mr. Ezra Champion and Mrs. Mary Bumpas both of Lyme were Lawfully married together on the 24th of October AD 1752: Pr me Stephen Johnson Pastor of the first Church in sd Lyme Dated in Lyme 19 January A.D. 1769

Hannah Champion Daughter of Ezra & Mary Champion was born August 23rd 1753
Stephen Champion Son of Ezra & Mary Champion was born March 16th 1755
Ruben Champion Son of Ezra & Mary Champion was born February 16th 1757
Thankfull Champion Daughter of Ezra & Mary Champion was born June ye 23rd 1759
Dan Champion Son of Ezra & Mary Champion was born August 29th 1761
Ezra Champion Son of Ezra & Mary Champion was born August 28th 1763
Lydia Champion Daughter of Ezra & Mary Champion was born February 11th 1765
John Champion Son of Ezra & Mary Champion was born Decemr 21st 1768
Polley Champion Daughter of Ezra & Mary Champion was born January 26 1770
Joshua Champion Son of Ezra & Mary Champion was born August 22nd 1773

August the 10th AD 1757: Then I married Cyrus Lee to his now wife Mary Huntly - Test Samll Ely Justice of the Peace

Molley Lee Daughter of Cyrus and Mary Lee was born December 21st AD 1759
Lydia Lee Daughter of Cyrus and Mary Lee was born November 5th AD 1761
William Lee Son of Cyrus and Mary Lee was born October 24th AD 1763
Lory Lee Daughter of Cyrus & Mary Lee was born April ye 18th AD 1766
Nabby Lee Daughter of Cyrus & Mary Lee was born Septemr 29th AD 1768

Mr. Asel Roland and Mrs. Mary Champion widdow was married February the 16th Day by Richd Wait Justice of Peace

Lyme January the 27th 1768: These may Certifye that Ithamer Smith of Lyme was married to Sarah Sawyer of sd Lyme the 11th Day of November 1762: by me Benjamin Lee Justice of the Peace

Lita Smith Daughter of Ithamer and Sarah Smith was Born February 7th 1765
Luce Smith Daughter of Ithamer & Sarah Smith was born January 31st 1767
Simeon Smith Son of Ithamer & Sarah Smith was Born March 26th 1769
Jabez Smith Son of Ithamer & Sarah Smith was Born March 2nd 1771
Theode Smith Daughter of Ithamer & Sarah Smith was Born March 20th 1773
Elisabeth Smith Daughter of Ithamer & Sarah Smith was Born September 16th 1775-

[page 126] These may Certifie whome it may Conscearn that Mr. William Dewolf and Miss Elisabeth Roland both of Lyme were Lawfully Married together on the 6th Day of December A.D. 1764: by me John Lay 2nd Justice of the Peace

Zeporah Dewolf Daughter of William and Elisabeth Dewolf was born June 29th A.D. 1766
Billey Dewolf Son of Willm and Elisabeth Dewolf was born February 26th A.D. 1768
Martha Dewolf Daughter of Willm & Elisabeth Dewolf was born Decemr 15 1769
Elisabeth Dewolf Daughter of Willm & Elisabeth Dewolf was Born Novemr 3rd: 1771
Josiah Dewolf Son of Willm & Elisabeth Dewolf was Born ye 17th Day of January A.D. 1774
Elisabeth Dewolf Daughter of Willm & Elisabeth Dewolf Died Septemr 2nd Day A.D. 1776
Josiah Dewolf Son of Willm & Elisabeth Dewolf Died the 6th Day of September A.D. 1776
Josiah Dewolf Son of Willm & Elisabeth Dewold was Born August 24th Day A.D. 1777
Elisabeth Dewolf Daughter of Willm Dewolf & Elisabeth his wife was Born June 8th 1781
Sussannah Dewolf Daughter of William & Elisabeth Dewolf was born Decemr 22nd 1782

Lyme April 11th 1769: These may Certifie that Elisha Smith of Lyme was married to Azubah Tinker of sd Lyme the 15th Day of October 1769 by me Benjamin Lee Justice of Peace

Phebe Smith Daughter of Elisha and Azubah Smith was Born Sept 29th: 1768
Lusinda Smith Daughter of Elisha & Azubah Smith was born April 25th A.D: 1772

These may Certifie whomsoever it may Conscearn that Mr. Ruben Chadwick and Mrs. Martha Miller both of Lyme were Lawfully Married together the 11th Day of December A.D 1767 pr me Stephen Johnson Pastor of the first Church of Christ in sd Lyme
Russell Chadwick Son of Ruben & Martha Chadwick was born Decemr 20th A.D. 1769
Joseph Chadwick Son of Ruben & Martha Chadwick was born January 26th A.D. 1772
Cate their Daughter was born March 28th day A.D. 1774
Reuben their Son was born the 27th day of March A.D. 1779
Naby their Daughter was born the 9th day of February A.D. 1781
Betsey their Daughter was born the 1st day of April A.D. 1784
Thomas their Son was born the 16 day of September A.D. 1786

[page 127] These may Certifie that Stephen Huntly of Lyme in New London County was Married to Phebe Tubbs of sd Lyme the 2nd Day of April 1764 pr Benja Lee Justice of Peace June 1st 1768
Catharine Huntly Daughter of Stephen and Phebe Huntly was born February 10th 1765
Lucinda Huntly Daughter of Stephen & Phebe Huntly was born May 2nd A.D. 1767
Catharine Huntly abovesaid Died the 24th Day of December A.D. 1770
Lucinda Huntly abovesaid Died the 4th Day of Decemr A.D. 1774
Stephen and Phebe Huntly had a Son born March 9th 1775: and Died the Same Day
Phebe Huntly Wife of sd Stephen Huntly Departed this life the 14th Day of March A.D. 1775

Lyme in New London County November 27th 1777: These may Certifie whome:ever it May Consearn that Mr. Stephen Huntly of sd Lyme was Joyned in Marriage with Mrs. Lydia Brockway of Lyme aforesaid the abovesaid pr. Ezra Selden Just Paece
Stephen Huntly Son of Stephen & Lydia Huntly was born January 27th A.D. 1779
Recorded the 15th of May: 1779: by John Lay 2nd Regr.

Lyme the 9th of Decemr 1768: These may Certifye that Joseph Huntly was Married to Lydia Sawyer the 4th Day of May 1768: and both of Lyme Pr Benjamin Lee Justice of Peace
Abraham Huntly Son of Joseph & Lydia Huntly was born March 30thA.D. 1769
Olive Huntly Daughter of Joseph & Lydia Huntly was born October 6th A.D: 1771
Joseph Huntly Son of Joseph & Lydia Huntly was born July 19th A.D: 1775
Hope Huntly Son of Joseph & Lydia Huntly was born January 15th A.D: 1778

These May Certifie whomesoever it may Conscearn that that Mr. Lemuel Rogers and Mrs. Hannah Miller both of Lyme were Lawfully Married together 10th Day of December A.D. 1760 Pr me Stephen Johnson Pastor of the first Church in sd Lyme Dated in Lyme 27th June A.D. 1769
Sarah Rogers Daughter of Lemuel and Hannah Rogers was born Fryday July 9th 1762 and Died February the 11th 1765
Hannah Rogers Daughter of Lemuel & Hannah Rogers was born Monday August 6th 1764
Sarah Rogers Daughter of Lemuel & Hannah Rogers was born January 30th A.D. 1767
Lemuel Rogers Son of Lemuel and Hannah Rogers was born June 8th Day A.D. 1769
Robert Rogers Son of Lemuel & Hannah Rogers was born June 5th A.D. 1771
Nathan Rogers Son of Lemuel & Hannah Rogers was born the 21st February A.D: 1774
Ezra Rogers Son of Lemuel & Hannah Rogers was born February 23 on Fryday: 1776

[page 128] on the 3rd Day of March: A.D. 1768 then I married George Ransom to his now Wife Anna Tiffany Test - Samll Ely Justice of the Peace
Amasa Ransom Son of George and Anna Ransom was born January 31st A.D. 1769
Irena Ransom Daughter of George & Anna Ransom was born October 12th A.D. 1770
Lydia Ransom Daughter of George & Anna Ransom was born February 19th A.D. 1772
Azubah Ransom Daughter of George and Anna Ransom was Born July 2nd A.D. 1773
Keturah Ransom Daughter of George and Anna Ransom was born October 28th A.D. 1774

Anna Ransom Daughter of George and Anna Ransom was born February first: A.D. 1776
George Washington Ransom Son of George & Anna Ransom was born November 7th A.D. 1777
Nathan Tiffany Ransom Son of George & Anna Ransom was born 13th of July A.D: 1779
Sarah Ransom Daughter of George & Anna Ransom was born Septemr first Day A.D. 1781

Septemr 23rd 1737   Gideon Watrous and Martha Beckwith both of Lyme were Married together by me George Griswold Pastor of the 2nd Church in Lyme
Gurden Watrous Son of Gideon and Martha Watrous was born February 3rd A.D. 1738
Anna Watrous Daughter of Gideon & Martha Watrous was born Novemr 15th A.D. 1739
Gideon Watrous Son of Gideon and Martha Watrous was born April 22nd A.D. 1742
Jacob Watrous Son of Gideon and Martha Watrous was Born March 26th A.D. 1744
Oliver Watrous Son of Gideon & Martha Watrous was Born August ye 17th 1746
Richard Watrous Son of Gideon & Martha Watrous was Born November 30th A.D. 1748
Asa Watrous Son of Gideon & Martha Watrous was born April 15th A.D. 1751
Naomy Watrous Daughter of Gideon & Martha Watrous was born April 8th A.D.1753
Sylvanus Watrous Son of Gideon & Martha Watrous was born: October 9th A.D. 1755
Irena Watrous Daughter of Gideon & Martha Watrous was born October 15th A.D. 1757
Allen Watrous Son of Gideon & Martha Watrous was born November 15th A.D. 1759
Billey Watrous Son of Gideon & Martha Watrous was born June ye 6th A.D. 1765
Anna above named Died (the Wife of Jessie Minard) 31st of August A.D. 1767
Jacob Watrouse above said Died February 9th: A.D. 1769

Lawrrane Johnson was Married to Lydia Comstock the 3rd Day of March 1777: both of Lyme as it appears by Benjamin Lee Esqr Deceased Record of Marriges.
Christopher Johnson Son of Lawrrence and Lydia Johnson was born January 8th A.D. 1779
Samll Johnson Son of Lawrrence & Lydia Johnson was born January 8th A.D. 1781
Lydia Johnson Wife of ye abovesaid Lawrrance Johnson Died the 19th Day of August A.D. 1783

Lyme in New London County May the 20th A.D. 1784: then Lawrence Johnson was Married to Grace Harris boath of Lyme by me Eleazer Mather Just Pace
Daniel Johnson of Lawrance & Grace Johnson was Born March 4th A.D. 1785
Lawrence the Son of Lawrence and Grace was born on the 23rd day of Novr 1786
Ira Son of the said Lawrence and Grace was born on the 25 day of April 1789
Peria Son of the said Lawrence & Grace was born on the 25 day of March 1791
Timothy Son of the said Lawrence and Grace was born on the 4 day of September 1793
Lydia daughter of the said Lawrence & Grace was born on the 5 day of September 1795
Grace their daughter was born on the 29 day of April 1801
Phebe their daughter was born on the 4th day of June 1804

[page 129]   In Lyme in the Colony of Connecticut on the 14th Day of November: 1765 Samll Mather Junr and Lous Griswold boath of Lyme were Married to Each other by me: Matthew Griswold Assist   Certified Pr Matthew Griswold Assist.
Anna Mather Daughter of Samll and Lous Mather was born Decemr 11th 1766
Thomas Mather Son of Samll & Lous Mather was born October 10th 1768
Samuel Son of the said Samll & Lois was born the 4th day of Jany 1771
Phebe daughter of the said Samll & Lois was born the 22nd day of July 1772
Mehitable daughter of the said Samuel & Lois was born on the 14 day of November 1774
Henry Son of the said Samuel & Lois was born on the 31 day of July 1777
Fanny daughter of the said Samuel & Lois was born on the 13 day of Decr 1779
Richard Son of the said Samuel and Lois was born on the 10 day of May 1782
James Son of the said Samuel and Lois was born on the 14 day of March 1785
Peggy daughter of the said Samuel and Lois was born on the 16 day of July 1787
Lydia daughter of the said Samuel and Lois was born on the 11 day of Augt 1790
Lois the Wife of the said Samuel died on the 17 day of November A.D. 1804

Henry Son of the said Samuel & Lois died on the 24th day of August 1802
Richard Son of the said Samuel & Lois died on the 2d day of August 1805

Simeon Wood and Elisabeth Tubbs were Married to Each other August 12th 1760: by the Reverend Mr. George Griswold: as appears by the Evidence of James Huntly and Jason Lee both of sd Lyme who were then present
Elisabeth Wood daughter of Simeon & Elisabeth Wood was born Septemr 23rd 1761
Caroline Wood Daughter of Simeon & Elisabeth Wood was born Decemr 7th 1763
William Wood Son of Simeon & Elisabeth Wood was born March 22nd 1766
Eleazer Wood Son of Simeon & Elisabeth Wood was born June 5th 1768

These are to Certifie whomesoever it may Conscearn that Stephen Dewolf and Sarah Greenfield boath of Lyme were Lawfully Married together May 16th A.D. 1776: by me Stephen Johnson Pastor of the first Curch in sd Lyme. Dated in Lyme 4th June: 1778
Sarah Dewolf Daughter of Stephen & Sarah Dewolf was born January 10th A.D. 1777
Mrs. Sarah Dewolf the Wife of Stephen Dewolf above said Died January 12th A.D. 1777

These Certifie whome it may Consearn that Mr. Stephen Dewolf & Mrs. Theody Anderson boath of Lyme were Lawfully Married together the first Day of December the first Day of December A.D. 1782 by me Stephen Johnson Pastor of first Church in sd Lyme
Jeramiah Dewolf Son of Stephen & Theody was born February first 1784
Lucy Daughter of the said Stephen & Theody was born the 30th day May 1787
Stephen Son of the said Stephen & Theody was born the 14th day of October 1789
Theody Daughter of the said Stephen & Theody was born 9th of Novr A.D. 1793
Winthrop Buck Son of the said Stephen and Theody was born 4th of Septr A.D. 1795
Lydia daughter of the said Stephen & Theody was born on the 13th day of June 1798
Theody Wife of the said Stephen departed this Life on the 20th day of July 1798

[page 130] Curtiss Comstock of Lyme was Married to Esther Canfield of Saybrook February 20th 1755: as appeared: by the Evidence of Jabez Comstock and Danll Lord: who were then and there present
John Comstock Son of Curtiss & Esther Comstock was born November ye 12th 1756
Hezekiah Comstock Son of Curtiss & Esther Comstock was born February ye 7th 1759
Esther Comstock Daughter of Curtiss and Esther Comstock was born May ye 20th 1762
Curtiss Comstock Son of Curtiss and Esther Comstock was Born October 25th 1764
Giles Comstock Son of Curtiss & Esther Comstock was Born January 3rd 1767
Sarah Comstock Daughter of Curtiss and Esther Comstock was born February 20th 1769

Lyme November 9th 1769: These may Certifye that Benjamin Lee Junr and Mary Dorr 2nd were Joyned in Marriage on the 23rd of August 1761 - pr. George Dorr Justice of the Peace
Stephen Lee Son of Benjamin Lee Junr and Mary his Wife was born October 4th A.D. 1761
Sarah Lee Daughter of Benja Lee Junr & Mary his Wife was born Decemr first AD 1762
Mary Ann Lee Daughter of Benja Lee Junr & Mary his Wife was born May 9th A.D. 1765
George Lee Son of Benjamin Lee Junr & Mary his Wife was born August 23rd A.D. 1767
Lucy Lee Daughter of Benja Lee Junr & Mary his Wife was born July 23rd A.D. 1769
Zenos Lee Son of Benjamin Lee Junr & Mary his Wife was born August 31st A.D. 1771
Joseph Lee Son of Benjamin Lee Junr & Mary his Wife was born March 13th A.D. 1774
Charles Lee Son of Benjamin Lee Junr & Mary his Wife was Born August 17th 1776
Lydia Lee Daughter of Benjamin and Mary Lee was Born February 24th 1779
Benja Lee Son of Benjamin & Mary Lee was Born March first A.D. 1781

These are to Certifie whomsoever it may Conscearn that Mr. Roswell Beckwith and Mrs. Lydia Dorr both of Lyme were Lawfully Married together the 13th Day of January A.D. 1780 by me Stephen Johnson Pastor of the first Church in sd Lyme Dated Lyme 15th Day of August A.D. 1780

1780
Barach, Beckwith Son of Roswell & Lydia was born the 3d Day of November A.D. 1780
Betty, Daughter of said Roswell & Lydia was born the 5th Day of November A.D. 1782
Huldah, Daughter of said Roswell & Lydia was born the 14th day of November A.D. 1785
Eunice, Daugher of the said Roswell & Lydia was born the 14th day of December A.D. 1787
Roswell, Son of the said Roswell & Lydia was born the 8th day of October A.D. 1789
George, Son of the said Roswell & Lydia was born on the 20th day of February A.D. 1792

[page 131]   William Mack of Lyme was Married to Ruth Gee of sd Lyme the 12th Day of June: 1759
Delight Mack Daughter of Willm and Ruth Mack was born February 11th A.D. 1762
Dorcas Mack Daughter of Wm and Ruth Ma .k was born February 16th A.D. 1764
Ebenezer Mack Son of Willm & Ruth Mack was born January 26th Day A.D 1766
Abigail Mack Daughter of William and Ruth Mack was born Novemr 2nd 1770
Molley Mack Daughter of Willm & Ruth Mack was born February ye 8th 1773
William Mack Son of William and Ruth Mack was born April ye 6th A.D. 1775
Elijah Mack Son of Willm and Ruth Mack was born July 7th A.D. 1778
William Mack Son of Willm & Ruth Mack Died June 18th A.D. 1785

These may Signifie and Certifie that John Pirkins was Married to Hester Ayer on the 11th Day of Decemr 1766 by me George Beckwith Pastor of a Church in Lyme
Esther Pirkins Daughter of John & Esther Pirkins was Born January 9th: 1769
Stephen Pirkins Son of John & Esther Pirkins was Born Decemr 18th 1770
Stephen Pirkins above said Died April: 18th 1770
Ruth Pirkins Daughter of John & Esther Pirkins was Born August 22nd A.D: 1772
John Ayer Pirkins Son of John & Esther Pirkins was Born September 8th A.D. 1774
Elisabeth Pirkins Daughter of Esther & John Ayer Pirkins was Born December 9th A.D. 1777
Lucy Pirkins Daughter of John & Esther Pirkins was Born November 29th A.D. 1779
Seth Son of said John & Hester was born on the 30th day of April A.D. 1784
Ziporah their Daughter was born on the 16th day of August A.D. 1786
Daniel Champion their Son was born on the 30th day of October A.D. 1788

Mr. James Greenfield and Mrs. Nabby Daniels both of Lyme in New London County were Lawfully Married to Each other on the 30th Day of May: A.D. 1776 by John Lay 2nd Just Pace
Sarah Greenfield Daughter of James & Nabby Greenfield was born May 25th A.D 1777
Ezra Greenfield Son of James & Nabby Greenfield was born Novemr 28th 1779
Polley Greenfield Daughter of James & Nabby Greenfield was Born March: 29th 1782

Richard Greenfield Son of James & Nabby Greenfield was Born Novemr 9th 1784
Edward Lay Greenfield Son of James & Naby Greenfield was Born 13th Febry: 1788
Edward Lay Son of said James & Nabby died the 9th day of February 1789
Edward Son & Lucy Daughter of James & Naby being twins was born the 18th day of October 1790
Susannah Daughter of the said James & Naby was born on the 28th day of Jany: 1794
Abigail Daughter of the said James & Nabby was born on the 15th day of March 1797

[page 132]   To all Conscearned: this May Certifye that according to the best of my Remembrance Joshua Rogers and Phebe Fox boath of Lyme in New London County were Joyned in Marriage on or about the 18th of Nover A.D 1765. I am sure I Married them and make no Doubt but that was the time   Certified pr George Dorr Justice of Peace
Elias Rogers Son of Joshua and Phebe Rogers was born November 24th A.D. 1766
Ezra Rogers Son of Joshua and Phebe Rogers was born May 6th Day A.D 1768
Ursula Rogers Daughter of Joshua and Phebe Rogers was born February 4th: 1770

Daniel Mirick Way, Son of Daniel Shaw Way & Molley Mack was born on the 29th day of January A.D. 1791

Mr. Ezra Minor, and Miss Polley Mack was legally joined in Marriage on the 13th day of October by Elder Jason Lee A.D 1793

These are to Certifye whomesoever it may Concearn that Mr. Abel Hall and Mrs. Caroline Brockway both of Lyme were Lawfully Married together th 19th Day of October: AD 1769 pr me Stephen Johnson Pastor of the first Church in sd Lyme. Dated in Lyme 30th March A.D. 1770

Isaac Hall Son of Abel and Caroline Hall was born July 9th A.D 1774
William Hall Son of Abel and Caroline Hall was born the 27th Day of June A.D. 1778
Caroline Hall Daughter of Abel & Caroline Hall was born April 23rd A.D: 1780
Polley Hall Daughter of Abel & Caroline Hall was Born March 8th A.D: 1782
Lous Hall Daughter of Abel and Caroline Hall was Born August 30th A.D: 1784
Hannah Hall Daughter of Abel & Caroline Hall was Born August: 16th A.D 1786
Abel Hall Son of Abel & Carolina Hall was born July 13th A.D 1788
Caroline Hall Wife as above departed this life on the 9th day of September 1807
Abel Hall Junr Died in New York on   day of
Abel Hall the Elder departed this life one 20th day of December A.D 1816 aged 73

These may Certifye whomsoever it may Conscearn that Mr. Jehoada Mather and Mrs. Eunice Miller boath of Lyme were Lawfully Married together the 20th of December A.D. 1764 Pr me Stephen Johnson Pastor of the first Church in sd Lyme Dated in Lyme 19th Decemr 1769

Lay Mather Son of Jehoiada and Eunice Mathers was born April 10th A.D. 1768
Ezra Mather Son of Jehoiada and Eunice Mather was born January 27th A.D 1770
Martha Mather Daughter of Jehoiada & Eunice Mather was born April 7th 1772
Dan Mather Son of Jehoiada & Eunice Mather was Born the first of October: 1774
Sarah Mather Daughter of Jehoiada & Eunice Mather was born Septemr 21st 1776
Eunice Mather Daughter of Jehoiada & Eunice Mather was Born October 28th A.D. 1778

Nathan Beebe Miller Son of Thompson Miller was born the 13th Day Decr A.D. 1782

[page 133] Lyme ye 20th of April 1770: These may Certifie that Mr. Jonathan Gillet of Lyme formerly of Colchester was Married to Phebe Marvin the 11th of January 1748 by me Benja Lee Justice of Peace

Sarah Gillit Daughter of Jonathan & Phebe Gillit was born October 23rd A.D. 1749
Reynold Gillit Son of Jona and Phebe Gillit was born April 23rd A.D. 1750
Martin Gillit Son of Jona & Phebe Gillit was Born the 19th of July A.D. 1752
Jona Gillit Son of Jonathan & Phebe Gillit was Born Decemr 17th A.D. 1753
Joseph Gillit Son of Jona and Phebe Gillit was Born Novemr 5th A.D 1756
Dan Gillit Son of Jona & Phebe Gillit was Born Novemr first A. D 1758
Elisha Gillit Son of Jonathan & Phebe Gillit was Born March 29th A.D 1760
Ezra Gillit Son of Jona & Phebe Gillit was Born June 21st AD 1762
Joshua Gillit Son of Jona & Phebe Gillit was Born October 16th A.D 1766
Shadrach Gillit Son of Jona & Phebe Gillit was Born October ye 23rd A.D 1769
Phebe Gillit Wife sd Jonathan Departed this life January 8th AD 1776

These are to Certifie whomsoever it may Conscearn: that Mr. William Noyes & Mrs. Eunice Marvin boath of Lyme were Lawfully Married together ye 8th Day of April A.D. 1756 Pr me Stephen Johnson Pastor of the first Church of Christ in sd Lyme Dated in Lyme this 8 Day of February: AD: 1771

John Noyes Son of Wm and Eunice Noyes was born Decemr 18th AD 1756
Joseph Noyes Son of Wm & Eunice Noyes was born Septemr 7th AD 1758
Wm Noyes Son of Wm and Eunice Noyes was born October 30th A.D 1760
Matthew Noyes Son of Wm & Eunice Noyes was born February 26th A.D. 1764
William Noyes Esq. deceased on the 11th day of February 1807

Doctr John Noyes deceased on the 11th day of August 1808

These are to Certifie whomsoever it may Conscearn that Mr. Enoch Reed and Mrs. Phebe Peck both of Lyme were Lawfully Married together the 7th Day of January A.D. 1762 Pr me Stephen Johnson Pastor of the first Church of Christ in sd Lyme Dated in Lyme this 8th Day of February A.D. 1771
Joseph Reed Son of Enoch & Phebe Reed was born May ye 17th: Day A.D. 1762
Hepzibah Reed Daughter of Enoch & Phebe Reed was born March 17th A.D 1764
Caroline Reed Daughter of Enoch & Phebe Reed was born April first A.D 1766
John Reed Son of Enoch & Phebe Reed was Born July ye 20th A.D. 1768
Mary Reed Daughter of Enoch & Phebe Reed was Born Novemr 26th: A.D 1770
Rebeckah Reed Daughter of Enoch & Phebe Reed was Born January 3rd A.D 1778

[page 134] February 1739 Married Abraham Pirkins to Elisabeth Ely: a true copy February 2nd 1770 George Beckwith Pastor
Francis Pirkins Son of Abraham & Elisabeth Pirkins was born Decemr 14th A.D.1741/2
William Pirkins Son of Abraham & Elisabeth Pirkins was born October 20th A.D 1743
Abraham Pirkins Son of Abraham & Elisabeth Pirkins was born August 7th A.D 1745
Elisabeth Pirkins Daughter of Abraham & Elisabeth Pirkins was born January 4th A.D 1748
Danll Pirkins Son of Abraham and Elisabeth Pirkins was born January 15th A.D 1750
Abigail Pirkins Daughter of Abraham & Elisabeth Pirkins was born February 5th 1752 and Died in December in the year 1764
Samuel Pirkins Son of Abraham and Elisabeth Pirkins was born April 14th 1754
Sarah Pirkins Daughter of Abraham & Elisabeth Pirkins was born June 20th 1756
Joseph Pirkins Son of Abraham & Elisabeth Pirkins was born May 18th 1760
Benjamin Pirkins Son of Abraham & Elisabeth Pirkins was born June 10th 1762
Abigail Pirkins Daughter of Abraham & Elisabeth Pirkins was born March ye 27th 1764 and Died August 18th 1764
Elisabeth Pirkins Wife of sd Abraham Pirkins Died

These may Certifie that Mr. Samll Selden Junr and Mrs. Sarah Marvin both of Lyme were Lawfully Married together the 24th Day of Novemr A.D 1774 Pr me Stephen Johnson Dated Lyme April 7th 1777
Reynold Marvin Selden Son of Samll and Sarah Selden was born January ye 10th 1777 and Died March 29th 1777
Sarah Selden Wife of sd Samuel Died January 22nd A.D. 1777

New London County Ssr Lyme May 8th A.D 1770: these may Certifye that on the Last Day of Decemr A.D 1769: George Dorr Junr of Lyme and Molley Lovitt of New London were Lawfully Joynd in Marriage Pr George Dorr Justice of the Peace
Deborah Dorr Daughter of George Dorr Junr and Molley Dorr was Born October 26: 1770
George Dorr Son of George and Molley Dorr was Born January the 9th 1773 and Died October the first 1774
George Dorr Son of George and Moley Dorr was Born May the 6th 1775
Molley Dorr Daughter of George & Molley Dorr was Born May the 5th 1778 and Died September the 9th 1778
Molley Dorr Daughter of George & Molley Dorr was Born November ye 18th 1779
Joseph Dorr Son of George and Molley Dorr was Born November ye 16th 1782

[page 135] These may Signifie & Certifye that Fredrick Mather of Lyme was on the 16th Day of October 1765: married to Elisabeth Pirkins of the same town by me George Beckwith Minister of the Gospel
Anna Mather Daughter of Fredrick and Elisabeth Mather was Born August 24th 1766
Elisabeth Mather Daughter of Fredrick & Elisabeth was Born Decemr 23rd 1769

These are to Certifye whomsoever it may Conscearn that Mr. Ezra Hall and Mrs. Sarah Gillit both of Lyme were Lawfully Married together the 20th Day of April AD 1769 Pr me Stephen Johnson Pastor of the first Church of Christ in sd Lyme Dated in Lyme 14th January 1772

Ama Hall Daughter of Ezra and Sarah Hall was born Septemr 13th A.D. 1771
Phebe Hall Daughter of Ezra and Sarah Hall was born April 24th A.D. 1773
Jonathan Hall Son of Ezra and Sarah Hall was born April 16th A.D. 1775
Hephzibah Hall Daughter of Ezra & Sarah Hall was born April 25th A.D 1778
Ezra Hall Son of Ezra and Sarah Hall was Born February 28th A.D. 1780
Hephzibah Daughter of Ezra and Sarah Hall Died 6th Septemr A.D 1780
Ezra son of the sd Ezra died at Sulliven in the State of New York on the 8th day of Augt 1806 in the 27 year of his Age.

These is to Certifie that Joseph Burtt was Married on the 4th of November in ye year A.D. 1753: to Elisabeth Peck Daughter of Mr. William Peck Late of Lyme Deceasd - by George Beckwith Pastor

Elisabeth Burt Daughter of Joseph & Elisabeth Burtt was born February 6th 1755
Jemima Burt Daughter of Joseph & Elisabeth Burtt was born August 5th 1756
Wm Peck Burt Son of Joseph and Elisabeth Burtt was born Decemr 10th 1758
Ruhamah Burt Daughter of Joseph & Elisabeth Burtt was born January 31st 1762
Joseph Burtt Son of Joseph and Elisabeth Burtt was born January 28th 1766 and Died Died November the 11th 1767
Margaret Burt Daughter of Joseph and Elisabeth Burt was born Decemr 28th 1767
Joseph Burt Son of Joseph and Elisabeth Burtt was Born October first: 1769
Benjamin Burt Son of Joseph and Elisabeth Burt was born April 16th 1771
Zebulon Burt Son of Joseph and Elisabeth Burt was born March 8th 1773
Sarah Burt Daughter of Joseph & Elisabeth Burt was born April 27th A.D 1775
Israel Burt Son of Joseph and Elisabeth Burt was born 15th January A.D: 1783

[page 136]   These may Certifye that Ezra Mack of Lyme was on the 21st of August: 1770 was Married to Lydia Gibbs of the Same Town by me -- George Beckwith Minister of the Gospel

Lydia Mack Daughter of Ezra & Lydia Mack was Born June 10th A.D. 1771
John Mack Son of Ezra and Lydia Mack was born February ye 15th Day A.D. 1773
Nabbe Mack Daughter of Ezra and Lydia Mack was Born January ye 23rd Day A.D. 1775
Charles Mack Son of Ezra and Lydia Mack was born ye 12th of Decemr A.D. 1777
Asenath Mack Daughter of Ezra & Lydia Mack was born 19th Day of January A.D. 1780
Debbe Mack Daughter of Ezra & Lydia Mack was born May the Second: A.D 1782
Elane Mack Daughter of Ezra and Lydia Mack was Born October 19th A.D 1786
Polly Mack Daughter of said Ezra and Lydia was born Sept 26th A.D 1789
Ezra Son of said Ezra and Lydia was born on the 11th of Augt 1791

To the Clerk of the Town of Lyme. Sr I hereby Certifie you that Sylvanus Smith of Lyme Molley Shipman of Saybrook were Joyned in Marriage by me the Subscriber on the 4th of October: 1769 William Hart Pastor of the first Church in Saybrook

Ezra Smith Son of Sylvanus & Molley Smith was Born November the 2nd A.D. 1770
Elisabeth Smith Daughter of Sylvanus & Molley Smith was born August ye 3rd Day A.D. 1772
Ama Smith Daughter of Sylvanus & Molley Smith was Born Septemr ye 15th Day A.D. 1774
Lucy Smith Daughter of Sylvanus and Molley Smith was Born May 16th Day 1777
Polley Smith Daughter of Sylvanus & Molley Smith was Born February 20th 1780
Sylvanus Smith Son of Sylvanus & Molley Smith was Born Decemr 4th 1784

John Ely Son of Daniel and Ama Ely was born September 24th A.D 1737
Lucretia Ely Daughter of Danll & Ame Ely was born November 21st A.D 1738 and Died November 22nd 1738

LYME, CONNECTICUT, VITAL RECORDS

Ama Ely Daughter of Danll and Ame Ely was Born January 29th A.D. 1740
Lucretia Ely Daughter of Danll & Ama Ely was Born November 6th A.D. 1742
Christopher Ely Son of Danll & Ama Ely was Born December 7th A.D: 1743
Elisha Ely Son of Danll & Ame Ely was Born July 21st Day A.D: 1748
Recorded the 23rd Day of November 1771: by John Lay 2nd Clerk

These are to Certifie that Mr. Sylvanus Smith and Miss Elisabeth Wait boath of Lyme were Lawfully Married together the first Day of October A.D. 1767 by me - Stephen Johnson Pastor of the first Church in Sd Lyme
Elisabeth Smith Wife of said Sylvanus Smith Departed this Life the 28th Day of May: 1768

[page 137] These may Certifie whomsoever it may Conscearn that Mr. Samuel Hill and Mrs. Edith Bayley both of Lyme were Lawfully Married together the the Second day of January A. D 1769 Pr me - Stephen Johnson Pastor of the first Church of Christ in Lyme Dated in Lyme this 7th Day of February 1772
Christopher Hill Son of Samll and Edith Hill was Born January 28th A.D 1771
Edward Hill Son of Samll & Edith Hill was Born October 4th A.D. 1772
Edward Hill Son of Samll & Edith Hill Died October 4th A.D 1773
Edward Hill Son of Samll & Edith Hill was born Septem ye 7th A.D in 1774
Mary Ann Hill Daughter of Samll and Edith Hill was born March 24th 1777
Mehetabel Hill Daughter of Samll & Edith Hill was born March 26th 1779
Roxana Hill Daughter of Samll & Edith Hill was born January 9th 1782
Sarah Hill Daughter of Samll & Edith Hill was born January 28th 1784
Edith Hill the wife of Samuel Hill Died November 16th 1814

These may Certifye that Mr. Henry Roland Junr and Mrs. Phebe Huntly both of Lyme in New London County were Lawfully Married to Each other on the 28th Day of May A.D 1772 by me - John Lay 2nd Justice of the Peace

These Certifie that Mr. Elisha Merrow Junr and Mrs. Elisabeth Joram boath of Lyme in New London County were Lawfully Married to Each other on the 6th Day of Novemr 1777 by me John Lay 2nd Justice of ye Peace

[page 138] Lyme May 31st A.D 1771: These may Certifie that Ensign Elihu Ely and Mrs. Anna Ely both of Lyme were Lawfully Joyned in Marriag on the 30th of May abovesaid. Certified by me George Beckwith Clerk
Caroline Ely Daughter of Elihu & Anna Ely was born March ye 8th A.D 1772
Joseph Elihu Ely Son of Elihu & Anna Ely was born October the 15th A.D. 1773
Anna Ely Daughter of Elihu & Anna Ely was Born December 16th 1775

Mehetable Daughter of Elihu & Anna Ely was born August 31st 1778
Elihu Son of Elihu & Anna was born November 30th 1780
Richard Son of Elihu & Anna was born January 31st 1783
Oliver Son of Elihu & Anna Ely was born April 4th 1785
Phebe Daughter of Elihu & Anna was born 1st August 1787
Elias Son of Elihu & Anna was born 26th June A.D. 1790
Mr. Elihu Ely died June 25th 1815 in the 78 year of his Age

These may Signifie and Certifye that on the 17th Day of June 1770: Titus Hayes of Lyme was Married to Deborah Beckwith of the Same Town by me George Beckwith Pastor
Richard Hayes Son of Titus and Deborah Hayes was born April 26th 1771
Abigail Hayes Daughter of Titus & Deborah Hayes was born January 12th A.D: 1773
Titus Hayes Son of Titus and Deborah Hayes was Born February ye 26: A.D 1776

New London April 11 1772 these Certifie that Mr. Andrew Griswold of Lyme and Mrs. Eunice Prince of New London was Married March 31st 1768 by me David Jewit Pastor
Martha Griswold Daughter of Andrew and Eunice Griswold was born Octr 16th 1769
Mary Griswold Daughter of Andrew & Eunice Griswold was born March 4th 1773
William Griswold Son of Andrew & Eunice Griswold was Born Decemr 12th 1774

Andrew Griswold Son of Andrew & Eunice Griswold was Born January 30th 1777 and Died the 27th of February: 1777

[page 139] Bettey Miner Daughter of Ebenezer and Bettey Minor was born May 25th: 1751
Lucy Miner Daughter of Ebenezer & Bettey Miner was Born July 24th A.D 1752
Jonathan Miner Son of Ebenezer & and Bettey Miner was Born May 19th A.D. 1754
Abigail Miner Daugher of Ebenezer and Bettey Miner was Born Decemr first: 1755
Hannah Miner Daughter of Ebenezer & Bettey Miner was Born August first 1758
All the above named Children were Born at New London
Lydia Miner Daughter of Ebenezer Miner & Bettey his Wife was born August 22nd 1760
Charles Miner Son of Ebenezer & Bettey Miner was Born January 28th A.D. 1763
Ebenezer Miner Son of Ebenezer & Bettey Miner was Born Septemr 5th A.D 1764
Azriah Miner Son of Ebenezer & Bettey Miner was Born August 23rd A.D 1766
Huldah Miner Daughter of Ebnezer & Bettey Miner was Born April 20th 1769 and Died June the 8th 1769
Huldah Miner Daughter of Ebenezer & Bettey Miner was Born June 8th 1770

These are to Certifye whomsoever it may Conscearn that Mr. John Hayes and Mrs. Azubah Roland both of Lyme were Lawfully Married together the 20th Day of September A.D 1764 Pr me Stephen Johnson Pastor of the first Church in se Lyme Dated in Lyme November 27th A.D. 1772
Lydia Hayes Daughter of John and Azubah Hayes was born July 20th A.D. 1765
Polley Hayes Daughter of John & Azubah Hayes was Born February 4th 1768
Abner Hayes Son of John and Azubah Hayes was Born April 8th 1770
John Hayes Son of John & Azubah Hayes was Born August 23rd 1772

December 17th Day A.D. 1775: Then I Married Andrew Smith of Lyme to his now Wife Hester Beckwith: Test Samll Ely Justice Pace
Elijah Smith Son of Andrew and Hester Smith was Born February 24th A.D: 1777

Mr. Timothy Lester & Miss Judith Rogers was Joined in Marraige 25th of April 1781
Nathan Son of the said Timothy & Judath was born on the 19th day of January 1782
Jerimiah Son of the said Timothy was born on the 21 day of February 1784
Patty daughter of the said Timothy & Judath was born on the 21 day of May 1786
Jesse Son of the said Timothy & Judath was born on the 24 day of Septr 1788
Hannah daughter of the said Tim & Judath was born on the 4 day of October 1790
Parthenah their daughter was born the 18th of April 1792 & died the -- Novr 1799
Leviah their daughter was born the 7th of March 1795 and died Septr 1796
Joseph Hitchcock their son was born the 7th of April 1797. He died November 1799
Polly daughter of the said Timothy & Judath was born on the 31st of March 1799
Crandle son of the said Timothy & Judath was born on the 24th day of March 1802

[page 140] These are to Certifye whomsoever it may Conscearn that Mr. Lee Lay and Mrs. Lovisa Griswold both of Lyme were Lawfully married together the first Day of January A.D. 1771 by me Stephen Johnson Pastor of the first Church in sd Lyme Dated in Lyme 28th Septemr A.D. 1772
Susa Lay Daughter of Lee and Lovisa Lay was Born the 27th Day of Decemr A.D 1771
Thomas Griswold Lay Son of Lee and Lovisa Lay was born the 3rd of March A.D. 1775
Lovisa Lay Daughter of Lee and Lovisa Lay was born the 27th Day of March A.D. 1777
Alexander Lay Son of Lee & Lovisa Lay was born September 23rd A.D. 1779
Lee Lay Son of Lee and Lovisa Lay was born January: 16th A.D. 1782
Lous Lay Daughter of Lee & Lovisa Lay was Born April 2nd Day A.D. 1784
Gordius Lay Son of Lee and Lovisa Lay was Born April 6th 1787
Willoughby Lynde Son of Lee & Lovisa Lay was Born August 27th 1790
Willoughby Lynde Lay Died Sept 20th 1790
Willoughby Lynde Lay Son of Lee & Lovisa Lay was Born January 12th 1792
James Benjamin Lay Son of Lee & Lovisa Lay was Born December 9th 1794

Phebe Daughter of Lee & Lovisa Lay was Born December 9th 1797
Thomas Griswold Lay Died Sept 15th 1815
Lovisa Lay the Wife of Capt Lee Lay Died on the 5th day of February 1813
Capt. Lee Lay Died on the 13th day of February 1813
Susa the wife of Daniel Robbins Died 27th Feby 1813
December ye 7th Day A.D. 1768 then I married Mr. John Mather Junr to his now Wife Hephzibah Peck: Certified pr Samll Ely Justice of the Peace
Huldah Mather Daughter of John & Hephzibah Mather was born April 16th 1770
Elijah Mather Son of John & Hephzibah Mather was Born Decemr 17th 1772
Hephzibah Mather Daughter of John & Hephzibah Mather was born February 4th 1776
John Mather Son of John & Hephzibah Mather was Born September ye 27th: 1779
Luther Peck Mather Son of John & Hephzibah Mather was born February 3rd: 1782
Luther P. Mather Son of John & Hephzibah Mather Died May 24th 1783 aged one year 3 months & 21 days
Joseph Higgins Son of the said John and Hepzibah was born on the 3d day of December A.D. 1789

East Haddam February 23rd 1774 These may Certifie whome it may Consearn that Nathan Phelps and Jerusha Wade boath of Lyme were Joyned in marriage Novembr the 4th 1773 Pr me Grindal Rawson Clerk
Phebe Phelps Daughter of Nathan & Jerusha Phelps was born October ye 19th A.D. 1773
Joseph Phelps Son of Nathan & Jerusha Phelps was Born July 31st A.D. 1775
Rebeckah Phelps Daughter of Nathan & Jerusha Phelps was born June 2nd 1777
Betsee Phelps Daughter of Nathan & Jerusha Phelps was born April 7th 1779
Jerush Phelps Daughter of Nathan & Jerusha Phelps was born Novemr 15th 1780
Phanna Phelps Daughter of Nathan & Jerusha Phelps was born November the first A.D. 1783

[page 141] Lyme June the 22nd 1771: These may Certifie that Richard Roland was married to Jerosh Chadwick both of Lyme on the 27th Day of March 1764. Pr me Benjamin Lee Justice of Peace
Eunice Roland Daughter of Richd & Jerusha Roland was born Decemr 29th 1766
Catharine Roland Daughter of Richd & Jerusha Roland was Born April 2nd 1769
Richard Roland Son of Richd & Jerusha Roland was Born July 15th 1771
Martha Roland Daughter of Richd & Jerusha Roland was born June 8th 1773
Perthene Roland Daughter of Richd & Jerusha Roland was born July 29th 1775
Martha Roland Daughter of Richd & Jerusha Roland Died Decemr 13: 1775
Anna Roland Daughter of Richd & Jerusha Roland was Born February 15th 1778
Danll Roland Son of Richd & Jerusha Roland was born November 5 1780
Shaler Roland Son of Richd & Jerusha Roland was Born February 2nd 1783

I hereby Certifye all whome it may Conscearn that Jabez Watrous of Lyme and Hester Jones of Saybrook were Joyned together in Marriage by me the Subscriber on the 20th Day of August 1763 - William Hart Pastor of the first Church in Saybrook
Elias Watrous Son of Jabez & Hester Watrous was Born October 8th A.D. 1765
Elias Watrous Son of Jabez & Hester Watrous Departed this life Decemr 14: 1766
Elisha Watrous Son of Jabez & Hester Watrous was born January ye 9th A.D. 1769
Mr. Jabez Watrous above named Departed this life the 6th Day of May: 1784

These may Certifye that Mr. Turner Calkins and Mrs. Marcy Cooley both of Lyme were Lawfully married to Each other on the 21st of May A.D 1757 by John Lay 3rd Justice of the Peace
Asa Calkins Son of Turner and Marcy Calkins was born Septemr 2nd 1757
Absolom Calkins Son of Turner and Marcy Calkins was born March 18th 1759
Eunice Calkins Daughter of Turner & Mary Calkins was born Septemr 3d 1761
Matthew Calkins Son of Turner and Marcy Calkins was born February 9th 1764
Jemima Calkins Daughter of Turner & Marcy Calkins was born March 16th 1766

Stephen Calkins Son of Turner & Marcy Calkins was born April 8th 1768 and Died November 12th 1768
Sarah Calkins Daughter of Turner and Marcy Calkins was born Septemr 29th: 1769
Marcy Calkins Wife of sd Turner Calkins Died October 6th 1771

[page 142] These may Certifye whomesoever it may Conscearn that Mr. William Smith and Mrs. Mary Moore both of Lyme were Lawfully Married together the 8th Day of January AD 1772: Pr me Stephen Johnson Pastor of the first Church in sd Lyme. Dated in Lyme this 16th Day of March: 1773
Dan Smith Son of Willm and Mary Smith was Born Novemr 18th A.D 1772
Union Smith Daughter of Wm & Mary Smith was born Novemr 3rd A.D 1774
Azariah Smith Son of Willm & Mary Smith was born December 25th A.D 1777
William Moore Smith Son of Wm & Mary Smith was born December 13th AD 1782
Azariah Above mentioned was drowned on the 9th day of March A.D. 1799

These may Certifye whomsoever it may Conscearn that Mr. Ezra Miller & Mrs. Sarah Mather both of Lyme were Lawfully married together the 19th Day of February A.D 1761: by me Stephen Johnson Pastor of the first Church in sd Lyme. Dated in Lyme 3rd May: 1773
Sarah Miller Daughter of Ezra & Sarah Miller was Born Novemr 13th A.D. 1761
Phebe Miller Daughter of Ezra & Sarah Miller was born April 18th A.D 1764
Hephza Miller Daughter of Ezra & Sarah Miller was born June 4th A.D. 1769
Eunice Miller Daughter of Ezra & Sarah Miller was Born February 19th A.D. 1771
Lucy Miller Daughter of Ezra & Sarah Miller was Born July 8th A.D 1774
Martha Miller Daughter of Ezra & Sarah Miller was born April 24th A.D 1777

These are to Certifye whomsoever it may Consearn that Mr. Richd Lay and Mrs. Marcy Mather both of Lyme were Lawfully Married together the 18th Day of March A.D. 1773 Pr me Stephen Johnson Pastor of the first Church in sd Lyme. Dated in Lyme this 20th Day of May: A.D 1773
Fredrick Lay Son of Richard & Marcy Lay was born the 9th Day of December: 1774 and Died the 23rd Day of December A.D. 1775
Marcy Lay Daughter of Richard and Marcy Lay was born 23rd of February 1787
Richard Son of said Richard & Marcy was born the first day of July A.D. 1789
Joseph Son of the said Richard & Marcy was born the 12th day of April A. D 1792
Marcy Lay Wife of Richard Lay departed this life on the 9th day of May 1795
Mr. Richard Lay & Mrs. Esther Biggs was Legally Joined in Marraige the 20th Novr 1797
Lucy daughter of the sd Richd & Esther was born on the 5th day of April A.D. 1799

[page 143] New London County Ss Lyme June 17th A.D 1773: then Caleb Wood of Lyme was married to Dorothy Bacon of sd Lyme Pr Eleazer Mather Justice of Peace

Ephraim Sawyer & Jamimah Hill was legally joined in marriage Novr 20th A.D 1774
Betsy Daughter of the said Ephm & Jamimah was born on the 1st November 1775
Polly Daughter of the said Ephm & Jamimah was born on the 22d November 1777
David Son of the said Ephm & Jamimah was born on the 6th February A.D. 1780
Temperance Daughter of the said Ephm & Jamimah was born on the 30th December A.D 1784
John Son of the said Ephm & Jamimah was born on the 14th September 1789
Ephraim & Jamimah being twins, was born on the 10th day of February A.D. 1792

These Certifye that Mr. Wm Rufus Hyde and Mrs. Elisabeth Starlin boath of Lyme were Lawfully Married to Each other on the Evening next after the 3rd Day of October 1773: by John Lay 2nd Justice of Peace
Willm Rufus Hyde Son of Wm Rufus and Elisabeth Hyde was born Decemr ye 10th Day: 1775
Elisabeth Hyde Daughter of Wm Rufus and Elisabeth Hyde was born January 14th 1780
Alexander Hyde son of Wm Rufus and Elisabeth Hyde was born March 16th 1782
William Rufus Hyde Died ye 13th of November A.D. 1783

LYME, CONNECTICUT, VITAL RECORDS

These may Certifie whome it may Conscearn that James Comstock of Lyme and Thankfull Crosbey of East Haddam were Joyned in Marriage May 9th A.D 1763 Pr Grindal Rawson Clerk Alis Pastor of the 3rd Church of Chrt in East Haddam East Haddam: May 11th 1773

Ruth Crosbey Comstock Daughter James & Thankfull Comstock was born April 4th 1766
Joab Comstock Son of James and Thank Comstock was born ye 4th April A.D. 1768
Elisabeth Comstock Daughter of James & Thankfull Comstock was born April 1st A.D. 1770
Mr. James Comstock above said Died July ye 23rd A.D. 1773

[pages 144 and 145 missing from book]

[page 146] These may Signifye that on the 19th Day of Septemr 1773 Abijah Mack was Married to Eunice Rogers boath of them of Lyme -- by George Beckwith Pastor

Elishabe Mack Daughter of Abijah and Eunice Mack was born May 11th A.D. 1774
Mehetable Mack Daughter of Abijah & Eunice Mack was born Decemr 5th A.D. 1775
Sarah Mack Daughter of Abijah & Eunice Mack was born August 4th A.D. 1777
Jonathan Mack Son of Abijah and Eunice Mack was born October 2nd 1780
Elisabeth Mack Daughter of Abijah & Eunice Mack was born January 22nd 1783
Joseph Mack Son of Abijah & Eunice Mack was born August 21st 1785

Mr. Elisha Lee and Mrs. Abigail Murdock were Joyned in Marriage October 4th 1761: A true Copy of Record pr. me John Devotion Saybrook June 12th 1773

Phebe Lee Daughter of Elisha and Abigail Lee was Born May ye 23rd A.D 1762
Elisha Lee Son of Elisha and Abigail Lee was Born March ye 18th 1764
John Murdock Lee Son of Elisha and Abigail Lee was Born May ye 7th 1766
Enoch Lee Son of Elisha and Abigail Lee was Born August ye 7th 1768
James Lee Son of Elisha and Abigail Lee was Born September 18th 1770
Jonathan Lee Son of Elisha and Abigail Lee was Born February 26 1772
George Washington Son of Elisha & Abigail was Born June 25th 1775
Fanne Lee Daughter of Elisha and Abigail Lee was Born March 25th 1781
Richard Lee Son of Elisha & Elisabeth Lee was Born September 26th 1783
Abigail Lee Daughter of Elisha & Abigail Lee was Born July 11th 1786

These may Certifie all whome it may Consearn that Mr. Benajah Ames and Luce Scovel boath of East Haddam were Lawfully Joyned in Marriage Novemr 15th 1762 Pr Grindal Rawson Clerk East Haddam March 20th 1771 this above Certificate was given of sd Marriage to Mr. Ames Test Rawson Grindal Clerk

Rachel Ames Daughter of Benajah and Luce Ames was Born June 11th A.D. 1765
Luce Ames Daughter of Benajah and Luce Ames was Born October 13th 1767
Alice Ames Daughter of Benajah & Luce Ames was Born August 23rd 1770
Mary Ames Daughter of Benajah and Luce Ames was Born July 28th 1772

David Fithin Sill; and Sarah Griswold, was Joyned in Marriage May 1st day 1767
Polly Sill their daughter was born June 27th day A.D. 1768 Monday
Thomas Sill their Son was born November 26th A.D 1769 Sunday
Lois Sill their daughter was born August 29 A.D. 1771 Thursday
John Sill their Son was born June 14th A.D. 1773 Monday
David Sill their Son was born January 8th A.D. 1775 Fryday and died the 19th day of June A.D. 1775

Carried into the other book

[page 147] These may Certifie all whome it may Conscearn we the Subscribers were Eye witnesses to Danel Peck's Marriage with his Wife Jerusha Yearington of Stonington at presson December 25th in the year 1764: Dated February 15th 1774 Abel Hall Daniel Hall

Elisha Peck Son of Daniel and Jerusha Peck was born Febry 3rd A.D 1766'
Jerusha Peck Daughter of Danll and Jerusha Peck was born January first 1768

Daniel Peck Son of Danll & Jerusha Peck was Born October 21st 1769
Ruth Peck Daughter of Danll & Jerush Peck was Born Septemr 19th 1771
Ezekiel Peck Son of Danll & Jerush Peck was born Decemr 11th 1773
Asenah Peck Daughter of Danll & Jerusha Peck was born August 7th 1776
Clarrissa Peck Daughter of Danll & Jerusha Peck was born January 12th A.D. 1780

These are to Certifye whomsoever it may Concearn that Mr. Sylvanus Higgins and Mrs. Elisabeth Clark both of Lyme were Lawfully Married together the 15th Day of July A.D 1773 Pr me Stephen Johnson Pastor of the first Church in sd Lyme Dated in Lyme this 17th Day of March A.D 1774

Marcy Remeck Higgins Daughter of Silvanus & Elisabeth Higgins was born May 6th 1774

[page 147] Eleazer Hudson and Hannah Miller both of Lyme in New London County were Lawfully Married to Each other on the 23rd Day of February 17766 -by me John Lay 2nd Just Paec

Elias Hudson Son of Eleazer and Hannah Hudson was born Septemr 22nd A.D. 1766
Elisha Hudson Son of Eleazer & Hannah Hudson was born February ye 5th AD 1769
Lous Hudson Daughter of Eleazer & Hannah Hudson was born April ye 4th A.D. 1771
Mary Hudson Daughter of Eleazer & Hannah Hudson was Born May 16th A.D. 1774
Samuel Hudson Son of Eleazer & Hannah Hudson was born August ye 28th A.D. 1776
Eleazer Hudson Son of Eleazer & Hannah Hudson was born Novemr 25th A.D. 1779
Elisha Hudson Son of Eleazer and Hannah Hudson Died October 8th A.D. 1780
Elisabeth Hudson Daughter of Eleazer & Hannah Hudson was Born February 18th 1782 and Died March 8th A.D. 1782
Elisha Hudson Son of Eleazer & Hannah Hudson was Born February 19th 1783

[page 148] Lyme 29th of April A.D. 1774 These may Certifye that on the Last Day of February A.D. 1774 Martin Bathrick [Beckwith] and Anna Horton both of Lyme were Lawfully Joyned in Marraige: Pr George Dorr Justice of the Peace

Mr. Stephen Hudson and Mrs. Patence Bishop was legally Joined in Marraige on the 26 day of July 1795
Anna Daughter of the said Stephen & Patience was born 3d May 1796
Joseph Son of the said Stephen & Patience was born 14 Decr 1798
Patience Wife of the said Stephen died on the 19th day of March 1800

These may Signifye and Certifie that Jacob Sawyer was on January 12th 1742/3 married to Rose Bennet boath of Lyme: pr me George Beckwith Pastor
Jacob Sawyer Son of Jacob and Rose Sawyer was Born June 12th A.D. 1745
Phebe Sawyer Daughter of Jacob and Rose Sawyer was Born February 10th 1747
Matthew Sawyer Son of Jacob and Rose Sawyer was born January the 30th 1751
John Sawyer Son of Jacob and Rose Sawyer was Born February ye 8th 1753
Asa Sawyer Son of Jacob and Rose Sawyer was Born July 30th A.D. 1756

These may Signifie and Certifie that Jacob Sawyer Junr was on March the 16th 1769: Married to Sarah Wrathbone both of Lyme pr me George Beckwith Pastor
Diadamy Sawyer Daughter of Jacob & Sarah Sawyer was born Decemr 25th 1769
Thankfull Sawyer Daughter of Jacob & Sarah Sawyer was born Novemr 25th 1771
Desire Sawyer Daughter of Jacob & Sarah Sawyer was born March 9th 1774
Sarah Sawyer and Lucy Sawyer Daughters of Jacob and Sarah Sawyer (being twins) were born July 25th A.D. 1776

Lyme May 13th 1787: then Mr. Lot Peck of Lyme was Married to Mrs. Polley Kent of sd Lyme by me Daniel Miner Pastor of the Strit Congl Church
Stephen Son of the said Lot & Polley was born the 5th day of June A.D. 1789
Nathaniel Son of the said Lot & Polley was born the 15th day of May A.D. 1791
Nathaniel above mentioned died the 31 day of January 1794
Bettey their daughter was born 9th March 1793 & died 9th February 1794
Nathaniel their Son was born on the 19th day of October 1795

LYME, CONNECTICUT, VITAL RECORDS

Charles Son of the said Lot & Polly was born 15 day of February 1797
Betey daughter of the said Lot & Polly was born 26 day of May 1799

[page 149] These may Signifye and Certifye that Mr. Timothy Marvin was on the 30th Day of May 1765: Married to Mrs. Sarah Pirkins both of Lyme by me George Beckwith Pastor of a Church in sd Town
Lucy Marvin Daughter of Timothy and Sarah Marvin was Born March ye 14th A.D. 1766
Picket Marvin Son of Timothy & Sarah Marvin was Born February ye 5th A.D 1768
Asahel Marvin Son of Timothy & Sarah Marvin was Born Septemr ye 16th A.D 1769
Timothy Marvin Son of Timothy & Sarah Marvin was Born August ye 3rd A.D. 1771
Sarah Marvin Daughter of Timothy & Sarah Marvin was Born July the 7th A.D. 1773

These may Certifye whomesoever it may Conscearn that Mr. Mather Peck and Mrs. Esther Coult both of Lyme were Lawfully Married together the 25th Day of April A.D 1771 pr me Stephen Johnson Pastor of the First Church in Christ in Lyme. Dated in Lyme June first AD. 1774
Lucy Peck Daughter of Mather & Esther Peck was Born May ye 5th A.D 1772
Mary Coult Peck Daughter of Mather & Esther Peck was Born March ye 12th A.D 1774
Joseph Peck Son of Mather & Esther Peck was Born April 26th A.D. 1776
Esther Peck Daughter of Mather & Esther Peck was born October 17th 1778
Abigail Peck Daughter of Mather & Esther Peck was born February 4th 1781
Miriam Peck Daughter of Mather & Esther Peck was born Septemr 9th 1783
Mather Peck Son of Mather & Esther Peck was born January 12th 1786
Mrs. Esther Wife of Mr. Mather Peck died the 1st day of Sept A.D. 1786
Mr. Mather Peck was Married to Mrs. Rhuiami Howell 19th Novr A.D. 1786
David Howell Son of the said Mather & Rhuiami was born 20th August 1787
Mr. Mather Peck was Married to Mrs. Azubah Watrous on the 5th day of August 1790
Jerusha Daughter of the said Mather & Azubah was born 1 day of June 1791
Jesse Son of the said Mather and Azubah was born 6 day February 1794
Reheumah their daughter was born on the 12 day of July A.D. 1800
          Pr Benjamin Lee Justice of Peace
William Storey Son of Samll and Mary Storey was born Novemr ye 12th A.D. 1774

Lyme February 17th 1774. These may Certify that Samuel Story of Lyme was Married to Mary Minard of said Lyme pr Benja Lee Just Peace
William Son of said Samuel & Mary was born November 12th A.D 1774

[page 150] William Westcot Munsell Son of Timothy and Elisahba Munsell was born at New London on January 24th 1770
James Munsell Son of Timothy & Elishaba Munsell was born June 28th 1773 at Lyme
Anna Munsell Daughter of Timo & Elishaba Munsell was born Septemr 7th A.D 1775
Anna Munsell Daughter of Timothy & Elishaba Munsell Died June 18th 1777
Timothy Son of the said Timothy & Elishabah was born 16th day of April A.D. 1778
John Andross Son of the said Timothy & Elishaba was born on the 9th July A.D. 1781
Sally Anne Daughter of the said Timothy and Elishaba was born on the 23d Octr 1784

16 June 1774 Isaac Tubbs Son of Isaac and Sarah Tubbs was born the 8th Day of June A.D. 1753

Mrs. Esther Emmons formerly Wife of Mr. Thomas Lord deceasd Feby 3d A.D. 1792

These may Certifie that Mr. Marvin Lord of Lyme in the State of Connecticut was Lawfully Married to Mrs. Emelia Woolcot of East Windsor in said Connecticut on the 30th Day of May 1771 Test Joseph Perry Minister of the Gospel in said East Windsor East Windsor April 8th 1778
Roger Woolcott Lord Son of Marvin & Emelia Lord was born January 13th AD 1778
Emelia Lord Daughter of Marvin & Emelia Lord was born February 5th Day 1780
Topheas Lord Daughter of Marvin & Emelia Lord was born March 17th Day 1782
Marvin Son of the said Marvin & Emelia Lord born Jany 29th 1784 died Feby 7th day A.D. 1784

Polly Daughter of the said Marvin and Emelia was born on the 3d Day of Jany 1786
Marvin Son of the said Marvin and Emelia was born on the 5th day of April 1788
Ursula Daughter of said Marvin and Emelia was born on the 7th day of Jany A.D. 1792
Betsy Daugther of the said Marvin & Emelia was born on the 11 day of August A.D. 1794

[page 151] These are to Certifye whomsoever it may conscearn that Mr. Ezra Lee & Mrs. Deborah Mather both of Lyme were Lawfully Married together the 14th Day of Novemr A.D 1771 by me Stephen Johnson Pastor of the first Church in sd Lyme Dated in Lyme this 30th of Septemr AD 1774
Samll Holden Lee Son of Ezra and Deborah Lee was Born August 5th A.D 1772
Elisabeth Lee Daughter of Ezra & Deborah Lee was Born August 31st A.D 1774
Luce Lee Daughter of Ezra & Deborah Lee was Born May ye 8th A.D. 1777
Lucy Lee abovesaid Died October 25th 1778
Lucy Mather Lee Daughter of Ezra & Deborah Lee was born Novemr 10th 1779
Polley Lee Daughter of Ezra and Deborah Lee was Born April 16th 1782 and Died the 7th Day of May 1782
Phebe Lee Daughter of Ezra and Deborah Lee was born June 6th A.D. 1783
William R. H. [Richard, Henry] Son of the said Ezra & Deborah was born 17th Sept A.D 1787
Margerit Stoughton being their Daughter was born on the 11th day of Novr 1794

Mr. Elias Mather & Mrs. Lucinda Lee both of Lyme were Lawfully Married together: 17th Day of October A.D. 1771 Pr me Stephen Johnson Pastor of the first Church in Lymee Dated in sd Lyme 2nd of March 1775
Andrew Mather Son of Elias & Lucinda Mather was born September 26th A.D. 1772
Clarissia Mather Daughter of Elias & Lucinda Mather was born August 10th A.D. 1774
Elias Mather Son of Elias & Lucinda Mather was born June ye 25th A.D. 1776
William Lee Mather Son of Elias & Lucinda Mather was Born August first 1779
Sylvester Mather Son of Elias & Lucinda Mather was Born February 8th 1782
Nathanll Green Mather Son of Elias & Lucinda Mather was Born Novemr 25th 1784 and Died the 4th of April 1785
Charles Mather Son of Elias & Lucinda Mather was Born June 9th 1787
Capt. Elias Mather died the 30th day of August A.D. 1788

New London County Ss Lyme Decemr 4th A.D. 1770 Mr. George Roland and Mrs. Freelove Daviss both of sd Lyme were Lawfully married to Each other by me John Lay 2nd Just Paece
Mary Roland Daughter of George & Freelove Roland was born Decemr 14th A.D. 1771
Isaac Daviss Roland Son of George and Freelove Roland was born February 2nd A. D 1774
Benjamin Roland Son of George & Freelove Roland was born January 28th A.D. 1777 and Died the 13th Day of Februar 1777
Willm Roland Son of George and Freelove Roland was born 11th Day of May 1779
George Roland Son of George & Freelove Roland was Born July 25th A.D. 1781

Mr. Noah Beebe was Joined in Marraige to Mrs. Hannah Luther on the nineth day of June 1805 and on the 22nd day of May 1806 the said Noah Beebe was Joined in Marraige to Mrs. Preserve Avery as appears by Certificates from Lawfull Authority.

[page 152] William Matson of Lyme was Married to Eunice Skinner of Colchester June ye 9th A.D 1763
William Matson Son of William & Eunice Matson was born April ye 8th A.D. 1764
David Matson Son of William & Eunice Matson was born January 29th A.D 1766
Ely Matson Son of William & Eunice Matson was born February the 11th A.D 1768
Aaron Matson Son of Willm & Eunice Matson was born May the 6th A.D 1770
Eunice Matson Daughter of William & Eunice Matson was born November 27th A.D 1774
one Daughter sd Wm and Eunice had was born January ye first 1773 and Died the 6th Day of the same January 1773
William Matson Son of Wm and Eunice Matson Departed this life August 30th A.D. 1771

William Matson Son of Wm and Eunice Matson was Born April 19th A.D. 1780
Eunice the Daughter of William & Eunice Matson Died Sept 22nd 1803
William Matson Died Octr 24 1804
Eunice Matson widow of William Matson Died Decr 19 1814

These may Certifie whomsoever it may Concearn that Mr. Martin Miner and Mrs. Elisabeth Davis both of Lyme were Lawfully Married together June 11th A.D. 1772 Pr me Stephen Johnson Pastor of the first Church in sd Lyme Dated in Lyme 14th January A. D. 1776
Marvin Miner Son of Martin and Elisabeth Miner was born February ye 8th A.D. 1774
Joanna Miner Daughter of Martin & Elisabeth Miner was born January 18th A.D. 1776
Elisabeth Miner Daughter of Martin & Elisabeth Miner was born April 10th 1778
Lous Miner Daughter of Martin & Elisabeth Miner was born January 21st 1781
Jenne Miner Daughter of Martin & Elisabeth Miner was born January 13th 1783
Lurena Miner Daughter of Marin & Elisabeth Miner was born April 20th 1785
William Son of said Martin & Elisabeth was born the 25th day of May A.D. 1788

Lyme November ye 22nd 1773: These may Certifie that Nathaniel Tillitson of Lyme was married to Elisabeth Tillitson of sd Lyme the first Day of March 1770 by me Benjamin Lee Just of Peace
Nathan Tillitson Son of Nathll & Elisabeth Tillitson was born Septemr 20th 1770
Eunice Tillitson Daughter of Nathll & Elisabeth Tillitson was born March 7th 1772
Joseph Tillitson Son of Nathll & Elisabeth Tillitson was born May 28th 1773
Abigail Tillitson Daughter of Nathll & Elisabeth Tillitson was born May 17th 1775
Lydia Tillitson Daughter of Nathll & Elisabeth Tillitson was born January 7th 1777
Jonathan Tillitson Son of Nathll & Elisabeth Tillitson was born January 23rd 1779
Nathaniel Tillitson Son of Nathll & Elisabeth Tillitson was born January 22nd 1781
Bettey Tillitson Daughter of Nathll & Elisabeth Tillitson was born Novemr 28th 1782
Charlotte Tillitson Daughter of Nathll & Elisabeth Tillitson was born February 14th 1785
Nathaniel Tillitson above said Departed this life on ye 14th of Septemr A.D. 1785

[page 153]   Norwich Novemr 17th 1773: These Certifie that Zenos Beckwith of Lyme and Anna Harriss of New London were Joyned in Lawfull marraige on the 23rd Day of June A.D 1768 Pr Wm Whiting Justice of Peace
Christopher Beckwith Son of Zenos & Anna Beckwith was born March 29th 1769
Esther Beckwith Daughter of Zenos & Anna Beckwith was born June 6th 1770
Stephen Beckwith Son of Zenos & Anna Beckwith was born Decemr 13th 1771
Joseph Beckwith Son of Zenos & Anna Beckwith was born Septemr 4th 1774
Elisabeth Beckwith Daughter of Zenos & Anna Beckwith was born March 21st 1776
Deborah Beckwith Daughter of Zenos & Anna Beckwith was born Decemr 14 1778
Harris Beckwith Son of Zenos & Anna Beckwith was born Decemr 30th 1780
Thomas Beckwith Son of Zenos & Anna Beckwith was Born February 10th 1783

Lyme the 4th of January: These may Certifye that Eusebious Bushnell was married to Borredill Lathimer the 13th Day fo Septemr 1772 Certifyed Pr Benja Lee Justice of Peace
Hannah Bushnell Daughter of Eusebious & Borredill Bushnell was Born Decemr 14th A.D. 1773
Clerianea Bushnell Daughter of Eusebious & Borredill Bushnell was Born October 9th 1775

These are to Certifie whomesoever it may Conscearn that Mr. Silvanus Clark & Miss Eunice Anderson both of Lyme were Lawfully married together the 28th Day of May A.D. 1775 pr me Stephen Johnson Pastor of the first Church in sd Lyme Dated in Lyme 4th March: 1776
Eunice Clark Wife of sd Silvanus Clark Died the 25th of August A.D. 1776

These Certifie whome it may Conscearn that Mr. Sylvanus Clark and Mrs. Elisabeth Kent Boath of Lyme were Lawfully Married together the first Day of August A.D. 1779 by me Stephen Johnson Pastor of the first Church of Christ in sd Lyme
Eleazer Clark Son of Sylvanus & Elisabeth Clark was Born May 30th A.D. 1780
Wm Kent Clark Son of Sylvanus & Elisabeth Clark was Born Decemr 14th 1781
Eunice Clark Daughter of Sylvanus & Elisabeth Clark was Born Novemr 11th 1784
Henery Son of Silvenus & Elisabeth Clark was born June 15th A.D. 1789
Abigail Daughter of said Silvenus & Elisabeth Clark was born March 2d day A.D. 1792
Charles Son of the said Silvs and Elisabeth was born the 2d day of April A.D. 1794

[page 154] These are to Certifie whomesoever it may Conscearn that Mr. John Ayer and Mrs. Clerinea Lay both of Lyme were Lawfully Married together on the 4th Day of November AD 1773 pr me Stephen Johnson Pastor of the first Church in sd Lyme Dated in Lyme 5th March: A.D: 1776
Lay Ayer Son of John & Clerinea Ayer was born March 8th A.D 1778
Lydia Ayer Daughter of John & Clerina Ayer was born November 26th A.D. 1779
Hannah Ayer Daughter of John & Clerina Ayer was born February 10th A.D. 1782
John Ayer above Named Departed this life on the 8th Day of January: A.D: 1784
John Ayer Son of John & Clerrney Ayer was Born July 2nd A.D 1785

These are to Certifye Whomesoever it may Concearn that Mr. Reynold Gillet and Miss Martha Marvin both of Lyme were Lawfully Married together the 9th Day of June: AD: 1774 Pr me Stephen Johnson Pastor of the first Church in sd Lyme Dated in Lyme 26th April: 1776
Huldah Gillet Daughter of Reynold & Martha Gillet was born April 10th 1775 and Died the 4th Day of August AD: 1775
James Gillit Son of Reynold & Martha Gillit was Born June 27th A.D. 1776
Jonathan Gillit Son of Reynold & Martha Gillit was Born Septemr 14: 1779 and Died the 7th of March A.D 1784

Mr. William Gee and Mrs. Abigail Mack both of Lyme were Lawfully married to Each other on the first Day of January: A.D 1761
Abigail Gee Daughter of William & Abigail Gee was born January 26th Day A.D. 1762
Zopher Gee Son of William & Abigail Gee was Born August 28th A.D. 1763
Sarah Gee Daughter of William & Abigail Gee was born October ye 21st A.D. 1765
William Gee Son of William & Abigail Gee was born October 13th Day A.D. 1767
Elisabeth Gee Daughter of Wm and Abigail Gee was born June 13th A.D. 1769

[page 155] These may Certifye that Mr. Nathan Avery and Miss Als Pearson both of Lyme in New London County were Lawfuly Married to Each other on the 9th Day of April: A.D: 1776 by John Lay 2nd Just Pace

Mr. Abner Brockway and Mrs. Catharine Marvin was Legally Joyn'd in Marraige on the 7th day of September A.D 1775
Cate daughter to the said Abner & Catharine was born the 6th day July 1776
Lucina their daughter was born 17th Sept 1778 & died March the 26th day 1779
Marvin Son of the said Abner & Catharine was born the 8th day of July 1780
Jemmy Son of the said Abner & Catharine was born the 23d day of May 1782
Abner Son of the said Abner & Catharine was born the 19th day of August 1785
Pickett Son of the said Abner & Catharine was born the 10th day April 1788

These are to Certifye whomesoever it may Conscearn that Mr. Roswell Clark and Parnall Peck both of Lyme were Lawfully Married together the 9th Day of May A.D: 1771 Pr me Stephen Johnson Pastor of the first Church of Christ in Lyme Dated in Lyme 30th July: AD: 1776
Peter Peck Clark Son of Roswell & Parnal Clark was born June 14th A.D: 1772
Roswell Clark Son of Roswell & Parnall Clark was born April 22nd A.D. 1774
William Clark Son of Roswell & Parnal Clark was born April 18th A.D. 1776

Mary Clark Daughter of Roswell & Parnal Clark was born March: 24: 1780
Lusena Clark Daughter of Roswell & Parnal Clark was born January 17th 1782

These Certifye that Mr. Silas Miller & Mrs. Lous Smith both of Lyme in New London County were Lawfully Married to Each other on the first Day of April: A.D: 1773 by me John Lay 2nd Just Paec
Lucindia Miller Daughter of Silas & Lous Miller was born November 9th A.D. 1773
Nathan Miller Son of Silas & Lous Miller was born the 15th of Septemr A.D. 1775 and Died the 24th of Septemr 1775
Nathan Miller Son of Silas & Lous Miller was Born April 5th A.D. 1777
Silas Miller Son of Silas & Lous Miller was born January 20th 1779
Munsell Miller Son of Silas & Lous Miller was Born January 12th 1781
Munsell Miller Son of Silas & Lous Miller Died November 12th A.D. 1782
Munsell Miller Son of Silas & Lous Miller was born November first A.D. 1783

[page 156] This is to Certifie that the Revernd Stephen Johnson of Lyme in Connecticut was Married to Miss Abigail Leveritt of Roxbury on the 28th Day of May: 1776 haveing been first Published according to the Laws of this Colony by the Subscriber: William Gordon Pastor of the 3rd Church in Roxbury June the 3rd 1776 Recorded July 22nd 1776 by John Lay 2nd Regr.

These may Certifye that John Merrow of Lyme was Married to Hannah Mather of sd Lyme on the Evening after the 4th Day of June: A.D 1775 pr me Eleazer Mather Just Paec
John Oliver Merrow Son of John & Hannah Merrow was born August 26th A.D. 1775

These may Signifye and Certifie that on the 18th Day August A.D: 1774 Mr. Lee Peck was Married to Miss Elisabeth Marvin boath of Lyme by me George Beckwith Clerk

These Certifye that Mr. John Peck Junr and Miss Rebeckah Smith both of Lyme were Lawfully Married together the 3rd Day of November A.D. 1774 pr me Stephen Johnson Pastor of the first Church in sd Lyme Dated in sd Lyme 13th Novemr A.D. 1776

Stephen Peck Son of John and Rebeckah Peck was born Decemr 20th AD 1775
Lucy Peck Daughter of John and Rebeckah Peck was born August 10th AD 1778
Elisha Peck Son of John and Rebeckah Peck was born ye 25th Day of Febry 1781
Clarry Peck Daughter of John & Rebeckah Peck was born March 9th 1785
John Peck Son of John and Rebeckah Peck was born August 8th 1787
Seth Peck Son of John and Rebeckah Peck was Born
Charles Peck Son of John and Rebeckah Peck

[page 157] These are to Certifie whomsoever it may Conscearn that Dan Chadwick and Hannah Huntly both of Lyme were Lawfully married together the 28th Day of May AD 1775 Pr me Stephen Johnson Pastor of the first Church in sd Lyme Dated in Lyme 17th February: 1777
Molley Chadwick Daughter of Dan and Hannah Chadwick was Born April 18th AD 1776
Dan Chadwick Son of Dan and Hannah Chadwick was Born Decemr 22nd AD 1777
Elias Chadwick Son of Dan & Hannah Chadwick was Born May 15th AD 1780 and died July 3rd 1780
Lois daughter of the said Dan & Hannah was born on the 18th day of September 1781
Elias son of the said Dan & Hannah was born on the 7 day of January 1784
Elizabeth daughter of the said Dan & Hannah was born 14 June 1786
Abigail daugther of the said Dan & Hannah was born 17 day of April 1790
Anna daughter of the said Dan & Hannah was born 4 day of Feby 1792
Dan the Elder departed this life on the 27th day of August 1798

Jonathan Avery of Lyme and Preserved Smith of New London were Lawfully married to each other on the 8th Day of December AD: 1760: by the reverend Mr. George Griswold Pastor of the Second Church in sd Lyme as appears by sd Church Record
Abraham Avery son of Jonathan & Preserved Avery was born Septemr 18th AD 1763

Samuel Sill and Eunice Dorr was Lawfully Joyn'd in Marraige on the 18th day of December AD 1788 by Ezra Selden Justice of the Peace
Ursula Daughter of the said Samuel & Eunice was born 4th Octr AD 1789
Samuel Dudley Son of the said Samll & Eunice was born the 25th of Decr AD 1790
Elisabeth Daughter of the said Samuel & Eunice was born 30th of Novr AD 1792
Fanny Daughter of the said Samuel & Eunice was born the 4th day of April AD 1796
Shadrach Son of the said Samuel & Eunice was born on the 15th day of July AD 1799

These are to Certifie whomsoever it may Concearn that Mr. Stephen Johnson Junr & Mrs. Anna Lord both of Lyme were Lawfully married together the first Day of Septemr AD: 1774 pr me Stephen Johnson Pastor of the first Church in sd Lyme: August 9th 1776
Diodate Johnson Son of sd Stephen & Anna Johnson was born February 8th 1778
Betsey Johnson Daughter of sd Stephen & Anna Johnson was born August 6th 1780
Cate Johnson Daughter of sd Stephen & Anna Johnson was born Febry 22nd 1783
Diodate Johnson Son of sd Stephen & Anna Johnson Died 9th of Decemr 1783
Sally Bank Daughter of Capt Stephen & Mrs. Anna Johnson was born 25th Jany 1785
Anna Daughter of the said Stephen & Anna Johnson was born 22nd Feby 1787

[page 158] These Certifie whomsoever it may Concearn that Mr. John Griswold and Mrs. Sarah Johnson both of Lyme were Lawfully Married together the 5th Day of November A.D. 1772 Pr me Stephen Johnson Pastor of the first Church of Christ in sd Lyme Dated in Lyme 6th April: AD: 1778
Diodate Johnson Griswold son of John & Sarah Griswold was born Decemr 16th AD 1773
Ursula Woolcot Griswold Daughter of John & Sarah Griswold was born Decemr 2nd AD 1775
Elisabeth Griswold Daughter of John & Sarah Griswold was born October 15th AD 1778
Sarah Griswold Daughter of John & Sarah Griswold was born August 12th 1781
John Griswold Son of John & Sarah Griswold was born August 14th AD 1783
Mary Ann Griswold Daughter of John & Sarah Griswold was born February 25th AD 1786
Charles Chandlor Son of John & Sarah Griswold was born Novr 9th AD 1787

These may Signifye and Certifie that Mr. Dan Marvin was on October 14th 1762 married to Mrs. Mehetabel Selden both of Lyme by me George Beckwith Pastor
Reynold Marvin Son of Dan and Mehetabel Marvin was born July 21st AD 1763
Dan Marvin Son of Dan & Mehetabel Marvin was born October 15th AD 1765
Reynold Marvin Son of Dan & Mehetabel Marvin Died Decemr 10th AD 1767
Reynold Marvin Son of Dan & Mehetabel Marvin was Born March 21st AD 1769
Sarah Marvin Daughter of Dan & Mehetabel Marvin was Born September 21st 1771
Selden Marvin Son of Dan and Mehetabel Marvin was Born November 24th AD 1773
James Marvin Son of Dan and Mehetabel Marvin was Born May 16th A.D. 1776
Capt. Dan Marvin Departed this Life December the 30th A.D. 1776
James Marvin Son of Dan and Mehetabel Marvin Died Novemr 6th A.D. 1779

These are to Certifie whomesoever it may Conscearn that Mr. Francis Ingraham and Mrs. Lucretia Tinker [married Samuel Peck Oct 18 1781] boath of Lyme were Lawfully Married together the 24th Day of Novemr A.D. 1773: by me Stephen Johnson Pastor of the first Church in sd Lyme. Dated Lyme 26th June 1778
Married U Marvin D. Lay
Olive Ingraham Daughter of Francis and Lucretia Ingraham was born Septemr 6th 1774
Lucy Ingraham Daughter of Francis and Lucretia Ingraham was born August 31st 1776

John Giles was married to Ruth Ransom the 1st day March 1778
Susannah their Daughter was born the 23d day Augt 1778
John their Son was born the 27th day of March A.D. 1780
John their Son died October the 25th day A.D 1780
John their Son was born the 21 day of August 1781
Isaac their Son was born the 29 day of March 1783

Susannah their Daughter died the 12th day June 1789
Abner Son of the said John and Ruth was born the 16th day of March A.D. 1791

These Certifie that Mr. Jasper Champen and Mrs. Bettey Chadwick boath of Lyme in New London County were Lawfully Married to Each other on the first Day of January A.D 1761 by me John Lay 2nd Just Paec

Waity Champion Daughter of Jasper and Bettey Champion was born Septemr 27th 1761
Elisabeth Champion Daughter of Jasper & Bettey Champion was born November 6th 1763
Lucinda Champion Daughter of Jasper & Bettey Champion was born September 22nd 1764
Lovice Champion Daughter of Jasper & Bettey Champion was born Feby 18 1767
Lucey Champion Daughter of Jasper & Bettey Champion was born April 6 1769
Eunice Champion Daughter of Jasper & Bettey Champion was born July ye 16th 1772
William Champion Son of Jasper & Betty Champion was born March 20th 1777
Sands Champion Son of Jasper & Bettey Champion was born July: A.D: 1789

These may Signifie & Certifie that Abraham Emmerson was in Novemr 1750: married by me to Deborah Lord boath of Lyme by me - George Beckwith

Abraham Emmerson Son of Deborah and Abrm Emmerson was Born Septemr 19th 1752
Mary Emmerson Daughter of Abraham & Deborah Emmerson was born May 9th 1755
Deborah Emmerson Daughter of Abraham & Deborah Emmerson was Born February 29th 1756
Theophilus Emmerson Son of Abraham & Deborah Emmerson was Born August 26th 1758
Joseph Emmerson Son of Abraham & Deborah Emmerson was Born August 24th 1762
Broadstreet Emmerson So of Abraham & Deborah Emmerson was Born April 22nd 1765 and Died about the month of October 1765
Judith Emmerson Daughter of Abraham & Deborah Emmerson was Born July 17th 1766
Abigail Emmerson Daughter of Abraham & Deborah Emmerson was Born Septemr 13 1769
Mary Emmerson Daughter of Araham & Deborah Emmerson Died Decemr 22 1769
Deborah Emmerson Wife of the above said Abraham Emmerson Died January 9th 1770
Theophilus Emmerson Son of Abraham & Deborah Emmerson Died Novemr 3rd 1776 in Captivity
August 9th 1773: then I married Abraham Emmerson to his now Wife - Mary Rathbone. Certified by Samll Ely Just Peace
Elisabeth Emmerson Daughter of Abraham & Mary Emmerson was born March 23rd 1778 and Died the 23rd Day of March: 1779

These are to Certifie that Thomas Rathbone and Mary Wait boath of Lyme were Lawfully Married togethor the 5th Day of May: A.D. 1763 by me Stephen Johnson Pastor of the first Church in Lyme Dated in Lyme 7th May A.D. 1779
John Rathbone Son of Thomas & Mary Rathbone was born February ye first 1764
Ebenezer Rathbone Son of Thomas & Mary Rathbone was born March 12th 1766
Thomas Rathbone Son of Thomas & Mary Rathbone was born March 19th 1768

[page 159] Mr. James Burnham & Miss Mihitable Bennett was Legally Join' in Marrage on the 23d of November A.D. 1780 pr George Beckwith Pas
Polly their Daughter was born the 11th Novr 1781 and died the 20th Jany A.D. 1782
John Bennett Son of the said James & Mihitable was born on the 12th day of June A.D. 1783
Phebe Daughter of the said James & Mihitable was born on the 28th day of June 17[86]

To all whome these Presents may Concearn that Noah Miller of Lyme and Sarah Crocker of New London were Lawfully married in February [ ] by me is hereby Certified by me Mathw Graves Minister   New London January 5th 1779
Recorded January 7th 1779 by John Lay 2nd Regr

Sarah Miller Daughter of Noah & Sarah Miller was born Novemr 9th A.D. 1778
John their Son was born on the 7th day of June 1780
Cate their Daughter was born on the 11th day of April A.D. 1783
These are to Certifie that Mr. Samuel Beckwith and Miss Polley Greenfield Boath of Lyme were Lawfully Married together the 21st of June A.D. 1781 Pr me Stephen Johnson Pastor of the first Christ said Lyme Dated Lyme 6th
Abigail Beckwith Daughter of said Samll and Polley Beckwith was born February 12th 1782
Richard Greenfield Beckwith Son of Samll & Polley Beckwith was born March 1st 17
Hannah Daughter of Samuel & Polley Beckwith was born Decr 19th A.D. 1790
Salley Mehaley Daughter of the sd Samll & Polly was born on the 26 Septr 1793
Sally Daughter of the said Samuel & Polly was born on the 26 day of Sept 1793

This may Certifie that Mr. Nathem Latimer Junr of Lyme and Mrs. Anna Dodge of Colchester were legaly Joyned in Marriage on the 10th Day of Decemr A.D 1778 before me John Watrous Justice Peace
Jonathan Latimer Son of Nathan and Anna Latimer was born on ye 11th of Novemr 1781
Ensin George Chadwick Junr was Married to Miss Welthy Brown 7th Decr 178[0]
Robert Son of said George & Welthy was born July 28th A.D 1781
Fanny Daughter of said George & Welthy was Born 5th May 1783

[page 160] These Certifie that Mr. Henry Roland of Lyme in New London County was Lawfully Married to Mrs. Phoebe Huntly of sd Lyme the 28th Day of May 1772 by me John Lay 2nd Justice of the Peace
Palmer Roland Son of Henry Roland Junr & Phoebe his wife was born July 16th 1773
Amos Roland Son of Henry Roland Junr & Phoebe his wife was born July 16th 1775

These are to Certifie whomesoever it may Concearn that Mr. Robert Denison and Mrs. Esther Wade both of Lyme were Lawfully Married together the 6th Day of February A.D. 1777 by me Stephen Johnson Pastor of the first Church in se Lyme Dated in Lyme 8th of March A.D 1779
Nabby Denison Daughter of Robert & Esther Denison was born March ye 16th A.D. 1779
Joseph their Son was born on the 10th day of November A.D. 1780
Charles their Son was born on the 28th day of September A.D. 1782
Andrew their Son was born on the 15th day of January A.D. 1785
Robert their Son was born on the 4th day of January A.D. 1788

This may Certifie etc: that Doctor Samuel Mather and Mrs. Ellis [Alice] Ransom were married October first 1761   Test Ephraim Little Clericus   Colchester April 20th 1780
Alice Mather Daughter of Samll & Alice Mather was Born October 4th A.D. 1762
Sarah An Mather Daughter of Samll & Alice Mather Was Born Septemr 13 1766 and died August 27th A.D. 1767
Sarah An Mather Daughter of Samll & Alice Mather was Born June 19th A.D. 1772
Lous Mather Daughter of Samll & Alice Mather was Born February 8th 1776
Lewey Mather Daughter of Samll & Alice Mather was born Novemr 21st A.D. 1777
Samll Boerhame Mather Son of Samll & Alice Mather was born Septemr 27th 1780
Mrs. Elles Mather died on the   day of
Doct Samuel Mather was married to Mrs. Sally Anderson on the 9th day of January in the year 1806
John Watrous their son was born on the 21 day of Jany 1807

These Certifie whome it may Conscern that James McCrackin and Elisabeth Smith was legally Joyned in Marraige by me   Nezriah Bliss Justice Peace
Thomas McCrackin Son of James and Elisabeth McCrackin was born Septemr 12th 1782
William McCrackin Son of James & Elisabeth McCrackin was born April 5th 178[4]

[page 161] Mary Tillilson the Wife of Jacob Tillitson and Mary Tillilson the Wife of Lee Tillitson boath of Lyme Testifie and Say that they are [thus wing] to the age [of]
Bershaba Chapman Daughter of Samll Chapman of sd Lyme and that she [--] said Bershaba was Eighteen years old Some time in the moth of November [1780] by the best of their knowledge

New London County Ss Lyme December 20th A.D. 1780 then and there Personally Appeared the above said Mary Tillitson Wife of sd Jacob Tillitson and Mary ye Wife of Levey Tillitson and made Solomon Oath to the Tru[th] of the abov . . . . Deposition before me Eleazer Mather Just Paec Recorded the 22nd Day of Decemr A.D. 1780 by John Lay 2nd Regr

Barshaba Chapman Daughter of Samll and Esther Chapman was born in the Town of Lyme the first Day of November 1763: Recorded the 11th of January 1781 by order of Samll Chapman of Lyme: by John Lay 2nd Regr.

To all whome it may Concearn Know ye that Mr. Seth Smith of Lyme and Mrs. Hannah Murdock Widdow of Saybrook, boath in the County of New London were Joyned together in Wedlock on the 17th Day of May: 1780 Pr me John Devotion Pastor of the 3rd Church in Saybrook Saybrook May 30th 1781

William Lay Smith Son of Seth & Hannah Smith was Born ye first Day of May 17--
John Lay Smith Son of Seth & Hannah Smith was Born December 21st A.D. 17 --
Eliza Daughter of the said Seth & Hannah was born December 27th A.D. 1795 being Sund[ay]
Eliza above mentioned departed this life on the 23d of October 179--

These Certifye that Mr. Moses Marvin and Mrs. Zilpha Gill boath of Lyme were Lawfull Married together the 30th Day of March A.D. 1780 by me Stephen Johnson Pastor of the first Church in sd Lyme Dated Lyme 13th of March 1783
James Marvin Son of Moses and Zilpah Marvin was born January 24th 17[81]
Daniel Marvin Son of Moses & Zilpah Marvin was born February 18th 17 --

[page 162] These are to Certifye that Mr. Andrew Sill and Mrs. Ellenor Dorr Boath of Lyme was Lawfully Married together June 20th 1773 by me Stephen Johnson Pastor of the first Church in sd Lyme Dated in Lyme 25th Decemr 1780
Abel Sill Son of Andrew and Ellenor Sill was born August 8th A.D. 1774
Jonathan Palmer Sill Son of Andrew & Ellenor Sill was born January 8th A.D. 1776
Andrew Sill Son of Andrew and Ellenor Sill was born March 31st A.D. 1778
Phebe Sill Daughter of Andrew and Ellenor Sill was born March 26th A.D. 1781

These are to Certifie that that Mr. Gearshom Watrous and Mrs. Mehetable Ransom boath of Lyme were Lawfully Married together the 11th Day of April A.D. 1776 Dated Lyme April 7th 1781 Pr me Stephen Johnson Pastor of first Church in sd Lyme
Their first Child was a Son and was Born ye 11th of January 1777 and died ye 17th Day of the Same January
Phineas Watrous Son of Gearshom & Mehetable Watrous was born July 12th 1778
Polley Watrous Daughter of Gearshom & Mehetable Watrous was born October 26 1781
Christopher Watrous Son of Gearshom & Mehetable Watrous was born Decemr 17th 1782
Mehetable Watrous Daughter of Gearshom & Mehetable Watrous was born May 20th 1786

Marlborough March 17th 1786: These may Certifie that Joseph Smith of Lyme was Joyned in Marriage with Elisabeth Darby of Hebron upon the 31st Day of October A.D. 1782 pr me David Huntington Pastor of the Chh in Malborough
Erastus Smith Son of Joseph & Elisabeth Smith was Born April 13th Day 1783

Polley Smith Daughter of Joseph & Elisabeth Smith was Born July ye 30th 1785
Ambrous Smith Son of Joseph & Elisabeth Smith was Born April 12th 1788
Betsey Daughter of the said Joseph & Elisabeth was born December 4th day A.D. 1790
Joseph Son of the said Joseph & Elisabeth was born on the 10th day of June A.D.1793

[page 163] These are to Certifye that Mr. Nathan Tinker and Mrs. Mehetable Beckwith boath of Lyme were Lawfully Married together the 17th Day of February A.D.1780 by me Stephen Johnson Pastor of the first Church in sd Lyme Dated in Lyme April 28th 1781
Lurena Tinker Daughter of Nathan & Mehabel Tinker was Born August 24th 1780
Allen Tinker Son of Nathan and Mehetabel Tinker was Born Decemr 30th 1781
Elisabeth Tinker Daughter of Nathan & Mehetabel Tinker was born July 18th 1783
Jonathan Tinker Son of Nathan Tinker and Mehetabel his wife was born June 14th 1785
Anna Daughter of the said Nathan & Mehetable was born the 12th day June 1788
Mary Daughter of the said Nathan & Mehetable was born the 3d Decr 1790
Nathan Tinker died on the - day of April A.D. 1792
Nathan Son of the said Nathan & Mehilable was born Septr 30th A.D. 1792

Nehemiah Mack and Mrs. Eunice Beckwith Boath of Lyme was Lawfully Married to Each other on the 5th Day of February A.D. 1749; as Certified by Evidence etc.
Mehetable Mack Daughter of Nehemiah and Eunice Mack was Born April 4th 1752
Nehemiah Mack Son of Nehemiah & Eunice Mack was Born May 18th 1754
Benjamin Mack Son of Nehemiah & Eunice Mack was Born Septemr 15th 1756
David Mack Son of Nehemiah & Eunice Mack was Born January 4th 1759
Eunice Mack Daughter of Nehemiah & Eunice Mack was Born February 20th 1761
Hezekiah Mack Son of Nehemiah & Eunice Mack was Born January 20th 1763
Silas Mack Son of Nehemiah & Eunice Mack was Born October 4th 1765
John Mack Son of Nehemiah & Eunice Mack was born October 25th 1768
Elisabeth Mack Daughter of Nehemiah & Eunice Mack was Born July 24th 1770
Mehetabel Mack Daughter of Nehemiah & Eunice Mack Died Septemr 16th 1776
Eunice Mack Daughter of Nehemiah & Eunice Mack Died July 16 1780

These are to Certifie whome it may Conscearn that Stephen Mather and Elisabeth Peck Boath of Lyme were Lawfully Married together the 5th day of Septemr A.D. 1782 by me Stephen Johnson Pastor of ye first Church of Christ in sd Lyme. Recorded ye 20th Day of January 1783 by John Lay 2nd Regr
Elijah Mather Son of Stephen & Elisabeth Mather was Born February 14th A.D. 1783

[page 164] These lines are to Certifie that Benjamin Mack and Nabby Lord was Lawfully Married by me Danll Miner Pastor of the Congregational Church in Lyme the 29th Day of January 1781: I say by me as Witness my hand this 9th Day of April A.D. 1782 Daniel Miner
Benjamin Mack Son of Benjamin & Nabby Mack was born Decemr 6 1781

Adonijah Marvin Baker was born on the 14th day of June A.D. 1776

These Certifie that Robert Sanders and the Widdow Hannah Rogers boath of Lyme in New London County were Lawfully Married to Each other on the 6th Day of September: A.D. 1779 by me John Lay 2nd Just Paec
Jean Sanders Daughter of Robert & Hannah Sanders was born April 5th 1780

These may Certifie that Mr. Hallam Latimer of Lyme and Mrs. Marcy Dodge of Colchester were legally Joyed in Marriage on the 17th Day of September A.D. 1778: before me John Watrous Jus Paec
David Latimer Son of Hallam & Marcy Latimer was Born May 7th 1779
Marcy Latimer Daughter of Hallam and Marcy Latimer was Born Decemr 3rd 1781 and Departed this life August 27th A.D. 1782

LYME, CONNECTICUT, VITAL RECORDS

Peter Latimer Son of Hallam and Marcy Latimer was Born August first: 1783
Peter Latimer above said Departed this Life May ye 11th A.D 1784
Nicolas Hallam Latimer Son of Hallam & Marcy Latimer was Born october 17th 1785 and Died ye 22nd of October 1786
Lucy Latimer their Daughter was born August 16 1787
Frances Latimer their Daughter was born March 6th 1790

Stephen Tucker was Legally Married to Elisabeth Wade on the 24th day of June 1767
James their Son was born on the 25th day of May A.D. 1769
Atwell their Son was born on the 17th day of February A.D. 1772
Esther their Daughter was born on the 8th Day of May A.D. 1775
Stephen their Son was born on the 6th Day of December A.D. 1780
Stephen Tucker Departed this life on the 13th Day of March A.D. 1792

[page 165] These may Certifie whomesoever it may Concearn that Ezekiel Miner and Margreet Wait boah of Lyme were Lawfully Married ye 11th Day of June A.D. 1747 pr me Stephen Johnson Pastor of first Church in Lyme
Eias Miner Son of Ezekiel and Margreet Miner was Born February 7th A.D. 1749
Martin Miner Son of Ezekiel and Margreet Miner was Born September ye first A.D. 1750
Sarah Miner Daughter of Ezekiel & Margreet Miner was born July 7th A.D. 1752
Anderson Miner Son of Ezekiel & Margreet Miner was born July 9th A.D. 1754
Ezra Miner Son of Ezekiel and Margreet Miner was born October ye 2nd A.D. 1756
Seth Miner Son of Ezekiel and Margreet Miner was born ye 6th Day of October 1758
John Miner Son of Ezekiel & Margreet Miner was born ye 25th Day of January 1761
Lorena Miner Daughter of Ezekiel & Margreet Miner was born ye 18th of April A.D. 1763
Sarah Miner Daughter of Ezekiel & Margreet Miner Died July 18th A.D. 1765
Sarah Miner Daughter of Ezekiel & Margreet Miner was born at Simsbury July 13th A.D. 1766
Ezra Miner Son of Ezekiel and Margreet Miner [died] ye 20th of July: AD 1766
Margreet Miner Wife of Sd Ezekiel Miner Died September 13th Day A.D. 1767

These Certifie that Mr. Ezekiel Miner of Lyme in New London County and Mrs. Margreet Reed widdow and Relect of Mr. Ahimaz Reed late of sd Lyme Deceasd were Lawfully Married to Each other on the 24th Day of November: 1768 by me John Lay 2nd Just Paec
Ezra Miner Son of Ezekiel & Margreet Miner was born September: 12th A.D: 1769
Abner Miner Son of Ezekiel & Margreet Miner was born October 23rd A.D: 1771
Margreet Miner Wife of sd Ezekiel Miner Died ye 16th Day of July A.D. 1775
Ezekiel Miner Died May 20th A.D. 1780

Mr. Joseph Miner of Lyme Died the 30th Day of May: A.D: 1781
Mrs. Grace Turner Miner Relect of Mr. Joseph Miner Died June 6th A.D. 1784

These are to Certifie whom so ever it may Conscearn that Mr. Ezra Ingraham and Miss Bettey Robins boath of Lyme were Lawfully married together the 15th Day of January A.D: 1784 by me Stephen Johnsn Pastor of first Church in sd Lyme
Ethelenda Ingraham Daughter of Ezra and Bettey Ingraham was Born Decemr 30th: 1784
Ethelinda Daughter of Ezra & Betsey Ingraham died on the 24th day of April 1787
Ethelinda Daughter of Ezra & Betsey Ingraham was born Novr 14th day A.D. 1787
Samuel Son & Abigail Daughter, of said Ezra & Betsey being twins, was born on the 17th Day of May Anno Domini 1790
Betty Daughter of said Ezra & Betsey was born 16th day of Aug 1792
Anne Daughter of the said Ezra & Betsey was born 31 day of July A.D. 1796

[page 166] These Certifie that on the 5th Day of April 1761 in Lyme in the State of Connecticut Mr. Elisha Robins & Mrs. Elisabeth Tinker were Married to Each other by me the Subscriber according to the laws of this State Certified this 13th Day of April 1778 Pr Matthew Griswold D: Governor
Eunice Robins Daughter of Elisha & Elisabeth Robins was Born November 18th 1762
Elisabeth Robins Daughter of Elisha & Elisabeth Robins was Born April 5th 1764
Elisha Robins Son of Elisha and Elisabeth Robins was born August 8th 1767 and Died Decemr 18th 1767
Mary Robins Daughter of Elisha & Elisabeth Robins was born June 8th 1768
Abigail Robins Daughter of Elisha & Elisabeth Robins was born August 30th 1771
Elisha Sheffield Robins Son of Elisha & Elisabeth Robins was Born August 31st 1777 and Died the 24th of Novemr: 1781
Elisha Robins Son of Elisha & Elisabeth Robins was born ye 10th of November: 1782
Elisabeth Robins Wife of said Elisha Died December 11th 1782. She was forty three years old the 16th Day of May 1782

Mr. Elisha Robins was married to Mrs. Lydia Cooley 15th Jany 1784
Lydia Daughter of the said Elisha & Lydia was born October the 28th day A.D. 1784
Thomas Anderson Son of the said Elisha & Lydia was born the 9th day of March A.D. 1787
Joseph Son of the said Elisha & Lydia was born the 28th day of May A.D. 1789
William Son of the said Elisha & Lydia born on the 27th day of July A.D. 1792

These Certifie that we the Subscribers Saw Mr. Jason Lee of Lyme married to Mrs. Abiah Brown on the 21st Day of January in the year 1762 by the Reverend Mr. Lord of Norwhich: Dated in sd Lyme the 22nd Day of May A.D. 1784. Samuel Griswold - Mary Griswold
Joseph Lee Son of Jason & Abiah Lee was Born January ye 26th A.D 1763 and Departed this life Decemr 4th AD 1763
Joseph Lee ye 2nd Son of Jason & Abiah Lee was born Septemr 30th A.D. 1764
Polley Lee Daughter of Jason & Abiah Lee was Born January ye 17th A.D. 1767
Joseph Lee Son of Jason and Abiah Lee Died January ye 25th A.D. 1768
Eunice Lee Daughter of Jason & Abiah Lee was born January 28th A.D. 1769
Jason Lee Son of Jason and Abiah Lee was Born January 26th A.D. 1771
Bettey Lee Daughter of Jason & Abiah Lee was born January ye 7th A.D. 1773
Harris Lee Son of Jason and Abiah Lee was Born May ye 29th A.D. 1775
Anna Lee Daughter of Jason & Abiah Lee was born March 12th A.D. 1778
Samuel Lee Son of Jason and Abiah Lee was born August ye 8th A.D. 1780 and Departed this life March 9th A.D. 1782
Harris Lee Son of Jason and Abiah Lee Departed this life June ye 26th A.D. 1783
Sollomon Lee Son of Jason and Abiah Lee was born October ye 13th A.D. 1783

John Griffing of Lyme was married to Phebe Taber of New London on the 11th Day of June 1761 by Mather Biles Pastor of a Church at New London as certified by Evidence

[page 167] These may Signifie and Certifye that Mr. William Ely was on the 8th of September 1783 Married to Miss Alice Mather Boath of Lyme by me George Beckwith Pastor

Joseph Walker was Married to Selah Cooley on the day of --
Walter Son of the said Joseph & Selah was born on the 11th day of June A.D. 1787
John Cooley Son of the said Joseph and Selah was born on the 11th October 1789
Amos Son of the said Joseph and Selah was born on the 6th day of June A.D. 1791
James Son of the said Joseph and Selah was born on the 25th day of October A.D. 1795

Lyme April 19th A.D: 1757: then I Married Darious Peck of sd Lyme to his now Wife Elisabeth Beckwith -- Samuel Ely Justice of Peace -- the foregoing as a copy Extracted for Samll Ely Esqre Record of Marriages
Martin Peck Son of Darious & Elisabeth Peck was Born October 8th A.D. 1759

Elisabeth Peck Daughter of Darious & Elisabeth Peck was Born December 10th A.D. 1761
Darious Peck Son of Darious & Elisabeth Peck was born February the 2nd A.D. 1764
Simeon Peck Son of Darious & Elisabeth Peck was born January ye 31st A.D. 1766
Andrew Peck Son of Darious & Elisabeth Peck was Born February the Second A.D. 1768
John Moore Peck Son of Darious & Elisabeth Peck was Born February first A.D. 1770
Huldah Peck Daughter of Darious & Elisabeth Peck was Born August ye 31st A.D. 1772
William Peck Son of Darious & Elisabeth Peck was Born July ye 18th A.D. 1774
Elisha Peck Son of Darious & Elisabeth Peck was Born May the 16th A.D. 1777
Timothy Peck Son of Darious & Elisabeth Peck was Born August the 15th A.D. 1779
Matthew Marvin and Elisabeth Demming boath of Lyme in the County of New London were Lawfully Married to Each other on the 30th Day of May A.D. 1771 as Certified by Evidence
Joseph Marvin Son of Matthew and Elisabeth Marvin was Born March 26th A.D. 1772
Mehetabel Marvin Daughter of Matthew & Elisabeth Marvin was Born October 26th A.D. 1773
Mary Marvin Daughter of Matthew & Elisabeth Marvin was Born Novemr 16th A.D. 1775
David Marvin Son of Matthew & Elisabeth Marvin was Born November 2nd A.D. 1777
Elisabeth Marvin Daughter of Matthew & Elisabeth Marvin was Born Novemr 12th A.D. 1779
Abigail Marvin Daughter of Mathew & Elisabeth Marvin was Born December 31st A.D. 1782
Rosalind Marvin Daughter of Matthew & Elisabeth Marvin was Born January 26th A.D. 1785
Lurania Marvin Daughter of Matthew & Elisabeth Marvin was born 18th of April A.D. 1786
Jonathan Deming Son of said Mathew & Elisabeth was born 11th Septr 1789
Mrs. Elisabeth Marvin widow of Matthew Marvin died June 22d A.D. 1839 aged ninety two years --

[page 168] Mr. Elijah Bingham of Lyme in New London was married to Mrs. Mary Banning Brockway of sd Lyme on the 14th of April 1761 by Samll Ely then a Just Paec as is Certified by Evidence
Theody Bingham Daughter of Elijah and Mary Bingham was Born 21st Septemr 1761
Roswell Bingham Son of Elijah and Mary B Bingham was Born 28th of January 1763
Walter Bingham Son of Elijah and Mary Bingham was Born 15th February 1765
Malenda Bingham Daughter of Elijah & Mary Bingham was Born 12th of May 1767
Silas Bingham Son of Elijah and Mary Bingham was Born 24th of March 1769
Theody Bingham Daughter of Elijah & Mary Bingham Departed this life 20 April 1771
Said Bingham had a Son born 24th of June 1771 & Died 28th of the sd June 1771
Sluman Bingham Son of Elijah and Mary Bingham was born 31st of May 1772
Polley Bingham Daughter of Elijah & Mary Bingham was born 16th of August 1775
Claratha Bingham Daughter of Elijah and Mary Bingham was Born 14th Novemr 1777
Nathan Bingham Son of Elijah and Mary Bingham was Born 5th of May 1780
Pheby Bingham Daughter of Elijah & Mary Bingham was Born first Septemr 1782
Claratha Bingham above named Departed this life ye 25th August 1783
Phebe Bingham above named Departed this life 6th October 1783

These Certifie that Gabriel Ely of Lyme in New London County was Lawfull Married to Eunice Marrimon of Harwington in Litchfield County on the 11th Day of August: 1779 as appeared by the Evidence of Joseph Hayden, George Marvin an Ruben Barber etc.
Polley Ely Daughter of Gabriel and Eunice Ely was Born March 23rd 1782
Silas Peck Ely Son of Gabriel and Eunice Ely was born November ye 7th 1783
Rachel Ely Daughter of Gabriel and Eunice Ely was born Septemr 6th 1785
Joseph Marrimon Ely Son of Gabriel & Eunice Ely was born June 18th 1788
William, Son of the said Gabriel & Eunice Ely was born August 4th A.D. 1790
Erastus Son of the said Gabriel & Eunice was born December 25th A.D. 1792

Fanny daughter of the said Gabriel & Eunice was born on the 22d of March 1795
Teressa daughter of the said Gabriel & Eunice was born on the 5th day of June AD 1798
These Certifie that Gurdon Ely on the 30th day of July A.D. 1783 Lawfully Joyned in Marriage with Parnal Phelps by Ezra Selden Just of the Peace Lyme July 30th 1783
Mahala Ely Daughter of Gurdon and Parnal Ely was born ye 3rd Day of Oct: 1784 and Died the 27th Day of July: 1785
Clarissa Daughter of the said Gurdon & Parnal was born August 17th 1786
Ammi Son of said Gurdon & Parnal was born December 16th 1789
Ruth Daughter of sd Gurdon & Parnal was born July 17th 1792
Martha Dauthter of the said Gurdon and Parnal was born June 23d AD 1794
Gurdon Son of the said Gurdon and Parnal was born Novr 1st A.D 1796
Silame daughter of the sd Gurdon & Parnal was born August 11th A.D. 1798

[page 169] taken from the Records of the late Benjamin Lee Esqr that Samuel Comstock was married to Esther Lee February ye 2nd: 1769 Test Lemmuel Lee
Christopher Comstock Son of Samuel and Esther Comstock was born June 16th 1769
Elisabeth Comstock Daughter of Samuel and Esther Comstock was Born October 14 1770
Samuel Comstock Son of Samuel & Esther Comstock was born August the 29th 177-

Lyme May the 12th Day: A.D: 1778 then Mr. Elijah Selden was Lawfully Joyned in Marrared with Mrs. Eunice Comstock Certified pr me Ezra Selden Justice of Peace
had a Son Born June 13th 1799 and Died June 24th 1779
Elijah Selden Son of Elijah and Eunice Selden was Born the 26th Day of August: 1780
Charles Selden Son of Elijah and Eunice Selden was Born Tuesday the 11th Day of June 1782
Ezra Selden Son of Elijah and Eunice Selden was Born Sunday the 21st day of August 1785
Eunice Daughter of Elijah and Eunice Selden was Born Sunday the 6th day of July A.D. 1788
Lura Daughter of said Elijah & Eunice was born the 12th day of April A.D. 1791
Eunice Wife of said Elijah departed this life on the 14th day of October A.D. 1791
Mr. Elijah Selden was Legally joyned in Marraige to Mrs. Hannah Tracy Septr 25th A.D. 1792

New London County Ss: Lyme December 5th Anno Domini: 1776: then Azariah Beebe of Lyme was Marraied to Diedamy Marvin of sd Lyme Lyme pr me Eleazer Mather Just Paec
Adonijah Marvin Beebe Son of Azariah and Diedamy Beebe was Born October 12th A. D 1777
Betsee Beebe Daughter of Azariah and Diedami Beebe was Born October 11th 1780
Azariah Beebe Son of Azariah & Diedami Beebe was Born March ye 28th 1783
Richard Beebe Son of Azariah & Diedami Beebe was born April the 23rd A.D. 1785

Abel Rogers of Lyme was married to Hannah Rogers of sd Lyme on the 19th Day of February 1784 as Certifie by Evidence
Ebenezer Rogers Son of Abel and Hannah Rogers was Born March 4th Day: 1785
Elisabeth Rogers Daughter of Abel & Hannah Rogers was Born January 2nd Day 1787
Susannah Daughter of the said Abel & Hannah was born September 28th day A.D. 1789
Christopher Son of the said Abel and Hannah was born the 22d day of March AD 1793
[page 169] Hannah daughter of said Abel & Hannah was born on the 19 March 1797
Joseph son of the said Abel & Hannah born on the 13 day of Feby 1800
Abel Moor son of the said Abel & Hannah born 11 May 1801
Gideon Mather their son was born the 3d April 1804

[page 170] Ebenezer Chapman and Elisabeth Huntly boah of Lyme were Lawfully Married to Each other the 17th Day of June: AD: 1755
Eunice Chapman Daughter of Ebenezer and Elisabeth Chapman was born Jany 1st Day 1756

Edward Chapman Son of Ebenezer & Elisabeth Chapman was Born July first 1760
John Chapman Son of Ebenezer & Elisabeth Chapman was Born July 15th 1762
Bershaba Chapman Daughter of Ebenezer & Elisabeth Chapman was born July 16th 1764
Robert Chapman Son of Ebenezer & Elisabeth Chapman was born May first 1766
Ezekiel Chapman Son of Ebenezer & Elisabeth Chapman was born March 12th 1768
Phebe Chapman Daughter of Ebenezer & Elisabeth Chapman was born August 9th 1770 and Died the --
Ruth Chapman Daughter of Ebenezer & Elisabeth Chapman was born August 15th 1772
Elisabeth Chapman Daughter of Ebenezer & Elisabeth Chapman was born April 2nd 1774
Asael Chapman Son of Ebenezer & Elisabeth Chapman was Born February 26 1776
Moses Chapman Son of Ebenezer & Elisabeth Chapman was born January 10th 1778
Susa Chapman Daughter of Ebenezer & Elisabeth Chapman was born February 28th 1782
Ebenezer Chapman Departed this life September 12th A.D: 1785
John Chapman Son of sd Ebenezer Chapman Died September ye 27th 1783

Colchester January 23rd 1784 these may Certifie that Elisha Lay of Lyme and Mary Olmsted of Colchester were Lawfully Joyned together in marraige the 30th Day of March: 1783   Test - Robert Robbins
Elisha Lay Son of Elisha and Mary Lay was born August 10th A.D 1783
Stephen Lay Son of Elisha and Mary Lay was born December 3rd A.D. 1786
John Olmstead Son of the said Elisha & Mary was born on the 17th day of Septr A.D 1789
Sarah Daughter of the said Elisha and Mary was born on the 9th day of Octr AD 1791
Lucy Daughter of the said Elisha & Mary was born on the 3rd day of Decr AD 1793
Lucy Lay departed this life on the 16 day of July in the year 1807
Mary Wife of the sd Elisha Lay died on the 5th day of August 1807 aged 54

Lyme January the 31st A.D 1785: then I the Subscriber married Luther Reives, and Anna Person boath of sd Lyme to Each other   Test Seth Ely Justice of ye Peace
Benjamin Son of Luther & Anna Reives was Born 23rd of Febry 1787
Rumsey Son of the said Luther & Anna was born the 18th day of April 1789
Sarepta Daughter of the said Luther & Anne was born on the 13th of June 1792
Polley Daughter of the said Luther & Anne was born on the 5th of April 1795
Hannabal Son of the said Luther was born on the 9th day of Jany 1797
Anne daughter of the said Luther & Anne was born the 1st day of Octr 1799

[page 171]   Lebbeus Peck and Lydia Lee boath of Lyme in New London County were Lawfully Married to Each other on the 17th Day of June: 1784
Catharine Peck Daughter of Lebbeus and Lydia Peck was born April 20th 1785
Polley Peck Daughter of Lebbeus and Lydia Peck was Born February 4th 1787

These may Certifie that I married Edward Chapman 2nd to Barshaba Chapman July the 3rd 1781   Jason Lee
Caleb Chapman Son of Edward Chapman & Barshaba his wife was born February 23rd 1782
John Chapman Son of Edward and Barshaba Chapman was born May 21st AD 1785
Ebenezer Chapman Son of Edward & Barshaba Chapman was born January ye 14th 1788

Edward Chapman was married to Molley Huntly May 26th: 1765

Mr. John Lay departed this life April 14th AD 1788 - in the 92d year of his age (father of Elisha Lay and Grandfather of Stephen Lay [1697/91])

These may Certifie that I married Ebener Mack to Polley Harvey Harvey August 12th 1787
Esther Mack Daughter Daugher of Ebenezer and Polley Mack was born June 10th 1788

Silvah Kimball Daughter of John Kimball & Reuhannah his Wife was born November the 15th AD 1763

[page 172] These are to Certifye that Elisha Champion and Miss Phebey Miller boath of Lyme were Lawfully Married the 27th Day of November AD 1783 pr me Stephen Johnson Pastor of the first in sd Lyme
Judah Champion Daughter of Elisha and Phebey Champion was born November 11th 1784
Hephzibah Champion Daughter of Elisha and Phebe Champion was Born the 30th Day of June 1786
Lurana Daughter to the said Elisha & Phebe was born 9th May 1789
Elisha Son of the said Elisha & Phebe was born on the 2d day of June AD 1791
Phebe daughter of the said Elisha & Phebe was born on the 19th April AD 1795
Harrion [Harriet] their daughter was born on the 19 day of November 1804

This is to Certifye all Consearned that Matthew Griswold Junior Esqr was Married to Miss Lydia Ely on the 4th Instant pr David Higgins Minister of the Gospel Lyme September 5th 1788

These may Certifye that Ebenezer Booles and Moley Gilbert were Married to Each other on the 9th Day of February: 1786 by me Richard Wait Junr Just Paece
Polley Booles Daughter of Ebenezer and Molley Booles was Born July the first AD 1786
Fanny Booles Daughter of Ebenezer and Molley Booles was Born Novemr 3rd 1788

Ruel Wilson Son of George & Susannah Wilson was born on the 26th day of April AD 1775
William Willson was born on the 15th day of February A.D 1780
Susannah Wilson was born on the 14th day of February AD 1784
David Wilsen was born on the 10th day of December AD 1786

[page 173] April 21st 1776: was Married John Daniels and Lucretia Watrous by the Revnd Mr. Stephen Johnson
Watrouse Daniels Son of John & Lucretia Daniels was Born May the 19th Day 1779 and John Daniels Son of John & Lucretia Daniels was also Born the 19th Day of May 1779 they they being twins
Lucretia Daniels Wife of sd John Daniels Died June the first 1779
Watrous Daniels Died September the 15th 1779
John Daniels Son of John and Lucretia Daniels Died April 11th 1780
John Daniels and Jemiah Clark boath of Lyme were Lawfully Married to Each other on the 18th Day of April 1780 by John Lay 2nd Just Paec
Jemime Daniels Wife of Sd John Daniels Died January the 14th 1781
March 13th 1782 John Daniels and Eunice Beckwith were Lawfully Married to Each other by the Reverend Mr. Stephen Johnson
Lucretia Watrous Daniels Daughter of John and Eunice Daniels was born April 19th 1783
Eunice Daniels Wife of Sd John Daniels Died September ye 12th 1784
This may Certifye that John Daniels and Esther Wait was married to Each other on the 19th Day of September: 1786 by me Richd Wait Junr Just of Peace
John Watrous Daniels Son of John & Esther Daniels was Born March 7th 1788

This may Certify that I Married Mr. Nathan Griffing to Miss Catharine Johnson Octr the 16th day AD 1788   Jason Lee Elder
Their children as appears by the family bible of their son Jasper were as follows
Jasper born Aug. 29, 1790
Lucy born Feb. 16 1794
Mary born Nov 29 1795
John born June 1 1798
Nathan Griffing died Apr 24 1836 age 76 yrs 5 mos
Catharine widow of Nathan Griffing died Nov 26 1846 age 84
    Attest William Marvin Town Clerk Jan. 22, 1919

Mr. William Peck & Mrs. Judith Marvin was Married together on the day of
Reynold Marvin, their Son was born on the 21st day of March AD 1780
Frankling, Son of the said Judath & Willm was born on the 3d of August AD 1781

Judith, Daughter of the said Wm & Judith was born on the 6th day of Decr AD 1782
Nathaniel their Son was born on the 14th day of October AD 1787

[page 174] Caleb Champlin and Anna Ely was Lawfully Joyned in Marraige on the 27th Day of February AD 1786
Christopher their Son was born on the 6th Day of February 1787
John their Son was born on the 18th day of November AD 1788

[page 174] Silvanus Avery & Mary Luther was Joyn'd in Marraige June 6th 1782
Benjamin Son of the said Silvanus & Mary was born on the 15 March 1788
Betty Daughter of the sd Silvanus & Mary was born on the 12 day April 1793
Olive Daughter of the sd Silvanus & Mary was born the 2 day of June 1796
Silvanus Son of the said Silvanus & Mary was born the 2 day of October 1799
Nancy daughter of the sd Silvanus & Mary was born the 31 day of August 1801
Lucy daughter of the sd Silvanus & Mary was born the 8 day of May 1805

Allen Chadwick & Hannah Brooks Joyn'd in Marraige 5th Decr 1766
James Son of the said Allen & Hannah was born Septr 4th day AD 1767
William Son of the said Allen & Hannah was born Feby 9th day AD 1769
Allen Son of the said Allen & Hannah was born March 1st day 1771
Martha their daughter was born on the 30th day of January 1773 and the said Martha died the 7th day of February 1773
Martha their daughter was born on the 8th day of July 1774
Nathaniel Son of the said Allen & Martha was born 2d Day April 1776
Gurdon Son of the said Allen & Hannah was born on the 26th day March 1778
Ama Daughter of the sd Allen & Hannah was born the 5th day April 1780
Bette Daughter of the said Allen & Hannah was born 8th of Feby 1782
Isaac Son of the said Allen & Hannah was born the 24th of May 1784
Hannah Wife of said Allen died on the 23d of July 1790

[page 175] John Belote & Dorcas Mack was Lawfully Joynd in Mareaige on the 12th day of February AD 1787
Harris Son of the said John & Dorcas was born the 2d June 1787
John Son of the said John & Dorcas was born the 21st May 1789
Isaac Son of the said John and Dorcas was born the 22d Augt 1791
Betsy daughter of the said Jno & Dorcas was born the 16th day of March 1794
Abigail Peck daughter of the said John & Dorcas was born the 29th day of Augt 1796
Ruth daughter of the said John & Dorcas was born the 29th day of July 1798
William Maxon son of the sd John & Dorcas was born the 10th day of Augt 1800

Elias Brockway & Lovica Champin was Joynd in Marriage
Christopher Son of the said Elias & Lovice was born the 9th day of April AD 1787
Jasper Son of the said Elias & Lovice was born the 20th of April AD 1790
Ellice Daughter of the said Elias & Lovice was born the 18th of June AD 1793
Betsey Daughter of the said Elias & Lovice was born the 20th of September 1795
Elias Son of the said Elias & Lovice was born on the 25 of Novr AD 1797
William Champion their son was born on the 15 day of August 1799
George son of the said Elias & Lovice was born the 18 day of December 1804
Charles son of the said Elias & Lovice born on the 13 of June 1807
James Madison their son was born on the 27 day of May 1809
Lovisa daughter of the said Elias & Lovica was born on the 10th May 1811

Henry Cone Son of Henry & Watestill Cone was born the 7th day of February A.D. 1789
Harry Cone
Henry Cone
Silas their Son was born on the 7th day of August 1791
Andrew Diodate Griswold was born on the 8 day of Feby 1794
William Prince their Son was born on the 23d of August 1796
Charles Smith their Son was born on the 5th of November 1798

Oliver Bray their Son was born on the 3d of May 1801
Elihu Lyman their Son was born on the 1t of Novr 1803

[page 176]   James Sullard and Lydia Dewolf was Legally Joyn'd in Marraige on the 13th day of April 1780
Stephen Dewolf, Son of the sd James & Lydia born Decr 13th AD 1780
Ellis Daughter of the said James & Lydia was born May 30th AD 1783
Lucy Daughter of the said James & Lydia was born Novr 16th AD 1787

The births & deaths of the Children of Lieut John Harris
Lois daughter of John & Harris was born Novr 11th AD 1754
Lemuel Son of said John etc was born Octr 15th AD 1757
David Son of the said John etc was born Septr 25th A.D 1761
Ireane daughter of the said Jno etc was born Octr 3rd AD 1763
Josiah Son of the said Jno etc was born Jany 1st AD 1766
Polly daughter of the said Jno etc was born Feby 21st A.D 1768
John Son of the said Jno etc was born Jany 31st AD 1770
Ireane died June 16th 1776 Lois died April 7th AD 1777
Lemuel died Octr 11th 1780 David died Feby 25th AD 1785

The births of the Children of William Banning as appears from a Copy taken from a bible, by Lucy Eldest Child of said Banning & sworn to by said Lucy before Benja Perkins Just Paec
Lucy Banning was born on the 8th day of May A.D. 1770
Azubah Banning was born on the 28th day of Novr AD. 1771
William Banning was born on the 26th of August 1773
Benja Banning was born on the 26th of Feby AD 1775
Temperance Banning was born the 14th of June AD 1776
Elisha Banning was born on the 29th of Jany 1778
Amasa Banning was born on the 4th day of Octr 1779
Clarissa Banning was born on the 2d day of June 1781
Calven Banning was born on the 2d day of June 1785
Septr 1792 Recorded & compaired pr David F. Sill Register

[page 177] Mr. DAvid Ramon was legally Married to Miss Elisabeth Tucker on the 30th day of November AD 1780
Dorcas their Daughter was born on the 11th day of September AD 1781
Hetty their Daughter was born on the 1st day of October AD 1783
Joseph & Benjamin their Sons was born the 24th day of July AD 1786
Richard their Son was born on the 21st day of August AD 1788
David their Son was born on the 9th day of July AD 1791
Benjamin died on the 3d day of May AD 1793

Stephen Chadwick & Leoamy Rogers was married 8 day of Decr 1781
Polly their daughter was born on the 26th day of February AD 1782
John Son of the sd Stephen & Leoamy was born the 19th day of Octr 1784
Samuel Son of the said Stephen & Leoamy was born the 20th day of June 1786
Elisha Son of the said Sephen & Leoamy was born the 2d day of June 1788
Richard Son of the said Stephen & Leoamy was born the 25th day of Decr 1790
Amy Daughter of the said Stephen & Leoamy was born the 20th day of May 1793
Ezra Son of the said Stephen & Leoamy was born the 3rd day of May 1796
Seth Son of the said Stephen & Leoamy was born the 7 day of Augt 1798
Stephen Son of the said Stephen & Leoamy was born the 18 day of June 1801

[page 178]
John S. Matson

LYME, CONNECTICUT, VITAL RECORDS

Volume 2 1790 - 1832
Lyme Records
Births, Marriages, Deaths

[p 1] Doctr William Lord & Miss Anna Mather both of Lyme was Legally Joyn'd in Marriage on the 4th day of September 1790

Mr David F. Sill was Joined in Marriage to Miss Sarah Griswold 20th May 1768
Polly Daughter of the said David & Sarah was born 27 day of June 1768
Thomas Son of the said David & Sarah was born 26 day of Nov -- 1769
Lois daughter of the sd David & Sarah was born 29th of August 1771
John son of the said David & Sarah was born 14th of June 1773
David son of the said David & Sarah was born 8th of January 1775
David died on the 19th day of June 1775 being about 5 months old
John was drowned at Hartford on the 26 day of Aug.t 1794 Aged 21
Polly died on the 9th day of January 1802 ---
Col David F. Sill Esqr departed this Life January the 8th 1813 in the 80th year of his age. --
Mrs. Sarah Sill died November 20th 1815

Mr Enoch Lord Jun.r & Miss Esther Durfey of New London was Legally Joyn'd in Marriage on the 3 day of June A.D. 1790
Thomas Durfey Son of the said Enoch & Esther was born on the 17th Day of Feby 1792
Phebe W Daughter of the said Enoch & Esther was born on the 12th Day of Jany 1794
Sally Read daughter of the said Enoch & Esther was born on the 12th Feby 1796
Nancy M. Daughter of the said Enoch & Esther was born the 26th Augt 1798
Polly Y daughter of the said Enoch & Esther was born the 27th Septr 1800
Betsy G daughter of the said Enoch & Esther was born the 27th Nov.r 1802
Eunice Noyes their daughter was born the 6th Dec.r 1804
William Marvin their son was born the 21st of Dec.r 1806
George W. Lee their son was born on the 13 day of Sep.r 1808

[p 2] Thomas Way Junr and Ame Merrick was Legally Joyn'd in Marriage on the first day of September AD 1753
Jane Elisabeth Daughter of the said Thomas & Ame born 27th May 1754
Grace daughter of the said Thomas and Ame was born 25th July 1755
Elisha son of the said Thomas and Ame was born June 13th 1757
Eunice Daughter of the said Thos. & Ama was born May 1st 1759
Thomas son of the said Thomas & Ame was born June ye 8th 1761
Ame Daughter of the said Thos & Ame was born March 14th 1763
John son of the said Thomas and Ame was born Decr 30th 1764
Delight Daughter of the sd Thos. & Ame was born February 5th 1767
Merick son of the said Thomas & Ame was born Decr 16th 1768
Daniel Shaw son of the said Thos & Ame was born June ye 28th 1772
Merrick Way died Oct.r 2d 1789 in the 11th year of his age
John Way died Nov.r 21 1785 in the 21 year of his age
Grace Way died July 10th 1760 in the 5th of his age

Lieut. Elisha Way and Miss Eunice Crocker was Legally Joyn'd in Marriage on the tenth day of January 1782
Elisabeth Daughter of the sd Elisha & Eunice born June 17th 1783
Eunice Daughter of the sd Elisha & Eunice was born Jany 3d 1786
Esther Daughter of the said Elisha & Eunice, born June 10th, 1788
Ame Daughter of the said Elisha & Eunice born December 20th 1790

[p. 3] Capt. Cullick Ely Junr & Miss Azubah Sill was Legally Jon'd in Marriage on the Second day of February AD 1790
Lucia S. Daughter of the said Cullick & Azubah was born Octr 17th AD 1791
Azubah Lee their daughter was born on the 29th day of September 1793

Sophia daughter of the sd Cullick & Azubah was born 25 day of July 1795
Russel and one other son who died at 12 days also born 13 day of Jany 1798
Elizabeth their daughter was born on the 13 day of September --- 1799
Lucia S died on the 6th day of November --- 1805

Mr. Ezra Gillet and Miss Amy Miner was Legally Joyn'd in Marriage on the 30th day of April AD 1789
Jonathan son of said Ezra & Amy was born June 6th day 1790
Sally daughter of said Ezra & Amy was born the 8 June 1793
Ezra son of the said Ezra and Amy was born on the 26th day of Jany 1802

[p. 4] Mr. Giles Tiffany & Miss Esther Peck was Legally Joyn'd in Marriage on the 25th day of October AD 1790

M.r Josiah Beckwith was Legally Joined in Marriage to Miss Mehetable Pearson on the 13th day of Septr 1770
Andrew their son was born on the 24th day July 1771
Anna their daughter was born on the 15th day June 1773
Richard Pearson their son was born the 30 day of August 1775
Josiah their son born 12 Augt 1779 & died 13 May --- 1780
Hannah their daughter born on the 13 day of March 1781
Mehetable their daughter was born on the 30 of August 1783
Eunice their daughter was born the 26 day of Feby 1786
                                                          1785
Josiah their son was born the 26th day of August 1789

Mr. Richard Lord was Legally Joyn'd in Marriage to Miss Nancy Mitchell of Saybrook on the 9th Day of December AD 1790
William Mitchell Son of said Richard & Nancy was born November 9th AD 1791
Richard Lynde son of said Rich. & Nancy was born 5th Decr 1793
Stephen Johnson Son of said Rich. & Nancy was born 26 March 1797
Sarah Ann daughter of the said Richard & Nancy was born 15th June 1799
John Mitchel their son was born the 18th day of November 1802

[p. 5] Lieut. Calvin Selden was legally Joyned in Marriage to Miss Phebe Ely on the 20th Day of September AD 1790
Roxana Daughter of the said Calvin & Phebe was born 19th May 1791
Exra Son of the said Calvin and Phebe born 17th Aug.t 1793

Capt. Abner Lord Junr & Miss Mary Selden was legally Joyned in Marriage on the 7th Day of November AD 1782
Betsy Daughter of said Abner & Mary was born Friday July 16th 1784
Tempe Lord their Daughter was born Monday April the 3d AD 1786
Sophia Daughter of the said Abner & Mary was born May 19th AD 1788
Polly Daughter of the said Abner & Mary was born Monday April 19th AD 1790
Abner son of the said Abner & Mary was born Monday Augt 6th AD 1792

[p. 6] M.r Ebenezer Mack & Miss Polly Harvy was Legally Joyn'd in Marriage on the 12th day of Aug AD 1787
Esther their Daughter was born on the 10th day of June 1788
Polly their Daughter was born the 2d day of Augt AD 1790
Salmon Son of the said Eb.r and Polly was born 20th day of July AD 1792
Charmis Son of the said Ebr and Polly was born the 6th day of March 1795
Chabris son of the said Ebenr & Polly was born the 5th of November 1797
Cornelius son of the said Ebenezer & Polly was born the 16th day of March 1800

Capt. Thomas Way Junr was Legally Joyn'd in Marriage to Miss Polly Lee on the 11th day of October 1787

Ezra Maynard was Joined in Marriage to Miss _____
Selden their son was born the 5th of May -- 1795
Orran their son was born on the 29th of March 1797
Ezra their son was born on the 16th day of June 1799
Whitman their son born the 4th of October 1804

[p. 7] M.r Benjamine Colt was Legally Joyn'd in Marriage to Miss Elisabeth Denison the 24th Day of December AD 1788
Nancy Daughter of said Benj & Elisabeth born 28 Octr 1790
Benjamine Gardner, Son of said Benja & Elisabh was born Jany the 10th AD 1793
Mary Sears their Daughter was born on the 19th day of Feb.y 1797
John Denison their son was born on the 13th day of August 1799
Joseph, Harris their son was born on the 10th day of August 1801
George Robert their son was born on the 24th day of Octr AD 1804

Mr Reynold Johnson was Legally Joyn'd in Marriage to Miss Phebe Smith, on the 12th day of February AD 1789
James Son of the said Reynold & Phebe was born 3rd August 1791
Elijah Son of the said Reynold & Phebe was born 7th Jany AD 1794
Benjamine their Son was born on the 17th of September AD 1795
Lucinda Daughter of the said Reynold & Phebe was born 30th of March AD 1796
Lilles Green Daughter of the said Reynold & Phebe was born 14th of August AD 1798
William son of the said Reynold & Phebe was born 23d November AD 1800
Charles B. son of the said Reynold & Phebe was born 23 of Jany AD 1804

[p. 8] Mr. John Ely and Miss Mary Lord both of Lyme was Legally Joyned in Marriage on the 25th Day of January AD 1791

Mr Silas Sill and Miss Hannah Griswold was legally Joined in Marriage on the 9th day of December AD 1779
Richard their Son was born on the 29th day of July AD 1781
Sarah their Daughter was born on the 5th day Aug.t 1785
George Griswold their Son was born on the 26th day of Jany AD 1792
Horace Son of said Silas & Hannah was born 5th March 1794
Polly daughter of the said Silas & Hannah was born 10th August 1796
Richard died at Albany September 10th 1809 and was buried in the family burying Ground of Col Francis nicol in Bethlehem 8 miles below Albany
Sally died at New York January 12th 1810 & was buried in the old Presbyterian Church Yard

Mr. Marvin Huntly & Miss Carolina Lord was legally Joyn'd in Marriage on the 9th day of April AD 1789
Sally Daughter of the said Marvin & Carolina was born May 10th 1790
Marvin Lord son of the said Marvin & Carolina was born the 25th Octr 1792
Hariot daughter of the said Marvin & Carolina was born 13th July 1795
a son of the said Marvin & Carolina was born 9th of May 1797 & died 14th June 1797
Marvin Lord their son died on the 8 day of June 1794
Asenath their daughter was born on the 8 day of Augt 1798
Marvin son of the said Marvin & Carolina was born the 10th Augt 1802
Carolina their daughter was born on the 15th day of Jany 1803
Abel Lord their son was born on the 12th day of June 1805
Lydia their daughter was born the 7 day of Augt 1807
Carolina wife of the said Marvin died the 25 day of Augt 1807
The said Marvin was Married to Mary Douglass 3d March 1808
Joseph Douglass son of Marvin & Mary born Sept. 23d 1809
Mary their Daughter born July 12, 1813

[p. 9] Mr Reu Huntly & Miss Abigal Mack was legally Joyned in Marriage on the 18th day of September AD 1788
Sally daughter of the said Reu & Abigal was born June 8th AD 1789
Spicer Mack son of the said Reu & Abigal was born the 1 day of April 1792
Lodwick Mack Huntly was born on the 7th day of March 1797
Reu Huntly & Eliza Booge was Joined in Marriage Feby · 1793
Phebe daughter of the said Reu & Eliza was born the 14th July 1793
Charles son of the said Reu & Eliza was born the 29th of Oct.r 1795

Ambrous Mack son of Abigail Mack born 11th Augt 1804 & died 3d Nov 1804

Mr Elisha Moor was married to Miss Elisabeth Smith Novr 14th AD 1771
Mr Elisha Moor died on the 3d of December AD 1773
Euncie, Daughter of said Elisha & Elisabeth was born 3d April 1774

Record of Doct.r Daniel Calkins' family after his removal to Lyme
Mary Wife of the said Daniel died on the 23 day of May AD 1777
Daniel Calkins was Married to Elisabeth Moor January 1 AD 1778
Ethelinda daughter of the said Danel & Elisabeth was born Oct 4th AD 1778
Daniel the Son of said Danel & Elisabeth was born April 1st AD 1780
William Smibert son of said Danel & Elisabeth was born May 15th AD 1781
Amos Son of the said Danel & Elisabeth was born March 18th AD 1782
Elisabeth Daughter of said Danel & Elisabeth was born July 15th AD 1785
Sarah Daughter of the said Danel & Elisabeth was born Oct.r 27, 1787
Elisha Son of the said Daniel & Elisabeth was born March 6th 1789
Doctr Daniel Calkins departed this life on the 19 day of June 1792 ocationed by the kick of a Horse ···

[p. 10]   Revd David Higgins & Miss Eunice Gelbert was Legally Joyned in Marriage on the 17 day of January AD 1788
David Son of said David & Eunice was born Aug. 2 AD 1789
James Gilbert Son of said David & Eunice was born Feby 22 AD 1791

Cap.t Silvester Mather and Miss Betsey Wait was Lawfully Jony'd in Marriage on the 22 Day of May AD 1788
Nancy Daughter of the said Silvester & Betsey was born May 2 AD 1790
George Son of the said Silvester & Betsy was born Dec.r 24th AD 1791
Lois G their daughter was born the 28 day of July 1794
Richard son of the said Silvester & Betsy was born the 31st day of Octr 1798
Sylvester their son was born on the 29th day of June 1801
Henry their son was born on the 4th day of July 1803
William their son was born on the 14 day of August 1808

[p. 11]   Gurdon Watrous jun was Legally Joyn'd in Marriage to Miss Lucy Huntly on the 1st day of November 1787
Richard Son of the said Gurdon & Lucy was born Octr 27th 1788
Daniel Son of the said Gurdon & Lucy was born 29th Oct. 1791 & died Oct. 30. 1792
Amos Huntly son of said Gurdon & Lucy was born 11th day of Octr AD 1792
Allen Son of the said Gurdon & Lucy was born 3 day of April AD 1795
Dan Huntly Son of the said Gurdon & Lucy was born 25th April AD 1797
Oliver Son of the said Gurdon & Lucy was born the 20th of March 1800
Erastus son of the said Gurdon & Lucy was born the 27th of April 1802

M.r Reynold Huntly was Legally Joyn'd in Marriage to Miss Jerusha Mack on   day of   AD 1780
William Son of the said Reynold & Jerusha was born 22 May AD 1781
Lydia Daughter of said Reynold & Jerusha was born 9h Sept AD 1782
Reynold son of said Reynold & Jerusha was born 30th April AD 1784
Stanton son of said Reynold & Jerusha was born 12 Novr AD 1786

112 LYME, CONNECTICUT, VITAL RECORDS

Jerusha departed this life the 10th day of February AD 1787
M.r Reynold Huntly was Legally Joyn'd in Marriage on the 26th day of August AD 1787 to Mrs Esther McNight
Fanny Daughter of said Reynold & Esther was born 19th June AD 1788
Daniel their Son was born on the 15th day of August AD 1792
Reynold Huntley Sr. died at Manlius Center, N.Y. Sept. 9 1839 age 83 years. (Taken from tombstone inscription)

[p. 12] Rev. Edward Porter & Miss Dolly Gleason both of Farmington was Legally Joyn'd in Marriage on the 26th day of Nov.r AD 17 [   ]

Mr. Neal Courtney and Mrs Lydia Mack was legally joined in Marriage on the 6th day of September AD [   ]
Alanson Son of the said Neal & Lydia was born November 28 [   ]

Mr. Ezra Lay and Lydia Ingraham was Lawfully Joyn'd in Marriage on the 10th day of December AD 1789
Demiss Harriot their daughter was born on the 9th day of Feby [   ]
Horace Son of the said Ezra & Lydia was born on the 27th day of Jan. [   ]
Francis Ingraham son of the said Ezra & Lydia was born 14th September [   ]
Ezra son of the said Ezra & Lydia was born the 4th day of Octr [   ]
Ezra the son died on the 12th day of October [   ]
Horace died on the 22d day of October [   ]
Lydia wife of the said Ezra departed this life 1st day of Decr [   ]
Dimis Harriot above mentioned died on the 14th day of February AD [   ]

[p. 13] M.r Silas Brooks was Legally Joyn'd in Marriage to Mrs. Elisabeth Beckwith on the 22nd day of Oct.r AD 1786
Silas Son of the said Silas & Elisabeth was born on the 22d of January 1788
Joseph Son of the said Silas & Elisabeth was born on the 17th of August AD 1789
John Son of the said Silas & Elisabeth was born the 12th of April AD 1791
Hannah their Daughter was born on the 18th day of Septr AD 1792

Cap.t Enoch Lee & Miss Hester Calkins was Legally Join'd in Marriage on the 20th day of January AD 1793
Mary Daughter of the said Enoch & Hester was born Decr 2d AD 1793
Delia Daughter of the said Enoch & Hester was born 17th of Jany AD 1796
Albert son of the said Enoch and Hester was born 11th March 1799
Irving son of the said Enoch and Hester was born 19th of Augt 1801
Hiram son of the said Enoch & Hester was born 12th of May 1805
Carolina daughter of said Enoch & Hester was born 25th day of Jany 1809

[p. 14] M.r Thomas Mather & Miss Nabby Mather both of Lyme was Legally Joyn'd in Marriage on the 27th day of November AD 1791
Thomas son of the said Thos. & Nabby was born on the 10th of June AD 1794
Oliver son of the said Thos. & Nabby was born on the 15th October 1796

Capt Thomas G. Wait & Miss Hannah Calkins was legally Joyn'd in Marriage on the 4th Day of July AD 1790
Maria their daughter was born September 10th day AD 1792
Lois daughter of the said Tho.s & Hannah was born 15th April AD 1793
Emile daughter of the said Thos. & Hannah was born 15th April AD 1795
Thomas Griswold son of the said Thos. & Hannah was born 30 Septr 1798
Richard son of the said Thos. & Hannah was born 8th Aug.t 1800

[p. 15] Mr. William Sill and Miss Jamima Starling was legally Joyn'd in Marriage on the 21st Day of January AD 1789
Amy Daughter of the said Willm & Jamima was born 24th Decr AD 1789
William Travis son of said Wm & Jamima was born Feby 8th AD 1792
Jerusha daughter of the said Wm & Jamima was born the 18th of June 1795

Polly Matson daughter of the said Wm & Jamima was born 30th of May 1797
Lucy daughter of said Wm & Jamima was born the 20th of April 1799
Clarrissa daughter of th said Wm & Jamima was born the 30 of March 1801

Mr Israel Ely and Miss Eunice Noyes both of Lyme was Legally Joyned in Marriage on the 15th day of May AD 1792
Eunice Daughter of the said Israel & Eunice was born Feby 12th AD 1793
Hannah Daughter of the said Israel & Eunice was born Aug.t 1st AD 1794
Judah Son of the said Israel & Eunice was born May 6th AD 1796
Israel Noyes their Son was born on the 15 day of Feby 1798
Calvin son of the said Israel & Eunice was born on the 4th Novr 1799
Anna their daughter was born on the 22d Octr 1802

[p. 16] Mr. Samuel Comstock was Legally Joyn'd in Marriage to Mrs Esther Lee on the 2d day of February AD 1769
Samuel Son of the said Samel & Esther was born August 29th 1772
Josephus Son of the said Samel Esther born Jany 2d AD 1777
Lucinda Daughter of the said Sam.el & Esther born April 10th AD 1779
Eleanor Daughter of the said Sam.el & Esther born Feby 20th AD 1781
Esther Daughter of the said Sam.el & Esther born May 2d AD 1783
Lee Son of the said Samuel & Esther was born Augt 25th AD 1785
John L. son of the said Sam.el & Esther was born Septr 25th AD 1787
Christopher son of the said Sam.el & Esther born Nov.r 7th AD 1789

Mr. Lynde Champen was legally Join'd in Marriage to Mrs. Hepzibah Chadwick on the 18th day of January AD 1785
Daniel son of the said Lynde & Hepzibah was born the 5th of March AD 1786
Hepzibah wife of the said Lynde departed this life April 20th AD 1786
Mr Lynde Champen was legally Join'd in Marriage to Ms Anne Rowland on the 23d day of June AD 1788
Charles Son of the said Lynde & Anne was born on the 9th of April 1789
Lynde Son of the said Lyne & Anne was born on the 7th of Decr AD 1790

[p. 17] Mr. Elisha Fitch was legally Join'd in marriage to Mrs Nancy Champlen on the 23d day of April AD --- 1787
Ladowick Son of the said Elisha & Nancy was born 9th of Feby 1788
Nancy Daughter of the said Elisha & Nancy was born 4 July 1790
Sally Daughter of the said Elisha & Nancy was born 16th March 1793

Mr Selden Warner was legally Join'd in Marriage to Mrs Dorothy Selden both of Lyme on the 5th day of June 1788
Selden Son of the said Selden and Dorothy was born March 15th AD 1789
Andrew Son of the said Selden and Dorothy was born Decr 29 AD 1790
Joseph Son of the said Selden and Dorothy was born Decr 3d AD 1792
Richard son of the said Selden & Dorothy was born 19 October AD 1794
William Henry the son of said Selden & Dorothy was born 18th Feby --- 1797
Mathew Griswold son of the said Selden & Dorothy was born 6th March 1799

[p. 18] Capt. John Burnham and Miss Betsy Smith both of Lyme was Lawfully join'd in marriage on the 18th of July AD 1792
Nancy Smith Burnham their daughter was born 4th of Feby AD 1794
Polly daughter of the said John and Betsy was born the 4th of August 1797
Polly daughter of the said Jn and Betsy died on the 10th day of May 1799
Betsey wife of the sd John Burnham died on the 25th day of Augt 1803

Mr. Calven Spencer was legally Married to Miss Mehehitable (Brainard) on the 1 day of November AD 1789
Nancy Daughter of sd Calvin and Mehitbe was born April 20th AD 1791
Hovy Daughter of sd Calvin and Mehitable was born Jany 16th AD 1793

114   LYME, CONNECTICUT, VITAL RECORDS

Jedediah son of the sd Calvin & Mehibable was born 29th Augt 1794
Calvin son of said Calvin & Mehitable was born 7th April 1796
Elijah son of the said Calvin and Mehitable was born 26 Decr 1798
Charles son of sd Calvin & Mehitable was born 20th Novr 1800

[p. 19] Majr Ezra Wait was legally join'd in Marraige to Miss Luica Miller on the 23d February AD 1792
Carlos Adolphus their son was born 12th Feby 1794
Ezra Smith son of said Ezra and Lucia was born 9th Novr AD 1795
Ezra Smith son of said Ezra & Lucia deceased the 5th day of Octr 1796
Lucia wife of said Ezra deceased on the 24th day of November 1796

Mr. Lay Mather and Miss Caroline Wade both of Lyme was legally join'd in Marriage on the 20th day of September AD 1792

[p. 20] This certifies that Peter Peck Clark & Miss Polly Smith both of Lyme were Married together on the 2d day of Octr AD 1793
            By David Higgins V.D.M.
Recorded this 7th day of October AD 1793
            pr David F. Sill Town Clerk

Capt Richard Mather and Miss Eunice Moor both of Lyme was legally Joined in Marriage on the 23d day of Octr AD 1790

Mr Elihu Huntly was Joined in Marriage to Mrs Naomia Brockway
Gideon their son was born on the 15th August 1777
Seth their son was born on the 1st May 1779
Jedidiah Brockway was born on the 1st May 1783
Sarah their daughter was born on the 28th May 1785
Deberoh their Daughter was born on the 8 March 1787
Mehitable their daughter was born on the 14 Jany 1789
Baruck their son was born on the 29th Jany 1792
Barna [bas] B. their son was born on the 23d May 1794
Amos their son was born on the 1st July 1796

[p. 21] Capt William Tinker 2d & Miss Elisabeth Turner of Montville was Legally Joyn'd in Marriage on the 30th day of November AD --- 1786
Mathew Son of the said Willm & El--- was born July 27th AD 1790
Lydia their Daughter was born the 25th day of June AD 1792
Sabra Daughter of the said Wm & Elisabeth was born 18th Augt 1794

Mr William Gee Junr was legally Joined in Marriage on the 27th day of Novr AD 1788 to Miss Sally Tinker ---
Sally Daughter of said Wm & Sally was born Feby 15th Ad 1790
William Son of the said William & Sally was born Jany 9th AD 1793
Silas Son of the said William & Sally was born on the 23d of Septr 1794
Matthew Son of the said Wm & Sally was born on the 14th day of Jany 1798
Polly daughter of the said Wm & Sally was born on the 7th day of March 1802
Elinda their daughter was born on the 25 day of Jany 1805
Betsy daughter of the said Wm & Sally was born the 20 day of June 1808

[p. 22] Mr Pardon Ryon was legally Joyn'd in Marriage to Miss Rebecca Minor July the 19th AD 1792
Pardon Son of the said Pardon & Rebecca was born July 8th AD 1793
Mercyann daughter of the said Pardon & Rebecca was born the 2d Octr 1796
James Son of the said Pardon & Rebecca was born on the 5th Jany 1799
Harriot W. daughter of the said Pardon & Rebecca was born on the 8th Jany 1801
Emmeline their daughter was born on the 7th day of Feby 1805
Maryette --- was born the 12 day of May 1807

Eliza Caroline their daughter was born 1st day of May 1809
Fanney Almena their daughter was born the 7 September 1811
Mr Pardon Ryon Died --- 31st March 1813
Mrs Rebecca Ryon Died --- 5th April 1813

David Moody Jewett Esq. was Married to Miss Neaome Hurlbut, of New London on the 28th day of Octbr AD 1790
Phebe Taber, Daughter of the said David & Neame was born June 18th AD 1791
Nancy Daughter of the said David & Neamae was born April 18th AD 1793 and departed this life on the 31st day of October AD 1793
David Jewett Son of the said David & Neaome was born 16th Octr 1794
John Griffing their son was born on the 2d of Decr AD 1796
David their Son departed this life on the --- 1797

[p. 23] Mr. Richard Wait junr was Legally Joined in Marriage to Miss Polly Wade January 29th AD 1794

Mr. Nathaniel Matson was Legally Join'd in Marriage to Miss Polly Sill on the 8th day of October D _____ 1791
Polly the wife of Natha Matson Died   January   1802
This certifies that on the 25th day of September AD 1806 Mr. Nathaniel Matson and Miss Anna Ely both of Lyme were Lawfully joined in Marriage.
            David Huntington
            minister of the Gospel
Amos Polly Son of Amos Polly was born 1 July AD 1789

[p. 24] Mr Moses Sill of East Windsor was Legally Joined in Marriage to Miss Assenath Coult Jany 19th AD 1794

Mr Asahel Roland junr Legally Join'd in Marriage to Miss Hannah Greenfield the 16th day of October AD 1791
Carolina Daughter of the said Asahel & Hannah was born Decr 13th 1791
Asahel son of the said Asahel & Hannah was born 11th February 1796
John Greenfield son of the said Asahel & Hannah was born 28th Feby 1799
[Mary daughter of Asahel & Hannah] (see L.R. Vol 36 P. 80)

[p. 25] Mr Thomas Lonergan was Legally Joined in Marriage to Miss Fanney Bournes on the 4th day of October _____ AD 1790
Polly Daughter of the said Thomas & Fanney was born ---
Atteis [Alles] Daughter of said Thomas & Fanney was born ---

Mr Zelophead Ely was Legally Join'd in Marriage to Miss Elisabeth Starling on the 5th day of November AD 1793
Jacob Son of said Zelophd & Elisabeth was born August 30th AD 1794
Lyman Son of the said Zelophd & Elisabeth was born June 21st AD 1796
Elisabeth daughter of the said Zelophd & Elizabeth was born July 27 AD 1798
John Russel their son was born on the 24th of Septr -- 1800
Parnel their daughter was born the 13th of Augt 1802
Hiram their son was born on the 28th day of July 1805

[p. 26] Mr Jedediah [H.] Lewis was Legally joined in Marriage to Miss Sabra Lee Nov.r 24th AD 1793 by Elder Jason Lee

Mr. Alfred Wills of Whitestown in the State of New York was legally Joined in Marriage to Miss Abigail Lee of Lyme on the 17th day of January in the year 1804

Mr. Joseph Mather & Miss Zelinda Gould both of Lyme was married together December 27th AD 1792
            Certified Pr David Higgins V D M --
David Son of the said Joseph & Zelinda was born Octr 22d AD 1793

James Gould Son of the said Jos & Zelinda was born Octr 9 AD 1795
Moses Son of said Joseph & Zelinda was born the 3d Jany 1798
Joseph Son of said Joseph & Zelinda was born the 8 day of May 1800

[p. 27]   Mr. Ezra Chadwick was legally Joined in Marriage to Miss Sally Lay on the 30th day of January AD 1784
Lurany Daughter of the said *Danel & Sally was born Jany 30th 1785
Hepzibah their Daughter was born the 18th day of March 1787
Phebe their Daughter was born the 17th of Octr AD 1790
Charles Chauncy their Son was born 3rd of Octr AD 1793
*(Prob. Ezra "Danll" in Original)
Mr Eusebus Dodge was legally Joined in Marriage to Miss Anne Merchant on the 2 day of February AD 1794
Certified by Matthew Griswold Jun. Justice of the Peace
John Son of the said Eusebus & Anne was born March 24th AD 1795
Jeremiah son of the said Eusebus & Anna was born 25 of March 1798
Nancy their daughter was born on the 2d day of May 1800
Polly their daughter was born on the 29th day of June 1803
Eusebus their son was born on the 22d day of May 1806

[p. 28]   Capt John Hughs was Legally Joined in Marriage to Miss Jamima Burnham on the 7th day of Jany 1788
Joseph Higgins their Son was born March 31 day 1794
Polly daughter of the said John & Jamimah was born March 1797
John Gordon son of the said John & Jamimah was born 1th Jany 1802
Betsey Maria Daughter of the said John & Jemima was born Feby 20th AD 1808

This may Certify all concerned that Stephen Otis and Lucy Wedger both of Lyme were married together on the first day of May AD 1794 By David Higgins V.D.M.
Haydon Son of the said Stephen and Lucy was born Novr 23 AD 1794
Stephen Son of the said Stephen and Lucy was born Septr 27th AD 1796
Edward Son of the said Stephen and Lucy was born Feby 6th 1798
Charlotte Daughter of said Stephen & Lucy was born May 29 1806

Capt James Ransom was married to Mrs Abigail Comstock on the 8 day of February 1810

[p. 29]   Mr George Waid Junr was legally Joined in Marriage to Miss Martha Mather on the 4th day of December 1791.
Dan Son of the said George & Martha was born 10th August 1794
Harriot daughter of the said George & Martha was born 22d August 1800
Eunice daughter of the said Geo. & Martha was born the 19th Sept 1802
Almira daughter of said George & Martha born ----
Martha Ann daughter of said George & Martha
Wade born ---

Mr Samuel Perkins was legally Joined in Marriage to Miss Polly Jewett both of Lyme on the 18th Decr 1780
Polly Daughter of the said Samel & Polly was born Septr 25th AD 1781
Polly died on the 18th day of July   AD 1783
Joseph their Son was born 7th Augt 1783 & died 10th March AD 1786
Polly their Daughter was born on the 14th day of July AD 1785
Samuel their Son was born on the 2d day of May   1787
Lucretia their Daughter was born 11th Jany 1791 & Died 24th Feby 1791
Rogers Son of the said Samel & Polly was born 9th May 1792
Sophia their Daughter was born on the 7th March 1794

[p. 30]   Mr John Brown and Miss Anne Brockway both of Lyme was legally joined in marriage Septr 18th AD 1794 as appears by a Certificate from William Noyes Esqr

Naby daughter of the sd Jn & Anne was born on the 4th Augt 1795
Harry son of the said John & Anne was born on the 3rd Novr 1797
William son of the sd John & Anne was born on the 22d Augt 1801
John son of the sd John & Anne was born on the 24th Octr 183 [1803]

Mr. Isaac Tillitson was married to Miss Content Fox of New London on the 29th day of August --- AD 1789
Isaac son of the said Isaac & Content was born 12th April AD 1790
Chauncy their son was born on the 25th day of Augt AD 1793
Reuben their son was born on the 26th day of March 1795

[p. 31]   Mr. Peter Pearson was legally joined in marriage to Miss Parnial Corah on the 15th day of November --- AD 1781
Richard son of the said Peter & Parnal was born 9th Jany AD 1783
Phebe daughter of the sd Peter & Parnial was born 8th Novr - AD 1784
Anna their Daughter was born on the 15th day of Feby - AD 1787
Peter their Son was born on the 25th day of February AD 1789
Rachal their Daughter was born on the 3rd day of Jany AD 1791
Julany their Daughter was born on the 7th day of March 1793
Abijah their son was born Aug 14, 1795
Sarah their daughter was born June 22, 1798
Mary their daughter was born June 21, 1804
Births of three children named above taken from original family records in possession of Chas. W. Pierson
Nov. 10, 1927   Attest William Marvin, Town Clerk

Mr. Jason Lee Junr and Miss Jane Griswold both of Lyme was legally joined in Marraige on the 18th day of Feby AD 1795
Joseph Woodbridge Son of the said Jason & Jane was born 28 Jany 1796
Matthew Griswold their son was born on the 4th day of June 1799
William Bramble was married to Abigail Shipman
Daniel Son of William & Nabby Bramble was born 4th Feby - 1792
William Son of the sd Wm & Nabby was born on the 23rd Decr - 1793
Nabby daughter of the sd Wm & Nabby was born on the 12th Decr - 1795
Polly daughter of the sd Wm & Nabby was born on the 9th Jany 1798
Frankling son of the sd Wm & Nabby was born on the 16th July 1800
Jeheal son of the said Wm & Nabby was born on the 2nd Augt 1802
Hester daughter of the sd Wm & Nabby was born on the 17th July 1804
Orrin Shipman their son was born on the 15th day of Septr 1807

[p. 32]   Mr. Abner Beckwith of Lyme was legally married to Miss Hannah Comstock of Montville on the 29th of Feby AD 1782
Abner son of the said Abner & Hannah was born Decr 24th AD 1784
Hannah wife of said Abner Departed this Life Decr 25th AD 1784
Abner Beckwith was legally joined in marraige to Miss Parnal Ingraham on the 16th day of January -- AD 1787
Samuel Ingraham their son was born August 3d AD 1788

Mr. Gurdon Avery was legally joined in marraige to Miss Eunice Powers on the 1st day of January AD 1792
Eunice Daughter of the said Gurdon & Eunice was born 4 Feby AD 1793
Gurdon their son was born on the 19th day of June AD 1795

[p. 33]   Mr Joseph Lee & Miss Sally Champion both of Lyme was legally joined in marraige March 30th day AD 1795

Mr George Champlin was joined in marraige to Miss Eunice Anderson on the 26 day of January 1800
George their son was born on the 30 day of August 1802

Maryann their daughter was born the 17th day of March 1805
Daniel A. their son was born on the 26th day of August 1807
Abigail their daughter was born on the 22 day of August 1810
John Gardiner their son was born on the 19 day of February 1813
Henry their son was born on the 26 day of February 1815
Henry above said died on the 12th day of December 1816
Nathan their son was born on the 11th of November 1817
Eunice their daughter was born on the 27th of July 1820

Mr Joseph Smith & Miss Eunice Smith both of Groton was legally joined in Marraige on the 4th day of April A.D 1790
Gilbert Tenant, their son was born on the 1st day of Novr AD 1791
Joseph Denison, their son was born on the 4th of May AD 1794
Mr. Joseph Smith, 4th died August 15th 1797
Eunice Burnham, formerly wife of Joseph Smith, 4th, died August 17th 1809

[p. 34] Mr. Nathan Boon and Miss Sally Peck was legally joined in marriage on the 10th day of June - AD 1795
Mr. Joseph Tillotson & Lucinda Munsell was legally joined in marriage on the 21st day of January, AD 1795
Joel their son was born on the 16th day of January AD 1796
Joseph, son of said Joseph & Lucinda was born 5th April 1798

[p. 35] Mr. Nathaniel Shaw Woodbridge and Miss Lois Mather, was legally joined in marriage May 5th AD 1796

Mr. John Cook Smith and Miss Amy Chapman was legally joined in marriage 25th Feb. 1796 as appears by a certificate from Elder Jason Lee
John, son of said John and Amey was born 27th day of March 1797
Daniel, son of the said Jno and Ame was born 26th Dec. 1798
Lucy daughter of the sd Jono & Ame was born the 25th of Feby. 1801
Reuben, son of the said John & Ame was born 5th day of May, 1803
Ame wife of the sd John C Smith died on the 10 day of April 1805

[p. 36] Mr. Caleb Wood and Miss Lois Chapman was legally joined in marriage on the 15th day of Decr 1796 as appears by certificate from Elder Jason Lee

Richard McCurdy Esqr. and Miss Ursula Wolcott Griswold daughter of Mr. John Griswold was legally joined in marriage on the 10th Sepr 1794 as appears by certificate from Lathrop Rockwell, Minr of this church in Lyme
John Griswold, son of the said Richard & Ursula was born 28th Novr AD 1795
Charles Johnson son of the said Rich'd & Ursula was born 7th Decr 1797
Robert Henry, son of the said Richard & Ursula was born 24th April 1800
Richard Lord, son of the sd Richard & Ursula was born 29th May 1802
Alexander Lynde son of the sd Rich'd and Ursula was born 19th July 1804
Saryann their daughter was born on the 25th day May 1807

[p. 37] Mr. Clark Peck of Bloomfield in the state of New York and Miss Carolina Hall of Lyme was legally joined in marriage on the 18th day of January AD 1797, as appears by certificate from Lathrop Rockwell Pastor of the sd Church in Lyme

Mr. Harvy Roberson was legally joined in marriage to Miss Martha Fellows on the ---
William Fellows their son was born on the 6th of March 1803
Ephanoditus their son was born on the 1st day of December 1804

Mr. Alpheus Thompson of Montville was legally joined in marriage to Miss Maryann Phebe Reed of Lyme on the 4th day of May in the year 1790, as per certificate
Fanney Daughter of the sd Alpheus & Phebe was born 31th May 1791
Isaac, their son was born on the 7th day of June AD 1794
Lyna, their daughter was born on the 23rd of Octr 1796

Erastus, their son was born on the 5th day of June 1803
Maryan Phebe, wife of the said Alpheus died the 19th day May 1805

Mr. David Perkins and Miss Eunice Rogers was legally joined in marriage on the 1st day of Feb'y 1797 as appears by a certificate from Elder Jason Lee

[p.38]   Mr. Rufus Huntly was legally joined in marriage to Miss Hannah Freeman on the 22d day of February AD 1797 as appears by certificate from Elder Jason Lee

This certifies that George Appleby and Clarine B. Tucker was joined in marriage on the 26th day of January 1815
By me, Nathn Matson, Justice of Peace

[p. 39]   This certifies that Elisha Watrous & Martha Griswold both of Lyme was married Decr 5th AD 1795
by me William Williams Just Pae

This certifies that Mr. Enoch Lay & Miss Hannah Lay was joined in marraige on the 12th day of June AD 1806
by me David F. Sill, Justice of Peace

Mr. Shadrack Gillet and Miss Elizabeth Peck both of Lyme was joined in marriage on the 27th day of November AD 1792
Reynold son of the said Shadrack & Elizabeth was born on the 10th April 1793
Shadrack son of the said Shadrack & Elizabeth was born on the 13th Jany 1795 and died on the 23rd day of October ---- 1796

Moreley Clark son of John Clark was born the   June 1796

[p. 40]   Mr. Tory Maxon and Miss Betey Champlin was married 3 August 1782
Amos Champlin their son was born on the 3d day of May AD 1783
Nathan son of the said Tory & Betsy was born on the 16th of April AD 1785
Betsey Daughter of the said Tory & Betsy was born June 19th AD 1792

Twins   (Salley Latimer their daughter was born on the 16th day of March 1796
         (and Phebe Peck their daughter was born on the said 16 day of March 1796

This may certify all concerned that Mr. Charles Ely & Miss Betsey Perkins both of Lyme were married together on the 22nd of Decr AD 1796
by David Higgins V.D.M.

[p. 41]   Mr. Nathaniel Shaw Woodbridge & Miss Eliza Mumford was legally joined in marriage on the 24th day of June AD 1790
Polly S. daughter of the said Nathl & Eliza was born 26th day of June 1791
Lucretia M. daughter of the said Nathl & Eliza was born 10th day of Octr 1792

Eliza, wife of the said Nathaniel departed this life Feby 21st 1795
Nathaniel S. Woodbridge was legally joined in Marriage to Miss Lois Mather on the 5th day of May AD 1796
Nathaniel S. Woodbridge son of the said Nathl & Lois was born on the 17th day of February --- AD 1797
Nathaniel S. Woodbridge the Elder died June 17th AD 1797

Mr. William Coult and Miss Anne Denison was legally joined in marriage on the 2d day of October --- AD 1796
William Ely, Son of the said Willm & Anne was born 24th June 1797
Abigail Matson daughter of the sd Wm. & Anne was born 6th July 1800
Anna Maria daughter of the said Wm. & Anna was born the 9th of July 1802
Anna Maria died on the 5th day of Oct. 1802 aged three 3 months
Anna wife of the said Wm. died the 11th of Oct. 1802 aged 29 years and 6 months
Mr. William Coult was joined in marriage to Miss Mary Marvin on the 11th day of November 1807

120   LYME, CONNECTICUT, VITAL RECORDS

[p. 42]   Mr. Richard Royce was legally joined in marriage with Miss Eunice Ames on the 12th day of February AD 1797

Mr. Elijah Wattrous was married to
Joshua M. their son was born on the 22nd day of August in the year 1800
Urrin their   was born on the 7th day of January 1805
Eleazer their son was born on the 27th day of April Anno Dom 1807

Mr. Matthew Rowland was legally joined in marriage to Miss Saley De Wolf both of Lyme on the 23 day of April AD 1797
Maria daughter of the sd Mat & Sally was born on the 7th day of July 1798
Richard son of the sd Matthew & Sally was born on the 26 day of July 1800

[p. 43]   Mr. Dudley Sterling and Miss Phebe Sill was legally joined in marriage November 16th 1797

Mr. Noah Beebe Junr and Miss Sybal Rathbun was legally joined in marriage on the 26th day of August   AD 1784
Olive daughter of the said Noah & Sybal was born 14th Septr AD 1787
Fanny daughter of the said Noah & Sybal was born 13th Augt AD 1790
Caty daughter of the said Noah & Sybal was born 19th AD 1792
Amasa son of the said Noah & Sybal was born 25th July AD 1794
William Lord Son of the said Noah & Sybal was born 8th Augt AD 1796

Jon son of Uzel & Mehitable Johnson was born on the 24 of March 1794
Huldah daughter of the sd Uzel & Mehitable was born on the 1st of April 1797
David, son of the sd Uzel & Mehitable was born on the 17th of May 1800
Daniel, son of the sd Uzel & Mehitable was born on the 28th of June 1802
Rhoda, daughter of the sd Uzel & Mehitable was born on the 4th of March 1805

[p. 44]   Mr. Asa Jones was joined in marriage with Polly Moor on the --- day of April in the year AD 1791
Asa, son of the said Asa & Polly was born on the   day of April 1792
Polly daughter of the said Asa & Polly was born on the 26th September 1793
Amasa, son of the said Asa & Polly was born on the 17 of Jany 1796
Hannah, daughter of the said Asa & Polly was born on the 16 of Jany 1798

Mr. Nathaniel Mather was legally joined in marriage with Miss Eunice De Wolf on the 19th day of Feb'y 1795
Joanna their daughter was born Decr 11 AD 1795
Nathaniel their son was born on the 12 day of August 1799
Nancy Maria their daughter was born 27 March 1804
Francis William their son was born the 30 June 1807
Joanna Mather died Dec. 17 1826 aged 31 years.

[p. 45]   Mr. William Lay junr of Lyme was joined in marriage to Miss Betsy Parsons of East Hampton the 9th day of Octr AD 1792
Abigail daughter of the said Wm. & Betsy was born 20th Feby 1795
Polly daughter of the said Wm. & Betsy was born 5th April 1796
Patty daughter of the said Willm & Betsy was born 30th July 1798
Robert Parsons, son of the sd Wm. & Betsy was born 20th Septr 1800
Betsy, daughter of the sd Willm and Betsy was born on the 13th day of June 1805

Mr. Smith Watrous was joined in marriage the 2d of June 1794 to Miss Eunice Marvin -----
Eunice, daughter of the sd Smith & Eunice was born 26th May 1795
Lee Marvin, their son was born on the 28th day of Octr 1796

[p. 46]   George Bigelow Swaney was born 4th July AD 1774

James Denison Son of John &   Denison was born Feby 10th 1813
Phebe Denison daughter of the above born Sepr 5th 1815

William Denison their son born Octr 6th 1816
John Denison their son born Jan'y 7th 1819
Richard & Nancy, twins born March 30th 1823

Mr. John Munsell junr was joined in marriage with Miss Azubah Huntly on the 25th day of Decr AD 1783
Azubah, their Daughter was born on the 25th day of Septr AD 1784
Mehitable, their Daughter was born the 5th day of May AD 1789
Betsey, their Daughter was born on the 10th March 1791
John, their Son was born on the 10th day of Feb'y AD 1793
Joseph, their Son was born on the 17th day of Decr 1796
Sherman, son of the said John & Azubah was born 20th Septr 1799

[p. 47] Mr. Richard Sparrow of Harrison County in the State of Virginia was legally joined in marriage to Miss Union Smith of Lyme on the 13th day of May AD 1798 by Lathrop Rockwell Pastor of the First Church in Lyme
Mary Howland, daughter of the said Richard & Union was Born on the 7th day of March in the year ---- 1799

Capt. Nehemiah Smith was joyned in marriage with Miss Betsy Gee on the 22d day of June ---- AD 1788
Erastus, Son of the said Neh & Betsy was born May 1st day 1791
Charles, Son of the sd Nehemiah & Betsy was born 24th of Jany 1793
Betsy, daughter of the sd Nehemh & Betsy was born 24th of April 1795
Sukey, daughter of the sd Nehemh & Betsy was born 13th of Augt 1796
James, son of the sd Nehemiah & Betsy was born 10th March 1799
Abigail, daughter of the sd Nehemiah & Betsy was born 18th Septr 1800

[p. 48] Mr. Zopher Gee was married to Miss Esther Beckwith on the 13th Day of November Ad 1788
John son of the said Zopher & Esther was born 30th of Augt --- 1789
Salmon Son of the sd Zopher & Esther was born the 16 of Octr --- 1792
Esther Daughter of the sd Zopher & Esther was born the 16 day of July --- 1794
Esther wife of the sd Zopher died on the 31 day of August 1794
Zopher Gee was married to Lura Jones of Hebron Septr the 10th 1795
Anson Son of the said Zopher & Laury was born the 3rd of Jany 1799
Samuel Son of the sd Zopher & Laura was born the 9th of Feby 1801
Lury their daughter was born on the 26 day of March 1805

Mr. Nathan Tinker was joined in marraige to Miss Sarah Gee on the second day of December ---- AD 1784
Nathan son of the sd Nathan & Sarah was born on the 31t Day of April 1785
Salmon son of the sd Nathan & Sarah was born the 22d day of Novr 1788
Sarah wife of the said Nathan died on the 14th day of Decr 1788
Salmon son of the said Nathan & Sarah died on the 15th day of Jany 1789
Nathan Tinker was married to Lucy Smith on the 21st of March 1790
Anna daughter of the sd Nathan & Lucy was born on the 4th of July · 1791

Sally daughter of the sd Nathan & Lucy was born on the 8h of Feby 1793
Anne daughter of the sd Nathan & Lucy died on the 6th of Septr 1793
Charles son of the said Nathan & Lucy was born & died 26 of Octr 1795
Luramey daughter of the sd Nathan & Lucy was born the 6 of Jany 1797
Charles their son died on the 17th day of July   1796

[p. 49] Mr. Jasper Huntly was married to Miss Azubah Mack on the 31st day of December AD 1768
Sarah daughter of the sd Jasper & Azubah was born July 26th 1771
Hannah daughter of the sd Jasper & Azubah was born 20th Novr 1773
Ezra son of the said Jasper & Azubah was born the 1st day of Jany 1777

Azubah daughter of the said Jasper & Azubah was born 23 Novr 1782
Jasper son of the said Jasper & Azubah was born the 13 day of Novr 1790
Hannah their daughter died on the   day of Novr 1790
Azubah their daughter died on the   day of June 1784
Jasper their son died on the 6th day of December 1790
Jasper Huntley senior died on the 12th day of June 1816

Mr. Silas Robbins was married to Hannah Peck on the 13th day of December 1781.
Rufus son of the said Silas & Hannah was born 27 Sepr 1783
Abner son of the said Silas & Hannah was born 6 Augt 1786
Lura daughter of the sd Silas & Hannah was born 19 Novr 1788
Phebe daughter of the sd Silas & Hannah was born 10 May 1792
John Son of the said Silas & Hannah was born 20th Augt 1794
John their Son died on the   day of February 1797

[p. 50]   Mr. Silvanus Tinker and Miss Joanna Dishon was legally joined in marraige on the 22nd day of Octr 1789
Sally Tinker their daughter was born on the 26th Augt 1791
Polly daughter of the sd Silvs & Joanna was born 27th April 1794
Lucy Smith daughter of the sd Silvs & Joanna was born 16 Jany 1798
Joanna daughter of the sd Silvs & Joanna was born 22d of Feby 1801
Fanny C. Tinker their daughter was born 27th Octr 1805
Eliza B. Tinker their daughter was born 25th Octr 1808
Catherine C. Tinker their daughter was born 24th Octr 1813

Mr. David Lay and Miss Lucy Ingraham both of Lyme was legally joined in marraige on the 8th day of February 1798
Oliver Ingraham son of the said David & Lucy was born 16th November 1799
Sarahann their daughter was born on the 22nd of May 1803
Laura their daughter was born on the 24 of May 1806
Lucy their daughter was born on the 19 of Septr 1810
George Cowles son of David & Lucy born 25th Novr 1815
Sarahann daughter of David & Lucy died 27th Feby 1813

[p. 51]   Mr. Stephen DeWolf and Miss Nabby Beckwith was legally joined in marriage on the 3d day of Jany AD 1799

Mr. Abner Rowley was Joined in marraige to Miss Anne Wade on the 22d day of December AD 1796
Lydia the daughter of sd Abner & Anne was born the 29th Octr 1798
Thomas son of said Abner & Anne was born the 2d of May 1800
Joseph son of said Abner & Anne was born the 3d day of April 1804
Anna their daughter was born on the 3d day of Feby 1806
Anna wife of the said Abner died on the 21st Novr 1810 in the 36 year of her age.
The said Abner Rowley was born on the 22d day of September 1771

Mr. John Parsons was married to Miss Lois Wait Octr 1 AD 1786
Joanna daughter of the said Jno & Lois was born on the 31 July 1787
Abigail daughter of the said John & Lois was born on the 12 Octr 1788
Phebe daughter of the said John & Lois was born on the 15 April 1790
William son of the said John & Lois was born the 30th July 1791
Lucy daughter of the said Jno & Lois was born the 9 July 1793
Lydia daughter of the said Jno & Lois was born the 14 July 1795
Marshfield son of the said Jno & Lois was born on the 11 March 1798
A son born & died on the 19th day of August 1800
Richard Wait son of the sd John & Lois born 19th Augt 1801
Thomas Griswold their son was born on the 19th Novr 1803
John son of the sd John & Lois was born the   day of Decr 1805
George son of the sd Jno & Lois was born the 2d day of Jany 1808

Elizabeth daughter of the sd John & Lois was born the 30th July 1810
Lucy Parsons daughter of John & Lois Parsons died on Tuesday May the 12th AD 1818

[p. 52]   Mr. Zadock Darrow was married to Miss Lucy Lord both of Lyme on the 25th day of June AD 1791
Lucy Way daughter of the said Zadock & Lucy was born 30th Oct. 1792
Sally Lord daughter of the said Zad'k & Lucy was born 24th Dec. 1794
Emma daughter of the sd Zadock & Sally was born 19th March 1797

Mr. James Ely and Miss Catharine Hayes was legally joined in marriage on the 30th day of June 1768
Richard Hayes their son was born on the 28th March 1769
James, son of the sd James & Cath was born 26th February AD 1771
Dorcas, their daughter was born on the 30th Octr 1773
Phebe their daughter was born on the 30th Novr 1775
Aaron, son of the sd James & Catharine was born 16th Octr 1778
John, son of the sd James & Catharine was born 7th March 1781
Cate, their daughter was born on the 26th May 1783
William their son was born on the 13th July 1785
Calvin their son was born on the 24th March 1788
Calvin, deceased on the 24th day of November AD 1790
Dorcas, their daughter deceased on the 8th day of March 1795

[p. 53]   Mr. Seth Ely Junr was married to Miss Phebe Marvin on the 14th day of April 1799 as appears by a certificate from Mr. Higgins.

This certifies that James F. Nason and Lydia Tibbetts were legally joined in marriage on the evening of the 30th September AD 1832 by the undersigned.
John S. Rogers, Justice of Peace

Mr. Samuel Hudson was married to Rhoda Rogers both of Lyme on the 20th day of April AD 1798, By Daniel Minor

Capt. Oliver Peck & Mrs Amy Lee both of Lyme were legally joined in marriage on the 29th day of Aug. 1797
3 augt.) Oliver son of the said Oliver & Amy was born on the 12th Novr 1798
1801   )

[p. 54]   Mr. Elisha O. Ely & Miss Fanny Ely was legally joined in marriage on the 6th day of May ---- 1798

Mr. Daniel Tillotson was legally joined in marriage to Miss Lucy Lewis on the 22nd day of October AD 1790
Elizabeth their daughter was born on the 4th day of March AD 1792
James, son of the said Daniel & Lucy was born the 13th Septr 1794
Epheraim their son was born on the 5th day of December 1796
Salome, their daughter was born on the 2d day of August 1799

Mr. David Rogers was legally joined in marriage to Miss Betsy Chadwick on the 22nd day of March 1797
Ezekiel son of the said David & Betsy was born 22nd day of Feby 1798
John, son of the sd David & Betsy was born 2d day of April 1800

[p. 55]   Mr. John M. Lee & Miss Anne Beckwith was joined in marriage on the 3rd day of February ---- 1788
Nancy daughter of the said Jno & Anne was born 18th Novr 1790
John son of the said John & Anne was born 21st Novr 1793
Savelion son of the said John & Anne was born 13th Octr 1796
Julia daughter of the said John & Anne was born 7th April 1799
Edwin, their son was born on the 25th day of July 1801
Elisha their son was born on the 25th day of January 1804

Orlando E. their son was born the 8 day of June 1807
Richard Theodore their son was born the 7 day June 1810
Abel Huntington son born May 24th 1812
Abby Frances daughter born June 18th 1816

Mr. Elias Hudson was married to Miss Lucinda Miller on the 25th day of June in the year 1799
Nancy daughter of the sd Elias & Lucinda was born 3d June 1799
Louisa S. Hudson of sd Elias & Lucinda born Feby 13th 1806
Silas M. their son born Jan'y 5th 1809

Hipzebah Chadwick, daughter of Allen & Mary Chadwick was born 29th March 1797

John Thompson was married to Susanah Willson
George their son was born the 17th day of October AD 1802
Mary Ann Thomsn their Daughter was born 15 March 1810

[p. 56]   Mr. Gurdon Watrous was joined in marriage to Miss Theody Beckwith on the 16th day of Novr AD 1762
Gurden, son of the sd Gurdon & Theody was born on the 5th day of May 1764
Huldah, daughter of the sd Gurdon & Theody was born 15th April 1766
Daniel, son of the sd Gurdon & Theody was born 27th April 1769
Theody, daughter of the said Gurdon & Theody was born 28th Septr 1771
Rhoda daughter of the said Gurdon & Theody was born 12 May 1774
Theody, wife of the said Gurdon died on the 28th day of June 1775
Gurdon Watrous was again married to Elizabeth Paton 21st June 1778
Gideon son of the sd Gurdon & Elizabeth was born on the 28th June 1779
Asa, son of the sd Gurdon & Elizabeth was born on the 28th July 1781
Polly, daughter of the sd Gurdon & Elizabeth was born on the 17th June 1783
Asa, son of the sd Gurdon & Elizabeth died on the 14th day of Sept 1785
Gilbert, son of the sd Gurdon & Elizabeth was born on the 16th Octr 1785
William, son of the sd Gurdon & Elizabeth was born on the 30th Novr 1787
Silvanus, son of the sd Gurdon & Elizabeth was born the 5th April 1790
Elizabeth, daughter of said Gurdon & Elizabeth was born 25th Feb'y 1793
Benjamin, son of the sd Gurdon & Elizabeth was born the 21st Decr 1796

Mr. William Ely Pearson was married to Miss Mehitible Reeve of Long Island on the ----
Samuel son of the said Wm. & Mehitable was born 14th Octr 1782
Elisha son of the said Wm. & Mehitable was born 27th May 1785
Sarah daughter of the sd Wm & Mehitable was born the 2d July 1788
Reeve, son of the sd Wm & Mehitable was born the 7 May 1792
Mehitable, daughter of the sd Wm. & Mehitable was born the 19th Decr 1794

[p. 57]   Mr. David Matson was legally joined in marriage with Miss Lois Sill on the 25th day of January 1797
Wed 1st   John Sill son of the said David & Lois was born 15th day of Novr 1797
      2d   George son of the said David & Lois was born 27th day of July 1799
      3d   Polly, daughter of the said David & Lois was born 29th July 1801
      4th   Richard, son of the said David & Lois was born 29th Sepr 1803
      5th   Eunice, daughter of the said David & Lois was born 15 Decr 1805
            Richard their son died at Albany the 16th December 1807
      7th   David son of sd David & Lois on the 30th day of August 1812
      6th   Richard was born on the 18th day of January AD 1810

Mr. Stephen Starling was legally joined in marriage with Miss Polly Brown on the 24th day of September AD 1798
One child stillborn was born 1 Oct. 1799
Stephen, their son was born on the 5 May 1801

John, their son was born the 16 day of Octr 1803
*Erratta - David Matson is misplaced.

[p. 58] Mr. George Beckwith Junr was married to Miss Penelope Beckwith both of Lyme on the - day of May AD 1785
Penelope, daughter of the said Geo. & Penelope was born 26th July 1785
Allen, son of the said Geo. & Penelope was born 12th Augt AD 1786
Fabius, son of the said Geo. & Penelope was born 5th Feb'y AD 1788
Polly, daughter of the said Geo. & Penelope was born the 3rd Novr AD 1789
Patience, daughter of the said Geo. & Penelope was born the 20th July AD 1791
Erastus, son of said Geo. & Penelope, was born the 11th May AD 1793
George, son of the said Geo. & Penelope, was born the 24th Dec. AD 1794
Maria, daughter of the sd Geo. & Penelope was born the 26th Dec. AD 1796
Emmilu, daughter of the sd Geo. & Penelope was born the 29th Septr AD 1798
Eliza, daughter of the sd Geo. & Penelope was born the 4th April AD 1800
Mr. Joshua Griffing was married to Miss Betsy Johnson both of Lyme on the 14th day of Feb'y 1781
Johnson, son of the sd Joshua & Betsy was born 17th April 1782
Anne, daughter of the sd Joshua & Betsy was born 8th April 1784
Joseph, son of the sd Joshua & Betsy was born 25th June 1794
Charles, son of the sd Joshua & Betsy was born 8th August 1796
William, son of the sd Joshua & Betsy was born 29th Decr 1798

[p. 59] Mr. Joseph Strickland was married to Miss Phebe Lewis on the first day of March AD 1792, as appears by certificate
Nancy, daughter of the sd Joseph & Phebe was born 16th day of Feb'y 1793
Charles William, their son was born on the 27th day of May AD 1795
Fanny, daughter of the said Joseph & Phebe was born the 13th day of June 1797
Eliza, daughter of the said Joseph & Phebe was born the 26th day of June 1799
James Lewis, son of the said Joseph & Phebe was born the 3 of October 1801
Mariette daughter of the sd Joseph & Phebe was born 11 June 1804

Mr Samuel DeWolf was married to Miss Susannah Keeney both of Lyme on the 17th day of January AD 1782
William, son of the sd Saml & Susannah was born the 6th October 1782
Jabez, son of the sd Saml & Susannah was born the 29th Feb'y 1784
Joseph, son of the sd Saml & Susannah was born the 9th Decr 1785
Phebe, daughter of the sd Saml & Susannah was born the 15th Septr 1787
Hannah, daughter of the sd Saml & Susannah was born the 1st March 1790
Sally, daughter of the sd Saml & Susannah was born the 12th March, 1792
Martha, daughter of the sd Saml & Susannah was born the 26th April 1794
Polly, daughter of the sd Saml & Susannah was born the 20th March 1796
Samuel, son of the sd Saml & Susannah was born the 1st July 1798
Daniel, son of the sd Saml & Susannah was born the 8th May 1800
Josiah, son of the sd Saml & Susannah was born the 2nd Feb'y 1802
Anne, daughter of the sd Saml & Susannah was born the 25th Septr 1803

[p. 60] Mr. Stephen Miner was born on the 10th day of November 1756
Miss Lydia Allen was born on the 7th day of July AD 1763
Mr. Stephen Miner was married to Miss Lydia Allen on the 28th day of August 1783
Elizabeth, daughter of the said Stephen & Lydia was born 31st May 1784
Daniel, son of the said Stephen & Lydia was born 21st Novr 1785
Mercy, daughter of the sd Stephen & Lydia was born on the 1st Decr 1787
Nancy, daughter of the sd Stephen & Lydia was born the 28th Octr 1789
Allen, son of the said Stephen & Lydia was born the 18th Septr 1791
Fanny, daughter of the sd Stephen & Lydia was born the 17th Octr 1793
Polly, daughter of the sd Stephen & Lydia was born the 22d Jany 1796

Stephen, son of the said Stephen & Lydia was born on the 17th May 1798
Charles, son of the said Stephen & Lydia was born on the 17 June 1800
Mr. Daniel Clark was married to Miss Mary Baker on the 31st day of March AD 1768
Lucindia, daughter of the sd Daniel & Mary was born 24th Jan'y 1769
Silence, daughter of the sd Danel & Mary was born 11th May 1770
Dudley, son of the said Danel & Mary was born 4th Feb'y 1772
Phebe, daughter of the sd Daniel & Mary was born 11th Decr 1773
Daniel, son of the sd Daniel & Mary was born 18th Feb'y - 1776
Mary, daughter of the sd Danel & Mary was born 5th March - 1778
Arnold, son of the sd Daniel & Mary was born 12th Aug - 1779
Susannah, daughter of the sd Danel & Mary was born 14th Novr 1782
Reuben, son of the sd Daniel & Mary was born 14th Feby 1785
Asahel, son of the sd Daniel & Mary was born 10th April 1788

[p. 61] Mr. Dudley Clark was married to Miss Edey Bump on the 9th day of January AD 1791
Richard, son of the sd Dudley & Edey was born 22d May 1791
Patty, daughter of the sd Dudley & Edey was born 22d April 1793
Sally, daughter of the sd Dudley & Edey was born 2d April 1795
Arnold, son of the sd Dudley & Edey was born 26th July 1797
Dudley, son of the sd Dudley & Edey was born 20th July 1799
Polly, daughter of the sd Dudley & Edey was born 6th March 1801

Mr. Harris Tinker was legally joined in marriage to Miss Elizabeth Deshon on the 15th day of November AD 1792
Elizabeth, daughter of the sd Harris & Elizabeth was born 24th day of Augt AD 1793
Harris, son of the said Harris & Elizabeth was born 5th of June AD 1797
Joseph Deshon, son of the said Harris & Elizabeth was born the 4th of August 1800
Harriot, their daughter was born the first day of April 1803
Teressa, their daughter was born the 14th day Octr 1807

[p. 62] Mr. Thomas Griswold was joined in marriage with Miss Ethelinda Caulkins on the 19th day of April AD 1801 as appears by a certificate from Moses Warren Junr Esq.

Mr. William Champion of Lyme, State of Connecticut, and Esther Ross of Westerly in the State of Rhode Island was lawfully joined in marriage before me
Paul Maxson, Justice of Peace Westerly February 15, AD 1801
James Ross, their son was born the 22d day of Feb'y 1802
William Sands, their 2d son was born the 13th day Jan'y 1804
Cynthy Maria, their daughter was born on the 27th day of Octr 1806
Calolina Matildea their daughter was born 19th Feb'y 1809
Henry Lorenzo their son born Feb'y 6th AD 1811
Charles Frederick their son born Feb'y 21st 1813

[p. 63] Mr. William Dessent Hockridge was born in the County of Essex in England on the 25 day of March   1776 and was married to Miss Huldah Rogers on the 8th day of January 1797
William son of the said Wm & Huldah was born 28th May 1798
John Dessent their son was born on the 12th day of Feby 1801
Charles their Son was born on the 13th day of Novr 1802
William Dessent Hockridge was drowned at Sea the 26 Decr 1802

Mr. William Hall of the city of New York was legally joined in marriage to Miss Sarah Sill on the 8 day of December 1806
Caroline their daughter was born on the 5th day of Septr 1807
Mrs. Sarah Hall died at New York 12th January 1810
Mr. William Hall & Miss Mary T. Haines were married to Each other 17th June 1811

William Son of said William & Mary born 16th March 1812
Sarah Daughter of sd Wm & Mary was born 1st Sept 1813

Mr. Jonathan Hall was joined in Marraige with Miss Betsy Lord both of Lyme on the 8th day of April AD 1800
Jonathan son of the sd Jono & Betsy was born the 17th April 1801
Ezra son of the said Jono & Betsy was born on the 6th of Jany 1803
Reuben Lord their son was born on the 4th day of Feby 1805

[p. 64] Samuel Holden Parsons was born 14th May 1737 D S
Mehitable Mather was born on 5th March 1743 d
Mr. Samuel H. Parsons & Miss Mehitable Mather both of Lyme was legally joined in Marraige on the 10th Septr 1761 N S
William Mather son of the sd Samel & Mehitable was born 5th July 1762
Lucy daughter of the sd Samel & Mehitable was born 8th Novr 1764
Thomas son of the sd Samel & Mehitable was born 12th Decr 1767
Enoch son of the sd Samel & Mehitable was born on the 5th Novr 1769
Mehitable daughter of the sd Samel & Mehitable was born on the 24th Decr 1772
Phebe daughter of the sd Samel & Mehitabel was born on the 25 Jany 1775
Samel Holden son of the sd Samel & Mehitabel was born on the 31st Dec 1777
Margaret Ann their daughter was born at Reading 15th Feby 1780
Margaret Ann died of Measels at Middletown 28th Augt 1783
Margaret their daughter born at Middletown on the 1st June 1785
Thomas died at Lyme of a disentary on the 8 day of Decr 1778
Genel Samel H. Parsons was drowned in the Big Beaver River near the Connecticut reserve on the 17th day of Novr 1789 Aged 52 years six months & 16 days & buryed on the bank of sd river near its conflux with the Ohio river
    Recorded at the particular request of William W Parsons
    David F. Sill Register

Mr. George Bissell was legally joined in Marraige to Miss Parnal Minor on the 22d day of August AD 1801 as appears by a certificate from Elder Jason Lee

Mr. Thomas Pilgraim was legally Joind in Marraige to Miss Dorcas Ransom on the 31st day of May 1801
Benjamin son of the sd Thomas & Dorcas was born 5th Feby 1802
Lydia their daughter was born on the 5 of Novr 1803
Thomas J. their son was born on the 19th of Novr 1805

[p. 65] Mr. Allen Smith was born on the 20th of July in the year 1762
Miss Hannah Peck was born on the 13 day of April 1767
The said Allen Smith & Hannah Peck was Joined in Marraige on the 22d Novr 1786
Lucretia daughter of the said Allen & Hannah was born the 4th day of February 1788
Esther daughter of the said Allen & Hannah was born the 2d day of Januy 1790
Nathaniel son of the said Allen & Hannah was born the 24th day of May 1791
Deborah daughter of the said Allen & Hannah was born the 27th day of Decr 1794
Sears Peck Son of the said Allen & Hannah was born the 3d day of July 1798

Mr. Abel Smith was legally joined in Marraige to Miss Polly Gee on the   day of August 1798 as appears by Certificate from M. Warren Esq.

Edward Rowland son of Evi Rowland was born on the 22d day of Feby 1778
Joseph Brooks was born the 1st April in the year 1796
William Bump was born on the 28th day of Novr 1787
William Comstock was born on the 9th March 1782

[p. 66] Mr. Dan Huntly was legally Joined in Marraige to Miss Lovice Peck on the 15th day of February 1780
Elizabeth daughter of the said Dan & Lovice was born 25th day of Feby 1794

Mr. Abner Rowley was married to Anna Wade on the 22d day of December 1796
Lydia their daughter was born 29th October 1798
Thomas their son was born the 2d May 1800

Mr. William Watrous was legally Joined in Marraige to Miss Betsey Reed September 16th AD 1798
Harry Watrous son of said William and Betsey was born October 27th AD 1799

Mr. Silas Brown was Joined in Marraige to Miss Sarah Tinker on the 2d day of January 1803
Thomas their son was born on the 19th day of Octr 1803
Samuel Prentice their son was born on the 24th day of Feby 1805
George Beckwith their son was born on the 8th day of June 1807
George Beckwith above died about 24 Octr 1808
George Beckwith son of the said Silas was born 24th July 1809
Carolina Canady their daughter was born the 19 day Octr 1811
Anson Sandford their son was born the 9th Octr 1814
Charles Nathan Was born Oct 4th 1819

[p. 67] Mathias Wesner Baker was married to Neomi Bates on the 16th day of April in the year 1789
Mathias Wesner son of the said Mathias & Neomi was born 7 April 1790
Mary daughter of the sd Mathias & Neomi was born 2d Decr 1791
Sophia daughter of the said Mathias & Neomi was born 6th May 1793
Elizabeth daughter of the sd Mathias & Neomi was born 11th April 1795
John Herman son of the sd Mathias & Neomi was born 9th July 1796
Lucy daughter of the said Mathias & Neomi was born 15th Feby 1798
George Herron son of the said Mathias & Neomi was born 10th April 1799
Catherine daughter of the said Mathias & Neomi was born 21st Feby 1801

Mr. Thomas Smith was legally joined in marriage to Miss Azubah Wade on the 30th day of January 1799
Thomas Merrit son of the said Thos. & Azubah was born the 11th of Novr 1799
Maryann their daughter was born the 3d of Decr 1803

Hiram Still son of Pember W. Still was born 26th Novr 1802
Eliza, daughter of sd Pember & Susanah was born 31 July 1804
Hannah, their daughter was born the 9 day of December 1807

[p. 68] Mr. Alexander Allen was legally joined in marriage to Miss Mary Chadwick on the 7th day of October AD 1800
Betsy, daughter of the sd Alexr & Mary was born on the 16th day of July 1801

Mr. Reynold Lord was legally joined in marriage to Miss   Loomis of Colchester on the 23rd day of April 1802

Mr. Elijah Mack & Lydea Tillotson was legally joined in marriage (as certified by Elder Lee) the 4th of April 1799
Dorcas, daughter of the sd Elijah & Lydia was born the 25th day of Feb'y 1800
William, son of the sd Elijah & Lydia was born the 7 day of July 1802
Joshua Tillotson, their son was born on the 16th Septr 1804

Mr. Roswell Champion was legally joined in marriage to Miss Jamimah Mather on the 21 day of February 1788
Sylvester son of the sd Roswell & Jamima was born the 11th Novr 1788
Henry, son of the sd Roswell & Jamemah was born the 13th July 1790
Roswell, son of the sd Roswell & Jamemah was born the 9th of March 1793
Daniel, son of the sd Roswell & Jamemah was born the 26th of Decr 1798
John, son of the sd Roswell & Jamemah was born the 17 of April 1801

[p. 69] Mr. Ezra Mather & Miss Phebe Wade was legally joined in marriage the 8th day of November A.D. 1795
Ezra, son of the said Ezra & Phebe was born the 11th Octr 1797
Phebe, daughter of the sd Ezra & Phebe was born the 27th of Octr 1799
Orlando, son of the sd Ezra & Phebe was born the 28th of May 1802
Robert Miller, their son was born on the 6th March 1804
Orlando, their son died on the 5th day of Septr 1804
Orlando[2], their son was born the 5 of October 1807
Mr. Ezra Mather died February 27th 1808

[p. 70] Mr. Samuel Buckingham 3d of Saybrook was legally joined in marriage to Miss Johanna Matson of Lyme on the 8th day of March in the year 1798

This certifies that on the 1st day of Jan'y 1800 Mr. Alexander Hyde was joined in marriage to Miss Mary Burnham by me Lathrop Rockwell

Mr. Stephen D. Sellard was legally joined in marriage to Miss Polly Spencer on the 15th day of April in the year 1802
Calvin Spencer their son was born on the 28th day of February 1803

Mr. Joseph Reed was married to Miss Phebe Reed
Abigail, daughter of the sd Joseph & Phebe was born the 20th Decr 1784
Sally, daughter of the sd Joseph & Phebe was born the 14th Decr 1786
Caroline daughter of the sd Jos & Phebe was born the 22d of April 1789
Nancy & Laura their daughters was born on the 4th of June 1791
John, son of the said Joseph & Phebe was born the 18th of Decr 1793
Henry, son of the said Joseph & Phebe was born the 11th day of May 1796
Emelia, daughter of the sd Joseph & Phebe was born 13th day of Feb'y 1799
Charles William, their son was born on the 18th day of Decr 1802

[p. 70] Mr. John G. Jewitt of East Haddam & Lois Lay of Lyme are joined in marriage to each other on the 6th of Feb'y 1803

Mr. Gideon Waterhous was joined in marriage to Miss Phebe Rhodes on the 12th day of February 1803

[p. 71] Mr. Charles Smith & Lois Parsons was joined in marriage to each other on the 11th day of March 1801
Mary, daughter of the sd Charles & Lois was born 25th of Decr 1801
Frances, daughter of the sd Charles & Lois born May 10 1804
Eunice Burnham, daughter of sd Charles & Lois born Sept. 8, 1806
Julia, daughter of the sd Charles & Lois born Oct. 16, 1809
Wm. Parson,s son of sd Charles & Lois born 2nd June 1813
Lois Smith, wife of Charles Smith died Augt. 24th 1819
This certifies that on the 28th of March 1821 Charles Smith of Lyme was by me married to Phebe Parsons 2nd of Sd Lyme according to the laws of the State of Connecticut for the solemnization of marriage
Test. Lathrop Rockwell, Clerk
Charles Henry son of Charles & Phebe Smith born May 14 1822

[p. 72] Mr. Stephen Tinker was joined in marriage to Miss Polly Strickland on the 28th day of April AD 1796
Maria, daughter of the sd Stephn & Polly was born 26th of March 1797
Lyndia, daughter of the sd Stephn & Polly was born the 20th of Feb'y 1799
Emily, daughter of the sd Stephn & Polly was born the 23d of April 1801
Stephen, son of the sd Stephen & Polly was born on the 23d of July 1803

Mr. Elijah Mather was joined in marriage to Miss Sally Lord both of Lyme on the 5th day of October in the year 1797

Reuben Lord son of the sd Elijah & Sally was born on the 15th of Feb'y 1800
Sally Miranda their daughter was born on the 18th of Oct 1801
Elijah Peck, son of the sd Elijah & Sally was born on the 22nd of May 1803
Cap't Ichabod Smith was legally joined in marriage to Miss Abigail Marvin on the   day of   179
and on the   day of   the sd Abigail was delivered of two children one of which died the other is
Abigail Marvin daughter of the sd Ichd & Abigail was born the 20th of Aprl 1802

[p. 73]   Mr. Stephen Peck & Miss Elizabeth Johnson was legally joined in marriage on the 23d day of August AD 1801
Mrs. Elizabeth Peck above mentioned died on the 7th of Novr 1803

Mr. Ezekiel Huntly & Miss Ruth Miner was legally joined in marriage on the 8th day of September AD 1803
William their son was born the 19th day of July 1804

Mr. Richard Leech & Hepzebah Mather were joined in marriage on the 27th day of November AD 1799
Elisha Ely son of the sd Rich & Hepzh was born the 2d of Septr 1800
Richard Montgomery their son was born 30 of May 1803
Elisha Ely abovementioned died the 9th day of Decr 1802

Cap't Joseph Burnham was legally joined in marriage with Mrs. Eunice Smith on the 10th day of May AD 1798
Samuel Guardner their son was born on the 17th of June 1799 and died on the 18 day of said June 1799
James son of the sd Joseph & Eunice was born the 2d Septr 1800
William Joseph their son was born 1st May 1809
Mrs. Eunice Burnham died August 17th 1809

[p. 74]   Mr. Josef Ransom was legally joined in marriage to Miss Charlotte Benham on the 18th day of Novr 1798
Louisa their daughter was born on the 1st day of Sepr 1800
Vincent their son was born on the 1st day of March 1802
Eliza, their daughter was born on the 18th day of Novr 1803
Joel Benham son of the sd Jose & Charlotte was born 19th April 1805

Mr. James Gillet was legally joined in marriage to Miss Elizabeth Peck on the 29th day of November A.D. 1798
    as appears by a certificate from Lathrop Rockwell
Dudley Peck, son of the sd James & Elizabeth was born on the 30th day of Novr 1799

Mr. Ezekeil Wade was joined in marriage to Miss Lydia Way on the   day of   in the year
James son of the said Ezekeil & Lydia was born the 29th of Octr 1801
Sarah, daughter of the sd Ezekeil & Lydia was born on the 7th of April 1804

[p. 75]   Mr. Moses Mather was joined in marriage to Miss Sally Champion on the 21 day of June 1801 by Elder Jason Lee.
Sally, daughter of the sd Moses & Sally was born the 19th day of May 1802
Sally, wife of the sd Moses died on the 14th day of June 1802
Sally, their daughter died on the 19th day of Augt. 1802
This certifies that Mr. Moses Mather & Miss Hannah Champion was lawfully married together pr George Atwell Elder
Lyme Octr 12, AD 1802
Sallyann daughter of the said Moses & Hannah was born 30th Decr 1803

Mr. Reuben Champion was legally joined in marriage to Miss Esther Chadwick on the 27th day of December 1780
Betsy, daughter of the sd Reuben & Esther was born 27th Septr 1781
Susannah, daughter of the sd Reuben & Esther was born 12th Novr 1783
Anne, daughter of the sd Reuben & Esther was born 16th of Octr 1785
Reuben, son of the said Reuben & Esther was born 12th of Decr 1787
Amon, son of the said Reuben & Esther was born 1 day of Feb'y 1790
Israel, son of the said Reuben & Esther was born 16th of July 1792
Esther, their daughter was born on the 5th day of Decr 1794
Carolina, their daughter was born on the 20 day of April 1801

[p. 76]   Mr. Stephen Champion was legally joined in marriage to Phebe Moshier on the 28th day of January AD 1776
Sally, daughter of the sd Stephen & Phebe was bcrn the 11th day of Novr 1777
Hannah, their daughter was born on the 1st day of Jan'y 1779
Charlotte, their daughter was born on the 10th day of June 1782
Sebree, son of the said Stephen & Phebe was born the 25th day of Augt 1785
Fanny, their daughter born 9th May 1789 & died the 9th of March 1791
Fanny, their daughter was born on the 3rd day of April 1791
Phebe & Polly, twins their daughters was born on the 5th of April 1794
Lydia, their daughter was born on the 6th day of March 1797
Miranda, their daughter was born on the 30th day of July 1799
Chauncy, their son was born on the 4th day of April 1802

Mr. Rufus Sturtevent was joined in marriage to Miss Mary Manning on the   day of
Anna, their daughter was born 5th September 1795
Harriot, their daughter was born the 28 of January 1798
Josiah, their son was born on the 12th of May 1800
Mary, their daughter was born on the 10th of May 1802
George Foster their son was born on the 4 of March 1805

[p. 77]   Mr. William Clark was married to Miss Jamimah Rogers on the 22d day of January AD 1807

Mr. William Wait was legally joined in marriage to Miss Rebecca Avery on the 24th day of January 1805

Mr. Darius Harden was married to Irane Scofill on the 28th day of October 1802
Nancy, their daughter was born on the 10th March 1804
Eliza, daughter of the said Darius & Irenea born 4 Octr 1805
Darius, their son was born on the 23d day of Sepr 1807
George W. their son was born the 7 day of Jan'y 1810
Irane their daughter was born the 24 of August 1812

[p. 78]   Mr. Daniel Jacobs was joined in marriage to Miss Polly Chadwick on the 14 day of June 1798
Erastus, their son was born the 3d day of Septr 1801
William, their son was born the 8 day of Septr 1803
Mary, their daughter was born the 12 day of July 1805

Roger Griswold Esquire was joined in marriage to Miss Fanny Rogers of Norwich on the 27th day of Octr 1788
Augustus Henry son of the sd Roger & Fanny was born the 27th Octr 1789
Charles Chandler son of the sd Roger & Fanny was born the 8th Feb'y 1791
Matthew son of the sd Roger & Fanny was born on the 13th Septr 1792
Frances Ann, their daughter was born on the 15th Jan'y 1795
Roger Woolcott, son of the sd Roger & Fanny born on the 15th March 1797
Eliza Woodbridge, their daughter was born on the 7th April 1799

Marian, their daughter was born on the 4th of Jan'y 1802
William, son of the sd Roger & Fanny was born the 22d March 1804

Mr. John Murdock was joined in marriage to Miss Hepzibah Miller on the 20 February 1793
John son of the sd John & Hepzibah was born the 7th May 1796
Lucy Miller their daughter was born on the 27 Feb'y 1799

Amos Tinker to married to   Tucker
Lynde their son was born 25 December AD 1785
Rachel, their daughter was born on the 21st Octr 1787
Polly, their daughter was born on the 10th March 1791
William their son was born on the 15th April 1795
Henry Mather their son was born on the 8th January 1799
Sally, their daughter was born on the 11th October 1803

[p. 79] Mr. Benjamin Beckwith was married to Lucy Watrous on the 12 day of February 1805
Maryan their daughter was born the 15th Novr 1805

Mr. Seth Lee was legally joined in marriage to Miss Anna Hill on the 22 day of March 1798
Christopher, son of the said Seth & Anne was born 13th Jan'y 1799
Seth Lee son of the said Seth & Anna was born 17 Octr 1800
Elizaann daughter of the sd Seth & Anna was born 20 Augt 1802
Betsy daughter of the said Seth & Anna was born 18 Decr 1804
Richard, son of the said Seth & Anna was born 30th October 1806
Abby Wells daughter of the said Seth & Anna was born 23 March 1809
Mary, daughter of the said Seth & Anne was born 14 Augt 1811

Mr. John Tubbs was married to Miss Elizabeth Bush 13 June 1785
Abigail daughter of the said John & Eliza was born on the 19 May 1786
Hannah daughter of the sd John & Elizabeth was born on the 25 Septr 1788
Jamima daughter of the sd John & Eliza was born on the 2d of July 1791
John G. son of the said John & Eliza was born on the 26th Decr 1794
Job son of the said John & Eliza was born on the 23rd April 1797
Eliza daughter of the sd Jno & Eliza was born on the 13 Decr 1805
Elizabeth Tubbs wife of John Tubbs died Ap'l 12 1822

[p. 80] Marriage of Majr William Sterling
Maj'r William Sterling was married to Miss Jerusha Ely of Saybrook on the 11th day of September AD 1794
Robert Ely son of the sd Wm & Jerusha was born 20th March 1796
Thomas Sill son of the sd Wm & Jerusha was born 5th April 1798
Willm Erastus son of the sd Wm & Jerusha was born 9th June 1801
Jerusha Lay their daughter was born on the 25 May 1803
Robert died on the 7th day of March 1806

Mr. John Mather Junr was married to Miss Sally Cleveland Royce on the 9th day of May AD 1804
John Oliver, son of the sd John & Sally born on the 25th day of March 1805
Elisha Royce their son was born on the 21 day of Novr 1806

Capt. Joseph Smith 2d was legally joined in marriage to Ms Lucy Harris of New London on the 28th day of August 1794 as appears by a certificate from Mr. Henry Channing.
Emelia daughter of the sd Joseph & Lucy was born on the 10th Octr 1795
Almira daughter of the sd Joseph & Lucy was born the 11th of Feb'y 1797
Sophronia their daughter was born on the 18 day of Jany 1799
Carlos Adolphus son of the sd Jos. & Lucy was born the 10 of July 1801
Livingston Harris their son was born on the 7th day of July 1803
Nelson Hamilton their son of the said Jos. & Lucy was born the 5 Aprl 1806

Abby Carolina their daughter was born 18 day of March 1808
Leonard Whiting their son was born the 23d day of April 1810

[p. 81]   Mr. Uzal Johnson & Miss Mehitable Baker was joined in marriage on the   day of
Thomas, son of the said Uzal & Mehitbl was born 27 of Feb'y 1792
Phebe, their daughter was born on the 12 Jany 1794
Sally, their daughter was born the 12 Feby 1796
Nancy, their daughter was born the 26 Augt 1798
Polly, their daughter was born the 27 Septr 1800
Betsy their daughter was born the 25 Novr 1802

Mr. Walter Goold was joined in marriage to Miss   Latimer
Lydia, their daughter was born on the 23rd day of Octr 1785
Betsy, their daughter was born on the 22 day of Decr 1786
Henry Latimer, their son was born on the 12 Day of Octr 1788
Walter H., their son was born on the 12 day of Septr 1790
Ethelinda, their daughter was born on the 15 day of Septr 1792
Charles C. Pinckney, their son was born the 4 day of Octr 1794
Hosmer Johnson their son was born the 25 day of April 1798
Horace Octavius their son was born the 12 day of Augt 1800
Gardner, their son was born on the 24 day of Octr 1802
Saly Christophers, their daughter born the 7 day of March 1805

[p. 82]   Mr. Abner Beckwith and Miss Joanna Clark both of Lyme was legally joined in marriage on the 23rd of Septr 1806

Mr. Asahel Chapman was married to
Eliza their daughter was born on the 21st day of Septr 1800
John their son was born on the   day of Feby 1803
Plyney their daughter was born the   day of   1805

Mr. Matthew Cooley was married to Miss Prudence Ray 21 Octr 1798
Matthew Bull is the first child
John How their son was born the 12th day of Decr 1801
Job Miller Walker their son was born the 15 day of May 1806
Matthew Bull their son was born the 25 day of May 1800
Samuel Ingraham Watrous their son was born 11 March 1808
                                                                1810
Mr. Joseph Waid was legaly joined in marriage to Miss Hannah Sanders on the 2d day of August 1812

[p. 83]   Mr. David Wait was legally joined in marriage to Miss Sophia Eliza Wood on the 20th day of April AD 1806
Mary Lay their daughter born February 25th AD 1807
Richard son of David & Sophia born July 13th 1808 and died October 10th 1808
Richard son of David & Sophia was born September 1st 1809
Elizabeth Hale their daughter was born August 14th 1811
Emily Maria their daughter was born July 3d 1813

Mr. William Lord was joined in marriage to Miss Harriot Ely on the 20th day of May AD 1802
William Russell their son was born on the 27th Augt 1803
Harriot Ely their daughter was born on the 8 day of April 1805
David Ely their son was born on the 5 day of Feb'y 1807

[p. 84]   Mr. John Maynard Junr. was married to Miss Lydia Havens on the 23d day of Novr AD 1791

Fanny their daughter was born on the 8th of Octr 1792
Nancy their daughter was born on the 4 of Decr 1793
Charlotte their daughter was born the 7th of March 1794 [must be error]
John Beebe their son was born the 15th of Decr 1796
Jerusha their daughter was born the 2d of Septr 1798
Polly their daughter was born the 7th of May 1800
Lydia their daughter was born the 15th of Jany 1803
Harriot their daughter was born the 20 of Decr 1806
(Also Betsey C - Mar Chas D. Sherman) [written in at later date]

The ageses of the children of James Goold & Mary his wife
Elisha Goold son of the sd James & Mary was born 28 March AD 1771
William Goold son of the sd James & Mary was born 17 Decr AD 1773
Polly, their daughter was born on the 11th day of August 1777
Sally, their daughter was born on the 26th day of Decr 1779
Sophia their daughter was born on the 1 day of Jany 1782
Alford son of the sd James & Mary was born 12 of May 1784
Naoma their daughter was born the 28 of Feb'y 1786
James, their son was born the 12 day of Novr 1789
Betsy, their daughter was born the 8 day of Septr 1792
Nabby, their daughter was born the 1st day of March 1795

[p. 85] Mr. Edward Hill was joined in marriage to Miss Betsy Lee on the 26th day of November AD 1801
Christopher Edward their son was born on the 21st February 1803
Elizabeth Lee their daughter was born on the 9 day of December 1804
Maryann Phebe their daughter was born on the 26th day of June 1807
Lucia Marvin their daughter born 22d January 1810
Margaret Jane their daughter was born 3d May 1812
William Henry their son was born 15th January 1816

Capt. Matthew Peck was joined in marriage to Miss Lois Hall on the 18th day of September AD 1808
Phebe Dorr their daughter born 1st Octr 1809
Mary Haines their daughter was born 26th June 1811
Lucy Burnham their daughter born 11th January 1814

Mr. Mather Rogers was joined in marriage to Miss Sally Wicks on the 29 February 1800
Polly daughter of the sd Mather & Sally was born the 24 Octr 1800
Esther daughter of the sd Mather & Sally was born the 2d Octr 1804
Sally daughter of the sd Mather & Sally was born 9 March 1807
Carolina their daughter was born on the 19th day of Augt 1809

[page 86] Capt. Richard Huntly was legally joined in marriage to Miss Sally Kimbell on the 21 day of May in the year 1807
Sophia daughter of the sd Richard & Sally was born on the 29th Decr 1808
Elijah Kimball, son of sd Richard & Sally was born on the 9th May 1811
Emiline Deliverance their daughter born on the 29th Septr. 1813
John Whittlesey, their son was born on the 6th day Augt 1816

Mr. Elkanah Huntly was joined in marriage with Miss Anna Bishop on the 14 day of November 1799
Nancy daughter of the sd Elkanah & Anna was born the 1st Octr 1800
James son of the sd Elkanah & Anna was born the 18th Feby 1802
Jonathan Bishop their son was born on the 23 day of Jany 1804
Emela their daughter was born on the 4th day of June 1806
Sally, their daughter was born on the 4th day of August 1808
5 other children

[page 87] Mr. Elijah Rogers was joined in marriage to Miss Hannah Beckwith on the 22d day of Octr 1807
William Ely their son was born on the 9 of April 1809

Mr. Samuel Harvey & Miss Marsilva Ely were on the 16 day of March legally joined in marriage ----
Samuel their son was born on the 16th day of Feby 1807
Betsy their daughter was born on the 23d day of April 1809

Mr. Ezra W. Miller was legally joined in marriage to Miss Sally Terry on the 15th day of August 1809

Isaac Jones of Sayrook was married to Eunice Champion of Lyme on the 1 day of December in the year 1806
Alexander their son was born on the 11 April 1807

[page 88] Mr. David Caulkins was joined in marriage to Miss Polly Peck on the 1st day of January 1806
Maryann their daughter was born on the 19th Feby 1807
Lydia Lee their daughter was born on the 2d Feby 1809
Emiline their daughter was born on the 21st April 1811
Ann Catharine Tinker their daughter was born on the 10th Sept. 1813
Stephen Lee, their son was born on the 8th June 1816

Mr. Gideon Watrous 2d of Lyme was married to Miss Phebe Rhodes of Barrington on the 12th Feby ---- 1803
John Rhodes, their son was born on the 12 day of April 1804
George Payton their son was born on the 15th day of May 1807

[page 89] Captn Mechail Huntly & Miss Marcy Remick Higgins was joined in marriage on the 26 day of October AD 1806
Their son Silvanus Higgins was born on the 11th day of Decr 1808
Their son Giles Leonard was born on the 17th day of Augt 1810
Their son Joseph William was born on the 21 day of April 1812

Mr. Theophilus Morgan of Groton was legally joined in marriage Miss Mary Hinkley of Stonington on the 10 of May 1795
Mary, daughter of the sd Theopu & Mary was born 10th March 1796
Henry, son of the sd Theopu & Mary was born 30 March 1797 and died on the 18 day of April ---- 1797
Alva, son of the sd Theopu & Mary was born on the 7th June 1798
Sidne, son of the sd Theopu & Mary was born on the 30 August 1800
Carolina, their daughter was born on the 22nd day of Decr 1801
Charlott Miranda daughter was born on the 4 day of July 1804
Corville their daughter was born the 22nd day of June 1806 and died on the 10 day of October ---- 1806
Jennet, their daughter was born the 23 Novr ---- 1807
Theophilus, their son was born the 26 day of Decr 1809 and died on the 11th day of January 1810

[page 90] Capt. Thomas Sill was married to Miss Mehitable Mather on the 6th day of November 1799 by the Revd David Higgins
John Griswold their son was born on the 3d day of Septr. 1800
Phebe Mather their daughter was born on the 27 Novr 1801
Henry Mather their son was born on the 2d day of Octr 1803
Margaret their daughter was born on the 14th day of Septr 1805
Nancy their daughter was born on the 7th day of Decr 1807
Sarah Griswold was born on the 25th day of December 1809

Mary their daughter was born January 26th AD 1812
Frances their daughter was born July ---- AD 1814

Samuel Summers son of Miss Dolly Higgins was born on the -- day of January 1803

[page 91]   This certifies whom it may concern that on the 2nd Day of January 1810 Mr. Henry Perkins of New London and Miss Mary Shaw Woodbridge of Lyme were lawfully joined in marriage by me David Huntington Minister of the Gospel.

Sarah Douglas their Daughter was born 2nd Decr 1812

Mr. Allen Tinker was joined in Marriage to Miss -- on the day of ----
Charles son of the said Allen was born the 17 of Decr 1803
Mary Ann their daughter born the 17 November 1806
Daniel their son born the 17 day of January 1811

This certifies that Joseph Dowsett and Betsy Tillotson were united in marriage by me this 4th day of Nov. 1810
         Andrew Griswold
         Justice of the Peace
Taken from Vol 3, Page 260 Births
Marriages and Deaths
by William Marvin Registrar

[page 92]   Mr. Issac Watts Sill was married to Miss Mercy Wilcox Beckwith on the 2nd day of February 1811

Mr. Jasper Brockway and Miss Hannah Crandle was joined in marriage on the 4th day July 1812 as appears by certificate from Jesse Babcock Elder

Lavica Ann Brockway their daughter Born Augst 23d 1813
Julia Emeline their Daughter born April 2nd 1815
Horrace Gardiner their son born January 7th 1817
Robert Smith their son born August 20th 1818
Henry Brayman their son born April 20th 1820
Carlos Marcena their son born Feby 15th 1822

[page 93]   Mr. Jonathan Sisson Junr was married to Miss Holdridge on the -- day of Jany 1806
Elizabeth their daughter was born the 7th day of January 1808
Nathan H their son was born on the 28 day of Novr 1809
Mary their daughter was born on the 20 day of June 1812

Mr. Stephen Collins was married to Miss Thedy Crocker on the 12th day of December AD 1800
Jonathan Miner their son was born 1st August 1803
Dan their son was born 3rd Augt 1805 and died in the same month
David Crocker their son was born 30th July 1807
Sally Anderson their Daughter was born 4th Feby 1810
Thomas Mason their son was born 4th Feby 1813
Thedy the wife of Stephen Collins died 3rd April 1813

[page 94]   John Frederick Harrison was born April 6 AD 1786
Jane Shelden Brockway was born Oct 29th AD 1787
Said John & Jane was married to each other May 29th 1811

These may certify that Mr. Thomas W. Strickland & Miss Freelove Fitch were joined together in marriage Sept. 8th 1813
        By me Asa Wilson Elder

[page 95]   Joseph Miner and Hannah Johnson was married March 12th 1786
Prentis son of said Joseph & Hannah born Decr 14th 1791

Gilbers son of said Joseph & Hannah was born Sept 11th 1793
Esther daughter of said Joseph & Hannah born Augt 2nd 1795

Mr. Lee Comstock and Miss Phebe M. Miller was married April 2d AD 1811
This certifies that Denison Cranda and Lucy Moore were married at Lyme November 13th AD 1832
       By Peter Comstock Justice of Peace

[page 96] This may certify that Mr. Matthew Tinker and Miss Mary Miller were joined together in marriage September 19th 1811
       By me Asa Wilcox Eldr
Eliza Ann L. Tinker their daughter born 2nd June 1812
William Tinker 3rd son of Matthew and Mary Tinker was born April 2nd 1816

Mr. James Ransom Junr & Miss Elizabeth Clark was joined in marriage Feby 2nd 1786
Henry their son was born March 23rd 1787
Frances their daughter was born April 17th 1789
Clarisia their daughter was born March 7th 1791
Olive their daughter was born March 13th 1793
Clark their son was born July 15th 1794
Elias their son was born Sept 6 1796
Horace their son was born July 11th 1798
Elias their son died Dec 3d 1799
Orin their son was born June 30th 1800
Lydia Clark their daughter born May 22 1802
Elizabeth their daughter born May 2 1804
Sarah Ann their daughter born October 27th 1805

New London County ss Lyme 12th January 1815
I do hereby Certify that on the evening of the day & year above written Nathan Sanders and Jerusha Maynard both of said Lyme were joined together in marriage by me
       Charles Griswold Justice of Peace
Lydice their Daughter Born January 25th 1816
W Palmer their Son born October 22nd 1817
Phebe their Daughter born Sept 15 1821
Almira their daughter born Novr 29 1823

Mr. Reuben Havens and Miss Candace Denison was joined in Marriage -- day of January AD 1800
David Henry their son was born 13th Octr 1800
Dorcas Ursula their Daughter was born 28th Jan 1805
Henry Wolcott their son was born 27th Sept 1807
Mary Hannah their Daughter was born 27th Augt 1812
Candace the wife of said Reuben died Dec 20th Feby 1815
Charles McCurdy son of the said Reuben was born Aug 5th 1818

[page 98] This certifies that on the 21st day of March 1815 Benjamin Johnson of Lyme was by me married to Esther Comstock of sd Lyme according to the laws of the State of Connecticut for the Solemnization of Marriage
       Test Lathrop Rockwell, Clerk
Mary Ann daughter of Benjn & Esther Johnson was born March 12th AD 1816

This may certify that James Fitch and Nancy Strickland were joined together in marriage Feby 1st 1815
       By me Asa Wilcox Eldr

[page 99] Richard Pearson and Indiania Comstock were married --- December 20th 1813

Seabury Champion and Lucy Tinker were married to each other Septmr 1st 1811
Orren their son was born June 9th 1812
Fanny their daughter was born Feby 26th 1817

William Matson of Lyme and Rhoda Newton of Colchester were married April 30th 1807
William Newton their son was born Octr 22, 1811

James Darrow Junr & Sarah Champlin were married on the -- 19th day Decr 1807
Frances Champlin their daughter born 17th Octr 1808
Frances C. died 10th Jany 1810
Francis James their son was born 7th March 1810
Sarah Maria their daughter born 4th Augt 1811
Mary Lucinda their daughter born 10th Novr 1813

[page 101] I certify that Doc. Richard Noyes of Lyme State of Connecticut and Miss Martha Noyes of Westerly was joined in marriage on the 31st of March AD 1814 according to the laws of this state of Rode Island
           Jesse Babcock Edr
Wester Rode island March 31st AD 1814
John Noyes son of Richard & Martha born 22d January 1815

To all whom it may concern this is to certify that Benjamin Reeve & Patty Sill were joined in marriage at Lyme agreeably to the laws of the State of Connecticut on the 19th day of November AD 1809
       By me David Turner Justice of Peace
Julia Sill Reeve their daughter born Octr 31st 1810
Lucian Bonaparte Reeve born March 8th 1813
Sarah Ann Reeve their daughter born June 9th 1815

[page 102] Persia Johnson & Zilpha Bramble were married on the 29th day of March 1813
John their son was born June 28th 1814

William Huntly was married to Sarah Huntly by Jason Lee (according as sd Sarah states) on the 31st Augt 1788
Azubah their daughter was born on the 26th July 1789
Betsy their daughter was born on the 2d Feby 1792
Polly their daughter was born on the 6 day Sept 1794
William & Peter their sons (twins) born 10th Octr 1796
Stephen Mack their son born 21st Novr 1799
Erastus their son was born 30th April 1803
Harry their son was born 8th of December 1805
Lois their daughter was born 20th December 1808
Metilda their daughter born 4th March 1812
William Huntly died on the 3rd April 1813

[page 103] Benjamin Albee & Lydia Otis were married on the July 17th 1808
Benjamin their son was born on the 29th Januy 1810
William their son was born on the 10th Octor 1812
Calvin their son was born on the 1st June 1815
John Danford their son was born August 8th 1818

I hereby certify that Horace Wait and Martha Raymond of Lyme were married at New London on the 12th day of October 1816
          Abel McEwen pastor of the Cong.
          Chh New London

[page 104]   John Christopher Ely was married to Eunice Noyes on the 5th day of January
    AD 1811
John Noyes Ely their son born Novr 16th 1811
Esther Jane their daughter born Decr 30th 1812
Joseph Christopher their son born June 22d 1814
James Lawrence their son born April 23rd 1816
Capt. Christopher Ely died January 20th 1817 in the 74th year of his age

John Chadwick & Mercy Lay were married 9th Novr 1806
Benjamin their son was born the 13th April 1808
Frederick William their son born the 4th Septr 1811
Polly their daughter was born the 10th January 1816
Elisa Jane daughter was born the 15th May 1821
Joseph their son was born the 28th Novemr 1823

[page 105]   Thomas Neligan & Jerusha Boon was married 15 May 1803
Michael their son born on the 9th Octr 1806
William H. their son born on the 31st Jany 1809
Thomas their son born on the 17th Feby 1811

Abigail A. Bump daughter of Isaac & Susan Bump was born September 12th 1812
Ebenezer R. Bump son of Isaac & Susan Bump born June 24 1814
Mary Ann A Bump daughter of Isaac & Susan Bump born June 24 1817
John Bump son of Isaac & Susan Bump born Sept 21st 1820
Elizabeth M. Bump daughter of Isaac & Susan Bump born May 22, 1823
Penelope B. Bump daughter of Isaac & Susan Bump born January 8, 1826
Nancy H. Bump daughter of Isaac & Susan Bump born August 18, 1828
Caroline Bump daughter of Isaac & Susan Bump born May 1st 1830
Adalade Bump   ]
Ellen Bump   ]   daughters of above born Augt 20 1835

Robert B. Chadwick & Fanny Marvin Wood were married June 20 1808
Wealthy Ann their daughter born Nov. 7th 1809
Mary Lay their daughter born May 1st 1814

[page 106]   George Taylor was married to Polly Wood the -- AD 18 --
William Taylor son of George & Polly Taylor was born December 23d AD 1816
Phebe was born January 23d AD 1821
Joseph was born July 10th AD 1823
John was born March 26th AD 1826
Amos Sanders son of William & Mehitabel Sanders was born August 9th AD 1820
Hannah Sanders daughter of the above born Feb 7th 1822

Daniel son of Wm & Abigail Chappel born 10th July 1793
Enoch son of sd Wm & Abigail was born 28th March 1796
Julia Ann daughter of Wm & Abigail was born 5th March 1801

[page 107]   Mr. Jared Watrous and Miss Phebe Champion both of Lyme were joined in
    marriage on the 26th Novr 1816 by Seth Smith, Justice of Peace

John Hamilton and Hetty Warren was married December the 15, 1817

This may certify that Mr. Jonathan G. Lewis and Miss Sarah P. Strickland were joined to-
    gether in marriage January 22nd 1828 by Mr. Thos. W. Strickland, Just. of Peace

[page 108]   Lynde L. Tinker & Penelope Spencer was married Nov. 11th 1804
Frederick Augustus son of Lynde L & Penelope born 24 August 1805
Elisabeth daughter Lynde & Penelope born Nov. 4th 1806
Maria, daughter Lynde & Penelope born July 8th 1809
George, their son was born Novr 10th 1811

140 LYME, CONNECTICUT, VITAL RECORDS

Julia, their daughter born Sept. 16th 1813
Lynde, their son born March 8th 1815
Mary their daughter born June 11th 1817
Lynde L. Tinker was born Decr 25 1785

Watrous Maynard & Elisabeth Clark was married October the 31st AD 1816
James Henry their son was born Jan'y 14th 1818
John Maynard their son was born August 9th 1833

[page 109]   Moses H. Warren and Mary F. Miner was married December 25th 1817
John Moore 2nd and Emily Crane were married at Killingworth February 22nd 1815
John Alexander Moore son of the above was born March the 1st 1816
Elias Crane Moore born August 23d 1817

[page 110]   Ezra Peck & Eunice Clark were married in May -- 1808
Wm. K.C. Peck, son of the above born March 13th 1809
Charles C. Peck son of the above born Nov. 20, 1811
Horace E. Peck son of the above born May 3, 1813
Eleazer C. Peck son of the above born March 11, 1816
Maria E. Peck, daughter of the above born 13 Augt. 1818
Orrin Miller Peck born son of the above born 8th May 1821
Ezra M. Peck died in the city of New York Sept. 5, 1839 - AE 55 ys.
William K. Peck son of Ezra & Eunice Peck died at Rising Sun Indiana June 17th 1846 AE 37
Orrin Miller Peck son of Ezra & Eunice Peck died at Charleston, South Carolina March 21st 1848 AE 26

Christopher Brockway & Christian Chapel were married June 22nd 1806
Julian, daughter of Chr & Christian born Decr 16, 1807
Eunice, daughter of sd Chr & Christian born Jany 6th 1810
Charles Elias Livingston son of Chr. & Christian born Nov. 15, 1811
Ezra C. son of Chr & Christian born March 6th 1814
Maryett, daughter of Chr & Christian born March 19th 1816
Christopher Jr. their son born May 25th 1818
Joseph S. their son born June 3d 1820
Elisabeth Hannah their daughter born June 11th 1822
Sarah Caroline their daughter born October 19th 1824

[page 111]   Joshua R. Warren & Harriot Way were married May 12th AD 1816
Mahitable their daughter born July 22nd AD 1817
William Watts Jones Warren their son born April 14th 1819
Mahitable their daughter died April 7th 1821
John Warren their son born April 21st 1821
Eunice Harriet their daughter born June 16th 1823
Sarah Mahitable their daughter born Jan'y 10th 1825
Caleb Raymond their son born June 25th 1829
Thomas Jefferson son of the above born April 7th 1831
Ellen E. Warren daughter of the above born July 27th 1833
Jane Warren daughter of the above born May 15th 1835

Samuel S. Warner was married to Abby Champlin Feb'y 23d 1819

[page 112]   Nath'l Clark & Mahittable A. Peck were married 28 day of May AD 1800
Henry King Peck Clark son of the above Nathaniel and Mahittable was born Novr 13 AD 1802
Lucy Ann daughter daughter of the above born Novr 30th AD 1805
William Sheldon son of the above born Sept 3d AD 1808
Ruth Mary daughter of the above born Feby 26th AD 1812
Sarah Lord daughter of the above born Oct 24 AD 1817

This may certify to whoom it may concern that Hanibal Reeve was lawfully married to Miss Eliza H. Lattimer on the 8th day of April 1818 by me
John Whittlesey Minister of the Gospel Both of Lyme

[page 113]   Houghton Spencer & Amilia Sarah Strutt were married in the year 1807
John Ward Spencer son of the above Houghton and Amilia Sarah was born at Lyme Oct 11th AD 1817
Daniel Rogers son of Susan Thompson Alias Susan Rogers born Decr 15, 1816
David Rogers son of the above Susan was born April 30th 1819

Champlin Lester & Sally Miner were married April 9th 1807
Champlin Lester was born March 16 1785
Sally Miner was born April 24th 1786
William Lester, son of Champlin & Sally Lester was born January 20th 1808
Charles Chancey son of Champlin & Sally Lester was born July 1st 1809
    and died July 28 1809
Also a son born & died Sept 24 1811
Mary Ann daughter of the above Champlin & Sally born February 1st 1813
Charles son of the above born June 29 1815
Horrace Bissell son of the above born Augt 6th 1817
Horrace died Oct. 24th 1819
Henry Miner son of the above born May 21st 1819

[page 114]   This certifies that on the 22nd day of April Dan Marvin of Lyme was by me married to Hepzibah Leach of Lyme according to the laws of the State of Connecticut for the solemnization of marriage
                        Test Lathrop Rockwell Clerk
Amos Dosett died 12th Oct AD 1819

                    Lyme May 22nd 1820
To all whoom it may concern this is to certify that on the 21st instant I solemnized a marriage between Mr. Calvin Spencer and Miss Fanny Miner both of Lyme East Society   George W. Appleton Pastor of the 1st Baptist Church in Lyme East Society

[page 115]   Gilbert S. Smith of Lyme and Maria Smith of Groton were married February 23 1818
Ellen Maria their daughter was born September 28th 1819
Clarinda Frink their daughter born May 7th 1822

This may certify that Mr. Elihu Chadwick & Miss Elizabeth Russell were joined together in marriage Feb'y 19th 1815 by Mr. Asa Wilcox Elder
Nancy Miner daughter of Elihu & Elizabeth Chadwick born Decr 20 1815
Daniel Russell son of the above Elihu and Elizabeth Chadwick born Feb'y 10th 1817
Israel son of the above born April 12th 1820
Mary Elizabeth their daughter born Feb'y 10th 1822

[page 116]   Doctr John L. Smith and Miss Fanny Strickland were married May 14th 1820 both of Lyme by certificate of George W. Appleton   Chas. Smith Register
Eliza Ann Smith daughter of John L. & Fanny Smith was born February 22nd 1821
1st Seth Smith son of John L. & Fanny Smith was born October 14th 1823
2nd ---- son of John L. & Fanny Smith was born June 16th AD 1836

[page 117]   To all whoom it may concern this may certify that I solemnized a marriage between Mr. Ezra Maynard Junr & Miss Charlotte Maynard both of lyme
        George W. Appleton
            Pastor of the Baptist Church
Mary Louisa Daughter of Ezra Junr & Charlotte Maynard born January 13th 1822

This may certify that Ansel Bouge and Mary C. Beebe were married on the 24th of Decr 1820 by Me Samuel B. Mather, Justice of the Peace
Lucretia Ann Bouge daughter of the above Ansel Mary was born June 8th 1821

[page 118]   This may certify that on the 10th day of Decr 1820 Jonathan C. Brown and Hannah Congdon both of Lyme were married by me Samuel B. Mather Justice of Peace

   Lyme December 28th 1820
To all whoom it may concern
This may certify that on the 28th day of December 1820 I solemnized a marriage between Mr. Ezra Chappell and Miss Rachel A. Bouge both of Lyme
      George Appleton Pastor
      of the first Baptist Church in
      Lyme East Society

[page 119]   To all whoom it may concern this is to certify that Mr. John G. Jewett and Miss Phebe P. Stark both of Lyme were joined in marriage at Mr. Nathan Stark's agreeable to the laws of the State of Connecticut on the eve of the 16th day of January AD 1821
  by Wm. Palmer Minister of the Gospel

To all whoom it may concern this may certify that on the 14th of January 1821 I solemnized a marriage between Mr. Matthew Gee and Miss Polly Rogers both of Lyme
      Geo. W. Appleton Pastor of the 1st
      Baptist Church in Lyme

This certifies that Matthew Gee and Eunice Chadwick both of Lyme were united in marriage Sept. 1st 1829 by the subscriber
      Chester Colton Pastor of the 1st
      Church in Lyme

[page 120]   Married at Lyme on the 19th day of October 1820 Lathrop Rockwell to Lucy Osborn both of this place Abel McEwen Pastor of the
      Congregational Church New London

This certifies that on the 18th day of June 1820 Enoch Waid of Lyme was married to Laura Miner both of Lyme according to the laws of the State of Connecticut for the solemnization of marriage
      Test Lathrop Rockwell Clerk

This may certify that Enoch Waid was married to Maria Fox on the 22nd instant by me. Lyme October 24th 1829   William Noyes Junr Justice of Peace

[page 121]   This certifies that on the 22nd day of August 1820 Daniel Chadwick was by me married to Nancy Waite both of Lyme according to the laws of the State of Connecticut for the solemnization of marriage
      Test Lathrop Rockwell Clerk

This certifies that on the 12th day of Novr 1820 Elisa W. Mather was by me married to Mary Ann Smith both of Lyme according to the laws of the State of Connecticut for the solemnization of marriage
      Test Lathrop Rockwell Clerk

This certifies that on the 19th day of December 1820 Charles W. Wait was by me married to Mary Smith both of Lym according to the laws of the state of Connecticut for the solemnization of marriage   Test Lathrop Rockwell Clerk

[page 122]   This certifies that on the 8th day of February 1821 Thomas Rathbum of East Haddam was by me married to Ann Ingraham of Lyme according to the laws of the

State of Connecticut for the solemnization of marriage
Test Lathrop Rockwell Clerk

[page 123]   These may certify that Niles H. Tooker and Lucy Darrow were united in marriage by me Lyme October 1820
Ebenezer Brockway   Justice of Peace

These may certify that William Lane and Jemima Self were united in marriage Lyme Oct 1820   Ebenr Brockway   Justice of Peace

[page 124]   This certifies that Mr. Ezra Brockway and Miss Leonora Brockway were legally married on the 9th Feby 1821 by Josiah Havens, Minister of the Gospel

This certifies that Mr. Israel Matson and Miss Phebe Ely were legally married on the 12th of Feby 1821 by me Josiah Hawes Minister of the Gospel

[page 125]   This certifies that Mr. John Elmore and Miss Phebe Sterling were legally joined in marriage on the 15th Feby 1821 by me Josiah Hawes, Minister of the Gospel

This may certify that Henry H. Hess was married to Mary Tinker of Lyme County of New London on the evening of the second of this month by me William Noyes Junr Justice Peace

[page 126]   New London County
SS Lyme 23d March AD 1821
Then I the Subscriber lawfully married Benjamin Banning of East Haddam to Dotice Bramble of Lym   Joseph E. Ely Justice of Peace

This may certify that Israel Otis and Deborah Maria Babcock both of Lyme were on the 4th day of March AD 1821 married by me Samuel B. Mather Justice of the Peace

[page 127]   Lyme April 5th 1821
This may certify that on the 10th of March last I solemnized a marriage between Edward Moore and Mary Chappell both of Lyme
George M. Appleton Pastor
of the Baptist Church East Society

Lyme April 5th 1821
This may certify that on the 20th March that I solemnized a marriage between William Latham of Hebron and Eunice Miner of Lyme
George Appleton Pastor   1 Baptist Church East Society

[page 128]   William Noyes Jr. & Hannah Townsend were married at Albany Jany 5th 1812
Catherine Banks Noyes daughter of William and Hannah Noyes born September 27th 1813
Sarah Banks their Daughter born March 3d 1815
William their Son born August 15th 1816
Mary Ann their Daughter born February 1st 1818
Helena Decay their Daughter born August 7th 1819
William James son of the above William & Hannah born May 31st 1821
Mathew son of the above Wm & Hannah born May 31st 1828
Stephen Lord Son of the above Wm & Hannah born ---

[page 129]   Nancy Judson Appleton Daughter of George Ward M Appleton was born Feb 21st 1820

This may certify that Thomas T. Mulford of New Haven in the State of Ohio and Phebe Steward of Lyme in the State of Connecticut were this 25th day of March 1821 lawfully joined in marriage by me S. G. Thatcher Justice of the Peace

[page 130] Sylvester Wooster was married to Louisa C. Hayden of Saybrook June 22nd 1818
Sylvester Wooster Junr was born June 7th 1819
Sylvester Wooster Junr Died Augt 28th 1820

Alvin Babcock was (by his own evidence born June 2nd 1803

[page 131] John Hart Jr. and Nancy Mather were married June 25th 1811
Sylvester M their son born May 29th 1812
Elizabeth Ann their Daughter born June 17th 1814
John Alexander their son born July 5th 1816
Sylvester M their son died Decr 7th 1816

This certifies that Capt. Gardiner Gallop of Salem and Miss Phebe Sill of Lyme were married by me April 19th AD 1821
    Josiah Hawes Lyme

[page 132] Doctor Thomas Miner & Miss Phebe Mather were married May 8th AD 1810
Phebe Wife of Dr. Thos Miner died Feby 5th AD 1811

This certifies that James S. Graham & Mary Ingraham were married by me August 11th AD 1821
    Josiah Hawes Lyme

[page 133] This certifies that that Samuel Daniels & Jerusha Miller were married by me August 11th AD 1821   Josiah Hawes Lyme

Francis J. Lay was married to Maria Norton of Albany June 20th 1821
Mary Elisabeth daughter of the above Francis J & Maria Born at Albany June 19th AD 1824
[page 134] William B. Tooker & Nancy Tinker were married October 19th 1818
Samuel W. their son was born July 3d 1820

This certifies that on the 23d day of Sept. 1821 Enoch L. Chappel of Lym was by me married to Lucy Ann Tucker of sd Lyme according to the laws of the State of Connecticut for the solemnization of marriage
Test Lathrop Rockwell Clerk

[page 135] This certifies that on the 22nd day of August 1821 John McCrary of Lyme was by me married to Mary Ann Rowland of sd Lyme according to the laws of the State of Connecticut for the solemnization of marriage
    Attest Lathrop Rockwell Clerk

Amos C. Maxon was born May 3d AD 1783
Elizabeth Tinker the wife of Amos C. Maxson was born July 18th AD 1783
Amos C Maxon & Elizabeth Tinker were married August   AD 1807
John P. Maxon son of Amos & Elizabeth was born May 12th 1808
Nancy their Daughter born June 16 1810
Elizabeth their Daughter born June 15 1812
Nathan Tinker their son born July 31 1814
Fabius Beckwith their son born Oct 6 1816
Amos Champlin their son born Feb 8th 1821

[page 136] This certifies that on the 30th month of Sept 1821 George D. Clark of Lyme was by me married to Phebe Havens of S/D Lyme according to the laws of the State of Connecticut for the solemnization of marriage
    Test Lathrup W. Rockwell Clerk

This certifies that Solomon Sampson and Elizabeth W. Clark were lawfully married on this- -day of August 1821
    by me Samuel B. Mather Justice of Peace

[page 137] This may certify that Shubel Bogue and Anne Beebe of Lyme were lawfully married on the 9th day of Sept. 1821 by me Samuel B. Mather Justice of Peace

To all whoom it may concern
This may certify that on the 24th day of Sept 1821 I solomized a marriage between John Rogers Jr. and Harriet Huntley both of Lyme
    Geo. W. Appleton Pastor of the Baptist Church East Society

[page 138] Lyme October 28th 1821
To All it may concern
This may certify that on the evening of the 28th ultimo I solemnized a marriage between Mr. Charles Tinker and Miss Mahala Beckwith both of Lyme
    Geo. W. Appleton Pastor of the 1st Baptist Church in East Lyme Society

[page 138] This certifies that on the 24th day of Nov. 1821 Gurdon Hungerford of East Haddam was by me married to Maria Rowland of Lyme
    Attest Lathrop Rockwell Clerk

[page 139] This certifies that Elisha Pratt and Lurinia Robbins were married by me Novr 7th AD 1821   Josiah Hawes

This certifies that George Havens was by me married to Harriot Champion both of Lyme on the 6th day of Decr 1821
    Attest Lathrop Rockwell Clerk

[page 140] This certifies that Dr. Abraham Blatchley of Guilford and Miss Jemima Marvin of Lyme were married by me Dec 14th AD 1821   Josiah Hawes

This certifies that Mr. Richard Chadwick 2nd and Miss Mary Sill were joined together in marriage July 20th 1817 by me Asa Wilcox Elder
Emeline Sill Chadwick daughter of Richard & Mary Chadwick was born February 5 AD 1818
Ambrose Niles Chadwick their son born Nov 6 1819
Sarah Harvey their daughter born Apr 15th AD 1821
Louisa Ann their daughter born Feb 5 1823

[page 141] This may certify that Timothy Johnson and Rachel Ransom were legally married on the 5th day of Decr 1821 by Seth Lee Pastor of the Strict Congregational Church of Lyme   Certified by Seth G. Lee Church Clerk

To all whoom it may concern
This is to certify that Dr. John L. Rogers and Miss Matilda Lord both of Lyme were joined in marriage at Mr. L. Lords agreeably to the Laws of the State of Connecticut on the eve of the 10th day of February in the year of our Lord 1822 by me
    William Palmer
    Minister of the Gospel
Colchester Feb 10 1822

[page 142] This may certify that on the 20th day of Feby 1822 Mr. William Beckwith and Miss Martha Graham both of Lyme were joined in marrage agreeable to the laws of the State of Connecticut by me   Chestr Smith Justice of peace

John Beckwith & Nancy S. Burnham were married January 25th 1814
Elizabeth Smith their daughter born April 8th 1816
Nancy S. Beckwith wife of John Beckwith died Octbr 29 1818
John Beckwith & Phebe Parsons married Apr 24th 1820
Nancy B. Beckwith their daughter born Apr 16 1821

[page 143] Giles Manwaring & Sophia Tinker were married January 31st 1807
Ralph Denison son of Giles & Sophia Manwaring was born July 10th 1808
William M. their son born April 10th 1810
Esther Ann B their Daughter born 25 July 1812
Giles their son born July 20th 1814
Martha Sophia their daughter born Oct 10th 1816
Abby G their Daughter born 10th Sept. 1819
John Anderson their son born Jan'y 27 1823

This certifies that George R. Griffin of East Haddam and Annie Johnson of Lyme were married by me Feby 14th AD 1822   Josiah Hawes

[page 144]   This certifies that on the 3d day of March 1822 Thomas M. Smith was by me married to Hannah Rogers both of Lyme
    Test Lathrop Rockwell Clerk

This certifies that on the 7th day of April 1822 William Youngs was by me married to Hannah Rowland both of Lyme
    Attest Lathrop Rockwell Clerk

[page 145]   This certifies that Marshfield S. Parker and Azubah Marvin both of Lyme was joined in marriage by me April 9th 1822 Josiah Hawes
John Marvin Parker their son born April 9th 1823
Marshfield Sterling Parker their son born March 19th 1826
William Mather Parker their son born July 20th 1828
Ann Maria Parker their daughter born Sept 16th 1830
Jane Louisa Parker their daughter born Sept 27th 1839
Henry Lord Parker their son born Jan 11th 1843
Seymour Landon Parker their son born Septem 1st 1845

This certifies that on the 28th day of May 1822 Matthew Marvin was by me married to Sarah R. Lord both of Lyme
    Test Lathrop Rockwell · Clerk

[page 146] This certifies that on the 22nd day of May 1822 Charles J. McCurdy was by me married to Sarah Ann Lord both of Lyme   Test. Lathrop Rockwell Clerk

This certifies that on the 10th day of July 1822 Charles C. Griswold was by me married to Elizabeth Griswold both of Lyme   Attest Lathrop Rockwell Clerk

[page 147]   This certifies that on the 5th Day of August 1822 George W. Bump was by me married to Sally C. Haynes both of Lyme   Charles Smith Justice of Peace

This may certify that I solemnized a marriage at Lyme August 11 1822 between David Phelps and Nancy Miller both of Lyme
    George W. Appleton Pastor of the first Baptist Church

[page 148]   This certifies that William Bartman and Mary McCoy both of Lyme were joined in marriage June 10th 1822 by me Joseph Vail Minister of Hadlyme

[page 148]   This certifies that Elisha Robbins and Amanda Howard both of Lyme were by me married on the 8th day of Sept AD 1822
    Charles Smith Justice of Peace

[page 149]   Lyme October 4, 1822
This may certify that on the evening of the 3d of Oct I solemnised a marriage between Mr. Ruel Beckwith 2nd and Miss Julia Ann Chappell both of Lyme East Society Geo. W. Appleton Pastor of the 1st Baptist Church in Lyme East Society

Lyme October 3d 1822
This may certify that on the evening of the 22nd September I solemnised a marriage between James Dill Esq. of New York and Miss Eliza Champlin of Lyme E. Society
  Geo. W. Appleton
  Pastor of the 1st Baptist Church in Lyme East Society

[page 150] Sarah Taylor & Mary Jane Daughters of Elisha & Sarah Ingraham were born at North Killingworth May 29 1819
Asa Saunders Son of the above Elisha & Mary was born at Lyme the 9th of April 1822

This certifies that on the 9th day of August 1822 Simeon Whipp was by me married to Catherine N Tucker both of Lyme
  Attest Lathrop Rockwell Clerk

[page 151] This certifies that on the 15th day of July 1822 I married Erastus Rogers and Delight [Judd] both of Lyme
  Ezra Pratt Justice of Peace

This certifies that Philip Morgan of Waterford and Sarah Ann Lord of Lyme were married by me Sept. 19th 1822 Josiah Hawes

[page 152] This certifies that on the 14th day of January AD 1823 Simon Bailey of Haddam was by me married to Huldah Phelps of Lyme
  Charles Smith Justice of Peace

This certifies that on the 9th day of Feby 1823 John H. Sumner of Middletown was by me married to Betsey Conkling of Lyme
  Attest Lathrop Rockwell Clerk

[page 153] This certifies that on the 13th of January 1823 I solemnised a marriage between Mr. Jabez Swan of Lyme and Miss Larua Griffin of East Haddam
  George W. Appleton
  Elder Lyme Et Society

This certifies that on the 13th day of Feby 1823 Joseph Miller and Eliza Maynard both of Lyme was by me married
  Attest Charles Smith Justice of Peace

[page 154] This certifies that on the 2nd day of March 1823 Daniel S. Brayman of Groton was by me married to Mary W. Havens of Lyme
  Test Lathrop Rockwell Clerk

This certifies that on the 18th day of March 1823 Samuel S. Fowler of Albany state of New York was by me married to Emma S. Marvin of Lyme
  Attest Lathrop Rockwell Clerk

[page 155] This certifies that on the 18th day of March 1823 Silas Lester was by me married to Mary O. Huntley both of Lyme
  Attest Lathrop Rockwell Clerk

Henry Selden Son of Daniel & Maria Spencer born June 30th 1822
John Harvey son of the above Danl & Maria born Feby 26 1824
Daniel Washington their son born Feby 17th 1826
Hannah Maria their daughter born August 12th 1829

[page 156] This certifies that Dr. Ambrose Niles of Lyme and Frances Marvin of Hartford were married by me April 2nd AD 1823 Josiah Hawes

This may certify that Mr. Ruel R. Strickland and Miss Harriot Tinker were joined together in marriage April 6th AD 1823 by me Thos W. Strickland Justice of Peace

[page 157] Lyme May 10th 1823
This may certify that on the 14th of April last I solemnized a Marriage between Mr. Richard Chadwick and Mrs. Hannah Lay both of Lyme
    Elder George W. Appleton
    Lyme East Society

This certifies that Silas Bramble & Amy Sawyer both of Lyme were by me married April 27th AD 1823   Josiah Hawes

[page 158]   To whom it may concern
This is to certify that Mr. Charles Tiffany of Williston State of Vermont and Miss Naomi Jewett of Lyme State of Connecticut were joined in marriage at Widow Naomi Jewetts agreeably to the Laws of the State of Connecticut on the 16th day of June in the year of Lord 1823
    by me William Palmer Minister of the Gospel
Colchester June 16th 1823

    Lyme May 25th 1823
This may certify that on the evening of the 25th May I solemnized a marriage between Mr. Ezra B. Fox and Miss Sally Maria Waid the former of East Haddam the latter of Lyme
    Elder Geo W. Appleton
    Lyme East Society

[page 159]   This may certify that on the 12th Inst I solemnized a marriage between Mr. Nathaniel Wheeler of Montville and Miss Phebe Ladd of Lyme East Society
Lyme August 31st 1823 Elder George W Appleton

This certifies that Mr. William B. Niles and Miss Julia Ely both of Lyme were married by me July 27th AD 1823   Josiah Hawes

[page 160] Ezekiel Rogers and Mary Beckwith were married Novr 7th 1819
Josiah Nelson their son born January 4th 1821
Peter Beckwith their born October 9th 1822
Henry Newell their son born 8th March 1827

To all whoom it may concern
This is to certify that Selden Rogers and Betsey Huntley both of Lyme were Joined in Marriage at Mr. Silas Huntley agreeably to the Laws of the State of Connecticut on the evening of the 28th of September in the year of our Lord 1823 by me John S. Rogers Justice of the peace   Lyme Sept. 28th AD 1823

[page 161]   This certifies that on the 31st day of October AD 1823 Walter Flynn of New York and ---- Bowman of Lyme were joined in Marriage by me Charles Smith Justice of Peace

Andrew Beckwith and Lucinda Hudson were married May   1816
Margarett Lucinda Daughter of Andrew & Lucinda Beckwith was born March 6th 1817
Harriet Miller Daughter of the above Andrew & Lucinda was born Sept. 26 1819

[page 162] This may certify that Mr. Edmund Smith of Windham and Miss Harriet Coats of Lyme were joined in marriage Jan'y 4th 1824 by Ebenr Loomis, Pastor - Baptist Church New London

To all whoom it may concern this is to certify that Mr. John Tibbits of East Windsor and Miss Lydia Johnson of Lyme were joined in marriage at Widow Johnson's on the 30th day of December 1823 by Seth Lee Lyme Decr 30th 1823

[page 163]   This is to certify that on the 21st day of Decr AD 1823 Charles W. Harison & Elisabeth A Sawyer both of Lyme were joined in marriage by me Simon Shaler Elder

This may certify that Aaron E. A. Skinner and Clarisa Graham both of Lyme were lawfully married on the 20th day of Novr 1823 by me Samuel B. Mather, Justice of Peace

[page 164]   To all whom it may concern
This certifies that on 7th day of April 1824 Mr. Benjamin Phelps and Miss Rachel Waid both of Lyme were by me married
   Attest: Charles Smith Justice of Peace

This certifies that Mr. Similius Ely of Lyme and Miss Maria Anne Stannard of Guilford were married by me March 2nd AD 1824   Josiah Hawes

This certifies that Similleus B. Ely and Elisabeth P. Ely both of Lyme were married by me October 4th 1842
Recorded October 8th 1842   C. E. Murdock
By Joshua R. Warren, Regr.

[page 165]   This certifies that on the 8th day of April 1824 John M. Champion was by me married to Sophia M. Lay of Lyme

   Attest Lathrop Rockwell, Clerk

This certifies that I married Joseph Peck 3d to Ann Gilbert both of Lyme on June 14th 1824
   Attest Lathrop Rockwell Clerk

[page 166]   This certifies that John Gordon Hughes and Julia Ann Bill were married by me June 20th AD 1824 both of Lyme   Josiah Hawes, Lyme

This certifies that Abner S. Ely of Lyme and Fanny Griffin of East Haddam were married by me June 24th AD 1824   Josiah Hawes

[page 167]   This certifies that Herman Young was married to Clarissa C. Brooks both of Lyme Oct 20th 1823 by me Christopher Comstock Just of Peace

This certifies that Mr. George H. Armstrong of Norwich was married to Miss Lydia Miller of Lyme July 18th 1824 Christopher Comstock Just of Peace

John M. Young son of Benjamin H. Young & Lucy his wife was born May 23, 1820 Taken from Vol 3, p 63
   Attest William Marvin, Town Clerk

[page 168]   Lyme July 17th AD 1824
I then married Mr. Samuel Rogers and Miss Betsey Chapel   Alfred Burnham Minister of the Gospel

This certifies that on the 14th day of July 1824 Mr. Jonathan Sisson and Miss Hope Spencer both of Lyme were by me married
   Nathan Weldman Pastor of the 1st Baptist Church in Lyme

[page 169]   This certifies that on the 18th day of July 1824 Mr. Charles Pilgrim of New York was by me married to Miss Mary James of Lyme
   Attest Nathan Wildman Pastor of the 1st Baptist Church in Lyme

[page 169]   This certify that Calvin S. Manwaring and Nancy Tinker were joined in marriage at Lyme on the 12th day of February AD 1824 by me Peter Comstock Justice of Peace

[page 170]   This certifies that Ladock D. Beckwith and Jedidah Spencer both of Lyme were by me married at said Lyme on the 5th day of Septr AD 1824 by Nathan Wildman Pastor of the 1st Baptist Church in Lyme

To all whoom it may concern
This certifies that Mr. John Wood and Mrs. Esther Lee of Lyme Connecticut were joined in marriage agreeable to the laws of the State of Connecticut on the 16th day of Novr in the year of our Lord 1824 by me Lyme Nov 16th 1824 Seth Lee, Minister of the Gospel

[page 171]   This certifies that Seth M. Peck and Sarah Pierson both of Lyme were married by me Sept 8th AD 1824   Josiah Hawes

This certifies that Stephen Sterling Jr. and Sally M. Marvin both of Lyme were married by me December 9th AD 1824   Josiah Hawes

[page 172]   This may certify that Chancey Champion and Mary Ann Lay of Lyme were joined in marriage on the 18th day of October AD 1824 by me Peter Comstock Justice of Peace

This may certify that Charles Spencer and Julia Ryon both of Lyme were by me married on the 21st day of October 1824 by Nathan Wildman Pastor of the 1st Baptist Church in Lyme

[page 173]   This may certify that Joseph Brooks and Mary Ryon both of Lyme were by me married on the 24th day of October 1824 Nathan Wildman Pastor of the 1st Baptist Church in Lyme

This may certify that Enoch Howard and Joanna Cables both of Lyme were married on the 24th day of October 1824 by me Nathan Wildman Pastor of the 1st Baptist Church in Lyme

[page 174]   To all whoom it may concern
This is to certify that Mr. Charles H. Daniels of Lyme and Miss Mary Darrow of New London were joined in marriage at the house of John S. Rogers agreeably to the laws of the State of Connecticut on the Eve of the 16th January AD 1825
Lyme 16th Jan'y by me John S. Rogers, Justice of Peace 1825

To all whoom it may concern
This is to certify that Mr. George R. Peck and Miss Elisabeth S. Lee both of Lyme Connecticut were joined in marriage agreeable to the laws of the State of Connecticut on the 12th day of January in the year of our Lord 1825 by me
Lyme Jan'y 12, 1825   Seth Lee Minister of the Gospel

[page 175]   New London County SS Lyme March 23rd AD 1828
Then Elisha M. Comstock of Waterford was duly married to Hetty R. Hamilton of Lyme by Moses Warren Justice of Peace

This may certify that Mr. Enos Gates and Miss Maryann Payne were joined together in marriage Jan'y 2nd 1828 by me Thomas W. Strickland   Justice of Peace

[page 176]   This may certify that Andrew M. Danolds of Richmond in Virginia and Caroline Clark of Lyme in Connecticut was lawfully married on the 6th day of Decr 1824 by me Samuel B. Mather   Justice of Peace
Caroline wife of Andrew M. Danolds died Feb'y 11th 1826
Roxanna P.M. Donald their daughter born Oct. 7th 1825

This certifies that Nathan Smith and Hannah Stark both of Lyme were joined together in marriage March 14th 1825 by me Asa Wilcox Elder

[page 177]   Elizabeth Rogers wife of Rowland Rogers died Feb'y 27th 1825

Joseph Noyes and Sarah Griswold Gurley were married May 14th 1823
Mary Gurley Noyes their daughter born Decr 13th 1824
Jane Elizabeth Noyes born February 23rd 1827

[page 178]   Sarah R. Comstock daughter of Peter and -- Comstock born Sept 28th 1806
Hetta Eliza their daughter born March 4th 1808
Mary Ann their daughter born Dec. 24th 1809
Hannah R. their daughter born Nov. 20th 1811
Moses W. their son born June 20th 1814
Peter A. their son born April 20th 1817
William H. their son born March 20th 1819

Lois W. their daughter born August 24th 1820
John J. their son born June 24th 1822
Sarah Raymond their daughter died June 4th 1821

I hereby certify that on this 29th day of Decr 1823 I joined in marriage Daniel Prentice and Lucretia Smith both of Waterford
Lyme 29th Decr 1823   J.R. St. John

[page 179]   Lyme June 19th 1823
I this day joined in marriage Nehemiah Haynes of Waterford and Mary Manwaring of Lyme
J. R. St. John

Lyme July 13th 1823
This certifies that I this day joined in marriage Roger W. Griswold and Juliett Griswold of this place   John R. St. John

[page 179]   Lyme 13th October 1823
This certifies that on the 8th day of Oct. AD 1823 I married Henry Lee to Julia Miller both of this place   J. R. St. John

[page 180]   Lyme 13th October 1823
I hereby certify that I this day joined in marriage John Tubbs of Lyme and Lucy Smith of Waterford   J. R. St. John

Lyme Decr 7th 1824
I this day married Adam Manwaring Jr. to Susan Harding both of Lyme
J. R. St. John

[page 181]   Lyme Decr 9th 1824
I this day joined in marriage Rufus A. Smith of New London & Frances Manwaring of Lyme
J. R. St. John

Lyme January 19th 1825
I this day joined in marriage Christopher Lathrop of Boston and Dimmiz Truman of this place   J. R. St. John

Lyme July 1st 1824
I hereby certify that I this day joined in marriage Lee Comstock of Lee Roy and Sarah W. Caulkins of this place   J. R. St. John

[page 182]   Elisha C. Caulkins was married to Abby Chapman March 16th AD 1816
Elizabeth A. Caulkins their daughter born Sept. 19, 1817
Juliet G. Caulkins their daughter born Feby 23d 1820
Epaphraz C. Caulkins their son born March 16 1824
Juliett Griswold daughter of Elisha C. & Abby Caulkins died Nov. 9th 1825

Lyme July 8th 1825
This certifies that on the 23rd day of June 1825 I married Mr. James Kelsey Jr. of Saybrook & Miss Louise Millard of Lyme
Henry Stanwood

This certifies that Peter Chapman and Eliza Harding were married by me September 12th 1824
Joshua R. Warren Justice of Peace

[page 183]   This may certify that Mr. Richard Ransom and Miss Mary Miller both of Lyme were lawfully married by me this day   Wanton A. Weaver   Justice of Peace

This certifies that Elisha M. Huntley and Mary Tinker both of Lyme were joined in marriage by me on the 24th day of May AD 1824   Nathan Wildman

[page 184] To whom it may concern This certifies that on the 11th day of Sept AD 1825 Mr. Daniel Steward and Miss Sarah Tinker both of Lyme were legally joined in marriage by me Nathan Wildman
Calvin M. Steward son of Daniel & Sarah Steward was born April 2nd 1832

This may certify that Osmond Darrow and Sarah Loomis were lawfully joined in marriage at Lyme Octr 26th 1825 by me
Francis Darrow, Minister of the Gospel

[page 185] This may certify whoom it may concern that Mr. Hazard Wilcox and Polly Wright both of Lyme were lawfully married by me this evening Lyme 2nd Oct. 1825
Wanton A. Weaver Justice of Peace

To whoom it may concern this certifies that on the 25th day of June 1822 Simion Morgan and Phebe Clark both of Lyme were by me married according to law
Joel Loomis Justice of Peace

[page 186] To whoom it may concern this certifies that on the 21st day of Oct. 1819 Samuel Russel and Sally Ransom both of Lyme were by me lawfully joined in marriage
Joel Loomis Justice of Peace

To whom it may concern this certifies that on the 10th day of Novr 1824 Selden Bartherick and Lydia Randall both of Lyme were by me married according to the laws of this state
Joel Loomis Justice of Peace

[page 187] To whom it may concern this certifies that on the 9th day of October 1821 Shadrack Gillet and Grace Dean both of Lyme were by me married according to the laws of this state
Joel Loomis Justice of Peace

This certifies that on the 10th day of Novr 1819 Selden Maynard & Lydia Maynard both of Lyme were by me married agreeable to the laws of this state
Joel Loomis, Justice of Peace

[page 188] To whom it may concern This certifies that on the 14th day August 1818 Orrin Maynard and Dorcas Mack both of Lyme were joined in marriage by me
Joel Loomis Justice of Peace

To whoom it may concern this certifies that on the 20th day of October 1820 Stephen Tucker and Catherine Havens both of Lyme were by me married according to the laws of this state   Joel Loomis Justice of Peace

[page 189] This certifies that on the 13 day of December 1825 Prentice Comstock of Lyme was by me married to Lynda M. Banning of sd Lyme according to the laws of the State of Connecticut for the solemnization of marriage
Test Lathrop Rockwell Clerk

[page 189] This certifies that on the 5th day of May 1825 William Stanner of Kingsbridge State of New York was by me married to Mary Stammers of Lyme according to the laws of the State of Connecticut for the solemnization of marriage
Test Lathrop Rockwell Clerk

[page 190] This certifies that Victor M. Johnson of Lyme and Laura M. Jewett of East Haddam were married by me Decr 8th AD 1825   Josiah Hawes

Lyme Nov 23d 1825 This certifies that Jared Watrous and Mary Denison were married by me this day Nathan Wildman

[page 191] Lyme Decr 25th 1825
This certifies that Benjamin Gardiner Jr. of New London and Ethelinda Gee of Lyme were duly joined in marriage this day in Lyme by me   Elias Sharp Elder

This certifies that Jason Rogers and Abby A. Maynard were married by me Nov. 24th 1825 in sd Town of Lyme   Nathan Wildman

Elisha H. Smith was born Novr 4th AD 1805
Alvin Smith born August 5th 1809
John M. Smith born Decr 8th AD 1811

[page 192]   Mr. Isaac Stanton of Stonington was married by me to Mrs. Nancy H. Smith of Lyme   January the 15 1826   Nathan Wildman

To whom it may concern   This is to certify that Mr. Abijah Pierson and Miranda Huntley both of Lyme were joined in marriage at Mr. Silas Huntley Lyme agreeably to the laws of the State of Connecticut on the 13th day of Novr AD 1825 by me   Seth Lee, Minister of the Gospel

[page 193]   This is to certify that on the 25 of September AD 1825 Jabez Comstock and Margaret A. Brockway both of Lyme were joined in marriage by me
      Simon Shailer   Pastor of the Baptist Churck in Haddam

To all whom it may concern   This may certify that Mr. David G. Royce and Miss Eunice B. Beebee both of Lyme were joined in marriage agreeable to the laws of the State of Connecticut on the 11th day of Septr AD 1825 by me
      Seth Lee   Pastor of Strict Congregational Church Lyme

[page 194]   This certifies that on the 27th day of March AD 1826 I married Anson C Merritt of Stonington to Miss Betsey Tinker of Lyme
      Charles Smith   Justice of Peace

This certifies that on the 17th June AD 1826 I married Mr. James H. Pratt to Mrs. Nancy Jones both of Saybrook   Charles Smith   Justice of Peace

[page 194]   This certifies that Watrous B. Smith of East Haddam was by me married to Sarah Rogers of Lyme on the 7th day March 1826
      Attest Lathrop Rockwell, Clerk

[page 195]   This certifies that on the 29th day of Decr 1825 Amos Maxon was by me married to Sally Clark both of Lyme   Test Lathrop Rockwell   Clerk

This certifies that Mr. Richard W. Parsons and Miss Clarissa L. Griffing both of Lyme were married by me   Feb 27th 1826   Henry Stanwood

[page 196]   This certifies that Ashel Miller and Julian Brockway both of Lyme were by me married agreeable to the laws of this state on the 6th day of July 1826 Nathan Wildman

Elias Barrell was born at Scituate Mass. June 18, 1791
This certifies this Elias Barrell and Lydia Latham both of Lyme were by me joined in marriage on the 20th of June 1826 according to the laws of the State of Connecticut for the solemnization of marriage   Lyme June 20th 1826   Test Lathrop Rockwell Clerk
James Elias son of Elias and Lydia
Barrell was born May 30 1827
Charles son of Elias & Lydia
Barrell was born April 21, 1829

[page 197]   This certifies that Thomas D. Lord and Caroline Bulkley both of Lyme were married by me July 16th AD 1826   Lyme July 26th AD 1826
      Josiah Hawes Pastor of 3 Church in Lyme

This certifies that on the 6th day of July 1826 Charles E. Hart was by me married to Phebe M. Sill both of Lyme according the laws of the State of Connecticut for the solemnization of marriage   Test Lathrop Rockwell   Clerk

[page 198]   This certifies that Similius Lord and Lucy Rogers both of Lyme were married by me August 3rd AD 1826   Lyme   August 10th 1826   Josiah Hawes

I certify that I joined in marriage Agreeable to the laws of this State David Andrews of Saybrook and Rebecca Rogers of Lyme at Lyme July 2nd 1826
      Oliver Willson   Pastor of Second Baptist Church in Montville

Azariah Beebe died Nov. 20 1826 age 46 yrs.

[page 199] New London County SS Lyme 5th August 1826
Be it remembered that on this 5th August 1826 Henry Harrison and Patty Sawyer both of Lyme aforesd were joined in wedlock by and before me.
Richard E. Selden 2nd Justice of Peace

New London County SS Lyme 9th July 1826
Be it remembered that on this 9th July 1826 Albert Huntly of Lyme aforesd and Almira Field of Killingworth in the county of Middlesex were joined in wedlock by and before me.   Richard E. Selden 2nd Justice of Peace

[page 200] This certifies that on the 30th day of Sept 1825 I married Dan Gilbert to Mary Ann Champlin both of Lyme   Attest Charles Smith Justice of Peace

This certifies that William Wilson of Marlboro & Elisabeth M. Chadwick of Lyme were married by me Oct 8th AD 1826   Josiah Hawes

This certifies that Ezra Brockway of Lebanon and Lucy Ann Steward of Lyme were married on the 14th Sept. 1826 by me Nathan Wildman

[page 201] This certifies that Ashel Miller and Julian Brockway both of Lyme were married by me on the 6th day of July AD 1826   Nathan Wildman

This certifies that James Loomis and Eliza H. Comstock both of Lyme were by me married on the 8th day of October AD 1826   Nathan Wildman

This certifies that Silas Havens and Miss -- Griffin both of Lyme were married by me on the 24th day of Sept. 1826   Nathan Wildman

[page 202] To all whoom it may concern This certifies that Mr. Abel Keeny and Miss Maria Cobb both of Lyme were joined in marriage at Mr. Isaac Cobbs agreeable to the laws of this State of Connecticut on the evening of the 14th of Sept. in the year of our Lord 1826 by me John L Rogers Justice of Peace

This certifies that on the 7th day of Nov 1826 Albert James was by me legally married to Mary Rich both of Lyme   Test Lathrop Rockwell Clerk

[page 203]   Edward Greenfield Ann Lay were married June 2nd 1814 John their son born July 27 1815
Charles William their son born May 30 1817
Sarah Ann their Daughter born Augt 13 1819
James Scott their son born Oct 11th 1821
Harriet Louisa Their Daughter born Apl 11th 1824
Janett Care their Daughter born Augt 2nd 1826
Russel Case their son born December 24th 1829

This certifies that Mr. Joel Steel of Bloomfield State of New York and Miss Caroline Ely of Lyme State of Connecticut were married by me AD 1816 May 26th
Lyme July 8th AD 1827   Josiah Hawes Pastor of the 3d Church in Lyme

[page 204]   This certifies that on the 1st day of Nov. 1826 John W. Quinn was by me married to Sarah M. Haven both of Lyme   Test Lathrop Rockwell Clerk

[page 204] This certifies that Richard M. Champlin was by me married to Helena West both of Lyme on the 2nd day of Jany 1827
Lyme Jany 3d 1827   Attest Lathrop Rockwell Clerk
Harriet daughter of Richard M and Helena Champlin was born Dec 6 1828
Richard Champlin son of Richard M. and Helena Champlin was born Aug. 19, 1832

This certifies that John H. Taggers of Boston was by me married to Lucretia Dart of Lyme on the 15th day of Jany 1827   Test Lathrop Rockwell Clerk [page 205] This may certify that Mr. Cyrus Cook and Miss Mehitable A Shipman were joined together in marriage. Lyme March 22nd 1827 by me Thomas W. Strickland Justice of Peace

This certifies that Chrstopher Haynes and Maria Bump both of Lyme were married by me Feb. 11th 1827   Josiah Hawes Lyme

[page 206] This certifies that Horace Ely and Rhoda Tooker both of Lyme were married by me Jan 3d 1827   Josiah Hawes

This certifies that Jesse Stannard of Saybrook & Sally Phelps of Lyme were married by me on the 25th April AD 1827   Charles Smith Justice of Peace

To whoom it may concern This certifies that on the 27th April AD 1827 Mr. Watson Clark and Miss Sarah Ann Nowley both of East Haddam were married by me   Charles Smith Justic of Peace

[page 207] I hereby certify that I married Joseph Clark of East Haddam to Louis Miller of Lyme they having been previously published in Pleasant Valey meeting House Lyme 7th July 1826   Ezra Pratt Justice of peace

This certifies that on the 8th of April 1827 Whitman Tibbets and Julia Ann Chadwick were lawfully married by me Jonathan Comstock Justice of peace for N London County

[page 208] This certifies that Mr. Asa Park Edgecomb of Groton and Miss Mary Bill of Lyme were married by me June 27th AD 1827   Josiah Hawes

This certifies that Mr. Matthew Griswold Jr and Miss Phebe H. Ely both of Lyme were married by me July 5th AD 1827   Josiah Hawes

[page 209] This may certify that Joel Johnson of Chatam and Emeline Ursula Huntley of Lyme were joined in marriage June 7th 1827 by me Joseph Vail Minister of Hadlyme

This certifies that Franklin M. Brown and Ede A Miller both of Lyme were married by me July 15th AD 1827   Josiah Hawes

[page 210] This certifies that on the 23d day of Novr AD 1827 I married Samuel Ingraham to Harriet Ingraham both of Saybrook   Attest Charles smith Justice of Peace

To whoom it may concern This certifies that on the 29th day of Novr AD 1827 I married Mr. King Miller of Saybrook to Miss Mahitable Dart of Lyme   Attest Charles Smith Justice of Peace

[page 211] This certifies that on the 30th day of Sept AD 1827 I married James L Strickland to Mary Ann Comstock both of Lyme   Attest Nathan Wildman Pastor of Baptist Church in Lyme

This certifies that on the -- day of July AD 1827 I married Edwin Smith to Mary E. Tubbs both of Lyme   Attest Nathan Wildman Pastor of the First Baptist Church in Lyme

[page 212] New London County SS Lyme Decr 9th 1827 Be it remembered that on the day aforesaid Wm Huntley of Lyme and Lorain Fields of Killingworth were Joined in marriage according to the Laws of this State by & before me   Richd E. Selden Jr. Justice of Peace [Also entered on page 223]

New London County SS Lyme 5th Novr 1827 Be it remembered that on the day aforesaid John A. King of Southhold Long Island and Caroline Saunders of Lyme aforesaid were joined in marriage according to the Laws of this State by & before me. [also entered on page 224]   Richard E. Selden Jr. Justice of Peace

[page 213] This certifies that Mr. George Mitchel and Parnal Beckwith both of Lyme were married on the 1st day of December 1827 by me Samuel B. Mather Justice of Peace

This certifies that Thomas J. Hitt of North Kingston Long Island State of New York and Deborah Miller of Lyme Connecticut were married by me Janry 23d 1828
Josiah Hawes

The name of the groom in the above certificate of Marriage should read "Thomas J. Hill" and his residence "North Kingston" Rhode Island"
Lyme Sept 6th 1912   Attest William Marvin Town Clerk

[page 214]   I hereby certify that Samuel Saunders Jr and Julia Ann Huntley both of Lyme were lawfully married by me March 2nd 1828
Tubal Wakefield   Minister of the Gospel

This may certify that Mr. Austin Spencer & Miss Charlotte C. Spencer both of Lyme were joined in marriage Nov 12th 1827 by me Joseph Vail East Haddam Nov. 25th pastor of the Church in Hadlyme 1827

[page 215]   This certifies that on the 5th day of January AD 1828 I married Eliaz Smith of Waterford to Eunice Lester of Lyme   Joseph Chadwick Justice of peace

This is to certify that on the 31st day of December 1827 Aaron Watrous of Saybrook & Laura E Luther of Lyme were joined by me in marriage   Simon Shaler pastor of the Baptist Church in Haddam

[page 216]   I certify that I joined in marriage agreeable to the laws of this State Joshua Moor & Lois Hamilton both of Lyme this 10th day of Sept in the year of our Lord 1827   Oliver Wilson   Sept 16th 1827   pastor of the 2nd Baptist Church in Montville

To the clerk of the town of Lyme, I do hereby certify that Ebenezer Nichols of East Haddam and Margaret Ely of Lyme were lawfully married by me Tubal Wakefield minister of the Gospel   Lyme Feb. 10th 1828

[page 217]   This certifies that David M. Jewett of Lyme and Ann Rathbone of Salem were married by me March 26th AD 1828   Josiah Hawes

This certifies that Martin Lester & Abby C. Rowland both of Lyme were married by me April 7th 1828   Josiah Hawes

This certifies that Capt. Nathaniel Conklin and Mahitable Miner both of Lyme were married by me April 15th 1828   Josiah Hawes

[page 218]   Nathaniel M. Brown and Eliza D. Brockwy both of Lyme were married by me May 1st 1828   Josiah Hawes
Worthington Dunham their son was born February 8th 1829
Jane Miles their daughter was born November 13th 1832
Jenett Eliza their daughter was born October 5th 1833
Ellen Laura their daughter was born April 8th 1837
Peter Wilber their Son and   )
Kathleen their Daugher (twins)) born January 29th 1843

I do hereby certify that George E. Niles of Prattsburgh New York and Mary Russel of this place were lawfully married by me Lyme May 14th 1828
Tubal Wakefield Minister of the Gospel

[page 219]   This certifies that Alvin Babcock and Mary Closson both of Lyme were married by me June 15th 1828   Joshua R. Warren Justice of peace

This may certify that Romanta Ives and Charlotte Forsyth were lawfully joined in marriage at Lyme May 27th by me   Francis Darrow Minister of the Gospel

[page 220]   I do hereby certify that Ely Tiffany and Almira Smith were lawfully married by me Lyme July 6th 1828   Tubal Wakefield Minister of the Gospel

This may certify that M. Job Tubbs and Miss Fanny C. Tinker both of Lyme were lawfully joined in marriage on the 17th January 1827 Salem January 29th 1827 Nathaniel Miner Pastor of Congregation church in Chestefield Society

[page 221] This certifies that Samuel Brown and Salome Niles both of Lyme were married by me July 21st AD 1828   Josiah Hawes

This may certify that on the 23rd of July 1828 Alanson Wright of East Haddam and Emily A Banning of Lyme were joined in marriage by me -- Hadlyme Augt 4th 1828 Joseph Vaill Minister of the Gospel Hadlyme

[page 222] This certifies that Leonard Beebe and Phebe Beckwith were married August 24th 1828 by Henry Wightman

This certifies that Charles Beckwith and Betsy Shipman were duly joined in marriage on the evening of the 25th of September 1828 by me John Rogers Justice of Peace

[page 223] This certifies that Nathaniel M. Wait and Mehitable Chadwick both of Lyme were united in marriage in conformity to the law on the 14th day of October 1828 by the Subscriber Chester Colton Minister of the Gospel

[page 224] I hereby certify that Hammond Powers of Saybrook was married to Clarissa Lewis of Lyme December 15th 1828   Abel McEwen pastor of the Congregational Church New London

[page 225] This may certify that Gideon Rogers 2nd and Eliza Rogers were lawfully joined in marriage at Lyme December 18th 1828 by me
Francis Darrow Minister of the Gospel

This certifies that William W.S. Gillett and Huldah Waid both of Lyme were married by me- Lyme January 18th 1829   Joshua R. Warren Justice of peace

[page 226] This certifies that William H. Johnson and Eliza Ann Perkins both of Lyme were married by me January 5th AD 1829   Josiah Hawes

This certifies that Nathaniel Baker of East Haddam & Delia Babcock of Lyme were married by me January 4th AD 1829   Josiah Hawes

[page 227] This certifies that William Smith & Hannah M. Ely both of Lyme were married by me Dec. 28th AD 1828   Josiah Hawes

This certifies that Daniel Johnson and Melinda Austin both of Lyme were married by me August 10th 1828   Nathan Wildman Pastor of the 1st Baptist Church in Lyme

[page 228] This certifies that William C. Howard & Eliza W. Congdon both of Lyme were married by me October 26th 1828 Nathan Wildman Pastor of the 1st Baptist Church in Lyme

This certifies that Clark G. Stillman of Westerly Rhode Island & Electa Howard of Lyme were married by me October 30th 1828 Nathan Wildman Pastor of the 1st Baptist Church in Lyme

[page 229] This certifies that Henry H. Clark & Almena Loomis both of Lyme were married by me November 19th 1828 Nathan Wildman Pastor of the 1st Baptist Church in Lyme

This certifies that John I Manwaring & Harriet Anderson both of Lyme were married by me November 27th 1828 Nathan Wildman Pastor of the 1st Baptist Church in Lyme

Charles Francis Manwaring Son of John I and Harriet Manwaring born May 29th AD 1830
Sarah Ellen daughter of the above born January 9th 1832
Harriet Jane daughter of the above born Sept 7th 1833

[page 230] This certifies that Asabel Rowland & Abby Greenfield both of Lyme were married by me January 25th 1829 Nathan Wildman Pastor of the 1st Baptist Church in Lyme

This certifies that James Haynes of Lyme and Mary Hand of Long Island were united in marriage on the 22nd day of January 1829 by the Subscriber Chester Colton Pastor of the 1st Congregational Church in Lyme

[page 231] This certifies that Atwell Tucker Junr and Hannah Chadwick alias Gulliver married by me April 20th 1829   Joshua R. Warren, Justice of Peace

I do hereby certify that David Maynard and Nancy Page were lawfully married by me -- Lyme April 19th 1829   Tubal Wakefield Minister of the Gospel

[page 232]   I certify that Atwell Tucker and Lucy Waid were lawfully married by me 26th April AD 1829   Ezra Pratt, Justice of Peace

This certifies Joseph A. Sobuck and Sally Warhead were married by me April 28th 1829   Peter Comstock, Justice of Peace

[page 233] Mr. Elisha Smith and Mary Gorton were married December 26th 1808
William Angus their son was born October 8th 1809
Mary Gorton their daughter born March 10th 1812
Edmund, their son born October 21st 1815
John Gorton their son born September 24th 1819
Elisha their son born February 2nd 1822
Frances Elisabeth their daughter born March 13th 1824
Charles Henry their son born October 27th 1828

This certifies that Silas Wood and Eliza Peck both of Lyme were married by me March 29th AD 1829   Josiah Hawes

[page 234] This certifies that Daniel Anderson and Ethelinda Ingraham both of Lyme were united in marriage as the law directs on the 28th of May 1829 by the subscriber Chester Colton pastor of the 1st Con. Ch. in Lyme

This certifies that George Miller and Jerusha Ann Cobb were married by me July 8th 1829   Tubal Wakefield

[page 235] This certifies that Elisha Miller Jun'r and Caroline Page were married by me July 8th 1829   Tubal Wakefield

This certifies that Joseph Higgins Mather of Saybrook and Sarah Selden Jewett of Lyme were married by me August 9th 1829   Tubal Wakefield Minister of the Gospel

[page 236] This certifies that Stephen I. Lord and Sarah A. McCurdy both of Lyme were united in marriage on the 24th August 1829 by the subscriber Chester Colton Pastor of the 1st Church in Lyme

This certifies that Ambrose Burdick of East Haddam and Mary Ann Luther of Lyme were joined in marriage by Alvan Ackley Minister of the Gospel

[page 237] This certifies that on the 30th day of August 1829 Dan W. Mather and Elisabeth Clark both of Lyme were united in lawful marriage by me Herman L. Vaill Minister of the Gospel & Pastor of the 2nd Congregational Church in Lyme

This certifies that on the 7th day of September 1829 Lester Clark 2nd and Mary Ann Lester both of Lyme were united in lawful marriage by me Herman L. Vaill

[page 238] This certifies that Almus Pratt of Deep River and Sally A. Collins of Lyme were joined in marriage on the 11th of October 1829 by the subscriber Chester Colton Pastor of the 1st Church in Lyme

This certifies that Nathaniel Matthews of New London and Betsy Bramble of Lyme were married by me November 2nd AD 1829   Josiah Hawes

[page 239]   This certifies that Richard Royce and Sally M. Mather were joined in marriage on the 26th of November 1829 by the subscriber   Chester Colton Pastor of a Church in Lyme

Be it remembered that on this 27th day of December 1829 Timothy Pratt of Saybrook and Nancy Saunders of Lyme were joined in marriage according to the laws of this state by and before me.   Richard E. Selden Junr Justice of Peace

[page 240]   This certifies that Orlando Miner and Belinda Otis both of Lyme were married by me December 8th AD 1829   Josiah Hawes

This certifies that Charles Sloman and Betsey Maynard both of Lyme were married by me March 21st AD 1830   Nathan Wildman Pastor of the 1st Baptist Church in Lyme
Catharine Ann Sluman born Jan'y 13th 1831
Mary Eliza Sluman born Jan'y 28th 1833
John Andrew Sluman born Sept. 19th 1834 died July 13th 1841
Charles Alexander Sluman born Aug. 11th 1836 Died Oct. 28th 1836
Charles Henry Sluman born Sept. 12th 1837
Niles Alexander Sluman born March 28th 1840
William Eagles Sluman born March 25th 1842 D. June 5 1862
Infant Male Sluman born April 2nd 1843 D Apr 5th 1843
Joseph Ely Sluman born Feb'y 10th 1845 D. Oct. 9th 1845
Joseph Albert Sluman born Feby 12th 1846
Evelyn Maria Sluman born April 7th 1848 died April 7th 1849
Betsey Maria Sluman born March 8th 1852
Charles D. Sluman departed this life November 12th 1869
Betsey Maynard Sluman departed this life May 16th 1889

[page 241]   This certifies that William G. Gorton and Eliza R. Warren both of Lyme were married by me March 3rd AD 1830   Nathan Wildman Pastor of the 1st Baptist Church of Lyme
Esther Ann daughter of the said William & Eliza was born Decemr 14th 1830
Sarah Mehitabel daughter of the said William & Eliza was born February 16 1833
John Son of the said William & Eliza was born October 19, 1834

This may certify that George Washington Phelps of East Haddam and Sally Reed of Lyme were united in the bonds of marriage on the 14th of April 1830 by the subscriber Chester Colton Pastor of the 1st Congregational Church in Lyme

[page 242]   This certifies that Elihu Strong and Christiana Beckwith were duly joined in marriage agreeably to the law of the State of Connecticut on the evening of the 4th of April AD 1830 by John S. Rogers Justice of the Peace

This Certifies that John E. Rogers of Norwich and Sarah M. Chapel of Lyme were married by me May 9th AD 1830   Nathan Wildman Pastor of the 1st Baptist Church in Lyme

[page 243]   This certifies that George Miller Avery of Waterford and Abby Eliza Wait of Lyme were united in marriage on the 18th of May 1830 by the subscriber Chester Colton Pastor of the 1st Church in Lyme

This certifies that John W. Allen and Harriet C. Mather were united in marriage on the fifth of July 1830 by the subscriber   Chester Colton Pastor of a church in Lyme

[page 244]   This certifies that on the 2nd day of August 1830 Josiah Kellogg of Wilmington N.C. and Lydia M. Utley of Lyme were united in lawful marriage by me   Herman L. Vaill
Samuel Vine Kellogg son of the above was born March 17th AD 1832

This certifies that on the 24th of August 1830 Charles Chadwick and Mary A. Rowland both of Lyme were united in lawful marriage by me. Herman L. Vaill

[page 245] This certifies that Alexander Keables and Roxana Maynard both of Lyme were married by me June 29th AD 1830 Nathan Wildman Pastor of the 1st Baptist Church in Lyme

This certifies that Samuel Talcott of Hebron and Asenath Morgan of Lyme were married by me September 7th AD 1830   Josiah Hawes

[page 246] This certifies that Calvin Huntley and Betsey Rogers both of Lyme were married by me October 31st 1830 Nathan Wildman Pastor of the 1st Baptist Church in Lyme

This certifies that Silas C. Beebe and Mercy A. Wait both of Lyme were married by me November 28th 1830 Nathan Wildman Pastor of the 1st Baptist Church in Lyme

[page 247] This certifies that Gerrish Bracy and Eliza Miller both of Lyme were married by me November 30th 1830   Joseph Chadwick Justice of Peace
New London County Ss Lyme 25th November 1830 Be it remembered that on the day aforesaid Harvey Hall of Colchester and Sally Mott of Groton were joined in marriage by and before me Richd E. Selden Junr Justice of Peace

[page 248] This certifies that William Brockway and Nancy F. Post were married by me December 15th 1830   Josiah Hawes
Thomas Clark Brockway son of Wm & Nancy Brockway born Septemr 18th 1831
Richard William Brockway son of Wm & Nancy Brockway born February 25th 1835

Nancy Jane Sheldon Harrison daughter of the said Wm. & Nancy was born August 1st 1836

Lyme October 22d 1837 this day William Brockway & Hannah Martin both of this town were legally joined in marriage by me Harvey Bushnell Minister of the Gospel
Ebenezer Brockway son of Wm & Hannah Brockway was born Oct. 17th 1838

This certifies that Adin Tooker and Mary A. Miller were married by me Decr 29th AD 1830   Josiah Hawes

[page 249] This certifies that George Hazard Chadwick and Mary H. Sparrow were united in marriage on the 19th day of December 1830 by the subscriber
Chester Coton Pastor of a Church in Lyme

This certifies that David Royce and Elisabeth Forsyth were married by me February 2nd 1831   Nathan Wildman

[page 250] Lyme February the 25th AD 1831
This certifies that Mr. John Babcock of Lyme and Miss Julia Ann Hubbard of East Haddam were joined in marriage agreeably to the laws of the State of Connecticut on the evening of the 25th of February AD 1831 by me   John S. Rogers Justice of Peace

This certifies that Joel Beckwith of Lyme and Sybil Starkey of Saybrook were united in marriage on the 3rd of March 1831 by the subscriber   Chester Colton pastor of a Church in Lyme

[page 251] This certifies that on the 27th day of March 1831 Jonathan T. Mack and Jane D. Ransom both of Lyme were united in lawful marriage by me Herman L. Vaill Minister of the Gospel

This certifies that Abel L. Huntley and Lydia B. Reed both of Lyme were married by me March 16th AD 1831 Nathan Wildman Pastor of the 1st Baptist Church in Lyme [page 252] This certifies that George W. Harding and Eunice C. Brockway were married by me March AD 1831   Nathan Wildman Pastor of the 1st Baptist Church in Lyme

This certifies that Darius Harding and Sally M. Rogers both of Lyme were married by me April 17th AD 1831   Nathan Wildman Pastor of the 1st Baptist Church in Lyme

[page 253] This certifies that LeRoy Mowry of Troy and Catharine B. Noyes of Lyme were united in marriage on the 17th of April 1831 in conformity to the laws of this state by the subscriber   Chester Colton Pastor of a Church in Lyme

This certifies that Abiel Stark Junr of Lyme and Jane Alice Ely of Pleasant Valley State of New York were married by me April 3rd AD 1831   Josiah Hawes

[page 254] This certifies that on the 22nd of May 1831 Calvin Nebb of Lyme and Hannah Gardner of Preston were united in lawful marriage by me   Herman L. Vaill

This certifies that Reuben Smith and Nancy Harding both of Lyme were married by me February 28th 1831   Nathan Wildman

[page 255] This certifies that William Beckwith and Caroline Champion both of Lyme were married by me May 24th 1831   Nathan Wildman

This certifies that Winthrop DeWolf and Hepsibah C. Anderson of Lyme were united in marriage on the 20th of June 1831 by the subscriber Chester Colton Pastor of a Church in Lyme

[page 256] This certifies that William F. Griswold and Sarah B. Noyes of Lyme were united in marriage on the 9th of June 1831 by the subscriber Chester Colton Pastor of a Church in Lyme

This certifies that Seth Chadwick & Caroline Rowland both of Lyme were married by me July 5th 1831   Nathan Wildman

[page 257] This certifies that William D. Davison and Abby C. Manwaring both of Lyme were married by me July 10th 1831   Nathan Wildman

This certifies that Harvey Tooker and Mary Maynard both of Lyme were married by me June 12th AD 1831   Josiah Hawes

[page 258] This certifies that Henry Jones and Phebe S. Marvin both of Lyme were married by me July 24th 1831   Josiah Hawes

This certifies that Silas Tucker and Lucy Havens both of Lyme were united in marriage on the 3rd of July 1831 by the subscriber   Chester Colton Pastor of a Church in Lyme

[page 259] New London County Lyme 23d July 1831
James Bogue and Laura Sawyer have been married together this day by me Zebulon Brockway Jr. Justice of Peace

New London County Lyme 23d July 1831
Jabez H. Bogue and Joanna Denison have this day been married together by me Zebulon Brockway Jr. Justice of Peace

[page 260] New London County Lyme 23d December 1830
Gurdon Grayham and Elisabeth Otis have this day been married together by me Zebulon Brockway Jr. Justice of Peace

This certifies that Benjamin Barter of New London and Mary Miller of Lyme were married by me July 29th 1831   Nathan Wildman Pastor of the 1st Baptist Church in Lyme

[page 261] This certifies that Selden P. Marvin and Phebe Reed both of Lyme were joined in marriage on the 1st of September 1831   Chester Colton Pastor of a Church in Lyme

This certifies that Ebenezer W. Comstock of Norwich, New York and Juliaett Champion of Lyme Connecticut were united in marriage on the 10th of October 1831 by the subscriber   Chester Colton Pastor of a Church in Lyme

[page 262]   This certifies that Peter Comstock and Maria Warren both of Lyme were married by me October 27th AD 1831   Nathan Wildman

This certifies that John Smith and Delia Mack both of Lyme were married by me October 2nd AD 1831   Nathan Wildman

[page 263]   This certifies that Silas Clarke of Watertown, New York and Sarah Elisabeth Ely of Lyme were married by me October 7th AD 1831   Josiah Hawes

This certifies that Amasa H. Gillett of Hebron and Lucy Ann Banning of Lyme were married by me September 28th AD 1831   Josiah Hawes

[page 264]   New London County Ss Lyme 17th October 1831
Be it remembered that on the day aforesaid Timothy Peckham Jun of South Kingston Rhode Island was united in marriage to Harriet Rand of Lyme aforesaid by and before me.   Richd E. Selden Jun Justice of Peace

This certifies that Jesse H. Jerome of New London and Betsy Gee of Lyme were duly joined in marriage by me November 6th 1831 Elias Sharpe Elder

[page 265]   This certifies that John Bartlet of New Orleans and Mary A. Hill of Lyme were joined in marriage on the 7th day of November AD 1831 by the subscriber   Chester Colton   Pastor of a Church in Lyme

This certifies that George R. Coult and Catherine Caulkins both of Lyme were joined in marriage on the 17th day of November AD 1831 by the subscriber   Chester Colton   Pastor of a church in Lyme

[page 266]   This certifies that Samuel A. Wait and Mercy A. Chadwick both of Lyme were joined in marriage on the 24th day of November AD 1831 by the subscriber -- Chester Colton   Pastor of a Church in Lyme

This certifies that Sylvanus H. Huntley and Lydia L. Caulkins were united in marriage on the 15th of December 1831 by the subscriber   Chester Colton Pastor of a Church in Lyme

[page 267]   This certifies that Orrin F. Smith of New London and Emma A. Loomis of Lyme were married by me November 3rd 1831   Nathan Wildman

This certifies that Diodate G. Wilson of Hebron and Lucina Rogers of Lyme were joined in marriage agreeably to the law of the State of Connecticut on the 14th day of March AD 1832 by the undersigned   John S. Rogers Justice of Peace

[page 268]   This certifies that John Erastus Selden was born February 22nd AD 1829

This certifies that Horace Ely and Clarrissa Marvin both of Lyme were married by me May 1st AD 1832   Josiah Hawes

[page 269]   This certifies that David P. Otis of Waterford and Hannah R. Comstock of Lyme were married by me March 21st AD 1832   Nathan Wildman

This certifies that Joseph B. Chadwick and Parthenia Lord both of Lyme were married on the 25th June 1832 by the subscriber   Chester Colton   Pastor of a church in Lyme

[page 270]   This certifies that Richard H. Miller and Elisabeth Stebbins both of New London were united in marriage July 8th 1832 by the subscriber   Chester Colton   Pastor of a Church in Lyme

This certifies that John Clark and Julia Ann Champion both of Lyme were united in marriage July 14th 1832 by the subscriber   Chester Colton   Pastor of a Church in Lyme [page 271] I hereby certify that Mr. Jonathan R. Martin and Miss Hannah B. Crocker both of Lyme were lawfully joined in marriage the sixteenth day of August Eighteen hundred thirty two by me Frederick Wightman Pastor of the first Baptist Church in Lyme

I hereby certify that Mr. Levi B. Chapel and Miss Sarah Latham were lawfully joined in marriage the eleventh day of September AD 1832 by me Frederick Wightman Pastor of the 1st Baptist Church in Lyme

[page 272] I hereby certify that Ira A. Bush and Matilda P. Manwaring were lawfully joined in marriage the twentieth day of September one thousand eight hundred and thirty two by me Frederick Wightman Pastor of the 1st Baptist Church of Lyme

Russel Bogue and Sila Tillitson married April 2nd 1822 by Samuel B. Mather Esq. The above is copied from the family records by F. Fosdick T. Clerk   Lyme January 23rd 1864

This certifies that Reuben L. Hall and Abby W. Lee both of Lyme were united in marriage September 11th 1832 by the subscriber Chester Colton Pastor of a Church in Lyme

Lyme 3rd Book of Marriages From 1832

[p. 1] I hereby certify that Stephen L. Rowland and Lydia E. Havens both of Lyme were lawfully joined in marriage the 8th day of November one thousand eight hundred and thirty two by me
        Frederick Wightman Pastor of the 1st Baptist Church in Lyme

I hereby certify that Charles F. Starkey of Essex and Frances M Congdon of Lyme were lawfully joined in marriage the twentieth day of November eighteen hundred and thirty two by me
        Frederick Wightman Pastor of the 1st Baptist Church in Lyme

[p. 2] I hereby certify that Justin L Beckwith and Mary A Crocker both of Lyme were lawfully joined in marriage the twenty-second day of November one thousand eight hundred and thirty two by me
        Frederick Wightman Pastor of the 1st Baptist Church in Lyme

This certifies that Elias Ely Esqr of New York and Elisa Nichols of Lyme were married by me November 5th AD 1832   Josiah Hawes

[p. 3] This certifies that Henry Steward and Georgiana Sterling both of Lyme were Married by me December 20th AD 1832   Josiah Hawes

This certifies that on the 6th Day of January 1833 Ulysses McCrery and Lydia Rowth both of Lyme were united in lawful marriage by me -   Herman S. Vaill -

[p. 4] I hereby certify that Horace B. Manwaring and Sophia Huntley, both of Lyme were lawfully joined in marriage the eleventh day of December one thousand eight hundred and thirty two
        by me Frederick Wightman Pastor of the 1st Baptist Church in Lyme

New London County SS Lyme January 30th AD 1833 this certifies that I this day married Dan Tinker and Czrina Austin both of said Lyme   Joshua R. Warren Justice of Peace

[p. 5] This certifies that Mirachi Huntly and Abby I Bush both of Lyme were married January 2nd AD 1833 by me   Joseph Strickland Justice of Peace

This certifies that James F. Shepherd of Windham and Betsey I Haynes of Lyme were united in marriage on the 6th day of January 1832 by the subscriber
        Chester Colton Pastor of a Church in Lyme

[p. 6] I hereby certify that Jonathan Page and Rachel Waid both of Lyme were lawfully joined in marriage the twenty seventh day of January eighteen hundred and thirty three -
by me   Frederick Wightman Pastor of the 1st Baptist Church in Lyme

This certifies that Samuel L. Comstock & Harriet B. Miner both of Lyme Ct were lawfully married by me this 17th of March 1833   R. S. Crampton V.D.M.

[p. 7] This certifies that Samuel Gilbert and Almira Maynard both of Lyme were married by me March 7th AD 1833   Elijah Willard

Oliver I. Lay of Lyme and Mary A. Whittlesey of Saybrook were married June 6th AD 1827

    Sarah Ann Lay their daughter born February 10th 1829
    Adeline Lay their daughter born September 18, 1830
    Mariette I Lay their daughter born October 14 1831

[p. 8] This certifies that John D. Clark of east haddam and Jane E. Tucker of lyme were united in marriage April 14, 1833 by the subscriber
        Chester Colton Pastor of a church in Lyme

I hereby certify that Mr. Edmund W. Smith of Middletown and Miss Frances S. Miner of Lyme were lawfully join'd in marriage, the 6th of May 1833 by me
        Frederick Wightman Pastor of the First Baptist Church Lyme

[p. 9] This certifies that David Prigh of Attica N.Y. and Eunice Lord of Lyme were married July 15th 1833 by the subscriber   Chester Colton Pastor of a church in Lyme

Seth Henry Wait son of John J. and Mary Anne Wait was born April 11th 1833

Thomas Spencer Champion was born Sept. 12th 1825

[p. 10] This certifies that on the 6th day of October 1833 Solomon J. Adams of Rodman N.Y. and Nancy Bush of Lyme Con. were united in Lawful marriage by me
                                                Herman L. Vaill Minister of the Gospel

This certifies that Silas E. Coy of Meriden was married to Lorinda Willard of Lyme on the 15th day of September 1833 by me
                                                Elijah Willard Elder in the Methodist Episcopal Church

[p. 11] This certifies that Rev. Willys Warner of Yale College and Elizabeth A. Hart of Lyme were united in marriage on the 9th of October 1833 by the subscriber
                                                Chester Colton Pastor of a church in Lyme

This certifies that Abraham P. Ely and Philina Griffin of North Lyme were united in marriage on the 22nd of September 1833 by the subscriber
                                                Chester Colton Pastor of a church in Lyme

[p. 12] This certifies that George W Fox and Emariah C Hardin were married by me October 21th 1833   Nathan Shailor Pastor of the Baptist Church in Chesterfield

This certifies that Richard Beebe and Hannah Congdon were married by me October 21th 1833   Nathan Shailor Pastor of the Baptist Church in Chesterfield

[p. 13] This certifies that Samuel S Alison and Frances A Pilgrim both of Middletown were united in marriage October 27th 1833 by the subscriber
                                                Chester Colton Pastor of a church in Lyme

I hereby certify that Austin F Perkins and Mary M Way both of Lyme were lawfully joined in marriage the twenty sixth of November, one thousand eight hundred and thirty three by me   Frederick Wightman Pastor of the first Baptist Church of Lyme

[p. 14] I hereby certify that Oliver Closson and Juliaette Tinker both of Lyme were lawfully joined in marriage the twenty-eight of November one thousand eight hundred and thirty three by me   Frederick Wightman Pastor of the first Baptist Church in Lyme

This certifies that Enoch S Lay and Mary A Champion of Lyme were united in marriage November 24th 1833 by the subscriber   Chester Colton Pastor of a Church in Lyme

[p. 15] This certifies that Edward N Bates of Haddam and Rebekah A. Champion of Lyme were united in marriage November 28th 1833 by the subscriber
                                                Chester Colton Pastor of a Church in Lyme

This certifies that on the 1st day of January 1834 Orlando E Lee and Lydia A Miller both of Lyme were united in lawful marriage by me
                                                Herman L. Vaill, Pastor of the 2nd Cong. Church of Lyme

[p. 16] This certifies that William Peck and Eliza Wood both of Lyme were married by me December 29th AD 1833   Josiah Hawes

I hereby certify that Simon R. Paine and *Lacy A Gorton both of Lyme were lawfully joined in marriage the ninth day of January Eighteen hundred and thirty four by me.
                Frederick Wightman Pastor of the First Baptist Church in Lyme

[p. 17] This certifies than Enoch Lester 2nd and Mary Lester both of Lyme were lawfully married on the 19th day of January AD 1834 by me   John Dwyer, Justice of the Peace

This certifies that Charles D Manwaring of East Haddam and Elisabeth Hughes of Lyme were united in marriage February 17th, 1834 by the subscriber
                                                Chester Colton, Pastor of a church in Lyme

[p. 18] This certifies that Chauncey Bliss of Marlborough and Esther Slate of Lyme were united in marriage march 2nd 1834 by the subscriber
         Chester Colton Pastor of a church in Lyme

This certifies that Alexander L McCurdy and Josephine Lord of Lyme were united in marriage March 17th 1834 by the subscriber Chester Colton Pastor of a church in Lyme

[p. 19] This certifies that Samuel Chadwick and Fanny Rogers both of Lyme were married November 25th AD 1810 by me Andrew Griswold, Justice of the Peace

 Mary Ann, their daughter was born August 25th AD 1811
 Fanny Elisabeth daughter was born January 19th 1814
 Samuel their son was born February 4th 1816
 Frances Jemima their daughter born March 3d 1818
 Juliaett their daughter born November 29th 1820
 William Augustus their son was born March 24th 1823
 Fanny Elisabeth Chadwick died February 4th AD 1815
 Frances Jemima Chadwich died February 25th AD 1831
 Mr. Samuel Chadwick died July 8th AD 1833 aged 47 years

This certifies that Philo Parmelee was married to Sarah P Johnson by me in Lyme March the thirtieth in the year of our Lord one thousand eight hundred and thirty four
         Benjamin G. Goff minister of the Gospel

[p. 20] I hereby certify that Bulkley Edwards of Middletown and Abigail Topliff of Lyme were lawfully joined in marriage the tenth day of April one thousand eight hundred and thirty four by me Frederick Wightman Pastor of the first Baptist Church in Lyme

I hereby certify that Francis B Lee of Bosrah and Mercy G Huntley of Lyme, were lawfully joined in marriage the twenty seventh of April, one thousand eight hundred and thirty four by me. Frederick Wightman Pastor of the first Baptist Church in Lyme

[p. 21] This certifies that Joseph Page and Adaline Waid of Lyme were united in marriage on the 16th of April 1834 by the subscriber Chester Colton Pastor of a Church in Lyme

This may certify that Griswold Holmes of Montville and Mary A. Forsyth have this day been united in marriage Lyme May 20th 1834
         Mark Mead Minister of the Gospel

[p. 22] This certifies that Ralph Taintor of Colchester and Phebe Lord of Lyme were married by me June 2nd A.D. 1834 Josiah Hawes

This certifies that Horace A. Brockway and Rhoda Griffin both of Lyme were married by me June 9th A.D. 1834 Josiah Hawes

[p. 23] I hereby certify that Samuel Woods of Asburnham Mass. and Elisa Ann * Lapiare of Lyme were lawfully joined in marriage the tenth day of June one thousand eight hundred and thirty four by me. Frederick Wightman Pastor of the first Baptist Church in Lyme

This may certify that Thomas Lewis of Norwich, Chenango County and State of New York and Mary Moore of Lyme were joined in marriage on the 19th day of June A.D. 1834 by me
         Peter Comstock Justice of Peace

[p. 24] I hereby certify that Mr. Guy M. Beebe and Miss Dotia Otis were legally married by me Sabbath eve Augt 31st 1834 Andrew M. Smith Pastor 2d Baptist Church of Lyme

I hereby certify that Joseph Tinker of the State of New Hampshire and Betsey Chapel of Lyme were lawfully joined in marriage the twenty second day of September one thousand eight hundred and thirty four by me
      Frederick Wightman Pastor of the first Baptist Church in Lyme

[p. 25] This certifies that Reubin Lord Junr of Lyme and Sarah Weaver of Batavia N.Y. were united in marriage Sept. 23rd 1834 by the subscriber
         Chester Colton Pastor of a church in Lyme

I hereby certify that William Humes of Sterling and Emily Huntly of Lyme were lawfully joined in marriage the eighth day of October one thousand eight hundred and thirty four by me
Frederick Wightman Pastor of the first Baptist Church in Lyme

[p. 26] I hereby certify that Daniel G. Rogers and Lucy Ann Otis both of Lyme were lawfully married the 12th day of October one thousand eight hundred and thirty four by me
Frederick Wightman Pastor of the first Baptist Church in Lyme

I hereby certify that John J. Reynolds and Betsey Wade both of Lyme were legally married by me Sabbath eve Oct. 12th 1834   Andrew M. Smith Pastor 2nd Bap. Ch. h. Lyme

[p. 27] I hereby certify that Mr. William H. Stark and Miss Mary Ann Raymond both of Lyme were legally married by me Monday October 13th 1834.
Andrew M. Smith Pastor 2nd Bap. Ch.h. Lyme

This certifies that Morris Hinsdale of LeRoy New York and Martha A. Waid of Lyme were united in marriage October 21st 1834 by the subscriber
Chester Colton Pastor of a church in Lyme

[p. 28] I hereby certify that Silas Carter of Killingworth and Betsey Huntly of Lyme were lawfully joined in Marriage the first day of November one thousand eight hundred and thirty four by me.   Frederick Wightman Pastor of the first Baptist Church in Lyme

This certifies that Joseph Durfey of Groton and Lucy Ann Burnham of Lyme were united in Marriage on the 24th of November 1834 by the subscriber
Chester Colton Pastor of a Church in Lyme

[p. 29] This certifies that Southmayd Miner was married to Sarah Banning by me December the ninth A.D. one thousand eight hundred and thirty four
Benjamin G. Goff Minister of the Gospel

I hereby certify that Jeremiah Bush and Nancy Beckwith both of Lyme were lawfully Joined in marriage the twenty first day of December one thousand eight hundred and thirty four by me   Frederick Wightman Pastor of the first Baptist Church in Lyme

[p. 30] September 9th 1834 George F. Langworthy of Stonington and Julia Ann Chadwick of Lyme appeared before me the undersigned and I married them according to law.
J.S. Anderson

I hereby certify that Harris Crocker of Waterford and Sabra Manwaring of Lyme were lawfully joined in marriage the thirtieth of January one thousand eight hundred and thirty five by me   Frederick Wightman Pastor of the first Baptist Church in Lyme

[p. 31] I hereby certify that Daniel Manwaring of Lyme and Mary Beebe of Waterford were lawfully joined in marriage the first day of March one thousand Eight hundred and thirty five by me.   Frederick Wightman Pastor of the first Baptist Church in Lyme

I hereby certify that Thomas J. Way and Mary A. Bump both of Lyme were lawfully joined in marriage the twenty second day of February, one thousand eight hundred & thirty five by me   Frederick Wightman Pastor of the first Baptist Church in Lyme

[p. 32] Lyme March 29th 1835 This day Alfred Lester and Lucy Peck both of this Town were legally joined in marriage by me   Harvy Bushnell Minister in 3rd Society Lyme

Lyme March 30th 1835 This day Charles H. Dean of Stonington and Ede Brown of Lyme were legally joined in marriage by me   Harvy Bushnell

[p. 33] Lyme March 23rd 1835 This day Horace Chapel and Caroline L. Banning both of this Town were legally joined in marriage by me.   Harvey Bushnell

Victoria G. Chapel daughter of Horace and Caroline L. B. Chapel was born Aug. 31. 1846

168   LYME, CONNECTICUT, VITAL RECORDS

This certifies that Alfred L. Wells of New York and Sarah G. Sill of Lyme were united in marriage on the 13th of April AD 1835 by the subscriber
           Chester Colton Pastor of a church in Lyme

[p. 34] This certifies that Livingston H. Smith of Norwich and Abby M. Wait of Lyme were united in marriage on the 14th of April 1835 by the subscriber
           Chester Colton Pastor of a church in Lyme

This certifies that Livingston H. Smith of Norwich Ct. and Louisa S. Wait of Lyme Ct. were united in marriage March 26th 1839 by the subscriber
           Chester Colton Pastor of a Church in Lyme

This certifies that Richard L. Griswold of New York and Louisa G. Mather of Lyme were united in marriage 25th of May 1835 by the Subscriber
           Chester Colton Pastor of a Church in Lyme

[p. 35] This certifies that William J. Banning and Lucy Lay of Lyme were united in marriage on the 4th of June 1835 by the Subscriber   Chester Colton Pastor of a church in Lyme

Lyme June 1st 1835 This day Samuel M. Birdsey of Middletown and Elisabeth M. Miller of this place were legally joined in marriage by me
           Harvey Bushnell Minister of the Gospel

[p. 36] Lyme June 2nd 1835 This day Ulysses Hayden of Essex and Elisabeth E. Lord of Lyme were legally joined in marriage by me   Harvey Bushnell Minister of the Gospel

This certifies that at Lyme on the 31st day of May A.D. 1835 Mr. Lay Ayer of Lyme was married to Mrs. Mary Smith of Waterford by   John Dwyer Justice of the Peace

[p. 37] This certifies that Israel Havens and Irene Harding were united in marriage June 15th 1835 by the subscriber   Chester Colton Pastor of a church in Lyme

Lyme August 2nd 1835 This may certify that Ozias H. Bogue and Phebe Johnson both of this town have this day been united in marrige   Mark Mead Minister of the Gospel

[p. 38] I hereby certify that Norman Daniels of Hartford and Eveline Crocker of Lyme were lawfully married the ninth day of August one thousand eight hundred and thirty five by me   Frederick Wightman Pastor of the first Baptist Church in Lyme

I hereby certify that on this day August 16th 1835 The marriage of Lewis Emerson to Sophia Pilgrim both of Lyme were performed by me according to law
           George Carrington Pastor of the Congregational church in Hadlyme

[p. 39] This certifies that John Hart and Margaret Sill both of Lyme were united in marriage on the 25th of August 1835 by the subscriber
           Chester Colton Pastor of a Church in Lyme

This certifies that Shadrack Sill and Laura Lay both of Lyme were united in marriage on the 3rd of September 1835 by the subscriber   Chester Colton Pastor of a Church in Lyme

[p. 40] I hereby certify that Mr. Charles E. Tiffany of Williston Vermont and Miss Frances M Jewett of Lyme were legally married by me September 22nd 1835
           A. M. Smith Paster 2d Baptist Church Lyme

Lyme September 21th 1835 This day Erastus Selden and Laura Comstock both of this place were legally joined in marriage by me.   Harvy Bushnell

[p. 41] This certifies that Ira Tillotson and Betsey M Lay both of Lyme were united in marriage September 20th 1835 by the subscriber   Charles Colton Pastor of a Church in Lyme

This certifies that on the 13th day of September 1835 Daniel Howard Junr and Cordelia Dowsett both of Lyme were united in lawful marriage by me   Herman L. Vaill

[p. 42] This certifies that on the 14th day of September 1835 David C. Manwaring of Waterford and Frances S. Clark of Lyme were united in lawful marriage by me
           Herman L. Vaill

I certify that on this day Sept 14th 1834 the marriage of Benjamin H. Catlin of Haddam to Amelia D. Spencer of Lyme was performed by me according to law.
    George Carrington Junr Pastor of the Congregational Church in Hadlyme

[p. 43] Lyme October 11th 1835 this day Charles E. Smith of New York & Mary E. Brockway of this place were legally joined in marriage by me.
    Harvy Bushnell Minister of the Gospel

Lyme October 18th 1835 this day John H Dayton of Sagharbour N.Y. and Frances J. Nicols of this place were legally joined in marriage by me
    Harvy Bushnell minster of the Gospel

[p. 44] This certies that on the 18th day of October instant Chauncy Prentice and Caroline Latham, both of Lyme were united in lawful marriage by me.
    Herman L. Vaill Pastor of the Cong. Church in East Lyme
Dated Lyme Oct 22 1835

Lyme November 4th 1835 This day James L Brown of Mansfield and Eliza I Emerson of this town were legally joined in marriage by me. Harvey Bushnell Minister of the Gospel

[p. 45] This may certify that Joseph W. Huntly & Mary E. Reed both of this town have this day been united in marriage Lyme November 10th 1835 Mark Mead V.D.M.

This certifies that Norris Rathbun of East Haddam and Luna L Swan of Lyme were united in marriage on the 23rd of November 1835 by the Subscriber.
    Chester Colton Pastor of a church in Lyme

[p. 46] This certifies that Griswold Chappell of Lyme and Hannah C Lesheur of Pomfret were united in marriage on the 9th of November 1835 by the subscriber
    Chester Colton Pastor of a church in Lyme

This certifies that Elisha Havens and Lucy A Champion both of Lyme were united in marriage on the 25th of ___ 1835 by the subscriber
    Charles Colton pastor of a church in Lyme

[p. 47] I certify that on this day Nov 26th 1835 the marriage of Arnold Buckingham of East Haddam to Cornelia Luther of Lyme was preformed by me according to law.
    George Carrington Pastor of the congregational church of Hadlyme

I hereby certify that Thomas Twist Jr. of Windham Ct. and Harriet Beckwith of Lyme Ct. were lawfully joined in marriage the twenty seventh of November one thousand eight hundred and thirty five by me.
    Frederick Wightman Pastor of the first Baptist church in Lyme

[p. 48] I hereby certify that Gershom Main of Windham Ct. and Eliza D Tinker of Lyme Ct. were lawfully joined in marriage the 27th day of December one thousand eight hundred and thirty five by me Frederick Wightman Pastor of the first Baptist Church in Lyme

I hereby certify that Alva West and Susan Gilbert were lawfully joined in marrige on the 8th day of January AD 1836 by me. Stephen L Peck Justice of Peace

[p. 49] I certify that on this day December 27th 1835 the marriage of Edward Josephus Osborn of Saybrook to Fanny Pilgrim of Lyme was performed by me according to law
    George Carrington associate Pastor of the Congregational Church Hadlyme

This certifies that William Armstrong of New London and Sarah Manwaring of Lyme were united in marriage on the 21st of January 1836 by the subscriber
    Chester Colton Pastor of a church in Lyme

[p. 50] I hereby certify that Ezra M. Champion and Elizabeth Jane Richardson were lawfully married the twentieth of January one thousand eight hundred & thirty six by me
    Frederick Wightman Pastor of the first Baptist Church in Lyme

I hereby certify that Benjamin Manwaring and Freelove Beckwith both of Lyme were lawfully joined in marriage January the tenth one thousand eight hundred and thirty six by me
       Frederick Wightman Pastor of the first Baptist Church in Lyme

[p. 51] Lyme February 3rd 1836 This day Obed B. Ely of this Town and Emma Giddings of Richland Michigan were legally joined in marriage by me
       Harvey Bushnell minister of the Gospel

I hereby certify that Ichabod Ryon and Maria E. Morgan both of Lyme were lawfully joined in marriage the sixth day of March one thousand eight hundred and thirty-six by me.
       Frederick Wightman Pastor of the first Baptist Church in Lyme

[p. 52] Salem October 19th 1835 This may certify that on the 19th day of October 1835 Mr. Nelson Guy Loomis of Salem Conn.t and Miss Laura Ann Gorton of Lyme, Conn.t were united in the bonds of matrimony in the presence of a large number of witnesses by me
       Charles Thompson Pastor of the Congregational Church & Society in Salem

This certifies that Almon Bacon and Margaret S. Clark both of Lyme were united in marriage the 29th of February 1836 by the subscriber
       Chester Colton Pastor of a church in Lyme

[p. 53] I hereby certify that Erastus Rogers and Anna C. Beebe both of Lyme were legally married by me January 15th 1836 Andrew M. Smith Pastor 2nd Baptist Church Lyme

This certifies that Morgan Lewis and Sarah Ann Chapman were joined in marriage on the 27th day of March 1836 by me   Lodowick Bill Justice of Peace

[p. 54] I hereby certify that William A. Smith and Mary Ann Gorton both of Lyme were lawfully joined in marriage the fifth day of April one thousand eight hundred and thirty six by me   Frederick Wightman Pastor of the first Baptist Church in Lyme

I hereby certify that on this day March 6th 1836 the marriage of Stephen White of Haddam to Betsey Lewis of Lyme was performed by me according to law
   George Carrington Associate Pastor of the Congregational Church in Hadlyme

[p. 55] This may certify that Christopher H. Lee of Lyme and Susan M. Howe of Bozrah have this day been united in marriage by me. Mark Mead Minister of the Gospel
  Lyme July 14th 1836

I hereby certify that Elisha H. Smith & Maria Brockway both of Lyme were lawfully joined in marriage the 26th day of June one thousand eight hundred thirty six by me
       Frederick Wightman Pastor of the first Baptist Church in Lyme

[p. 56] I hereby certify that Albert L. Chapel & Julia E. Tillotson both of Lyme were lawfully joined in marriage the twenty eighth of June one thousand eight hundred & thirty six by me   Frederick Wightman Pastor of the first Baptist Church in Lyme

I hereby certify that Asa Holt and Polly Smith both of Waterford were lawfully joined in marriage the seventh day of August One thousand eight hundred and thirty six by me
       Frederick Wightman Pastor of the first Baptist Church in Lyme

[p. 57] I hereby certify that Nathan E. Green and Mary Ann Beckwith both of Lyme were lawfully joined in marriage the thirty first day of July one thousand eight hundred and thirty six by me. Frederick Wightman Pastor of the first Baptist Church in Lyme

I certify that on this day September 12th 1836 the marriage of Daniel A. Shepard of Cleaveland Ohio to Louiza M. Gates of Lyme was performed by me according to law
    George Carrington Associate Pastor of the Congregational Church Hadlyme

[p. 58] This certifies that James Wood and Azubah Dolph of Saybrook were united in marriage on the 18th of September 1836 by the subscriber
       Chester Colton Pastor of a church in Lyme

Lyme 31st 1836   This day Walter H. Wilkie & Caroline Warner both of this place were legally joined in marriage by me   Harvey Bushnell Minister of the Gospel

[p. 59] This certifies that on the 30th day of October 1836 Joseph Beebe of Waterford and Frances Beckwith of Norwich were united in lawful marriage by me
Herman L. Vaill Minister of the Gospel

This certifies that Otis P. Bailey of Boston and Eliza Appleby of Lyme were united in marriage on the 9th of October 1836 by the subscriber
Chester Colton Pastor of a church in Lyme

[p. 60] This certifies that Richard N. Watrous of Chester and Ann Janette Austin of Lyme were united in marriage on the 16th of October by the subscriber
Chester Colton Pastor of a Church in Lyme

This certifies that Billings P. Learned of Lockport New York and Mary A. Noyes of Lyme were united in marriage on the 1st of November 1836 by the subscriber
Chester Colton Pastor of a Church in Lyme

[p. 61] This certifies that John A. Russ of Mansfield and Ruth A. Reed of Lyme were united in marriage on the 24th of November 1836 by the subscriber
Chester Colton Pastor of a Church in Lyme

This certifies that Abel Smith of the Town of Preston State of New York and Susan Jerome of the town of Salem Connecticut were married by me on the 15th day of January 1837
Daniel Stewart Justice of the Peace

[p. 62] Nathan Jewett Junr and Lucretia Stark were legally married by me Tuesday morning February 7th 1837
Andrew M. Smith Pastor Baptist Church Colchester Borough

This certifies that Richard L. Lord and Esther A. Lord of Lyme were united in marriage January 31st 1837 by the subscriber -
Chester Colton Pastor of a Church in Lyme

[p. 63] This certifies that Samuel B. Dast of Saybrook and Adaline Hand of Lyme were united in marriage on the 23rd of February 1837 by the subscriber -
Chester Colton Pastor of a Church in Lyme

I hereby certify that Francis A. Porter of Waterford and Harriet Meloney of Lyme were lawfully joined in marriage September the fourth one thousand eight hundred and thirty six by me   Frederick Wightman Pastor of the first Baptist Church in Lyme

John M. Young son of Benjamin H & Lucy Young was born May 23d A.D. 1820

[p. 64] I hereby certify that Alanson Hedden of Stonington and Laura M. Gorton of Lyme were lawfully joined in marriage the twenty fifth of February one thousand eight hundred and thirty six by me . . . . . . Frederick Wightman Pastor of the first Baptist Church in Lyme

This certifies that George Appleby and Maria Waid were joined in marriage on the 12th March 1837 by me   Alvan Ackley Minister of the Gospel

[p. 65] This certifies that Timothy Peckham of South Kingston R.I. and Harriet Rand of Lyme were married by me October 21st AD 1831
Richard E. Selden Jr. Justice of the Peace

This certifies that William Bunnel of Stonington and Phebe Church of s. Stonington were married by me November 3rd A.D. 1833
Richd E. Selden Junr Justice of the Peace

[p. 66] This certifies that Eleazer Spencer of Saybrook and Betsey Saunders of Lyme were married by me May 4th A.D. 1834   Richard E. Selden Junr Justice of the Peace

This certifies that Ira Watrous of Saybrook and Emily Saunders of Lyme were married by me June 15th A.D. 1834   Richard E. Selden Junr Justice of the Peace [p. 67] This certifies that Russel W. Babcock and Wealthy Emmons both of Lyme were married by me November 8th A.D. 1835 Richard E. Selden Junr Justice of the Peace

This certifies that Jared Daniels and Eleanor Bogue both of Lyme were married by me June 10th A.D. 1836 Richard E. Selden Junr Justice of the Peace

[p. 68] This certifies that William Beckwith of Waterford and Mary Blake of Lyme were married by me February 11th A.D. 1837 Richard E. Selden Junr Justice of the Peace

Lyme February 12th 1837 this day Edward C. G. Brockway and Adaline Damon both of this place were legally joined in marriage by me
H. Bushnell Minister of the Gospel

[p. 69] Lyme April 2d 1837. this day Lorenzo Congdon and Clarissa Miner both of this Town were legally joined in marriage by me
Harvy Bushnell Minister of the Gospel

This may certify that James M. Beebe and Sarah M. Hall were this day united in marriage and the ceremony performed by me Lyme April 20th 1837 Chauncy G. Lee

[p. 70] This certifies that Reuben C. Tinker and Almira Waid of Lyme were united in marriage March 28th 1837 by the subscriber Chester Colton Pastor of a Church in Lyme

This certifies that John Maynard and Mary Daniels of Lyme were united in marriage April 16th 1837 by the subscriber Chester Colton Pastor of a church in Lyme

[p. 71] This certifies that Ebenezer R. Bacon of Lyme and Eliza W. Warren of Waterford were united in marriage May 7th 1837 by the subscriber
Chester Colton Pastor of a Church in Lyme

To whom it may concern. This is to certify that Mr. Charles H. Brockway and Miss Frances A. Luther both of Hadlyme Ct. were joined in marriage at her father's house in H-L. according to the laws of the State of Connecticut on the 28th day of May in the year of our Lord one thousand eight hundred and thirty seven by me William Palmer V.D.M. Chester May 29th 1837

[p. 72] Lyme July 6th 1837 This day William Tinker of Westfield Massachusetts and Eleanor Jane Bill of Lyme Connecticut were legally joined in marriage by me
Harvey Bushnell Minister of the Gospel

Married at Lyme May 24th 1837 Mr. Reuben Huntly to Mrs. Phebe Huntly both of the Town of Lyme Certified by Daniel Stewart Justice of Peace

[p. 73] I hereby certify that Welcome A. Browning of Scio Allegany County of New York and Betsey Moore of Lyme were lawfully joined in marriage the third of September Eighteen hundred and thirty seven by me Frederick Wightman Minister of the Gospel

I certify that on this day July 9th 1837 the marriage of John Bogue of Lyme to Lydia Mitchell of Saybrook was performed by me according to law
George Carrington Associate Pastor of the Congregtional Church in Hadlyme

[p. 74] Lyme August 28th 1837 This day Francis Wilcox of Salem and Harriet Griffin of this Town were legally joined in marriage by me. Harvy Bushnell Minister of the Gospel

This certifies that John C. Woodstock of Killingworth and Adaline Pilgrim of Lyme were united in marriage on the 15th of October 1837 by the subscriber
Chester Colton Pastor of a church in Lyme

[p. 75] This certifies that Ebenezer Mack and Sophronia Harding both of Lyme were united in marriage Oct 17th 1837 by the subscriber
Chester Colton Pastor of a Church in Lyme

This certifies that William J. Lord and Mehitabel S. Slate both of Lyme were united in marriage Nov. 29th 1837 by the subscriber Chester Colton Pastor of a Church in Lyme

[p. 76] Lyme October 22nd 1837 this day William Brockway and Hannah Martin both of this Town were legally joined in marriage by me.
                                            Harvy Bushnell Minister of the Gospel

This certifies that John Eldridge of Chatham Massachusetts and Mary Ann Chadwick of Lyme were married by me January 28th A.D. 1838
                                            Joshua R. Warren Justice of the Peace

[p. 77] This certifies that Joseph H. Lay and Elizabeth A. Maxon were united in marriage February 4th 1838 by the subscriber   Chester Colton Pastor of a Church in Lyme

Mr. Eusebius Clark and Miss Caroline Congdon both of Lyme was lawfully married on the 2d day of January A.D. 1838 by   John Dwyer Justice of the Peace

[p. 78] Lyme January 21st 1838. This day William C. Way and Frances S. Lester both of this Town were legally joined in marriage by me
                                            Harvy Bushnell Minister of the Gospel

This certifies that Adrial Huntly & Wealthy Ann Congdon both of Lyme were united in Marriage March 14th 1838 by the subscriber
                                            Chester Colton Pastor of a Ch.h. in Lyme

[p. 79] This certifies that Thaddeus P. Fanning of Bozrah and Sarah A. Greenfield of Lyme were united in marriage March 4th 1838 by the subscriber
                                            Chester Colton Pastor of a Church in Lyme

This may certify that John Reed Brockway and Harriet N. Gillett both of Lyme were joined in marriage at Lyme Grassy Hill Society on the 13th day of March 1838 by
                                            E. Loomis Minister of the Gospel

[p. 80] Married at Lyme on the 11th of March 1838 Mr. John Rogers to Mrs. Hannah Chapman both of Lyme   Certified by Daniel Stewart Justice of the Peace

Married at Lyme on the 29th day of April 1838 Epaphroditus Miller to Catharine Rogers both of Lyme   Certified by Daniel Steward Justice of Peace

[p. 81] This certifies that Lester H. Maynard and Mahala Brooks both of Waterford Ct. were united in marriage May 28th 1838 by the subscriber
                                            Chester Colton Pastor of a Church in Lyme

This may certify that Nathan Burdick & Maryette Tinker were lawfully joined in marriage at Lyme June 3d 1838 by me   Francis Darrow Minister of the Gospel

[p. 82] New London County S.S. Lyme June 10th 1838   This may certify that Mr. Peter Mason of New London and Miss Lois Chapel of Lyme were at the above date legally joined in marriage by the undersigned authority
                                            Certified by   Jared Turner Justice of the Peace

New London County S.S. Lyme June 11th 1838   This may certify that Mr. Calvin Beckwith of New London and Miss Lucretia Chapel of Lyme were on the 11th day of June 1838 legally joined in marriage by the undersigned authority.
                                            Certified by   Jared Turner Justice of the Peace

[p. 83] This certifies that Maxamilian Oretel of New York and Mary Greenfield of Lyme Ct. were united in marriage July 18th 1838 by the subscriber
                                            Chester Colton Pastor of a Church in Lyme

This certifies that George W. Avery of New London and Sarah M. Greenfield of Lyme Ct. were united in marriage July 18th 1838 by the subscriber
                                            Chester Colton Pastor of a Church in Lyme

[p. 84] This certifies that Niles Taylor of Norwich and Eliza Bailey of Lyme were united in marriage July 8th 1838 by the subscriber   Chester Colton Pastor of a Church in Lyme

174   LYME, CONNECTICUT, VITAL RECORDS

I hereby certify that this day April 8th 1838 the marriage of Asa Sheldon Jr. of Hopkinton Rhode Island to Christiana F. Waterhouse of Lyme was performed by me according to law. George Carrington Associate Pastor of the Congregational Church Hadlyme

[p. 85] Lyme June 10th 1838 this day Asa S. Lee & Mary Bailey both of this town were legally joined in marriage by me.   Harvy Bushnell Minister of the Gospel

This may certify that Elisha Palmer and Ellis Loomis were lawfully joined in marriage at Lyme Nov. 30th 1837 by me   Francis Darrow Minister of the Gospel

[p. 86] This certifies that David Hogue of Debuque Iowa Territory and Lucy G. Wells of Lyme were united in marriage Aug.t 9th 1838 by the subscriber
                    Chester Colton Pastor of a Church in Lyme

This certifies that Isaac Cobb and Fanny Grumley of Lyme Ct. were united in marriage August 12th 1838 by the subscriber   Chester Colton Pastor of a Church in Lyme

[p. 87] This may certify that Edward Tompkins and Juliaette E. Chadwick were lawfully joined in marriage at Lyme May 29th 1838 by me
                    Francis Darrow Minister of the Gospel

I certify that on this day September 30th 1838 the marriage of Amasa Day of Auburn N.Y. to Ursula M. Gates of Lyme was performed by me according to law
     George Carrington Associate Pastor of the Congregational Church in Hadlyme

The marriage was performed at the house of James Gates in the presence of James Gates his wife his two other children and two younger persons.   G.C.

[p. 88] This certifies that Mr. Ezra Beckwith of Waterford and Miss Julia Ann Gates of East Haddam were joined in marriage in Lyme according to the laws of the State of Connecticut on the 16th day of September 1838. by me   Erastus Denison Minister

To whom it may concern. This is to certify that Mr. Samuel Hart of Durham and Miss Lydia R. Davison of Lyme Connecticut were joined in marriage at her Fathers in Lyme Ct. according to the laws of the State of Connecticut on the twenty eighth day of October in the year of our Lord one thousand eight hundred and thirty eight
     E. Lyme October 28th 1838   By me   William Palmer V.D.M.

[p. 89] To whom it may concern this is to certify that Mr. William D. Smith and Miss Eunice M. Davison both of this town were joined in marriage at her Fathers in Lyme Ct. according to the laws of the State of Connecticut on the twenty eighth day of October in the year of our Lord one thousand eight hundred & thirty eight   By me William Palmer VDM
     E. Lyme Oct 28th 1838

This certifies that Mr. Henry G. Pratt of Saybrook and Miss Caroline E. Brockway of Lyme were joined in marriage in Lyme according to law on the 30th day of October 1838
                    By   Erastus Denison Minister

[p. 90] I hereby certify that Richard Clark of Salem and Jane E. Tooker of Lyme were married by me on the 18th of November 1838   Hiram Walden Minister of the Gospel

I hereby certify that Timothy A Laplass of Lyme and Emeline T. Gardner of East Haddam were married by me December 2nd 1838   Hiram Walden Minister of the Gospel

[p. 91] I hereby certify that Joel Clark of Salem and Olive Tooker of Lyme were married by me December 2nd 1838   Hiram Walden Minister of the Gospel

To whom it may concern. This is to certify that Mr. Eben Dart of Waterford and Miss Juliette Hurlbut of Lyme Ct. were joined in marriage at Mr. Hurlbuts Lyme according to the laws of the State of Connecticut on the 25th of December in the year of our Lord one Thousand eight hundred and thirty eight   By me   Wm. Palmer VDM

[p. 92] To whom it may concern. This is to certify that Mr. John W. Crary of Lebanon Ct and Miss Sally Huntley of East Lyme Ct were joined in marriage at Mr. E. Huntleys E. Lyme Ct according to the laws of the State of Connecticut on the 13th day of January in the year of our Lord one thousand eight hundred and thirty nine   By me   Wm Palmer VDM
    E. Lyme Jan 13th 1839

To whom it may concern. This is to certify that Mr. Charles D. Williams of Middletown and Mrs. Betsey Reed of this town were joined in marriage at Loomis Boarding house E. Lyme according to the laws of the State of Connecticut on the 24th of February in the year of our Lord one thousand eight hundred and thirty nine by me   Henry R. Knapp
    E. Lyme, Feby 24th 1839

[p. 93] This certifies that John Noyes and Ann Colton both of Lyme Ct were united in marriage on the 5th of February 1839 by the subscriber
                            Chester Colton Pastor of a Church in Lyme

This certifies that George W Lord and Emily E Moore both of Lyme Ct were united in marriage on the 5th of March 1839 by the subscriber.
                            Chester Colton Pastor of a Church in Lyme

[p. 94] This certifies that William P. Peck and Mary Caton both of Lyme Ct were united in marriage March 24th 1839 by the subscriber
                            Chester Colton Pastor of a Church in Lyme

This certifies that Frederick Champion and Mahala Tinker both of Lyme Ct. were united in marriage March 29th 1839 by the subscriber
                            Chester Colton Pastor of a Church in Lyme

[p. 95] This certifies that James Haynes and Harriet Beckwith both of Lyme Ct. were united in marriage April 9th 1839 by the subscriber
                            Chester Colton Pastor of a Church in Lyme

To whom it may concern. This to certify that Mr. Seth Smith of Victor N Y and Miss Cordelia Loomis of E. Lyme Ct were joined in marriage at Mr. Joel Loomis E. Lyme Ct according to the laws of the State of Connecticut on the first day of April in the year of our lord one thousand eight hundred and thirty nine   By me   Wm Palmer V.D.M.

[p. 96] This certifies that William T. Banning and Mary Ann Ransom both of Lyme Ct were united in marriage April 30th 1839 by the subscriber
                            Chester Colton Pastor of a Church in Lyme

This certifies that Archibald R. Havens of Shelter Island and Caroline A. Hughes of Lyme Ct. were united in marriage May 22d 1839 by the subscriber
                            Chester Colton Pastor of a Church in Lyme

[p. 97] This certifies that Henry Brewer of Cortland N. Y. and Mary A. Lee of Lyme Ct were united in marriage June 4th 1839 by the subscriber
                            Chester Colton Pastor of a Church in Lyme

This certifies that Charles M. Havens and Abby Robbins both of Lyme Ct were united in marriage July 2nd 1839 by the subscriber   Chester Colton Pastor of a Ch.h. in Lyme

[p. 98] Lyme June 23rd 1839 I hereby certify that James Clark and Sophia Tooker both of Lyme were this day joined in marriage by me.   Hiram Walden Minister of Gospel

This certifies that Erastus C. Goodrich of Lima New York and Sarah L. Clark of Lyme Connecticut were united in marriage October 10th 1839 by the subscriber
                            Chester Colton Pastor of a Church in Lyme

[p. 99] Eleazer S. Ely of Lyme Connecticut and Martha Campbell of the City of New York were married October 17th 1833
    William H. Ely their Son was born June 15th A.D. - 1834
    Abby Lee Ely their daughter was born August 19th - 1836

176 LYME, CONNECTICUT, VITAL RECORDS

 Mary Florence their daughter was born Decemr 25th - 1838
 Eliza Morgan their daughter was born May 27th - 1841

To whom it may concern This is to certify that Mr. George Thomas of Norwich and Miss Matilda L. Banning of Lyme Ct were joined in marriage at the home of Prentice Comstock according to the laws of the State of Connecticut on the 3rd day of November in the year of our Lord one thousand eight hundred and thirty nine
 Lyme Nov 3d 1839   By me Wm Palmer V.D. M.

[p. 100] New London County S.S. Lyme November 3rd 1839 I then married John C. Bogue and Lucy E. Littlefield both of Lyme   Samel S. Warner Justice of Peace

This certifies that John Champion of Lyme Ct and Lucy M. Clark of Middletown were united in marriage Nov. 3rd 1839 by the subscriber
          Chester Colton Pastor of a Church in Lyme
 Recorded Decemr 12th 1839 By Joshua R. Warren Regr

[p. 101] I hereby certify that William H. Miner of East Haddam and Harriet N. Luther of Lyme have this day been joined in marriage by me
 Lyme Decemr 9th 1839   Hiram Walden Minister of the Gospel
 Recorded January 1st 1840 By Joshua R. Warren Regr

This may certify that George Miller and Sarah Way both of this town were legally united in marriage on the 22nd instant - Lyme 23d March 1840
   Nathaniel Miner Pastor of the second Congregational Church of East Haddam
 Recorded March 23d 1840 By Joshua R. Warren Regr

[p. 102] New London County S.S. Lyme 4th February 1840 Be it remembered that on the day of the date aforesaid Charles Miner and Huldah Condol both of Lyme were united in marriage according to the law by and before me   Richard E. Selden Jr. Justice of Peace
 Recorded April 6th 1840 By Joshua R. Warren Regr

[p. 103] To whom it may concern This is to certify that Mr. Wm H. Beebe of Waterford and Miss Frances Caulkins of Lyme Ct were joined in marriage at her fathers in Lyme Ct according to the laws of the State of Connecticut on the 19th day of April in the year of our Lord one thousand eight hundred and forty.   By me Wm Palmer V.D.M.
 E. Lyme April 20th 1840

This certifies that Joseph Beebe & Nancy B. Hughes both of Lyme Ct were united in marriage April 12th 1840 by the subscriber   Chester Colton Pastor of a Church in Lyme
 Recorded May 7th 1840 By Joshua R. Warren Regr

[p. 104] This certifies that Thomas Hall of Rhode Island and Nancy M Youngs of Lyme Ct were united in marriage by the subscriber April 19th 1840
         Chester Colton Pastor of a Church in Lyme
 Recorded May 7th 1840 By Joshua R. Warren Regr

This certifies that Benjamin Franklin Chapel and Nancy Waid both of Lyme Ct were united in marriage May 12th 1840 by the subscriber
         Chester Colton Pastor of a Church in Lyme
 Recorded June 10th 1840 By Joshua R. Warren Regr

[p. 105] This certifies that William P Brockway and Elizabeth B Tinker both of Lyme were joined in marriage at Lyme on the 23rd day of August 1840
         By E Loomis Minister of the Gospel
 Recorded August 24th 1840 By Joshua R. Warren Regr

This may certify that Morrison R Wait of Maumee Ohio and Amelia C Warner of Lyme Ct were united in marriage Sept 21, 1840 by the subscriber
        Frederick Gridley Pastor of the Cong Church in East Lyme
 Recorded October 22, 1840 By John Noyes Regr

[p. 106] New London County Ct., Lyme Sept 20 1840 I then married George C Emerson of Lyme and Rachel L Carter of Morris County New Jersey.
        Certified by Saml S Warner Justice of Peace
 Recorded Oct 21 1840 By John Noyes Regr

This may certify that on the 15th of Nov. AD 1840 Christopher B Chapman of New London and Emeline E Maynard of Waterford were joined in marriage by
        Richd L Lord Justice of the Peace
 Recorded Nov 23 1840 By John Noyes Regr

[p. 107] This may certify that Ezra N Lester and Nancy Otis both of Lyme were legally joined in marriage at Lyme on the 25th day of November 1840
       By E Loomis Minister of the Gospel
 Recorded Decr 1st 1840 By John Noyes Regr

This certifies that Joel Miner and Mary H Peck both of Lyme Ct were united in marriage Novr 23d, 1840 by the subscriber   Chester Colton Minister of the Gospel
 Recorded Dec 14, 1840 By John Noyes Reg

[p. 108] This certifies that Enoch Noyes and Catharine Lord both of Lyme Ct were united in marriage Decr 10th 1840 by the subscriber   Chester Colton Minister of the Gospel
 Recorded Decr 14 1840 By John Noyes Regr

This certifies that James Bill and Anne Lord both of Lyme were by me united in marriage Sept. eighteen hundred thirty nine   Phillips Payson
 Recorded Decr 28th 1840 By John Noyes Reg.

[p. 109] This certifies that Allen Griffin and Sarah E Lord both of Lyme were united in marriage by me June thirteenth, eighteen hundred thirty nine   Phillips Payson
 Lyme Dec 28th 1840 Recorded Dec 30th 1840 By John Noyes Regr

This certifies that Joseph Martin and Elisa A Dickinson both of Lyme were united in marriage by me May twenty fourth, eighteen hundred and forty Phillips Payson
 Lyme Dec 28th 1840 Recorded Dec 30th 1840 By John Noyes Regr

[p. 110] This certifies that William Daniels of Waterford and Nancy Havens of Lyme were united in marriage by me June twenty first eighteen hundred forty.
             Phillips Payson
 Lyme Dec 28 1840 Recorded Dec 30 1840 By John Noyes Regr

This certifies that David Austen Martin and Roxanna I Bradbury, both of Lyme, were united in marriage by me June twenty fourth eighteen hundred forty Phillips Payson
 Lyme Dec 28 1840 Recorded Dec 30 1840 By John Noyes Regr
 Lucy Martin daughter of David Austin and Roxanne Martin was born Aug. 5, 1841

[p. 111] This certifies that Moses Wright of Tecumseh Michigan and Emiline Royce of Lyme were united in marriage by me June 10, 1840   Phillips Payson
 Lyme Dec 1840 Recorded Dec 30 1840 By John Noyes Reg

[p. 112] This certifies that Abel Beckwith and Mary Anne Lester, both of Lyme were united in marriage by me Sept 1 1840   Phillips Payson
 Dec 28th 1840

This Certifies that John Sterling and Hannah Randall both of Lyme were united in marriage by me Nov 19 1840   Phillips Payson
 Lyme Dec 28 1840 Recorded Dec 30 1840 By John Noyes Reg.

This may certify that at Lyme on the 31st of January AD 1841 Thomas C Daniels of Waterford and Eliza Dart of Lyme were united in marriage by
        Richard L. Lord Justice of Peace
 Recorded Feb 1 1841 By John Noyes Reg

[p. 113] This certifies that Albert Royce of East Lyme and Frances Fidelia Beckwith of Lyme were by me united in marriage Jan 20 1841   Phillips Payson
Recorded April 20 1841 By John Noyes Reg

This certifies that Timothy Ely of Middletown Ct and Sarah Anne Stark of Lyme were united by me in marriage April 27 1841 North Lyme May 10th 1841   Phillips Payson
Recorded May 10 1841 By John Noyes Reg

[p. 114] This certifies that Richard S Griswold of New York and Frances A Mather of Lyme were united in marriage May 31st 1841 by the subscriber
Chester Colton Minister of the Gospel
Recorded June 1 1841 By John Noyes Reg

This certifies that John Appleby and Emily S Robbins both of Lyme were married by me in the evening of Aug 1 1841 Lyme Aug 2nd 1841
D. S. Brainerd Pastor of the 1st Cong. Church in Lyme
Recorded Aug 3 1841 By John Noyes Reg

[p. 115] This certifies that William H Cobb of Lyme and Miss Ruth Phillips of Waterford were joined in marriage by me Aug 29 1841
D. S. Brainerd Pastor of 1st Cong Church in Lyme Ct
Recorded Aug 30 1841 By John Noyes Reg

This certifies that Mr. Thomas Grumley of Saybrook and Miss Eunice B Waide of Lyme were joined in marriage by me Aug 29 1841
D. S. Brainerd Pastor of 1st Cong Church in Lyme Ct
Recorded Aug 30 1841 By John Noyes Reg

[p. 116] This certifies that Mr. Valentine A Miller and Miss Mary Ann Rowland were joined in marriage by me Aug 30 1841   D S Brainerd Pastor of 1st Cong Church in Lyme
Recorded Sept 1 1841 By John Noyes Reg

I certify that on this day August 10 1841 I have solemenized according to law the marriage of John Hale of Guilford to Ann L Comstock of Lyme
George Carrington Pastor of the Congregational Church Hadlyme
Recorded Sept 2, 1841 By John Noyes Reg

[p. 117] I hereby certify that James B Cook of Orwell Vermont and Lucretia Caulkins of Lyme were lawfully joined in marriage the sixth day of October eighteen hundred and forty one by me   Frederick Wightman Pastor of the Baptist Church in Haddam
Recorded Oct 7th 1841 By Joshua R Warren Reg

This may certify that on the 17th day of October AD 1841 Jonathan Green of Lyme and Sarah Ann Beckwith of Waterford were united in marriage by
Richard L Lord Justice of Peace
Recorded Oct 25th 1841 By Joshua R Warren Reg

[p. 118] This is to certify that William W. J. Warren and Maria E. Peck both of this town were united in marriage by me on the 2nd November instant.
D. S. Brainard Pastor of First Cong. Church Lyme Ct.
Lyme Novr 3d 1841 Recorded Nov. 10th 1841 By Joshua R. Warren Reg.r

Walter S. Warren was born July 31st 1842
William W. S. Warren Jr and Maria E. Warren was born April 13th 1844
Joshua R. Warren 2nd was born March 5th 1850
Jennie E. Warren was born Jan. 7, 1858 See Vol 5 p. 4

I certify that on this day October 27th 1841 the marriage of Abraham W. Willey of East Haddam to Catherine S. Brockway of Lyme has been solemnised by me according to law
George Carrington Pastor of the Associated Church Hadlyme
Recorded Novem. 25th 1841 By Joshua R. Warren Reg.

[p. 119] This certifies that I married Mr. Thomas Beebe of Waterford and Miss Sarah Caulkins of Lyme November 25th 1841   Amos D. Watrous Minister of the Gospel
Recorded Decemr 23d 1841 By Joshua R. Warren Reg.r

To all Whom it May Concern, I hereby certify that in the town of Lyme on the 9th day of November AD 1841 I lawfully joined together in Holy Matrimony Abby Fosdick of the town of Lyme State of Connectti and Allen M. Sisson of the town of Salem Connecticut
       Wilson Cogswell Minister of the Gospel
Recorded January 3d 1842 By Joshua R. Warren Reg.r

[p. 120] To all Whom it May Concern. I hereby certify that in the town of Lyme on the 18th day of December AD 1841 I lawfully joined in Holy Matrimony Clarissa Miner and John Way Jun.r both of the town of Lyme and State of Connecticut
       Wilson Cogswell Minister of the Gospel
Recorded January 3d 1842 By Joshua R. Warren Reg.r

This certifies that I married Mr. Eleazer C. Peck and Miss Eunice H Warren both of Lyme January 11th 1842 Lyme Jany 19th 1842   Amos D. Watrous Minister of the Gospel
Recorded February 7th 1842 By Joshua R. Warren Reg.r

>   Charles E. M. Peck was born October 29th 1842
>   Orin M. Peck was born May 22nd 1844
>   Joshua W. Peck was born February 8th 1846
>   Harriet E. Peck was born April 27th 1847
>   Sarah E. Peck was born April 4th 1851

[p. 121] This certifies that I married Mr. Cornelius Chapman and Maryann Appleby both of Lyme January 30th 1842   Amos Watrous
Recorded February 26th 1842 By Joshua R. Warren Reg.r

This certifies that I married William G. Rowland and Mary J. Lester March 6th 1842 both of Lyme   Amos D. Watrous
Recorded March 16th 1842 By Joshua R. Warren Reg.r

[p. 122] This certifies that I married Mr. Elisha M. Sawyer of Lyme and Ursula Brainard of Haddam March 27th 1842   Amos D. Watrous Minister of the Gospel
Recorded April 25th 1842 By Joshua R. Warren Reg.r

This certifies that I married Mr. James S. Morris of New York and Miss Amelia L. Gulliver of Lyme April 3d 1842   Amos D. Watrous Minister of the Gospel
Recorded April 25th 1842 By Joshua R. Warren Reg.r

[p. 123] On the 30th of March 1842 Mr. William Patten of Salem and Miss Louisa Harrison of Lyme were by me lawfully joined in marriage   C. E. Murdock
Recorded April 28th 1842 By Joshua R. Warren Reg.r

This certifies that I married Mr. Orlando Champion and Nancy L. Richardson both of Lyme May 2nd 1842   Amos Watrous Minister
May 30th 1842 Recorded June 1st 1842 By Joshua R. Warren Reg.r

[p. 124] This certifies that the Rev. Davis S. Brainerd and Miss Ann Maria Chadwick were united in marriage on the 24th instant at the house of her father Capt. Daniel Chadwick in Lyme by me   David D. Field Minister of the Gospel & Pastor of the Church in Haddam
Dated at Lyme May 25th 1842 Recorded June 1st 1842 By Joshua R. Warren Reg.r

This certifies that Mr. Leander King and Miss Harriet E. Moore both of Lyme were married by me June 5th AD 1842   Amos D. Watrous Minister of the Gospel
Lyme June 6th 1842 Recorded June 6th 1842 By Joshua R. Warren Reg.r

[p. 125] This is to certify that Ezra Ingham of Saybrook and Jane L. Grumley of Lyme were united in marriage by me the   day of December 1841
       D. S. Brainerd Pastor of 1st Cong Church
Recorded June 6th 1842 By Joshua R. Warren Reg.r

This is to certify that Andrew Ure Jun.r of Patterson New Jersey and Abby G. Rowland of Lyme were united in marriage by me the 31st day of January 1842
D. S. Brainerd Pastor 1st Cong. Church Lyme Ct.
Recorded June 6th 1842 By Joshua R. Warren Reg.r

[p. 126] This certifies that I married Mr. John Lay and Mrs. Lydia Cone both of Lyme June 17th 1842   Amos D. Watrous Minister of the Gospel
Recorded June 28th 1842 By Joshua R. Warren Reg.r

This certifies that I married Mr. Henry Spencer and Miss Elizabeth Mulholland of England June 26th 1842 Lyme June 27th 1842   Amos D. Watrous Minister of the Gospel
Recorded June 28th 1842 By Joshua R. Warren Reg.r

[p. 127] New London County SS Lyme June 21st 1842 Be it remembered that on the day of the date aforesaid Alanson Bramble of Lyme and widow _____ Huntley of East Haddam were united in marriage according to law by and before me
Richard E. Selden Jr. Justice of Peace
Recorded July 22d 1842 By Joshua R. Warren Regr

I hereby certify that Mr. John L Kirtland of Saybrook and Miss Elizabeth S Beckwith of Lyme were married by me at said Lyme on the 24th instant according to law.
F. W. Chapman Pastor of the Congregational Church of Deep River, Con.
Lyme July 25th 1842 Recorded July 25th 1842 By Joshua R. Warren Regr

[p. 128] On the 7th of July 1842 Selden M Hayden and Rosetta Harrison were by me lawfully joined in marriage   C. E. Murdock
Recorded Augt 1st 1842 By Joshua R Warren Regr

This is to certify that Asabel Clark and Juliaette Chadwich were lawfully joined in marriage by me on the 25th day of July AD 1842   Thomas W Swan Justice of the Peace
Recorded August 16th 1842 By Joshua R Warren Regr

[p. 129] This is to certify that Mr. James P Terry of Somers and Miss Catharine A Matson of Lyme were united in marriage by me August 16th 1842
D. S. Brainerd Pastor of the 1st Cong Chruch in Lyme Ct
Recorded August 18th 1842 By Joshua R Warren Reg.r

This is to certify that John D Clark and Mary Tefft were united in marriage by me August 21st 1842   D S Brainerd Pastor of the 1st Cong Church 1st Soc. Lyme
Recorded August 31st 1842 By Joshua R Warren Reg.r

[p. 130] This is to certify that John Bump and Elizabeth Beckwith both of Lyme were united in marriage by me September 4th 1842
D. S. Brainerd Pastor of the 1st Cong Church & Society Lyme
Recorded Septem 24th 1842 By Joshua R Warren Reg.r

This is to certify that Stephen Prentice of East Lyme and Mary Clark of Lyme were joined in marriage by me September 25th 1842
D. S. Brainerd Pastor of the 1st Cong. Church & Society Lyme, Ct.
Recorded Septem 24th 1842 By Joshua R Warren Regr

[p. 131] This certifies that John Bates and Betsy Wood both of Lyme were joined in marriage by me August 29th 1842   C E Murdock
Recorded October 8th 1842 By Joshua R Warren Regr

This certifies that Richard B Daniels and Mary A Bramble both of Lyme were joined in marriage by me September 18th 1842   C E Murdock
Recorded October 8th 1842 By Joshua R Warren Regr

[p. 132] This certifies that Giles Staplins and Mrs. Harriet Harding were united in marriage by me on the 23d instant Lyme October 28th 1842
D. S. Brainerd Pastor of 1st Cong. Church & Society Lyme Ct
Recorded October 28th 1842 By Joshua R. Warren Reg.r'

This is to certify that Edward Champion and Mary Dart both of Lyme were united in marriage by me on the 24th instant Lyme October 24th 1842
D. S. Brainerd Pastor of the 1st Cong. Church & Society Lyme Ct.
Recorded October 28th 1842 By Joshua R. Warren Reg.r

[p. 133] On the 21st of November 1842 Oscar Avery of Groton and Phebe A. Ely of Lyme were by me lawfully joined in marriage   C. E. Murdock
Recorded Novemr 23d 1842 By Joshua R. Warren Reg.r

New London County S.S. Lyme 13th December 1842 Be it remembered that on the day of the date aforesaid Comfort Hewlet and Eliza Banning (Johnson) both of East Haddam were united in marriage by and before me.   Richard E. Selden Jr. Justice of Peace
Recorded January 2d 1843 By Joshua R. Warren Reg.r

[p. 134] This certifies that Nehemiah D. Tinker and Roxana Beckwith both of Lyme were lawfully married on the 25th December 1842
Attest P. Brockett Pastor of the Baptist Church Lyme
Recorded January 9th 1843 By Joshua R. Warren Reg.r

This certifies that Sylvester W. Slate of Lyme and Mary Jane R. Hurlbut of East Lyme were lawfully married on the first day of January 1843
Attest P. Brockett Pastor of the Baptist Church Lyme
Recorded January 9th 1843 By Joshua R. Warren Reg.r

[p. 135] This certifies that Frederick B. Banta of New York and Hannah B. Tucker (Tinker written in pencil) of Lyme were lawfully married on the 8th of January 1843
Attest. P. Brockett Pastor of the Baptist Church Lyme
Recorded January 9th 1843 By Joshua R. Warren Reg.r

This certifies that William Bushnell of Saybrook and Nancy M. Clark of Lyme were lawfully married on the 15th day of January AD 1843
Attest P. Brockett Pastor of the Baptist Church Lyme
Recorded February 7th 1843 By Joshua R. Warren Reg.r

[p. 136] This is to certify that Mr. James Chapel of East Lyme Ct. and Miss Hannah Maynard of Lyme Ct. were legally joined in marriage in the above town of Lyme on the twenty second day of January in the year of our Lord one thousand eight hundred and forty three - By me the subscriber
Thos Dowling Pastor of the Baptist Church North Lyme, Ct
Recorded February 9th 1843 By Joshua R. Warren Reg.r

On the 1st of September A.D. 1842 I Joined in Marriage Shubael F. Bartlett M.D. and Fanny R. Griswold both of Lyme
Shubael Bartlett Pastor of the second church E. Windsor Conn.
Recorded February 18th 1843 By Joshua R. Warren Reg.r

[p. 137] This certifies that Joseph Sanders of Lyme in New London county was married to Ann Maria Reynolds of said town in said county this 4th day of March 1843 by me
Erastus W. Caulkins Justice of Peace
Recorded April 3rd 1843 by Joshua R. Warren Reg.r

I hereby certify that Fredric W. Comstock and Dorcas H. Waterhouse both of Lyme were joined in marriage by me April 30 1843
Stephen Alonzo LoPer Acting Pastor of the Congr. Church in Hadlyme
Recorded May 22, 1863 by Joshua R. Warren Reg.r

[p. 138] This certifies that Dan W. Mather of Lyme and Mary Ann M. Nash of Saybrook were lawfully married June 4th 1843
Attest P. Brockett Pastor of the Baptist Church Lyme
Recorded June 12th 1843 By Joshua R. Warren Reg.r

This certifies that Cornelius Banta and Henrietta Gulliver both of Lyme were lawfully married June 11th 1843   Attest P. Brockett Pastor of the Baptist Church of Lyme
Recorded June 12th 1843 By Joshua R. Warren Reg.r

[p. 139] I hereby certify that Francis M. Palmer of East Haddam and Margaret A. Nichols of Lyme were this day lawfully joined together in Marriage by me Lyme June 28th 1843
     Alexander Burgess Minister of St. Stephens Church East Haddam
Recorded July 11th 1843 By Joshua R. Warren Reg.r

[p. 139] This certifies that Nathan Howard of East Lyme and Cornelia Meigs of Lyme were lawfully married on the 25th day of June 1843
     Attest P. Brockett Pastor of the Baptist Church Lyme
Recorded August 3d 1843 By Joshua R. Warren Reg.r

[p. 140] This certifies that Francis W. Glover and Abigail Brockway both of Lyme were lawfully married on the 2nd of July 1843
     Attest. P. Brockett Pastor of the Baptist Church Lyme
Recorded August 3d 1843 By Joshua R. Warren Reg.r

This certifies that Horace Champion and Jane M. Maynard both of Lyme were lawfully married on the 6th July 1843   Attest. P. Brockett Pastor of the Baptist Church Lyme
Recorded August 3rd 1843 By Joshua R. Warren Reg.r

[p. 141] This certifies that William Tucker and Mary Ann Banta were lawfully married July 23rd 1843   Attest P. Brockett Pastor of the Baptist Church Lyme
Recorded Aug. 3d 1843 By Joshua R. Warren Regr

This certifies that A. W. Richardson of New York and Mahitabel Pilgrim of Lyme Connecticut were lawfully married on the 17th September 1843
     Attest P. Brockett Pastor of the Baptist Church Lyme
Recorded September 18th 1843 By Joshua R. Warren Reg.r

[p. 142] This certifies that Dudley R. Chesebro of Stonington and Jane R. Tinker of Lyme were lawfully married on the 24th September 1843
     Attest. P. Brockett Pastor of the Baptist Church Lyme
Recorded October 21st 1843 By Joshua R. Warren Reg.r

This certifies that J. P. Beckwith of East Lyme and Lucy C. Beckwith of Lyme were lawfully married on the 30th October 1843
     Attest. P. Brockett Pastor of the Baptist Church Lyme
Recorded Novem. 22d 1843 By Joshua R. Warren Reg.r

[p. 143] This certifies that Lathrop E. Slate Junr and Mary L. Champion both of Lyme were lawfully married on the 31st October 1843
     Attest P. Brockett Pastor of the Baptist Church Lyme
Recorded Novem 22d 1843 By Joshua R. Warren Reg.r

I hereby certify that Henry J. Comstock and Caroline S. Brockway were joined in marriage by me Nov. 15th 1843 Hadlyme Nov. 22d 1843
     Stephen Alonzo Loper Acting Minister of the Congregational Church Hadlyme
Recorded Decem. 4th 1843 By Joshua R. Warren Reg.r

[p. 144] This certifies that Mr. Edwin Sweitser of Philadelphia and Miss Clementine Lombard of Lyme were lawfully married on the tenth of March 1844
     Attest Pierpont Brockett Pastor of the first Baptist Church Lyme
Recorded March 26th 1844 By Joshua R. Warren Register

I hereby certify that Joseph Holmes of East Haddam and Maria K. Selden of Lyme were united in marriage by me on the 21st day of May AD 1844
     Stephen Alonzo Loper Acting Pastor of the Cong.l Church in Hadlyme
Recorded June 10th 1844 By Joshua R. Warren Register

[p. 145] This certifies that Jonathan Buck and Adaline Rice both of Lyme were lawfully married on the 10th of June 1844
                Attest Pierpont Brockett Pastor of the first Baptist Church in Lyme
    Recorded July 2d 1844 By J. R. Warren Reg.r

This certifies that George D. Clark and Adaline Havens both of Lyme were lawfully married on the 30th of June 1844
                Attest. Pierpont Brockett Pastor of the first Baptist Church in Lyme
    Recorded July 2d 1844 By J. R. Warren Regr

[p. 146] New London County SS Lyme 28th July 1844 be it remembered that on the day of date aforesaid John W. Rand of Lyme and Harriet Maria Bailey of Chatham County of Middlesex were united in marriage according to law by and before me
                Richard E. Selden Jr. Justice of Peace
    Recorded August 11th 1844 By Joshua R. Warren Reg.r

This certifies that Hezekiah Cosford of England and Hannah Sanders of Lyme were lawfully married by me August 18th 1844
                Attest. Pierpont Brockett Pastor of the first Baptist Church Lyme
    Recorded Augt 22d 1844 By Joshua R. Warren Regr

[p. 147] I hereby certify that the Rev. T. S. Vaill of Mercer County Illinois and Elizabeth S. Comstock of Lyme Connecticut were united in marriage by me in the Parish of Hadlyme August 1st 1844   Stephen Alonzo Loper Acting Pastor of the Cong.l Church Hadlyme
    Recorded August 27th 1844 By Joshua R. Warren Reg.r

New London County S S Lyme 24th November 1844 Be it remembered that on the day of the date aforesaid John Tooker Jr. and Delia Slate both of Lyme were united in marriage by and before me according to law   Richard E. Selden Jr. Justice of Peace
    Recorded Dec 10th 1844 By Oliver J. Lay Regr

[p. 148] This certifies that Mr. William H. Fox of East Lyme and Miss Susan B. Andrews of Saybrook Ct. were legally joined in marriage in the town of Lyme on the 16th of December in the year of our Lord one thousand eight hundred and forty four by me the subscriber
                Thomas Dowling Pastor of the Baptist Church North Lyme Ct.
    Recorded Jany 1st 1845 By Oliver J. Lay Regr.

This certifies that John A. DeWolf and Zylpha A. Johnson both of Lyme were lawfully married on the 29th December 1844
                Attest P. Brocket Pastor of the Baptist Church Lyme
    Recorded Jany 1st 1845 By Oliver J. Lay Regr.

[p. 149] I hereby certify that Capt. Ebenezer E. Brockway and Miss Lucy S. Bill both of Lyme were lawfully married by me in Lyme on the fourteenth day of January 1845 New London January   Thos. J. Greenwood Minister of the Gospel
    Recorded January 21st 1845 By Oliver J. Lay Regr.

This is to certify that Calvin Reed of Lyme and Deborah Benjamin of Preston were united in marriage by me on the twenty eighth day of November 1844
                D. S. Brainerd Pastor of the 1st Cong. Church Lyme Ct.
    Recorded Feby 19th 1845 By Oliver J. Lay Reg.

[p. 150] This certifies that Benjamin Brockway and Deborah Howard both of Lyme were united in marriage by me on the 16th day of January 1845
                D. S. Brainerd Pastor of the 1st Cong. Church Lyme Ct.
    Recorded Feby 19th 1845 By Oliver J. Lay Regr.

This is to certify that Ruel B. Huntley of East Lyme and Abby A. Bump of Lyme were united in marriage by me on the nineteenth day of February 1845
                D. S. Brainerd Pastor of the 1st Cong. Church Lyme Ct.
    Recorded Feby 19th 1845 By Oliver J. Lay Reg.

[p. 151] This certifies that James Lombard and Margaret O. Salter both of Lyme were lawfully married on the 30th day March 1845
    Attest. Pierpont Brockett Pastor of the first Baptist Church Lyme
Recorded April 29th 1845 By Oliver J. Lay Regr.

This certifies that Josiah W. Crocker of Waterford and Elizabeth A. Tiffany of Lyme were united in marriage by me April 14th 1845
    Stephen A. Loper Acting Pastor of the Congl Church in Hadlyme
Recorded May 1st 1845 By Oliver J. Lay Regr.

[p. 152] This certifies that Thomas S. Swan of East Haddam and Charlotte A. Rogers of Rome, Ohio were united in marriage by me on the 12th inst. May 12th 1845
    D. S. Brainerd Pastor of the first Cong. Church in Lyme Ct.
Recorded May 12 1845 By Oliver J. Lay Regr.

This certifies that Henry B. Noyes of Elmira New York and Sarah L. Holdrege of Lyme were joined in marriage by me on the 14th inst. Lyme May 15th 1845
    D. S. Brainerd Pastor of the 1st Cong. Church iñ Lyme Ct.
Recorded Lyme May 24th 1845 By Oliver J. Lay Regr.

[p. 153] New London County SS Lyme 10th May 1845 Be it remembered that on the day of the date aforesaid Samuel Holmes of East Haddam and Widow Cornelia Buckingham (formerly Cornelia Luther) of Lyme were united in marriage by and before me according to law.   R. E. Selden Justice of Peace
Recorded May 25th 1845 By Oliver J. Lay Regr.

This certifies that Richard W. Lee Esqr and Mrs. Betsey Chapman both of Lyme were lawfully joined in marriage by the subscriber June 19th 1840
    Oliver Brown Minister of the Gospel
Recorded August 29th 1845 By Oliver J. Lay Regr.

[p. 154] This certifies that Mr. Seth B. Dickinson of Hebron and Miss Mariette Howard of East Lyme were lawfully joined in marriage by the subscriber November 25th 1840
    Oliver Brown Minister of the Gospel
Recorded August 29th 1845 By Oliver J. Lay Regr

This certifies that Mr. James F. Saunders of Lyme and Miss Mariette Crowell of East Lyme were lawfully joined in marriage by the subscriber
Sept. 20th 1841   Oliver Brown Minister of the Gospel
Recorded August 29th 1845 By Oliver J. Lay Regr.

[p. 155] This certifies that Mr. Barach Johnson and Miss Mary A. Way both of East Lyme were lawfully joined in marriage by the subscriber. Oct. 14th 1841
    Oliver Brown Minister of the Gospel
Recorded August 29th 1845 By Oliver J. Lay Regr.

This certifies that Mr. David Baker of East Haddam and Miss Elizabeth Miner of Lyme were lawfully joined in marriage by the subscriber Oct 17th 1841
    Oliver Brown Minister of the Gospel
Recorded August 29, 1845 By Oliver J. Lay Regr.

[p. 156] This certifies that Mr. John B. Welles of Auburn of New York and Miss Roxana H. Lee of East Lyme Conn. were lawfully joined in marriage by the subscriber
Oct. 18th 1841   Oliver Brown Minister of the Gospel
Recorded August 29th 1845 By Oliver J. Lay Regr.

This certifies that Mr. David Quinby and Miss Roxana Spencer both of Lyme were lawfully joined in marriage by the subscriber
Feby 6th 1842   Oliver Brown Minister of the Gospel
Recorded August 29th 1845 By Oliver J. Lay Regr.

[p. 157] This certifies that Mr. Jared W. Watrous and Miss Caroline M. Peck both of Lyme were lawfully joined in marriage by the subscriber.
Dec. 26th 1842   Oliver Brown Minister of the Gospel
    Recorded August 29th 1845 By Oliver J. Lay Regr.

This certifies that Mr. Andrew Lathrop of Colchester and Miss Laura A. Royce of East Lyme were lawfully joined in marriage by the subscriber
April 2d 1844   Oliver Brown Minister of the Gospel
    Recorded August 29th 1845 By Oliver J. Lay Regr

[p. 158] This certifies that Mr. Horace B. Royce of East Lyme and Miss Lucretia M. Hughes of Lyme were lawfully joined in marriage by the subscriber
April 16th 1844   Oliver Brown Minister of the Gospel
    Recorded August 29 1845 By Oliver J. Lay Register

This certifies that Mr. Henry B. Chapel of East Lyme and Miss Mary A. Herrick of Waterford were lawfully joined in marriage by the subscriber
Feby 23d 1845   Oliver Brown Minister of the Gospel
    Recorded Aug. 29th 1845 By Oliver J. Lay Regr.

[p. 159] This certifies that Mr. Noah Harding and Miss Nancy Maria McCreary both of Lyme were lawfully joined in marriage by the subscriber.
March 9th 1845   Oliver Brown Minister of the Gospel
    Recorded Aug 29th 1845 By Oliver J. Lay Register

New London county S S Lyme 15th June 1845. Be it remembered that on the day of the date aforesaid Henry I. Bogue and Elisabeth S. Bogue both of Lyme were united in marriage by and before me according to law.
                                    Richard E. Selden Jr. Justice of Peace
    Recorded July 5th 1845 By Oliver J. Lay Regr.

[p. 160] I hereby certify that I married Jewett D. Baker of East Haddam and Abby Ann Hayden Miner of Lyme
Lyme August 21st 1845   Samuel D. Sill Justice of Peace
    Recorded August 30th 1845 By Oliver J. Lay Register

I hereby certify that Joseph Selden and Caroline Lord both of Lyme were united in marriage by me on the 4th day of September A.D. 1845
                        Stephen Alonzo Loper Pastor Cong.l Church Hadlyme
    Recorded Sept. 29th 1845 By Oliver J. Lay Regr.

[p. 161] This may certify that John M. Parker of Sag Harbor (New York) and Lucretia M. Tiffany of Lyme were lawfully joined in marriage in the meeting house in North Lyme August 17th 1845 East Haddam Aug.
    Nathaniel Miner, Pastor of the Second Congregational Church in East Haddam
    Recorded Oct 10th 1845 By Oliver J. Lay Reg.

I hereby certify that Frederick L. Swan of East Haddam and Laura A. Tiffany of Lyme were united in marriage by me October 9th 1845
    Hadlyme Oct 9th 1845 Stephen A. Loper Pastor of Congregational Church Hadlyme
    Recorded October 20 1845 By Oliver J Lay Regr.

[p. 162] This certifies that Mr. Horace Way and Miss Nancy Phelps both of Lyme were lawfully joined in marriage by the subscriber Sept 23d 1845
                                    Oliver Brown Minister of the Gospel
    Recorded November 10th 1845 By Oliver J. Lay Register

This certifies that Mr. Timothy H. Peck and Miss Irene E. Gillett both of Lyme were lawfully joined in marriage by the subscriber Sept 30th 1845
                                    Oliver Brown Minister of the Gospel
    Recorded November 10th 1845 By Oliver J. Lay Register

[p. 163] This certifies that I married Aaron S Brockway and Mary E. Anderson October 26th 1845 both of Lyme   Amos D Watrous Minister of the Gospel
Recorded November 4th 1845 By Oliver J. Lay Register

This certifies that Martin Doly of Ypsilanti Michigan and Eunice B. Banning of Lyme Connt were united in marriage by me on the 9th inst
           D S Brainerd Pastor of the 1st Cong Church in Lyme, Ct.
Lyme Dec 9th 1845   Recorded Dec 9th 1845 By Oliver J. Lay Regr.

[p. 164] I hereby certify that Amasa Day of East Haddam and Sarah S Spencer of Lyme were united in marriage by me November 27th AD 1845 Hadlyme Dec 4th 1845
           Stephen Alonso Loper Pastor of Congl Church in Hadlyme
Recorded Feby 2d 1846 By Oliver J. Lay Regr.

This may certify that David B. Date & Mary Hughes 2d were lawfully joined in marriage by me this day Lyme January 13th 1846   Samuel Griswold
Recorded February 9th 1846 By Oliver J. Lay Regr.

[p. 165] Lyme March 18th 1846 Judah Lord and Mary L Beckwith both of Lyme were this day legally joined in marriage by me.   Samuel Griswold Pastor
Recorded March 30th 1846 By Oliver J. Lay Regr.

New London County SS Lyme 29th March 1846 Be it remembered that on the day of the date aforesaid William Brockway of Saybrook and Mary Boo of Amsterdam in the kingdom of Holland were united in marriage by and before me according to law
           Richard E Selden Junr Justice of Peace
Recorded March 30th 1846 By Oliver J. Lay Regr.

[p. 166] This certifies that I married James Pilgrim and Frances Hughes March 26 1846 both of Lyme April 7th 1846   Amos D Watrous
Recorded April 15th 1846 By Oliver J. Lay Regr

This certifies that Mr James R Morgan of Waterford and Miss Jane Gray Raymond of Lyme were legally joined in marriage this day by me Lyme May 26th 1846
           Samuel Griswold Minister of the Gospel
Recorded June 23d 1846 By Oliver J Lay Register

[p. 167] This certifies that I married Calvin B Champion and Ann R Slate June 30th 1846 both of Lyme   A D Watrous
July 16th 1846 Recorded July 16 1846 By Oliver J. Lay Regr.

This certifies that I married Charles W Rogers and Caroline A Dean July 12th 1846 both of Lyme Lyme July 16 1846   A D Watrous
Recorded July 16th 1846 By Oliver J. Lay Register

[p. 168] This certifies that Elihu H. Palmer of Salem & Phebe L. Lester of Lyme were legally joined in marriage by me on the 19th of July 1846 Lyme Aug. 13 1846
           Samuel Griswold Minister of the Gospel 2d Eccl Soc. Lyme
Recorded Aug. 13th 1846 By Oliver J. Lay Register

This certifies that William H. Harrison & Louisa Clark both of Lyme were legally joined in marriage by me on the 19th day of July 1846
           Samuel Griswold Minister of the Gospel 2d Eccl Soc. Lyme
Lyme Aug. 13th 1846   Recorded Aug. 13th 1846 By Oliver J. Lay Register

[p. 169] This certifies that Charles M. Taintor of Shelburn Franklin Co. Mass & Mary Lord of Lyme were by me this day legally joined in marriage Lyme August 18th 1846
           Samuel Griswold Minister of the Gospel 2d Eccl. Soc. Lyme
Recorded Sept 15 1846 By Oliver J. Lay Regr.

This certifies that Orin Luther & Catharine Banning were united in marriage by me on the evening of the 11 inst Lyme October 12th 1846
                        D. S. Brainerd Pastor of the 1st Cong. Church in Lyme Ct.
Recorded October 24th 1846 By Oliver J. Lay Regr

[p. 170] Sylvester W. Fox & Mary Latham both of Lyme were this day legally joined in marriage by me
                    Samuel Griswold Minister of the Gospel 2d Eccl. Society Lyme
Lyme Oct. 11 1846   Recorded Nov. 10th 1846 By Oliver J. Lay Regr.

I hereby certify that Dudley B. Wells and Susan M. Waterhouse of Lyme were united in Marriage by me Nov. 10 1846 - Hadlyme Nov. 10, 1846
        Stephen Alonzo Loper Pastor of the Congl Church in the Parish of Hadlyme
Recorded Dec. 7th 1846 By Oliver J. Lay Regr.

[p. 171] This is to certify that Gad B. Baldwin of Brooklyn and Sarah A. Miner of Lyme were united in Marriage by me on the evening 30th inst.
                D. S. Brainerd Pastor of the 1st Cong.l Ch. in Lyme
Lyme Nov 30th 1846   Recorded Dec. 19 1846 By Oliver J. Lay Regr.

This is to certify that William A. Banta and Catharine Tucker both of Lyme were united in marriage by me on the 6th inst Lyme Dec. 7th 1846
                D. S. Brainerd Pastor of the 1st Congl Ch. in Lyme
Recorded Dec. 19 1846 By Oliver J. Lay Regr

[p. 172] This certifies that Dr. Seth Smith of New London and Mary E. Lay of Lyme were united in marriage by me on the 15th inst. Lyme Dec. 29th 1846
                D. S. Brainerd Pastor of the first Congl Ch in Lyme
Recorded January 5th 1847 By Oliver J. Lay Register

This is to certify that I married Mr. Samuel M. Mott of Norwich to Miss Frances E. Gilbert of Lyme March 14, 1847
Lyme March 23 1847   Amos D. Watrous
    Recorded March 24 1847 By Oliver J. Lay Regr

[p. 173] This certifies that I married John Daniels and Nancy Hall both of Lyme April 2d 1847   Amos D. Watrous
    Recorded April 3 1847 By Oliver J. Lay Regr.

This certifies that William Grover of Chatham and Eunice Avery of Lyme Connecticut were lawfully joined in matrimony by the subscriber April 4, 1847
                Chester Tilden Pastor of the Baptist Church North Lyme
Recorded April 5, 1847 By Oliver J. Lay Regr

[p. 174] I hereby certify that on the 14th day of Feb 1847 James Bliss and Ann Hudson both of Lyme New London County Conn were married by me Lyme May 18th 1847
                              Daniel Anderson Justice of Peace
   Recorded May 26th 1847 By Oliver J. Lay Regr

I hereby certify that on the 2nd day of May 1847 Wm Dawes Jr. and Abby Bogue both of Lyme New London County Conn. were married by me Lyme May 18 1847
                              Daniel Anderson Justice of the Peace
   Recorded May 25th 1847 By Oliver J. Lay Regr

[p. 175] I hereby certify that Henry Bramble and Mary A Slate were joined in marriage by me April 25 1847
Hadlyme May 1 1847   Stephen A. Loper Pastor of Congl Ch. Hadlyme
   Recorded May 3d 1847 By Oliver J. Lay Regr.

LYME, CONNECTICUT, VITAL RECORDS

To whom it may concern this may certify that George C. Vergason of Norwich and Jane B. Holt of Preston both of Connecticut were lawfully joined in marriage by the subscriber May 13th 1847
       Chester Tilden Pastor of the Baptist Church North Lyme
Recorded May 31st 1847 By Oliver J. Lay Regr.

[p. 176] This certifies that Charles E. L. Brockway of Saybrook and Caroline M. Rogers of East Lyme both of Connecticut were lawfully married by the subscriber May 16, 1847   Chester Tilden Pastor of the B Church North Lyme
Recorded May 31st 1847 By Oliver J. Lay Register

I have this day June 6th 1847 married Mr. Emerson Mixter of Tolland to Miss Frances E. Huntley of Lyme all in the State of Connecticut
       A. D. Watrous Minister of the Gospel
Recorded June 28th 1847 By Oliver J. Lay Regr.

[p. 177] This certifies that Lorrillard Spencer of West Chester N. York & Sarah J. Griswold of Lyme were united in marriage by me on the 30th ult (June)
Lyme July 16 1847   D. S. Brainerd Pastor of first Cong. Church in Lyme Connt
Recorded July 16 1847 By Oliver J. Lay Regr

This certifies that Richard A. Hungerford of East Haddam and Elizabeth C. Laplass of Lyme were lawfully joined in marriage July 4th 1847
       Chester Tilden Pastor of the Baptist Church North Lyme
Recorded Sept 13 1847 By Oliver J. Lay Regr

[p. 178] This may certify that Edward G. Hyde of New Orleans La. and Sarah W. Lord of Lyme were this day legally joined in marriage by me Lyme Sept 2 1847
       Samuel Griswold Minister of the Gospel
Recorded Sept 30 1847 By Oliver J. Lay Regr

This certifies that Frederick G. Richardson of New York and Caroline C. Pyne of Williamsburg Long Island were lawfully joined in wedlock by the subscriber Oct. 2d 1847
       Chester Tilden Pastor of the B Church N. Lyme
Recorded Oct. 14 1847 By Oliver J. Lay Regr.

[p. 179] To whom it may concern I hereby certify that Bartlett P. Sampson of North Lyme and Frances C. Crocker of East Lyme were lawfully joined in marriage by the subscriber Oct. 10th 1847
       Chester Tilden Pastor of the Baptist Church North Lyme
Recorded Oct. 25 1847 By Oliver J. Lay Regr.

To whom it may concern I hereby certify that Edgar Brockway and Lovica B. Luther both of Lyme were lawfully joined in marriage by the subscriber Oct. 24th 1847
       Chester Tilden Pastor of the Baptist Church North Lyme
Recorded Oct. 25th 1847 By Oliver J. Lay Regr.

[p. 180] To whom it may concern this may certify that Henry N. Damon of Lyme and Nancy K. Hayden of Essex both of Connecticut were lawfully joined in marriage by the subscriber Oct. 4th 1847
       Chester Tilden Pastor of the B. Church North Lyme
Recorded Oct. 25th 1847 By Oliver J. Lay Regr

This certifies that Charles Hayden of Essex and Amelia Damon of Lyme both of Connecticut were lawfully joined in marriage by the subscriber Oct. 4th 1847
       Chester Tilden Pastor of the B. Church North Lyme
Recorded Oct. 25th 1847 By Oliver J. Lay Regr.

[p. 181] This certifies that I married Mr. Ebenezer L. Roberts and Miss Clara R. Bacon Oct. 13th 1847   Amos D. Watrous
Recorded Nov. 1 1847 By Oliver J. Lay Regr.

I hereby certify that I married Elisha Miner of Lyme and Fanny Palmer of Salem Oct.
11th 1847   Samuel D. Sill Justice of Peace
    Recorded Nov. 1st 1847 By Oliver J. Lay Regr

New London County SS Lyme October 10th AD 1847 I then married George E.
Mather and Mary J. Bogue both of Lyme in New London County
                                  Certified by Samuel S. Warner Justice of Peace
    Recorded Nov 1st 1847 By Oliver J. Lay Regr.

This is to certify that Mr. Calvin King and Miss Susan Dorr both of Lyme were united
in marriage by me March 8 1847
                       Roger Albiston Minister of the Methodist Church
    Recorded Nov 8th 1847 By Oliver J. Lay Regr.

[p. 182] This is to certify that Mr. Wm Maynard and Miss Harriet Maynard both of
Lyme were united by me in marriage March 14th 1847   Roger Albiston
    Recorded Nov 8th 1847 By Oliver J. Lay Regr.

This certifies that Mr. Samuel Dorr Clark and Miss Mercy A Champion both of Lyme
were united by me in marriage Nov 1847   Roger Albiston
    Recorded Nov 8 1847 By Oliver J. Lay Regr.

[p. 183] This certifies that Mr Edmund Huntley of Norwich and Miss Sarah E Gilbert of
Lyme were united by me in marriage July 27th 1846   Roger Albiston
    Recorded Nov 8th 1847 By Oliver J Lay Regr

This certifies that Mr Silas Bramble and Mrs. Betsey Lay were united by me in marriage
August 1st 1847   Roger Albiston
    Recorded Nov 8th 1847 By Oliver J. Lay Regr.

[p. 184] This is to certify that Mr Orlando R Glover of Carbondale Pa and Mrs Maria E
Keables of New London were united by me in marriage Oct 24 1847
                                                                    Roger Albiston
    Recorded Nov 8th 1847 By Oliver J Lay Regr

This certifies that on the 17th day of October AD 1847 Albert Davis of Harbor Island
Lincoln County Maine and Eveline C Dwyer of East Lyme were united by me
                                  Daniel Anderson Justice of the Peace
    Recorded Dec 1 1847 By O J Lay Regr.

[p. 185] This certifies that Frederick Fosdick and Lucy Stark both of Lyme Connecticut were joined in marriage as the law directs by the subscriber November 25th 1847
             Chester Tilden Pastor of the 1st Baptist Church North Lyme
    Recorded Dec 11 1847 By Oliver J Lay Regr

To whom it may concern this certifies that James J Champlin and Lucinda Fosdick
both of Lyme Connecticut were lawfully joined in marriage by me the subscriber Nov
3d 1847   Chester Tilden Pastor of the 1st Baptist Church North Lyme
    Recorded Dec 11 1847 By Oliver J. Lay Regr

[p. 186] This certifies that Mr. Levi Bliss of Boston Mass and Miss Elizabeth P.
Johnson of Lyme were on the 21st day of Nov. last by me legally joined in marriage
                   Samuel Griswold Minister of the Gospel 2d Eccl Soc Lyme
    Recorded December 15 1847 By Oliver J. Lay Regr.

This certifies that Mr Peter Pierson and Mrs. Betsey Russell both of Lyme were this day by
me legally joined in marriage Lyme Nov 16th 1847
                   Samuel Griswold Minister of the Gospel 2d Eccl Soc Lyme
    Recorded Dec 15th 1847 By Oliver J. Lay Regr

[p. 187] This may certify that Mr Milton L. Winslow of Sunderland Mass & Miss Caroline A Miner of Lyme Ct were joined in marriage in Lyme Ct Nov 1st 1847 according to the laws of the State by me. Lyme Dec 13th 1847
                    William A Smith Minister of the Gospel
Recorded Dec 18th 1847 By Oliver J Lay Regr.

This is to certify that Theodore La Mott of Chester and Emily Champion of Lyme were united in marriage by me on the 19th day of March 1848
                    D S Brainerd Pastor of the 1st Cong Church Lyme Ct
Recorded March 24th 1848 By Oliver J. Lay Regr.

[p. 188] This is to certify that Daniel Chadwick Junr and Ellen Noyes both of Lyme were united in marriage by me on the 21st day of March 1848
D S Brainerd Pastor of the 1st Cong Church in Lyme Ct
Recorded March 24 1848 By Oliver J Lay Regr

This certifies that Martin Sawyer and Eunice A Tinker both of Lyme Connecticut were lawfully joined in marriage by the subscriber March 30th 1848   Chester Tilden
Recorded April 12th 1848 By Oliver J. Lay Regr.

[p. 189] I hereby certify that Joseph Luther of Lyme and Lydia Ann Cone of East Haddam were joined in marriage as the Law directs by the subscriber April 2d 1848
                    Chester Tilden
Recorded April 12th 1848 By Oliver J. Lay Regr

This certifies that William Johnson and Emeline J. Bogue both of Lyme were married as the law directs by the subscriber July 16th 1848
                    Chester Tilden Pastor of the Baptist Church Lyme
Recorded Aug 1st 1848 Oliver J. Lay Register

[p. 190] This certifies that William Taylor of Lyme and Betsey Jones of Saybrook, Connecticut were lawfully married by the subscriber Sept 1st 1848
Recorded Oct. 6-1848 By Oliver J. Lay Register   Chester Tilden

State of Connecticut County of New London & Town of Lyme Sept 26th A.D. 1848 I hereby certify that I have this day united in marriage John M. Crosby of said State County & Town and Mary Elizabeth Johnson of said State County of Hartford and Town of Wethersfield having before so doing been certified of the consent of the parents of the said Johnson & of the due and legal publishment of the intention of marriage of the said parties in said Town of Wethersfield
                    John S. Wallis Justice of the Peace
Recorded Oct 16 1848 By Oliver J. Lay Regr.

[p. 191] State of Connecticut County of New London and Town of Lyme Sept 26th AD 1848 I hereby certify that I have this day united in Marriage Stephen P. Harlow of the said State County of Hartford & Town of Wethersfield & Laura R. Crosby of said State County of New London & Town of Lyme aforesaid having before so doing been certified of the consent of the parent of the said Crosby & of the due and legal publishment of the intention of marriage of the said parties in the Town of Wethersfield.
                    John S. Wallis Justice of the Peace
Recorded Oct 16th 1848 By Oliver J. Lay Register

This certifies that Marshfield Sterling Parker Junr and Jane Amelia Brockway both of Lyme were this day legally joined in marriage by me.
Lyme Sept 28-1848   Samuel Griswold
Recorded Oct. 27th 1848 By Oliver J. Lay Register

[p. 192] I hereby certify that William E. Marvin of Greenfield P.A. and Catherine F. Spencer of Lyme Ct. were united in marriage by me in the Parish of Hadlyme on the 2d of Nov. 1848 Hadlyme Nov. 2d 1848
                    Stephen A. Loper Pastor of the Congregational Church in Hadlyme
Recorded Nov. 7 1848 By Oliver J. Lay Register

I hereby certify that Griswold Chapell and Mehetabel Lord both of Lyme Connecticut were lawfully joined in marriage Nov. 5th 1848   Chester Tilden
   Recorded Nov. 7th 1848 By Oliver J. Lay Regr.

[p. 193] This certifies that John W. Platts of Milwaukee Wisconsin and Sarah L. Perkins of Lyme were united in marriage by me on the 22d day of August 1848 Lyme Nov. 17th 1848
                        D. S. Brainerd Pastor of the 1 Cong. Ch. in Lyme Ct.
   Recorded Nov. 17 1848 By Oliver J. Lay Register

This certifies that John E. Waite and Lucy Ann Dowsick both of Lyme were united in marriage by me on the 24th day of Sept. 1848
24th day of Sept 1848   D. S. Brainerd pastor of the first Cong. Ch. in Lyme Ct.
   Recorded Nov. 17th 1848 By Oliver J. Lay Regr.

[p. 194] I hereby certify that Selden Chadwick & Cordelia Otis of Lyme were united in Marriage by me in the Parish of Hadlyme on the 26th day of November A.D. 1848
Hadlyme 26th Nov. 1848   Stephen A. Loper Pastor of Cong.l Church Hadlyme
   Recorded Dec. 25th 1848 By Oliver J. Lay Register

This certifies that Ralph B. Clark of Colchester and Sarah Ann Caulkins of North Lyme State of Connecticut were lawfully joined in marriage by the subscriber Dec. 26th 1848   Chester Tilden Pastor of the Baptist Church.
   Recorded Jany 9th 1849 By Oliver J. Lay Regr.

[p. 195] This certifies that I have this day joined in marriage Mr. Thomas F. Prentice of Waterford and Miss Mariette Dwyer of East Lyme Lyme Dec. 31 1848
                        Marvin Leffingwell Pastor of M. E. Church
   Recorded Jany 29th 1849 By Oliver J. Lay Regr.

State of Connecticut County of New London & Town of Lyme Jany 26th AD 1849 I hereby certify that I have this day joined in marriage Erastus Bramble Jr. & Hellen Miner both of said Town of Lyme having been first certified of the publishment of said parties in the society in said Town where they reside & the consent of the parents of said Hellen to said marriage she the said Helen being a minor
                        John S. Wallis Justice of the Peace
   Recorded Feby 2 1849 By Oliver J. Lay Regr.

[p. 196] This certifies that Frederick Birdsey of Middletown and Laura A. Miller of Lyme were by me this day legally joined in marriage Lyme Jany 16th 1849
                        Samuel Griswold Minister of the Gospel
   Recorded Feby 12th 1849 By Oliver J. Lay Regr.

To whom it may concern - this may certify that Cornelius Mack and Harriet Watrous both of East Lyme Connecticut were lawfully joined in marriage by the subscriber March 28th 1849   Chester Tilden Late Pastor of the Baptist Church North Lyme
   Recorded April 2d 1849 By Oliver J. Lay Regr.

[p. 197] This certifies that Andrew J. Edwards and Alice Wright both of the Town of Lyme were married by me on the 15th day of April A.D. 1849 in the Town of Lyme
                        Wm Harris Minister of the Gospel
   Recorded May 7 1849 By Oliver J. Lay Regr.

This may certify that Mr. Seth Monroe Brockway and Miss Lucy Ann Ely both of Lyme were on the 20th inst. by me legally joined in marriage in Lyme May 22d 1849
                        Samuel Griswold Minister of the Gospel
   Recorded May 23 1849 By Oliver J. Lay Regr.

[p. 198] I hereby certify that Elihu Geer of East Hartford and Eliza P. Selden of Lyme were joined in marriage by me in the parish of Hadlyme on the 16th of May AD 1849
Hadlyme June 11, 1849   Stephen A. Loper Pastor of Congl. Church Hadlyme
Recorded June 13th 1849 By Oliver J. Lay Regr.

This certifies that Joseph Dimmock of Sandwich Massachusetts and Sarah H. Wing of Lyme were joined in marriage by me on the 28th inst.
Lyme Ct March 28th 1849   D. S. Brainerd Pastor of the 1st Congl Ch in Lyme
Recorded June 27th 1849 By Oliver J. Lay Regr.

[p. 199] This certifies that Daniel E. Dodge Jr. of Waterford and Amelia A. Saunders were joined in marriage by me on the 30th inst.
Lyme Ct. May 31st 1849   D. S. Brainerd Pastor of the First Cong. Ch. In Lyme
Recorded June 27th 1849 By Oliver J. Lay Regr.

This certifies that Ephraim H. Douglass and Jane Collins both of New London were joined in marriage by me on the 10 inst. Lyme Ct. June 10 1849
D. S. Brainerd Pastor of the First Cong. Ch. Lyme
Recorded June 27th 1849 By Oliver J. Lay Regr.

[p. 200] This certifies that Mr. Jedediah F. Brockway and Mrs. Elizabeth E. Hayden both of Lyme were on the 1st of July inst. by me legally joined in marriage
Lyme July 23d 1849   Samuel Griswold Minister of the Gospel
Recorded July 24 1849 By Oliver J. Lay Regr.

This certifies that Dr John Noyes & Mrs. Anna Sill were joined in marriage by me on the 21st Inst.
Lyme Ct June 22d 1849   D. S. Brainerd Pastor of the First Cong. Ch. in Lyme
Recorded June 27th 1849 By Oliver J. Lay Regr.

[p. 201] This certifies that Mr Edward Covell of Elmira New York and Miss Georgeanna L Parsons of Lyme were united in marriage by me on the 23d Inst
Lyme Ct Aug 24th 1849   D. S. Brainard Pastor of 1st Congl Ch Lyme Ct.
Recorded Sept. 20 1849 By Oliver J. Lay Regr.

This certifies that Seth Gillett of East Windsor and Catharine Whipp of Lyme were joined in marriage by me on the 12th inst
Lyme Ct Sept 19 1849   D. S. Brainard Pastor of 1st Congl Ch in Lyme Ct
Recorded Sept 20 1849 By Oliver J Lay Regr

[p. 202] I hereby certify that on the 30th day of Sept 1849 at my dwelling House in the Town of Lyme in the County of New London Richard N Denison and Emeline Robbins both of said Lyme were lawfully joined in marriage by me
Wm Marvin Justice of the Peace
Recorded Oct 1 1849 By Oliver J. Lay Regr.

This certifies that Elizur Hill of Hartford and Sarah A Rand of Lyme were married by me on the 28th day of August 1849 in the Town of Lyme
Wm Harris Minister of the Gospel
Recorded October 1st 1849 By Joshua R Warren Regr

[p. 203] This is to certify that on the 30th September 1849 David L Phelps of Saybrook and Delia M Slate of Lyme were joined in marriage by me
Simon Shailer Pastor of the Baptist Church in Haddam
Recorded October 1st 1849 By Joshua R Warren Regr

I hereby certify that on the 26th day of September 1849 Ezra Jones Post and Charlotte Rust were duly joined in marriage in the Town of Lyme by me.
Sylvester Nash Rector of St Johns Church Essex, Ct.
Recorded October 15th 1849 By J R Warren Regr

[p. 204] Lyme October 14th 1849 I hereby certify that I joined in marriage Hazard B Willcox of Lyme and Elisabeth Harvey of East Haddam
        Lyme October 26th 1849 Samuel D. Sill Justice of Peace
Recorded October 26th 1849 By Joshua R. Warren Regr

This certifies that Norman Perego of Windham Ct and Ann Tucker of Lyme were married by me November fifth one thousand eight hundred and forty eight
     Joseph B Damon Pastor of the Baptist Church 1st Society in Lyme
Recorded October 30th 1849 By Joshua R Warren Regr

[p. 205] This certifies that Charles E Peck and Ann Morrison both of Lyme were married by me July 9th AD 1848 Joseph B Damon Pastor of the Baptist Church 1st Society in Lyme
Recorded October 30th 1849 By Joshua R Warren Regr

This certifies that Elihu B Southworth of   and Lydia Lay of Lyme were married by me October 1st AD 1848
    Joseph B Damon Pastor of Baptist Church 1st Society in Lyme
Recorded October 30th 1849 By Joshua R Warren Regr

[p. 206] This certifies that Robert Champion and Susan A Dart both of Lyme were married by me October 15th 1848
    Joseph B Damon Pastor of the Baptist Church 1st Society in Lyme
Recorded October 30th 1849 By Joshua R Warren Reg.r

This certifies that Calvin Havens & Lydia Maynard both of Lyme were married by me February 5th AD 1849 Joseph B Damon Pastor of the Baptist Church 1st Society in Lyme
Recorded October 30th 1849 By Joshua R Warren Regr

[p. 207] This certifies that Timothy Wright of Glastenbury Ct and Mary E. Clark of Lyme were married by me April 5th A.D. 1849
    Joseph B. Damon Pastor of the Baptist Church 1st Society in Lyme
Recorded October 30th 1849 By Joshua R. Warren Regr

This certifies that Nathan Champlin & Phebe Dow both of Lyme were married by me April 30th 1849 Joseph B. Damon Pastor of the Baptist Church 1st Society in Lyme
Recorded October 30th 1849 By Joshua R. Warren Regr

[p. 208] This certifies that Giles Lester of Norwich and Joanna Maynard of Lyme were married by me April 1st A.D. 1849
    Joseph B. Damon Pastor of the Baptist Church 1st Society in Lyme
Recorded October 30th 1849 By Joshua R. Warren Regr

This certifies that John M. Huntley & Delia Caulkins both of Lyme were married by me September 25th A.D. 1849
    Joseph B. Damon Pastor of the Baptist Church 1st Society in Lyme
Recorded October 30th 1849 By Joshua R. Warren Regr

[p. 209] This certifies that Roswell W. Tinker of New London and Evelin B. Tinker of Lyme were married by me October 30th 1849
    Joseph B. Damon Pastor of the Baptist Church 1st Society in Lyme
Recorded October 30th 1849 By Joshua R. Warren Regr.

I hereby certify that Mr. Junius Marvin and Miss Adaline C. Raymond both of Lyme were united in marriage by me on the 2nd of December A.D. 1849 Hadlyme Dec. 4th 1849
    Stephen A. Loper Pastor of Congregational Church in Hadlyme
Recorded Decemr 6th 1849 By Joshua R. Warren Regr

[p. 210] This certifies that Elihu Smith and Mary Ann Appleby were joined in marriage by me on the second instant D.S. Brainerd Pastor of the first Cong. Church in Lyme Ct.
Lyme Ct December 7th 1849 Recorded January 23d 1850 By Joshua R. Warren Regr

LYME, CONNECTICUT, VITAL RECORDS

This certifies that Mr. Thomas M. Chamberlian of Williamstown Massachusetts and Miss Harriet D. Royce of Lyme Connecticut were by the subscriber lawfully joined in marriage October 1st 1846
             Oliver Brown Minister of the Gospel
Recorded February 6th 1850 By Joshua R. Warren Regr

[p. 211] This certifies that Mr. Francis M. Miner of East Lyme and Miss Maria A. Fox of Lyme were by the subscriber lawfully joined in marriage March 28th 1847
             Oliver Brown Minister of the Gospel
Recorded February 6th 1850 By Joshua R. Warren Regr

This certifies that Mr. Gurdon L. Maynard of East Lyme and Miss Betsey N. Ransom of Lyme were by the subscriber lawfully joined in marriage Novr 30 1848
             Oliver Brown Minister of the Gospel
Recorded Feby 6th 1850 By Joshua R. Warren Regr

[p. 212] This certifies that Mr. Frederick L. C. Brockway and Miss Marion A. Peck both of Lyme were by the subscriber lawfully joined in marriage April 9th 1848
             Oliver Brown Minister of the Gospel
Recorded February 6th 1850 By Joshua R. Warren Regr

This certifies that Mr. Edward Congdon and Miss Sarah Colt both of Lyme were by the subscriber lawfully joined in marriage April 17th 1849
             Oliver Brown Minister of the Gospel
Recorded Feby 6th 1850 By Joshua R. Warren Regr

[p. 213] This certifies that Mr. George Franklin Tillotson of Lyme and Miss Laura E. Caulkins of East Lyme were by the subscriber lawfully joined in marriage December 7th 1849
             Oliver Brown Minister of the Gospel
Recorded Feby 6th 1850 By Joshua R. Warren Regr

This certifies that Mr. George Tucker and Miss Lucy Way both of Lyme were by the subscriber lawfully joined in marriage October 15th 1849
             Oliver Brown Minister of the Gospel
Recorded Feby 6th 1850 By Joshua R. Warren Regr

[p. 214] This certifies that Mr. Edgecomb J. Beckwith and Miss Maria A. Culver both of Lyme were by the subscriber lawfully joined in marriage Feby 3d 1850
             Oliver Brown Minister of the Gospel
Recorded Feby 6th 1850 By Joshua R. Warren Regr

This certifies that Amos C. Maxon and Phebe Pierson were joined in marriage by me on the seventh instant Lyme Feby 8th 1850
        D. S. Brainerd Pastor of the first Cong.. Church in Lyme Ct.
Recorded February 26th 1850 By Joshua R. Warren Regr

[p. 215] This certifies that John H. Broadwick and Elizabeth B. Havens both of Sagharbor Long Island were joined in marriage by me on the 20th instant
Lyme February 20th 1850 D. S. Brainerd Pastor of the first Cong. Church in Lyme Ct.
Recorded February 26th 1850 By Joshua R. Warren Regr

This certifies that Timothy D. Avery of Lyme and Mrs. Jane Burnham of Salem were by the subscriber this day lawfully joined in marriage Lyme November 15th 1846
             Oliver Brown Minister of the Gospel
Recorded March 1st 1850 By Joshua R. Warren Regr

[p. 216] This certifies that Mr. Gurdon Clark and Miss Mary E. Maynard both of East Lyme were by the subscriber this day lawfully joined in marriage. Lyme February 13th 1850
             Oliver Brown Minister of the Gospel
Recorded March 1st 1850 By Joshua R. Warren Regr

This certifies that Mr. Alfred P. Beckwith and Miss Sarah C. Brockway both of Lyme were by the subscriber this day lawfully joined in marriage Lyme February 19th 1850
                            Oliver Brown Minister of the Gospel
   Recorded March 1st 1850 By Joshua R. Warren Regr

[p. 217] This certifies that Henry Robbins and Sarah M. Cone were joined in marriage by me on the 7th instant Lyme April 8th 1850
              D. S. Brainerd Pastor of the first Cong. Church in Lyme Ct
   Recorded April 10th 1850 By Joshua R. Warren Register

This certifies that Fitch C. Smith and Lois C. Watrous were joined in marriage by me on the 26th Lyme April 6th 1850   D. S. Brainerd Pastor of the first Cong. Church in Lyme Ct.
   Recorded April 10th 1850 By Joshua R. Warren Regr

[p. 218] This certifies that James Ferlong and Isabella B. Appleby of Lyme were joined in marriage by me on the nineteenth instant
Lyme Ct April 20th 1850   D. S. Brainerd Pastor of the first Cong. Church in Lyme
   Recorded May 16th 1850 By Joshua R. Warren Register

This certifies that Lieut S. B. Buckner of the U.S.A. and Mary J. Kingsbury were joined in marriage by me on the 2nd instant Lyme Ct. May 16th 1850
              D. S. Brainerd Pastor of the first Cong. Church in Lyme Ct.
   Recorded May 16th 1850 By Joshua R. Warren Regr

[p. 219] This certifies that John R. Morgan and Lydia M. Day were joined in marriage by me on the 15th instant Lyme Ct May 16th 1850
              D. S. Brainerd Pastor of the first Cong. Church in Lyme Ct.
   Recorded May 16th 1850 By Joshua R. Warren Regr

This certifies that Mr. Israel Havens and Miss Prudence M. Clark both of Lyme Connecticut were married June 2nd 1850 by me
                      John F. Blanchard Minister of the Gospel
   Recorded June 19th 1850 By Joshua R. Warren Regr

[p. 220] This certifies that Mr. Joseph Church and Miss Elizabeth Bogue both of Lyme Connecticut were married June 16th 1850 by me
                      John F. Blanchard Minister of the Gospel
   Recorded June 19 1850 By Joshua R. Warren Regr

This may certify that Mr. Noyes W. Palmer of Salem and Miss Diadamia P. Ely of Lyme were this day lawfully joined in marriage by me
                      W. M. Meech Minister of the Gospel
   Recorded Sept 23rd 1850 Joshua R. Warren Regr

[p. 221] This certifies that Mr. George W. Davison and Miss Mary Ann Wood both of Lyme were this day lawfully joined in marriage at Lyme by me
Sept 10th 1850   W. M. Meech Minister of the Gospel
   Recorded September 23rd 1850 By Joshua R. Warren Regr

This certifies that Augustus W. Morgan and Abby A. Damon were joined in marriage by me on the second instant Lyme June 3rd 1850
              D. S. Brainerd Pastor of the 1st Cong. Church in Lyme
   Recorded Septemr 27th 1850 By Joshua R. Warren Regr

[p. 222] This certifies that Charles Beckwith and Ann Burrow both of Lyme were joined in marriage by me on the 21st instant Lyme July 22nd 1850
              D. S. Brainerd Pastor of the first Cong. Church in Lyme
   Recorded Sept 27th 1850 By Joshua R. Warren Regr

This certifies that Mr. Amasa S. Buckingham and Miss Mary L. Tribble were joined in marriage by me on the 2nd instant Lyme Ct. Sept. 17th 1850
                    D. S. Brainerd Pastor of the first Cong. Church in Lyme Ct.
    Recorded Septemr 27th 1850 By Joshua R. Warren Regr

[p. 223] This certifies that in the parish of Hadlyme Lyme on the evening of Sunday Sept 1st 1850 Joel M. Gloyd of Maumer City Ohio and Mary E. Warner daughter of Samuel S. Warner of Lyme Conn. were legally married by me
                    Amos Cheesebrough Ordained Minister of the Gospel
    Recorded Sept 27th 1850 By Joshua R. Warren Regr

This certifies that Mr. Benajah P. Bill & Miss Louisa M. Peck both of Lyme were by the subscriber this day lawfully joined in marriage Lyme Sept. 17th 1850
                    Oliver Brown Minister of the Gospel
    Recorded October 2nd 1850 By Joshua R. Warren Regr

[p. 224] North Lyme Sept. 17th 1850 This may certify that Thomas B. Peck and Hepzibah S. Tooker both of this place were on the 16th instant married by the undersigned
                    James Noyes
    Recorded October 21st 1850 By Joshua R. Warren Regr

I hereby certify that Mr. Charles Erastus Kirtland of Westbrook and Miss Emeline E. Beckwith of Lyme were lawfully joined in marriage on the 4th day of November 1850
                    Wm A. Hyde Officiating Minister
    Recorded November 25th 1850 By Joshua R. Warren Register

[p. 225] This certifies that William G. Lane of Sandusky Ohio and Elizabeth D. Griswold of Lyme were joined in marriage by me on the 30th instant Lyme Ct. October 31st 1850
                    D. S. Brainerd Pastor of the First Cong. Church in Lyme Ct.
    Recorded Decemr 4th 1850 By J. R. Warren Register

This certifies that Horace P. Clark of Lyme & Eleanor A. Hastings of New York City were joined in marriage by me on the first instant Lyme Ct. Dec. 4th 1850
                    D. S. Brainerd Pastor of the first Cong. Church in Lyme
    Recorded Decemr 4th 1850 By J. R. Warren Register

[p. 226] William Braddick of Essex and Lucy Tinker of Lyme were united in marriage Dec. 30th 1850 by Rev. E. F. Burr   E. F. Burr
    Recorded January 22d 1851 By Joshua R. Warren Regr

This certifies that Mr. William Stone and Miss Mary Ann Swan both of Lyme Ct. were this day lawfully joined in marriage by me Lyme Oct. 28th 1850
                    W. W. Meech Minister of the Gospel
    Recorded February 17th 1851 By Joshua R. Warren Regr

[p. 228] This certifies that Stephen Chadwick and Fanny Davenport both of Lyme were lawfully joined in marriage by me November 7th 1830
                    Oliver Coats Justice of the Peace
    Emmia Maria Chadwick Daughter of Stephen & Fanny Chadwick born November 15th A.D. 1831
    Elisha Ambrose Chadwick Son of Stephen & Fanny Chadwick born Decemr 20th 1834
    Hesekiah Ewin Chadwick Son of Stephen & Fanny Chadwick born December 26th A.D. 1840
    Recorded May 6th 1851 by Joshua R. Warren Regr

[p. 231] This may Certify that Samuel S. Sawyer and Frances Gulliver both of Lyme were joined in marriage by me on the 4th day of June A.D. 1837
                    M. S. Parker Justice of the Peace
    Recorded August 18th 1851 By Joshua R. Warren Regr

[p. 260] This certifies that Joseph Dowsett and Betsey Tilletson were united in marriage by me this 4th day of Nov. A.D. 1810   Andrew Griswold Justice of the Peace

To the Town Clerk of the Town of Lyme   I Caroline Brockway of said town hereby certify that I was present with Lucy D. Brooks wife of Augustus O. Brooks at the time of the birth of Marrion J. Brooks.   Marion J. Brooks was born August 26th 1850
Signed Caroline Brockway

[p. 261] State of Connecticut County of New London SS Lyme Sept. 14th 1867 Hannah Bogue of said Lyme having been duly sworn deposes & says that she was present with Eliza Bogue wife of Samuel M. Bogue at the birth of Mary E. Bogue & also at the birth of Minerva S. Bogue both of which occurred at said Town of Lyme as follows - viz Mary E. Bogue was born on December 28th 1849   Minerva S. Bogue was born on August 1st 1860 & further deponent saith not sworn to before me this 14th day Hannah Bogue of Sept AD 1867   John W. Marvin Notary Public

[p. 263] New London County ss May 4th 1834 Be it remembered that on the day of the date aforesaid Eleaser Spencer of Haddam and Betsey Saunders of Lyme were united in marriage by and before me   Richard E. Selden Jr. Justice of Peace
Taken from Justices' Records Recorded Nov. 26th 1907 by William Marvin Reg

New London County ss Lyme 26th April 1840 Be it remembered that on the day of the date aforesaid Giles Ingraham of East Haddam and Emily Rau of Lyme were united in marriage by and before me   Richard E. Selden Jr. Justice of Peace
Taken from Justice's Record Recorded Nov 26th 1907 by William Marvin Reg.

New London County ss Lyme 29 August 1841 Be it remembered that on the day of the date aforesaid Edward Hewlet of East Haddam and Francisca Motte of Lyme were united in marriage according to law before me   Richard E. Selden Jr. Justice of Peace
Taken from Justice's Record Recorded Nov. 26th 1907 by William Marvin Reg.

[p. 264] Jasper Griffing Married Mahala Terry Jan 10, 1840 Their children born at Lyme were as follows:
  Hilliard Griffing born Oct 27, 1840
  Francis Henry Griffing born Nov 18, 1843 - and died Dec 18 1854
  Almira Terry Griffing born Nov 5, 1847
  Catherine Ester Ann Griffing born June 30, 1845
  James Charles E. Griffing born Dec 10, 1852
  Jasper Griffing above named died Dec 27, 1866
  The foregoing record recorded from the Jasper Griffing family bible This 22d day of Jan. 1919 by William Marvin, Town Clerk.

1847-48 Report of Births in the 1st School Society in Lyme for the year ending on the 1st Monday of August 1848

Date of Birth	Name of Child	Name of Parents	Age Parents	Color	Occupation	Residence
1st District						
June 24th 1848	Georgiana Beckwith	Charles M. Beckwith	41	White	Farmer	Lyme, Ct.
		Betsey E. Beckwith	37	do		
Dec. 14 1847	Caroline Miller	George Miller	37	do	Carpenter	Lyme, Ct.
		Sarah Miller	26	do		
June 1848	Joseph S. Brockway Jr.	Joseph S. Brockway	28	do	Merchant	Lyme, Ct.
		Mary S. Brockway	30	do		
2nd District						
Jany 9 1848	Louisa Miner	Joel Miner			Farmer	Lyme, Ct.
		Mary Miner				
3rd District						
Dec. 30th 1847	William Appleby	Miss Isabella Appleby	7 mos.	do		Lyme, Ct.
Sept. 3d 1847	Name not known	John DeWolf		do	Shoemaker	Lyme, Ct.
		Ann DeWolf				
Jany 30 1848	Sarah M. Tillitson	Ira Tillitson			Farmer	Lyme, Ct.
		Betsey Tillitson				
Feby 20 1848	Thomas E. Johnson	Thomas Johnson		do	Laborer	Lyme, Ct.
		No name Johnson		colored		
March 8 1848	Jane Bump	John Bump		white	Laborer	Lyme, Ct.
		Elisabeth Bump				
March	George Appleby	Miss Mary Ann Appleby		white		Lyme, Ct.
July 3 1848	John Noyes	John Noyes			Physician	Lyme, Ct.
		Ann Noyes				
Aug 5 1848	Elisabeth W. Lord	William J. Lord		white	manufacturer	Lyme, Ct.
		Mehitabel S. Lord		white		
5th District						
Oct. 13, 1847	Phebe Slate	Lathrop E. Slate Jr.	31	do	Blacksmith	Lyme, Ct.
		Mary C. Slate	22	do		Lyme, Ct.
March 26 1848	James D. Havens	Charles M. Havens	30	do	House Carpenter	Lyme, Ct.
		Abby Havens	26	do		
Sept. 18 1847	Adeline C. King	Leander King	31	do	Shoemaker	Lyme, Ct.
		Harriet King	23	do		

Date of Birth	Name of Child	Name of Parents	Age Parents	Color	Occupation	Residence
Oct. 8th 1847	Sarah A. Champion	Horace Champion	27	do	Farmer	Lyme, Ct.
		Jane Champion	23	do	--	Lyme, Ct.
April 22 1848	Sarah Ann Way	Wm. C. Way	35	do	Farmer	Lyme, Ct.
		Frances Way	33	do	--	--
Jany 20th 1848	David C. Maynard	Richard E. Maynard	38	do	Cooper	Lyme, Ct.
		Almira Maynard	37	do	--	--
May 12th 1848	Lucy E. Fuller	George C. Fuller	33	do	House Carpenter	Lyme, Ct.
		Mary Ann Fuller	30	do	--	--
6th District						
May 1 --	James De Gray Haynes	Henry Haynes	30	do	House Carpenter	Lyme, Ct.
		Mary Haynes	27	do	--	--
Dec. 21 --	not named	Daniel Anderson	31	do	Farmer	Lyme, Ct.
		Frances Anderson	31	do	--	--
Dec. 6 --	not named	Stephen DeWolf	59	do	Farmer	Lyme, Ct.
		Julia DeWolf	46	do	--	--
7th District						
Feby 4 1848	Alfred Nelson Havens	Daniel C. Havens	6 mos.	white	Miller	Lyme, Ct.
		Mrs. - Havens		do	--	--
4th District						
Feby 16 1848	William Lombard	James Lombard	5 mos.	white	Manufacturer	Lyme, Ct.
		Margaret Lombard		do	--	Lyme, Ct.
		2nd School Society				
1st District						
July 14 1848	James Brockway	Ebeneser E. Brockway	33	white	Farmer	Lyme, Ct.
		Lucy S. Brockway	26	do	--	--
Nov. 24 1847	Ellen Bump	Ebeneser Bump	38	do	Farmer	Lyme, Ct.
		Minerva Bump	35	do	--	--
Dec 2d 1847	Isabella Ely	Samuel C. Ely	37	do	Merchant	Lyme, Ct.
		Frances Ely	30	do	--	--
April 7 1848	Henry W. Ely	William Ely	45	do	Farmer	Lyme, Ct.
		Emma Ely	43	do	--	--
Nov. 14 1847	Sarah E. Hughes	John G. Hughes	44	do	Stone cutter	Lyme, Ct.
		Julia Hughes	43	do	--	--

LYME, CONNECTICUT, VITAL RECORDS 200

Date of Birth	Name of Child	Name of Parents	Age Parents	Color	Occupation	Residence
Aug. 2d 1848	David E. Quinby, Jr.	David E. Quinby	30	do	Farmer	Lyme, Ct.
		Roxana Quinby	28	do		
June 11 1848	Mary Jane Stark	Abial Stark 2d	42	do	Farmer	Lyme, Ct.
		Jane A. Stark	40	do		
3rd District						
Feby 28 1848	Sarah E. Miner	Daniel S. Miner	35	white	Ship Carpenter	Lyme, Ct.
		Sarah M. Miner	35	do		
March 23d 1848	Frances A. Hungerford	Richard A. Hungerford	25	do	Pedlar	Lyme, Ct.
		Elisabeth C. Hungerford	22	do		
April 30th 1848	-- Hayden	Charles Hayden	25	do	Sailor	Lyme, Ct.
		Amelia Hayden	20	do		
Jany 8 1848	Francis Damon	Henry N. Damon	24	do	Coaster	Lyme, Ct.
		Nancy Damon	20	do		
Jany 15 1848	Robert L. Laplass	Robert H. Laplass	28	do	Farmer	Lyme, Ct.
		Nancy E. Laplass	28	do		
4th District						
Feby 6 1848	Martha Murdock	Ann Murdock	26	white	Housekeeping	Lyme, Ct.
6th District						
Oct. 8 --	Florence A. Sterling	John Sterling	44	do	Farmer	Lyme, Ct.
		Hannah S. Sterling	25	do		
Nov. 18 --	No name	David A. Martin	28	do	Carpenter	Lyme, Ct.
		Roxana Martin	26	do		
Aug 19h --	No name	E. D. Brockway	31	white	Merchant	Lyme, Ct.
		M. C. Brockway	31	do		
Oct. 13th 1847	Walter S. Ely	Calvin L. Ely	31	do	Cooper	Lyme, Ct.
(in pencil)		Oru E. Ely	30	do		
5th District						
Jany 7 1848	Joseph Selden Johnson	Barach Johnson	35	White	Farmer	E. Lyme, Ct.
		Mary Ann Johnson	26	do		

1848 & 9 Report of Births in the 1st School Society in Lyme for the year ending on the 1st Monday of August 1849

Date of Birth	Name of Child	Sex	Name of Parents	Age Parents	Color	Occupation	Residence
3rd District							
August 20th 1848	Jane Morley	Girl	Charles S. Morey Betsey Morley		white	House painter	Lyme
Dec. 1st 1848	Wm. Henry Freeman	Boy	Sophia Freeman Illegitimate		black		Lyme
Dec. 22 1848	Ann E. Terry	Girl	James Terry Catharine Terry		white	Minister	Lyme
January 3rd 1849	Willis Vernon	Boy	Edward Vernon Frances Vernon		white	Druggist	New York
February 2nd 1849	George Mather	Boy	George Mather Geruah Mather		do	Farmer	Lyme
April 2nd 1849	"	Girl	Ira Hyde E. Hyde		do	Miller	Lyme
May 1st 1849	"	Boy	C. F. Comstock Stillborn Elisa Comstock		do	Carpenter	Lyme
July 1st 1849	"	Girl	George Leete Jane Leete		white	Farmer	Lyme
July 14th 1849	Catharine Peck	Girl	Charles Peck Ann Peck		do	Farmer	Lyme
4th District							
Aug 28th 1848	William	Male	William I. Banning Lucy L. Banning		do	Manufacturer	Lyme
Dec. 24th 1848	"	Male	John Appleby Emily Appleby		do	Laborer	Lyme Lyme
May 15th 1849	"	Male	Cornelius Banta Henrietta Banta		do	Laborer	Unknown
Aug 1st 1849	E. C. Lombard	Male	James Lombard Margaret Lombard		do	Manufacturer	Lyme
5th District							
Septem 21st 1848	George Miller	Male	Alonso Miller Harriet Miller	24 21	white	Farmer	Lyme
March 15th 1849	Richard Robbins	Male	Henry Robbins	28 37	white	Mason	Lyme
May 30th 1849	Ellen G. Slate	Female	George R. Slate Elisabeth Slate	32	white	Farmer	Lyme

Report of Births in the 1st School Society in Lyme for the year ending on the first Monday of August 1849

Date of Birth	Name of Child	Sex	Name of Parents	Age Parents	Color	Occupation	Residence
6th District							
April 27th 1849	Harriet Emma	Female	Eleaser C. Peck	33	white	Agriculturist	Lyme
			Eunice Peck	26			
Jan.y 19th 1849	Anna Ophelia	Female	Elisha Havens	37	white	Agriculturist	Lyme
			Lucy Havens	30			
June 16th 1849	Not named	Female	Morgan Lewis	36	white	do	Lyme
			Sarah A. Lewis	31			
June 17th 1849	Not named	Female	Henry S. Gilbert	30	white	Stone cutter	Lyme
			Jane Gilbert	24			
7th District							
Feby 21st 1849	William Chappell	Male	Issac D. Chappell	31	white	Agriculturist	Lyme
			Harriet Chappell	29			
July 28 1849	Not named		John Wait	46	white	do	do
			Mary Ann Wait	37			
Jany 7th 1849	Not named stillborn	Female	Stephen Chadwick	48	white	Agriculturist	Lyme
			Fanny Chadwick	39			
Sept 1st 1848	Amon Champion		Chauncy Champion	47	white	do	do
			Mary Ann Champion	45			
May 6, 1849	Martha E. Champion	Female	Robert M. Champion	30	white	Agriculturist	Lyme
			Mary Ann Champion	21			
June 17 1849	Not named (stillborn)	Male	Isaac Peckham	37	white	do	do
			Fanny M. Peckham	35			
April 27, 1849	Frances E. Champion	Female	Edward Champion	25	white	do	do
			Mary Champion	25			
Feby 12, 1849	Theodore Hall	Male	Jesse Hall	32	white	Stone cutter	do
			Abby Hall	26			

Report of Births in the 2nd School Society in Lyme for the year ending on the first Monday of August 1849

Date of Birth	Name of Child	Sex	Name of Parents	Age Parents	Color	Occupation	Residence
1st District							
Oct. 27th 1848	Sarah E. Lord	Female	Samuel H. Lord	26	white	Farmer	Lyme
			Elisabeth C. Lord	22			
July 8th 1849	not named	Female	Edgecomb Beckwith	47	white	Laborer	Lyme
			Sarah Beckwith	37			

VOLUME 4 203

Date of Birth	Name of Child	Sex	Name of Parents	Age Parents	Color	Occupation	Residence
Sept 29 1848	Rebecca L. Bill	Female	James A. Bill Ann S. Bill	32 29	white	Book Publisher	Lyme
2nd District							
Nov. 16th 1848	Lucinda F. Champlin	Female	James S. Champlin Lucinda Champlin	not given	white	Not named	Lyme
Aug.t 17 1849	Brainard A. Banning	Male	Edwin H. Banning Emily Banning	not given	white	not named	Lyme
April 1st 1849	Nancy Elizabeth Reynolds	Female	Henry B. L. Reynolds Temperance Reynolds	not given	white	not named	Lyme
May 13 1849	Mary E. Banning	Female	William T. Banning Mary Ann Banning	not given	white	not named	Lyme
4th District							
Oct. 15 1848	Name unknown	Female	Daniel A. Baldwin Betsey Baldwin	40 to 50 30 to 40	white	Farmer	East Lyme
Jany 17 1849	Elbert Morton Beebe	Male	Joseph Beebe Nancy Beebe	30 30	white	Farmer	Lyme
Dec. 14 1848	Jane Maria Way	Female	John Way Sr. Clarissa Way	24 28	white	Farmer	Lyme
April 5th 1849	Not named	Male	William Frink Sarah Frink	40 to 50 30 to 40	white	Farmer	East Lyme
Nov. 12 1848	Name unknown	Female	George I. Mason, Jr. Martha Mason	20 to 30 20 to 30	colored	Farmer	Lyme
March 28 1849	Orris Rosanna Mason	Female	John Mason Clorinda Mason	27 25	colored	Laborer	Lyme
June 23 1849	Caroline Miner	Female	Charles Miner Huldah Miner	34 31	white colored	Laborer	Lyme
6th District							
Oct. 17 1848	Maria Lester	Female	Esra S. Lester Nancy Lester		white	Laborer	Lyme
April 7, 1849	Not named	Male	Jonathan M. Swan Dimis Swan		white	Carpenter	Lyme
April 16 1849	James Ely	Male	Noah Harding Nancy M. Harding		white	Farmer	Lyme

LYME, CONNECTICUT, VITAL RECORDS

Report of Births in the 1st School Society in Lyme for the year ending on the first Monday of August 1849

Date of Birth	Name of Child	Sex	Name of Parents	Age Parents	Color	Occupation	Residence
1st District 1st Society							
1848 December 7	John L. Rowland	Male	William G. Rowland Mary Loisa Rowland	32 25	white white	Farmer --	Lyme, Ct. Lyme, Ct.
1849 June 6	Charles S. Miner	Male	Charles H. Miner Betsey F. Miner	28 26	white white	Carpenter --	Lyme, Ct. --
1849 March 13	Clarissa B. Champion	Female	John Champion Lucy M. Champion	34 34	white white	Farmer --	Lyme, Ct. Lyme, Ct.
1849	Charles M. Chadwick	Male	Daniel Chadwick Jr. Elen Chadwick	24 24	white white	Attorney at Law --	Lyme, Ct. --
1849 June 15	Not named	Female	John Hart Margaret Hart	60 40	white white	merchant --	Lyme, Ct. --
1848 Nov. 7	John L. Dorr	Male	John Dorr Nancy Dorr	25 24	white white	Farmer --	Lyme, Ct. --
1848 Oct.	Margaret Jane Fuller	Female	Joseph I. Fuller Catharine Fuller	31 24	white white	Joiner --	Lyme, Ct. Lyme, Ct.
1848 Aug 31	Anna M. Brainard	Female	Davis S. Brainard Anna Brainard	35 26	white white	Clergyman --	Lyme, Ct. --
1849 July 12	Not named	Male	J. B. Damon Martha Damon	39 35	white white	Clergyman --	Lyme, Ct. --
1848 Sept. 5	Modina Lay	Female	Joseph H. Lay Elisabeth A. Lay	35 37	white white	Shoe Maker --	Lyme, Ct. --
1849 Feby 22	David Morley	Male	David Morley Caroline W. Morley	34 25	white white	Carriage Maker --	Lyme, Ct. --

Report of Births in the 1st School Society in Lyme for the year next preceding the first day of August A.D. 1850

Date of Birth	Name of Child	Sex	Name of Parents	Age Parents	Color	Occupation	Residence
1st District							
1849 Nov 1	George Rowland	Male	William G. Rowland Mary Ann Rowland	35 24	white white	Farmer --	Lyme Lyme
2nd District							
1849 Dec 11	Mary M. Tinker	Female	William Tinker Nancy Tinker	not given not given	white white	Farmer --	Lyme --
3rd District							
Aug 29	Thomas Johnson	Male	Thomas Johnson Mary Ann Johnson	36 24	Black do	Laborer --	Lyme --

Date of Birth	Name of Child	Sex	Name of Parents	Age Parents	Color	Occupation	Residence
4th District							
1849 Oct. 27	James Monroe Willey	Male	A. W. Willey Catharine S. Willey	not given not given	white white	Woolen Manufacturer	Lyme
Dec 14	Martha A. Appleby	Female	John Appleby Emily Appleby	do	white white	Laborer	Lyme Lyme
5th District							
1849 Sept. 4	John B. Beckwith	Male	William J. Beckwith Mary Jane Beckwith	37 29	white white	Farmer	Lyme
4th District							
1849 Dec 10	Jerusha Eva Bogue	Female	James Bogue Laura Bogue	46 35	white white	Laborer	Lyme Lyme
1850 April 24	Richard Lay	Male	Joseph H. Lay Elizabeth Lay	34 39	white white	Shoemaker	Lyme Lyme
May 1	not named	Male	Joseph S. Brockway Mary S. Brockway	29 31	white white	Merchant	Lyme Lyme
May 6	Caroline Tribble	Female	John Tribble Caroline Tribble	30 22	white white	Mariner	Lyme Lyme
2nd District							
1850 April 26	Elihu Smith	Male	Elihu J. Smith Mary Ann Smith	49 27	white white	Shoemaker	Lyme
May 25	Francis Lord	Male	William J. Lord Mehitabel Lord	37 33	white white	Manufacturer	Lyme
June 23	Charles J. Morley	Male	Charles S. Morley Betsey A. Morley	34 32	white white	Painter & Glaser	Lyme
July 12	Ira Beebe	Male	Ira Beebe Judith Beebe	26 22	white white	Gold Digger in Calif.	East Lyme East Lyme
4th District							
1850 July 26	Martha Jane Denison	Female	Richard N. Denison Emeline Denison	27 17	white white	Farmer	Lyme Lyme
1850 Feby 7	Abigail A. Way	Female	William C. Way Frances S. Way	37 34	white white	Stonecutter	Lyme Lyme
7th District							
1850 Feby 30	Nancy Susan Champion	Female	Ezra M. Champion Elisabeth I. Champion	36 34	white white	Farmer	Lyme Lyme

LYME, CONNECTICUT, VITAL RECORDS

Date of Birth	Name of Child	Sex	Name of Parents	Age Parents	Color	Occupation	Residence
May 21	Lucy Jane Reed	Female	James E. Reed Emaline Reed	not given not given	white white	Farmer	Lyme Lyme
June 16	Richard Wm Peckham	Male	Isaac H. Peckham Frances M. Peckham	not given not given	white white	Farmer	Lyme Lyme
1850 July 10	Kathleen C. Champion	Female	Edward Champion Mary Champion	not given not given	white white	Farmer	Lyme Lyme
Feby 23	Alexander S. Wait	Male	Samuel A. Wait Mercy Wait	45 39	white white	mariner	Lyme Lyme
6th District							
1850 June 30	George H. Champlin	Male	William Champlin Phebe Champlin	not given not given	white white	Shoemaker	Lyme Lyme
1850 June 30	Francis P. Champlin	Male					
1850 March 30	John W. Haynes	Male	Henry Haynes Mary Haynes	not given not given	white white	Carpenter	Lyme Lyme
1850 March 30	Richard G. Haynes	Male					
2nd District							
1850 April 6	John Brockway Parker	Male	Marshfield Parker, Jr. Jane A. Parker	24 26	white white	merchant	Lyme
1850 July 15	William H. Reynolds	Male	Henry B. S. Reynolds Temperance Reynolds	24 28	white white	Farmer	Lyme
1850 March 5	Joshua Raymond Warren	Male	Wm W. I. Warren Maria E. Warren	31 31	white white	Physician	Lyme Lyme
4th District							
1850 June 23	No name	Male	George W. Tucker Lucy Tucker	21 21	white white	Laborer Laborer	Lyme Lyme
6th District							
No date	No name	Female	Seth M. Brockway Lucy A. Brockway	21 21	white white	not stated	Lyme Lyme
No date	No name	Female	Ebeneser D. Brockway Mary Brockway	21 21	white white	Merchant	Lyme Lyme
1850 May 3	James Lester	Male	Alfred Lester Lucy Lester	21 21	white white	not stated	Lyme Lyme
1850 July 30	Ludowick Bill	Male	James A. Bill Ann Selden (Lord) Bill	33 31	white white	Farmer	Lyme Lyme
1850 Feb. 14	Josiah Beckwith	Male	Edgecomb Beckwith, Jr. Maria Beckwith	-- --	white white	laborer	Lyme Lyme

Date of Birth	Name of Child	Sex	Name of Parents	Age Parents	Color	Occupation	Residence
1st District							
1850 Dec. 25	Florence Griswold	Female	Robt H. Griswold	--	white	Mariner	Lyme
			Robt H. Griswold	--	white		Lyme
1	Caroline Morley	Female	David Morley			carriage maker	Lyme
3rd District							
1850 Nov. 1	Lyman Chapman	Male	Charlie Chapman	51	white	Farmer	Lyme
			Amy Chapman	46	white		Lyme
4th District							
1850 Sepr 10	Sarah Banning	Female	Elisabeth R. Pratt	--	white	--	Lyme
Dec. 2		Female	William I. Banning	--	white	manufacturer	Lyme
6th District							
1850 Nov.	William Harding	Male	Noah Harding	--	white	farmer	Lyme
			Maria Harding	--			Lyme
1850 Dec.	George Martin	Male	Jonathan R. Martin	--	white	farmer	Lyme
			Hannah Martin	--	white		Lyme

Report of Marriages in the 1st School Society for the year ending on the 1st Monday of August 1848

Date	Names of Persons	Age	Color	Occupation	Place of Birth	Residence	Name of Minister or Magistrate	First or other Marriage
1st District								
March 21st 1848	Daniel Chadwick, Jr.	23	white	attorney at law	Lyme Ct	Lyme Ct	Rev. Davis S. Brainerd	first
	Ellen Noyes	23	white	--	Lyme Ct	Lyme Ct	Rev. Davis S. Brainerd	first
Oct. 24th 1847	Orlando R. Glover	27	white	Inn Keeper	Essex Ct	Lyme Ct	Rev. Roger Albiston	first
	Maria C. Keables	27	white	Inn Keeper	Norwich Ct	Lyme Ct	Rev. Roger Albiston	first
Oct 13th 1847	Ebeniser L. Roberts	24	white	Joiner	Stockbridge, Mass.	Meriden Ct	Rev. Amos D. Watrous	third
	Clarissa R. Bacon	23	white	--	Lyme Ct	Meriden Ct	Rev. Amos D. Watrous	first
July - 1848	Charles E. Peck	--	white	Farmer	Lyme Ct	Lyme Ct	Rev. J. B. Damon	first
	Ann Morris	26	white	--	Ireland	Lyme Ct	Rev. J. B. Damon	first
5th District								
Nov. 21 1847	Horace R. Brockway	26	white	Painter	Lyme Ct	Lyme Ct	Rev. L. G. Leonard	do
	Jennett C. Greenfield	21	white	--	Lyme Ct	Lyme Ct		do
Sept 5th 1847	George E. Mather	26	white	Farmer	Lyme Ct	Deep River	S. Selden Warner Esq.	do
	Mary J. Bogue	23	white	--	Hadlyme Society	--	S. Selden Warner Esq.	do
March 19 1848	Theodore La Mott	28	do	Iron Founder	Vermont	Lyme	Rev. D. S. Brainerd	
	Emily Champion	19	do	--	Vermont	--		
Oct. 14 1847	Joseph Fuller	30	do	House Carpenter	New York	Lyme	Rev. Mr. Steene	
	Catharine Kearney	24	do	--	New York	Lyme		
7th District								
Oct. 16 1847	Samuel Bushnell	21	white	Mariner	Saybrook	Saybrook	Rev. Mr. Crane	first
	Phebe Dart	21	do	--	Lyme	Saybrook	Rev. Mr. Crane	first
Oct. 16 1847	Henry Ross	21	white	Farmer	Saybrook	Saybrook	Rev. Mr. Crane	first
	Lucretia Dart	19	do	--	Lyme	--	Rev. Mr. Crane	first
Nov. 21 1847	James Barrel	21	white	Mason	Saybrook	Saybrook	Rev. Mr. Crane	first
	Mary Bracy	17	do	--	Lyme	Saybrook	Rev. Mr. Crane	first
July 4 1848	Robert M. Champion	25	do	Book Agent	Lyme	Lyme	Married in Philadelphia	first
	Mary Ann Murphy	25	do	--	New York	Lyme	Married in Philadelphia	first
2nd Society								
Sept 3rd 1847	Edward G. Hyde	45	white	Merchant	Norwich Ct	New Orleans	Rev. Saml Griswold	2d
	Sarah M. Lord	22	do	--	Lyme	New Orleans		1st
Nov. 14 1847	Peter Pierson	59	do	Farmer	Lyme	Lyme	Rev. Samuel Griswold	2nd
	Betsey Russel	49	do	--	Lyme	Lyme	Rev. Samuel Griswold	2nd

Date	Names of Persons	Age	Color	Occupation	Place of Birth	Residence	Name of Minister or Magistrate	First or other Marriage
April 1 1848	Martin Sawyer	25	do	Farmer	Lyme	Lyme	Rev. Chester Tilden	1st
	Eunice A. Tinker	26	do		Lyme		Rev. Chester Tilden	1st
Oct. 24 1847	George N. Phelps	35	do	Farmer	Lyme	Lyme	Rev. Walter Wilkie	1st
	Abby E. Warner	27	do		Lyme	Lyme	Rev. Walter Wilkie	1st
Sept 4 1847	Charles Hayden	25	do	Sailor	Westbrook	Lyme	Rev. Chester Tilden	1st
	Amelia Damon	20	do		Lyme	Lyme	Rev. Chester Tilden	1st
Oct 4 1847	Henry N. Damon	24	do	Coaster	Lyme	Lyme	Rev. Chester Tilden	1st
	Nancy Hayden	30	do		Westbrook	Lyme	Rev. Chester Tilden	1st

Report of Marriages in the 2nd School Society for the year ending on the 1st Monday of August 1848

Date	Names of Persons	Age	Color	Occupation	Place of Birth	Residence	Name of Minister or Magistrate	First or other Marriage
4th District								
Oct 11 1847	Elisha Miner	19	white	Farmer	Lyme	Lyme	Samuel D. Sill Esq	first
Oct 11 1847	Fanny Palmer	16	do		Lyme	Lyme	Samuel D. Sill Esq	first
5th District								
April 1st 1848	Frederick L. C. Brockway	29	do	Farmer	Lyme	Lyme	Rev. Oliver Brown	first
	Mary Ann Peck	24	do		Lyme	Lyme	Rev. Oliver Brown	first
Oct. 10 1847	Bartlett P. Sampson	26	do	Farmer	Lyme	East Lyme	Rev. Chester Tilden	first
	Frances C. Crocker	20	do		East Lyme	East Lyme	Rev. Chester Tilden	first

Report of Marriages in the 1st School Society in Lyme for the year ending on the 1st Monday of August 1849

Date	Names of Persons	Age	Color	Occupation	Place of Birth	Residence	Name of Minister or Magistrate	First or other Marriage
Oct 27 1848	William J. Beckwith	34	white	Agriculturist	Lebanon Ct	Lyme	Rev. William Dixon	First
	Mary J. Havins	27	white		Sag Harbor N.Y.			First
April 29 1849	Nathan Champlin	32	white	Agriculturist	Lyme	Lyme	Rev. Joseph B. Damon	First
	Phebe D. Clark	13	white		Lyme			First
Oct 15 1848	Robert Champion	24	white	Agriculturist	Lyme	Lyme	Rev. Joseph B. Damon	First
	Susan Dart	19	white		Lyme			First
1849 May 30	Daniel E. Dodge	32	white	Mariner	Chatham Ct	Waterford Ct	Davis S. Brainard	first
	Amelia A. Sanders	20	white		Lyme Ct	Waterford Ct		first
	Elderkin Waite	35	white	Stone Cutter	Lyme Ct	Lyme Ct	Davis S. Brainard	first
	Lucy A. Dowsick	35	white		Lyme Ct			
	John Noyes	34	white	Physician	Lyme Ct	Lyme Ct	Davis S. Brainard	Second
	Edward Anna Sill	34	white					Second
	Ephriam Douglass	25	white	Town Clerk	New London Ct	New London	Davis S. Brainard	first
	Jane Collins	25	white	New London	New London Ct	New London		first

Report of Marriages in the 2nd School Society in Lyme for the year ending on the first Monday of August 1849

Date	Names of Persons	Age	Color	Occupation	Place of Birth	Residence	Name of Minister or Magistrate	First or other Marriage
1st District								
July 1st 1849	Jedediah F. Brockway	32	white	Farmer	Lyme	Lyme	Rev. Samuel Griswold	First
	Elisabeth E. Hayden	32	white	::	Lyme	Lyme	::	Second
Nov. 5 1848	Griswold Chapel	::	white	Farmer	Lyme	Lyme	Rev. Chester Tilden	Second
	Mehitabel Lord	::	white	::	Lyme	Lyme	::	First
2nd District								
Sept. 28, 1848	M. S. Parker Jr.	22	white	Merchant	Lyme	Lyme	Rev. Samuel Griswold	First
	Jane A. Brockway	22	white	::	Lyme	Lyme	::	First
Apl 17 1849	Edward Congdon	43	white	Tailor	Lyme	Lyme	Rev. Oliver Brown	First
	Sarah Colt	38	white	::	Lyme	Lyme	::	First
Sept. 1 1849	William Taylor	32	white	Farmer	Lyme	Lyme	Rev. Chester Tilden	::
	Betsey Jones	35	white	::	Lyme	Lyme	::	::
4th District								
Sept 9, 1848	George J. Mason Jr.	::	colored	Farmer	Lyme	Lyme	William Marvin Esq.	First
	Martha Condol	::	colored	::	Lyme	Lyme	::	First
May 20 1849	Seth M. Brockway	28	white	Coaster	Lyme	Lyme	Rev. Samuel Griswold	First
	Lucy Ann Ely	20	white	::	Lyme	Lyme	::	First
June 6 1849	Seth L. Peck	23	white	Tanner	Lyme	Lyme	not named	First
	Eunice Gallup	28	white	::	North Stonington	Lyme	::	First

Report of Marriages in the 1st School Society in Lyme for the year next preceeding the first day of August A.D. 1850

Date	Names of Persons	Age	Color	Occupation	Place of Birth	Residence	Name of Minister or Magistrate	First or other Marriage
1st District								
1849 Sept 19	Seth Gillett	::	white	Wheelright	Windsor	New Haven	Davis S. Brainerd	first
	Catharine Whipp	::	white	::	Lyme	New Haven	::	first
No date	Orrin Havens	::	white	Farmer	New London	New London	Davis S. Brainerd	First
	Martha Merriman	::	white	::	Lyme	New London	::	First
2nd District								
1849 Aug 23	Edward Covell	30	white	Merchant	Elmira N.Y.	Elmira N.Y.	Davis S. Brainerd	first
	Georgiana Parsons	19	white	::	Stonington Ct	Elmira N.Y.	::	first
3rd District								
1849 Sept 25	John M. Huntley	19	white	Farmer	Lyme	Lyme	Joseph B. Damon	first
	Delia A. Caulkins	18	white	::	Lyme	Lyme	::	first

VOLUME 4   211

Date	Names of Persons	Age	Color	Occupation	Place of Birth	Residence	Name of Minister or Magistrate	First or other Marriage
Nov. 18	Elihu J. Smith	49	white	Shoemaker	Stamford Ct	Lyme	Davis S. Brainerd	Second
	Mary A. Appleby	27	white	--	Lyme	Lyme	--	Second
7th District								
1849 Nov. 15	John Anson Baker	27	white	Farmer	Lyme	Lyme	Francis Darrow	first
	Mary M. Havens	15	white	Farmer	Lyme	Lyme	--	first

Report of the 2nd School Society in Lyme for the year next preceding the first day of August A.D. 1850

Date	Names of Persons	Age	Color	Occupation	Place of Birth	Residence	Name of Minister or Magistrate	First or other Marriage
2nd District								
1849 Dec 3	Junius Marvin	29	white	Farmer	Lyme	Lyme	-- Soper	first
	Adaline C. Raymond	29	white	--	Lyme	--	--	first
4th District								
1849 Oct 15	George W. Tucker	20	white	Laborer	Lyme	Lyme	Oliver Brown	first
	Lucy J. Way	20	white	--	Lyme	Lyme	--	first
6th District								
no date	William S. Ransom	28	white	Merchant	not known	New London	not stated	first
	Elisabeth Brockway	27	white	--	--	Lyme	--	first
1st District								
1850 April 19	James Furlong	--	White	Farmer	Ireland	Lyme	Davis S. Brainard	first
	Isabel Appleby	--	White	--	--	--	--	
No date	Orrin Havens	--	White	Farmer	New London	New London	Davis S. Brainard	first
	Martha Merriman	--	White	--	Lyme	New London	--	
5th Dist.								
1850 Apr. 7	Henry Robbins	30	White	Mason	Lyme	Lyme	Davis S. Brainard	second
	Sarah M. Cone	22	White	--	Lyme	Lyme	--	
June 2	Israel Havens	43	White	Farmer	Lyme	Lyme	John F. Blanchard	Third
	Prudence Clark	44	White	--	Lyme	Lyme	--	
6th Dist.								
1850 March 26	Fitch C. Smith	44	White	Farmer	Lyme	Lyme	Davis S. Brainard	first
	Lois Watrous	32	White	--	Lyme	Lyme	--	
1850 June 2	Augustus W. Morgan	25	White	Farmer	Lyme	Lyme	Davis S. Brainard	first
	Abby Ann Damon	23	White	--	Lyme	Lyme	--	
1850 Aug.	Charles Beckwith	--	White	Farmer	Lyme	Lyme	Davis S. Brainard	first
	Ann Burrows	--	White	--	Lyme	Lyme	--	

Date	Names of Persons	Age	Color	Occupation	Place of Birth	Residence	Name of Minister or Magistrate	First or other Marriage
1850 Sept.	Amasa S. Buckingham Mary S. Tribble		White White	Mechanic	Saybrook	Saybrook	Davis S. Brainard	first
1850 Sept.	Noyes W. Palmer Desdamia P. Ely		White White	Laborer	Lyme Lyme	Salem Lyme	William W. Meech	first
1850 Sept. 10	George W. Davison Mary Ann Wood		White White	Mason	Lyme Lyme	Lyme Lyme	William M. Meech	first
1850 Sept. 16	Thomas B. Peck Hepsibah S. Tooker		White White	Farmer	Lyme Lyme	Lyme Lyme	James Noyes	first
1850 Oct. 28	William Strong Mary Ann Swan		White White	Manufacturer	Lyme Lyme	Lyme Lyme	William W. Meech	first

Report of Deaths in the 1st School Society in Lyme For the year ending on the 1st Monday of Aug. 1848

Date	Name	Age	Color	Occupation	Place birth	Residence	Reputed Cause
Bk 4 Deaths							
1st Dist.							
Dec. 19, 1847	Ady Clark	79	White		Lyme	Lyme	consumption
April 4, 1848	Harriet Havens	47	White		Lyme	Lyme	Erysipelas
Aug. 9, 1847	George Mather	3	White		Lyme	Lyme	
July 4, 1848	Mrs. Ann Noyes	30	White	Physician's wife	England	Lyme	
July 6, 1848	John Noyes	2 days	White		Lyme	Lyme	
May 16, 1848	Miss Mary or Polly Read	80	White	wife Chas. Lay	New York	Lyme	from fractured limb
March 5, 1848	Mrs. Margaret Lay	36	White	agriculturist	R. Island	Lyme	Asthma consumption
Aug. 1, 1847	Abraham Clark	65	White	do	Lyme	Lyme	Asthma
Oct. 20, 1847	Winthrop DeWolf	40	White		Lyme	Lyme	lung fever
Janu 1, 1848	Mercy Dorr	20	White		Lyme	Lyme	unknown
Dec. 23, 1847	Not named	2 days	White		Lyme	Lyme	Fits
Dec. 6, 1847	Not named	3 days	White		Lyme	Lyme	Fits
June 16, 1848	Natanel M. Waite	48 yrs.	White	Farmer	Lyme	Lyme	liver complaint
March 30, 1848	Wissam Anderson	48	White		Flushing, L.I.	Lyme	consumption
Aug. 28, 1847	Elisha E. Morgan	6	White		Lyme	Lyme	croup
Jany 14, 1848	Betsey Spencer	72	White		Lebanon	Lyme	Apoplexy
Nov. 10, 1847	James M. Brockway	26	White	Shoemaker	Lyme	Lyme	Typhus fever
Feby 13, 1848	Robert W. Lay	34	White	Pedlar	Lyme	Lyme	Smallpox
Sept. 27, 1848	Abner S. Ely	13	White		Lyme	Lyme	lap of the intestines
Jany 6, 1848	David W. Morgan	35	White	Farmer	Lyme	Lyme	inflammation of the bowels
Sept. 4, 1847	Capt. Dan Marvin	81	White	Farmer	Lyme	Lyme	old age
Aug. 19, 1847	Mrs. Hepsibah Marvin	72	White		Lyme	Lyme	disentery
Jany 3, 1848	Mrs. Mary Reed widow of Geo. Reed	99	White		Lyme	Lyme	old age
Aug. 16, 1847	Sarah Smith	90	White		Saybrook	Lyme	old age
Sept. 1847	George G. Ely	1	White		Lyme	Lyme	serofula & consumption

Report of Deaths in 1st School Society in Lyme For the year ending on the 1st Monday of Aug. 1849

Date	Name	Age	Color	Occupation	Place birth	Residence	Reputed Cause
Sept. 28, 1848	Richard E. Reed male	45	White	laborer	Lyme	Lyme	consumption
Jany 9, 1849	Sylvanus Bogue male	78	White	laborer	Lyme	Lyme	old age
Jany 8, 1849	Infant child male I Appleby		White		Lyme	Lyme	
Sept. 26, 1848	David M. Peck male	23	White	laborer	Lyme	Fairhaven	fever

LYME, CONNECTICUT, VITAL RECORDS

Date	Name	Age	Color	Occupation	Place birth	Residence	Reputed Cause
Nov. 18, 1848	George Moore male	56	White	mariner	London	Lyme	dropsy
Jany 21, 1849	Samuel West male	77	White	farmer	Chatham	Lyme	old age
March 15, 1849	Martha Robbins female	26	White	--	Waterford	Lyme	childbirth
April 3, 1849	Mary Brown female	68	White	--	N. York	Lyme	fever
July 26, 1849	Hannah Havens female	38	White	--	Lyme	Lyme	dropsy
Aug. 9, 1848	Marvin A. Leffingwell male	5 mo.	White	--	E. Lyme	Lyme	consumption
Nov. 23, 1848	Phebe Morgan female	82	White	--	Lyme	Lyme	consumption
March 30, 1849	John Gilbert male	60	White	farmer	Lyme	Lyme	consumption
1st Dist.							
July 2, 1849	Mary Chapman female	75	White	--	Lyme	Lyme	Palsy
May 1, 1849	Lucy Clark female	99	White	--	Lyme	Lyme	old age
Dec. 10, 1848	Reuben Champion male	92	White	Farmer	Lyme	Lyme	old age
Nov. 24, 1848	Mehitabel Johnson female	79	White	--	Lyme	Lyme	old age
Dec. 20, 1848	Sophia Raymond female	56	White	--	Lyme	Lyme	consumption
Nov. 30, 1848	Ursula Chadwick female	42	White	--	Montville	Lyme	consumption
Aug. 27, 1848	Seth H. Wait male	15	White	Mariner	Montville	Lyme	cause unknown
Nov. 22, 1848	Lucinda Champlin female	27	White	--	Lyme	Lyme	affection woes nervous affection
Nov. 30, 1848	Lucinda F. Champlin female	14 days	White	--	Lyme	Lyme	affection woes nervous affection
June 20, 1849	Oliver Spencer male	50	White	Farmer	Lyme	Lyme	--
Jany 17, 1849	Deborah Smith female	70	White	--	East Haddam	Lyme	--
April 12, 1849	Alice M. Sluman female	1	White	--	Lyme	Lyme	--
	Dudley Emerson male	20	White	Farmer	Lyme	Lyme	consumption
March 29, 1849	Julia Ann Morgan female	28	White	--	Lyme	Lyme	consumption
July 8, 1849	Ursula Sill female	59	White	--	Lyme	Lyme	disease of the heart

(Excerpts) Report of Deaths in 1st School Society in Lyme for year next preceding first day of August A.D. 1850

1st Dist.							
1849, Aug. 11	George R. Waite male	29	White	sawyer	Lyme	Albany	consumption
Oct. 1	William H. Tillotson Male	32	White	mail driver	Lyme	Lyme	inflammation of the bowels
7	Mary Ann Avery female	54	White	dressmaker	Lyme	Lyme	inflammation of the bowels
3rd Dist.							
1849, Oct. 4	John H. Sewia male	7	Black	--	Lyme	Lyme	consumption
Nov. 18	Hannah Pierce female	47	Black	--	unknown	Litchfield	typhus fever
6th Dist.							
1849, Oct. 30	Aaron Brockway male	40	White	painter	Lyme	Lyme	consumption

Date	Name	Age	Color	Occupation	Place birth	Residence	Reputed Cause
2nd Dist.							
1849, Dec.	Maria Smith female	40	White	seamstress	Lyme	Lyme	fits
4th Dist.							
1849, Sept. 25	Albert M. Beebe male	8 months	White	--	Lyme	Lyme	Disentary
1849, Oct. 6	Ansel Ely Way male	2½ yrs.	White	--	Lyme	Lyme	Disentary
1849, Oct. 9	Walter Irvin Royce male	4 yrs.	White	--	Lyme	Lyme	Dysantary
Sept. 9, 1848	Simion Morgan male	70	White	Farmer	Middletown	Lyme	consumption
Jany 12, 1849	John L. Rowland male	1 month	White	--	Lyme	Lyme	not stated
April 2, 1849	Richard S. Griswold male	39	White	Merchant	N.York City	Lyme	consumption
April 22, 1849	Sarah D. Platt female	24	White	music teacher	Salem, Ct.	Milwaukee, Wisconsin	consumption
1850, May	Infant not known female	3 weeks	White	--	Lyme	Lyme	inflammation of bowels
2nd Dist.							
1850, Feb. 13	Usial Maynard Male	46	White	Farmer	Waterford	Lyme	Consumption
March 19	Thomas L. Dimiock Male	3 months	White	--	Lyme	Lyme	Consumption
1850, March 20	George Mather Male	1	White	--	Lyme	Lyme	Lung Fever
4th Dist.							
1850, April 14	-- Bogue female	80	White	--	unknown	Lyme	Old Age
5th Dist.							
1850 June 23	Elisha S. Robbins Male	78	White	Farmer	Lyme	Lyme	Erysypilas
6th Dist.							
1850 June 20	Jared Watrous Male	72	White	Farmer	Lyme	Lyme	Fall from a horse
1850 May 6	Mary Tinker Female	90	White	--	Lyme	Lyme	Old Age
1850 Apr. 30	John N. Haynes Male	30 days	White	--	Lyme	Lyme	Inflammation of the lungs
1850 Apr. 30	Richard G. Haynes Male	30 days	White	--	Lyme	Lyme	Inflammation of the lungs
1850 June 6	Susannah Waite Female	88	White	--	Lyme	Lyme	Old Age
1856 June 30	Nancy Susan Champion Female	30	White	--	Lyme	Lyme	Consumption
1850 March	Lucy Rogers Female	81	White	--	East Haddam	Lyme	Old Age
1850 April	Phebe Johnson Female	59	White	--	not given	Lyme	Palsy
1850 April 9	John Brockway Parker Male	3 days	White	--	Lyme	Lyme	not stated
not stated	Maria Griswold Female	46	White	--	not named	Lyme	Consumption
1850 June 3	Lucretia Morgan Female	62	White	--	Lyme	Lyme	Consumption
1850 July 28	Jonathan Gillet Male	60	White	Farmer	Lyme	Lyme	Consumption
not stated	Luisa Peck Female	57	White	--	Lyme	Lyme	Erysypelas

LYME, CONNECTICUT, VITAL RECORDS

Date	Name		Age	Color	Occupation	Place birth	Residence	Reputed Cause
1st School Society								
1850 Dec. 3	Harriet Dwyer	Female	23	White	--	East Lyme	Lyme	Consumption
1850 Dec. 28	Henry Perkins	Male	70	White	Farmer	Plainfield, Ct.	Lyme	Palsy
3rd Dist.								
1850 Oct. 5	Edward L. Sheffelin	Male	65	White	Druggist	New York	New York	Dropsy
6th Dist.								
1850 Sept. 30	Charlotte Maynard	Female	83	White	--	Lyme	Lyme	Dropsy
7th Dist.								
1850 Sept. 29	Amon Champion	Male	60	White	Farmer	Lyme	Lyme	Dysantary
1850 Oct. 5	John M. Cummings	Male	74	White	Farmer	Nova Scotia	Lyme	Dysantary
1850 Dec. 5	Waitstill Cone	Female	89	White	--	Lyme	Lyme	Old Age

VITAL RECORDS
Extracted from Lyme Land Records

Jan. 28, 1733	the birth of the children of John Agect alias Adsot [or Adsit] ye [ ]	LLR2:180
	Lyme Sarah Ageet was born ye 10 of Augst 1717	LLR2:180
	Samuel Ageet was born the 30 of October 1719	
	Mary Ageet was born ye 28 of August 1723	
	Benjamin Ageet was Born the 26 of October 1728	
	Stephen was born the 20 of August 1730	
May 21, 1726	John Alger was born the : 1 : day of August 1694	LLR2:140
	John Alger was married to Temperance Tillotson	
Temperance	the 13 day of December 1722	
Tillotson wife	Their son Nathan Alger was born the 2nd day of October 1723	
of John Alger	Joanna Alger their daughter was born the 3 day of August 1725	
was born 15	their son Mathew was born ye 20 day of March 1726/7	
August 1704	Temperance Alger wife of John Alger Dyed ye 8th September	
Sept 15 1727	17[27] Dates cut off	
	the children of John Alger and Mary his wife is as follows	
Dr 16, 1731	John Alger's Son John by his second wife was born 14 December 173[0] Dates cut off	
	their son Benjamin Alger was born ye 19 day of March AD 17[33] Dates cut off	
	their son John Dyed July ye 23 1735	
	Their daughter Mary was born ye 13th day of November 1735	
	Mary Alger Dyed ye 11 of March 1736	
	Their Second Daughter Mary was born ye 20 day of January [1737] Date cut off	
	John Alger was born ye 19th of March 1739	
	Silas Alger was born August ye 13 1742	
	Seth Alger son of John and Mary Alger was born 2nd Day of February 17 [45/6] Date cut off	
	Nathan Alger son of John Alger dead the 7th Day of December 174[5] Date cut off	
	John and Mary Alger their children born ye 28 Day of September 17[48] Date cut off and Died the same day	
	Benjamin Alger son of John and Mary Alger Died April 23 17[52] Date cut off	
	Jonathan Algur & Grane [Irene] Way Were Married Together April 7th [9] 1740	LLR6:282
	Elisabeth Algur was born ye first day of January 1740/1	
	Elisabeth Algur dyd ye 7th of March 1740/1	
	Elisha Algur was born ye 5th of April 1742	
	Elisha Algur dec. April 12 1742	
	George Algur was born ye 24th of Feb. 1742/3	
	Elizabeth widow of Roger Alger - Late of Lyme Decd formerly ye wife of William Haris [Har[r]is] Dyed in July in ye year 1729 Atested by Benjamin DeWolf	LLR2:364
May 8, 1733	Joseph Alger was married unto Mary Huntly the 27 day of April 1733	LLR2:104
	the births of ye Children of Joseph Alger and Mary his wife is as follows	
	viz their son Joseph was born ye 22 day of Aprill AD 173[sic3]	

March 17 11/12	Roger Alger Senior was married) by me Joseph Peck Recorder unto Elizabeth his now wofe) LLR2:466 By Joseph Peck Justis

Roger Alger Juner was born 25 July in ye year 1687
Roger Alger junor was married to Sarah Stoten ye 8
   februy 1708   LLR:2:231
their son Jofeph Alger was born the 1 Day of December 1709
Ruth Alger was born ye 18 Day of January 1712
Jonathan their son was born ye 14 of April 1714
David Alger was born ye 1 Day of August 1716
Roger their son was born ye 17 Day of February 1719
Simeon was born ye 17 Day of August 1721 [1722]
Sarah Alger their daughter was born ye 27 September 1726
James Alger was born ye 30 Day of December 1728
David Alger Died ye 22 day of May 1732
Roger Alger Died the 2nd Day of August AD 1759

	Thomas Andreuson was married unto Hanah Peck 25 June 1696 LLR2:129
June 97	Hannah Anderson was borne The 31 May 1697
	Hanah Anderson Deceased the 13 June 1697
April 98	a second Hanah Anderson wase borne the 7 Aprill 1698
	Hanah Anderson deceased the 18 Aprill 1698
Oct. 1712	The birith and Death of the Children of Thomas LLR2:366 Anderson and Hana his now wife

Sarah Anderson was borne the 22 Apprill 1703 [also LLR2:129]
Hanah Anderson the third was borne the 25 July 1705
John Anderson was borne the 26 August 1712
Thomas Anderson was born the 26 Febe 1714 and
   Dyed March the 29 1715
Mr. Thomas Anderson died the first Day of May AD 1746
Mrs. Hannah Anderson wife of Mr. Thomas Anderson Dyed ye
   25th Day of feby AD 1734/5   aged sixty years five months and
   11 days   LLR6:5
John S. of Capt. Thomas & Margaret   LLR16:239

21 Aprill 1701	John Andrus was mared to Rachell [DeWolfe] [d. of Edward] the 2 Desembr 1696 LLR:2:234

the birth and Death of the children of John Andrus and
   Rachell his wife
Thomas Andrus was Borne the 15 [25] July 1697
Abegall Andrus was Borne the 13 March 1697 [sic]
John Andrus was Borne the 6 April 1700
Hana Andrus was Borne the 23 January 170 1/2

Danill Ayer & Ester Champion were married together ye 17th of
   April AD 1740   LLR7:75
Saris [Siris] Ayer was born ye 22d of March AD 1741
Mary Ayer was Born ye 30th Day of November AD 1742
Esther Ayer was born the 3rd Day of April 1745
Siris Ayer Died ye 5th Day of October AD 1745
Danll Ayer Son of Danll and Esther Ayer was born November ye
   1st 1747 and Died ye first Day of Decemr 1747
Lebbeus Ayer Son of Danll and Esther Ayer was born ye 11th
   Day of Decsmr AD 1748

John Ayer son of Danll & Esther Ayer was born January 16th
AD 1750/51
Daniel Ayer born July 15 1757
[scrap of paper pinned to page in LLR 7:75]

Bradford, the widow Katherine died ye 6th day of November
[1733]   LLR2:40

Mary Darrow Blague was born ye 23 day of April 1737 [d. of
Jermiah]   LLR2:46

Sarah Blague Daughter of Jeremiah Blague was born ye first Day
of June 1735

May 6, 1730   Daniel Beckwith was married: to Ruth Rice ye 4 Novomber 1728
[d. of Jonathan] [Royce]   LLR2:324
their son Jonathan was born the 3 Day of September 1729
Daniel Beckwith was born ye 21 Day of October being born on
tusday   1731
Samuel Beckwith was born ye 12 of March A.D. 1733
Matthew Beckwith was born ye 28 of June AD 1736
Ruth Beckwith was born October ye 5th AD 1737
Lydia Beckwith was born January ye 16th (15) Day AD 1739/40
Ruth Beckwith Wife of the above sd Daniel Beckwith Died the 30th
Day of June AD 1757

James Beckwith was married to Rebeccah Lamb the fifteenth day
of October 1717
Their daughter Sarah was born 20 of March 1722
Their Son James was born the first day of Aprill - 1725
Rebeckah was born 30 June 1728

Feb 3 1697/8   Jeames Beckwith was married to Sarah his wife   LLR2:133
The birth and Death of the Children of Jeames Beckwith and
Sarah his wife - Jeames Beckwith was borne the 1 of May 1695
Marthu [Martha] Beckwith was borne the 8 August 1697
Danell Beckwith was borne the 13 of October 1699
Daniell Beckwith Deceasd February 1700

December 1704   Sarah Beckwith Was borne 23 December 1701
Daniell Beckwith a second Daniell was borne 26 October 1704

[   ] 1707/8   Renald Beckwith was borne 15 February 1706/7
[   ] 1709   Samuel Beckwith was borne 24 Maye 1709
August 1711   Elizabeth was born the 23 July 1712
John Beckwith was born ye tenth Octobr 1713
Mary Beckwith was born ye third January 1716/7   LLR2:133

Feb 1705   Jona[h] Beckwith was married to Rebecka [DeWolf??] his now
wife: the 26th Aprill 1696   LLR2:321
The birth and the Death of the children of Jona Beckwith and
Rebecka his wife
John Beckwith was borne the = 11 = 22 [11] febuary 1697
[Ensign John Beckwith d. Aug. 22 1740]
Samuell Beckwith was borne the = 11 = 7 Aprill 1699
Jona[h] Beckwith was borne the = 11 = 11 febuary 1701

[Rev.]   Greg [George] Beckwith was borne the = 11 = 28 Aprill 1703
Rebecka was borne -- the = 11 = 10 Desember 1704

26 June 1679	The Birth and nams of the children of Joseph [z] B[eckwith] and Susana his wife Sarah Berkett was Borne LLR1:50 14 Ap[ril] [1677] Joseph Berket was Borne: 15 Aprill 1679 Thomas Beckwith of Lyme and Sarah Lewis of Haddam were married on ye 16th of Novembr AD 1725 LLR6:116 Mary Beckwith Daughter of Thomas Beckwith was born ye 23d of January AD 1726/7 Abnor Beckwith was born ye 16th of Septt AD 1728 Ventel Beckwith was born ye 14th of March AD 1735 Sarah Beckwith was born ye 8th of May AD 1737 Deborah Beckwith daughter of Thomas & Sarah Beckwith was born ye 29th of August 1742
June 1699	Joseph Beckwith Juner was married unto Marah his now wife this 18 day of May 1699 LLR2:200 [she is called Marah Lee dau. of Thomas] Joseph Beckwith the Son of the above sd was born 1 June 1700
July 1700	Thomas Beckwith was borne the first of July 1702 Ezekiah Beckwith was borne 5 September 1704
November 1706	Mary Beckwith was borne 20 Augst 1706
May 10 1733	Susannah was born ye 14 of may 1708 Mary ye second was born 3 of April 1710 Lydia their daughter was born Feb. 16 1712/3 Elijah Beckwith was born 15 December 1715 Nathan Beckwith was born 22 Febr 1717/8 Dorithy Beckwith was born ye 19 September 1720 Stephen Beckwith was born 6th day of March 1722
	The birth and names of the Children of Mathew LLR1:61
1679	Berkworthi his Daughter Elizabeth was Born 4 february 1678 Ruth was born the 14 March 1680/81
1685	Sarah was borne 15 [25] December 1684
July 4 1729	Mathew Beckwith the Son of Mathew and Elizabeth Beckwith was born the 13 Day of Aprill 1667 LLR2:355 [ ] coppy taken out of Guilford Records october ye 15th 1719 A.D. T F Samuel Hill Town Clerk
July 1727	Mathew Beckwith senior dyed the 4 [14] day of June 1727 LLR2:47 Matthew Beckwith ye 3d was married: Eleshaba [Rayner, d. of Josiah] his wife feb ye 17 1721 their son Abigah was born ye 25 Aprll 1722 elishaba their Daughter was born the 4 day of february ye 1723/4 their daughter Lois was born ye 1 day of July 1725 their Daughter Diadame: was born ye 8 November 1728 their daughter Eunis was born ye 14 of May 1733 Sarah Beckwith was born ye 22d Day of April 1737
	Caleb Benits Wife died ye 12 Day of November 1732 LLR2:458 Caleb Benit ye son of Caleb Benit is eighteen year old ye 26 of Marcl, 1721 LLR2:457 Caleb Benit Juner was married unto Rebeckah Mack LLR2:15 Thankfull their daughter was born ye 1 [2] Day of March 1727/8 Their son Caleb was born ye 12 Day of January 1729/30

EXTRACTED FROM THE LAND RECORDS 221

Henory Benet was married unto Sarah Champean   LLR1:6
[25th] desember 1673 This was Recorded by order
[   ]Leitenante grant this 27 Genuary 1673
Birth of Henory Benets children
[Caleb] Benet was borne the 11 october 1675
[Rose] Benet was borne the 15 November 1677

20 Jenuary 1680   The Death and Berth of Henory Benetts child[ren]   LLR1:50
John Benett was borne the 26 Desember 1680
9 maye 84 Sarah Benett was borne 7 Agust 1683
Loue Benet was borne 19 March 1685

9 July 88   Dorete benet was borne 19 Maye 1688
30 July 91   Henory Benet was borne 29 July 1691
Henry Bennet Sener Dyed January the 17, 1726[/7]   LLR2:347
Sarah Bennit wife to the above Henry Bennit dyed the 31 of
March 31, 1727   March 1727

Henry Beit Junr was married to Abegall pike his wife   LLR2:51
the 15 Day of Aprill 1713
Phebe their Daughter was born ye 4 August 1716
Henry ye son was born ye 19 Januar 1714
Abegall was born ye last day of Novembr 1718
Abegall ye wife of Henry Benit Decd ye 24 Decembr 1717
Phebe their daughter Decd ye first of Janaur 1717
Abegall Decd ye last of June 1717
Henry Benit was married to Mary Moos his wife ye 13 of November
1718   [Moss see NE Register]
Rose ye Daughter was born ye 19 Janaur 1719/20 [1720/1]
Pheby Bennot their daughter was born ye 5th Day of July 1726

Hennery Bennit Juner and abigarl Morse were married   LLR6:100
together on ye 22d Day of febeuary AD 1732/3
Mary Bennit was born ye 3 Day of October AD 1734
Abigarl Bennit was born 20th Day of September AD 1736
Ruth Bennitt was born ye 20th of Janerary 1738/9
Lucy Bennitt was born ye 6th of Decembr 1740
Dorothy Bennitt was born ye 7th [17] of Augest 1742
Lydia Bennet Daughter of Henry Bennet Junior was born ye 6th
Day of October 1744
Henry Bennet son of Henry Bennet jr. and Abigail his wife was born
ye 18th day of April 1747
Sarah Bennet Daughter of Henry Bennet Jur and Abigail his wife
was born ye 8th day of July AD 1749
Phebe Bennet Daughter of Henry Bennet Junr and Abigail his wife
was born the 28th day of March 1752

1709   John Benet was married to Marah [Mary Huntly] now wife the
2 January 1706   LLR2:51
The birth and death of the Children of John Benet and Marah his
wife
Samuell was borne the 14 December 1707
Abbegall was born the 6 Aprill 1709
Sept 1710   John was borne the 18 August 1710
Jane was borne the 25 May 1714
Mary was born the 30 May 1716
Sarah was born the 29 January 1719
Elijah was born the 20 May 1722
Jedadiah was born the 24 June 1724

[?] 18, 1730	John Benit dyed ye 15th day of December 1730	
	Mary Benit daughter of John Benit died Aprill 21 1731	
	Samuel Benit was married to Hannah Wade ye 3rd of August 1733 [1732]	LLR2:442
	The birth of ye children of Samll Benit is as follows viz his son Samuell Benit was born ye 13 Day of August AD 1734	
January 29, 1673	William Briggs the son of John Brigs and [M----] Briggs his wife was borne the 30 [July] 167[ ]	LLR1:50
1680	Peter Briggs wase Borne the 5 Feb 1680	
19 May 1680	The birth and death of children of John Borden and Hanah his wife	LLR1:86
	Jeane Borden was borne the 11 January 1680	
March 90	John Borden junier was maryed unto Marah his wife the 13th March 1689/90	LLR2:45
Feb 14 1693/4	The births and Death of the children of John Borden and his wife	
	Marah Borden was Borne the 30 Desember 1690	
	John Borden was Borne the 4 March 1693 [1692/3]	
30 May 1704	Hanah Borden was borne the 28 Aprill 1695	
	Sarah Borden was borne the 17 Aprill 1698	
	Martha borden was borne the 11 Septem 1700	
	Samuell borden was borne the 15 Aprill 1704	
	John Baling [Borden] Deceast the 11 March 1708/9	
1726	John Borden was married to Rebeckah Roalon [Roulen] his wife the 14 day of July 1715	LLR2:208
	their son Joseph was born the 27 day of July 1716	
	Elisha Borden was born the 8 day of April 1728 [1718]	
	Ezekill Bordon was born the 20 day of June 1720	
	Hannah Borden was born the 31 day of March 1723	
	William Bordon was born the 26 day of October 1725	
	John Borden was born ye 1 [23] Day of October 1730	
[ ]y 16 1730	John Borden Dyed the 13 day of December 1730	
	Rebekah Borden his wife died ye 19th Day Decembe 1730	
	Samull Bordon was married to Mary Fox ye 11 Day of February A.D. 1728/29	LLR4:52
	Their daughter Mary was born ye 13 January 1729/30	
	Ephram Brockway was married to Susanna Carrier ye february 7, 1727/6	LLR2:352
	Their son Ephram was born ye 31 March 1728	
	Asa was born ye 11 Day of July 1730	
	The children of John Brockway:	LLR2:109
	Breget was Born the eighth day of August 1708	
	Walston Brockway was Born ye 25 Decm 1711	
	Mary was Born ye third of July 1713	
	Jane [Jean] was Born ye sixth of Feabuary 1717	
	John Brockway was born ye 4 July 1721	
	Phebe Brockway was born february 1 1724/5	
	Naomi Brockway was born ye 3 Day of May 1727	
[?] 26, 1733	John Brockway the son of Willm Brockway was married unto Elizabeth Banning the 1 Day of March 1727	LLR2:318
	The birth of the children of ye above John Brockway	
	Elizabeth his daughter was born ye 2 Day of Aprill 1728	

EXTRACTED FROM THE LAND RECORDS 223

his son John was born ye 28 Day of July 1729
Ebenezer was born the 15 Day of October 1731
Sarah Brockway Daughter of John Brocway 2nd and
    Elizabeth his wife was born ye 15 Day of March AD 1734
Mary Brockway Daughter of John Brockway 2nd Elizabeth
    his wife was born ye 26th Day of April AD 1738
Elizabeth Brockway Wife of John Brockway 2nd Deceasd
    the 26th Day of April AD 1738
John Brockway second was Married to Sarah Scovil ye 22nd
    of March 1739
Elihu Brockway Son of John Brockway and Sarah his Wife was
    born the 23rd Day of March AD 1740
Dorothy Brockway Daughter of John Brockway and Sarah his
    wife was born ye 3rd day of June AD 1742
Ezekiel Brockway Son of John Brockway ye 2nd and Sarah
    his Wife was born ye 8th Day of May A.D. 1745

Richard Brockway was married to Rachell his now wife   LLR2:294
    [ ] 25 October 1697
The birth and death of the Children of Richard Brockway
    and Rachell
Rachell was borne the 17 Augste 1698
Hanah was borne the 14 Augste 1700
Sarah was borne the 25 June 1703
Ruth was borne the 20 June 1706

28 January 1701 [ ]   Lydea was borne the 17 Aprill 1709
Richard was born the 4 Aprill 1711
Jedidiah was born the 23 October 1713
Deborah 7 December 1716
Rachel ye wife of Richard Brockway Departed this life ye
    9th of April 1718
The above [ ] Richard Brockway was married to Elizabeth Tiffany
    [d. Consider Tiffany] his second wife the 5th of May 1720.
Elizabeth their first child was born the 22 June 1721   LLR2:294
their twins were born the 1 February 1723 one of which
    is a son, and his name is Consider, the other is a

17 february 1725/6   daughter her name is Abigail
Silence their daughter was born 13 Aprill 1726
Unice their Daughter was born ye 24 August 1732
Nathan Brockway was born May 7 AD 1736
Tiffany Brockway was born ye 9th Day of August AD 1740
Elisabeth [1st wife Samuel Waller] daughter of Richard and
    Elisabeth brockway died the 30th Day of March AD 1742
Consider Brockway son of Richard and Elisabeth _____ye
    17 Day of February 1747/8

William Brockway was married unto Elizabeth his wife the
    8 March 16 [92]   LLR2:2
The birth of the Children of William Brockway

[from Brockway gen]   William was borne 26 December 1693
John was borne 10 Maye 1697
Richard was borne 11 September 1699
Elizabeth was borne 2 March 1701/2
Ebenezer was borne 29 October 1704

William Brockway Junr was married to Prudence prat the 3
    octbr 1716   LLR2:2

	[Hannah] Brockway was born ye 30 Day of November 1718 William was born ye 22 of Febr 1723
January 20 1683	The births and Deaths of the Children of Wolston Brockway and Hana his wife LLR1:26 Hanah Brockway was borne the 14 September 1664 William Brockway was borne the 25 July 1666
Sent to the Clerk	Wolston Brockway was borne the 7 February 1667 Marah Brockway was borne the 16 January 1669 Briget Brockway was borne the 9 January 1671 Richard Brockway was borne the 31 September 1673 Elizabeth Brockway was borne the 24 May 1676 Sarah Brockway was borne the 23 Septem: 1679 Debrah Brockway was borne the 1 May 1682
15 May: 88	good wife Brockway deceased the 6 February 1687
	The birth and Death of the Children of [Wolston Jr.] LLRII:9 Margaret his wife Wolston was Borne 26 October 1689 Samuell was Borne 10 February 1691/2 Jonathan was Borne 10 [20] Maye 1694 Debrah was Borne 11 November 1696 Edward was Borne 8 March 1699/8 [1698/9] Marget was Borne 17 Aprill 1701 Ephram was Born 4 Aprill 1703 Wolston Brockway Junior was married to Margaret [d. of Lewis Jones of Saybrook] October 4, 1688
Written in the margin	John, son of Wolston & Hanna b 168[?] [on LLR3:3 are 2 deeds from Wolston to his son John both dated 1716]
May, 1675	Abraham Brunson and Hana Brunson was married the LLR1:37 second of September 1674 by Mathew Griswold Anna Brunson was Borne the 5 october 1675
[ ] 1676	the Daughter of Abraham son Brunson Abram Brunson the sonne of Abraham Brunson was borne
[ ] 80	the 29 March 1677. Mary Brunson was born 21 January 167[ ] Mary Brunson was born the 21 March 1680 Elizabeth Brunson was Borne the 12 August 1682
[[1733	Stephen Calkins Children born in Lyme are as follows LLR2:81 his son Stephen Calkins was born ye 13 Day of March 1731/2 Sarah Calkins was born ye 14th Day of July 1734 Turner Calkins was born ye 5th Day of November 1736
June 11 1713	Thomas Chadwicks Juner Daughter Jerusha Chadwick was born ye 13 of May 1713 LLR2:304 Thomas Chadwick Senr Died ye 3 Aprill 1731
	Henery Champeau Senr was married unto Debrah Jones his now wife the 21 March 1697/8 LLR2:108 [Henery] Champeau Deceast the 17 of February 1708/9
	The Birth and Death of the Children of Henry Jr. and Susanna Champion LLR2:5 Josuah was borne the 28 September 16 [ ] Henery [ ] borne the 5 January 16 [ ] Susanna [ ] borne the 25 February 16 [ ]

EXTRACTED FROM THE LAND RECORDS 225

	Samuel borne the 18 June 169 [ ] Als[e] borne the 15 [16] March 1694 Rachel was borne the 2 December 1697 Abegull was borne the 25 June 1699 St[even] was borne the 15 July 1702 Mary was borne the 14 October 1704 Henery Champeon Deceased about the middle of July 1704

Sept 30 1729	Henry Champon was married to Sarah Peterson ye 11th July
	1708 LLR2:440
	their first Child mehatabell was born on ye Sabbath Day
	  ye 4 September 1709
	their second Child sarah Champon was born on Saturday
	  Auguset ye 15 day in ye year 1713
	their third Child was born on Monday october 28 1717 her name
	  is Esther Champon
	their fourth Child Henry Champion was born on thursday ye
	  20th day of March in ye year 1729

Febr ye 19
1731
	Joshua Champon was married unto Mary Mott [sometime] in
	  May 1712 LLR2:266
	the birth of ye Children of Joshua Champon & Mary his wife
	  is as follows
	[ ] their daughter mary was born 9 day of Aprill A.D. 1713
	Hannah their Daughter was born ye 1[31] day of august AD 1715
	Joshua their son was Born ye 6 February 1718/17
	Samuell their Son was born ye 17 December 1722
	Susanna their daughter was born ye 8 May AD 1725
	Phebe their Daughter was born ye 12 October 1728
	Ezra their Son was born ye 21 February 1731/30
	Mary Champon ye wife of ye above [?] Joshua Champon
	  Dyed ye 29 March 1730/31

May 12 1733	Joshua Champion was married to his second wife Sarah
	  Griffing ye 15 March 1732/3 LLR2:266
	Sarah Champion Daughter of Joshua and Sarah Champion was
	  born ye 18th day of March 1734
	Jasper Champion Son of Joshua and Sarah Champion was
	  born ye 30th Day of July 1739 [37]
	Ruth Champion Daughter of Joshua and Sarah Champion was
	  born ye 22nd Day of June 1744
	Samuel Champion Son of Joshua and Sarah Champion was born
	  ye 15th Day of January 1746/7

May 10 1684	Thomas Champeon was married unto hanah Brockwaye the
	  23 of August 1682 LLR1:115
	The Birth and Death of the Children of Tho Champeon and
	  hanah his wife

Sent to the Clarke	hanah Champeon was borne the 13 February 1683
[ ] Maye 88	Sarah Champeon was borne the [3] 8 March 1687/8
[ ] March 90/91	Thomas Champeon was borne the 21 January 1690
	Marah borne last of July [16] 93: Henery borne 2 May [16]95 Debrah borne 26 Aprill [16]97; Elizabeh borne 1 July 16[99]
	Thomas Champeon was married to Elizabeth [wade d. John] his wife ye 21 of June 1709 LLR2:231 The Birth of ye Children of Thomas Champeon and his wife

Elizabeth Champion was borne ye 15 of March 1710
Thomas was Born ye third of March 1712
Hannah was Born ye 16 of July 1715
John was Born ye 23 of January 1717/18
Lucy was Born ye 30 of Sepr [1720]
Phebe was born ye 25 of June 1726
Nathan was born ye 23 of June 1723   LLR2:231
Phebe Champeon [   ] dyed 14 day of September 1726
bridget was born ye 16 day of May 1728
Parnal their daughter was born ye 28 April 1731

April 1705   Thomas Champeon senior deceased the 5th of Aprill 1705

Edward Church and Mary Clemants [d. of William] were married
    together ye 3d day of March 1742/3   LLR7:583
Loas Church Daughter of Edward Church was born ye 15th Day
    of March · A.D. 1743/4
Susannah Church Daughter of Edward & Mary Church was born
    ye 18th Day of March AD 1745/6

Eleaer Clark of Lyme & Abigail Clark of Nantucket, were
    married together on ye 15th of Octobr AD 1741   LLR7:161
Simon Clark was born ye 26th of Sept 1742
Seth Clark Son of Eleazer and Abigail Clark was born ye
    25th of August 1745
Eunice Clark Daughter of Eleazer and Abigail Clark was born ye
    8th Day of May AD 1747
Jemima Clark Daughter of Eleazer and Abigail Clark was born
    ye 15th January 1748/9
Abigail Clark, Wife of [   ] Eleazer Clark died the 10th Day
    of September 1750
Nathanell Clarke was married unto Sarah Lay his wife the
    December 3 1696 [widow of Simon DeWolfe]   LLR2:170
The Birth and the Death of the children of Nathanell
    Clark and Sarah his wife
John Clark was borne --- the 21 December 1697
Nathaniell Clark was borne the 11 September 1699
Thomas Clark was born)
Samuel Clark was borne)   Vol 4 p. 307, 309, 310
William Clark was borne)
Eleazer [prob. son of Nathanell and Sarah DeWolfe]   [these were
    in New London Probate Records   obviously written
Sarah [see LL R4:124 DeWolf prob. stepdaughter]   in later]

Nathaniell Clark was married to phebe [Smith d. Richard Jr.]
    his wife Novembr 1720
Silas their son was born ye first Octobr 1722

May 30, 1728   Elijah was born the 20 day of August 1724
Mary was born the 31 day of January 1725/6
Elizabeth was born the 19 January 1727/8
Nathanil was born the 5 Day of Aprill 1730

Thomas Clark was married unto Rebeckah Waterus of Lyme ye
    25 Day of November Anno [25th] 1730   LLR2:359
the birth and Death of ye Children of Thomas Clark
    Rebeckah his wife is as follows
their son Isaac was born ye 31 Day of March AD 1732 [1731]

1731	William Clark was married unto hannah Peck November ye 30th Day 1731	LLR2:281

the birth and death of ye children of William Clark & Hannah his wife
their first Child being a daughter her name is Elizabeth

1734   Clark was born ye 24 September 1732; on the Sabath day mornin of 7 of ye clock
Sussana Clark was born ye 18 Day of August 1734 on ye beginning of ye Sabath
Lucy Clark was born Dec 13th 1736
Hannah Clark was born ye 22nd Day of May 1739
Sarah Clark was born January ye 22nd 1741/2
Sheldon Clark was born ye 10th Day of February 1743/4

	John Clerk was married to mindwell his wife ye 3d of March 1719/20	LLR3:338

William their Son was born ye 4th Febr 1720/21

The birth of ye Children of William Clement in Lyme
William Clemmant ye son of William Clemment was born

[?]   ye 20 Day of September ye 20 1728
his son John was born ye [worn] Day of ----- 1731

	John Cobb was born ye first day of Jany 1735/6	LLR7:157

Simon Cobb was born ye 27th of August 1737
Ann Cobb was born ye first day of August 1739

	Westall Cogswell was married unto martha his now wife the 24 May [1697]	LLR2:228

The birth and death of the Children of Westall Cogswell and martha his wife
Sarah Cogswell was borne the 4 June 1698
Hanah Cogswell was borne the 23 Sept. 1700
Steven Cogswell was borne the 25 March 1702
Sarah Cogswell Deceased the 30 November 1704

Jan 1704/5   Martha the wife of Westall Cogswell Deceased the 17 January 1704/5
Martha Cogswell Deceased the 27 January 1705

Sarah Colten Daughter to Thomas Coulten was borne the 25 of September 1678
Capt. Thomas Colton of Longmeadow Mass married Sarah Griswold Sept. 11 1671

	The Deth and birth of the Children of Danell Comstock and alse his wife [Alse]	LLR4:129

marah was borne the 4th Aprill 1685

[   ] March   Ann was borne the: 13 March 1686/7
89/87

	Daniel Comstock died December ye 15 1725	LLR4:128
	The Birth of John Comstocks children	LLR1:12

Abbegall Comstock was Borne 12 Aprill 1662
Elizabeth Comstock was Borne 9: June 1665
William Comstock was Borne 9: January 1669
Christian Comstock was Borne: 11 December 1671 [m. Robert Mentor]
Hanah Comstock was Borne: 22 February 1673

LYME, CONNECTICUT, VITAL RECORDS

John Comstock was Borne: 31 Sept. 1676
Sammell [Gamwell] Comstock was borne: 6 July 1678
The Birth of ye children of John Comstock   LLR2:427
Jonathan was born ye 4th of May: 1712
John was born ye 5th of July 1714

John Comstock son of Wm Comstock was married unto
    Rebeckah Bates Feb. 17, 1725 The birth   LLR2:171
    of ye children of ye John Comstock is as follows · viz
Phebe Comstock was born ye 16 of November AD 1727
Curtise Comstock was born ye 8 of October 1729
Rebecka Comstock was born ye 11th of February 1732/3
Abigail Comstock, Daughter of John Comstock and
    Rebeckah his wife was born ye 18th Day of July AD 1735
John Comstock above named Departed this life March 28 AD 1769

William Comstock was married to naomy daughter of Benj. Niles
    the 10 September 1695   LLR2:10
[Abegail] Comstock wa borne: the 9: August 1696
[William] Comstock was borne the 15 June 1698
William Comstock above Departed this life ye 15th day of
    March A.D. 1728

Matthew Cooley of Lyme and Jemimah [Jemima] Rogers of New
    London were married together ye 22 Day of
    August AD 1734   LLR6:53
Mercy Coley Daughter to Matthew Coley was born the
    31 Day of May AD 1735
Absalom Cooley was born ye 5th Day of Febr AD 1737/8
Matthew Cooley was born ye 24th Day of February 1739/40
Paul Cooley was born the 15th Day of April 1742
John Cooley son of Matthew & Jemimah Cooley was born ye
    24 Day of May 1744
Molley Rogers Cooley Daughter of Matthew & Jemimah Cooley
    was born ye 29 Day of August 1746
Job Cooley son of Matthew & Jemimah Cooley was born ye
    first Day of November 1748
N.B. the remainder of Cooley children recorded in Book of
    marriages

Benjamin Coult was married to miriam Harris his now wife
    Daughter of Thomas Harris formerly of Lyme in Connecticut
    Coloney Latly this 26 day of may: 1724 [Poughkeepsie] county
    of Sopus [now part of Dutchess County]
their Son John was born the 19 day of May 1725
their son Joseph Coult was born ye 13 day of february 1727/26
Mary Coult was born the 4 Day of December 1728

Samuel Coult was married unto Abigall Marvin ye 7 November
    1734   LLR2:462
Their Daughter Patthene Coult was born 9th day of June 1736
Martain Coult was born ye 27 Day of July AD 1738
Samll Colt was born ye 14th Day of February 1740/41
Samll Colt Senr died ye 23rd Day of February 1742/3

Ebeneazer Darrow was married to Abi Rogers the 17th Day of
    Aprill ano domini 1727   LLR2:177
The birth of ye Chilldren of Ebenezer Darrow and abi his wife

EXTRACTED FROM THE LAND RECORDS 229

[ ] 27
1729/8
[ ] 30 1730

their son Zadok was born ye 25 Day of December 1728
Sarah was born ye 6 Day of November 1730
Abi their Daughter was born ye 27 Day of August 1732
Elizabeth Darrow was born ye 20 of octobr 1734

The bearth and death of ye Children of John &   LLR6:177
Patience Denison
Samll Denison was born August ye 21 AD 1733
Patience Denison was born June ye 7th AD 1735
Samll Denison Dyed December ye 3d AD 1736
John Denison Dyed December ye 13th AD 1736
John Denison was born February ye 6th AD 1736/7
Samuell 2d was born [added later Deed Samll Denison from Father
Mr. John Denison dated 1775 LLR14:174]

Edward DeWolfe Sr: the birth of his Children   LLR1:38

3 June 1675

Simon DeWolfe was borne: 28: November 1671
Charles DeWolfe was borne: 18: September 1673
Benjamin De Wolfe was born ye 3d December 1695

Josiah DeWolfe was married to Anna Waterman his wife:
4: of November 1713   LLR2:90
Josiah DeWolfe ye Son was born ye 20th of December 171[4]
Josiah their second son was born ye first of Sept 171[6]
Simon was born ye: 22: of January 171[8]
Jabez was Born ye 23 of June 172[1]
Judith was born: ye ninth of Febe 172[4]
Daniel was born the 20 day of November 172[6]
Elizabeth was born the 18 Day of August 173[0]

Josiah Dewolf Junr and Martha Ely were married together
Septt ye 13th 1739   LLR7:79

Simon DeWolfe was mared unto Sarah Laye the   LLR2:107
12 of November 1682
the Birth and Death of the Children of Simon DeWolf and
Sarah his wife
Simon DeWolfe was born: the 18 November 1683
Sarah DeWolfe was borne: the 2 Desember 1685
John DeWolfe was borne the 17 Aguste 1687

[ ]25:89

Josiah DeWolfe was borne the 15 November 1689
phebe DeWolfe was borne 20 January 1691 [m. Joseph Mather]

[ ]93

Danell DeWolfe was borne the 29   2
Desember 1693
Simon DeWolfe Sener Deceased the 5th September   LLR2:61
1695

[ ] February
1706
24 October
1702

Simon DeWolfe: Deceased the 24: January 1708   LLR2:183
7
Steven DeWolfe Deceased the 17 October 1702   LLR2:144
The agge of the Children of Steven DeWolfe and
Hana his wife

24 October
1702

Debra was borne the 25 July 1690
Hana was borne - Augst --- 1693
Steven was borne January 1694
Benjamin was born october 1695
Lewes was borne 5 June 1698

	Phebe was borne 5 June 1701 Edward that he had by his first wif is 16 year old Last March [1701?]
	Edmund Dorr was married to Mary Griswold the 4 September 1719 their Son George was born at Hartford ye 4th of August 1720 LLR2:183 Edward Dorr was born ye 1 Day of November 1722 Mathew Dorr was born ye 14 Day of June 1725 Mary Dorr was born ye 10th Day of June 1727
July 31 1728	William Dowley son of Doctr Dowley and Martha his wife was born the 12 of march 1725/4 LLR2:408
	The Birth and Death of the Children of Joseph Dutton [ ] Marah his wife LLR2:9 Benjamin Dutten was borne the 10th Oc[tober] 1691
[ ] 1731	Daniel Elys Second Wife died ye 2 Day of Aprill 1731. She was ye Daughter of Mr. Samuel Wells of Hartford LLR2:295
[ ] 1729	Richard Ely Juner was married to Elizabeth Peck his now wife ye 23 day of January 1724 LLR2:223 Elizabeth their Daughter was born ye 11 of October 1724 Ester was born ye 22 day of may 1726 Ezra was born ye 6 day of January 1728 Mary Ely was born Octobr ye 21 1729 Elizabeth Ely ye Wife of ye above Richard Ely Died October ye 8th 1730
[ ] 12 1733	The above Richard Ely Juner was married unto Phebe Hubbard his second wife the 26 Day of October 1732 Richd Ely Son of Richd Ely Junr was born Septt 30th 1733 LLR2:223
[ ] [ ] 1736	Seth Ely was born Decembr ye 11th 1734 Elihu Ely was born November ye 18th 1736 Elihu Ely Decd Decembr ye 7 1736 Elihu Ely 2 was born Novembr ye 15th 1737 Josiah Ely was born July ye 20th 1739 Robert Ely was born June ye 26th 1741
Aprill: 14: 1684	Mrs. Elizabeth Ely Deceased the 12 November 1683 LLR1:53 Sent to the County Clark
June 1 1685	Mr. Richard Ely Sener Deceased the 24 November 1684 LLR1:53
April 14 1684	William Ely was married to Elizabeth Smith his wife [identified in Haddam Records as d. Simon] the 24 of may 1681 LLR1:52 The birth and Death of the Children of William Ely and Elizabeth his wife:
Sent to the Clark	Ann Ely was borne the 12 of March 1681/82 Elizabeth Ely was born the: 26: may 1683
October 25 1715	[ ] Mr. William Ely was married to Mrs. Hannah Thompson Daughter of Deacon William Thompson [of] Chebacko in Ipswitch by Mr. John Wise minister of ye Society [October 25, 1715] LLR:2:234 The birth of the children of ye above Wm Ely & Hannah his wife is as follows: Jacob Ely was born ye 19 of August at nine o'clock at night 1716

EXTRACTED FROM THE LAND RECORDS

Entered January ye 4:1733/4

James was born ye 11 of January at nine o'clock at night 1718/19
Martha was born the ye 27 of January at 10 o'clock in ye morning 1720/1
Deborah was born ye 8 of March at 3 o'clock afternoon 1723
Maryann was born May 18 at 5 o'clock in ye morning 1725
Samuel was born ye 4 of June at 10 o'clock in ye morning 1727
these six children baptized by ye Reverend Mr. Noyes
Ruh[   ]ammi a son born 24 August at 10 o'clock forenoon 1732 baptized by the Reverend Mr. George Beckwith
Their last child being a son still born of ye 29 of March 4 o'clock afternoon 1733
Mrs. Hannah Ely above mentioned (viz) ye wife of Mr. Wm Ely Dyed ye 3 of Aprill 1733

21 August 1712

Thomas Enes was married to marget [d. of Lewis Jones of Saybrook; widow of Walston Brockway, Jr.] his now wife 7th February 1710   LLR2:56
The birth and Death of their Children of Thomas and his wife marget:
Thomas Enes was born --- the --- 28 may 1712

the names and birth of ye Children of Daniel Galusiah   LLR2:203
Jonas Galusiah was born ye 12 March 1723/4
Sarah Galusiah was born ye 21 Day of June 172[6]
Jacob Galusiah was born March ye 9th 1720/1

Elizabeth Gilbart, Daughter of Danell Gilbart was born ye 20th Day of August AD 1735   LLR2:23

9 May: 841 Mathew Gilbert was married to Sarah Peak   LLR1.17
the 2: May: 1684 Sent to the Clark

Benjamin Graham was married to Anne Comstock his wife May ye second 1717   LLR2:187
Mary their Daughter was born ye eighth of Febr 1719
Benjamin was born the eighteenth Day of Jun 1723
Sarah Graham their Daughter was born May: the eight day 1726
Anne Graham wife to ye above Benjamin Graham Died Aprill 10 1729
sd Benjamin Graham was married unto Hannah Andros the 14 Day of August 1729
their son Martain [Mortain] was Born ye 18 September 1730
their Daughter Anne was born ye 25 September 1731

28 June 1707

Thomas Graves was married to Mary Hopson the 28 March 1703
The Birth and Death of the Children of Thomas Graves   LLR2:248
and his now wife mary
Elizabeth was born the 11 March 1704
Marke Graves was born the 4 March 1708

21 August 1710

Easter Graves was born the 4 may 1710
Abigail

Jasper Griffen was married to Ruth Peck 29 Aprill: 1696   LLR2:129
Ruth Griffing was born --- the 28 Desemb 1699
Jasper Griffing was born ---- the 21 January 1697
Hana Griffing was born ---- the 28 January 1698
Sarah Griffing was born ---- the 13 Aprill 1702
Joseph Griffing was born ---- the 6 Maye 1704
Lemuel was born ---- the 23 March 1706

	Hesikiah was born ---- the 21 January 1707/8
	Hesikiah Deceast ---- the 29 February 1707/8
	John Griffing Esqr Died 29th of September A.D. 1764
	Mrs. Hannah Griswold relict of John Griswold Esqr Died the 11th Day of May AD 1773
November ye 11 1728	mr. George Griswold was married to Mrs. Hannah Lynde of Saybrook June ye 22 1725 LLR2:216
	their Son George was born ye 19th of September 1726
	Elizabeth their Daughter was born ye 16 day of July 1728
	Lucretia Griswold was born ye 26 Day of March 1730
	Silvanus Griswold was born ye 3d Day of February 1732/3
	John Griswold was married to hannah Lee his wife June ye 23 1713 LLR2:195
	Mathew Griswold their son was born ye 25 of March 1714
	Phebe Griswold their Daughter was born ye 22 Day of Aprill 1716
	Thomas Griswold was born ye 15 Day of February 1718/19
	Hannah Griswold was born ye 10 Day of January 1723/4
	Luce Griswold was born ye 6th Day of July 1726
	Sarah Griswold was born ye 2d Day of December 1728
	Clerine was born ye 30 Day of may 1731
	Clerine Deyd ye 9 Day of Aprill 1732
	Clarene the second Daughter of ye above sd John Griswold was born Febr ye 9 1732/3
	Deborah Griswold was born ye first Day of March A.D. 1734/5
	John Griswold Son of John Griswold [?] Born May 15th AD 1739 and Died 4th January 1742
	Mathew Grisould was marrod to phebe Hyde his wife the 21 May 1683 LLR1:57
May 26 85	Phebe the Daughter of Math Griswould and Phebe his wife was borne the 15 August 84 [16]84
Aprill 27 1686	Elizabeth his second Daughter was borne 19 November [16]85
May 88	Sarah Griswould was borne the 19 March 1687
Sept 88	Mathew Griswould was borne the 15 September 1688
	Geog Griswold was borne the 13 Aguste 1692
	Mary Griswold was borne the 22 Aprill 1694
	John Griswold was born the 22 December 1690
	Mr. Mathew Griswold Deceased ye 13 day of Januy 1715/16
	Phebe Griswold Deceasd: The 29 November 1704 LLR2:194
	Ensign Samuell Griswold Deceased ye 9th day of June 1727
28 January 1701 1700	the Children of John Haiden and Marah his wife LLR2:201
	the birth and Death of them
	Ebenezer was borne 8 October 1698
	Jedediah was borne 14 Desember 1700
	Nehemiah was borne 16 January 1703/4
	George Hall and Eunice Gates were married together on ye 17th of Octobr · 1738
	Elisha Hall was born ye 7th of April 1740
28 Feb 1707/8	The birth and Death of the Children of William Haris LLR2:199 and Eliz[abeth Brockway d. of Wolston Sr.] his now wife
	Tabatha Haris was born the ---- 11 ---- 9 May 1702
	Sarah Haris was born the ---- 11 ---- 11 7 February 1704/5

	Easter Haris was born the --- 11 --- 11 ---11 August 1706
	Thankfull Haris was born e the --- 11 --- 11 ---23 February 1707/8
5 June 1707	Mosis Huntly [Jr.] was married unto Rachill haris: the 21 of January 1706/7
] 1704/5	Goodwife Harvy the wife of John Harvi Sen Deceased 9 Jan 1704/5 LLR2:138
	Mary Harvy Deceased ---- the ---- 10 Jan 1704/5
] 1704/5	Sarah Harvi Deceased ---- the ---- 13 Jan 1704/5
	John Harvy Senior Deceased 18 Jan 1705
	ye birth of John Harves Children: Elizabeth Harve born: 30: March 1708 LLR2:138
	Abigal harve born May ye 4th 1710 [m. ---Reed]
	Sarah harve born Aprill 1 1712
	John Harve born Aprill 7 1716
	Joshua Harve born March ye 3d 1718
	Joseph Harve Aprill 6 1720
	Benjamin Harve was born ye 28 July 1722

Thomas Harvy was married to Abbegale [Smith d. Richard Jr.] [widow Abigail Harvy m. Edw. Stocker] his now wife: the 25 November 1702

The Birth and Death of the Children of Thomas Harvy and abbegale his wife

Elizabeth was Born the 7 Day of May 1703
Elizabeth Deceast --- the --- 5 Day of october 1703
Joana --- was borne the: 7 Day of Aprill 1706
Thomas --- was born --- the: 27 Day of February 1708/9
Abegall was born the 13 of June 1712
John was born the 16 of November 1715
Richard Harve was born ye 1 of July 1719

Richd Hase and Patience Mack Were Married   LLR5:300
    Together on ye 24th Day of April 1735
There Son Silas Hase was born ye 15th Day of February 1735/6
Seth Hays was born ye 26th Day of December 1737
Richd Hays was born ye 30th Day of June 1740
John Hays was born ye 25th Day of May 1742
Cathrine Hays was born the 7th Day of November AD 1744
Titus Hayes son of Richard and Patience Hayes was born ye February ye first 1746/7
Philemon Hayes son of Richd & Patience Hayes was born ye 26th Day of February 1748/9
Joseph Hayes son of Richard and Patience Hayes was born May ye 15th AD 1751

October 27, 1731	Nathaniell Havens was married unto Elizabeth Beebe ye 7 day of July [M - 1732] LLR2:144

The Birth of ye Children of Nathanll Havens & Elizabeth [   ] their first Child being a daughter [   ] name of Sarah [   ] born [Mar. 29, 1733]

Nathan Havens Son of Nathll and Elizabeth Havens was born ye 2nd day of January [1735/6]

Anna Havens Daughter of Nathll and Elisabeth Havens born ye 10th Day of March 1737

Edward Havens Son of Nathll and Elisabeth Havens was born ye 26th Day of February [1738/9]

LYME, CONNECTICUT, VITAL RECORDS

	Peter Havens son of Nathll and Elisabeth Havens was born ye 4th Day of August [1741]
	Elisabeth Havens daughter of Nathll Havens and Elisabeth Havens was born ye 26 Day of [April 1744]
	Daniel Havens son of Nathaniel and Elizabeth Havens was born ye 29th day of January [1747]
[cut off] 31:1733	The age and birth of the Children of John Hazer that were born in Lyme LLR2:140
	his Son Thomas Hazon was borne in Lyme the 12 Day of Feby 1732/3
	His Daughter Hannah Hazon was born at Noridge or Norwich may ye 18 1731
	John Hazen Junr and Deborah Peck wear married Together on ye 10 Day of March AD 1737
	John Hazen ye 3d - Son of John and Deborah Hazen was born ye 10th Day Feberary AD 1737/8
	Macy Hazen was born ye 29th Day of March 1740
	Mary hazen ye Daughter of John Hazen was born ye fifth day of Janeuery 1734/5
	Benony Hillard and Martha Lord were married July 6th 1740
	Bozaleel Hillard was born Augest 30th 1741 LLR7:332
	Bettey Hillard was born 10th Day of September AD 1743
27 Jan 1686	Charls Hoges was married unto Ane his wife LLR1:135 the first of July 1686
	Sarah Spencer-formerly the wife of John Haltum above said Deceased the: 21 January 1704/5 LLR2:117
Novem 3 1729	Benjamin Hudson was married to mabel Roulen March 26 17 [1728]
	their Daughter Rebeckah Hudson was born ye 9: day of aprill 17[29]
	their Son Benjamin was born ye 15 Day of January 17[32/3]
	their Son Samuel was born ye 29 day of August 1735
	their Son Elezar was born ye 9th Day of June 1738
	mabel the Wife of Benjamin Hudson Died the 25th of February 174[1]
20 July 1706	Johnathan Hudson was maried unto Sarah [Tinker d. John] his wife the 17 June 1686 LLR1:135
March :1: 1687/8	The Birth and Death of the Children of Jonathan Hudson: and: Sarah: his wife LLR2:33
	Sarah Hudson: was borne the 27 of March 1687
	Debrah Hudson: was borne the :27 of october 1688
	Jonathan Hudson: was born the: 6 of January 1689
22 March 94/3	Hanah Hudson was borne the: 6 of Aprill 1693
[cut off] 30: 1726	John Hudson was married ye 14: of novem to hannah Roling 1721 LLR2:253
	John Hudson ye son was born the 26 of Septer 1723
	Hannah Hudson was born the 15 day of September 1725
	Rachel was born the 10 day of march 1727/8
	Richard Hudson was born ye ---- 1730
	Mary Hudson was born ye --- 17th --- of February 1736/7
	Rachel Hudson Dyed march ye 17th 1736/7
	Rachel Hudson was born ye 26 of July 1741

EXTRACTED FROM THE LAND RECORDS 235

	Richard Hudson was born ye 5th Day of May 1744
	John Hudson Died october 27th AD 1743
26 July 1702	The Birth and Death of the Children of Nathanell Hudson and
	Rachel [widow of Arter Schofil] his wife LLR2:252
	John Hudson was born the 2d of September 1696
	Nathanell Hudson was borne the 20th of October 1698
	Benjamin Hudson was borne the 18 of October 1700
	Thomas Hudson was borne the 1 of Aprill 1703
	Mary Hudson was borne 23 of August 1705
	Nathll Hudson [Jr.] and Lydia Tubes were married Together
	November:15:1721 LLR6:37
	There Daughter Lydia was born ye 7th Day of October AD 1722
	There Daughter Luce was born ye 12th Day of Septt AD 1725
	There Son Nathll was born ye 25th Day of Febeuery AD 1728/9
	There Son Richd was born ye 11th Day of December AD 1731
	There Son Elijah was born ye 29th Day of October AD 1735
August 4:1730	Thomas Hudson was married to Ester Graves ye 29 Aprill 1728
	Their daughter Ester was born ye 1 Day of September LLR2:220
	1729
	Thomas Hudsons Wife Died ye 12 Febr 1730/1, her name
	was Ester
	Aaron Huntly was maryed to Marah [Champion d. of Henry]
	Chamberlain his wife 22 February 1676 LLR2:78
Taken out of	The birth of the children of Aaron Huntly and Marah
the fist Book	his wife
of Reords folio	John Huntly was Borne the 22 November 1677 LLR1:60
60 By me	Elizabeth Huntly was borne the 16 March 1679
[ ]	Aaron Huntly was borne the 1 December 1680
5 May 21 1692	Danell Huntly was Borne the 25 Maye 1682
	Marah Huntly was Borne the 14 February 1685
	Jeane Huntly was Borne the 10 September 1686
	David Huntly was Borne the 17 March 1687/88
May:5:92	Solloman Huntly was Borne the 31 Maye 1691
19 Feb 1707/8	Aaron Huntly Junr was married to Debrah Dewolf the 27 July
	1707
10 Aprill 1710	Hana [Honor] was borne ---- the ---- 22 July 1708
6 Aprill 1711	Aaron was born the 14 September 1710
9 Desemb 1712	Sollomon was born ---- the 1 September 1712
	Deaborah was born the 20: of August: 1714
	Ruth was born the first Day of March 1716/17
	Stephen was born ye twenty eighth of February 1719
	phebe was born ye first of March 1721/2
	Easter was born ye 21 of May 1724
	Nathan was born ye 2d day of June 1726
	Jemima was born ye 30 day of august 1728
	Timothy was born ye 22 Day of October 1731
	Aaron Huntly Deceased ye 16 [26] Day of September 1748
	Aaron Huntly ye 3d and Mary Leach were married Together
	June 1738 LLR7:162
	Stephen Huntly was born on ye 25th of March 1740
	Naomy Huntly was born ye 14th Day of February 1742/3

Selvanius Huntly son of Aaron & Mary Huntly was born the last of August 1749
Ruben Huntly Son of Aaron & Mary Huntly born the 25th of September AD 1752
Beththeasel Huntly son of Aaron & Mary Huntly was born October 15th AD 1755
Zenas Huntly son of Aaron & Mary Huntly was born January 16th AD 1759
Aaron Huntly ye 3d above named Died the 18th Day of november: 1763

Benjeman Huntly and Lydia Beckwith was married together on ye 27th Day of April AD 1732   LLR5:307
their son curtice Huntly was born ye 5th Day of May AD 1735

Daniell Huntly was married to Hannah Brown ye 27 of July 1720   LLR2:291
Danl ye son was born ye 16 of August 1721
Jacob Huntly was born ye 5th day of June 1723
James Huntly was born ye 17 of Aprll 1725
Amos Huntly was born ye 31 of october 1727
Daniell Huntly Dyed ye 14 day of January 1732/3

Children of David Huntly son of Aaron Huntley senior and Mary [Tinker m. 24 oct.1742]   LLR2:295

Aprll 1711

Elihu   ]   LLR16:160
Mehitable]

[written in later]

By former wife
Ezekiel   ]   LLR5:545
Jonathan]   b. Mar. 9, 1728 See B.M. & D 1:57
[There was at least one more daughter and another son by former marriage]
David Huntley died Aug. 31, 1745 see B.M. & D. Vol. 1: P. 68

26 [decr] 1676   Said John Huntly Deceased the 16 day November 1676   LLR1:30

1702/3   John Huntly was married to Elizabeth [Pearson, dau. of Samuel and sister of Peter] his now wife: 2 Feb 1699   LLR2:295
The Birth and Death of the Children of John Huntly and Elizabeth his wife
John Huntly was Borne: the 19 october 1699
Elizabeth huntly was born the 2 January 1701/2
Mary huntly was borne the 20 June 1703
Petter huntly was borne the 4 march 1705
Joseph huntly was borne the 27 January 1707
Benjamin huntly was borne the 5 February 1709

is deud   Lucy huntly was born the 15 of December 1711
Samuel was born the 23 of Decembr 1713
Lucy huntly was born the 22: of Aprll 1716
Sarah huntly was born ye 17 of June 1718
Elizabeth was born ye 30 of Septr 1721

April 27 1727   John Huntly juner was married to Lydia Robins   LLR2:112
[d. Joseph]
their Son Hezekiah was born the 13 day of February 1725/6
Lydia Huntly Deceased April 21, 1728

June 19, 1728   John Huntly Deceased ye 25 Day of may 1728

EXTRACTED FROM THE LAND RECORDS

Feb. 1711/2	John Huntly [son of John Huntly] was born the 3d of June 1709	LLR5:307
June 13 1682	Mosis Huntly was mared unto Abigall Comstock widow of John Comstock the 18 January: 1680	LLR1:49
	the birth and Death of the Children of Mosis Huntly and Abigail his wife:	
	Mosis Huntly was borne the 31 Maye: 1681	
[ ] 21:1685	Mary Huntly was borne the 26 December 1683	
	John Huntly was borne the 9 September 1686	
5 June 1707	Mosis Huntly Junr was married unto Rachill haris: the: 21 of January 1706/7	LLR2:230
	The birth and Death of the Children of mosis Huntly and Rachell his wife	
28 october 1711	Abigall was borne the 22 August: 1708	
	William Huntly was born June 24 1712	
	Peter Huntly was married unto Mary Ransom 20 March 1729	LLR2:192
	their first child being a daughter was born 18 March 1730 her name is Patience	
	the wife of Peter Huntly Died ye 5 July 1732	LLR2:467
	Peter Huntly was married to his second wife viz Sarah Robins Febr 14 1732/3	
	the daughter of ye Peter and Sarah was born 26 Febr her name was Lois 1733	
	Sarah Huntly was born ye first Day of May AD 1736	
	Ezra Huntly was born ye 4th Day of October AD 1738	
	Hannah Huntly Daughter of Peter and Sarah Huntly was born ye 4 Day of August 174 [cut off]	
	Jasper Huntly Son of Peter and Sarah Huntly was born the 4th of September AD 1749	
	Samll Huntly & Ruth Huntly were married Together on ye 5th Day of May AD 1736	
	Solomon Huntly was born ye 19th Day of June A.D. 1737	
	Hepsebeth Huntly was born October ye 9th 1738	
	Benjamin Huntly Son of Samll & Ruth Huntly was born at New London March 8th 1740	
	Molley Huntly Daughter of Samll & Ruth Huntly was born at New London August 13 1743	
	Ruth Huntly Daughter of Samll & Ruth Huntly was born at New London March 6th 1745	
	Samuel Huntly Son of Samuel and Ruth Huntly was born the 11th Day of March 1747	
	Lemuel Huntly son of Samuel and Ruth Huntly was born the 7th Day of November 1748	
	Esther Huntly Daughter of Samuel and Ruth Huntly was born February 2nd 1750	
	Aaron Huntly Son of Samuel & Ruth Huntly was born the 4th of Novemr 1752	
	Hezekiah Huntly Son of Samuel and Ruth Huntly was born May ye 20th 1754	
	Mehepzibah Huntly Daughter of Samll and Ruth Huntly was born 2nd June 1756	

	Solomon Huntly Son of Samll & Ruth Huntly Died the 2nd Day of October 1759
	Solomon Huntly Son of Samuel and Ruth Huntly was born ye 7th of January AD 1761
Aprill 1711	Solomon Huntly was marry to Ruth his now wife 13 February 1710/11 LLR2:295
	Sollomon Huntly deceased before Feb. 11 1724
Feb. 3 1730/31	Jaritt [Javitt, Jared, Gerard] Ingraham was married to Marcey Taylor ye 27 Day of October 1729 LLR2:96
	Their son Javitt was born ye 4 Day of September 1730
	Patience Ingraham their Daughter was born ye 2 November 1732
	Elisabeth Ingraham their Daughter was Born November 14 173[4]
	Daniel Ingraham their son was born March 25th 1737
June 18 1730	Nathan Jewitt was married to Deborah Lord of Lyme the 23 Day of December 1729 the Nathan Jewitt belongs LLR2:422
	to ye town of Rowley In ye Mathasuess bay in New England the above Nathan Jewitt & Deborah Lord were married by me
	Stephen Whittlesey Justice of Peace
	Luce Jewit was born ye 14 of June 1730/1
	Joseph Jewit was born ye 13 of December 1732
	Nathan Jewit was born ye 20 of September 1734
	David Jewet their Son was born october ye 27th 1736
	Gibbins Jewet their son was born ye first Day of November 1738
	Hibbert Jewet was born ye 11th Day of May 1741
	Mary Jewet was born April ye 15th Day 1743
	John Johnson was born ye 20th Day of March AD 1737 LLR6:131
	son of John & Hannah Johnson [this line written in later]
Feb 1 1732	Benjamin Jones Malatow [mulatto] was married unto Abigail Menta Decembr 10, 172[8] LLR2:230
Decembr 17th 1745	Benjamin Jones son of Benjamin and Abigail was born ye 3rd Day of July Anno Domini 1737
	Edward Laye Records
	The birth and Death of the Children of Edward Lay Merah his wife
	John was borne 10 January 1697 LLR2:249
	Marah was borne the 15 august 1699
July 1705	Joseph was borne the 22 Aprill 1702
	Hipsabeth was borne the 17 Desember 1704
	A deed of gift from Edward Lay to his Son Robert Lay LLR5:528
	[Note: This establishes a Robert Lay as son of Edward]
	The: Burth of John Laye Junr drummer see 2d Book p. 351 and Sarah his wife (see 2d 173) LLR1:24
	Sarah: Laye was: Borne 4 febuary 1664
	Rebeikahe: Laye: was Borne 9th September 1666
	Edward Laye: was Borne 26 January 1668
Sent to the Clarke	Catterne Laye was Borne i 11th febuary 1671
May 28 1684	Marah Laye was borne: 21th march 1678
	Elizabeth Lay was borne: 18 Desem: 1681
3 may 1684	John Lay was borne 25 March 1683
	Abigall Lay was borne 9: Septem 1673
25 January 1684	Phebe Lay was borne 13: January 1684

EXTRACTED FROM THE LAND RECORDS

Jun 8 1686	John Lay Juner was maryd unto Johana [smith d. Richard Sr.] his wife the 26 of Maye 1686	LLR1:136
	The Birth and Death of the Children of John Lay Juner and his wife Johan[nah]	
6 Desember 1692	Johannah Was Borne the 8th of October 1687 John Wase Borne the 4 of October 1692	
	John Lay: Senior Deceased 18: Day of January 1674	LLR1:27
	John Lay was married unto Sarah Lee Decem 21 1712	LLR2:339
	ye birth of ye Children of ye above sd John Lay & Sarah his wife	
	Sarah Lay was born ye 10 Day of September 1715	
March 18 1733/4	Elizabeth Lay was born ye 4 Day of July 1720	
	Amos Lay was Born ye 19 Day of March 1722/3	
	Lucia Lay was Born august ye 8 Day 1726	
	Phebe was born ye 28 Day of march 1730	
	Sarah Lay the wife of ye above sd John Lay Died may 31 1732	
	ye above sd John Lay was married unto ye widow Ruth Robins [widow of Edward Robbins] the 10th Day of January 1732/3	
	their son Richard Lay was born ye 16 Day of october 1733	
	their son Icabod Lay was born ye 16th Day of October AD 1733	

John Lay ye 2d and Mary Lewis were married Together on
 ye ---- 14th ---- of May 1733   LLR6:252
William Lay was born march ye first 1733/4
Elisabeth Lay was born April ye ---- 13 ----1736
Jerusha Lay was born ye 11th of February 1739/40
Elisha Lay Son of John & Mary Lay was born ye first Day of
 September 1747
Elizabeth Lay Daughter of John & Mary Lay died ye 16th
 Day of August 1749
Mr. John Lay departed this life Apr. 14th AD 1788 in the
 92d year of his age. Taken out of 1st Book of B.M.D. p. 171
[These two lines were added later] [Grandfather of Stephen Lay]

The children of John Lay second Tavern Keeper   LLR2:420
John Lay was born ye 13 Day of Sept. 1714
Sarah Lay was born ye Second Day of June 1718
Elizabeth Lay was born ye seventh Day of Decembr 17 [faded
 or blank]

Lyme January 27th 1736/7 John Lay ye 3d and [H]annah Lee
 both of Lyme were joynd together in ye Holy State
 of marriage according to ye law and custom of this   LLR1:3
 Goverment by me Jonathan Parsons Pastr   LLR6:71
John Lay, (ye son of John Lay ye 3d and Hannah his wife)
 was born ye 29th Day of December AD 1737
Hannah Lay was born ye ---- 18th ----˙ of Feberary 1739/40

Benjamin Lee and Mary Ely were married Together ye 25th of
 March AD 1736   LLR6:279
Mary Ann Lee was born ye 13th of November AD 1738
Benjamin Lee son of Benjamin & Mary Lee was born ye 27th Day
 of February AD 1740/1
William Lee son of Benjamin & Mary Lee was born ye 8th Day
 of April AD 1743
Lucia Lee daughter of Benjamin & Mary Lee was born ye 17th Day
 of January AD 1745/6

	Martin Lee son of Benjamin & Mary Lee was born ye 14th Day of June 1748
	Esther Lee Daughter of Benjamin & Mary Lee was born July 27th Day 1753
	Abigail Lee Daughter of Benjamin & Mary Lee was born Nov. 30th Day 1752
	John Lee son of Benjamin & Mary Lee was born May 14 1755
	Elisabeth Lee Daughter of Benjamin & Mary Lee was born May the 25th AD 1757
	[Le]muel Lee son of Benjamin & Mary Lee was Born May the 3rd AD 1760
	Daniel Lee son of Benjamin & Mary Lee was Born July 5 AD 1762
September 9 1696	The Birth and Death of the Children of John Lee and his wife Elizabeth LLR2:128
	John Lee was marred unto Elizabeth Smith the 8 Febeuar 1692
	Sarah Lee was borne the 12 November 1693
	Elizabeth Lee was borne --- the --- 30 Aprill 1695
	Phebe Lee was borne --- the --- 2 March 1696
	Luci Lee was Borne the 20 June 1699
7 Desem 97	Jeane Lee was borne --- the --- 20 Maye 1701
	John Lee was borne --- the --- 17 maye 1703
	Joseph Lee was borne --- the --- 24 November 1705
12 March 1711/12	Mary Lee was born the 30 January 1707/8
	Elizabeth Lee was born the 16 May 1710
	Benjamin was born 4th September 1712
	Joanna was born ye 28 Aprll 1715
	John Lee was married to Lydiah Allen ye 14 of March 1723
	Elizabeth Lee was born ye 2d - day of november 1724 LLR4:48
Octr 28 1731	Lydia Lee was born ye 13 Day of august in ye year 1727
	Parthenia their daughter was born ye 15 day of october in ye year 1730
	Lydiah Lee ye wife of ye above John Lee Deyed ye 25 Day of October 1731
	John Lee a bove written was married unto Eunice Lee ye 17 Day of february 1731/2
	their son John Lee was Born the 25 Day of July anno Dom 1733
	Martain Lee was born July 26 1735
	Gils Lee was born ye 27 Day of July AD 1737
	Anna Lee was born ye first Day of August AD 1739
	Eunice Lee ye wife of John Lee Dyd April ye 20th 1741
	Saybrook Octobr ye 7th 1741: This may Certifye that Captt John Lee of Lyme was married to Mrs. Abigail Tully of Saybrook this Evening by me --- William Hart LLR7:222
	Joseph Lee was married to Mary Alin his now wife the 21 Day of August in ye year 1727 LLR2:406
	their son Lemuel Lee was born the seventh Day of November in the year Anno Domini 1728
	Samuell was born ye 15th October 1730
	Sarah Lee was Born ye 9th Day of August 1733
	Hester Lee Was born ye 22d Day of October AD 1735
	Joseph Lee Was born ye 27th Day of Janeuary AD 1737/8
	Jason Lee was born August ye 20th 1740
	Catea Lee was born ye 28th Day of March AD 1743

EXTRACTED FROM THE LAND RECORDS 241

Catea Lee Daughter of Joseph and Mary Lee Died ye 3rd Day of October 1748

Lemuel [Samuel] Lee Son of Joseph & Mary Lee Died January ye 4th AD 1748/9

[Capt.] Stephen Lee was married unto Abigail Lord Daughter of Mr. Richard Lord of Lyme December the 24th anno domini 1719 LLR2:413

entered March the 7th 1725/6

Hannah Lee was Born September the 21 anno domini 1720
Abigail Lee was Born August the 10th ano Domini 1722
Stephen Lee was Born May the 4th ano Domini 1724
Joseph Lee was born the 2 day of September 1726
Frederick Lee was born ye 14th Day of November 1728
Benjamin Lee was born ye 12th Day of December anno Domini 1730
Daniel Lee was born the 9th day of September anno domini 1732
Thomas Lee was born ye 26th Day of August anno dom 1734
and Jane Lee was born ye 26th Day of August AD 1734
Elisabeth Lee was born ye 18th Day of August AD 1736
Joseph Lee Died ye 10th Day of february AD 1736/7
Joseph Lee was born ye 23d Day of May 1738
Lydia Lee was born ye 20th Day of April 1740
Silas Lee was born ye 20th Day of April 1740
Silas Lee Dyed 27th April 1741 LLR2:414
Lydia Lee dyed March 6th 1741/2
Abigail Lee Wife to Capt. Stephen Lee Dyed Sept ye 19th 1742

Captt Stephen Lee of Lyme and ye widow Mary Pickitt of New London were married Together on ye 25th of Jan. 1742/3 LLR7:345

The Burth of Thomas Lees Children LLR1:10
John Lees was borne: September: 21: 1670
Thomas: Lees Jun was borne: Desember: 10: 1672
Sarah Lees was borne: January: 14: 1674
The Wife of Thomas Lees Deceased may: 21: 1676 [Ann]
Thomas Lees was married unto Marah DeWolfe 13th July [1676?]
Phebe Lees was borne was born April 14: 1677
[Marah] born April [23] 167[8]

Elizabeth Lee the Daughter of Thomas Lee and Marah his wife was borne: 20 October 1681 LLR1:145
William Lee was borne: 7 aprill 1684
Steven Lee was borne the --- 27 June 1686
Joseph Lee was borne the 14 maye 1688
benjamin Lee was borne the 8 october 1690
benjamin Lee Deceased the --- 12 october 1692
Steven Lee Deceased the 5 Desember 1694
Hannah Lee was borne the 25 Febuary 1694/5
Steven Lee was borne the 19 January 1698
Lidia Lee was borne the 18 February 1701

The Birth and Death of the Children of Thomas Lee alias Laigh LLR2:121
John Lee alias Laigh was borne the 21 September 1670
Thomas Lee alias Laigh was borne the 10 Desember 1672
William Lee alias Laigh was borne the 7 Aprill 1684

	Joseph Lee alias Laigh was borne the 14 maye 1688
	Benjamin Lee alias Laigh was borne the 22 Desember 1692
24 Feb 1705	Thomas Lee was married unto Elizabeth his now wife
	24 Jan 1695 LLR2:322

The Birth and Death of the Children of Thomas Lee and Elizabeth his wife
Mary Lee was born the --- 22 October 1698
Elizabeth Lee was born borne the --- 8 Aprill 1701
Ester Lee borne the --- 18 August 1703
Thomas Lee was borne the --- 19 Desem 1705

7 November 1710 Samuell Lee was borne the --- 7 July 1708
Eunice Lee was born the --- 18 Septr 1711
Elisha Lee was born the --- 7 march 1714

12 Jan 1704/5 Ensigne Thomas Lee Deceased 5 January 1704/5 LLR2:31
Joseph Lee Deceased 19 Jan. 1705

Mr. Thomas Lee Juner Dyed the 13 Day of October
1733 LLR2:211

William Lee was married to Mary Griffing: 1: november - 1715
LLR2:326

The birth of William Lee's children
Ezra Lee was born Janauy ye 7 1716/7
Lydia Lee was born ye second Day of March 1718/9
Abner was born ye firs of June 1721
Elias Lee was born november ye 27 1723
Abner Lee Dyed June the 2nd 1725
Abner Lee the second was born october 26 1726
Azubah Lee was born Aprill ye --- 24 --- 1729
Cyrus Lee the son of William Lee was born ye 26 Febr 1731/2

I ye subriber [Subscriber] having Receid Lawfull Certificate
of ye bans of matramony between James Lewis and LLR6:65
Phebe Mack both Lyme and at there Desire ye Said Persons
were Joyned Together in Wedlock and pronounced man and
wife according to ye Law of God and this Goverment
Febr ye 5th Day Anno Dom 1735/6 Attest, George Beckwith
Clerk

Phebe Lewis: Daughter of James and Phebe Lewis; was born ye
January ye 8th AD 1736/7
Cyrus Lewis was born febr 2d 1738/9
Ester Lewis Daughter of James & Phoebe Mack Lewis was born
May 22d 1741
Joanna Lewis was born March ye 4th 1742/3
Nehemiah Lewis son of James and Phebe Lewis was born ye 20
June AD 1745
Seth Lewis Son of James and Phebe Lewis was born ye 15 of
February 1747/8
John Mack Lewis son of James & Phebe Lewis was born
November ye 9th 1751

Dec 14 1727 William Lewis was married to Elizabeth Borden the
23 Day of February 1715 LLR2:222
The birth of the children of Lewis and Elizabeth his wife
Hannah was born ye 26 day of November 1716
Joseph was born ye 1 day [January] 1718

EXTRACTED FROM THE LAND RECORDS 243

	Jane was born ye 10 day of February 1720	LLR2:222
	Elizabeth was born ye 12 day of February 1722	
	Borden was born ye 14 day of January 1725	
Aprill 14 1731	William was born ye 11 day of June 1727	
	Ely was born ye 9th Day of March 1729/30	

The birth and Death of ye Children of Joseph Lord & Abigail
    Comstock his wife married March 11 1724/5   LLR7:366
Abigail Lord was born ye 3 day of February 1725/6
Joseph Lord was born ye 11th of March 1726/7
Benjamin Lord was born ye 3 of Janeuary 1728/9
Elijah Lord was born ye first Day of January 1730/31
Elisabeth Lord was born ye 19th of August 1732
Salvens Lord was born ye 21 of August 1734
Danill Lord was born ye 12th Day of October 1736
Mr. Joseph Lord Decs ye 25th July 1736

May 28 1684   The birth and Death of the Children of Richard Lord and
    Elizabeth his wife   LLR1:60
Elizabeth Lord was born the 28 October 168[3]

Janu 21 1725/6   Oxford negro man & Temprance molato girll the two
servants of Richard of Lyme were married together
the 21 D of Janury 1725/6 by ye Reverd moses noyes
the birth of the children of oxford and Temporance the two
servants of mr. Richard Lord Junr: I say the birth of
the children of the sd oxford and Temperance are as
follows:
Zachry their son was born the 23 day of october 1726
Luke was born ye 14th Day of may 1728
Jordan their Son was born ye 30 Day of october 1732

May 6 1728   Richard Lord was married to Elizabeth Lynd July 11 1720
Their son Richard was bon Apr. 1 17 1722
Susannah was born the 16 of Janeuery 1724
Enoch Lord was born the 15 day of December 1725
Elizabeth was born the 14 day of november 1727
Ann Lord was born the 22 Day of December 1729
Their son Linde was born ye [2] Day of Febreary 1732/3
Elizabeth was born ye 9th Day of November AD 1735

Samll Lord and Katharine Ransom were married   LLR6:184
    together on ye 26th Day of June AD 1735
Samll Lord Son of Samll & Katharin Lord was born ye 16 Day
    of July AD 1737
Phebe Lord was born ye 24th of Febr AD 1738/9
Nathan Lord was born ye 10th of April 1741
Nicholas Lord was born January ye 20th 1742/3
Jabez Lord their Son was born April ye 16th 1745
Betey Lord their Daughter was born April ye 9th 1747
[Peter-son?]
Merey Lord Daughter of Samll and Katharine Lord was born
    August ye 21th 1749

June 3 1729   Theopholus Lord was married unto Deborah Mack ye 8 Day
    of May Anno Domini 1728. The birth of their   LLR2:22
    Children is as follows:
their Daftor Lydia was born the 19 Day of March 1728/9

	Deborah Lord was born ye 26th Day of November 1730
	Sarah Lord was born ye 20 Day of February AD 1732/3
	Hulda Lord was born July ye 16 AD 1735
	Hephsabeth Lord was born June 22 AD 1737
	Elizabeth Lord was born July ye 5th AD 1739
23 January 1706/7	Thomas Lord was married to Mary his now wife: 22 Desem: 1698 LLR2:334
	the birth and death of the Children of Thomas Lord and Mary his wife
	Thomas was Borne the 22: September 1694
	Mary was Borne the 20 march: 1695
	Joseph was Borne the 17: october: 1697
	Theophilas was Born the 19: Desember: 1698
	Elizabeth: was Born the 1: October: 1701
	Daniell was Born the 19: Desember 1703
	Samuell was Born the 22: December 1705
3 March 1709/10	Abegal was Borne the maye 1708
	Martha was born the [was blank]
	David was born the 9 day of June 1715
	Thomas Lord Dyed the 22 day of June 1730
Jany 6 1727	Thomas Lord juner was married to Esther marvin LLR2:98 December 28 [1726]
	The birth of the Children of Thomas Lord and Esther his wife
	Esther Lord was born ye 19 Day of January 172[8/9]
	Mary Lord was born ye 27 Day of September 1730
	Abner Lord was born ye 9th of March 1733
	Matthew Lord was born ye 20th 1734
	Thomas Lord was born April ye 7th 1737
	Renold Lord was born August ye 12th 1739
	Matthew Lord Dyd October ye 29th 1736
	Renold Lord Dyd June ye 29 1740
	Tapheniah Lord was born June ye 5th 1741
	Barnabas Tuthil Lord was born the last Day of March 1743/4
	Samll Loveland and ye Widdow Susanah Roulin were married together ye 6th Day of March AD 1735
	There Son Samll Loveland was born on ye 12th Day of December --- AD --- 1735
	Ebenezer Mack Juner and Abigail Davis [prob. widow of Daniel Davis] were married together on ye 23 day of December AD 1736 LLR6:78
	William Worman Mack was born ye 26th of January 1737/8
	Abigail Mack was born ye 14th of March 1740
	Sophar [ia] Mack was born February ye 7th 1743/4
	Lydia Mack Daughter of Ebenezer Mack and Abigail his wife was born June 25th 1746
Desember 31 1697	John Mack[e] Records the Birthe and Death of his Children and his wife Sarah [Ben[n]it] LLR2:166
	Ebenezer Macke was born the 8 Desember 1697
	Marah Mack was born the 10 November 1699
	Rebecka Mack was born the 4 october (1)701
	Johana Macke was born the 17 Septem: 1703
13 J[un] 1706/7	Debrah Mack was born the 11 october 1706

EXTRACTED FROM THE LAND RECORDS 245

May [8] 1733

Mr. John Mack was married unto the Widow Abigail Danill the 4th Day of May 1733: ye birth of sd Macks children [ ] is as follows
their daughter Elizabeth mack was born ye 21 Aprill 1734
John Mack Juner was married to Love Benet his now wife 13 January 1703/4
The Birth of the Children of John Mack and Love his wife

18 October 1707

Sarah Mack was borne the 10 october 1704
Phebe mack was borne the 28 June 1707
Elisabeth Mack was borne the 4 of february 1712
patiance was Born the 3 Day of Aprill 1714
Ebeneazer was born the: 24: of February 1716
Lydia was born the: 4: of June 1718
John Mack was born the 26 Aprill 1720
Ezra Mack was born ye 1 of Aprill 1722
Nehemiah was born ye 5 of Januy 1724
Ester Mack was born ye 30 of Novembr 1725
Hezekiah Mack was born ye 20 day of January 1728
Dorithy Mack was born ye 11 day of December 1729
Love Mack [widow of John Mack] ye wife of ye above John Mack Dyed ye 25 Day of June 1732/3

Jonathan Mack was married unto Sarah Benit ye 24 Day of August A.D. [1727]   LLR2:7
their son Joseph was born ye 22 July [1729]
Jonathan their son was born ye 1 Day of July [1731]
Love Mack was born April 15th 1734
John Mack was born January 15th 1735/36
Elisabeth Mack was born ye 30th of December 1738
Josiah Mack was born January ye 25th 1740/41

Samuel Mack was born ye 3rd Day of May 1743
Sarah Mack Daughter of Jonathan Mack was born ye 8th Day of April 1745
Abijah Mack Son of Jonathan and Sarah Mack was born ye 30th Day of Septem 1746
Lous Mack Daughter of Jonathan & Sarah Mack was born November ye 30th 174[7]
Lydia Mack Daughter of Jona & Sarah Mack was born November 12 17[50]
Benjamin Marvin and Deborah Mather were married Together on ye 11th Day of November anno Dom 1742   LLR7:311

Elisha Marvin and Katharine Mather were married on ye 17th of May AD 1739
Pickitt Marvin was born ye 9th of March 1739/40
Elisha Marvin was born ye 19 Day of June 1742
Timothy Marvin Son of Elisha and Katharine Marvin was born ye 23rd day of May AD 1744
Joseph Marvin son of Elisha and Katharine Marvin was born Feb 14, 1755

James Marvin and Ruth Mather were married Together ye 26th of April 1737   LLR6:15
Ruth Marvin was born ye 25th of April AD 1738
Huldah Marvin was born ye 27th of June AD 1740
their son James Marvin was born the 3rd Day of March 1742/3

Moses Marvin Son of James and Ruth Marvin was born ye 14th day
   of April AD 1745
Martha Marvin Daughter of James and Ruth Marvin was born May
   ye 22nd Day AD 1748
Mr. James Marvin afore named Died April 3rd AD 1769
Lieut James Marvin Son of the foresaid James Marvin Died
   February 19th AD 1776

John Marvin and Sarah Graham was married to each other the
   7th Day of May: AD 1691
Their first Child being a Daughter was born April 12th AD 1692
   and died
Sarah Marvin Daughter of John & Sarah Marvin was born Febry
   25 1694
Mary Marvin Daughter of John & Sarah Marvin was born July
   23rd 1696
John Marvin Son of John & Sarah Marvin was born August
   9th 1698
Elizabeth Marvin Daughter of John and Sarah Marvin was born
   Novemr: 23: 1701
Joseph Marvin Son of John & Sarah Marvin was born June
   16th 1703
Benjamin Marvin son of John & Sarah was born March 14th 1706
Mehatabil Marvin Daughter of John & Sarah Marvin was born
   Septemr 12 AD 1709
Jemima Marvin Daughter of John & Sarah Marvin was born July
   20th 1711

John Marvin was married to mehitable Champen the 24 Feb.
   17[25/6]   LLR2:300

September 6   their Son John was born ye 30th day of January 1726/7
1727   their Daughter mehetabel marvin was born ye 27 June 1729
               their Son Adonijah their son was born ye 1 day of march 1731/2
               Elizabeth marvin was born ye 21 day of August 1734
               Easter Marvin was born ye 15 Day of April 1737

               Joseph Marvin was married unto Jane Lay ye 28 Day of
                  May 1730   LLR2:399
Dec. 29 1731   their dafter Hepsibeth was borne ye 11 march 1730/31

               Mathew Marvin was married unto Mary Beckwith ye 20th Day of
                  Aprill 1732
May 1732   Marvin was married by ye Reverd Jonathan   LLR2:299
                     Parsons Pastor of the first Society in Lyme
               The birth of the children of Matthew Marvin & Mary his wife
                  is as follows:
               Their son Seth Marvin was born ye 12 day of July at break
                  of Day 1733
               Their Daughter Eunice was born ye 2 Day of December 1735

10 January   The birth and Death of the Children of Renald Marvin and
1706/7   [Phebe] his wife [Renald Marvin was married to   LLR2:168
                  Martha Waterman June 30, 1709]
               Phebe was borne the 3 Desember 1696
children of   Daniell was borne the 24 February 1701/2
Phebe   Lidia was borne the 12 January 1703/4
               Easter was born the 3 of Apll 1707

EXTRACTED FROM THE LAND RECORDS 247

Children of Martha
- Martha was born the 3 of Apll 1710
- Elisha was born the 26 of Sept 1711 [d. 30 Nov. [1714]]
- James was born the 26 of May 1713
- Sarah was born the [8] of March 1715
- Elisha the Second was born ye 8 of March 1717
- Meriam was born the month of March 1719

Captt Renald Marvin Decst ye 18th of October 1737

21 Jan 1704/5 John Janer Junr [Tanner, Jr.] a servant to Renald Marvin Decesed the 6 January 1704/5   LLR2:53

Reynald Marvin Juner was married to the widdow Sarah Lay the 23 day of December 1725 ye birth of ye children of sd Marvin
Reynold their son was born ye 23 Day of october 1726
Phebe their Daughter was born ye 18 day of March Anno Dom 1727/8
Dan Marvin their son was born the 2 Day of January 1731/30
Lydia Marvin their Daughter was born the 14th Day of September AD 1733

March 5th 1726 Samuell Marvin was married to Susanah Graham of Hartford the 5th Day of May 1699: - the Birth of their children is as follows: LLR2:276
Samuell Marvin their eldest Son was born Febru 10 1699 or 1700
Zecheriah was Born the 27th Day of December 1701
Thomas was Born the 4 March 1703/4
Mathew was Born the 7 Day of November 1706
Abigail was Born the 13 day of September 1709
Elizabeth was Born the 2: day of June: 1712
Nathan was Born the 21 day of November 1714
Nehemiah was Born the 20 day of Februy 1716/17 in the time the Deep Snow
my twins were Born the 15 day of Aprill in the year 1721:
  The one a boy still born [15 April 1721]
  the other a Daughter her name is Mary [15 April 1721]

Deacon Samuell Marvin Died May ye 15th 1743

Zechariah Marvin was married to Abigail Lord ye 29 Day of March 1732
the account of ye birth and names of ye Children of Zecheriah Marvin & Abigail his wife is as follows viz
their Son Elihu Marvin was born ye 13 day of february 1732/3
There Son Zacariah Marvin was born ye 11th Day of August 1735
Susannah Marvin was born Novemr ye 12th 1738
Thomas Marvin Son of Deacon Zechariah & Abigail Marvin was born ye 12 of October 1737
Thomas Marvin Son of Deacon Zechariah & Abigail Marvin Died ye 15th Day of October 1737
2nd Thomas Marvin Son of Deacon Zechariah & Abigail Marvin was born ye 29th of May 1742
Daniel Marvin Son of Deacon Zechariah & Abigail Marvin was born ye 2nd of May 1745
Joseph Marvin Son of Deacon Zechariah & Abigail Marvin was born January 8th 1747

Silas Marvin son of Deacon Zechariah & Abigail Marvin was
born ye 19 of July AD 1750
Joseph Marvin son of Deacon Zechariah & Abigail Marvin Died
22nd Day of January AD 1750/1
Daniel Marvin Son of Deacon Zechariah & Abigail Marvin
Deceased ye 30th Day of January AD 1750/51

The birth of ye children of Joseph Mather and Phebe his
wife   LLR2:229
Joseph was born ye fifteenth of March 1715
Elleazer was born the 17 day of novembr 1716
Phebe was born the fifteenth of March 1718/19
John Mather was Born ye 13: July: 1721
Jerusha was born ye 11th day of february 1725/26
Samuel Mather was born 10 Day of November 1728
Benjamin Mather was born the 19 Day of September 1732
Ann Mather was born the 22 Day of September 1733
Simon Mather was born ye 21 of Febr 1736
Simon Mather died ye 26 of Febr 1736
Samll Mather died ye 7 of October 1739

January 20th 1737/8
This may Certifye all Whom it may Consarn that Joseph Mather
of Lyme and Anne Boothe of Kensington bouth of this
Colony of Connecticut were Joyned Together in Muriage
on ye 26th Day of Octobr Anno Dom 1737   LLR6:144
by me ye Subinber as Witnes my hand - William
Burnham Pastor of ye Chh in: Said Kensington
Recorded Janr 30th AD 1737/8

[ ] January 1711/12 Samuel Mather was married to Debrah [Wade d. of John] his
now wife the 1 Day of January 1711/12
Theair Son Richard mather was Born Decembr 22 1712
Marcy was Born ye: 14th: of november 1715
Deborah was born ye 15th of Januay 1717/18
Lucy mather was born ye 28: Decembr 1720
Mehetabal was born ye 28 Day of December 1723

The birth of the Children of Timothy and Sarah Mather   LLR3:37
Timothy: ye son was born the: 9: of octobr 1711
Joseph: ye son was born ye 23: of Febr 1713
Ruth Mather was born ye third of Dembr 1715
Catharane mather was born ye 11 Janna 1717
Moses mather was born ye 23 Febr 1719

Timothy Mather Juner and Sarah Lay were married   LLR5:307
together on ye 12th Day of February AD 1735/6
Timothy Mather, there Son was born April 3d 1737
Sarah Mather was born on ye 7th of May 1739
Jehoid Mather was born ye 16 of November 1740
John Noyes Mather was born ye 24th of Augest 1742
Eunice Mather was born ye 3rd Day of June 1744
Joanne Mather Daughter of Timothy Mather and Sarah his
wife was born ye 31st of March 1746
Joanna Mather Daughter of Timothy Mather and Sarah his wife
died January 19 1746/7
Ruben Mather Son of Timothy Mather Junr and Sarah his Wife
was born ye 26th Decembr 1747

Aseph Mather son of Timothy Mather and Sarah his Wife
was born ye 11th Day of August 1749
Lucy Mather Daughter of Timothy Mather Junr & Sarah his wife
was born May 11th 1751
Sarah Mather wife of Timothy Mather Junr Died May 25 AD 1761

[date?]
the birth of the Children of Robert miller
Mary miller his daughter was born Decembe 15th 1703
Hannah was born ye 15 February 1705
Noah miller was born ye 4 November 1710
John Miller was born the 6 August 1713
Nicodemas Miller was born ye 16 February 1715
Elisha Miller was born ye 6 march 1716
Eliphalett miller was born ye 4 october 1718

Jacob Miler was married [Martha Thompson d. of William]
ye 26: Aprll 1711   LLR3:318
their son Jacob was born ye 19 July 1712
Robert was born ye 19 March 1714/15
Tomson was born ye 24: June 1716
Martha was born ye 3 - march 1718

[?] 1729
Nathan miller ye son of Jacob miller was born the last day
of August 1722   LLR2:450

Clement Minor was married to East[her] Lee his wife 31
octob 1722   LLR2:191
Lucrecia ye Daughter of Clement & Esther miner was born
may ye 22 1724
Christopher minor the son of Clement and Ester minor was
born February ye 23 1726
Andrew minor was born ye 26 day of may 1728
Elisha minor was born ye 24 August 1730
Sabra Minor was born 2 Day of october 1732
Zenas miner was born ye Jan: 10 1734-5
Zenas Minor Dyed February ye 24th AD 1737/8   LLR2:190
Samll Minor was born August ye 21 1738
John Miner was born March ye 25th 1742
Joel Minor Son of Clement and Esther Minor was born
February 25 [1743/4]

The Birth of the children of William Miner & Anna
married   LLR2:132
William his son was Born the 27th of Aprll 1694
Clement was born ye 12th of Feber 1695/6
Joseph was born the 12 of December 1698
Susanna was born ye - 14: of Septembr 1699
Christopher was born the: - 17: of Aprll 1701
Thomas was born - the 5: of Janeuery 1702
Sarah was Born the 26 - of July 1704
Stephen was Born the: 9 of Aprll 1706
Samuell was Born the 26 of July 1708
Anne was Born the - 6 - of May 1710
John was Born the 15 - of Aprll 1712
Elihue was Born the 16: of: Octobr 1716
Silvester was Born ye 3 of: June 1714

	William Minor son of Clement Minor and Grandson of Thomas Minor of Stonington was born Nov. 6 1670 William Minor married Sarah, dau. of Joseph[2] Beckwith Anna was probably his second wife William Minors Wife died ye 9th Day of November 1732 LLR2:40
April 1709	Jeams Mose was marred unto marah his now wife the 15 october 1707 The Birth and Derth of the Children of Jeames Mosse and Marah his wife Marah Mosse was born the 22 September 1708
Jan 1709/10	Sarah Mosse was born the 7 Desember 1709
[?] 1711	Jeames Mose was born the 23 September 1711
	These may Cerifie all persons that John Mott of Lyme LLR2:56 in ye County of New London in ye Colony of Connecticut son of Samuell Mott and Annah Mott of ye Town of Westerly in Kings County in Colony of Rhode Island and Dauter of Edward Mott appeared in Westerly the fifth Day of october AD 1732 and were Lawfully Joyned in marriage before me --- John Richmond Justice
[?]	The Birth and Death of the Children of John Mott and LLR2:90 Marcy his wife Mary Mott was Borne the 5th January 1692/3
	A Deed of Gift: from: Wolston Brockway to his sone LLR2:77 Samuell Motte Jr. [confirms that Samuell Motte's wife Marah was really Marah Brockway, dau. of Wolston Sr.]
	Samuell Motte was married unto *Marah [Brockway d. of Wolston Sr.] his wife the 6: April [1692] Mary: was Borne: the : 10th March 1692/3 Samuell was borne: the: 1 Febuary 1694 Hanah was born 11 March 1696/7 John was born 25 Desember 1698 [Ex]perience was borne 8 march 1703/4 Lidea was borne 22 march 1706 Nathanill was borne 16 July 1707 Deborah was borne 1 June 1710
Aprill ye] 1732	Samuell Mott Juner was married unto --- Spencer July 31, 1717 LLR2:251 the birth of the Children of ye sd Samuell Mott is as follows Ebenezer their Son Ebenezer was born the 5 July 1718 Samuell their Son was born ye 29 Day of August 1720 Mary their Daughter was born the 15 October 1722 [second] Samuell their Son was born ye 10 Day of August 1724 Azariah their Son was born the 10 Day of January 1726 Sarah their Daughter was born the 13 Day of December 1728 Samuell ye 3rd their son was born ye 2 Day of Aprill 1731 Nathaniel Mott was Born ye 15 Day of Aprill 1733
	John Munsels Childrens berths &c LLR6:156 Abigail Munsel was born November ye 24th AD 1727 Mary Munsel was born April ye 7th AD 1729 Cattaran Munsel was born Septt ye 4th AD 1731 John Munsel was born July ye 16th Ad 1735

Thomas Munsel was born March ye 23 AD 1738
Joseph Munsel was born Febr ye 19 1739/40
James Munsel Son of John Munsel was born ye 20th Day of
April AD 1743
Timothy Munsel Son of John and Mary Munsel was born ye
24th Novemr AD 1745
Anna Munsell Daughter of John & Mary Munsell was born the
13th Day of February 1750
Mr. John Munsell Died January: 9th AD 1776

John Monsell ye son of Thomas Monsell was born   LLR7:126
August ye 19th in ye year 1690
Recorded Octobr 25 1740 Benjamin Fox

Octobr 18 1732   Thomas Monsell was married unto Deborah Rogers 10 January
172[8]   LLR2:176
their Son Thomas was born ye 7th Day of December 172[8]

Moses Noyes was married to Mary Ely his wife ye 15th
of Janur 1712/13   LLR2:169

Moses their son was born ye: 1: of Septembr 1714
Ruth Noyes was Born ye sixth of January 1716
Ruth Noyes Decd ye 5 Febr 1719
their second Daughter also called Ruth was born ye 23 Aprll 1722

Mr. Moses Noyes Esq. Departed this life the 10th Day of
october AD 1743

Doctr · John Noyes Dyed the 5 of August 1733

Nov. 14 1729   The Revd Mr. Moses Noyes Desd the tenth Day of November
1729   LLR3:26
The Birth of Mr. Mosis Noys Children   LLR1:33
Mosis Noys was Borne the: 1 August 1678
Feb 8   Ruth Noys was Borne the: 6 January 1681

John Oliver was married to Savy: Comstock his wife
Januaye 11 1714/15   LLR2:187

Feb 14:1731/2   The Reverend Mr. Jonathan Parsons was married unto Mrs.
Phebe Griswold the daughter of Mr. John Griswold
Esquire the Fourteenth day of December anno Dom
1731 by ye Reverend mr. George Griswold   LLR2:73
names and birth of ye Children of ye Reverend Mr.
Jonathan Parsons and Mrs. Phebe his wife is as followeth
(viz:) their Son Marshfield Parsons was born Februy
17th Day 1732/3
Jonathan Parsons was born ye 25th Day of April AD 1735
Samll Holden Parsons was born ye 14th of May AD 1737
Thomas Parsons was born April 28th AD 1739
Ezra Parsons was born January ye 2nd 1741/2
Ezra Parsons Died January 13 1741/2
Pheby Parsons was born ye 7th Day of october 1743
Phebe Parsons Died the 28th of April 1746

Samll Pearson of Lyme and mehittable Dudly of Saybrook Wear
Married Together ye --- 22 --- Day of June AD 1738   LLR6:288
Mehetabel Person [Pearson] above wife of said Samll Person
Died the 9th Day of September: 1759

Elijah Peck and Hepsebath Parsons [marked over Pearson]
[d. of Pieter Pierson] were married Together on ye
28th Day of April AD 1737   LLR6:161
Mary Peck was born ye 14th of May AD 1738
Mary Peck Deyed ye 18th of March AD 1739
Peter Peck was born ye first Day of February AD 1739/40
Peter Peck died ye 3rd Day of June AD 1741
Elijah Peck was born ye 28th Day of May AD 1742
Peter Peck 2nd was born ye 22nd Day of March AD 1744
Mehipsabah Daughter of Elijah & Mehep Peck was born ye
2nd Day of March 1745/6
Jedediah Peck Son of Elijah and Mehipsabah Peck was born
January 28th Day AD 1747/8
William Peck Son of Elijah & Mehipzebah Peck was born
March 22 Day AD 1750
Luther Peck Son of Elijah & Mehipzibah Peck was born March ye
20th AD 1752
Parnel Peck Daughter of Elijah & Mehipzibah Peck was
born Maye ye 13th AD 1754
Anna Peck Daughter of Elijah & Mehipzibah Peck was born May
the first 1756
Elizabeth Peck Daughter of Elijah & Mehipzibah Peck was born
May the 14th AD 1758 and Died April the 20th AD 1759
Elizabeth Peck Daughter of Elijah & Mehepzibah was born June
5th AD 1760
Elisha Peck son of Elijah & Mehipzibah was born April ye 3rd
AD 1762
The remainder of the Deaths of ye Peck and his Children are
Recorded in the Book of marriages Folio 64

Westerly, May ye 16th - 1739 - Then Jedediah Peck and
Tabatha Person [d. Peter Person] made their   LLR6:273
Personal appearance before me in Westerly & then
I Joynd them Together in ye bond of Marriage, I Say
by me
                John Maxson, an Elder of a babtis
                Church in Westerly
Recorded June
ye 6th 1739

The Birth and Death of the Children of Joseph Peck (born 1641)
and Sarah (born 1636) his wife taken out of the first
book of Records folio 17 This 23 July 1696: married   LLR2:129

[Family of Joseph and Sarah, obviously not Children of
above Joseph & Sarah]   LLR2:366
Sarah Peck was Borne the 4 August 1663
Joseph Peck was Borne the 12 March 1667
Elizabeth Peck was Borne: the: 9 September 1669
Debrah Peck was Borne the: 31 July 1672
Hanah Peck was Borne the: 14: September 1674
Ruth Peck was Borne: 19 August 1676
Joseph Peck Deceased the: 10 October 1677
Samuel Peck was Borne the: 29 July 1678
Joseph Peck was Borne the: 20: March 1680
David Peck was Borne: the: --- January 1687

EXTRACTED FROM THE LAND RECORDS 253

	Deakon William Peck Deceased: the: 4 October 1694 being 93 years old
	Elizabeth Peck wife of said Deacon Deceased the 5 Desember 1683
Desem 1706	Joseph Peck grand son was born - 13 Augst 1705
[ ] 1734	Benjamin Peck was married unto Sarah Champen ye 8 of February 1733/4 LLR2:245

Dan Peck was born ye: 11: Day of may 1735
Dan Peck Dyed October ye first 1736
Mehitable Peck was born ye 12th of January 1737/8
Benjamin Peck was born ye 26th of April - 1740 -
Dan Peck was born April ye first 1742
Elisabeth Peck was born the 21st Day of March AD 1743/4
Cyrus Peck Son of Benjamin and Sarah Peck was born ye 2nd Day of May AD 1746
Dan Peck Son of Benjamin and Sarah Peck died the 30th Day of October 1746
Elias Peck son of Benjamin and Sarah Peck was born ye 20 Day of June AD 1748
Sarah Peck Daughter of Benjamin and Sarah Peck was born February 21 1750
Lee Peck Son of Benjamin and Sarah Peck was born July fifth Day 1752
Esther Peck Daughter of Ben. and Sarah Peck was born Octobr 30: 1756
Sarah above named Daughter of Benjn & Sarah Peck Died April 14 1775

Jasper Peck was marned to Sarah Clark November   LLR2:219
24, 1731

	Their Daughter Sarah Clark was born ye 24 December 1732
Feb 4, 1733	Nathll Peck was born March ye 11th 1735

Jasper Peck was born Septt ye 20th 1737
Juda Peck was born January 22-th 1739/40
Renold Peck was born March ye 8 1742
Susanna Peck Daughter of Jasper and Sarah Peck was born ye 11th Day of August AD 1744

Joseph Peck juner was marryed to Susanna his now wife
the 3 October 1704   LLR2:129

Joseph Peck Juner his maredg is recorded in p 129   [LLR2:129]
[Joseph m Sarah 23 July 1696?]

	Joseph Son of sd Joseph peck was born the 13 Augst 1705
Sept 1720	Jasper Peck was born the 3 Febuary 1707/8

Sarah Peck was born the 17 march 1709/10
Han Peck was born 10 marsh 1712

Samuell Peck was mared to Elizabeth Lee 28 Desem:1699[8]
          LLR2:129
Elizabeth Peck the daughter of Samuel Peck Deceased the 15th January 1704
Elizabeth Peck the daughter of Samuell was born 26 Aprill 1702
A second Elizabeth was born this 14 May 1705
Samuell was born the 12 July 1707
William Peck was born the last Day of august 1709   LLR2:129
          12 July 1707/8 [seem to be 2 dates]
Benjamin Peck was born the 6 Day of March 1711

LYME, CONNECTICUT, VITAL RECORDS

Elizabeth Peck ye Wife of Mr Samuell Peck Died ye 29
August 1731   LLR2:129
Samuell Peck was married unto ye widow Martha Barbor of
Killingworth the 25 Day of January 1731[/2]
Martr Peck ye daughter of ye above namd Samuell Peck and
Martha his wife was born ye 4th day of June 1733
Samuell Peck died ye 28 day of June 1734/5

Samuell Peck juner was married to Aless Way his now wife
ye 7 day of November 1728   LLR2:234

Decr 24 1728

their son Samuell was born ye 7 September 1729
Abner was born the 27 Day of September 1731
Darius Peck was born ye 11 Day of September 1733
Carter Peck was born ye 22 Day of June 1737
Elisha Peck was born ye 27th of November 1739
Daniel Peck was born the 27th Day of March AD 1742

William Peck was married to Jememah marvin Janury
ye 25 1731/2   LLR2:126

[This is a copy of a deed in which it states]   LLR4:304
John Cresse & Hannah Cresse of ye County of Cape May
in the province of New Jersey being husband and
wife married in Lyme of New England the Seventeenth
day of July anno domini 1693. The sd Hannahs maiden
name was Perigo born march the 31 1674

September 17:
1683

Sent to
Clarke
May:10:84

[ ] 9/10

The Birth and Death of the Children of
Robert Perego and Marah his wife   LLR1:58
Hanna [anna] Perego was borne the 31 march 1674
Mary Perego was Born the: 1 Aprill: 1677
Abegall Peregoe was Borne the 21: July: 1681
Robert Peregoe was borne 18 Aprill 1683
Elizabeth Peregoe was born 30 october 1683

Petter Person was married unto Lidia [Mack d. of John
Senior [will of]] his now wife the [las---]   LLR2:9
phebe was born the second of march 1789/90
Samuell Person was born ye first of novembr 1712
Lydia was born ye 26 of march 1714
Lydia Decd ye last Febr [wife of Peter] 1716
Peter Person was married to Mary Lord [d. of Lt. Richard Lord]
the 20: of Sept: 1716
Richard was born ye 9 Decembr 1717
Hepsabah was born May ye first 1719
Tabatha was born may the 6 Day 1721
Peter was born the: 29 march 1724
Mary Person was born the 22 August 1726
Irene their Daughter was born ye 24 August 1732

Mary wife of Peter person Decd ye 25 of Aperll [ ]

[Peter] married wid Martha Peck [ ] of January 6 AD 1735/6

The birth of John Peters children   LLR1:46
Marah Petterson was borne: the: 18 february [1679]

Henery Petterson was mared unto marah [widow of Robert
Perigo] his wife the 15 Aprill 1683   LLR1:83
Sarah Petterson was borne the 20: october 1686

EXTRACTED FROM THE LAND RECORDS 255

	John Phelps and Dorithy Rathbun were married Together on ye 10th of Novbr 1737	LLR7:73
	Charles Phelps Son of John Phelps was born ye 22d of January 1738/9 [m. Elizabeth Tiffany d. of Lt. Nathan]	
	Sarah Pier [d. of Thomas] was borne the 25 August 1678	LLR1:46
	Marry Pier was borne the 18 may 1682	
	Hanah Pier was borne the 16 Feb. 1683	
Jan. 25 1690	Thomas Pier Juner was born the 16 March 1689	
1727	The Reverend mr. Samuell Pierpont died the 15 day of March 1722/3	LLR2:125
	William Pike was married to Abbegall Comstock	
May 10 1684	the 24 June 1679: sent to the [ ]	LLR1:113
May 26 1883	the birth of William Pikes Children	
	Abigal Pike was borne the 14 may: 1683	
	Abigal Pike Deceased the: 26: May: 1683	
November 84	William Pike was borne 9 September 1684	
	John Pike was borne the 9 September 1686	
	Danell Pike was borne the 5 October 1687	
	John Pike Deceased the 25 October 1686	
	Abegall Pike was born the 3 Maye 1690	
Sept. 1679	Peter Prat was maried unto Elizabeth Griswold that was Devost from John Rogers; they were married the 5 August 1679	LLR1:63
May 88	Petter Prate Deceased the 24 march: 1688	
	Samuel Prat was married to Elizabeth Peck 8 Desember 1686	LLR1:17
		LLR2:129
	David Prat was borne January 1687	LLR1:17
	The birth of ye Children of Joseph Ransom & Jane his wife	LLR2:267
	Mary was: Born ye 13th of May 1709	
	Mathew was Born: ye: 23: August 1711	
	Jane was born ye 24 June 1714	
	Catharin was Born ye 8 of March 1716/17	
	Joseph was Born ye 11 of July 1719	
	Phebe was Born: ye 24 of Decembr 1721	
	Stephe was born: ye 8th Day of may 1724	
	Matthew Ransom and Sarah Way were married Together on ye 16th of Decembr 1736	LLR7:41
	Lydia Ransom was born July ye 3d AD 1738	
	Lydia Ransom Dyd March 12 1740	
	Richd Ransom was born ye 13th of May 1740	
	Lydia Ransom was born June 26 1742	
	George Ransom Son of Matthew and Sarah Ransom was born April the 14th 1744	
	Elisha Ransom Son of Matthew and Sarah Ransom was born February 6th 1745	
	John Ransom Son of Matthew and Sarah Ransom was born February 23rd 1748	
	Irena Ransom Son of Matthew and Sarah Ransom was born Jan 4th 1750	

	Matthew Ransom Son of Matthew and Sarah Ransom was born 30th Septemr 1756 Danll Ransom Son of Matthew and Sarah Ransom was Born May ye 10th AD 1760 Matthew Ransom of Lyme foresaid Decd October 5th AD 1760 at Saragow [Oswego, N.Y.]
May 10 1684	Danell Rayment was marred unto Rebekah Laye the 15 of Aprill: 1684: Sent to the Clarke LLR1:129 Richard Rament was borne: the 9 January 1686
Jan 1700 1701	The Birth of the children of Josia Rainer and Sarah his wife LLR2:213 Elishabe was Borne ---- 4 Desembr 1700 John was Borne the 19 Apprill 1703
July 1703	Ebenezer was Borne the 13 March 1704/5 Siurll [Sybil?] was borne the 19 Septembre 1707
] 1710	Josiah was born the 8 Febuary 1709/10 Joseph was born the 10 June 1713 Sarah was born the 17 Aprll 1715 Diedamia Rayner was born ye 18 July 1719
	the birth of the children of Benjamin Reed & Sarah his wife LLR2:205 their twins being too Daughters viz margret & mindewell was born ye 20 Day of march 1729/30 Caraline was born ye -- 14th -- of January AD 1731/2 Sarah was born ye -- 22d of -- August AD 1734 Enock was born ye -- 26th of Septt AD 1736
	John Reed was married unto unto Debrah Niles his now wife January 1700 LLR2:300 The birth and Death of the Children of John Reed and Debrah his wife Benjamin was borne the 10th maye 1700 Marah was borne the 10 Aprill 1702 John was borne the 11 Febuary 1705/6 Jonathan was borne the 30 march 1707 Nathanyell was borne the 30 September 1711
[Novemb? 22 1712	John Reed died ye 23 Day of December 1732 Elizabeth Reed ye wife of John Reed Died ye 18 Day of Janur 1732/3
	John Reed Juner of Lyme, & Mary Welch of Colchester were married Together on ye 12th Day of May AD 1730 LLR5:346 There Daughter Elisabeth was born ye 18th of Janeuary AD 1730/31 There Son John Reed was born ye 9th Day of Novembr AD 1732 There Son James Reed was born ye 9th Day of August AD 1734
March 24 1733	Jonathan Reed was married unto Elizabeth Mack ye 24 December 1729 LLR2:61 Their son Jonathan was born ye 17th Day of September 172[1730?] Elizabeth Reed ye wife of above sd Jonathan Reed Dyed ye 18 Jan. 1732/3 Jonathan Reed was married to ye Widow Elizabeth Smith [widow of Daniel] ye 14th Day of March AD 1734 LLR6:58 Sd Reed was married by ye Reved Mr. Jonathan Parsons

EXTRACTED FROM THE LAND RECORDS

Daniel Reed was born ye 7th Day of March AD 1735
Animaaz [Anniaus] Reed was born ye first Day of November AD 1736
Elisabeth Reed was born ye 30th of August AD 1738
Pheby Reed was born ye 25th of November AD 1740
Nathaniel Reed was born -- June ye 27th -- AD 1743
Suse Reed Daughter of Jonathan and Sarah Reed was born ye 4th Day of November AD 1745

cut] ober 27 1680
March 20 1680
Feb 23 1682

the Death and birth of William Robesons Children   LLR1:73
William Robeson was borne the 24 october 1677
Marah Robeson was borne the 12 January 1680
William Robeson was born the 19 febuary 1682

Edward Robins was married to Ruth Smith [d. of John Smith] ye 23: october 1718   LLR2:460
Jerusha Robins the Daughter of Edward Robins was born September 11, 1719
John was born ye 1 Day of october 1726
Nathan was born ye 8 february 1728/9
Ruth Robins was born ye 17 Day of february 1731/30
Edward Robins Died ye 5 December 1731

[ ] 84

Jeane Robins Deseased the: 15 April 1684 Sent to the Clark [she was formerly wife of John Tillotson]   LLR1:12

John Robins was marred unto Elizabeth his wife the 20 Sept 1692   LLR2:4

Edward Robins was born the 10 June 1693

John Robins was married unto Ruth Alger ye 3d November 1732   LLR2:466
Ruth Robins died ye 15 of April 1733

June 97

Aprill 1701

Joseph Robins was marred unto: Sarah his wife [dau. of Isaac Waterhouse, Sen] the 10th June 1697   LLR2:95
Joseph Robins Juner was borne the 30 March 1698
Sarah Robins was borne the 22 Aprill 1700
Lidea Robins was borne the 9 october 1703
Ruth was born ye 22: Aprll - 1705
Sarah was borne: 10: march 1709
[m]ehetable was born ye 3d of Febe 1712
Easter was born ye 2 of febr 1715
Lucy ye 1 Feb 1718

Jonathan Rogers was married to Ales Champion December 1718   LLR2:331
Joseph Rogers their son was born 31 August 1719
Sarah their Daughter was born the 8 March 1721/22
Ales their Daughter was born ye 20 day of February 1723/4 [m. Jacob Sullard]
Lucresia was born 1 January 1725/6 [1724/5]
Jonathan was born ye 11 Day of July 1728
Jerusha was born ye 1 Day of August 1730
Ezekiel Rogers son of Jonathan and Ales Rogers was born ye 12 day of March AD 1734/5 [12 nov 1731]
Stephen Rogers son of Jonathan and Ales Rogers was born ye 15 day of March AD 1734/5
Jonathan Rogers died the Second Day of February A.D. 1746/7

10 Aprill 1705	Henery Roland was mearyed to Temperance his now wife: 24 September 1702	LLR2:270

The birth and Death of the Children of Henery Roland and Temperance his wife
Francis was borne the 11 September 1703
John was borne the 6 May 1706
Temprance was borne the 11 November 1708
Pacianes was born the 24 Febr 1710/11
Henry was born the 5 June 1712
Elizabeth was born the 3 Novembr 1714
Francis Dyed ye 17th of Decembr 1714
Sary was born ye 16 of March 1717

23 July 1701	The Birth and Death of the Children of Richard Roland and Rebecka his wife	LLR2:184
	Rebecka was Borne the 14 Aprill 1699	
	Hanah was Borne the 20 Desember 1701	
1726	Marah was Borne the 20 July 1704	
	Richard was borne the 1 march 1707/8	
	Mabell was borne the 17 August 1709	
	Uriah was born the 17 November 1710	
28 Desember 1702	Benjamin was borne the 1 august 1716 Asall was borne the 1 August 1718	

I ye Sabenber [Subscriber] having Recevd - Lawfull Certificate of ye bans of Mattrimony between Uriah [s. of Richard & Rebecca] Roland and Lydia Lee both of Lyme, and at their Desire ye Said Persons were Jonyd Together in wedlock and pronounced Man and Wife according to ye Laws of God and this Goverment october ye 13th Day AD 1737   LLR6:182
Recorded Decembr 29 AD 1737; attest, Jonathan Parsons, Pastr
William Roulin was born ye 5th Day of Decembr AD 1738
Lydia Roulin was born ye 13th of Decembr AD 1740
  [written under this]
The other children are shown by the will or Uriah Roland
Edward   Azuba
Daniel   Molly
Uriah
Phebe

Asel Rauling of Lyme and Zipparah Waller of New London were married on ye 14th of Decembr 1738 [in New London]   LLR7:377
[H]enery Rauling So of Asel & Zipparah Rauling was born the 10th Day of March 1739/40
Lucy Rauling was born ye - 5th Day of febr 1742/3
Elizabeth Roland their Daughter was born the 7th Day of January AD 1744/5
Elizabeth Roland Daughter of Asael & Zipparah died ye 5th Day of September Anno Domini 1746
Elizabeth Roland Daughter of Asael and Zipparah Roland was born ye 26th of July AD 1747
Hepzibah Roland Daughter of Asael and Ziporah Roland was born August 26 1750
Susannah Roland Daughter of Asael and Ziporah Roland was born April 17th AD 1752

EXTRACTED FROM THE LAND RECORDS

Hannah Roland Daughter of Asael and Ziporah Roland was born April 22nd AD 1755
Rebeckah Roland Daughter of Asael of Ziporah Roland was born 21st of April AD 1757
Zipirah Roland wife of Asael Roland Died 17th Day of April AD 1760

Benjamin Raulin and Eunice Wad were married Together on ye 10th Day of March AD 1736   LLR6:205
Richd Raulin Son of Benjm & Eunice Raulin was born Septt 4th 1737
Rebeckah Roland Daughter of Benjn & Eunice Roland was born October 30th 1739
George Roland Son of Benjamin & Eunice Roland was born April ye 18 1742
Eunice Roland Daughter of Benja & Eunice Roland was born Sepember 20th 1745
George Roland Son of Benja & Eunice Roland Died ye 16th Day of January 1745/6
Mary Roland Daughter of Benja Roland and Eunice his wife was born Decemr ye 13 1747
George Roland son of Benjamin & Eunice Roland was born September 29th 1749

John Roulin & Hannah Anderson were married together March 27 AD 1726   LLR5:340
Temperance Roulin was born ye 20th of febeuary AD 1726/7
Sarah Roulin Was born febeuery 19th AD 1728/9
Hannah Roulin born Janerary 17th AD 1730/1
Hannah Roulin Decsd Sept 4th AD 1731
Thankfull Roulin born ye 5th Day of June AD 1732
Thankfull Roulin Decsd June 18th AD 1732
John Roulin was born May ye first AD 1733 and decsd ye same Day
Nicalus Roulin was born April ye 17th AD 1734
Hannah Roulin Was born May ye 4th AD 1735
Elisabeth Roulin Was born March 9th AD 1737
John Roland son of John and Hannah Roland was born ye 5th Day of March AD 1739

May ye 5th 1736 Richard Shaw and John Beckwith   LLR6:70
saw Richard Roulin and Hannah Greenfield Lawfully married: at or near South: Hold:
       Richard Shaw
       John Beckwith
Recorded December ye 17th AD 1736
[ ] Stephen Lee Clerk

[birth of ye children of Sanders, Jr.]

Samuell Sanders Juner his daughter Ruhanna was born ye 8 July 1731   LLR2:301
his son John Sanders was born ye 16 Day of December 1733

James Sawer was married to Hezediah [He[r]ediah] Bartlet on ye 4th Day of April 1739   LLR7:131
Sarah Ward Sawer was born ye · 24th · of July · 1740

Jacob Sayer was married: June ye 22 1710: to Martha Loomer his wife   LLR2:92

His Daughter Martha was born ye: 7: of May 1711
His Son: James was born ye: 7: of Desember 1712

LLR7:381 deed in which Jacob Sawer names son Elias
LLR11:261 deed in which Elias Sawer refers to his late father Jacob

Arter Scofel was married unto Rachell his wife the
   [17 Dec. 1689]
The birth and deaths of the children of arter scofel and
   Rachel   LLR2:7
Arter Scofell was born the 3 February 1691/2
Jeames Scofell was born the 9 January 1693/4
Jeams Scofell Deceased the 16 Febuary 1693/4
Arther Scofell Deceased the 24 June 1694 [father]
      [Relationship supplied by H.W. Brainard]
Arter Scofel was married to Elizabeth his now wife
   the Febuary 1710/11   LLR2:295
Jeames Scofell their son was born ye 18 of January 1711
Elizabeth was born ye 26 of July in ye year 1715

John Scoffell and Sarah Algur were married on ye
   3 of November 1742   LLR7:308

James Scovell was married ye 10 Day of Octobr 1734   LLR5:177
Elisabeth Scofel was born Decembr · 30th · 1737
Sebbel Scofel was born June ye 11th 1740
Rhoda Scovel was born ye 9th Day of July 1743
Sibbel Scovel Daughter of James and Elisabeth Scovel Died
   ye 9th Day of November 1745
Sibel Scovil Daughter of James and Elisabeth Scovil was born
   ye 12th Day of July AD 1746
Irene Scovil 2nd Daughter of James and Elisabeth Scovil was
   born July 23 day 1749
Arter Scovil Son of James and Elisabeth Scovil was born April
   14th 1752
Isaac Scovil son of James and Elisabeth Scovil was born the
   5 Day of May 1756

[   ] 06   Stephen Scofell was marryed unto Sarah [Champion d. of
   Thomas & Hannah] his now wife the 4 November
   1705   LLR2:231
The birth and Death of the Children of Stephen Scofell
   and Sarah his wife
Stephen was borne the 20: Augste 1706
1708   Sarah was borne this ··· 11: Septem 1708

John Sears and Elisabeth Watrous were married on ye 13th Day
   of June AD 1734   LLR6:248
John Sears was born ye 4th Day of March AD 1734/5
Richd Sears was born July ye 30th AD 1738
Elisabeth Sears was born ye 9th of October 1741
Mary Sears Daughter of John & Elisabeth Sears was born ye
   24th Day of August AD 1744
Seth Sears Son of John & Elisabeth Sears was born ye 16th
   Day of October AD 1748

EXTRACTED FROM THE LAND RECORDS 261

This is to inform all whome it may Concern   LLR2:424
That John Sill of Lyme and Phebe Fithim [Fithian]
of Bridghampton was maried the 22 Day of December 1731
by me Ebeneezer White of Bridghampton

The birth of Joseph Sills children: Elizabeth Sill was
   born November: 20 --- 1707   LLR2:456
John Sill was born ye 14: febr 1709
phebe Sill was born Febr 10 - 1712-13
Joseph Sill was born 25 of Aprill 1715
Thomas Sill was born August 25 1717
Luce Sill born Decembr ye 1 - 1719
Jabez Sill & Richard Sill being twins waas born ye 4 august 1722
Elijah Sill was born ye 6 Day of November 1724
Sarah Sill was born ye 2 Day of January in ye year 1727/28
Elisha Sill was born ye 6 Day of Aprill in ye year 1730
Joseph Sill died Novr 10 AD 1765 in the 88th year of his age
Phebe Wife of said Joseph died on the 4th Jany 1772 in the
   86 year of her age

Captain Joseph Sill was mareed unto Sarah his wife
   the 12: feb 1677   LLR1:102
Joseph Sill the sone of Joseph Sill and Sarah his
   wife was borne the 6: January 1678
Zachariah Sill the son of Joseph Sill and Sarah his
   wife was born ye 2 Day of June - 1682
Capt Joseph Sill was married to the Wido Sarah Marvin
   Feby 12th Day 1677 & died Augs 6th 1696 in the 60th
   year of his age

Abraham Skiner was mared unto abigale his now wife the
   20th Day of June 1699   LLR2:192
The birth and Death of the Children of Abraham Skin [cut] and
   Abbigale his wife
Abraham: was borne - the - 9 Aprill 1700
Abigall was borne - the - 2 febuary 1701/2
Richard was borne - the - 4 october 1705
Abigale Skiner Deceast - the 21: febuary 1701/2
Abigale was borne - the - 9 Aprill 1708

August 8 1682   Richard Smith Junier was mareed unto Elizabeth [Lay, John]
   his wife the 17 Day of november 1677   LLR1:54
The birth and Death of the children of Richard Smith and
   Elizabeth his wife
Richard Smith was borne the 29 August: 1678
May 10:84   Abegall Smith was borne the 8 September 1682
Susana Smith was borne 4 febuary: 1684
Desem: 26: 84   Elizabeth Smith was born the 15 July - 1687
May 28: 90   Elizabeth Smith the wife of Richard Smith Deceased
   the 3th of Aprill 1690

20 Desem 1692   Danell Smith was born the 15: Aprill 1692
Daniel Smith Died march ye 22 1729/30

June 1698   Henery Smith was marred unto marah his wife: 15
   feb: 1689   LLR2:175
The birth and Death of the Children of Henery Smith and
   Marah his wife

	Johana was borne -- the 9th July 1688
	Sarah wase borne the -- 4th marth 1689
	Jeames Smith was borne -- 15 January 1693
	Marah wase borne the 24 Desember 1695
	Alls wase born the 9 June 1697
	Henery Smith Sener Deceased the 10th November 1701
Aprill 3	the birth of the Children of Mr. samuell Southworth that
1729	were born in Lyme LLR2:133
	Samuell Southworth was born ye 5 Day of May 1723
	the twins amos and abigail were born ye 15 march 1724/5
	Amos Dyed ye 14 of June 1725
	Mary was born ye 15 Day of May 1727
	The birth of the Children of Mr. Joseph Southworth LLR2:99
	Elizabeth was born 13 of febeuary 1711/12
	Constant was born 21 of Aprll 1715
	Elijah Smith and Elisabeth Beckwith were married Together on ye 28th day of November A.D. 1738
	Amon Smith was born ye 28th of March 1741 LLR6:267
	Elisha Smith Son of Elijah and Elisabeth Smith was born ye 6th day of July AD 1745
	Molley Smith daughter of Elijah and Elisabeth Smith was born ye 4th Day of July AD 1749 [1747]
	Enoch Andrew Jasper Elijah
febuary 14	Daniel Smith was married to Elizabeth Smith December
1728/9	7 17[26]
	their daughter Zillah was born ye 15 Day of October
	17[27] LLR2:182
	their son Richard was born ye 28 Day of December 17[28]
March 1701/2	Richard Smith Deceased 8 march 1701/2 LLR2:71
	Daniel Smith Died ye 22 Day of march 1729/30
Aprill 27,	James Smith was married to Elizabeth Way the 16 December
1727	1724 LLR2:175
	their son James was born ye 17 day of June 1726
	their Daughter Jerusha was born ye 29 Day of march 1731
August 19,	their Son Ithamer was born ye 20 Day of July 1734
1734	Parnal Smith was born ye 30th of July 1736
	Theodora Smith was born 30th Day of August 1738
	Simon Smith was born July ye 14 1740
	Nathaniel Smith was born the 4th Day of August 1745
	John Smith was marred unto marah his wife the 26: october: 1685 LLR1:87
	The birth and Death of the Children of John Smith & marah his wife
	martha was borne the 8th agust 1686 [m. Isaac Tubbs]

Josiah
Ruth
Elizabeth   LLR5:271
Quarles   LLR4:120   LLR6:147 [mentioned in will]
Samuel
Joseph
Jemimah

] 34	the birth and age of ye Children of Joseph Smith　　LLR2:189 his first Child being a son was born in Lyme his name 　　is Elisha Smith born ye 28 of may in ye year 1721 Benjamin Smith was born in East Haddam ye 17 Day of Aprill 1723 margret Smith was born at East Haddam may 22 1725 John Smith was born at East Haddam June ye 12 1727 Jesse Smith was born at East Haddam Septembr ye 2d 1729 Debrah Smith was born at East Haddam Aprill ye 7th Day 1731 Joseph Smith was born in Lyme ye 29 of october 1733
	Matthew Smith was married To Sarah Rogers ye 25 of 　　Febr 1719　　　　　　　　　　　　　　　　LLR3:368 their son Thomas was born ye 28: of novembr 1720 matthew was born ye · 26 · of Febr 1722/3 Jane was born the 19 day of february 1725/4 Rachel was born ye: 17 day of March 1729
Dec 24 1733	the above sd mathew Smiths twins were born ye 19th of September 　　1733 the one a son his name is James Rogers Smith, the 　　other is a Daughter her name is Sarah Stevens Smith Briant Smith was born: ye 27: of Aprll 1735
Aprill 27 1727	Thomas Smith was married to Elizabeth Robins ye 12 　　January 1726/7　　　　　　　　　　　　　　LLR2:175 The birth of the Children of Thomas Smith & Elizabeth his wife their Daughter Sarah was born the 13 november 1728 their Daughter Alis was born 13 Day of october 1731 Jane Ewens was born ye 2 Day of November 1733 Edward Smith was born March ye 12 1737 Henry Smith was born ye 19 of March 1739 David Carpenter Smith was born March 23: 1741 Elisabeth Smith their Daughter was born ye 27th Day of october 　　AD 1744 Alis Smith Dyed the 9th of August 1733
1704/5	Sarah Spencer formerly the wife of John Holtum above 　　Said Deceased the 21 January 1704/5 George Holtum Deceased the 21 January 1704/5
	Danell Sperry was married unto Debrah Peck: 3 Aprill: 　　1694　　　　　　　　　　　　　　　　　　LLR2:129
July 27, 1730	Daniel Starlin Junr was married to Ester Coult　　LLR2:199 　　the 14 day of May 1730 the birth of the Children of Daniel Starlin Junr and 　　Ester his wife William Starlin their Son was born ye 19 Day of August 1731 Easter and Anne; Starlin were both born ye 19 october 1736 William Starlin Decsd ye 30 of November 1736 [Easter] Starling Daughter of Daniel & Ester Starling Deceased 　　ye 14th Day of April AD 1751
	John Starlin was married to [Abigail Pratt of Colchester 　　Nov. · 1727]　　　　　　　　　　　　　　　LLR2:166 John Starlins wife Died ye 10 Day of may 1731
	Joseph Starlin was married unto Sarah Mack the 2d of 　　July 1730　　　　　　　　　　　　　　　　LLR2:464
May 2 1734	the birth and Death of ye Children of Joseph Starlin 　　& Sarah his wife

264 LYME, CONNECTICUT, VITAL RECORDS

their first Child Died being a daughter
their son Samuel Starlin was born ye 14th Day of october A.D. 1732
Sarah Stirlin was born July ye 22d 1734
Mary Starlin was born July ye 18th 1736
Joseph Starlin was born March ye 8th 1739
Hannah Starling Daughter of Joseph and Sarah Starling was born ye 5th of April 1741
William Starling son of Joseph and Sarah Starling was born ye 28th Day of May A.D. 1743
Phebe Starling Daughter of Joseph and Sarah Starling was born ye 26th Day of April 1745
Lydia Starling Daughter of Joseph and Sarah Starling was born ye first Day of April (sun about one hour High at night) AD 1747
The above named Joseph Starlin died Sept 19 1748 in the 42nd year of his age
The above named Sarah Starlin Died August 6th 1762

William Starlin died Jan. 22nd 1719 age 87 years   LLR2:269
(Inscription upon headstone) Attest W. Marvin Registrar
Oct. 9, 1905

Sterling, Wm. and Mary Sayer marriage contract
January ye fifth 1706/5   LLR3:240

Marah Stocker the wife of Edward Stocker Deceased: 28 December 1704   LLR2:198

?] 1704/5   Experience was borne the 13 march 1699
Edward was borne the 10 maye 1701
John was borne the 19 Aprill 1704
Mary was born: the 3 Aprill 1707
William was born the 6 octobr 1708
Martha Edward Stockers second Wife Dyed ye 31 Day of october 1732
Edward Stocker was married unto widow Abigail harvy ye 25 December 1733
[widow Abigail Harvy was dau. of Richard Smith & widow of Thomas Harvey]   LLR5:441

This reference is a Deed from Jacob Sullard and his wife proving that Allis (dau. of Jonathan Rogers & Alis Champion m. Jacob Sullard   LLR9:163

Consider Tiffany & Neomey [d of William and Neomey] Comstock were married together on ye 26th of November 1731
Consider Tiffany was born ye 15th of March 1732/3
Luther Tiffany was born ye 15th of April 1734
Neomey Tiffany was born ye 28th of Decembr 1737 [m Ezekial Huntley]
Samll Tiffany was born ye 13th of July 1740
[H]umphry Tiffany was born the 2nd Day of March 1743
Naomy the wife of Consider Tiffany Died ye 29th Day of May 1743

February ye 3 1728   The names of David Tillotsons Children and their birth   LLR2:250

David Tillotson was born ye 25 of January 1715
James Tillotson was born ye 20 of Aprill 1717
Simeon & Levi were both born ye 2d of may being twins 1719

EXTRACTED FROM THE LAND RECORDS 265

	Deborah was Born ye 26 Day of June 1721
	Mary was Born the 29 of march in ye year 1723
	Jonathan was born the 22 day of July 1726
	William Tillotson born ye 29' of october 1728
	Eunis Tillitson was born ye 18 July AD 1730
	Jacob Tillitson was born the 15th Day of December AD 1737
	Jacab Tileson [son of John] Deceased: the 22 November 1687
	LLR1:41
March: 13 1692/3	Jeams Tileson was marred unto Elizabeth [Scovil d. Arthur of Middletown] his wife the 20 Aprill: 1692 LLR2:96
	The berth & Death of the children of Jeames Tilesone and Elizabeth his wife
	Johannah Tileson was borne the 9th Januery 1692/3 [m. John Lewis]
	Jeames Tilleson deceased the 30 maye 1694
	John Tileson [the son of Jonathan] and Marah Jones LLR1:70 born 30 may [1686]
	John Tillson was born the [29 March] 1692
	David Tilleson was Born the 17 November 1694
	The birth and the Death of the Children of Jonathan Tillesone and marah his wife
	Jeames Tilleson was borne the 23 July: 1697
	Samuell Tilleson was borne the 20 September 1698
	Mary Tilleson was borne - 21 march 1700
	Temperance tilleson was borne 23 Augst 1704
	Jonathan Tilletson Sen Departed this Life: 3 october 1709
	Jonathan Tilletson was maried unto Rebecka Chamberlin the 19 August 1707 LLR2:351
Mar 6 1725/6	Samuell Tilletson was married Lydia Chadwick ye 5 of September October 1718 LLR2:338
	Their first child Samuell Tilletson was born the 14 day of September 1722
April [ ] 1727	Nathaniell Tilletson was born the 20 day of August 1724
	Joseph Tilletson was born ye 4 day of october 1726
Oct 24 1727	Eleazer was born the 22 day of October 1727
	Temprance their daughter was born ye 18 Day of Aprill 1730
	Nathan Tillitson was born ye 24 Day of June 1733
	Amos Tinker was married unto Luce Lee Januy ye 17 1716/17 LLR2:46
	the birth of ye Children of Amos Tinker and Luce his wife is as follows
	Joseph Tinker their Son was born ye 5 November 1717
	Amos Tinker their Son was born February ye 17 1719/20
	Lydia Tinker was born ye 5 November 1723
	Luce Tinker was born ye 9 february 1725/6
	Benjamin Tinker was born ye 6 may 1728
	Silranus Tinker was born ye 9 day of December 1730
	Partheny Tinker was born ye 25 November 1732
	Phenihas Tinker was born ye 6th day of febuary 1734/5
	Eunice Tinker was born March ye 31 1737
	Martain Tinker was born June ye 28 1739

	Johlel Tinker was born November ye 11 1741
	Bettey Tinker was born ye 4th Day of February 1744/5
May 9[1]684	Amos Tinker was mared to Sarah Duren the first of
	June 1682. Sent to the Clark LLR1:95
	The Death and Berth of the Children of Amase Tinker and
	Sarah his wife LLR2:64
January 13	
1693/4	John Tinker was Borne the 12th Febuary 1685
	Sarah Tinker was Borne the 19 July 1689
	Marah Tinker was Borne the 2 June 1692
	Samuell Tinker Juner was married unto Jemimah Smith Novemb
	19 1721 LLR2:103
	their Daughter Tamor was born ye 4 August 1722
	their Daughter Mary was born ye December: 1: Day Anno Domini 1724
	Samll their son was born ye 18 Day of June 1727
	Seth their Son was born ye 5 Day of November 1730
	Abigaill their Daughter was born ye 25 Day of Octobr 1732
Novem 1680	William Tomsome was mared unto Silla [delfa] [Philadelphia]
	Tileson the 19 July 1678 LLR1:81
?] 81	Rachell Thomson was borne the 18 october 1679
	Jeane Thomson wase borne the · the · 3: Desem 1681
may 84	Jeane Thomsone Deceased · 30 Jenuary 1681
	filadelfia [Philadelphia] Thomsone was borne 23 June 1683
?] 27	the birth of ye Children of Noah Tooker LLR2:53
1728	Dorkis Tooker the Daughter of Noah Tooker was born
	the 29 Day of September 1727
?] 11 1733	Tabor Tooker was born the 16 day of December 1729
	Thomas Tozer of Lyme & Debrah Bate of Saybrook were
	married together ye 23 day of May AD 1740 LLR7:34
	Elishame Tozer was born ye 3 Day of July 1741
	This may Certify whome it may Consern that Moses Trim of
	Lyme and Mahitable Pendal of Bolton wear Joyned in
	marriage by me ye Subinber Novembr 15th 1731 LLR6:148
	Recorded December 23d AD 1737
	Certifyed [ ] John Bissal Just. pacis
	the ages of ye Children of Isaac Tubs and marah [martha] his
	wife LLR2:423
Januy 21	Joseph Tubs was born ye 15 februy 1714
1729	Isaac Tubs was born ye 22 Day of Aprill 1716
	Elisha was born ye 16 march 1718
	Zephaniah was born ye 18 of august 1720
	Alpheas was born ye 30 of June 1723
	Abner was born ye 8 march 1725
	Ezeckell was born ye 13 July 1727
	Mary Tubbs Daughter of Isaac Tubbs and Martha Tubbs wife to
	Isaac Tubbs above written was born ye 2nd Day of April
	AD 1710
	Martha Tubbs Daughter of Isaac Tubbs and Martha [ ] Tubbs
	wife was born ye 11th Day of November 1712
	Isaac Tubbs Deceased ye 27th Day of March AD 1748/9

EXTRACTED FROM THE LAND RECORDS 267

Novembr 27 1730

Peter Tubs was married to Sarah Brockway
   the 10 Day of march 1723/4   LLR2:398
their Son Richard was born ye 16 Day of March 1724/25
their Daughter Lydia was born ye 16 Day of December 1727
Sarah was born ye 22 Day of Aprill 1729
Richard Tubs Dec ye 22 Day of September 1730

28 January 1701

The Children of Samuell Tubs and Elizabeth his wife   LLR2:206
The birth and Death of them
Samuell was born 15 September 1699

Janu 6 1727/8

John Tucker was married to Elizabeth Marvin ye
   28 Decembr 1727
Their Son John was born ye 29 Day of November An Domini 1730
Hannah their Daughter was born the 30th Day of August 1732
EED [EED on stone in Sterling Cem - a daughter]
   Tucker was born ye 12th Day of June 1740
Elizabeth Tucker was born ye 17th day of March 1735

Mr. Joshua Tucker Departed this Life October ye 2d
   Anno Dom 1731

Barnabas Tutle and Elisabeth Lord were married together ye
   13th Day of September AD 1726

March 1712

George Wade was married to his now wife Elizabeth
   [Durant] the 14 July 1708   LLR2:138
the birth and Death of the Children of Gorg Wade
   and his wife Elizabeth
mary Wade was born the 25 January 1710

July 26 1726

Hannah Wade was born the 2 May 1712
Elizabeth Wade was born the 16 of march 1714/3
eunice was born the 31 of Decem 1715
martha was born the 16 of Aprill 1718
George was born the 17 of January 1721/20
Joseph was born the 28 of october 1723
Elisabeth Wade [wife] to the above Georg Wade deyed
   the 11 day of December 1725
George Wade was married to Sarah Tucker ye 13: day of Aprill
   in the year 1726
Sarah Wade the above named wife of George Wade died the
   22 Day of December 1726
Mary Died ye 10 September 1727

?] 8 1730

George Wade was married to Widow Sarah Dowley 31 August
   1727
Mary the Daughter of ye Wade was born ye 1 Day of November
   1729
Sarah Wade was born May ye 25 1732
Asenah Wade was born ye 20th of January 1734/5
Elihu Wade was born July ye 11th 1737
Elisha Wade ws born July 20th AD 1740
Mr. George Wade above named Departed this Life the 28th
   Day of April 1762
[Children of John Wade Jun] [this was pencilled in after
   Wade entry]   LLR7:85
Durant Wade was born ye Seventh of April 1716
Ann Wade was born ye 13th of Decembr 1718

	Jonathan Wade was born ye 15th of febr 1720/1	
	Stephen Wade was born on ye 13th of Decembr 1724	
	Leucy Wade was born ye 27th of Octobr 1727	
12 Jan: 1704/5	Elizabeth Wade the wife of John Wade Deceased the: 6 December 1704	LLR2:139
] ye 8 1730	John Wade Sen Died the 24 March 1728	LLR2:138
2 october 1704	Thomas Waight was married unto mary [dau. of Abraham Bronson] his now wife the 16 augst 1704	LLR2:166
	the burth and Death of the Children of Thomas Waight and his wife: Sarah was born the 9 of June 1705	
	Thomas was born the ninth of octobe: 1706	
	John was born the first of Decembr 1707	
	Richard was born ye first of June 1711	
	Elisabeth was born ye 25 of Febr 1714	
	Joseph was born the 25 Day of Novemb 1715	
December	Sarah was born the 3 Day of July 1717	
ye 6 1726	Mary was born the 6 day of December 1718	
	Thomas Waight died the 27 day of June 1725	
	mary Waite Died ye 7 Day of may 1731	
novmber 30 1739	Richard Waite was married unto Elisabeth Marvin Daughter of Samuell Marvin the 8th Day of November AD 1733	LLR2:239
	The Birth of ye Children of Richard Waite and Elizabeth his wife is as follows	
	his Daughter Phebe Waite was born ye 21 Day of September 1734	
	Lous Wait Daughter of Richd and Elisabeth Wait was born Decembr the 3rd of 35	
	Richard Wait Son of Richd and Elisabeth Wait was born Novembr 28, AD ye 39	
	Elizabeth Wait Daughter of Richd and Elisabeth Wait was born August 12th 1741	
	Sarah Wait Daughter of Richd and Elisabeth Wait was born February 25 1745	
	Marvin Wait Son of Richd and Elisabeth Wait was born December 16th 1746	
	John Wait Son of Richd and Elisabeth Wait was born 21st of January 1749	
	Daniel Wait son of Richd and Elisabeth Wait was born February 2nd 1751	
	Wife of Richard Wait Departed this life 27th of May 1755	

Thomas Waite was married unto Elizabeth Lewis ye 21 Aprill 1731
Elizabeth their Daughter was born 1731
Johannah was born ye 29 of october 1733
Thomas Wait was born ye 25th Day of February AD 1735/6
Cloe Wait was born ye 20th Day of June AD 1738
Mary Wait was born ye 20th Day of August AD 1740
[Lee] Wait Son of Thomas & Elizabeth Wait was born ye 20th Day of August AD 1743
Esther Wait Daughter of Thomas and Elizabeth Wait was born April 16th 1746

EXTRACTED FROM THE LAND RECORDS 269

Tabitha Wait Daughter of Thomas & Elizabeth was Born 15th of March AD 1748

Elisabeth Waller Daughter of Richd and Elizabeth Brockway died ye 30th Day of March AD 1742 [1st wife of Samuel Waller] LLR2:294

John Waller was married unto Mary Durins [Doren, Durant] 28 Desember 1678 by Mr. Chapmane LLR1:95
The birth and Death of the Children of John Waller and Marah his wife
John Waller was born the: 11: November 1679

1688

William Warman was mared unto Abigail his wife the daughter of Mr. Laye Deceased on the third of August 1687 LLR2:41

The Death and berth of the Children of William Warman and Abbigal his wife

[ ] 1688

Abbigal Warman was borne the 7th of July 1692
William Warman was mared unto Abegall his wife the Daughter of Mr. Laye Deceased: one the third of August 1687

?] 25 1732

Gershim Waterus was married to Lydiah Smith the 5th of May 1720 LLR2:117
phinious his Son was Born ye first Day of July 1722
Parnal their Daughter was born ye 9 July 1725
Patience their Daughter was born ye 10 Day of february 1729/30

Isacke Waterus was married unto Sarah Pratt dau. of Wm. Pratt by Mr. Chapman the 20 Aprill 1671 LLR1:65

? January 15 1680

The Birth and Death of the Children of Isack Waterus and Sarah his wife
Elizabeth Watterus was Borne 22 March 1671
Sarah Watterus was Borne 24 febuary 1674
Lydia Watterus was Borne 20 Augst 1678
Isack Watterus was Borne 29 January 1680 Sent to the Clark

May 16 1683

Jabez Watterus was borne 16 Marche 1682/83
Samuell Watterus Was borne: 21 July 1685

Aprill 15 1785

Ruth Watterus was borne 31 July 1687
Rebecka Watterus was born 28 August 1693

[ ] June 98.

Gueshum Watterus: was borne 30: March 1696

The birth of ye Children of Isaac Watterus · elizabeth his wife LLR2:389
Elizabeth was Born ye 26 Decembr 1708
Rebeckah was bor ye 10 of febr 1710/11
Temperance was born ye 18 of Decembr 1714
Andrew: was born: ye 26: of June 1717
Jane was born the 17 Day of August 1719
Richard was born ye 18 September 1721
Anne was born ye 31 December 1723
Hannah was born ye 1 Day of December 1725

October 20 1729

Gersham Waterouse Son of Isaac Waterouse and Sarah his wife was born in the month of July in ye Year 1716 LLR2:144

270 LYME, CONNECTICUT, VITAL RECORDS

Abner Watrouse Son of Isaac Waterouse Junr and Sarah his
wife was born ye 19th Day of August AD 1727

Samuel Waterhoas ye son of Isaack Waterhous was born
the 13th of March 1712

Isaac Waterus ye son of Isaac Waterus Carpendr war: 21:
years old ye 31: of octobr 172[2] LLR2:441

Samuell Waterus was married to frances Brounson his
wife the fourth of octobr 1716
Their son Jedediah was born ye Eight of august 1717

Mr. Gererges Ways: childrens ages LLR2:200
John was born: ye 14th of July 1698
Thomas was born ye 18th of March: 1700

Mr. George Ways Children
November 20:   Elizabeth was born ye 31 of may 1702
1714   Elliph was born ye 10: of July 1704
Mehetabel was born ye 10 of July 1707
Ireney Way Daughter of George Way was born 4 Aprill
1723 LLR2:141
Lydia was born ye 5 Day of January 1725/6
Lydia Way above sd died ye 26 day of January 1725/6
Aless Way was born ye: 6 of December 1726
Lydia ye second was born ye 25 July 1729
Hanna Way was on ye 25 Day of Aprill 1732
The both of Mr. Thomas Ways Children Sr. LLR7:7
Joseph Way was born octobr ye 21tt in ye year 1724
Lous Way was born on ye 14th Day of Janeuery in ye year 1726/7
Recorded Sept   Eunice Way was born on the 18th Day of May in ye year 1729
11 1739   Thomas Way was born the 14th Day of June in ye year 1731
Elisabeth Way was born on ye 18th Day of Jeneuery in year 1733/4
Delight Way was born on ye 9th Day of August in ye year 1736
Marten Way was born on ye 9th Day of March 1738/9
Jane Way ye Wife of Thomas Way Died on ye 16th: Day of March
1738/9

The beath & Death of ye Children of Josiah & Margaret
Weeb [Webb] LLR7:313
John Weeb was born may ye 12th 1731
James Weeb was born June ye 15th 1733
Thomas Weeb was born June ye 10th 1735
Nathan Weeb was born Janeuary ye 25th 1739
Josiah Weeb Dyed Augest ye 24th 1741

Septr 12 1734   The birth of ye Children of Jonathan Weeks his children
born in Lyme is as follows LLR2:304
his Son Jonathan Weeks was Born ye 30 of may 1734
Jethro Week was born ye 9th Day of febeuary 1736/7

Isaac Willy was married to Rose Benit his wife ye 4
[14] December 1697 LLR2:23
Isaac their son was born ye [15] of Sept 1699
Sarah Willy was born ye 20 December 1700
John Willy was born ye 14 of September 1702
Hannah Willy was born the 11 of May 1704
Rachal Willy was born ye 22 of march 1708

EXTRACTED FROM THE LAND RECORDS

Abel Willy was born 28 August 1709
Miriam Willy was born ye 20 of march 1711
Deborah Willy was born ye 28 of August 1715   LLR2:23
Zachary Willy was born ye 24 of novembr 1716

Isaac Willy Juner and Deliverance Tallman Ware
   married on ye 12th Day of May AD 1727   LLR5:351
There Son Nathaniel Willy was born on ye 12th Day

Entered July
2d 1736
   of Febr AD 1727/8
There Daughter Deliverance Willy was born on ye 8th Day of
   Janeuary AD 1729/30
There Daughter Abigail Willy was born ye 18th Day of Janeuary
   A.D. 1729/30
There Son Bezella Willy was born ye 10th Day of Sept AD 1734
Derias Wille was born ye 3d Day of May AD 1737

[cut off] 1729
Edward White was married to Ruth Robins the 7 day of
   July 1728   LLR2:143

LYME, CONNECTICUT, VITAL RECORDS

MEMBERSHIP, BAPTISMS, MARRIAGES AND DEATHS FROM THE RECORDS OF THE FIRST CONGREGATIONAL CHURCH OF LYME CONNECTICUT

"Mr. Higgins kept a record of the church which opens with the statement that "for a long time no records have been kept of the church in this place neither are there any now to be found." This record was continued intermittently by some of his successors and the book contains much valuable information relating not only to the affairs of the church but in addition a large number of vital statistics of the locality, a considerable part of which are not of record elsewhere. Mr. Higgins upon leaving seems to have taken the book as it contains a record of marriages and funerals at which he officiated in and around Aurelius during 1802 and 1803. Fortunately it was returned soon after and years later was rebound in more durable form. Both for the convenience of the public, who frequently refer to it in connection with genealogical research and as a protection from fire, this valuable little volume has been kept in the town safe for the past twenty-five years." [1]

PASTORS OF THIS CHURCH UNTIL 1850

Rev. George Beckwith 1730-1785
Rev. David Higgins 1787-1801
Rev. David Huntington 1802-1811
Rev. Asahel Nettleton 1 year
Rev. Josiah Hawes 1814-1833
Rev. Harvey Bushnell 1835-1838
Rev. Philip Payson 1838-1841
Rev. Charles E. Murdock 1842-1844
Rev. James D. Moore 1844-
Rev. Daniel C. Tyler 1844-1845
Rev. Samuel Griswold 1845-1848
Rev. Enoch Fitch Burr 1848-1907 [2]

Note: History of the First Congregational Church of Old Lyme with membership, baptisms, marriages and deaths is to be published soon and will supplement information in this book.

---

1. Historical Address, William Marvin, First Congregational Church of Lyme, Aug. 22, 1926.
2. Ibid extracted from above pp 10-11.

EXTRACTED FROM THE CHURCH RECORDS

A Book of records for the Church in the 3d or North Society in Lyme Kept by David Higgins Pastor. January 1, 1788 December 1802 Now kept by David Huntington Pastor of the Church in North Lyme

[page 7] Revd George Beckwith
Dean Seth Ely
John Sterling
Richard Hayse
Ezra Selden
James Perkins
Elisha Marvin

William Brockway
David Beebe
Samuel McCary
Abner Lord

Harris Colt
Elisha Marvin Jr.

[page 8]
Grabiel Brockway [D. April 1807]
John Perkins

Ezra Brockway
Ezra Mack

James Ely

[p. 8] William Sterling
Samuel Sterling

Thomas Lord (D. April 1788)
Ezra Ely
Josiah Ely
Josiah Harvey

Elihu Harrison
Samuel Sill

Sarah his wife
Lydia his wife
Jane his wife
his wife
Hannah his wife

Catherine his wife
Desire Colt wd (d. June 3, 1800 to chch in Hadlyme)
Deborah Brainard wd
Ruhamah Ely wd
Esther Bradford wd
his wife
Sarah his wife

Temperance his wife (D. wd June 30 1794)

Elisabeth his wife (D. Nov. 6 1793 to Chch in Pittsfield)
Lois Brockway Wd
Huldah Rathborn (D. June 30, 1794)

Esther his wife (Esther Young alias Perkins D. Dec. 10 1795 to chch on Long Island at Southold)
his wife
Lydia his wife removed
Elisabeth Gould
Sarah Marvin
Mary Gould
Agness Meves (Reeves)
Sarah Butler (wife of Wm Butler D. Feb. 1795)

Catharine Lord wd
Hannah Waid Wd (D. June 6, 1794)
Jemima his wife

Elisabeth Gibbs (Feb 1788 D. to church at Wilberham)
Annah Ely

Esther Ely
Rebeckah Ely
Anna Ely

Stephen Ransom

Abigail Scovil
Sarah Lee (wife of Samuel Lee) (D.
June 27, 1788 to Chch of Christ
New London)

Tempson [Thompson]Miller
William McCary   Elizabeth his wife

[p. 8] Feb. 1788 Mrs. Elisabeth Gibbs was recommended to ye fellowship of ye chh at Wilberham
April 1788 Mr. Thomas Lord was recommended to communion (?) of ye church of Christ where providence sd call him
June 27 1788 Mrs. Sarah ye wife Lemuel Lee was recommended to the fellowship of ye chh of Christ at New London
Jany 1793 Eleazer Mather Jr. & Irene his wife Recommended to the fellowship of the chh in Jericho, State of Vermont
Oct. 30 Mrs. Deborah Lee recommended to fellowship with ye Chh where providence may place her
Nov: 6 Elisabeth Marvin recommended to the Chh in Pittsfield
June 6 1794 Widow Hannah Wade recommended to the Chh in Pittsfield
--30-- Widow Huldah Rathbon recommended to ye chh of God where providence may call her.

[p. 9] June 30 1794 Widow Temperance Lord was recommended to the fellowship of ye chh of Christ where providence may call her
Sept Col Abner Lord & Polly his wife recommended to the fellowship of ye Chh of Christ where providence may place them
Feb: 1795 Sarah Butler ye wife of Wm Butler recommended to ye fellowship of ye chh of Christ where providence may cast her
March 17 1799 George Mitchel & Lucy his wife recommended to ye fellowship of ye chh of Christ where providence may cast them
June 15 1795 Widow Thankful Brockway recommended to the church of Christ at Red [Hook?] state of New York
Dec. 10 Mrs. Esther Young alias Perkins to ye chh on Long Island at Southold under ye care of Mr. Goldsmith
Jan. 19 1796 Mr. John Perkins & wife recommended to ye church of Christ where providence may place them
Dec. 26 1796 Mrs. Hannah Comstock recommended to the church in Hadlyme
Sept: 20 1799 Widow Ann Ely recommended to the fellowship with the chh in Millington
June 3 1800 Widow Desire Colt recommended to fellowship with the church in Hadlyme
Oct: 26 1800 Widow Annah Mitchel recommended to the Church of Christ where providence may call her
April · 1807 Gamahel Brockway was recommended to the fellowship of the church of Christ wherever providence should place him.

[p. 10] A Catalogue of those who had been admitted to own the covenant before Oct. 17 1787

Cullick Ely   Eunice his wife
                                    Lois Selden Wd
Daniel Lord   Elisabeth his wife living
Samuel Mather   Allice his wife
Benjamin Lord   Hannah his wife
Wells Ely
Adriel Ely   Sally his wife
Giles Sill   Lucy his wife
Nimma Ely   Martha his wife
Benjamin Brockway

EXTRACTED FROM THE CHURCH RECORDS

Joseph Harvy
Timothy Marvin

Ambrose Niles

Richard Brockway
Eliphant Brockway
Ebenezer Banning
Elijah Ely
Abner Ely
Ebenezer Tiffany
Eleazer Mather Jr.

Polly Anderson Major Andr Wife
Mary his wife
Emerson

Mary Brockway
Desire Brockway
Dorothy his wife
Sarah his wife
Hepsibah his wife
Bridget his wife
Lucretia his wife
Irene his wife (D. Janr 1795 to chch
of Christ in Jericho, State of Vermont)

[p. 56] An Account when these Persons who had owned the convenant renewed it & joined in full communion
July 6 1788 Mary wife of Benjamin Lee
Sept. 28 1788 Lucretia wife of Ebenezer Tiffany
April 25, 1790 Adriel Ely & Sally his wife
July 4 Elisabeth the wife of Daniel Lord
November 7 Eleazer Mather Jr. & his wife
July 1 1792 Polly the wife of thos Anderson
Janr 20 1793 Capt. Timothy Marvin
June 16 Allice wife of Doct. Saml Mather
Sept. 1 Doct. Samuel Mather Widow Abigl Hayes
Thankful wife of Elipht Brockway

[p. 57] Professions of Religion Made
Decem 30 1787 Widow Annah Mitchel removed
June 8 1788 Kesiah ye wife of David Ely removed
July 20 1788 Abner Lord Junior & Polly his wife
Novem 28 1788 Phebe Renolds
January 4 1709 Elihu Ely
April 11 1790 George Beckwith Jr. & Patience his wife widow Azuba Sill
May 2 Phebe ye wife of Joseph Marvin and Esther Perkins removed
May 30 Betty Marvin [alias] Elisabeth Marvin removed
July 1 1792 Phebe Ely Daughter to Mr. Josiah Ely removed
July 29 Lucy the wife of George Mitchel removed
Oct. 21 Rebecka the wife of Henry Boon
Nov. 4 Mrs. Polly Ely wife of Capt. Chris Ely recomd from Chh at Killingworth
April 28 1793 Capt. Christopher Ely
May 5 Anne Lee Daughter of Benjm Lee alias Mary Ann Re
July 7 Abigail Ely Daughter of Esqr Seth Ely
Sept. 1 Elisabeth wife of Capt. Harris Colt re Lucretia Ely re
    Elisabeth Hayes, Lucy Mather re Sally Ely re
    George Mitchel removed
Oct. 6 Deborah Lee wife of Mr. Abner Lee Junior removed
Dec. 29 Eunice Higgins re Catharine the wife of Abner Brockway re
    Caroline Ely Nancy Denison
Janr 5 1794 Mr. James Goold
April 27 Richard Hayes Ely removed
    Col. Samuel Lee & his wife
    wife of Manassah Leach [Irena Ely]
    Ambrose Niles & his wife

Samuel Harvey & his wife Marcy Leia (Marsilva)
Reuben Lord and Benjamin Banning
George Richards the [   ]
Betty Kimberly Huntington
April 1810 Pheby Comstock - wife of Ezra B. Ely remd
Jimima Marvin Abram Ely Perkins
Betsey Lee now wife of Christopher Champlin

[p. 58] Jany 1811 Susan Brockway joined in full communion . . . .
[Wanda] Sill joined this church the last summer
Mary Tinker joined this church the last year
Jan 12 1812 Names of Persons admitted into the church in the year 1813
June Phebe Marvin
      Nancy Huntington   By the Revd A. Vail
      Betsy Brockway
Septr Rebeckah Bump
       Sarah Brockway
       Esther Starling   By the Revd Doct Symas
       Mahetabel Ely
       Clarrissa Marvin
Octobr Silas Brown and Susanna his wife
        John F. Harrison and Jane Shelden his wife
        Phebe Starling
        Phebe S. Starling
        Isaac W. Sill
        China Hungerford dismissed   by the Rev. Mr. Hotchky
        Phebe Sill
        Susanna Wood wife of Silas Wood
        Elizabeth M. Bump Daughter of J. Bump
        Lucretia Rogers
Nov. 14 John Ely and Lucy his wife
         Mercy Hide wife of Alexander Hide
         Mary Brockway wife of David Brockway   by the Rev. Mr. Vail
         Mary Niles and   ] children of
         Ambrose Niles Junr] Ambrose Niles
1814 Mrs. _____ Morgan
June 5 Erastus Sterling
        Azubah Marvin
        Nancy F. Brockway   by the Revd Mr. Hawes
        Lurania McCrery
        Betsy (R) Wood

[p. 140] A catalogue of those who were members of the church at the time of my settlement
Dea Seth Ely deceased Lydia his wife deceased
Dea Elisha Marvin deceased Elizabeth his wife deceased
    Ezra Selden Esqr and Hannah his wife deceased
        Jemima Sterling deceased
    Samuel Sterling deceased
        Annah Ely
    Josiah Ely deceased
        Anna Ely deceased
    Elihu Ely deceased
        deceased Phebe wife of Joseph Marvin
        Rebecca wife of Henry Boon deceased

Capt. Christopher Ely deceased
               Abigail Ely daughter of Esq Ely
               Elizabeth Hayes removed
Col Lemuel Lee removed and his wife removed
    wife of Manassah Leach deceased
Dea deceased Ambrose Niles & his wife Lois Niles Deceased Feb. 17 1833
Samuel Harvy deceased Sylvia his wife removed
Reuben Lord Benjamin Banning
removed Phebe Marvin now wife of Rev'd I F Huntington
Nancy Huntington Betsy Brockway
removed Rebecca Bump Sarah Brockway dismissed
Esther Sterling deceased Mehitabel Ely
Clarrissa Marvin
Silas Brown Lurania his wife Dec
John F. Harrison Jane Sheldon his wife deceased
removed Widow Phebe Sterling Phebe S. Sterling removed
removed Isaac W. Sill China Hungerford removed
Phebe Sill Susanna Wood wife of S. Wood
removed Elizabeth M. Bump Lucretia Rogers removed
John Ely deceased Lucy his wife
Mercy Hyde deceased Mary Brockway wife of D. B.
Mary Niles Ambrose Niles Deceased
Erastus Sterling removed Azubah Sill
Nancy F. Brockway - Lurania McCrery removed
Betsey R. Wood excommunicated Caroline Ely removed
Jemima Marvin removed Phebe Comstock deceased
Ezra Prall removed Fanny his wife removed
Josiah G. Ely Esqr dec Hannah Luther deceased

[p. 33] Professions of Religion
AD 1815 April 2d Louisa Huntington
AD 1815 April 2d Molly Butler deceased
AD 1815 August 27th Ursula Lord removed
AD 1817 Jan 8th the wife of Mr. Rodney Comstock removed
        Jan 8th the widow -- Ely
AD 1817 March 2 Col Seth Ely Esqr and his wife Phebe removed
        Mr. John McCrery removed
AD 1822 Nov 20 Wife of Mr. Abner S. Ely deceased
        Marshfield S. Parker
        Jerusha L. Sterling removed
        Erastus Sterling removed
        Azubah Marvin
        Ursula Sill
        Mary Lee deceased Oct. 5th 1835
        Ezra Pratt Removed
        Frances Pratt
        Betsey B. Wood Excommunicated

[p. 142] Admissions to this Chh by Recommendation
AD 1815 July 2d Mary Hawes wife of the Pastor from Chh in Cornwall
    Sept 1st Patience Ely wife of James Ely
    Caleb Millar & Wife from Chh in Hadlyme
AD 1825 Sept 2nd Mrs. Fanny Ely wife of Sheldon Ely from the Chh in
        Millington East Haddam
AD 1831 July 21st Lucy Lord wife of John Lord from 2d Baptist Church in Lyme - Received
    by letter

1835 May 3 Mary Ann Ely (sister of Elisha O. & Eliab Ely from the church in Hadlyme - letter of recommendation dated 29th Aug. 1834 but not presented for the consideration of the Church until May 3rd 1835
  Ms. Parker Clerk
June 14 Hannah W. Lord wife of John S. Lord by letter from church in Monson Massachusetts
July 5th Mary Martin & Hannah Martin by letter from church in Millington
Aug. 23 Joseph S. Lord by letter
1836 Jan 3rd Hannah B. Bushnell wife of Rev. Harvey Bushnell admitted by letter from 1st Church in Avon
1837 Feb. 5th Mary Tooker wife of Niles H. Tooker by letter from Baptist church Pleasant Valley
1840 May 3rd Bridget Dickinson from the Church in Westbrook
1842 July 2nd Lucy H. Murdock from the church in Hillsgrove Illinois
1845 Nov. 9th Mrs. Margaret Phillips from the church in Denton Orange County N. York
1846 May 3rd Mr Thomas Anderson & Rebecca his wife from the church in Setauket L. Island N York recommendation dated Oct. 15th 1841
1847 April 4th Mary C Brockway from church in Plainfield
1848 Jan 2nd Mrs. Elizabeth T. Lord from 1st Church in Saybrook
1850 June 16th Mrs. Adaline C. Marvin from church in Madison Georgia

[p. 143] Professions of Religion
AD 1824 July 4th Prudence Nichols
    July 4th Mary Ann Ely wife of Semalius Ely Excommunicated
    July 4th Phebe Brockway wife of Jedidiah Brockway
    July 4th Julia Ann Miller
    July 4th Caroline Buckley
    July 4th Mahitable Burnham Lord daughter of J. Lord
    July 4th Sally Otis daughter of Israel Otis dismissed
    July 4th Olive Dean
    July 4th Betsey Bramble living with Wm Marvin
    July 4th Delia Babcock belonging in the Valley
    July 4th Esther Franklin living at Mr. Miner
    July 4th Rachel Thompson living at Col J. Elys
    July 4th Penelope Bump daughter of John Bump
    July 4th Laura Anderson daughter of Maj. Anderson
    July 4th Emmiline Sill daughter of Jemima Sill
    July 4th Richard Ely
    July 4th Mary Ely wife of Richard Ely
    July 4th Allen W. Griffin
    July 4th Phebe Griffin wife of Allen W. Griffin
    July 4th Rhoda Griffin daughter of Allen W. Griffin
    July 4th Horace Ely deceased
    July 4th Sally Ely wife of Horace Ely deceased
    July 4th Phebe Ely daughter of Deacon Seth Ely removed
    July 4th Emily Marvin daughter of Deacon E. Marvin
    July 4th Azubah Parker wife of M.S. Parker
    July 4th Jerusha Sterling wife of Col Wm Sterling
    July 4th Gabdiel Rogers Ely son of Horace Ely
    July 4th John C. Ely
    July 4th Eunice Ely wife of John C. Ely
    July 4th Hannah Marilla Ely daughter of Olcott Ely
    July 4th Lucy Ann E[id]ens living at Capt Ariel Elys
    July 4th William Marvin
    July 4th Sophia Marvin wife of Wm Marvin
    July 4th Fredrick Beckwith

EXTRACTED FROM THE CHURCH RECORDS

    July 4th Dr. John Cotton Mather Brockway
    July 4th Elisabeth L. Brockway wife of Dr. Brockway
    July 4th Shadrac Sill
    July 4th Joseph Selden Lord son of Joseph Lord
    July 4th Erastus S. Lord
AD 1824 Sept. 5th Deborah Miller wife of Col Miller
     Deceased 5th Rhoda Butler
     5th Betsey Morgan
   Removed 5th Daniel Lord
   Removed 5th Almira Lord
     Nov. 7th Elias Peck Ely
     Nov. 7th Maria Ely Sterling
     Nov. 7th Phebe Hubbard
     Nov. 7th Sally Maria Howard
AD 1825   Jedidiah Brockway
     Emily McCrery
     Belinda Otis removed
AD 1827 March   Abner S. Ely
AD 1827   Heyden Otis removed
AD 1828 March   Julia Niles wife of William Niles
AD 1828 March   Prudence Pratt Daughter of E. Pratt Esqr removed
AD 1828 March   Elija Nichols removed
AD 1828 March   Caroline Warner
AD 1828 March   Caroline Banning
AD 1830 Sept. 5th Aeenath Morgan
AD 1830 Sept. 5th Nancy Morgan dismissed
AD 1830 Sept. 5th Arabella Ely deceased
AD 1831 July 31   Peter Lord Deceased
AD 1831 July 31   Joseph Lord Deceased
AD 1831 July   Wife of J. Lord
AD 1831 July 31   Jemima Harrison Deceased Feb. 4th 1835
AD 1831 July 31   James Lester
AD 1831 July 31   Annis Lester
AD 1831 July 31   William Niles
AD 1831 July 31   William Lord
AD 1831 July 31   Wm Smith
AD 1831 July 31   Sarah Lord
AD 1831 July 31   Laura Comstock
AD 1831 July 31   Catherine Perry
AD 1831 July 31   Betsey Bradberry dismissed
AD 1831 July 31   Charles Harrison Junor dismissed
AD 1831 July 31   Mary Lord
AD 1831 July 31   Seth Ely Jurer removed
AD 1831 July 31   Perkins Ely
AD 1831 July 31   Louisa Harrison
AD 1831 July 31   Mary Ann R Hawes removed
AD 1831 July 31   John Sterling
AD 1831 July 31   Joseph S. Hat[?] removed
AD 1831 July 31   Miranda Ely
AD 1831 July 31   Eliza Jack removed
AD 1831 July 31   Vashtte Tooker
AD 1831 July 31   Horace Ely 2d
AD 1831 July 31   Rhoda Ely
AD 1831 July 31   Henrry A. Ely
AD 1831 July 31   Mary Ely

AD 1831 July 31   Sarah Ely Decd 1835
AD 1831 July 31   Philuna Griffin
AD 1831 July 31   Abby Ely
AD 1831 July 31   Harres Lord
AD 1831 July 31   Reuben Lord 2d
AD 1831 July 31   Phebe H. Lord
AD 1831 July 31   Lucy Selden deceased
AD 1831 Sept 4th   Bethuel Williams
AD 1831 Sept 4th   Wife B. Williams
AD 1831 Sept 4th   Horace Brockway
AD 1831 Sept 4th   Roselina Jack
AD 1831 Nov. 5th   Abraham E. Perkins
AD 1831 Nov. 5th   Azubah Lord
AD 1831 Nov. 5th   Abel Moor
AD 1831 Nov. 5th   Lucy Peck
AD 1832 March 4th   David Ely
AD 1832 March 4th   George W. Sill dismissed

[p. 154] Professions of Religion
1835 Sept. 5 Lucy Martin   Rev. Mr. Bushnell
1836 April 3 Phebe   Rev. Mr. Bushnell
   May 1st Sarah Ely the widow of Marsh Ely decd
        died July 28, 1838
   June 5th Henry Jones & Phebe his wife ⎤ dismissed
            Betsey Brown
            Laura Anderson 2nd
            Sarah E. Lord   Rev. H. Bushnell
            Mary Ann McCrery
            Jane J. Harrison Decd
            George Ely Disd   ⎦
   July 3rd Theodsdia Beebe   ⎤   Rev. Harvey Bushnell
            Elizabeth Marvin   ⎦
1837 May 7th Francis Griffin
1839 May 5th Joseph L. Royce · Rev. Phillips Payson
1843 May 7th Mary Morgan Rev. Chas E. Murdock
1844 March 29th Samuel H. Lord   ⎤
                Phebe E. Griffin   Rev. James A. Moore
                Hepsibah S. Tooker ⎦
     May 19th Allen Griffin   ⎤
              Joseph L. Lord
              Erastus A. Lord Jun.
              David B. Date
              Mary S. Hughes
              Phebe C. Lord Disr
              Sarah W. Lord
              Harriet A. Lord   Rev. James A. Moore
              Judah Lord
              Rebecca Lord
              Mary L. Beckwith
              Mary Raymond
              Jane G. Raymond Disr
              Enoch D. Ely Dis   ⎦
     Dec. 8th Elisha Miller   ⎤
              Clarissa Miller   ⎦   Rev. Oliver Brown

[p. 155]
1847
  April 4th Seimilius B. Ely
      Elizabeth P. Ely   Rev. S. Griswold
      Edgcomb Beckwith
      Sarah Beckwith
1847
  April 4th Thaddeus H. Raymond
      Richard N. Denison
      Elizabeth Brockway   Rev. S. Griswold
      Ann Maria Smith
  May 2nd Sarah M. Sterling
      Silas B. Wood   Rev. S. Griswold
      Eliza Ann Wood
      Nathaniel M. Wood
1848
  March 5th Henry Steward - Rev. S. Griswold

[p. 164] Dismissions from the Church Recommendations to other Churches
1833 April Elisha Ely wife of Elias Ely to Dr. McCauley's Church city of New York
     May 18 Wid Phebe Sterling Congregational Church in Canaan
     June 2 Deac. Seth Ely his wife his son Seth & Daughter Abigail Congregational Church in Ripley N. York
     July 14 Miss Sarah Brockway Church in Westbrook
1835 Jan 18 George W. Sill Congregational Church in Yale College
     May 3rd Charles F. Harrison (not dismissed) but recommended by certificate to church in New York
     C. F. Harrison aftewards to wit on the 17th of May 1835 applied for a dismission from the church which was voted
     June 14 Phebe Selden to no particular church not knowing where she should be located but the church gave her a general recommendation
     Aug. 30th Shadrach Sill to no particular church not knowing where he should be located by a general letter of recommendation
1836 May 8th Abram E. Perkins & Mary his wife to the church in South Yarmouth Mass.
     July 3rd Mary Hawes & Mary Ann Howes to no particular church
     --10 Phebe H. Taintor to the church at Colchester
1837 Mar. 5 Joseph L. Lord to church in Plymouth, New York
     April 2nd James J. Lord to 1st church in Baffalo New York
     -- 9th David J. Ely to Presbyterian Church in Port Gibson Mississippi
     Sept 17th John C. Ely & Eunice his wife not dismissed but had a certificate of membership
     The certificate given John C. Ely not being satisfactory a dismission was afterwards to wit on the 12th of Nov. voted by the church
1838 May 13th Betsey Bradberry to Baptist church Pleasant Valley
     Sept. 23 Hannah B. Bushnell to no particular church.

[p. 165]
1840 May 3rd Roxana J. Frazier to Presbyterian Church in Brockport N. York
     June 21st Henry A. Ely to Presbyterian Church in Port Gibson Mississippi
1841 Feb. 20 Sally Southworth to Congregational Church in Deep River
     Sept. 6th Hanna W. Lord to church in Monson Mass.
     Oct. 17th Prudence Nichols to 1st Church in East Haddam
1842 June 12 Betsey Brockway to 2nd Church in Saybrook
1844 Feb. 4th Lucy H. Murdock to the Church in Meridan
     Oct. 27th George Ely to no particular church
     Nov. 17 Nancy Morgan to 1st Church in Saybrook

LYME, CONNECTICUT, VITAL RECORDS

    Dec. 8th Phebe A. Avery to church in Rochester N. York
1845 March 16 Julia Ann Millard to church in Warren Baltimore County Maryland
    Sept. 28 Saloma Babcock to Church in Clinton N. York
1846 March 22nd Phebe C. Selden to the church in Hadlyme
    June 7th Laura C. Selden to 1st Presbyterian Church in Sweden
    Monsoe Co. N.York
    Ursula Sill to church on Grassy Hill
    Dec. 13th Bethuel Williams & Martha Williams to the 2d Congregational church in N. London
    -- 27 Jane G. Raymond (alias) Morgan to first Congregational Church in New London
1847 Jan 24 Louisa Patten to congregational Church in Salem
    March 9th Henry Jones & Phebe S. Jones to Church in Salem
    May 23 Deac. Richard Ely Mary Ely & Mary E. Ely to no particular church
1848 July 17th Mrs. Mary Tooker to no particular church
    Sept 3d Mrs. Sarah W. Hyde to Dr. Spencers church Brooklyne N.Y.
    Oct. 1st Mrs. Emily Brink to church in LeRoysoille town of Pike Pennsylvania
1849 Feb. 21st Almira Trubee Church in Bridgeport Conn.
    Nov. 18th Mrs. Margaret Phillips to church in Plymouth Hollow Con.
1850 Jan. 23rd Mrs. Mary Tainfor to church in Shelbourne Mass.
    Feb. 9th Wm Smith & wife to church in Pettipaug
    March 4th Mrs. Mehetabel Chapel to church in Salem
    August 18th Mrs. Laura Eldridge to Presbyterian church in Sag Harbor N.Y.

[p. 166] List of Members of Congregational Church W. Lyme

Seimilius B. Ely
Elizabeth P. Ely
Edgcomb Beckwith
Sarah Beckwith
Thaddeus H. Raymond
Richard N. Denison
Elizabeth Brockway
Ann Maria Smith
Sarah M. Sterling
Silas B. Wood
Eliza Ann Wood
Nathaniel M. Wood
Henry Steward
Elisha Miller
Clarrissa Miller

Mary Martin
Hannah Martin
Mary C. Brockway
Elizabeth T. Lord died
    May 21st 1850
Adaline C. Marvin

Samuel M. Lord
Phebe E. Griffin
Hepsibah S. Tooker
Allen Griffin
Joseph L. Lord
Erastus A. Lord Jun
David B. Date
Mary S. Hughes
Phebe C. Lord dismissed
Sarah W. Lord dismissed
Harriet A. Lord
Judah Lord
Mary Lord dismissed
Rebecca Lord
Mary L. Beckwith
Mary Raymond
Jane G. Raymond dismissed
Enoch D. Ely dismissed

[p. 167] List of Members of the Congregational Church in North Lyme on the 1st of January AD 1844

Deac. Richard Ely Dismissed
Deac. Wm. Marvin
Reuben Lord Decd Dec. 4th 1849

Nancy Huntington
Elizabeth Huntington Decd Oct. 25 1845
Mehitabel Ely

Silas Brown
John A. Harrison
Marshfield S. Parker
Allen W. Griffin
John C. M. Brockway Decd
Erastus A. Lord Decd Dec. 14th 1850
Horace Ely
Horace A. Brockway
Jedidiah Brockway
Abner S. Ely
James Lester
Wm B. Niles Decd June 4th 1845
Wm Smith dismissed
Abram P. Ely
John Sterling
Henry Jones dismissed
George Ely dismissed
Francis Griffin
Joseph L. Royce
Nathan Damon Decd
John B. B. Lord
Betsey Matthews Deceased
Della Baker
Laura Selden dismissed
Mary Griffin
Louisa Patten dismissed
Miranda Ely
Sarah Lord Decd
Phebe L. Jones dismissed
Lucy Martin
Phebe A. Avery dismissed
Betsey Brown
Laura Anderson 2d
Mary Ann Ely
Jane J. Griffin Decd
Theodosia Beebe
Elizabeth Marvin
Mary Morgan

Clarrissa Ely
Phebe Gallop
Lucy Ely
Mary Brockway Decd
Louisa Huntington
Azubah Marvin
Ursula Sill dismissed
Betsey B. Wood
Susannah Wood
Frances Ely
Mary Martin
Hannah Brockway
Mary Tooker dismissed
Bridget Dickinson Decd
Phebe Brockway
Julia Ann Millard dismissed
Mehitabel B. Lord Dismissed
Esther Franklin
Laura Anderson dismissed
Mary Ely Dismissed
Phebe Griffin
Rhoda Brockway
Azubah H. Parker
Hannah M. Smith dismissed
Sophia Marvin
Elizabeth B. Brockway
Deborah Miller
Betsey Morgan Decd
Rhoda Ely
Mary E. Ely dismissed
Philura Ely
Azubah Lord
Lucy Lester
Emily McCrery dismissed
Caroline Wilkey
Caroline Banning
Nancy Morgan dismissed
Phebe Lord
Annis Lester
Sarah Griffin
Margaret Phillips dismissed

[p. 68] Baptism
Lewerett Huntington son to Josiah G. Ely and Elizabeth his wife Jany 12 1812
2nd Sabbath in June 1812 Lueratia Mimere Daughter of Samuel Hervy
    Baptized by the Revd Dart Griffing
1813
June Betsy Brockway daughter of Benjamin Brockway by the Revd Mr. Vail
        Eliza Ann daughter of Abraham Ely Perkins on acct of his wife
Sept Rebecka Bump wife of John Bump ⎤ by Rev. Doct Lyman
      Esther Starling ⎦
Oct. Silas Brown Lurania his wife and their children
      Thomas Samuel Prentis George Beckwith and Caroline Canada
      John Fredric Harrison and Jane Sheldon his wife
      China Hungerford wife of Amos Hungerford and her children ·

LYME, CONNECTICUT, VITAL RECORDS

  Justin Worthington, Horrace Harrison, Ann Maria, Emrne Eliza, Amos Franklin & Alonzo Cushman
  Phebe Sill Starling on her own acct and Harriot Alma and Marcus Aurchus Dualey children of the widow Phebe Starling
  Lucretia Rogers on her own acct
  George Worthington, Hannah Beckwith children of Isaac W. Sill
  Elizabeth Wood Clark an adopted child of Susanah Wood - by the Revd Mr. Hotchkiss
Novr 14th Lucy Ely wife of John Ely and Their children Horrace, William James, and John Griswold By the Revd Mr. Vail Senior

1814
June 5 Nancy Fidelia Brockway, Lurania McCrery, Betty Rogers Wood - Sally Maria [reljpes] Azubah Hervy, Phebe Sill, Ajahel Mather, Timothy Dwight, Abijah Perkins children of Ajahel Marvin and Azubah his wife --
  Erastus Sommer, Eliza Stow children of Erastus Starling
  Ansel Rodney a child of John Ely By the Revd Mr. Hawes

[p. 145]   Baptisms

A.D. 1815	April 20	Molly Butler on her own account
	April 9th	Frances Cornelia daughter of Erastus Sterling
	June 4th	Seth Baker son of Ely Perkins
	August 27th	Ursula Lord on her own account
	July 2nd	Deborah Ely child of Mr. Harvey
A.D. 1816	Aug. 25	William Burrit Son of the present pastor
A.D. 1817	Jan 5	Widow --- Ely on her own account
	12	Johnathon, Rossiana, Elizah, Calvin Lee children of Widow --- Ely.
A.D. 1817	March 2	Sarah Smith Comstock in the family of Rodney Comstock & on his Wife's account
A.D. 1817	March 9th	Selden Marvin, Elizabeth Colt, Phebe Hubard, Seth Elisha, Ebenezer Abigail Deborah children of Col. Seth Ely and Phebe his wife
A.D. 1817	May 4	Calvin Lynds, son of Widow John Ely
A.D. 1817	June 1	Abraham Ely, Son of Ely Perkins
A.D. 1817	June 29	Samuel Anderson son of Capt David Brockway
A.D. 1817	Sept. 21	Elisha Tomas, son of Widow Asabel Marvin
A.D. 1817	Sept. 21	Hannah a child living with Esq. Selden on Mrs. Seldon's account
A.D. 1817	Sept. 21	Reuben Son of Reuben Lord on his account
A.D. 1818	May 20	Charles Augustus Brewster, Son of Ezra Pratt
A.D. 1818	Aug. 23	Prince Beach Son of the present pastor
A.D. 1819	May 23	Sarah Elizabeth Daughter of Reuben Lord
A.D. 1819	May 30	Hannah Baker Daughter of Ely Perkins on Wife's account
A.D. 1820	July 30	Charles Nathan Son of Silas Brown
A.D. 1820	Aug 3d	Adaline & Addison Ezra children of N. Damon
A.D. 1820	Aug. 28	Marshfield Parker Son of Jedediah Lester on Wife's account
A.D. 1822	Nov. 20	Wife of Abner S. Ely on her own account
A.D. 1823	May 18th	Samuel Holmes Son of Reuben Lord
A.D. 1823	June 8th	Ezra Huntington Son of Ezra Pratt Esq.
A.D. 1823	June 29th	Hannah Ellen, Daughter of Capt. E. Sterling
A.D. 1824	July 4th	Junius Son of Wm & Sophia Marvin
A.D. 1824	July 4th	George Griffin Son of Wm & Sophia Marvin
A.D. 1824	July 4th	Phebe Brockway on her own account
A.D. 1824	July 4th	Caroline Buckley on her own account
A.D. 1824		Mahetable Burnham Lord on her own account
A.D. 1824		Sally Otis on her own account

EXTRACTED FROM THE CHURCH RECORDS

A.D. 1824 July 4th — Olive Dean on her own account

[p. 146]
A.D. 1824 July 4th — Betsey Bramble on her own account
A.D. 1824 July 4th — Delia Babcock on her own account
A.D. 1824 July 4th — Esther Franklin on her own account
A.D. 1824 July 4th — Rachal Thompson on her own account
A.D. 1824 July 4th — Emiline Sill on her own account
A.D. 1824 July 4th — Phebe Griffin on her own account
A.D. 1824 July 4th — Rhoda Beckwith Griffin on her own account
A.D. 1824 July 4th — Zebdial Rogers Ely on his own account
A.D. 1824 July 4th — Hannah Marilla Ely on her own account
A.D. 1824 July 4th — Lucy Ann Ewens on her own account
A.D. 1824 July 4th — John Cotton Mather Brockway on his own account
A.D. 1824 July 4th — Joseph Selden Lord on his own account
A.D. 1824 July 4th — Erastus Abel Lord on his own account
A.D. 1824 July 4th — John Marvin, Son of Marshfield & Asuhab Parker
A.D. 1824 July 18th — John Noyes, Esther, Jane, Joseph Christofer, William Noyes, Richard Noyes children of John & Eunice Ely
A.D. 1824 July 18th — William Horace, Sarah Elizabeth, Henry Adriel, Maria [?] Children of Horace & Sally Ely
A.D. 1824 July 18th — Joseph Leander Son of Erastus A. Lord
A.D. 1824 July 25 — Allen, Harriet Newel, Henry, Phebe Ellen, children of Allen W. Griffin and Phebe his wife
A.D. 1824 Aug. 1st — Richard Edwin, Elias Peck, Mary Emilene, Sarah Aurelia, David Josiah, Phebe Agusta, Zebulon Styles, Enoch Denison, children of Mr. Ely
A.D. 1824 Aug. 1st — Ulysses Hiram, Mary Emeline, Jedediah, Frederic Lord Cordin children of Jeddediah Brockway and Phebe his wife
A.D. 1824 Aug 1st — Bethiah Clay, Henry Brainerd, Prudence Brainard children of Henry Nichols and Prudence his wife
A.D. 1824 Sept. 5th — Bethey Morgan on his own account
A.D. 1824 Sept. 5th — Rhoda Butler on her own account
A.D. 1824 Sept. 5th — Daniel Lord on his own account
A.D. 1824 Sept. 26 — Mary Allice, Valentine Ansel Hepsibah Lucy, Elizabeth Marvin, Laura Ann, Griffin children of Valentine Miller on his wife's account

[p. 147]
A.D. 1824 Oct. 31 — John Griffin, Elizabeth children of Dr. John C. M. Brockway and Elizabeth Beckwith Brockway his wife
A.D. 1825 — Jeddediah Brockway on his own account
A.D. 1825 — Emily McCrery on her own account
A.D. 1825 — Eliza Dunham, Laura Ann, Horace Austin, Ebenezer Dunham, Mary Sophia children of Ebenezer Brockway Esqr. on his wife's account
A.D. 1826 — James Taylor son of Rev'd Noah C. [Saseton] and Emily his wife
A.D. 1826 May 7th — Augustus Son of Reuben Lord
A.D. 1826 July 9th — Jane Amelia Daughter of Dr. J.C.M. Brockway
A.D. 1826 July 16th — Marshfield Sterling Son of Marshfield S. and Azubah Parker
A.D. 1827 May 27 — Ellen Clarissa child of Wm Marvin and Shophia his wife
A.D. 1827 May 27 — Frances Elizabeth daughter of Abner S. Ely & Frances his wife
A.D. 1827 June 24th — Margaret Ann Daughter of Henry Nichols & Prudence his wife
A.D. 1827 June 24th — William Wallace Son of -- Mussel & Betsey his wife
A.D. 1829 May 31st — Jane Wood child of Ezra Pratt Esq. & Fanny his wife
A.D. 1829 July 26th — Caroline Brainerd Daughter W. Nichols & Prudence his wife

A.D. 1829 Aug 9th		William Mather Son of Marshfield S. Parker & Azubah his wife
A.D. 1829 Aug. 16th		Josiah Griffin Son of Abner S. Ely & Fanny his wife
A.D. 1829 Sept. 13th		Frances Daughter of Col John Ely & Eunice his wife
A.D. 1829 Sept 13th		Daniel Noyes Son of Col John C. Ely & Eunice his wife
A.D. 1830 May 9th		Ann Maria Daughter of Wm Smith & Hannah his wife
A.D. 1830 June 27th		Hannah Eliott Daughter of S. P Brown & Saloma once his wife
A.D. 1830 July 25th		William Joseph, Son of Wm Marvin & Sophia his wife
A.D. 1830 Sept 5th		Julia Ann Daughter of Wm Niles & Julia his wife on her account
A.D. 1831 June 26th		Maria Emeline Daughter of S.M. Brockway & Temperance his wife
A.D. 1831 July 31		Peter Lord on his own account
A.D. 1831 July 31		James Lester on his own account
A.D. 1831 July 31		Annis Lester on her own account wife of J. Lester
A.D. 1831 July 31		John A. Lord on his own account
A.D. 1831 July 31		William Smith on his own account
A.D. 1831 July 31		Laura Comstock on his own account
A.D. 1831 July 31		Charles Harrison Junr on his own account
A.D. 1831 July 31		Perkins Ely on his own account
A.D. 1831 July 31		Louise Harrington on her own account

[p. 148]

A.D. 1831 July 31		John Sterling on his own account
A.D. 1831 July 31		Miranda Ely on her own account
A.D. 1831 July 31		Philura Griffin on her own account
A.D. 1831 July 31		James Josiah Lord on his own account
A.D. 1831 July 31		Reuben Lord 2d on his own account
A.D. 1831 July 31		Phebe Higgins Lord on his own account
A.D. 1831 July 31		Jane Jemmima & Richard Rush children of C. Harrison
A.D. 1831 July 31		Wm. Horace, Lucy Ann, Rhode Catherine children of Horace Ely 2nd
A.D. 1831 Aug. 14th		Elizabeth Ely daughter of Joseph Lord
A.D. 1831 Aug. 14		Mary & Ann Selden children of Joseph Lord
A.D. 1831 Aug. 14th		Judah, William & Rebecca children of Joseph Lord
A.D. 1831 Aug. 14th		John Erastus Son of Laura Comstock
A.D. 1831 Aug. 14th		William Russel Son of Bradberry on wife's account
A.D. 1831 Aug. 14th		Roseana Jack daughter of Wm Bradberry on wife's account
A.D. 1831 Aug. 14th		Henry Selden & Agnes Newton children of ··· Bradberry
A.D. 1831 Aug. 14th		Samuel Sec. son of Bradberry on wife's account
A.D. 1831 Sept. 25th		Clarissa [Backles] daughter Bethuel Williams
A.D. 1831 Sept. 25th		Sophia Anne Maria daughter of B. Williams
A.D. 1831 Nov. 5th		Elizabeth Lord on her own account wife of A. Lord
A.D. 1831 Nov. 5th		Abel Moore on his own account
A.D. 1831 Nov. 5th		Lucy Peck on her own account
A.D. 1832 July 29th		Thomas Brockway Son of Wm Brockway & Nancy his wife
A.D. 1832 Aug 12th		Frances Ely Daughter of Wm Smith & Hannah his wife
A.D. 1832 Aug. 16th		Ann Maria Daughter of Marshfield S. Parker & Asubah his wife
A.D. 1832 Sept		Ambrose Ely Son of Wm Niles & Julia his wife

BAPTISMS

1833	July 29	Harriet Sophia Daughter of Wm Sophia Marvin by Rev. Mr. Crampton
1834	Aug. 10	Abner Sheldon Son of Abner S. & Fanny Ely Rev. J. Vaill
1835	June 28th	Hubert Son of Abram P. & Philura Ely Rev. H. Bushnell
	July 19th	Horatio Nelson Son of Saml M. & Temperance Brockway Rev. H. Bushnell
	Sept. 13th	Joseph Son of Reuben Lord 2nd & Sally his wife Rev. H.B.

EXTRACTED FROM THE CHURCH RECORDS   287

	Sept. 27th	John James Son of Horace & Rhoda Ely - Rev. H. Bushnell
	Oct. 4th	Elizabeth Mather daughter of James J. & Cornelia Lord Rev. H.B.
	Oct. 11th	Richard William Son of William & Nancy Brockway Rev. H.B.
	Oct. 11th	Mary Emily daughter of William B. & Julia Niles Rev. H.B.
1836	Jan 3rd	Frederick Agustus Son of John S. & Hannah W. Lord Rev. H.B.
	May 22nd	Francis Griffin Son of Wm & Sophia Marvin Rev. H.B.
	Oct. 9th	Harriet Elizabeth Daughter of H.A. & Rhoda B. Brockway Rev. H.B.
1837	Aug. 6th	Henry Marvin & Phebe Catharine children of Henry & Phebe S. Jones Rev. H.B.
	Sept. 3rd	Lucy Elizabeth Daughter of Erastus and Laura Selden Rev. H.B.
1838	July 8th	Mary Eliza daughter of Francis and Mary Griffin Rev. D. Lord

[page 149]

1838	Sept. 9	Enoch Marvin son of Wm B. & Julia Niles ⎤
		Elizabeth Spencer daughter of Samuel M. & ⎬ Rev. D.
		Temperance Brockway ⎦ Brockway
	Oct. 21st	John Smith son of John S. and Hannah W. Lord Rev. Mr. Bartlett
1839	July 7th	Ebenezar Son of Wm & Hannah Brockway Rev. Mr. Payson
1840	June 14th	Jane Louisa Daughter of M.S. & A.H. Parker Rev. Mr. Payson
1840	Sept. 24th	Israell Dunham son of S.M. & Temperance ⎤
		Brockway ⎬ Rev. Mr. Payson
1840	Sept. 24th	Edward Phillips son of Rev. Phillips &	
		Elizabeth Payson ⎦
1840	Sept. 27th	George Son of Francis & Mary Griffin Rev. P. Payson
1841	Sept. 4th	Ellen More Daughter of Allen & Sarah Griffin Rev. Mr. Brown
1842	Oct. 23rd	Wm. Mosely Son of Saml M. & Temperance Brockway Rev. Mr. Murdock
1842	Dec. 30	Mary Adalaide daughter of Ebenezer & Mary C. Brockway Rev. C. E. Murdock
1843	June 4th	Ellen Sophia daughter of Francis and Mary Griffin Rev. C. E. Murdock
1843	Sept. 1st	Allen Josiah Son of Allen & Sarah Griffin Rev. C. E. Murdock
1843	Sept. 4th	Celia Daughter of Wm & Hannah Brockway Rev. C. E. Murdock
1843	Nov. 3rd	Henry Lord son of M.S. & A.H. Parker Rev. C.E. Murdock
1844	May 19th	Mary Agusta daughter of -- & Phebe A. Avery Rev. James [Akins]
1845	June 29th	Caroline Lord daughter of Francis & Mary Griffin Rev. Mr. Thompson
1845		Eliza Morgan daughter of Allen & Sarah Griffin Rev. F. W. Chapman
1845	Oct. 12th	Mary Abba, Gilbert, Julia Eveline, James Monroe, and Sarah Maria children of Elisha & Clarrissa Miller Rev. Samuel Griswold
1846	Sept. 13th	Harriet daughter of Francis & Mary Griffin Rev. S. Griswold
1847	Sept. 4th	Elizabeth Agusta daughter of Erastus A. and Azubah Lord Rev. S. Griswold
1847	Nov. 7th	Eunice Ann, Silas Bates, Chas Henry & Wm Thomas children of Silas & Eliza Ann Wood Rev. S. Griswold
	Nov. 19	Sarah Catherine, Jane Elizabeth & Henry Perkins children of Abram P. and Philura Ely Rev. S. Griswold

1849	April 15	Sarah Elizabeth daughter of Samuel H. & Elizabeth T. Lord } Rev. E. B. Crane
	April 15	Reuben Lord Son of Allen & Sarah Griffin
	June 10th	Adelia Dunham, Eliza Emeline & Adel Barstow children of Ebenezer D. & Mary C. Brockway } Rev. N. Miner
	June 10th	Edward Thompson son of Mr. & Mrs. Phillips
	June 10th	Eveline Daughter of Francis & Mary Griffin
1850	Sept. 1st	Judah Holmes Son of Judah & Mary Lord Rev. Mr. Noyes
1850	Sept. 22	Alice daughter of Francis & Mary Griffin Rev. Mr. Noyes

[p. 159]

A.D. 1824 July 13th   John Noyes Esther Dan Joseph Christopher William Noyes Richard Noyes children of Col. John & Eunice Ely

A.D. 1824 July 15th   William Horace Sarah Elizabeth Henry, Adriel Maria Vail children of Horace & Sally Ely

[p. 79]

Marriages

Nov. 15 1789	Mr. Phiney Hays of Granby to Lucretia Jewett of Lyme
January 7 1788	Mr. John Hughes New York to Miss Jemmima Burnham Lyme
Jan. 10	Elijah Greenfield Auger to Lucindia Tubbs both of Lyme
Feb. 3	Amos Fox and Polly Fox both of Lyme
March 19 [ ]	Mr. Charles Otis to Mrs. Elisabeth Sweetland both East Haddam
April 3	Mr. Matson Smith to Miss Sarah Ann Mather both of Lyme
August 10	Timothy Tucker of Saybrook to Mary Perkins Lyme
Sept. 4	Matthew Griswold Junior Esqr to Miss Lydia Ely both of Lyme
Oct. 30	George Mitchel to Lucy Lee both of Lyme
Decemr 3	Mr. Ambrose Niles Junior to Miss Lois Brockway both of Lyme
January 21, 1789	Mr. William Sill to Miss Jemima Sterlin both of Lyme
April 23 1789	Samuel McCary to Widow Polly Woodward both of Lyme
Nov. 26 1789	Mr. Pardon Tillinghast of New London to Miss Amy Colt Lyme
Decm 3 1789	Samuel Clark Brockway to Sally Wade both of Lyme
Feb. 2, 1790	Mr. Cullick Ely Jr. to Miss Azubah Sill both of Lyme
March 4, 1790	John Phelps of Saybrook to Catherine Lord of Lyme
March 28	John Tucker of Saybrook to Vashti Harvy of Lyme
April 1, 1790	James Boague to Lydia Huntly both of Lyme
July 18	Daniel Stephenson of Springfield to Jansha (Jerusha) Mather of Lyme
August 5	Mr. Mather Peck to Mrs. Azuba Watrous both of Lyme
August 8	Abner Hayes to Azuba Banning both of Lyme
Sept. 30	Mr. Calvin Selden to Miss Phebe Ely both of Lyme
Sept. 30	Silas Miller of Colchester to Katty Jonston of Lyme
Oct. 4	Thomas Lonnargan to Lanny Swany both Irish
Oct. 10	Capt. William Rob of Wilksbury to Miss Betty Starlin Lyme
Oct. 24	Daniel Welch Colchester, Sarah Wright Lyme
Oct. 25	Giles Tiffany and Esther Peck both of Lyme
Oct. 28	David Moody Jewett Esqr East Haddam, to Miss Naomi Hurlbert Lyme
January 25 1791	Mr. John Ely & Miss Mary Lord both of Lyme
March 10	Dennis Drgon Transiant & Grace Beebe both of Lyme
April 26	Mr. Dan Marvin to Miss Huldah Mather both of Lyme
Nov. 27	Mr. Ezra Hullock Southold to Mrs. Lois Selden Lyme
Nov. 27	Mr. Thomas Mather to Miss Nabby Mather both of Lyme
Janr 8 1799	Judah Colt Esqr Ontario County State of New York to Miss Elizabeth Marvin Lyme

EXTRACTED FROM THE CHURCH RECORDS

[p. 80]
Feb. 2 1792	Mr. Martin Smith Newport Pennsylvenia to Miss Lucy Peck Lyme
Feb. 19	Doct. Thos H. Rawson East Haddam Miss Malinda Bingham Lyme
March 29	William Rogers & Lucenda Clarke both of Lyme
March 29	David Clarke & Phebe Clarke both of Lyme
Nov. 11	Mr. Joseph Alwell of Montville to Miss Ruth Stirling Lyme
Nov. 28	Libbeus Wright & Anne Pembleton both of Lyme
Dec. 16	Mr. Elihu Goold & Miss Sally Marvin both of Lyme
Dec. 27	Mr. Joseph Mather & Miss Zelinda Goold both of Lyme
Feb. 19 1793	Mr. Josiah Griswold Ely & Miss Betsy Sill both of Lyme
Feb. 19	Mr. Joseph Perkins of Bridgwater Vermont to Miss Patience Denison of Lyme Connecticut
March 22	Solomon Supio Jr. & Hannah Pembleton both Lyme
August 21	Mr. Abner Lee N York State to Miss Deborah Griffin Lyme
Sept. 30	Joshua Fox East Haddam Esther Blague Lyme
Oct. 2	Mr. Peter Peck Clark & Miss Polly Smith both Lyme
Oct. 10	Col Mashd Parsons & Mrs. Phebe Griffin both of Lyme
Nov. 4	Ammaniah Bates & Sarah Wright both of Lyme
Dec. 12	Elisha Beckwith East Haddam Lucy Beebe Lyme At Capt. A. Lees
Dec. 19	Mr. Edward Champlin Junr Miss Polly Brockway both of Lyme
Jan 1 1794	Mr. Thos Way Lemster Miss Bertha Perkins Lyme
Jany 19	Mr. Moses Sill East Windsor Miss Aseenith Colt Lyme
-- 29	Mr. Richard Wait Junr to Miss Polly Wade both of Lyme
Feb. 4	Solomon Lord & Sila Tiffany both of Lyme
March 6	Mr. James Harvey Miss Polly Rice both of Lyme
May 5	Stephen Otis & Lucy Widger both of Lyme
Feb. 18 1795	Mr. Matthias Fuller East Haddam Miss Huldah Marvin Lyme
Augt 31	David Huntly & Rachel Storey both of Lyme
Decem 9	Mr. Thomas Young Southold on Long Island and Miss Esther Perkins Lyme

[p. 81]
Decr 22 1795	Mr. Dyer Emmons East Haddam Miss Phebe Ely Lyme
Decr 24	Mr. Parmenius King Wilbraham Miss Rhoda Beebe Lyme
Decr 28	Mr. Samuel Comstock & Miss Betsy Perkins both of Lyme
Feb. 21st 1796	Elisha Emmons State of New York Phebe Perkins Lyme
May 3	Mr. Elisha Pratt Colchester & Miss Sally Sill Lyme
May 5	Nathaniel Shaw Woodbridge Esqr & Miss Lois Mather both of Lyme
May 12	Mr. Nathan Gillum of Chatham & Miss Martha Bidwell of Lyme
May 15	Capt. Timothy Marvin & Mrs. Azubah Sill both of Lyme
June 27	William Story & Phebe Beebe both of Lyme
July 6	Phineas Wright & Christiana Mentor both of Lyme
August 8	Mr. John J. Stoutenburgh of Clinton State of New York and Miss Sally Griffin of Lyme Connecticut
Sept. 16	Mr. John Otis & Miss Betsy Butler both of Lyme
Nov. 24	Mr. Holmes Marsh of East Haddam & Miss Ketura Boon
Decem: 6	Mr. Dyer Beckwith East Haddam & Miss Polly Emerson of Lyme
Decem: 17	Mr. Ebenezer Clark of Saybrook & Miss Abigail Mack of Lyme
Decem: 22	Mr. Charles Ely & Miss Betsy Perkins both of Lyme
January 19 1797	Mr. Ansyl Anderson & Miss Sally Smith both of Lyme

January 26	Mr. David Matson Windsor & Miss Lois Sill of Lyme
Feb. 12	Mr. Richard Rue & Miss Eunice Ames both of Lyme
April 6	Mr. Moses Deshon of Montville & Miss Lavina Goold of Lyme
Sept. 21	Mr. Asahel Marvin & Miss Azubah Sill both of Lyme
Oct. 5	Mr. Elijah Mather & Miss Sally Lord both of Lyme
Nov. 16	Mr. Eleazer Ely & Miss Dorcas Brockway both of Lyme
Nov. 16	Mr. Dudley Sterling & Miss Phebe Sill both of Lyme
March 29 1798	Mr. John R. Watrous of Colchester & Mrs. Lois Woodbridge of Lyme
May 10	Capt. Joseph Burnham & Mrs. Eunice Smith both of Lyme
May 17	Deacon Bezahel Beckwith East Haddam & Mrs. Lucinda Mather of Lyme
June 27	Silas Wood & Elizabeth (or Betty) Mack both of Lyme
Sept. 18	Elihu Smith and Fanny Mack both of Lyme

[p. 82]

Feb. 7 1799	Mr. Allen Willey of East Haddam to Miss Polly Brockway Lyme
April 7	Mr. Benjamin Banning & Miss Clarissa Corwin both of Lyme
-- 14	Mr. Seth Ely Junr & Miss Phebe Marvin both of Lyme
May 19	Mr. Pember Wade & Miss Anne Lord both of Lyme
27	Mr. Asa Minard & Miss Aseeniah Mack both of Lyme
June 6	Elias Leanord Negro & Mindy Freeman Negro of Lyme
-- 20	Mr. Huntley Marlow, New Hampshire & Miss Lucy Story Lyme
July 3	Mr. Jonah Cone Jr. East Haddam & Miss Polly Niles Lyme
-- 8	Mr. John Mack & Miss Betsey Pratt both of Lyme
Augst 15	Mr. Elihu Brockway & Miss Hepsibah Ely both of Lyme
Sept. 8	Jupiter or Jube David & Elisabeth Wood both of Lyme
Oct. 20	Mr. Marvin Banning of East Haddam Miss Allice Peck Lyme
Nov. 6	Mr. Richard Leach & Miss Hepsibah Mather both of Lyme
Janr 5 1800	Mr. Issac Thompson New London Miss Catharine Mumford Lyme
March 6	Mr. Sylvestor Chapman East Haddam & Miss Fanny Mather Lyme
-- 25	Mr. Samuel Ely & Miss Betsy Smith both Lyme
April 3	Mr. Silas Chadwick East Haddam Miss Sophia Gillet Lyme
-- 20	Mr. Ezra Rogers & Mrs. Deborah Ackley both of Lyme
July 19	Mr. Obiaiah Baxter of Yarmouth [?] & Miss Bridget Ely of Lyme
Augt. 24	Mr. Nathan Tiffany & Miss Lois Lord both of Lyme
-- 31	Mr. Joseph Emerson New London & Mrs. Eliza P. Greene Providence
Sept. 4	Aaron Indian & Taffena Tatson
-- 14	Christopher Shipman & Sarah Lee both of Lyme
-- 30	Mr. James Gates & Miss Jerusha Wood both of Lyme
Oct. 5	Mr. John Hart Wilkinson & Miss Lucy Scovil both of Lyme
-- 9	Mr. Alexander Allen of Glastonbury & Mrs. Mary Chadwick of Lyme

[p. 83]

Jany 14 1801	Mr. Amos Hungerford East Haddam & Miss China Harrison Lyme
Feb: 11 -	Mr. David Brockway & Miss Mary Anderson both of Lyme
Feb: 12 -	Thomas Beckwith & Polly Wade both of Lyme
Apl 2 -	Mr. Seth Harrison to Miss Clarrissa Banning both of Lyme

[18 entries June 30 1801 - May 15 1804 Pastorate of Rev. David Huntington in New York State]

EXTRACTED FROM THE CHURCH RECORDS

[p. 84]
Jany 1812 — Mr. Morrison Jack from St. Vincents to Miss Roxana Seldon of north Lyme
Mr. Dison [?] of Chatham to Hezakiah Comstocks daughter of Hadlyme Nov - 1811
Richard Evans to Betsey Williams - Dec. 1811

[p. 51] These by Josiah Hawes

January 23 AD 1815	Rev'd Alfred Mitchel of Norwich to Miss Lucretia Woodbridge Lyme
	Mr. Selden S. Warner Hadlyme to Miss Polly Brockway Lyme
	Mr. Reuben Lord to Miss Sarah Morgan both Lyme
Oct. 16	Mr. Leveritt F. Huntington to Miss Phebe Marvin both of Lyme
AD 1816 Jan 6th	Deacon George Beckwith Stockbridge Massachusetts to Miss Abigail Ely of Lyme
AD 1815 Nov 12th	Mr. Eliab Ely to Miss Ellis Sterling both of Lyme
AD 1816 May 26	Mr. Joel Steele Bloomfield State of New York to Miss Caroline Ely Lyme
AD 1816 June 23	Mr. Nathan Daman Ellington to Miss Lucina Brockway Lyme
AD 1816 Sept. 11	Mr. Israel Spencer to Miss Mary Niles both of Lyme
AD 1816 Oct 24	Theophilus Lord to Abigail Bramble both Lyme
AD 1816 Nov. 28	David Brown of Lyme to Miss Phebe Mosier Montville
AD 1817 July 6	Mr. Asa D. Post of Saybrook to Miss Nancy F Brockway Lyme
AD 1817 July 6	Mr. Waterous Clarke Nartlam (North Lyme?) to Miss Deborah Datte Lyme
AD 1817	Mr. Fredrick Beckwith to Miss Jerusha Sill boath Lyme
	Mr. Dan Marvin Jun to Miss Amanda Royce both of Lyme
	Mr. Wm. Clarke Bull Saybrook to Miss Susan S. Brockway Lyme
AD 1818 Jan 12	Mr. Henry Deshon Montville to Miss Olive Ransom of Lyme
Jan 19	Mr. Eli Bristol of Pens State of N York to Miss Lucinda Smith Lyme
April 1st	Bethuel Williams to Martha Ely both of Lyme
April 16	Mr. Theodore Gridley of Clinton N York to Miss Amy Ely Lyme
Septem 24	Joseph Spencer Esqr Rochester N York to Miss Elizabeth Selden of Lyme
AD 1819	Mr. Erastus A. Lord to Miss Azuba Royce both of Lyme
AD 1820 Feb 8th	Lewis Matson to Eunice Crosly Blacks of Lyme
AD 1820 March 2d	Capt. Zebulon Brockway Jun of Lyme to Miss Caroline L. Brockway of Troy New York
AD 1820 April 13th	Mr. Lanson Huntley to Miss Julia Tooker both of Lyme
AD 1820 April 20th	Dr. John C. M. Brockway to Elizabeth Griffin both of Lyme
AD 1821 Febry 9th	Mr. Ezra Brockway Junr to Miss Leonora Brockway Lyme
AD 1821 Febry 12th	Mr. Israel Matson to Miss Phobe Ely both of Lyme
AD 1821 Feb 13th	John Elmore Junr [?] to Miss Phebe Starling Lyme
AD 1821 April 19th	Capt. Gardner Gallup Salem to Miss Phebe Sill Lyme
AD 1821 June 7th	James S. Graham to Mary Ingraham both of Lyme
AD 1821 Aug 11th	Samuel Daniels to Jerush Miller both of Lyme
	Mr. Elisha Pratt to Miss Luranie Robbins both of Lyme
AD 1821 Dec 14th	Dr. Abraham Blatchley of Guilford to Miss Jemima Marvin of Lyme

[p. 152]
AD 1822	Mr. George R. Griffin of East Haddam to Miss Annis Johnson of Lyme
AD 1822 April 29	Mr. Marshfield Parker to Miss Azubah Marvin both of Lyme

AD 1822 Sept. 19		Mr. Phillip Morgan of Waterford to Miss Sarah Ann Lord of Lyme
AD 1823 April 16		Dr. Ambrose Niles of Lyme to Miss Frances Marvin of Hartford
AD 1823 April 27th		Silas Bramble & Amy Sewy [Sawyer] both Lyme
AD 1824 June 20th		John Gordon Hughes & Julia Ann Bill both Lyme
AD 1824 June 24th		Abner S. Ely of Lyme to Miss Fanny Griffin of East Haddam
		Mr. Stephen Sterling Junr to Miss Sally M. Marvin both of Lyme
AD 1825 Dec. 8th		Mr. Victor M. Johnson of Lyme to Miss Laura M. Jewet of East Haddam, Millington Society
AD 1826 July 16th		Mr. Thomas D. Lord to Miss C. Buckley both of Lyme
AD 1826 Aug 3d		Mr. Similius Lord & Miss Lucy Rogers both of Lyme
AD 1826 Oct 8th		William Wilson of Marlborough and Elisabeth M. Chadwick of Lyme
AD 1827		June 27th Mr. Asa Park Edgecomb of Groton to Miss Mary Bill of Lyme
AD 1827 July 5th		Mr. Matthew Griswold to Miss Phebe H. Ely both of Lyme
AD 1827 July 13th		Mr. Franklin Brown & Ede Miller both of Lyme
AD 1828 Jan		Mr. Thomas M. Hill North Kingston Long Island to Miss Deborah Miller of Lyme
AD 1828 March 26th		Mr. David M. Jewell of Lyme and Miss Ann Rathbone of Salem
AD 1828 April 7th		Mr. Martin Lester & Miss Abbe C. Rowland both of Lyme
AD 1828 April 15		Capt [Nathaniel] Conklin & Miss Mehitabel Miner both of Lyme
AD 1828 May 1st		Mr. Nathaniel M. Brown & Miss Eliza D. Brockway both Lyme
AD 1829 Jan 4		Mr. William Johnson & Eliza Ann Perkins both of Lyme
AD 1829 Jan 5th		Mr. Nathaniel Baker of East Haddam & Delia Babcock of Lyme
AD 1828 Dec 28th		Mr. William Smith & Miss Hannah M. Ely both of Lyme
AD 1829		Mr. Nathaniel Mathews New London to Miss Betsey Bramble Lyme
AD 1828 Dec 8th		Mr. Orlando Miner to Miss Belinda Otis both of Lyme
AD 1830 Sep 7th		Mr. Samuel Talcott of Hebron to Miss Aseenath Morgan of Lyme
AD 1830 Dec. 15th		Mr. Wm. Brockway to Mrs. Nancy Post both of Lyme
AD 1830 Dec. 29th		Mr. Adin Tooker to Miss Mary A. Miller both of Lyme

[p. 153]

AD 1831 June 12th		Harvey Tooker & Mary Maynard
AD 1831 July 24th		Mr. Henry Jones & Phebe S Marvin both of Lyme
AD 1831 Sept. 28th		Mr. Amassa H. Gillet Hebron & Lucy Ann Banning Lyme
AD 1832 Nov. 5th		Elias Ely Esq. New York & Eliza Nichols of Lyme
AD 1832 Dec. 27th		Henry Steward & Georgianna Sterling both of Lyme

EXTRACTED FROM THE CHURCH RECORDS

Burials 1787 - 1831

[p. 89]

Date	Name		Age
June 7 1788	Joseph Post	Saybrook	48
July 6 1787	Daniel Rathborn		17
Sept. 21 1787	Wd Rebecka Mott		102
Oct. 16 1787	Dean Joseph Colt		61
March 25 1790	Abner Griffin		49
Sept. 3 1790	Major John Griffin		53
March 16 1793	Wife Col Parsons		
April 25	An infant of Josh Griffins		
1795			
January 9	Wife of Jesse Beckwith		
Feb 24	Capt. Richd Mather		29
Apl 21	Mr. Jesse Beckwith		77
July 29	Mr. -- Mumford		84
Nov. 17 1787	Wife of Elijah Ely Katty		42
Decem 30	Widow Renah Harris		58
Jan. 5 1788	Humphry Tiffany		82
Jan 13 1788	An infant of Joshua Wrights		
Feb. 2 1788	An infant of Gordon Ely		
Feb. 27 1788	Widow Ruhama Ely		84
April 30, 88	Benjamin Luther		87
June 12 1788	Widow Esther Bradford		87
June 30 1788	Rebeckah Booge		19
August 16 1788	Sybbel Fox		52
August 16 1788	Zebulon child of Zebulon Brockway		1½
Sept. 17 1788	Esther wife of Capt. Chris. Ely		41
Oct. 7 1788	Sarah Mitchel widow		87
May 2 1789	Sarah Lord widow		74
Sept. 28 1789	Mr. James Perkins		86
Nov. 6 1789	Ephriam Sawyer Jr.		3
March 11 1790	An infant of Saml Griffins		
June 18 -	William McCary		61
July 22	Richard Hayes		81
Oct 10	John S. Terlin		87
Nov. 13	Abner Lord		57
Nov 25	Calvin son to James Ely		3
Feb 25 1791	Samuel McCary		88
March 26	Tempe Colt at Hudson		17
Janr 17 1799	Lucy, Peters wife		
Feb. 5	Mrs. [Jonathan] Emmons Wd		85
Feb. 7	Ziporah Perkins		5
Nov 25	Louis Brockway Widow		70
Feb. 3 1793	Warick Negro		70
Augt 1796	Russil Ely on West Indies		
Feb. 25	Hannah wife of Joshua Harvey		72
June 14	Sarah wife of David Beebe		60
July 14	wife of Gidn Beebe		
August 31	Mr. Ambrose Niles		70
Sept. 20	John a child of Lonsil? Brooks		3½
Sept. 22	Ebenzer Banning		
Oct 15	Joel Brockway		18
Nov. 1	Nancy Daughter to D.M. Jewett		1½

LYME, CONNECTICUT, VITAL RECORDS

[p. 90]

1793	Burials which I attended	
Nov. 4	Nathan Beebe Miller son to Thompson Miller aged	11 years
Oct. 24	Mr. Selden Marvin son to Dr. Marvin at Whitestown	23
Nov. 7	Mr. Stephen Emerson	75
Nov. 11	Mr. Eliphalet Brockway	54
Nov. 23	Capt. Ezra Ely	66
Decr 16	Mr. Samuel Rathbum	63
--	An infant daughter to Wm Sill	
Dec. 22	Revd George Beckwith - Burnt	90 2/3
31	Henry a child of Katta ? Ely fever & Canker	1
1794		
Feb: 1	a son of Wm Miller lamb-distemper	1
11	Calvin son to Richard Ely scarlet fever & Canker	1½
March 10	Benjamin Niles son to Capt. Ambrose Niles ditto	4½
19	Penelope Bump wife of John Bump smallpox	28
April 3	Mabel Butler daughter of John Butler fever & Canker	8½
14	Annah Sterlin wife of Saml Sterlin consumption	46
1795		
Feb: 12	An infant child of Saml & Eunice Sill	
March 10	Darcas Ely Daughter to Mr. James Ely consumption	
Oct. 5	Sarah Michel daughter of John Michel fever	21
Oct 24	Mrs. Sarah Marvin wife of Capt. Jim Marvin col & Alorbers	48
Nov. 17	Betty Miller daughter of Elisha Miller	3
1796		
Feb: 14	Stephen Ransom Cancer & consumption	73
June 4	Madm Sarah Beckwith old age	88
Sept.	Capt. Daniel Lord attended by Mr. Miner	59
Janr 9 1797	Hannah the wife of William Brockway Burn & a fit	
Jan: 31	James Fitch Stark a child of James Stark	3 months
Feb: 21	Alexander McCoy old age & Palsy	80
Feb: 22	Sally the wife of Daniel Ely child-birth	43
March 7	Capt. Harris Colt consumption on/Liver	66

[p. 91]

1797		
May 7th	Widow Lydia Griffin of Pattypague aged	85
May 22d	David Jewett son to David M. Jewet Esqr	2 2/3
June 18	Nathaniel Shaw Woodbridge Esqr consumption	26
July 1	an infant daughter of Erastus Selden	
Augt. 3	Miriam Burnham wife of Joseph Burnham	40
Augt. 29th	---- wife of John Rogers	24
July: 28	Thomas Sterling Drowned at sea	27
Nov: 29	--- wife of --- Dean of Millington Consumption	
Dec: 16	Rhuamana wife of Ebenr Tiffany nervous fever	69
1798 Deaths		
Janr - 17 -	widow --- Banning consumption	86
-- 26	Infant child of Cullick Ely's Jr.	
28	The wife of Henry Brown consumption	86
Feb: 25	Capt. William Brockway consumption	75
	Abigail Scovil consumption Abt	27
May 16	Mrs. --- Hathway --- consumption	28

EXTRACTED FROM THE CHURCH RECORDS

August 17	Allan Sullard Nervous Fever		17
Sept. 18	Mrs. Sarah Colt wife of Saml Colt chronic case		49
Nov: 16	Eleazer Mather Esqr Paralytic		82
1799			
January 13	Oliver a son to Ichobad Spencer conoulsion-fits		4
Feb. 13	Ebenezer Tiffany old age		83
Feb: 26	Deborah Brainard old age		98
March 24	Elijah Ely - drowned		57
	Rufus Porry - drowned		27
April 21	Robert Otis old age	about	92
26	Wd --- Wood old age	about	80
27	Elder Daniel Miner Palsy		63
May 28	Joseph Chapman killed by the fall of a tree		38
Spt: 18	Mr. Amma Ely swelling on his head		68
Oct: 4	Joseph Harvey Palsy & Putrid fever		80
Nov: 22	--- A child of Elihu Smith Inflamation in bowels		3 months
[p. 92]			
1799			
Dec: 4	Mrs. Catharine Marvin	aged	83
Oct:	An idiot child of Saml Sill		7
Dec: 28	A child of Dan Gillet		2
1800			
Janr 2	Mrs. Catharine Lord Consumption		82
-- 24	A child of Erastus Selden		7 months
Feb: 5	A child of Capt. Ambrose Niles		2 months
-- 16	A child of Ansyl Anderson worms & Fever		20 months
March 23	An infant child of Henry Brown Stillborn		
June 24	Joseph Lee Putrid - nervous fever		25
Oct: 13	Ebenr Rogers of the Gravel		74
22	Broadstreet Bacon consumption & old age		80
Decr 27	Fanny Dudley consumption		25
28	David Latimer mortification in his leg		21
1801			
Janr 24	Rebekah Ely consumption		20
Feb: 3	Valentine Miller consumption		62
	Grace Gillet wife of Dan Gillet consumption		43
May 2	Marvin Lord suddenly		55
June 1	An infant child of Wm Smith Jr.		

[p. 94]
Deaths AD 1806
1. a child of Benjamin Banning son					2 years
2. James Brockway (?) a native of this place died at E. Haddam
3. wife of Samuel Pecke - sudden - member of this church
4. daughter of John Maynard - 22
5. Mr. Abraham (?) Emerson 80
6. Robert Ely Hithing (?) aged 10 years
7. Amy Sill aged 16 years
8. Child of Ichabod Spencer aged five years
9. Ephriam Saunders aged 70
10. Capt Pratt very suddenly - 78 belonged to Saybrook - died here
11. Irabella Ely aged 26
12. Mr. Mackentosh

LYME, CONNECTICUT, VITAL RECORDS

Burials which I attended

1807
Jany 1   Molly Clark belonged to New Salem
Feb. 22   Isaac Butler aged seventy-five
    8-3   Sally Beckwith with a consumption
March 20   Mr. Joshua Hervey aged 89
                 Mrs. Brockway - of Mr. John Brockway - 75
                 Suddenly son of Isaac Sill's widow 5
                 Lucinda Rogers great Boy 14
April   child of Gideon Rogers & wife - 5 weeks old

Jan 2 1811 James Gould died of the Pleuresy
                 Jonathan Perkins of a consumption
                 Katharine Ely member died of a consumption at Dan Ely's
                 Abigail Ely died of a Typtus Fever 53
(Nov. 29 1811) wife of Capt. Ebenesar Brockway died with palsy
                 Samuel McCary's son - 10 years of age
                 Dinah - negro - Died of debility and old age about 90
                 David Comstock's child five weeks old died of fits
                 Allen W. Griffin's child stillborn
                 Jedidiah Brockway's twins - only few weeks old
                 Allan Bump's child Died of fits
                 Eloases (?) Ely child - soon after birth, or stillborn

[p. 158]   Funerals which I attended Time of Deaths Noted
AD 1815 March 23   the wife of Deacon Seth Ely
AD 1815 March 24   Benjamin Niles son of Deacon Ambrose Niles
AD 1815 June 25   Mr. Elihu Ely aged 77 of the typhus fever
AD 1816 Jan 17   A child of Elijah Brockway aged 5 months dropsy in head
AD 1816 March 17   Were lost in the Sound Capt. Elijah Ely's 3 children
AD 1816 March 17   Samuel Anderson Son of Maj Anderson lost in Sound
AD 1816 April 1st   Seth Barker child of Ely Perkins aged 10 months
AD 1816 April 4th   A daughter of Mr. Selden Warner aged 13 years Rickets
AD 1816 April 25   Mrs. Huntley wife of Seth Huntley
AD 1816 May 21st   Wife of Theophilus Lord typhus Fever aged 59 years
AD 1816 Aug. 30th   A child of Allen Griffin dead when born
AD 1816 Sept. 5th   Mahetabel Sill aged 27 consumption
AD 1816 Oct 20th   The wife of Gurdon Ely aged 61 [67] Typhus Fever
AD 1816 Oct 20th   The Widow Lay
AD 1817 Jan 22   A child of Charles Pilgrim aged 1 y measles
AD 1817   29   Capt. Christopher Ely aged 73 consumption
AD 1817 Feb 7th   Mr. Asabel Marvin aged 47 Fever
AD 1817 March 4th   Mr. John Reynolds aged 66 fever
AD 1817 April 3d   Mr. John Ely aged 36 Typhus Fever
AD 1817 April 30th   Child of Capt. John C. Ely aged 1 year
AD 1817 Sept 1st   Mrs. Johnson aged 86 once the wife of Rev. Mr. Johnson
                         pastor of chh [?]
AD 1817 Sept. 2   Wife of Mr. Samuel Stirling
AD 1817 Oct 19th   Mrs. Jemima Starling widow of Capt. Wm Starling aged 73
AD 1817 Oct 21   Deacon Elisha Marvin aged 75 consumption
AD 181[?]   Russel wood aged
AD 1818 April 1st   A child of Benjm Banning aged 8 years
AD 1818 April 19   Mrs. Mary Champlin aged 67 fever
AD 1818 June 3d   Mr. John Mitchel
AD 1818 June 4   Sarah Smith Comstock, Beebe aged 11 years [?]
                         daughter to Mr. Rodney Comstock consumption

EXTRACTED FROM THE CHURCH RECORDS 297

AD 1818	August 1st	Mr. Eleazar Ely aged 53 consumption
AD 1818	August 14th	Mrs. Ely wife of Mr. Cullick Ely aged 88 years
AD 1818	Sept. 21st	Abner Ely child of Abner S. Ely aged 15 months
AD 1818	Oct. 10th	Mr. Jacob Sterling aged 74 ashma
AD 1818	Oct 20th	Mr. George Warner aged 23 years fever
AD 1819	Feb. 18th	Annas Mitchel aged 64 consumption
AD 1819	Feb. 21st	Mrs. Peck
AD 1819	Feb. 15th	Mrs. Bettey Brockway wife of Mr. Benj Brock
AD 1819	May 25th	John Tucker aged

[p. 159]

AD 1819	Oct 21	Mrs. Betsey H. Bump wife of William Bump aged 40
AD 1819	Oct 5th	Miss Martha Ely sister to Mr. Gurdon Ely aged
AD 1820	Feb 7th	Mr. William Ely son of James Ely aged
AD 1820	Feb. 14th	A child of George Taylor Fanny aged 1 year
AD 1820	March 4th	Mrs. Rebecca Boon of Epilepsy aged
AD 1820	April 16th	David Wood son of [ ] Russel Wood aged 10 years
AD 1820	Oct 9th	Miss Hannh Ely sister of Mr. Gurdon Ely aged 55
AD 1820	Nov. 5th	Calvin Selden Esqr. aged 58 consumption
AD 1820	Dec. 16th	A child of --- Butler aged about 6 months
AD 1820	Dec	A child of Mr. Sylvester Cone few days old
AD 1820	Dec.	A child of Capt. Charles Harrison few days old
AD 1821	Jan 4th	Deacon Seth Ely Esqr. aged 86 years
AD 1821	[blot]	Moody Jewett by throwing himself from the house
AD 1821		Elisha Lord aged -- deranged and fever
AD 1821	1 July	Abraham Emerson fever aged 69 years
AD 1821		Lieut. Ichabod Spencer Dropsy
AD 1821		Dorcas Ely of consumption aged 18 years
AD 1821	Nov. 7	Miss Phebe Comstock aged 46 years
AD 1821	Nov. 30	Carloss Warner fever
AD 1822	Jan 30	Mr. Silas Wood
AD 1822	May 9th	Mr. Elihu Harrison aged 86 years
AD 1822	June 10th	Ebenezer Ely aged 11 years things evil son to Col Ely
AD 1822		Miss Mary Otis typhus fever aged
AD 1822	Nov. 6	Widow Butler old age aged 76
AD 1822	Nov. 6	Mrs. Phebe Marvin wife of Joseph Marvin
AD 1822	Nov. 6	Andrew Lord typhus fever aged 59
		son of Benj Lord aged 13 fever
AD 1822	Dec. 15	Maj. Thomas Anderson Palsy aged 76
AD 1823	Jan 2	A child of Mr. Boon
AD 1823	March 7th	The wife of Mr. Abner S. Ely of Dropsy aged 27
AD 1823	May 5th	The wife of Capt. Marshfied Leach aged 72
AD 1823	May 16th	Mr. Samuel Sterling aged 90 Palsy
AD 1823	June 22d	Miss Desiah Brockway aged 22 consumption
AD 1823		Benjamin Lord Junr. aged --- years fever
AD 1823	Oct. 21	Christopher Lord aged -- years fever
AD 1823	Oct. 24	Benjamin Lord senior aged -- years fever
AD 1823	Nov. 18	Augentus Lord aged 19 years fever
AD 1824	May	A child of David Brods soon after birth
AD 1824	May 31	Sally daughter of Robert Beckwith aged 4 years measls
AD 1824	July 5th	---son of
		-- Robinson aged 12 years

[p. 160]

AD 1824	Sept. 29	Eunice Sill aged 78
AD 1824	Oct. 17	Fanny Sill aged 27

AD 1824 Dec. 17   Uriah Clarke aged 24 Drowned
AD 1825   William Miner aged
AD 1825   Child of William Comstock aged 1 day
AD 1825   Wife of Wm Comstock aged 38 years
AD 1825 May 28   James Ely aged 81 Fever
AD 1825   Clarissa Dodett aged
AD 1825 Dec. 24   A child of Mr. Allaby aged 4 years
AD 1825 Dec. 29   Mrs. Lord mother of Reynold Lord aged 80
AD 1826 March   Miss Griffin Daughter of Benj Griffin
AD 1826 March   Widow Elihu Ely aged 82
AD 1826 Aug. 15th   Mrs. Sarah Ely wife of Mr. Horace Ely aged 48
AD 1826 Nov. 10th   Child of Benjamin Griffin aged 2 years
AD 1826 Nov. 6th   Widow Hudson aged
                       Mrs. Allaby [Maby]
                       Widow Jewet
AD 1827 May 3   Mr. Josiah Ely aged 76
AD 1827 May 17   Col William Starling consumption 59
AD 1827 May 23   A child of Barney Huntley whoping cough 2 y
AD 1828   A child of Mr. Smith
AD 1828   A child of Mr. -- Sampson
AD 1828 Dec. 25th   Mr. Richard Brockway aged 69 Dropsy
AD 1828 Dec. 28th   A child of Mr. Palmer aged few months
AD 1829 Feb. 3d   wife of Ichabod Spencer consumption aged 40
AD 1829 Feb 4th   Miss Esther Sterling Things-Evil aged 56
AD 1829 April 21st   Emma Ely daughter of Widow Dorcas Ely aged 24 years
AD 1829 Sep 13th   Mrs. Becket aged 70 died in Alms House
AD 1829 Oct 31   Widow Mary Anderson Aged 79
AD 1829 Dec 2d   Essi Ely son of Elisha Olcott Ely aged 21 years
AD 1829 Dec. 15th   Capt. Adriel Ely aged 84 years
AD 1830 May   Mrs. Peck
AD 1830 June 16th   Mrs. Tooker wife of Harvey Tooker aged 34 Dropsy
AD 1830 July 23d   Phebe H. Sterling aged 20 consumption
AD 1830   Widow Darrow aged 80
AD 1830 Dec. 26   Hiram Bill son of Lodowick Bill aged 20
AD 1831 June   A child of --- Hill
AD 1831 Sept.   Wife of Silas Brown aged 49 consumption
AD 1831 Octbr   Wife of Dr. Samuel Mather
AD 1831 Octbr   --- Wolfe consumption

Exerpts from the Selectmen's Book of Bills March, 1796 - Novr 6th 1809

May 1797	By a coffin for Thomson Miller's son 1 Dollar) By Ditto for McCoy 1.67)	2.67
	By extraordinary expenses on acct. of Alexr McCoy Nursing & funeral charges	17.17
August 1797	By Funeral expense for casar	3.60
	By Digging a Grave for Caesar Negro	1.00
	By coffin for Caesar Negro delivered at John Munsel	2.17
Feby 1798	By a coffin for Silas Wood's wife	1.--
Feby 1798	By Digging a Grave for Jabez DeWc"	1.--
1799 April	Lovina Brockway Born Feby. 12th 1792 to Thomas Way clothing included	26
	Ezra Brockway Born Jany 1, 1794 to Bridgham Lay clothing included	26
1799 June	By keeping and nursing Rachel Tinker from April 1st to May 4th - 199 and her Funeral expenses	11
1800 Jany	By making coffin for Sarah Jerom	2
	By digging a grave for Sarah Jerom	1
1800 April	By a coffin for Allen Chadwick 2.00 By ditto for Martha Leeve .43	2.43
	By digging grave for York Negro and Mary Marvin	2
	By a coffin for Joseph Belchers daughter	1
1800 June	By 4 qts rum for Mary Marvin's sickness and funeral 50 feet boards for her coffin Paint for ditto	1.00 .50 7
	winding sheet for Dan Chadwick	1.00 [d. 8-27-1798]
	By two loads of wood for Phinehes Wright in his last sickness	1
1800 Sept.	By coffin for Martha Tubbs	2
	By Digging Grave for Martha Tubbs and Stephen Hudson's wife [Stephen m Patience Bishop (m 7-26-1795)]	2
1800 Novr	Exra Brockway son of Woolston a med. visit	.50
1800 Decr	By Digging a Grave for Deborah Clark & other services	1.50
	By a coffin for Deborah Clark	2
1801 Jan'y	By a coffin for Gurdon Chadwick	2
1801 April	Lucy Alger died March 26th 1802	
	Hannah Hudson died March The -- 1802	
	Sarah Tubbs died April 26th 1801	

LYME, CONNECTICUT, VITAL RECORDS

1801 Novr	Jason Lee Junr Dr Contra By contracting by indenture to take bring up He Richard Baxter Manwaring a poor child to the age of 21 years which will be on the 10th day of April 1815	7
1801 Novr	By a coffin	2.00
	By digging a Grave for Jno Sanders Dec'd [John]	1.00
	By a coffin for David Havens	2.50
1802 May	By a coffin for Abigail [Reynolds] Blague [wife of James Blague]	2
1802 Novr 1	By a coffin for Jane Hacket	2
1803 Feby	By a coffin for Molly Phelps	2.17
1803 May	By a coffin for Mabel Hudson	2
1803 Nov.	Elizabeth McCrarey Dr Contra By keeping & supporting Lurana and Lucretia McCrarey Born May 8th 1797	11
1804 April	Elizabeth McCreasey Dr Contra By keeping Luceretia Beebe/alias/McCrarey 2 weeks at fifty cents	10.50
1804 August	By a coffin for Hannah Havens	2.50
1804 Augt	Peter Tubbs Dr Contra By keeping a child [son] of Joseph Youngs & your daughters [Lucy]	
1804 Decr 13	By grave clothes for Jno [John] Stocker Coffin for ditto	2.50 2.00
	By coffin for Ezekiel Beckwith	2.50
1805 Sept	By a coffin for Tim Saunders 94	2.11
1805 Septr	By a coffin for James Tucker By Digging a grave for Sarah Huntley	2.50 1
1805 Novr 4	By a Coffin for Elizabeth Clark	2.00
1806 Jany 15	By grave and herse for B. [Benja] White	
1806 April 7	By Coffin for Pomham	2
1806 June 2d	By Digging Grave for L. McIntosh	1
1806 Novr 3	By coffin for Jos [Joseph] Martin	.75
	By grave for [Thomas?] Towzer	1
1807 Feby	By grave cloaths for Isaac Butler	.83
1807 Feby	By carting corps of James Tucker from seaside to the [ ] Tucker's	2
1807 April 6	By grave hearse etc. Lucy Wade's funeral	2.50
1807 Sept 7	By coffin for Molly Tiffany	2.50
1808 April	By extra expense nursing Rich. Booge in his last sickness	6

MILITARY RECORDS

List of the Men who marched from Lyme "for the Relief of Boston in the Lexington Alarm," April, 1775:

Men's Names and Quality		Men's Names & Quality	Men's Names and Quality	
Joseph Jewett	Captain	Christopher Leach	Stephen Mosier	
David F. Sill	Lieut	Martin Wade	Allen McKnight	
Lee Lay	Lieut	Elisha Merron, Junr.	Samuel G. Dorr	
Daniel Lord	Ensign	William Lord	William R. Hyde	
Elisha Wade	Serjeant	John Coult, Junr.	Samuel DeWolf	
Ichabod Spencer	Serjeant	George Rowland	Giles Gilbert	
John Anderson, Junr.	Serjeant	Robert Dennison	Simon DeWolf	
Adriel Ely	Serjeant	Isaac Sill	Reynold Peck	
Elijah Selden	Serjeant	Adriel Huntly	Joshua Saunders	
Josiah Ely	Serjeant	Joseph Miner	Jacob Comstock	
Abraham Perkins	Serjeant	Benjamin Gale	Abner Brockway	
Josiah Ely	Corporal	Jonathan Miner	Lawrence Johnson	
Abraham Perkins, Junr	Corporal	Andrew Ely		
William Beckwith	Corporal	Micah Sill		
Joseph Sterling	Corporal	Stephen Ransom	Thomas Way, Junr.	Lieut.
Stephen Otis	Corporal	Daniel Havens	John Johnson	Ensign
John Saunders	Corporal	Elijah Phelps	Samuel Griswold	Serjeant
Ezra Sill	Private	John Congdon	Elisha Lee	Serjeant
Edward Dorr		Thaddeus Phelps	Andrew Griswold	Corporal
Job Tucker		Jasper Griffin, 3d	Enoch Smith	Private
Silas Marvin		Timothy Brainard	Stephen Sawer	Private
Stephen DeWolf		Levi Luther, Junr.		

from: RECORD OF CONNECTICUT MEN IN THE MILITARY AND NAVAL SERVICE DURING THE WAR OF THE REVOLUTION 1775-1783 pp. 16

LYME, CONNECTICUT, VITAL RECORDS

Colonial Wars

Burial Place	
Opposite Bill Hill School	Beckwith, Rev. George. Died 26 Dec. 1794 aged 92 (on tombstone) Church Record says he died 22 Dec. 1793. Served as Regimental Chaplain throughout French and Indian War. The original headstone was as follows: In memory of the Revd George Beckwith A.M. Pastor of the 3d Church of Christ in this town and late Member of the Corporation of Yale College Who died Dec. 26, 1794 in the 92d year of his age and 65th of his ministry Chaplain: References - State Library, War 5 - 276 Vols 9 & 10 of Conn. Historical Publications
Brockway's Ferry	Brockway, Edward - the son of Walston Jr. and Margaret, born 8 March 1698/9 Sergt 11 Co. 3d Regt in 1758. State Library War 5-2 1757. Conn. Hist. Col. Vol. 10, p. 69, 1758. Probably buried Brockway's Ferry.
	Brockway, Lieut John. Died 27 Nov. 1771 aged 81. Served in French and Indian War. 1st Co. 2 Regt in 1761. State Library Adams Papers. State Library War 9, 199.
	Brown, Nathaniel. Served in French and Indian War. His wife (1686-1777) is buried opposite Bill Hill School. Was in 4th Reg.t (4th Co) 1756. Conn. Hist. Col Vols 9 and 10. State Library War 6, 158B. & 731B.
	Clark, Thomas. His wife (1698-1734) buried in Ely Cemetery. He served in the French and Indian War in 14th Co. Col. Lyman's Reg.t in 1757. In 7th Co. 2d Reg.t in 1761. State Library - Adams Papers. State Library War 7, 31B & War 10, 31.
Selden Yard, Hadlyme	Comstock, James. Died 23 July 1773 in 38th year. Served in French and Indian War 6th Co. 3d Reg.t 1755 - Capt Hull's Co. in 1757. State Library War 7. 31B 32. State Library Adams Papers.
	Comstock, Samuel. His wife (1729-1750) is buried in Selden yard. He served in the French and Indian War, in 14th Co. Col. Lyman's Regt in 1757. 7th Co. 2d Regt in 1761. State Library Adams Papers. State Library War 7, 31B & War 10, 31.
Ely Ceme.	Ely, Daniel. Died in Service 9th Dec. 1762. Served in French and Indian War. State Library, War 10, 18.
Ely Ceme.	Ely, Joseph. Died 17 April 1762 in 46th Year. Served in French and Indian War. Was 2d Lieut. State Library War 5. 187 & War 7, 168.
Marvin Ceme.	Harvey, John. Died 23 Dec. 1767 in 92d year. Served in 2d Co. 2d Regt in French & Indian War in 1760. State Library, War 7, 70 and 9, 21 & Adams Papers

MILITARY RECORDS 303

Marvin Cemetery	Jewett, Cap.t Nathan. Died 10 Feb'y 1761 in 56d year. "Capt of a Milletary Company in Lyme" on stone. State Library War 5, 187 (1755) and War 6, 43B (1756)
Marvin Cemetery	Lord, John. Died 7 Jan. 1776 in 73d year. Served in French and Indian War in 3d Co. 3d Regt in 1756 --- 4th Co. 1st Regt in 1758 & 1762___ 12 Co. 1st Reg.t in 1759. 2d Co. 1st Regt in 1761. State Library, War 5, 320, 34A. War 9, 204. War 10. 19. 20A and Adams Papers.
Marvin Cemetery	Marvin, Capt. Elisha. Died 31 Dec. 1801 in 85th year. Military Service proven by will also inscription on his sword still preserved.
Marvin Cemetery	Selden, Samuel. Died 28 Feb. 1745 in 50th year. "Capt of 3d Co. of Foot in Lyme" on stone.

Revolutionary War

References given are all from the book Record of Connecticut Men in the War of the Revolution War of 1812 and War with Mexico.

Anderson, Thomas. Born Feb. 18, 1747 Died 15 Dec. 1822 aged 75 on stone. Vital Statistics say he was born 1749. Corp. 1st Co. 6th Regt 1775. Serg.t Jan 1, 1777. Appointed Lr. Mr. June 1778. 1st Lieut June 1779.

Marvin Cemetary Lieut Capt Dorrance Co. 1781-83. Member Society of Cincinnati. Pp. 72, 145, 146, 343, 348, 375 & 632.

Beckwith, Samuel. 1st Co. 6th Regt in 1775. Page 72. Has son buried in Pleasant View.

Beebe, Abner. In Capt Mather's Co. from Lyme at New London in 1776. Page 621. Has two wives buried in Selden Cemetary.

Bill, Benejah. Born 1760 Died 22 May 1842. Service shown only by pension - pp. 660-661.

Ely Cem. Bramble, Robert. Died 18 April 1845 aged 83. Capt. Mirl's Co. Waterbury's Brigade in 1781. Pp. 571, 655, 661.

Joshua-town Cemetary Brockway, Benjamin Born 1746. Died 17 Dec. 1830. Service shown in Pension list page 633.

Brockway, John. Born 1755, died 27 Nov. 1841. Service shown in Pension lists pp. 655-661.

Brockway, Capt. Zebulon. Born 1760 Died 16 March 1837. Service shown in pension list page 665.

Stone in Pleasant View Church, Edward. In Capt Holmes East Haddam Co. 4th Battalion. Killed in retreat from New York 15 Sept. 1776. Pp. 404, 400 -

Church, John. 3d Corp. Col Mather's Lyme Co. 1776. Capt Kirtland's Co. New London 1777 Pp. 613, 621. Wife buried in Selden Cemetary.

Selden Cemetary Comstock, Abner (Capt). Born 1727. Died 22 March 1811. In Capt Mather's Co. from Lyme 1776. Capt in Lt. Col Storr's Regt of Militia in Fall of 1776. Pp. 621, 631.

Dorr, Edmond. Served as mariner on State Man-of-War "Oliver Cromwell" at Saybrook in 1778. Page 597. Wife and daughter buried in Marvin Cemetary.

Ely Cemetary Ely, Aaron. Stone in Ely Cemetary as follows - In Memory of James Ely who died May 12 1776 age 47 years. Also his son Aaron who fell in battle near Kingsbridge in defence of American Independence in the year 1776 in the 24th year of his age.

Ely Cemetary	Ely, Adriel Born 1744 Died 13 Dec. 1829 age 85. Lexington Alarm 1775. 2d Lieut Capt Kirtland's Co. Wolcott's Regt New London Feb. 1777 Pp. 16, 613.
Ely Cemetary	Ely, Abner Born 1749 Died 2 Jan. 1805 age 56. Sergt 8 Co. 6 Regt. April 1775. commissioned Ensign 12 March 1777. 6th Reg.t Conn. Line 1777-1781. Pp. 76. 206.
Ely Cemetary	Ely, Capt. Christopher Born 1743 Died 28 Jan. 1817 in 74th year. Lieut 1st Co. 6th Regt. 1775. Capt. in 1777 in Col. Parson's Regt. Pp. 72, 99, 146.
Ely Cemetary	Ely, Major Daniel. Died 14th March 1776 in 83d year. Was in 1st Co. 6 Regt in 1775 (Probably also Colonial. as his father Daniel Ely was killed in service 9 Dec. 1762 in same Co. same Reg.t) page 72.
Ely Cemetary	Ely Elihu Born 15 Nov. 1737 Died 25 June 1815. Lieut in Capt Caulkins Co. from Lyme. Col. Latimer's Regt at Saratoga in 1777. Page 505.
Both in Ely Cemetary	Ely Elisha Died 12 July 1786 in 56th year. Surgeon's Mate in Col Parson's 10th Continental Reg.t in 1776. Appears as Surgeon of Col. Webb's (19th) Regt after July 29. On page 99 in book but omitted from printed index.
	Ely Josiah Born 20 July 1739 Died 27 April 1827. Lexington Alarm - page 16.
Marvin Cemetary	Griffin, Abner Born 29 March 1741 Died 23 March 1790. 2d Lieut under Col. John Ely State Regt under Spencer and Wolcott in Rhode Island and Conn. 1776-1777. Pp. 424.
Griffin Cemetary	Griffin Jasper Born 10 Dec. 1726 Died 21 Jan. 1818. In Capt Joseph Jewetts Co. from Lyme. 8th Regt 1775 - In battle of Long Island 1776. Pp. 89, 102.
	Griffin Jasper 3d Born 28 Feb. 1754 Died 19 Jan. 1777 age 23. Lexington Alarm. Page 16.
Marvin Cemetary	Griffin, Major John Born 10 May 1737 Died 2 Sept. 1791. Lieut in 1776 in Army on State "Man-of War" Oliver Cromwell" at Saybrook 1778. Pp. 100, 597 and 631.
Griffin Cemetary	Griffin, Joshua Born 25 Feb. 1752 Died 4 June 1831 In Capt Mather's Co. from Lyme. At Fort Trumbull, New London July 1776 Page 621.
Marvin Cemetary	Jewett, Capt Joseph Born 13 Dec. 1732 Died in service 29 Aug. 1776 Capt 8 Co. 8th Reg.t Capt of Lyme Co. at Lexington Alarm 1775. Mortally wounded and taken prisoner at Battle of Long Island 27 Aug. 1776 - died two days later. Pp. 16, 89, 101 Was son of Nathan and Deborah Jewett who are buried in Marvin Yard.
Pleasant View Cemetery	Lee, Capt. Abner Born 26 Oct. 1726 Died 3 Nov. 1809 In Sanford's Co. 5 Regt 1771 and 1783 Beebe's Co. Enos Regt on the Hudson in 1778. Pp. 346, 542.
Pleasant View Cemetery	Lee, Dan Died 7 Dec. 1831 age 71 Served in 1st Co. 6th Reg.t Serj.t of Co. for defence of Lyme in 1779. Pp. 72, 629, 635.
	Lord, Capt. Abner Born 9 March 1733 Died 12 Nov. 1790. Capt. from Lyme under Col. Ely. 4th Battalion 1776-1777. In Capt Mather's Co. at New London July 1776. Pp. 151, 424.
	Lord, Abner. Died 12 Sept. 1823 age 65. "A Patriot of and Soldier of the Revolution on Stone".

MILITARY RECORDS   305

Bill Hill School	Lord, Capt. Daniel. Born 12 Oct. 1736 Died 21 Sept. 1796 Ensign Capt. Joseph Jewetts Co. from Lyme Lexington Alarm 1775 Page 16.
Burnham Cemetery	Lord, Joseph. Born 11 March 1727. Died 13 March 1788. In Capt Mather's Lyme Co. at New London July 1776 Page 621.
Selden Cemetary	Luther, Levi. Died 28 July 1837 age 80. Under Capt Joseph Jewett of Lyme 8th Co. 8th Reg.t Pp. 89, 656.
Marvin Cemetary	Marvin Joseph Born 14 Feb. 1755 Died 18 Nov. 1839 In Capt Mather's Co. from Lyme at Fort Trumbull New London July 1776. Pp. 621, 656.
Bill Hill School	Mather, Samuel M.D. Died 17 May 1834 age 92. Appointed in October 1776 to go to Conn. Troops in the Jersey's with medicines, ect. Pages 628, 656.
Caulkins Yard	Otis Robert Born 10 May 1764 Died 7 Dec. 1826 Enlisted in Ely's Co. 1st Regt in 1777 for 3 years. Re-enlisted. At Peekskill and Valley Forge in 1781. Capt Donglas Co. 5th Regt Conn Line. In Virginia from April to November under the command of Marques de la Fayette Pp. 152, 349, 354.
Ely Cemetary	Perkins, Abraham Died 10 May 1786 in 73d year. Serjt in Capt Jewett's Co. at Lexington Alarm. Page 16. Perkins, Abraham Jr. Born 7 Aug. 1745 Died 15 April 1824. Corporal in Capt Joseph Jewett's Co. at Lexington Alarm 1775 Page 16.
Selden Cemetary	Phelps Samuel Died 5 June 1842 age 81. Served one year from March 1778 as mariner and carpenter on board Privateer Sampson, Capt. David Brooks, From Conn. River. Wounded in fight with British Sloop "Swallow" Moved to New York after the war but in Conn. in census of 1818. Pp. 631, 636.
Griffin Cem.	Rogers, Gideon Born 14 Jan. 1761 Died 5 June 1842 In 1st Regt Conn. Line 1779-80 Pp. 156, 656, 661.
Stone in Marvin Yard	Selden, Elijah Cap.t Jewett's Co. Lexington Alarm 1775. Sergt in 10th Continental Reg.t In Long Island, New York and up the Hudson to Peekskill. Serjt. Pp. 16, 100, 637. His wife is buried in Selden Cemetary. Selden Ezra Capt. Died in service 9th of December 1784 Serjt in Co. 1. 6th Reg.t 1775 2d Lieu.t Cont. 1776-1777 Adjutant and Capt 1st Reg.t 1777-1781. Wounded at Stony Point July 1779; furloughed home; re-joined his Regiment in 1780. Pp. 72, 99, 367, 242, 145-6. 338 & 374. Wife buried in Marvin yard.
Selden Cemetary	Selden Col. Samuel Died 11 Oct. 1776 in 52d year. Col. of 4th Reg.t in 1776 stationed on East River when British attacked New York 15 Sept. 1776. Taken prisoner on above date, above 34th St. and died a prisoner in New York City 11 October 1876. Page 403. On Headstone.
Selden Cem.	Selden, Capt. Samuel Born 1 Nov. 1748 Died 7 Sept. 1819 Lieu.t Col. Canfield's Reg.t at West Point 1781. Page 582.
Caulkins Cemetary	Sill, Isaac Born 20 April 1749 Died 19 Dec. 1806 In Capt. Joseph Jewett's Co. from Lyme at Lexington Alarm 1775. In Col Canfield's Militia Reg.t at West Point 1781. Pp. 16, 582.
Marvin Cem.	Sill, Micah Born 25 Dec. 1751 Died 10 Dec. 1782 In Capt. Joseph Jewett's Lyme Co. Lexington Alarm 1775. Page 16.

LYME, CONNECTICUT, VITAL RECORDS

Ely Cemetary	Spencer, Ichabod Lieut. Died 25 Sept. 1821 age 74 years. "An officer on the Revolutionary War" on headstone. In Capt Joseph Jewett's Co. 1775- Lexington Alarm. 2d Lieut 1778. First Reg.t at Penn. Valley Forge, Germantown, Ect. in assault at Stony Point 15 July 1779. 2d Lieut Capt Bingham's Co. 5th Reg.t 1781-1783. Lieut Provisional Reg.t of 1781. Pp. 16, 146, 242, 621, 636, ect.
Old Sisson Family Yard Norwich Road	Sisson, Capt. Jonathan Died 8 Dec. 1833 Age 80 Service only shown in pension list, of 1840 - pension to Elizabeth Sisson Lyme - age 86 in 1840. Her gravestone beside that of Capt. Jonathan's is as follows: In memory of Mrs. Elizabeth wife of Capt. Jonathan Sisson who died October 9, 1842 age 88.
Caulkins Cem.	Tillotson, Dr. George. born Nov. 4, 1754 Died 4 October 1838. In Cap.t Mather's Lyme Co. at Fort Trumbull, New London in July 1776. Pp. 621, 656.
Selden Cem.	Warner, Lieut John. Died 23 Feb. 1810 in 82d year. In Capt Holmes Co. Col. Selden's 4th Battalion - in 1776. Lieut in 2d Militia Reg.t Pp. 404, 625.
Selden Cem.	Warner, Selden. Died 1 March 1843 age 82 In Col Canfield's Militia Reg.t at West Point in Sept. 1781 - from East Haddam Pp. 582, 656.
Joshua- town Cem.	Wood, John Died 26 April 1845 age 88 Served as Seaman on State Man-of- War "Oliver Cromwell" from Saybrook 1778. Page 596, 661.

War of 1812

References given from same book as for Revolutionary Services   See page 11

The services of the soldiers from the Town of Lyme were divided between the following companies: viz:

Capt. Peter Lord - who was from south part of town
Capt. Samuel C. Selden - from Hadlyme
Capt. Lynde Reed - from New London
Capt. Charles P. Miller from New London
Capt. Charles Harrison from New London
and these Captains all served under Lt. Col. Asa Comstock Jr. of New London.

Name William Reynolds   Rank Private
enlisted January 18, Died in the Army
Military headstone in Hamburg Churchyard

Commander Peter Bradley   Reference Page 162
1813 25th Infantry the 3d of December 1813
Was the only soldier listed in the Regular Army, in the War of 1812.
The following were volunteers.

Anderson, Marsh E. Died 16 Nov. 1876 age 81 Buried Ely Cem. Private under Col. Samuel Selden. Page 5.

Beckwith Josiah. Died 16 Feb. 1813 aged 65. Buried in Burnham Yard Bill Hill. Private under Peter Lord. Page 13.

Brockway, David. Died 5 Feb. 1830 age 60. Buried Marvin Cem. Private under Miller - and Harrison. Page 21.

Brockway, Ezekiel Died 28 Feb. 1862 age 86. Buried Brockway's Ferry. Served under Selden - Private. Page 21.

MILITARY RECORDS

Brockway Ezra. Died 1876 80 Buried Selden Cem. Private under Selden, page 21

Brockway Jedidiah (Capt. on stone) Died 1852 age 66 Buried Selden Cem. Private under Selden.

Brockway Dr. John C.M. 1784-1846. Buried in Hamburg. Assistant Surgeon under Lt. Col. Asa Comstock, Jr. Page 21.

Brockway Richard C. Born 1 Oct. 1793. Died 15 Aug. 1838 Buried in Selden Cem. Musician under Selden. Page 22.

Brockway Rodney - Died 2 June 1837 age 52. Buried Marvin Cem. Corp. under Miller. Sergt under Harrison Page 22.

Comstock Oliver. Died 11 Feb. 1843 age 70 Buried Hadlyme Ferry. Private under Comstock Page 38.

Ely Abner S. Died 22 March 1866 age 76. Corp. and Sergt. under Selden. Buried in Hamburg page 50.

Ely Eliab - Died 29 Aug. 1853 age 74. Buried Ely Cem. Private under Lord. Page 50.

Ely Elias Died 8 Feb. 1873 age 83. Buried Ely Cem. Private under Lord. Page 50.

Ely John Died 17 April 1817 age 36 Buried Hamburg. Private under Miller and Harrison. Page 50.

Ely Marsh Major Died 2 Nov. 1835 age 74. Major under Comstock. Buried in Ely Cem. Page 50.

Gillet Dan M. Died 25 Aug. 1836 age 46. Buried Gillet Yard Grassy Hill. Private under Lord and Selden. Page 57.

Harrison, Charles Major (on stone) Died 1843 age 65. Buried Hamburg Cem. Corp. under Comstock. 1st Lieut under Miller. Page 63.

Harvey Samuel Died 4 Sept. 1819 age 37 Buried Selden Cem. Private under Lord and Selden. Page 63.

Huntley Silas. Died 6 Oct. 1832 age 55. Buried in Caulkins Cem. Sergt. under Reed. Page 71.

LaPlace Francis Died 1863 age 63. Buried Joshuatown Cem. Corp. under Selden. Page 79.

Lester James Died March 5 1891 age 99. Buried Hamburg Cem. "A Veteran of the War of 1812" on stone. Private under Miller and Harrison. Page 81.

Lord Peter Capt. Died 26 Dec. 1833 age 60 years. Inscription on Dr. Burr monument in Hamburg Cem. Captain under Lt. Col. Comstock. Page 83

Luther Ansel Died 1857 age 82. Buried Selden Cem. Sergt. under Selden. Page 84.

Luther John 1781-1864 Buried Luther Cem. Private under Harrison and Miller. Page 84.

Marvin William Died 15 Apr. 1876 age 88. Buried Hamburg Cem. Q.M. and Q.M. Sergt under Col. Comstock. Page 86.

Mitchell John Died 1857 age 79. Musician under Selden. Buried Selden Cem. Page 90.

Otis, Edward. Born 6 Feb. 1798 Died 8 May 1873 Buried in Marvin Cem. Private under Comstock Page 95

Peck Timothy Died 6 Nov. 1848 age 55 Buried Burnham Yard Bill Hill Sergt under Lord. Page 99

Phelps Roswell Died 29 Aug 1825 age 37 Sergt. under Selden Page 101 Buried in Selden Cem.

LYME, CONNECTICUT, VITAL RECORDS

Phillips Benjamin Died 12 Sept. 1813 at 24 Joshuatown Cem. Private under Selden

Ransom Richard Died 25 Aug. 1836 age 46. Buried Gillet Family Yard Grassy Hill. Private under Peter Lord. Page 105.

Royce David. served as private under Reed. His wife is buried in Caulkins Cem. with grave marked with plain stone at side. Page 110.

Royce Ruel Died 15 April 1829 age 86. Buried Caulkins Cem. Musician under Reed. Page 110

Selden Samuel C. Died 1852 age 65 Buried in Selden Cem. Captain under Col. Comstock Page 112.

Sill Samuel Died 14 Nov. 1871 age 80 Buried Pleasant View Cem. Private under Reed. Page 114

Sisson Oliver Died 14 Nov. 1871 age 85 Buried in Pleasant View Cem. Corp. under Miller and Corp under Harrison Page 114.

Smith Nathan Served as Sergt. under Harrison and Lieut. under Miller. Page 116. His wife is buried in Pleasant View Cem.

Spencer Austin Died 12 Dec. 1834 Buried Hadlyme Ferry Private under Comstock Page 118.

Spencer William 1788-1871 Buried Hadlyme Ferry Sergt. under Selden Page 118.

Stark, Abiel Died 26 July 1837 Buried Pleasant View Cem. Sergt. under Miller. Page 119.

Stark Christopher Died 7 Dec. 1879 age 91 Stone in Pleasant View Cem. where wife and child are buried. Private under Selden. Page 119.

Tittotson William Died 18 May 1834 age 51 Buried Caulkins Cem. Corporal under Reed. Page 125.

Warner Ebenezer Died 1871 age 81 Buried Joshuatown Cem. Musician under Selden. Page 130.

Warner Samuel Selden Died 1 April 1868 age 79 Adjutant under Col. Comstock. Buried Selden Cem. Page 131.

Willcox, Hazard. Died 17 March 1874 age 87 Buried Pleasant View Cem. Private under Reed. Page 136.

The War with Mexico

Records show only 4 from Lyme
References to Book - see page 11 (Record of Connecticut Men in the War of the Revolution, War of 1812 and War with Mexico.)

Cobb, Wm. H. Died 27 Nov. 1747 in service. Co F. 9th Reg.t Page 173 Stone in Hamburg Cem.

Harrison William B. Died 14 July 1848 in service. Co. D. 12 Infantry. Page 170 - Stone in Hamburg Cem.

Lord, George F. Served from 13 June 1844 to 13 June 1849 Co. C. 6th Inf. Page 176.

Peck Joshua Served 11 May 1848 to 20 June 1848 General Service Page 177

Civil War

Services generally engraved on headstones. All others are proven in the book: Record of Connecticut Men in War of Rebellion 1861-1860

Anderson Frank W. Died 27 June 1891 age 49 Sergt Co. 1, 9th Regt Conn. Vols. Buried Ely Cem. Page

Bogue Edwin H. Died Nov 1 1862 Co. K. 11th Regt Ct. Vol. Buried Selden Cem.

Bogue Joseph Died March 27, 1907 Age 68. Co. C. 26 Inf. Conn. Vol. Buried Pleasant View Cem.

Bogue Samuel L. Died 24 Sept. 1863 Co. F. 26th Reg.t Ct. Vol. Buried Selden Cem.

Brockway E. Plutarch Died Sept. 19, 1904 age 59 yrs. Co. M. 1st Ct. Cav. Ct. Vol. Buried Hamburg Cem.

Brockway William S. Died 26 Nov. 1874 age 76 Co. A. 10th Reg.t Inf. Ct. Vol. Buried Joshuatown Cem.

Bill John Oscar of Hartford, Ct. Died 10 July 1870 age 32 Co. A. 10th Reg.t Inf. Ct. Vol. Buried Hamburg Cem.

Bogue Jabez Died 5 June 1864 Co. I. 18th Inf. Co. K. 11th Reg.t Ct. Vol. Buried Selden Cem.

Bogue William H. 1844-1923 Co. F. 26th Regt Inf. Ct. Vol. Buried Griffin Cem.

Brockway Hugh B. 1829-1926 2d Lieut Co. D 1st Cav. Ct. Vol. Buried Hadlyme Ferry.

Brockway, Thomas Clark 1831-1895 Co. C. 18th Regt Ct. Vol. Buried Hamburg Cem.

Brooks Augustus Died in service 10 July 1863 Co. F. 26 Inf. Ct. Vol. Stone with wife in Hartford

Chapel John O. Was killed at Port Hudson June 14 1863 age 27. Co. a 26 Conn Pleasant View Cemetary

Comstock Charles S. Died 4 Feb. 1914 age 80 (in Essex) Co. D. 1st Regt C.V. Cav. Buried Selden Cem.

DeWolf John F. Co. K. 1st Conn. Cav Died at City Point Va. June 26, 1864 age 20 Buried Pleasant View Cem.

DeWolf Thomas E. Co. E. 18th Reg.t Ct. Vol. Wounded at Winchester Va. Died June 18, 1864 Ae 24 Buried Pleasant View Cem.

Ely Ansel R. Co. L. 1st Conn. Cav. killed at Five Forks Virginia April 1st 1865 - age 22 years. On stone Hamburg Cem.

Geer John A. 1821-1895 Corp. Co. F. 26th Regt. Ct. Vol. Buried Hadlyme Ferry Cem.

Hall, Charles H. Died April 23, 1917 74 Co. I. 18th Inf. Ct. Vol. Buried Joshuatown Cem.

Hall Harvey 1832-1907 Feb 27 '76 Co. I. 18th Inf. Ct. Vol. Buried Joshuatown Cem.

Hall, William S. Died 1894 age 53 Co. I. 18 Inf. Ct. Vol. Buried Joshuatown Cem.

Harrison, Corp. Charles W. Died 1901 Co. F. 26th Reg.t Ct. Vol. Buried Selden Cem.

Johnson Henry Phelps April 19, 1842 - Feb 23, 1923 Co. F. 26th Reg.t Ct. Vol. Buried in Selden Cem.

Johnson, William Henry Died 21 April, 1922 age 78 yr. Co. M. 2d Art. Ct. Vol. Buried Grassy Hill Cem.

Kingsbury - Col. Henry W. Col. 11 Conn. Killed 17 Sept. 1862 at Antietam, Md. Stone Hamburg, Cem.

Luther John Died 1901 age 75 Co. F. 26th Regt Ct. Vol. Buried Luther Cem.

Luther Orrin M. from East Haddam Died Aug. 1863 at Fort Sumpter. Co. F. 26th Reg.t Ct. Vol. Stone in Luther Cem.

Martin William. Died May 11, 1865 - Age 52 Co. A. 26th Regt Ct. Vol. Stone in Hamburg Cem.

Miner, Charles Died 6 Nov. 1880 age 68 Co. F. 26th Reg.t Ct. Vol. Buried in Caulkins Cem.

Miner, Charles H. Died New Orleans 13 Jan. 1863 @ 27 Co. F. 26th Reg.t Inf. Ct. Vol. Stone in Selden Cem.

Morgan John (Dr.) Born 17 Aug. 1845 Died 28 Aug. 1920 Co. C. 26th Regt Ct. Vol. Buried Selden Cem.

Palmer, Noyes W. Died 12 July 1863 in service. Co. F. 26th Inf. Ct. Vols. Stone in Hamburg Cem.

Parker, Capt. Henry L. Jan. 11-1843-Dec. 16 1892 Co. K. 10th Reg.t Ct. Vol. Buried Hamburg Cem.

Perkins Thomas D. Died at Fortress Monroe 10 July 1862 age 18 Co. D. 1st Conn. Art. Ct. Vol. Stone in Pleasant View Cem.

Phelps, John H. 1844-1917 Co. G. 13th Reg.t Ct. Vol. Buried Hadlyme Ferry Cem.

Phelps, Maro 1844-Nov. 1, 1926 86 Co. D. 22 Reg.t Ct. Vol. Buried Hadlyme Ferry Yard.

Rathbun, Benjamin 1845-1900 Nov. 28, 1905 60 Co. D. 12th Regt Conn. Vol. Buried Hadlyme Ferry Cem.

Reynolds John Died 19 Oct. 1864 Age 30 Co. C. 18th Reg.t Ct. Vol. Buried Griffin Cem.

Rogers, Niles S. Born 11 May 1840 Died 25 Oct. 1899 Co. F. 26th Reg.t Ct. Vol. Buried Grassy Hill Cem.

Sawyer, Charles. Died 4 March 1873 age 36 Co. M. 1st Regt Ct. Cav. Buried Hamburg Cem.

Slate, John T. 1841-Apr. 11 1911 69 Co. F. 26th Regt Ct. Vol. Buried Griffin Cem.

Sleuman William E. 1841-1911 Co. D. 1st Reg.t Ct. Vol. Co. D 1 Heavy Art. Buried Griffin Cem.

Tooker John 1818-1904 Co. F. 26 Regt Ct. Vol. Buried Joshuatown Cem.

Tucker, Chester Died Oct. 1 1903 Age 64 Co. L. 1st Regt Cav. Ct. Vol. Buried Pleasant View Cem.

Warner Ulysses S. Died 1 July 1863 in service Co. F. 26th Reg.t Ct. Vol. Stone Joshuatown Cem.

Warner, David W. Died 1895 - age 69 Lieut Co. C. 9th Inf. Ect. Buried Joshuatown Cem.

Way, Henry C. Died Jan. 1901 age 69 Co. C. 26th Regt Ct. Vol. Buried Griffin Cem.

Way Horace J. from Salem May 6-1827 -6 Sept. 1907 Co. C. 26th Regt Ct. Vol. Buried Pleasant View Cem.

Wood Nathaniel M. 1826-1863 Co. F. 26 Reg.t Ct. Vol. Buried Griffin Cem.

Wood John Norris 1847-1908 Co. M. 13th N.Y. Cav. Buried Hamburg Cem.

ADDENDA

LLR2:7A	John Benit ye son of Caleb Benit was married unto Mary Mose (cut off) (September _____) died December 6. Birth of children of the above Sd John and Mary his wife Joseph their son was born ye 20 Day of April _____ The above John Bennit died ye 6 day of Decembr ____( ) The above written Mary Benit wife of ye above sd John Benit Dyed _____
LLR4:74	A deed from Aaron Huntley to his son Aaron proves that Aaron Senior's wife was Marah Champion 2nd not Marah Chamberlain as named LLR 2:78 "- - - in my father Champion's lot"
LLR2:8A	Joseph Lord deceased the 25 of November 1687
LLR2:375	Petter Pratt was married to methitabell his now wife the 7th September August 2(___11) (year blotted out) (1709) Elizabeth Pratt their Daughter was born 24 Jualy 1711 Mehetabell prat thayr Daughter was boin 3 Day of octob: 1712 (Methitabell wife of Petter is named as dau. of Isaac Watrous. Sen._____ see LLR 2:40)
LLR2:300	omitted from entry Page 256 Samuel Reed son of John and Deborah (Niles) Reed borne 11 December 1709
LLR2:246 LLR2:362	Deed of sale from Richard Royce to Joseph Peck names wife of Richard Royce as Sarah Perego daughter of Robert
LLR2:252	Arter Shofel was borne the 3 of January 1691/2 (listed under children of Nathaniel Hudson and Rachel his wife) (son of Rachel by her first husband Arter Scovel) -- relationship supplied by H. W. Brainard
Vol 1:38	Rachel Presson Daughter of James and Anna Preson was born the 10th Day of Novembr 1789
LLR9:162	Margaret Woods deed from her father James Preston 12 April 1788 A.D.
Vol 1:150	Esther Marvin, Widow of Thomas Lord m [Jonathan] Emmons [of East Haddam] & d Feb 3, 1792 [in E. Haddam]
LLR1:54	Elizabeth m. Richard Smith Jr. Nov 17, 1677 [Elizabeth Lay dau. of John[1]]
LLR1:52	Elizabeth Smith m. William Ely, May 24, 1681 [dau. of Simon of Haddam identified in E. Haddam Records]

*indicates name appears more than once on a page.

ACKLEY, Lucy m Gideon Rogers, 64
ADAMS, Solomon J., 165
ADGIT (see under AGCET, ADSET)
ADSET, ADSIT, ADSOT
  Deborah d Stephen & Luce, 59
  Joseph s Stephen & Luce, 59
  Mary m Samuel Chadwick, 16
  Sarah d Stephen & Luce, 59
  Stephen s John, 217
  Stephen m Luce Chadwick, 59
AGET, AGECT, AGEET, AGGET
  Benjamim alias Adgit s John, 217
  Ebenezer s John & Abigail, 1, 2, 14*
  John m Abigail Graves, 14
  Mary d John, 217
  Molly d John & Abigail, 14
  Samuel s John, 217
  Sarah d John (1717), 217
  Sarah d John & Abigail, 14
  Stephen s John, 217
ALBEE, Benjamin m Lydia Otis, 138
  Benjamin s Benjamin & Lydia, 138
  Calvin s Benjamin & Lydia, 138
  John Danford s Benjamin & Lydia, 138
  William s Benjamin & Lydia, 138
ALGER, ALGUR
  Agnice w of Elijah Greenfield Alger, 37
  Ashbell s of Simeon & Mary, 23
  Benjamin s John & Mary, 217*
  Dan s Jonathan & Lydia, 10
  David s Roger & Sarah, 218*
  Elijah s Roger & Elizabeth, 6
  Elijah s Greenfield & Lucy, 11
  Elijah-Greenfield s Elijah & Agnice, 11, 37
  Elisha s Johnathan & Irene, 10
  Elisha s Jonathan & Irene, 10*, 217*
  Elisha s Jonathan & Lydia, 10*
  Elizabeth w of Roger died, 217
  Elizabeth d Jonathan & Irene 9, 217*
  Elizabeth d Jonathan & Irene, 9*
  Elizabeth d of Roger & Elizabeth, 6
  Elizabeth d of Greenfield & Lucy, 11
  Eunice d of Simeon & Mary, 23
  George s of Jonathan & Irene, 217, 10
  Greenfield m Lucy Wade, 11*
  Greenfield s Roger & Elizabeth, 6
  Greenfield m Mehetable Hayes, 11
  Hannah d Roger & Elizabeth, 6
  Irene d Jona & Lydia, 10
  James s Roger & Sarah, 218
  Joanna d John & Temperance, 217
  John m Mrs. Luce DeWolf, 56*
  John s John & Mary, 217
  John m Temperance Tillotson, 217
  John s John s & 2nd w Mary, 217*
  John (twin) s John & Mary, 217
  Jonathan m Grane (Irene) Way, 217, 9
  Jonathan s Roger Jr. & Sarah, 218
  Jonathan m Lydia Hudson, 10
  Jonathan s Jonathan & Lydia, 10
  Joseph m Mary Huntly, 217
  Joseph s Roger & Sarah, 218
  Joseph s Joseph & Mary, 217
  Joseph s Jonathan & Lydia, 10
  Lucy Wade Alger died, 299, 11
  Lydia d Jonathan & Irene, 10

ALGER, cont.
  Lydia m Stephen Smith, 65
  Mary d John & 2nd wife Mary, 217
  Mary II d John & 2nd wife Mary, 217
  Mary (twin) d John & 2nd wife Mary, 217
  Matthew s John & Temperance, 217
  Mehitable wife Roger died, 11
  Nathan s John & Temperance, 217*
  Nathaniel s Jonathan & Lydia, 10
  Patience d Greenfield & Mehitable, 11
  Richard Hayes s Greenfield & Mehitable, 11
  Roger Sr. m Elizabeth, 218
  Roger Jr. m Elizabeth Greenfield, 6
  Roger Jr. m Sarah Stolen, 218
  Roger s Roger Jr. & Sarah, 218*
  Roger s Greenfield & Lucy, 11
  Ruth m John Robins, 257
  Ruth d Jonathan & Lydia, 10
  Ruth d Roger & Sarah, 217
  Sarah d Roger Jr. & Sarah, 217
  Sarah d Jonathan & Irene, 10
  Sarah d Jonathan & Lydia, 10
  Sarah m John Scoffell, 260
  Seth s John & Mary, 217
  Silas s John & Mary, 217
  Simeon s Roger & Sarah, 218
  Simeon m Mary Hodge, 23
  Stoten s Simeon & Mary, 23
  Susannah d Jona & Lydia, 10
  Temperance w of John died, 217
  William s of Jonathan & Lydia, 10
  William Greenfield s Greenfield & Mehitable, 11
ALLEN, ALIN, Alexander m Mary Chadwick, 128
  Betsy d Alexander & Mary, 128
  John W. m Harriet C. Mather, 159
  Lydiah m John Lee, 240*
  Lydia b 1763, 125
  Mary m John Lee, 240
ALLISON, Samuel S. m Frances A. Pilgrim, 165
AMES, Alice d Benajah & Luce, 88
  Benajah m Luce Scovel, 88
  Bradish s John & Dorrilly, 53
  Dorrilly w John died, 53
  Eunice m Richard Royce, 120
  Eunice d John & Dorrilly, 53
  John m Dorrilly, 53
  John m Keturah Huntly, 53
  John Noyes s John & Keturah, 53
  Luce d Benajah & Luce, 88
  Mary d Benajah & Luce, 88
  Rachall d Benajah & Luce, 88
  Samuel m _____, 22
ANDERSON, Daniel, 199
  Daniel m Ethelinda Ingraham, 158
  Daniel s John & Elizabeth, 21
  Daniel s John & Elizabeth, 21*
  Elizabeth d John & Elizabeth 20, 58
  Eunice m Silvanus Clark, 92*
  Eunice m George Champlin, 117
  Eunice d John & Elizabeth, 21
  Frank, 309
  Hannah m Daniel Chadwick, 72
  Hannah m John Roulin, 259
  Hannah d Thomas & Hannah, 218*
  Hannah II d Thomas & Hannah, 218*
  Hannah III d Thomas & Hannah, 218

INDEX OF PERSONS 313

ANDERSON, cont.
  Hannah d John & Elizabeth, 21
  Hannah w of Thomas died, 218
  Harriet m John Manwaring, 157
  Hepsibah C. m Winthrop DeWolf, 161
  John s Capt. Thomas & Margret, 38, 218, 301
  John Jr. m Lydia Clark, 39
  John s of Thomas & Hannah, 218
  John m Elisabeth Minor, 20
  John s John & Elizabeth, 21, 301
  Lydia d John & Elizabeth, 21
  Lydia Anderson m John Cooley 1768, 50
  Margaret d of Capt. Thomas & Margret, 38
  Marsh E., 306
  Mary E. m Aaron S. Brockway, 186
  Mary d of Capt. Thomas & Margret, 38
  Rebecca w Thomas, 278
  Robert s Capt. Thomas & Margret, 38
  Sally m Dr. Samuel Mather, 97
  Sarah m John Beckwith, 21
  Sarah d Thomas & Hannah, 218
  Theody d John & Elizabeth, 21
  Theody m Stephen DeWolf, 79
  Thomas s Thomas & Hannah, 218
  Thomas s Capt. Thomas & Margret, 38, 303
  Thomas died, 218

  Thomas m Hannah Peck, 218
  Thomas Anderson Capt. m Mrs. Margret Reed, 38
  Wissam died, 213
ANDRAS, ANDRONS, ANDRUS
  Abegall d John & Rachell, 218
  Hannah (Hana) d John & Rachell, 218
  Hannah m Benjamin Graham, 231
  John m Rachell DeWolfe, 218
  John s John & Rachell, 218
  Thomas s John & Rachell, 218
  Unice m Joseph Giddings, 36
ANDREWS, David m Rebecca Rogers, 153
  Dorcase m James Ely, 8
  Susan B m William H. Fox, 183
APPLEBY, Eliza m Otis T. Bailey, 171
  George m Clarice B. Tucker, 119
  George m Maria Waid 1837, 170
  George m Maria Waid 1851, 171
  George s Miss Mary Ann Appleby, 198
  Isabella B. m James Ferlong, 195, 211
  John m Emily S. Robbins, 178, 201, 205
  Martha A. d John & Emily, 204
  Mary Ann m Cornelius Chapman, 179
  Mary Ann m Elihu Smith, 193, 205, 211
  William s of Miss Isabella Appleby, 198
APPLETON
  Nancy Judson d George W. & M___, 143
ARMSBY, Lucinda, 47
ARMISTEAD-OLMSTED
  Betsey d Joseph & Miriam, 57
  George Washington s Joseph & Miriam, 57
  Henry (Yeadon) s Joseph & Miriam, 57
  James Benson s Joseph & Miriam, 57
  Joseph m Miriam Wright, 57
  Joseph s Joseph & Miriam, 57
  Nicholas s Joseph & Miriam, 57
  Thomas Benson s Joseph & Miriam, 57
  William s Joseph & Miriam, 57

ARMSTRONG
  George H. m Miss Lydia Miller, 149
  Sarah d Sarah Armstrong, 9
  William m Sarah Manwaring, 169
AUSTIN, Ann Jenette m Richard Watrous, 171
  Czrina m Dan Tinker, 164
  Malinda m Daniel Johnson, 157
AVERY, ABraham m Elizabeth Noyes, 45
  Abraham s Abraham & Elizabeth, 45
  Abraham s Jonathan & Preserved, 94
  Ama m Thomas Merritt, 61
  Benjamin s Silvanus & Mary, 106
  Bettey d Silvanus & Mary, 106
  Elisha s Nathaniel & Rachel, 22
  Elizabeth d Abm & Elizabeth, 45
  Enoch s Abm. & Elizabeth, 45
  Eunice d Gurdon & Eunice, 117
  Eunice m William Grover, 187
  George Miller m Abby Eliza Wait, 159
  George W. m Sarah M. Greenfield, 173
  Gurdon m Eunice Powers, 117
  Gurdon s of Gurdon & Eunice, 117
  Hannah d Abraham & Elizabeth, 45
  John s Abraham & Elizabeth, 45
  Jonathan m Preserved Smith, 94
  Lucy d Silvanus & Mary, 106
  Margary m Abner Shipman, 57
  Mary d Abm. & Elizabeth, 45
  Mary Ann died 1849, 214
  Moses s Avery & Elizabeth, 45*
  Nancy d Silvanus & Mary, 106
  Nathan m Alice Pearson, 42
  Nathaniel, 22
  Olive d Silvanus & Mary, 106
  Oscar m Phebe A. Ely, 181
  Pearson Peck s Nathan & Alis, 42
  Preserved wife of Jonathan, 94
  Rachel w of Nathaniel, 22
  Rebecca m William Wait, 131
  Samuel s Abraham & Elizabeth, 45
  Silvanus m Mary Luther, 106
  Silvanus s of Silvanus & Mary, 106
  Temperance m John Moore, 17
  Thomas s Abraham & Elizabeth, 45
  Thimothy D. m Jane Burnham, 194
AYER, AYERS
  Bettey d Elisha & Abigail, 40
  Daniel m Betsey Smith, 31
  Daniel m Ester Champion, 218
  Daniel s of Daniel & Esther, 218*
  Elisha m Abigail Lee, 40
  Esther d Danill & Ester, 218
  Fanny d Elisha & Abigail, 41
  Hannah d John & Clerinea, 93
  Hester m John Pirkins, 80
  John m Clerinea Lay (Mrs.), 93*
  John s of Daniel & Ester, 219
  John s of John & Clerinea, 93
  Lay s of John & Clerinea, 93
  Lay m Mrs. Mary Smith, 168
  Lebbeus s Danill & Esther, 218
  Lucy d Elisha & Abigail, 41
  Lydia d John & Clerinea, 93
  Mary d Danill & Ester, 218
  Mary m Vinton Beckwith, 72
  Siris (Saris) d Danill & Ester, 218*

BABCOCK, Alvin, 144, 156
Deborah Maria m Israel Otis, 143
Delia, 278
Delia m Nathanial Baker, 157
John m Julia Ann Hubbard, 160
Russell W. m Wealthy Emmons, 172
BACON, Alman m Margaret S. Clark, 170
Clara, or Clarissa R. m Ebenezer L. Roberts, 188, 208
Dorothy m Caleb Wood, 87
Ebenezer m Eliza W. Warren, 172
BAILEY, BAYLEY, Edith m Samuel Hill, 84
Eliza m Niles Taylor, 173
Fanny m William Higgins, 43
Harriet Maria, 183
Mary m Asa Lee, 174
Otis P. m Eliza Appleby, 171
Simon m Huldah Phelps, 147
BAKER, Adonijah Marvin, 99
Catharine d Mathias & Neomi, 128
David m Elizabeth Miner, 184
Elizabeth d Mathias & Neomi, 128
George Herron s Mathias & Neomi, 128
Jewett D. m Abby Ann Hayden Miner, 185
John Anson m Mary M. Havens, 211
John Herman s Mathias & Neomi, 128
Lous m Jonathan Gilbert, 71
Lucy d Mathius & Neomi, 128
Mary m Daniel Clark, 126
Mary d Mathias & Neomi, 128
Mathias Wesner m Neomi Bates, 128
Mathias Wesner s Mathias & Neomi, 128
Mehitable m Uzel Johnson, 120, 133
Nathaniel m Delia Babcock, 157
Sophia d Mathias & Neomi, 128
BALDWIN, Daniel, 203
Gad B. m Sarah A. Miner, 187
BALING OR BORDEN, John & wife Hanah, 222
Jean d John & Hanah, 222
John Jr. & his wife Marah, 222
Children of John Jr. & Marah, 222
Hanah, Martha, John, Samuell, Marah, Sarah
John Baling died, 222
John Borden m Rebeckah Roalon (Roulen), 222
Children of John & Rebeckah, 222
Elisha,Ezekill, Hanah, John*,Joseph,William
Rebeckah died, 222
Samuel m Mary Fox, 222
Mary d Samuel & Mary, 222
BANKS, Sarah m William Noyes Junr., 66
BANNING, Amasa s William, 107
Azubah d William, 107
Benjamin m Dotice Bramble, 143
Benjamin s John Jr. & Margaret, 24
Benjamin s William, 107
Brainard s Edwin & Emily, 203
Calven s William, 107
Caroline, 279
Caroline L m Horace Chapel, 167
Catherine m Orin Luther, 187
Clarissa d William, 107
Ebenezer s John Junior & Jemima, 24
Edward, 203
Elisha s William, 107
Elisa m Comfort Hewlet, 181
Elizabeth m John Brockway, 222

BANNING, cont.
Emily A. m Alanson Wright, 157
Eunice B. m Martin Doly, 186
John Jr. m Margaret DeWolf, 24
John Jr. m Jemima Peck, 24
John s of John Jr. & Margaret, 24
Joseph s John Jr. & Jemima, 24
Linda, 152
Lucy d William, 107
Lucy Ann m Amasa H. Gillett, 162
Lynda M. m Prentice Comstock, 152
Margaret d John Jr. & Jemima, 25
Margaret wife of John Died, 24
Mary d William & Mary Anne, 203
Matilda L. m George Thomas, 176
Rureany d John Jr. & Margaret, 24
Sarah wife of Ebenezer, 275
Sarah m Southmayd Miner, 167
Sarah d John Jr. & Jemima, 25
Sarah d William & Elisabeth, 207
Temperance d William, 107
William s of John Jr. & Jemima, 24
William s William, 107
William J. m Lucy Lay, 168, 201
William T. m Mary Ann Ransom, 175, 203
William s William & Lucy, 201
William I., 207
BANTA, Cornelius m Henrietta Gulliver, 182, 201
Frederick B. m Hannah B. Tucker, 181
Mary Ann m William Tucker, 182
William A. m Catharine Tucker, 187
BARBER, BARBOR
Martha (widow) m Samuell Peck, 254
BARDNER, Gershom m Susannah Smith. 14
BARRELL, Barrell s Elias & Lydia, 153
Charles s Elias & Lydia, 153
Elias m Lydia Latham, 153
James s Elias & Lydia, 153
James m Mary Bracy, 208
BARTER, Benjamin m Mary Miller, 161
BARTHOLOMEW, Levi m Hannah Mack, 52
BARTHWICK, BARTHERICK
(Levi) Seldon m Lydia Randall, 152
BARTLETT, BARTLET
Herediah m James Sawer, 259
John Bartlet m Mary A. Hill, 162
Sarah Bartlet m William Waterouse, 13
Shubael F. M.D. m Fanny R. Griswold, 181
BARTMAN, William m Mary McCoy, 146
BATES, BATE, Deborah m Thomas Tozer, 266
Edward N. m Rebekah A. Champion, 165
John m Betsy Wood, 180
Neomi m Mathias Wesner Baker, 128
Patience m Nicudemus Miller, 15
Rebekah m John Comstock, 228
BEACH, Anne m Elihu Marvin, 59
BECKWITH, BECKETT
Abel m Lucy DeWolf, 65
Abel m Mary Ann Lester, 177
Abigail d Samuel & Polly, 97
Abigah s Matthew 3rd & Eleshaba, 220
Abijah m Susanah Leet, 4
Abner m Joanna Clark, 133
Abner s Abner & Hannah, 117
Abner s Thomas & Sarah, 117
Abner s Thomas & Mary, 220

INDEX OF PERSONS 315

BECKWITH, cont.
Absolam m Lydia Haynes, 31
Alfred P m Sarah Brockway, 195
Allen m Patience Beckwith, 65
Allen s Benjamin & Patience, 65
Allen s Geo. & Penelope, 125
Anderson s John & Sarah, 21
Anderson s Samuel & Sarah, 56
Andrew m Lucinda Hudson, 148
Andrew s Josiah & Mehetable, 109
Anna m Joseph Brown, 51
Anna d Josiah & Mehetable, 109
Anne m John Murdock Lee, 123
Asa s Abijah & Susanah, 4
Azubah d Jesse & Jerusha, 40
Barach s Roswell & Lydia, 80
Benjarnen m Lucy Watrous, 132
Betsa d Jesse & Esther, 75
Betsey (Shipman), 198
Betty d Roswell & Lydia, 80
Calvin of N.L. m Lucy Chappell, 173
Charles m Ann Burrows, 195, 211
Charles m Betsey Shipman, 157, 198
Christiana m Elihu Strong, 159
Christopher s Zenos & Anna, 92
Cyrus s Stephen & Jerusha, 23
Daniel m Ruth Rice, 219
Daniel s Daniel & Ruth, 219
Daniell 1st s Jeames & Sarah, 219*
Daniell 2nd s Jeames & Sarah, 219
Daniel 3rd m Jerusha Grant, 40
Daniel 3rd m Sarah _____, 40
David s Jona & Sarah, 33
Deborah m Titus Hayes, 84
Deborah m Reynold Peck, 51
Deborah d Thomas & Sarah, 220
Deborah d Zenos & Anna, 92
Diadame d Matthew 3rd & Elishaba, 220
Diadamy m Joseph Rogers, 17
Dorithy d Joseph Jr. & Marah, 220
Edgecomb, 202
Edgecomb J. m Maria A. Culver 194, 206
Elijah m Sarah Miller, 53
Elijah s Jesse & Esther, 75
Elijah s Joseph Jr. & Marah, 220
Elisabeth (Widow) m Silas Brooks, 112
Elishaba d Mathew 3rd & Elishaba, 220
Eliza d Watrous & Ruth, 39
Eliza d George & Penelope, 125
Elizabeth m John Bump, 180, 198
Elizabeth d Matthew, 220
Elisabeth m Darious Peck, 101
Elizabeth m Elijah Smith, 262
Elizabeth d Jeames & Sarah, 219
Elishaba d Matthew 3rd & Elishaba, 220
Elishabah m Joshua Champion Jr., 26
Elisabeth m John Kirtland, 180
Elizabeth d Zenos & Anna, 92
Elizabeth S. d John & Nancy, 145
Emeline E. m Charles Erastus Kirtland, 196
Emmilu d Geo. & Penelope, 125
Enis d Matthew 3rd & Elishaba, 220
Erastus s Geo. & Penelope, 125
Esther m Zopher Gee, 121
Esther m John Robbins, 48
Esther d Allen & Esther, 65

BECKWITH, cont.
Esther d Zenos & Anna, 92
Eunice m Guy Chadwick, 46
Eunice m John Daniels, 105
Eunice m Nehemiah Mack, 99
Eunice d Josiah & Mehetable, 109
Eunice d Roswell & Lydia, 80
Ezekiah (Hezekiah) s Joseph Jr. & Marah, 220
Ezekiel, 300
Ezra s Jesse & Esther, 75
Ezra of Waterford m Julia Ann Gates, 174
Fabius s Geo. & Penelope, 124
Frances Fidelia m Albert Royce, 178
Frances of Norwich m Joseph Beebe, 171
Freelove m Benjamin Manwaring, 170
George Rev., 302
George s Jona & Rebecka, 219
George Jr. m Penelope Beckwith, 125
George s Roswell & Lydia, 80
George s Geo. & Penelope, 125
Georgiana d Charles M. & Betsey E., 198
Hannah d Abel & Luce, 65
Hannah d John & Sarah, 21*
Hannah d Josiah & Mehetable, 109
Hannah w Abner died, 117*
Hannah d Samuel & Polly, 97
Hannah m Elijah Rogers, 135
Harriet of Lyme m Thomas Twist, 169
Harriet m James Haynes, 175
Harriet Miller d Andrew & Lucinda, 148
Harris s Zenos & Anna, 92
Hester m Andrew Smith, 85
Huldah d Roswell & Lydia, 80
Israel s Jesse & Esther, 76
J. P. of East Lyme m Lucy C. Beckwith, 182
Jeames m Sarah _____, 219
Jeames s Jeames & Sarah, 219
Jeames m Rebeckah Lamb, 219
James s James & Rebeckah, 219
Jerusha w Daniel 3rd died, 40*
Jerusha w Stephen died, 23
Jesse m Jerush Robbins, 40*
Jesse s Joseph & Jerusha, 40
Jesse Jr. m Esther Smith, 75
Jesse s Jesse & Esther, 75
Jesse d April 19, 1796 or 90?, 40
Joanna d Elijah & Sarah (Sally), 53
Joel m Sybel Starkey, 160
John m Sarah Anderson, 21
John s Jeames & Sarah, 219
John s Jona & Rebecka, 219
John 1st s Watrous & Ruth, 39*
John 2nd s Watrous & Ruth, 39
John m Nancy S. Burnham, 145
John m Phebe Parsons, 145
John B. s William J. & Mary Jane, 205
Jonah m Rebecka (DeWolf?), 219
Jonah s Jonah & Rebecka, 219*
Jonathan s Daniell & Ruth, 219
Jonathan s Jonathan & Sarah, 33
Joseph m Susana, 220
Joseph Berket s Joseph (2) & Susana, 220
Joseph Jr. m Marah Lee, 220
Joseph s Joseph Jr. & Marah, 220
Joseph s Jenos & Anna, 92
Joseph s Elijah & Sarah (Sally), 53

BECKWITH, cont.
Josiah, 306
Josiah s Edgecomb & Maria, 206
Josiah m Mehetable Pearson, 109
Josiah lst s Josiah & Mehetable, 109*
Josiah 2nd s Josiah & Mehetable, 109*
Justin L m Mary A. Crocker, 164
Ladock D. m Jedidah Spencer, 149
Lois d Matthew 3rd & Elishaba, 220
Lois d Matthew Jr. m John Huntley, 39
Loraine d John & Sarah, 21
Lucy C. m J.P. Beckwith, 182
Luranah d Allen & Esther, 65
Lydia m Benjamin Huntly, 236
Lydia d Joseph Jr. & Marah, 220
Lydia d Daniell & Ruth, 219
Lydia d Jonathan & Sarah, 33
Lydia Jr. m Elisha Miller, 18
Lydia d Elijah & Sarah (Sally), 53
Mahala m Charles Tinker, 145
Margaret d John & Sarah, 21
Margaret Lucinda d Andrew & Lucinda, 148
Maria d Geo. & Penelope, 125
Martha d Jeames & Sarah, 219
Martha m Gideon Watrous, 78
Martin s Abel & Lucy, 65
Martin m Anna Horton, 89
Mary d Joseph Jr. & Marah, 220
Mary 2nd d Joseph Jr. & Marah, 220
Mary d Jeames & Sarah, 219
Mary d Thomas & Sarah, 220
Mary m Matthew Marvin, 246
Mary (widow) m Capt. Daniel Starling, 6
Mary d Vinton & Mary, 72
Mary w Watrous died, 39
Mary m Ezekiel Rogers, 148
Mary Ann d Benjamin & Lucy, 132
Mary Ann m Nathan E. Green, 170
Mary Brainard d Watrous & Mary, 39
Mary L. m Judah Lord, 186
Mathew Sr., 220
Mathew s Matthew & Elizabeth, 220
Mathew 3rd m Eleshaba (Rayner), 220
Mathew Sr. d June 14, 1727, 220
Mathew s Daniell & Ruth, 219
Mehetable d Allen & Esther, 65
Mehetable m Nathan Tinker, 99
Mehetable d Josiah & Mehetable, 109*
Mercy Wilcox m Isaac Watts Sill, 136
Miranda d of Watrous & Ruth, 39
Nabby m Stephen DeWolf, 122
Nancy m Jeremiah Bush, 167
Nancy B. d John & Phebe, 145
Nancy S. w John died, 145
Nathan s Joseph Jr. & Marah, 220
Nathan s Jesse & Esther, 75
Nathaniel s Jesse & Esther, 75
Parnal m George Mitchell, 155
Patience d Allen & Esther, 65
Patience d George & Penelope, 125
Penelope m George Beckwith, 125
Penelope d George & Penelope, 125
Phebe m Nathan Robbins, 47
Phebe d Vinton & Mary, 72
Phebe w Jesse d Jan. 7, 1796, 40*
Phebe m Leonard Beebe, 157

BECKWITH, cont.
Polly d Geo. & Penelope, 125
Rebecka d Jona & Rebecka, 219
Rebeckah d James & Rebeckah, 219
Renald s Jeames & Sarah, 219
Rhoda d Abijah & Susannah, 4
Rhoda m Samuel Brooks, 73
Rice s Daniel & Sarah, 40
Richard Greenfield s Samuel & Polly, 97
Richard Pearson s Josiah & Mehetable, 109
Roswell m Lydia Dorr, 79
Roswell s Roswell & Lydia, 80
Roxana m Nehemiah D. Tinker, 181
Ruel 2nd m Julia Ann Chappell, 146
Ruth d Matthew, 220
Ruth died w. Daniel, 219
Ruth d Daniell & Ruth, 219
Sally (Mehaley) d Samuel & Polly, 97*
Samuel s Daniel & Ruth, 219
Samuel s Jone & Rebecka, 219
Samuel s Jeames & Sarah, 219
Samuel s John & Sarah, 21
Samuel, 303
Samuel m Sarah Dickens of New Shoreham, 56
Samuel m Polly Greenfield, 97
Samuel Ingraham s Abner & Parnall, 117
Sarah wife of Rev. George Beckwith, 273
Sarah d Mathew, 220
Sarah d Joseph & Susana, 220
Sarah d Jeames & Sarah, 219
Sarah d James & Rebeckah, 219
Sarah d John & Sarah, 21
Sarah d Jonathan & Sarah 33
Sarah d Matthew 3rd & Elishaba, 220
Sarah d Thomas & Sarah, 220
Sarah d Vinton & Mary, 72
Sarah Ann of Waterford m Jonathan Green, 178
Silas s Jona & Sarah Beckwith, 33
Silveness s Jesse & Esther, 75
Stephen s Joseph Jr. & Marah, 220
Stephen m Jerusha Watrouse, 23*
Stephen m Hannah Nuton, 23*
Stephen s Zenos & Anna, 92
Susannah d Joseph Jr. & Marah, 220
Susannah of New London m Daniel Huntley, 13
Temme d William & Luce, 49
Theody m Gurdon Watrous, 124
Thomas m Sarah Lewis, 220
Thomas s Joseph Jr. & Marah, 220
Thomas s Zenos & Anna, 92
Ventel child of Thomas & Sarah, 220
Vinton of Lyme m Mary Ayers, 72*
Wata d Samuel & Sarah, 56
Watrous m Mary Brainard, 39
Watrous m Ruth Robbins, 39
Watrous s Watrous & Ruth, 39*
William, 301
William m Martha Graham, 145
William m Caroline Champion, 161
William of Waterford m Mary Blake, 172
William H. m Frances Caulkins, 176
William J. m Mary J. Havins, 205, 209
Zenos m Ama Harriss, 92
BEEBE, Abner, 303
Adonijah Marvin s Azariah & Diedami, 103
Albert M. died 1849, 215

INDEX OF PERSONS 317

BEEBE, cont.
  Amasa s Noah & Sybal, 126
  Anna C. m Erastus Rogers, 170
  Anne m Shubail Bogue, 145
  Azariah s Noah & Edey, 31
  Azariah m Diedamy Marvin, 103
  Azariah s Azariah & Diedamy, 103
  Azariah died 1826, 12
  Borden s Jonathan & Hannah, 12
  Betse d Azariah & Diedami, 103
  Caty d Noah & Sybal, 120
  David, 273
  Edey d Noah & Edey, 31
  Elbert s Joseph & Nany, 203
  Elisha s Simeon & Anna, 33
  Elizabeth m Nathaniell Havens, 233
  Eunice B. m David Royce, 153
  Eunice d Noah & Edey, 31
  Fanny d Noah & Sybal, 120
  Guy M. m Dotia Otis, 166
  Ira, 205
  Ira s of Ira & Judith, 205
  Ira s Jonathan & Hannah, 12
  James M. m Sarah Melinda Hall, 172
  Jere (Zere) s Jonathan & Hannah, 12
  Jonathan m Hannah Lewis, 12
  Joseph of Waterford m Frances Beckwith, 171
  Joseph m Nancy B. Hughes, 176, 203
  Leonard m Phoebe Beckwith, 157
  Lydia d Noah & Edey, 31
  Mary of Waterford m Daniel Manwaring, 167
  Mary C. m Ansil Bouge, 142
  Molley d Noah & Edey, 31
  Noah m Edey Waller, 31
  Noah s Noah & Edey, 31
  Noah Jr. m Sybal Rathbun, 120
  Noah m Hannah Luther, 91
  Noah m Preserve Avery, 91
  Olive d Noah & Sybal, 120
  Patience m Edward Haven, 3
  Richard s Azariah & Diedarni, 103
  Richard m Hannah Congdon, 165
  Sarah wife of David, 273
  Silas C. m Mercy A. Wait, 160
  Simeon m Anna Terril, 33
  Thomas of Waterford m S. Caulkins, 179
  William H. of Waterford m Frances Caulkins, 176
  William Lord s Noah & Sybal, 120
  Zere s Jonathan & Hannah, 12
  Zeruiah d Jonathan & Hannah, 12
BELCHER, Joseph, 299
BELOTE, Abigail Peck d John & Dorcas, 106
  Betsey d John & Dorcas, 106
  Harris s John & Dorcas, 106
  Isaac s John & Dorcas, 106
  John m Dorcas Mack, 106
  John s John & Dorcas, 106
  Ruth d John & Dorcas, 106
  William Maxon s John & Dorcas, 106
BENHAM, Charlotte m Josef Ransom, 130
BENJAMIN, Deborah m Calvin Reed, 183
BENNET, BENIT BEIT, BENETT, BENNITT
  Abegall w Henry, 221
  Abegall d Henry Jr. & Abegall, 221*
  Abegall d John & Marah, 221
  Abigail d John m Robert Menter, 7

BENNET, cont.
  Abigarl d Hennery Jr. & Abigail, 221
  Bettey d Samuel & Hannah, 11
  Caleb s Henory & Sarah, 221
  Caleb s Caleb Jr. & Rebeckah, 220
  Caleb Jr. m Rebeckah Mack, 220
  Dorete d Henory & Sarah, 221
  Dorithy d Hennery Jr. & Abigarl, 221
  Elijah s Samuel & Hannah, 11
  Elijah s John & Marah, 221
  Eunice d Samuel & Hannah, 11
  Hannah d Samuel & Hannah, 11
  Henry (Henory) m Sarah Champion
    (Champean), 221*
  Henory s Henory & Sarah, 221
  Henry Jr. m. Abegall Pike, 221
  Henry s Henry Jr. & Abigail, 221
  Henry m Mary Moos ("Moss"), 221
  Henry Sr. d Jan. 17, 1726/7, 221
  Hennery Jr. m Abigarl Morse, 221
  Henry s Henry Jr. & Abigarl, 221
  Jane d John & Marah, 221
  Jean d Samuel & Hannah, 11*
  Jedadiah s John & Marah, 221
  John s Henory & Sarah, 221
  John m Marah (Mary Huntley), 221
  John s John & Marah, 221
  John died, 222
  John s Caleb m Mary Moss, 221
  Joseph m Sarah Calkins, 33
  Love d Hennory & Sarah, 221
  Love d Henry m John Mack Jr., 245
  Lucy d Hennery Jr. & Abigarl, 221
  Lydia d Hennery Jr. & Abigarl, 221
  Lydia d Samuel & Hannah, 11
  Mary d John & Marah, 221
  Mary d John died April 21, 1731, 222
  Mary d Hennery Jr. & Abigarl, 221
  Mary d Samuel & Hannah, 11
  Mary d Joseph & Sarah, 33
  Mihitabel m James Burnham, 96
  Nathan s Samuel & Hannah, 11
  Phebe d Henry Jr. & Abegall, 221*
  Phebe d Henry & Mary, 221
  Rose m Isaac Willey, 270
  Rose m Henry (Henory) & Mary, 221
  Rose m Jacob Sawyer, 89
  Ruth d Henory & Sarah, 221
  Ruth d Hennery Jr. & Abigarl, 221
  Samuel m Hannah Wade Aug. 3, 1732, 10
  Samuel m Hannah Wade Aug 3, 1733, 222
  Samuell s Samuel & Hannah, 222
  Samuel s John & Marah, 221
  Sarah d John & Marah, 221
  Sarah w Henry d., 221
  Sarah m John Mack, 244
  Sarah m Jonathan Mack, 245
  Sarah d Henry Jr. & Abigail, 221
  Thankfull d Caleb Jr. & Rebeckah, 220
  Zadock s Samuel & Hannah, 10
BIGGS, Esther m Richard Lay, 87
  William s William & Mary, 33
BILL, Benajah P. m Louisa Peck, 196, 303
  Eleanor Jane m William Tinker, 172
  James m Anne Lord, 177, 202, 206
  John Oscar, 309

BILL, cont.
Julia Ann m John G Hughes, 199
Lucy S. m Capt. Ebenezer E. Brockway, 183, 199
Ludowick s James A. & Anne S. L., 206
Mary m John Gordon Hughes, 149
Mary m Asa Park Edgecomb, 155
Rebecca d James & Ann, 203
BINGHAM, Claratha d Elijah & Mary, 102
Elijah m Mrs. Mary Banning Brockway, 102
Martha m Solomon Gee Junr, 73
Melinda d Elijah & Mary, 102
Nathan s Elijah & Mary, 102
Phebe d Elijah & Mary, 102
Polley d Elijah & Mary, 102
Roswell s Elijah & Mary, 102
Silas s Elijah & Mary, 102
Sluman s Elijah & Mary, 102
Theody d Elijah & Mary, 102
Walter s Elijah & Mary, 102
_____s Elijah & Mary, 102
BIRDSEY, BIRDSEYE
Frederick of Middletown m Laura A. Miller, 191
Samuel M of Middletown m Elizabeth M. Miller, 168
BISHOP, Abijah s Abraham & Patience, 12
Abraham, 12
Abraham m Hannah Champion, 13
Abraham s Abraham & Hannah, 13
Abraham m Sarah Gladding, 13*
Anna m Elkanah Huntley, 134
Elisha s Abraham, 13
Enos s Abraham & Sarah, 13
Hannah w Abraham, 13*
Hannah d Abraham & Sarah, 13
Isaac s Abraham & Sarah, 13
John s Abraham & Hannah, 13
Mary, 12
Mary d Abraham & Sarah, 13
Patience w Abijah, 12
Patience m Stephen Hudson, 89
BISSELL, George m Parnall Minor, 127
BLAGUE, Abigail Reynolds w James Blague, 300
David s of Jeremiah & Annah, 11
Esther d James & Abigail, 8
James m Abigail Reynolds, 8
James twin with Jonathan s of James & Abigail, 8
Jeremiah s James & Abigail, 8
John s James & Abigail, 8
Joshua s James & Abigail, 8
Mary m Rev. Stephen Johnson, 28
Mary Danow d Jeremiah, 219
Sarah d Jeremiah, 219
BLAKE, Mary m William Beckwith, 172
BLATCHLEY, Abraham Dr. m Jemima Marvin, 145
BLISS, Chauncey m Esther Slate, 166
James m Ann Hudson, 187
Levi m Elizabeth P. Johnson, 189
BOOGE, Eliza m Reu Huntley, 111
BOGUE, Bogue (female) died 1850, 215
Abby m Wm. Dawes Jr., 187
Edwin H., 309
Eleanor m Jared Daniels, 172
Elizabeth m Joseph Church, 195
Elizabeth S. m Henry J. Bogue, 185
Emeline J. m William Johnson, 190

BOGUE, cont.
Henry J. m Elizabeth S. Bogue, 185
Jabez H. m Joanna Denison, 161, 309
James m Laura Sawyer, 161
Jerusha Eva d James & Laura, 205
John m Lydia Mitchell, 172
John C. m Lucy E. Littlefield, 176
Joseph, 309
Mary E. d Samuel M & Eliza, 197
Mary J. m George E. Mather, 189, 208
Minerva L. d Samuel M. & Eliza, 197
Ozias H. m Phebe Johnson, 168
Russell m Sila Tillitson, 163
Samuel L., 309
Shubael m Anne Beebe, 145
Sylvanus died, 213
William H., 309
BOO, Mary m William Brockway, 186
BOOGE, Richard, 300
BOOLES, Ebenezer m Moley Gilbert, 105
Fanny d Ebenezer & Molley, 105
Polly d Ebenezer & Molley, 105
BOON, Betsey d Henry & Rebecca, 48
Charlotte d Henry & Rebecca, 48
Henry m Rebecca Smith, 48, 275, 276
Henry s Henry & Rebecca, 48
Hezekiah Smith s Henry & Rebecca, 48
Ichabod s Henry & Rebecca, 48
Jerusha d Henry & Rebecca, 48
Jerusha m Thomas Nelegan, 139
Keturah d Henry & Rebecca, 48
Nathan m Sally Peck, 118
Rebecca wife of Henry, 275, 276
Sally d Henry & Rebecca, 48
William s Henry & Rebecca, 48
Zurviah d Henry & Rebecca, 48
BOOTHE, Anne m Joseph Mather, 248
BORDEN, Elisha s John & Rebeckah, 222
Elizabeth m William Lewis, 242
Ezekill s John & Rebeckah, 222
Hannah d John & Marah, 222
Hannah d John & Rebeckah, 222
Jeane child of John & Hannah, 222
John Jr. m Marah _____, 222
John s John & Marah, 222
John m Rebekah Roulen, 222
John s John & Rebeckah, 222
John died 1730, 222
John died 1708, 222
Joseph s John & Rebeckah, 222
Marah d John & Marah, 222
Martha d John & Marah, 222
Mary d Samuel & Mary, 222
Rebeckah wife of John, 222
Samuel s John & Marah, 222
Samuel m Mary Fox, 222
Sarah d John & Marah, 222
William s John & Rebeckah, 222
BOUGE, Ansel m Mary C. Beebe, 142
Luretia Ann d Ansel & Mary, 142
Rachael A. m Ezra Chappell, 142
BOURNS, Fanny m Thomas Lonergan, 115
BOWMAN, _____ m Walter Flynn, 148
BRACY, Gerrish m Eliza Miller, 160
BRADBURY, Roxana J. m David O. Martin, 177
BRADDICK, William m Lucy Tinker, 196

INDEX OF PERSONS 319

BRADFORD, Hannah m Benjamin Robbins, 64
 Katharine w died 1733, 219
BRADLEY, Peter, Commander, 306
BRAINARD, BRAYNARD
 Anna III d Davis & Anna, 204
 Davis S. Rev. m Ann Maria Chadwick, 179, 204
 Mary m Watrous Beckwith, 39
 Mehetable m Calvin Spencer, 113
 Ursula m Elisha Sawyer, 179
BRAMBLE, Alanson m Widow Huntley, 180
 Betsey m Nathaniel Matthews, 159
 Daniel s William & Nabby, 117
 Dotice m Benjamin Banning, 143
 Erastus Jr. m Hellen Minor, 191
 Frankling s William & Nabby, 117
 Henry m Mary A. Slate, 187
 Hester d William & Nabby, 117
 Jeheal s William & Nabby, 117
 Mary A. m Richard Daniels, 180
 Nabby d William & Nabby, 117
 Orrin Shipman s William & Nabby, 117
 Phebe m Ezekeal Rogers, 41
 Polly d William & Nabby, 117
 Robert, 303
 Silas m Amy Sawyer, 148
 Silas m Betsey Lay, 189
 Timothy, 301
 William s William & Nabby, 117
 William m Abagail Shipman, 117
 Zilpha m Persia Johnson, 138
BRAYMAN, Daniel S. m Mary W. Havens, 147
BREWER, Henry m Mary A. Lee, 175
BRIGGS, BRIGS, Peter s John &M_____, 222
 William s John & M_____, 222
BROADRICK, John H. m Elizabeth Havens, 194
BROADWAY, BROCKWAY
 Caroline E. m Henry Pratt, 174
BROCKWAY (BROADWAY)
 Aaron S. m Mary E. Anderson, 186
 Aaron died 1849, 214
 Abagail (twin) d Richard & Elizabeth, 223
 Abagail m Frances W. Glover, 182
 Abner, 301
 Abner s William & Hannah, 57
 Abner m Catherine Marvin, 93, 275
 Abner s Abner & Catherine, 93
 Alice (see under Ellice), 106
 Anna d Walston & Anna, 3
 Anna d Anna, 27
 Anne m John Brown, 116
 Asa s Ephriam & Susanna, 222
 Asa s Johnathan & Phebe, 72
 Benjamin m Deborah Howard, 183, 303
 Betsey d Elias & Lovica, 106, 276, 277
 Bridget d Wolston & Hana, 224
 Breget d John, 222
 Brigget d Wolston & Anna. 3
 Bridget d Ezra & Dorcas, 50
 Bridget m Benjamin Hudson Jr., 32
 Carlos Marcena s Jasper & Hannah, 136
 Carolina d William & Hannah, 57
 Caroline m Abel Hall, 81
 Caroline S. m Henry J. Comstock, 182
 Caroline E. m Henry A. Pratt, 174
 Cate d Abner & Catharine, 93
 Catharine wife of Abner, 275*

BROCKWAY, cont.
 Catharine S. m Abraham Willey, 178, 205
 Charles s Elias & Lovica, 106
 Charles E.S. (L.) m Caroline Rogers, 188
 Charles Elias Levingston s Christopher & Christian, 140
 Charles H. m Frances Luther, 172
 Christopher s Elias & Lovica, 106
 Christopher m Christian Chappell, 140
 Christopher Jr. s Christopher & Christian, 140
 Consider twin with Abagail s Richard & Elizabeth, 223*
 David, 306
 Debrah d Wolston & Hana, 224
 Debrah d Wolston Jr. & Margaret, 224
 Deborah d Richard & Rachall, 223
 Dorothy d John II & Sarah, 223
 E.D., 200
 E. Plularch, 309
 Ebenezer s John & Elizabeth, 223
 Ebenezer D., 206
 Ebenezer s William & Hannah, 160
 Ebenezer E. Capt. m Lucy S. Bill, 183, 199
 Ebenezer s William & Elizabeth, 223
 Edgar m Lovica Luther, 188
 Edward s Wolston Jr. & Margaret, 224, 302
 Edward C.G. m Adaline Damon, 172
 Elias s Elias & Lovica, 106
 Elias m Lovica Champion, 106
 Elihu s John 2nd & Sarah, 223
 Eliza D. m Nathaniel Brown, 156
 Elizabeth m William Haris, 232
 Elizabeth m William S. Ransom, 211
 Elizabeth m Sam Waller, 269
 Elizabeth wife of Dr. John, 279
 Elizabeth wife of John 2nd died, 223
 Elizabeth d John & Elizabeth, 222
 Elizabeth d Richard & Elizabeth, 223
 Elizabeth d Richard & Hannah, 10
 Elizabeth d William & Elizabeth, 223
 Elizabeth d Wolston & Hana, 224
 Elizabeth Hannah d Christopher & Christian, 140
 Ellice d Elias & Lovica, 106
 Enos s Richard & Hannah, 10
 Ephraim s Walston Jr. & Margaret, 224
 Ephram m Susanna Carrier, 222
 Ephram s Ephraim & Susanna, 222
 Eunice d Richard & Elizabeth, 223
 Eunice d Christopher & Christian, 140
 Eunice C. m. George Harding, 161
 Exra, 299
 Ezekiel s John 2nd & Sarah, 223, 306
 Ezra, 299, 307
 Ezra m Dorcas Giddings, 50*
 Ezra m Leonora Brockway, 143
 Ezra m Lucy Ann Steward, 154
 Ezra C. s Christopher & Christian, 140
 Frederick L.C. m Marion A. Peck (Mary Ann), 194, 209
 George s Elias & Lovica, 106
 Gedeon s Jedediah & Sarah, 50
 Gedeon s Jedediah & Sarah b 1759, 50*
 Hanah d Wolston & Hana, 224
 Hanah m Thomas Champeon, 225
 Hana good wife Woltson died 1687, 224

BROCKWAY, cont.

Hanah d Richard & Rachall, 223
Hannah d William & Hannah, 57
Hannah d William Jr. & Prudence, 224
Henry Brayman d Jasper & Hannah, 136
Hettey d Richard & Hannah, 10
Horace A. m Rhoda Griffin, 166
Horace R. m Jennett Greenfield, 208
Horace Gardiner s Jasper & Hannah, 136
Hugh B., 309
Huldah m Sylvanus Lord, 58
Irena m William Miller, 73
James s Ebenezer & Lucy S., 199
James Madison s Elias & Lovica, 106, 213
Jean (Jane) d John, 222
Jane Amelia m Marshfield Sterling Parker Jr., 190, 210
Jane Sheldon m John Frederick Harrison, 136
Jasper s Elias & Lovica, 106
Jasper m Hannah Crandall, 136
Jedediah, Capt, 279, 307
Jedediah s Richard & Rachall, 223
Jedediah m Sarah Fox, 50
Jedediah F. m Elizabeth Hayden, 192, 210
Jemmy s Abner & Catharine, 93
Jesse s Jonathan & Phebe, 72
John Lieut., 302
John Dr., 279, 307
John, 303
John s John, 222
John s John & Elizabeth, 222
John s William & Elizabeth Banning, 222
John s Wolston & Hanna, 224
John 2nd m Sarah Scovill, 223
John Reed m Harriet Gillett, 173
Jonah s Jedediah & Sarah, 50
Jonathan s Walston Jr. & Margaret, 224
Jonathan m Phebe Smith, 72
Jonathan s Jonathan & Phebe, 72
Joseph S. s Christopher & Christian, 140, 198
Joseph S. Jr. s Joseph S. & Mary S., 205, 198
Julia Emeline d Jasper & Hannah, 136
Julian d Christopher & Christian, 140
Juliann m Ashel Miller (Julian), 153, 154
Leonora m Ezra Brockway, 143
Loas d Richard & Hannah, 10
Lovina, 299
Lovisa d Elias & Lovisa, 106
Lovica Ann d Jasper & Hannah, 136
Lucina d Abner & Catharine, 93
Lucey d Jedediah & Sarah, 50
Lydia d Richard & Rachall, 223
Lydia d Jedediah & Sarah, 50
Lydia m Stephen Huntley, 77
Marah d Wolston & Hana, 224
Marah m Samuell Mott, 250
Marget d Walston Jr. & Margaret, 224
Margaret A. m Jabez Comstock, 153
Maria m Elisha H. Smith, 1
Martin s of Jonathan & Phebe, 72
Martin 2nd s Jonathan & Phebe, 72
Marvin s Abner & Catharine, 93
Mary d of John, 222
Mary d John 2nd & Elizabeth, 223
Mary d William & Hannah, 57
Mary Banning m Elijah Bingham, 102

BROCKWAY, cont.

Mary E. m Charles Smith, 169
Mary C., 278
Maryette (Mariette) d Christopher & Christian, 140
Nancy, 276, 277
Nancy Jane Sheldon Harrison d Wm. & Nancy, 160
Naomi d John, 222
Naomia m Ehihu Huntley, 114
Naomy d Jedediah & Sarah, 50
Nathan s Richard & Elizabeth, 223
Patience m Gasper Dowzick, 42
Phebe wife of Jedidiah, 278
Phebe d John, 222
Phebe d Jonathan & Phebe, 72
Picket s Abner & Catharine, 93
Rachall d Richard & Rachall, 223
Rachall w Richard died, 223
Rachal d Jedediah & Sarah 1748, 50
Rachal d Jedediah & Sarah 1750, 50*
Richard m Rachall, 223
Richard s Richard & Rachall, 223
Richard m Elizabeth Tiffany, 223
Richard, 307
Richard 3d m Hannah Randall, 10
Richard s William & Elizabeth, 223
Richard s Wolston & Hana, 224
Richard William s Wm. & Nancy, 160
Robert Smith s Jasper & Hannah, 136
Rodney, 307
Rufus s Jonathan & Phebe, 72
Ruth d Richard & Rachall, 223
Samuel s Walston Jr. & Margaret, 224
Sarah, 276, 277
Sarah d John 2nd & Elizabeth, 223
Sarah m Peter Tub (b) s, 267
Sarah d Richard & Rachall, 223
Sarah d Walston & Anna, 3
Sarah d Walston & Hana, 3, 224
Sarah C. m Alfred Beckwith, 195
Sarah Caroline d Christopher & Christian, 140
Seth Monroe m Lucy Ann Ely, 191, 206, 210
Silence d Richard & Elizabeth, 223
Susannah d Jonathan & Phebe, 72
Temme d William & Hannah, 57
Thomas s William & Hannah, 57
Thomas Clark s Wm. & Nancy, 160, 309
Tiffany s Richard & Elizabeth, 223
Walston Jr. m Margaret Jones, 224
Walston s Walston Jr. & Margaret, 224
Walston s John, 222
Walston m Anna Brooks, 3
Walston twin with William s Walston & Anna, 3
Welthy m Noah Miller Jr., 73
William, 309
William m Mary Boo, 186
William 2nd m Hannah Clark, 57
William m Hannah Martin (Marvin), 160*, 173
William m Nancy F. Post, 160
William m Elizabeth _____, 223
William Jr. m Prudence Pratt, 223
William (twin) s Walston & Anna, 3
William s Wolston & Hana, 224
William s William 2nd & Elizabeth, 223
William s William Jr. & Prudence, 224

INDEX OF PERSONS 321

BROCKWAY, cont.
  William Champion s Elias & Lovica, 106
  William P. m Elizabeth Tinker, 176
  Wolston, 224
  Wolston s Wolston & Hana, 224
  Zebulon, Capt., 303
BROOKER, Sarah m John Marvin, 21
BROOKS, BROOK
  Anna m Walston Brockway, 3
  Anna m John Johnson Jr., 70
  Augustus, 309
  Clarissa C. m Heman Young, 149
  Fanny d Samuel & Rhoda, 73
  Hannah m Allen Chadwick, 106
  Hannah 3rd d Silas & Elizabeth, 112
  John s Silas & Elizabeth, 112
  Joseph s Silas & Elizabeth, 112
  Joseph b. 1796, 127
  Joseph m Mary Ryon, 150
  Mahala m Lester Maynard, 173
  Marian J. d Augustus & Lucy, 197
  Molly d Sam & Rhoda, 73
  Phebe d Samuel & Rhoda, 73
  Rhoda d Samuel & Rhoda, 73
  Samuel m Rhoda Beckwith, 73
  Samuel s Samuel & Rhoda, 73
  Silas m Elizabeth Beckwith, 112
  Silas s Silas & Elizabeth, 112
BROWN, Aaron s Joseph & Anna, 51
  Abiah m Jason Lee, 101
  Abigail d Jeremiah & Lydia, 29
  Anna d Joseph & Anna, 51
  Anson Sanford s Silas & Sarah, 128
  Bridgham s Jeremiah & Lydia, 29
  Carolina Canady d Silas & Sarah, 128
  Charles Nathan s Silas & Sarah, 128
  Ede m Charles H. Dean, 167
  Elizabeth d Jeremiah & Lydia, 29
  Ellen Loura d Nathaniel & Eliza, 156
  Franklin M. m Ede Miller, 155
  George Beckwith s Silas & Sarah 1807, 128*
  George Beckwith s Silas & Sarah 1809, 128
  Hannah m Daniell Huntley, 236
  Harry s John & Anne, 117
  James L. m Eliza Emerson, 169
  James Sheffield s Jeremiah & Lydia, 29
  Jane Miles d Nathaniel & Eliza, 156
  Janeet Eliza d Nathaniel & Eliza, 156
  Jeremiah m Lydia Smith, 29
  John m Anne Brockway, 116
  John s John & Anne, 117
  Jonathan C. m Hannah Congdon, 142
  Joseph m Ann Beckwith, 31
  Joseph s Joseph & Anna, 51
  Katharine (twin with Peter Wilbour) d Nathaniel & Eliza, 156
  Lurania, 277
  Lydia d Jeremiah & Lydia, 29
  Mary died, 214
  Nabby d John & Anne, 117
  Nathaniel, 302
  Nathaniel M. m Eliza Brockway, 156
  Peter Wilbour (twin with Katharine) s Nathaniel & Eliza, 156
  Polly m Stephen Starling, 124
  Ruth d Joseph & Anna, 51

BROWN, cont.
  Samuel m Salome Niles, 157
  Samuel Prentice Brown s Silas & Sarah, 128
  Silas m Sarah Tinker, 128
  Thomas s Silas & Sarah, 128
  Wealthy m Ensign George Chadwick Jr., 97
  William s Jeremiah & Lydia, 129
  William s John & Ann, 117
  Worthington Dunham s Nathaniel & Eliza, 156
BROWNING, Welcome A. m Betsey Moore, 172
BRUNSON, BROUNSON
  Abraham m Hana Brumson, 224
  Abram s Abraham & Hana, 224
  Anna d Abraham & Hana, 224
  Elizabeth d Abraham & Hana, 224
  Frances m Samuell Waterous, 270
  Hanna m Abraham Brunson, 224
  Mary d Abraham & Hana, 224
  Mary m Thomas Waight, 268
BUCK, Jonathan m Adaline Rice, 183
BUCKINGHAM
  Amasa S. m Mary Tribble, 196, 212
  Arnold m Cornelia Luther, 169
  Cornelia widow m Samuel Holmes, 184
  Samuel 3rd m Johannah Matson, 129
BUCKNER, S. Lieut. m Mary Kingsbury, 195
BULKLEY, Caroline, 278
  Caroline m Thomas D. Lord, 153
  Susannah m John Coult, 46
BUMP, Abby A. m Ruel B. Huntley, 183
  Abigail A. d Isaac & Susan, 139
  Adalaide (twin with Ellen) d Isaac & Susan, 139
  Caroline d Isaac & Susan, 139
  Ebenesar, 199
  Ebenezer R. s Isaac & Susan, 139
  Edey m Dudley Clark, 126
  Elizabeth M. d Isaac & Susan, 139
  Ellen (twin with Adalaide) d Isaac & Susan, 139
  Ellen d Ebeneser & Minerva, 199
  Freelove, 25
  George W. m Sally C. Haynes, 146
  Jane d John & Elisabeth, 198
  John s Isaac & Susan, 139
  John m Elizabeth Beckwith, 180, 198
  Maria m Christopher Haynes, 151
  Mary A. m Thomas Way, 167
  Mary Ann A. d Isaac & Susan, 139
  Nancy H. d Isaac & Susan m Charles Huntley, 139
  Penelope B. d Isaac & Susan, 139
  William b 1787, 127
BUNIPAS, Mary m. Ezra Champion, 76
  Isaac died, 25
BANNING, Benjamin m Dotice Bramble, 143
BUNNEL, Wm. m Phebe Church, 171
BURDICK, Ambrose m Mary Ann Luther, 158
  Nathan m Maryette Tinker, 173
BURNHAM
  Betsey d Josiah & Thankfull, 44
  Betsy d Joseph & Meriam, 18
  Betsy wife of Cap't. John died 1803, 113*
  Eunice widow of Cap't Joseph Smith died 1809, 130
  James m. Mehetabel Bennet, 96
  James s Capt. Joseph & Eunice, 130
  James s Josiah & Thankfull d. 1758, 44

BURNHAM, cont.
James s Josiah & Thankfull, 44*
James s Capt. Joseph & Eunice, 130
Jane m. Timothy D. Avery, 194
Jamima m Capt. John Hughes, 116
Jemima d Josiah & Thankfull, 44
John s Josiah & Thankfull, 44
John Capt. m Betsey Smith, 113
John Bennett s James & Mehetabel, 96
Joseph s Josiah & Thankfull, 44
Joseph m Meriam Coult, 18*
Joseph s Joseph & Meriam died 1780, 18*
Joseph s Joseph & Meriam b. 1780, 18*
Joseph Capt. m Eunice Smith, 130
Josiah m Thankfull Higgins, 44
Josiah s Josiah & Thankfull, 44
Lucy Ann m Joseph Durfey, 167
Marcy d Josiah & Thankful, 44
Mary (Mercy) m Alexander Hyde, 129, 276
Meriam wife of Joseph d. 1797, 19
Meriam Coult d Joseph & Meriam, 18
Nancy S. m John Beckwith, 145
Nancy Smith d Capt. John & Betsey, 113
Phebe d James & Mehetabel, 96
Polly d John & Betsey, 113*
Polly d Joseph & Meriam, 18
Polly born 1781 died 1782, 96
Rebecca d Joseph & Meriam, 19
Rebeckah d Josiah & Thankful, 44
Samuel s Josiah & Thankfull died 1759, 44*
Samuel s Josiah & Thankfull b 1762, 44
Samuel Gardiner s Joseph & Meriam, 18
Samuel Guardner s Capt. Joseph & Eunice, 130
William Joseph s Capt. Joseph & Eunice, 130
BURR, Enoch F., 272
BURROWS, Ann m Charles Beckwith, 195, 211
BURT, BURTT, Benjamin s Joseph & Elizabeth, 83
Elizabeth d Joseph & Elizabeth, 83
Israel s Joseph & Elizabeth, 83
Jemima d Joseph & Elizabeth, 83
Joseph m Elizabeth Peck, 83
Joseph s Joseph & Elizabeth d. 1767, 83
Joseph s Joseph & Elizabeth b. 1769, 83
Margaret d Joseph & Elizabeth, 83
Ruhamah d Joseph & Elizabeth, 83
Sarah d Joseph & Elizabeth, 83
Wm. Peck s Joseph & Elizabeth, 83
Zebulon s Joseph & Elizabeth, 83
BUSH, Abby J. m Mirichi Huntley, 164
Elizabeth m John Tubbs, 132
Ira A. m Matilda Manwaring, 163
Jeremiah m Nancy Beckwith, 167
Nancy m Solomon Adams, 165
BUSHNELL, Alexander m Cloe Wait, 65
Anna d Ephraim m Moses Dudley, 42
Clerianea d Eusebious & Borredill, 92
Daniel s Alexander & Cloe, 65
Eusebious m Borredill Lathimer, 92
Ephraim, 42
Hannah d Eusebious & Borredill, 92
Samuel m Phebe Dart, 208
Thomas s Alexder & Cloe, 65
William m Nancy Clark, 181
BUTLER OR BUTTLER
Hannah d Zeb & Anna, 65

BUTLER, cont.
Isaac, 300
Lord s Zebulon & Anna, 65
William m Sarah Lord, 40, 168
Zebulon Capt. m Anna Lord d. John Lord, 65
Zebulon s Zebulon & Anna, 65
CABLES, Joanna m Enoch Howard, 150
CALKINS, CAULKINS, CAULKINGS
Absalom s Tamor or Turner & Mary, 86
Amos s Daniel & Elizabeth, 111
Ann Catharine Tinker d David & Polly, 135
Asa s Turner (Tamor) & Marcy, 86
Catharine m George R. Coult, 162
Daniel m Elizabeth Moor (e), 111
Daniel s Daniel & Elizabeth, 111
Daniel Dr. died 1791, 111
David m Polly Peck, 135
Delia m John Huntley, 193, 210
Elisha s Daniel & Elizabeth, 111
Elisha C. m Abby Chapman, 151
Elizabeth d Daniel & Elizabeth, 111
Elizabeth m Silas Peck, 20
Elizabeth A. d Elisha C. & Abby, 151
Emiline d David & Polly, 135
Epaphrus C. s Elisha C. & Abby, 151
Ethelinda d Daniel & Elizabeth, 111
Ethelinda m Thomas Griswold, 126
Eunice m Jabez DeWolf, 46
Eunice d Tamor or Turner & Marcy, 86
Frances m Wm. H. Beebe, 176
Hannah m Capt. Thomas Wait, 112
Hester m Capt. Enoch Lee, 112
Jemima d Tamor or Turner & Marcy, 86
Juliet d Elisha C. & Abby, 151
Juliet Griswold d Elisha C. & Abby, 151
Laura E. m George Franklin Tillotson, 194
Lucia m Simon DeWolf, 49
Lucretia m James B. Cook, 178
Lydia Lee d David & Polly, 135
Lydia Lee m Sylvanus Huntley, 162
Marcy wife of Tamor or Turner died, 87
Mary Ann d David & Polly, 135
Mary wife of Dr. Daniel died, 111
Matthew s Tamor, Turner & Marcy, 86
Sarah d Daniel & Elizabeth, 111
Sarah m Joseph Bennet, 23
Sarah d Stephen, 224
Sarah m Thomas Beebe, 179
Sarah d Tamor, Turner & Marcy, 87
Sarah Ann m Ralph B. Clark, 192
Sarah W. m Lee Comstock, 151
Stephen m Stephen, 224
Stephen Lee s David & Polly, 135
Stephen s Tamor, Turner & Marcy, 87
Turner s Stephen, 224
William Smibert s Daniel & Elizabeth, 111
Zeruiah m Lowen Wait, 67
CAMPBELL, Martha m Erastus Ely, 175
CANFIELD, Esther m Curtiss Comstock, 79
CARRIER, Susanna m Ephram Brockway, 222
CARTER, Rachal m George C. Emerson, 177
Silas m Betsey Huntley, 167
CATLIN, Benjamin H. m Amelia D. Spencer, 169
CATON, Mary m William P. Peck, 175
CENTER, Martha m Edward Lay Jr., 24

INDEX OF PERSONS

CHADDOCK, CHADWICK
Abigail d Dan & Hannah, 94
Allen, 299
Allen s Allen & Hannah, 106
Allen s James & Martha, 16
Allen m Hannah Brooks, 106
Ama d Allen & Hannah, 106
Ambrose Niles s Richard & Mary, 145
Amy d Stephen & Leamy, 107
Ann Maria m Rev. Davis S. Brainard, 179, 204
Ann Maria d Capt. Daniel Chadwick, 179
Anna d Daniel & Hannah, 72
Anna d Dan & Hannah, 94
Anna d James & Anna, 14
Azubah d Guy & Eunice, 46
Benjamin s John & Mary (Mercy), 139
Bette d Allen & Hannah, 106
Bettey m Jasper Champion, 96
Bettey d Samuel & Mary, 16
Betsey m David Rogers, 123
Betsey d Reuben & Martha, 77
Brooks s James & Anna, 14
Cardina d Guy & Eunice, 46
Carolina m Sylvanus Mather, 19
Cate d Reuben & Martha, 77
Catharine relict of Daniel died, 72
Charles m Mary A. Rowland, 160
Charles Chauncey s Ezra & Sally, 116
Charles M s Daniel Jr. & Ellen, 204
Clarissa d James & Anna, 14
Dan, 299
Dan m Hannah Huntley, 94
Dan s Dan & Hannah, 94
Dan s James & Martha, 16
Dan the elder died, 94*
Daniel Ensign m Hannah Anderson, 72
Dan'll s Dan'll & Hannah, 72
Daniel d Feb. 1771, 72
Daniel m Nancy Waite, 142
Daniel Jr. m Ellen Noyes, 190, 204, 208
Daniel Russell s Elihu & Elizabeth, 141
Elias s Dan & Hannah died 1780, 94
Elias s Dan & Hannah b 1784, 94
Elihu m Elizabeth Russell, 141
Elisa Jane d John & Mary (Mercy), 139
Elisha s Nathaniel & Bettey, 73
Elisha s Stephen & Leoamy or Leony, 107
Elisha Ambrose s Stephen & Fanny, 196
Elizabeth d Dan & Hannah, 94
Elizabeth d Guy & Eunice, 46
Elizabeth d James & Martha, 16
Elizabeth M. m William Wilson, 154
Emeline Sill d Richard & Mary, 145
Emmia Maria d Stephen & Fanny, 196
Esther d Guy & Eunice, 46
Esther m Joseph Wade, 32
Esther m Reuben Champion, 131
Eunice m Matthew Gee, 142
Ezra s Dan'll & Hannah, 72
Ezra m Sally Lay, 116
Ezra s Stephen & Leoamy, 107
Fanny d George & Welthy, 97
Fanny d James & Anna, 14
Fanny Elizabeth d Samuel & Fanny, 166*
Francis Jemima d Samuel & Fanny, 166*
Frederick William s John & Mary (Mercy), 139

CHADDOCK, cont.
George Ensign Jr. m Wealthy Brown, 97
George Hazard m Mary H. Sparrow, 160
Gurdon, 299
Gurdon s Allen & Hannah, 106
Gurdon s James & Anna, 14
Guy m Eunice Beckwith, 46
Guy s Guy & Eunice, 46
Hannah w Allen died, 106
Hannah d James & Anna, 14
Hannah alias Gulliver m Atwell Tucker, 158
Hephzibah d Allen & Mary, 124
Hepzibah d Dan'll & Hannah, 72
Hepzibah d Ezra & Sally, 116
Hepzibah m Lynde Champen, 113
Hesekiah Erwin s Stephen & Fanny, 196
Isaac s Allen & Hannah, 106
Israel s Elihu & Elizabeth, 141
James m Anne Kent, 14
James s Allen & Hannah, 106
James m Martha Chadwick, 16
Jerusha d Guy & Eunice, 46
Jerush m Richard Roland, 86
Jerush d Thomas Jr., 224
John m Mary Lay (Mercy), 139
John s Stephen & Leoamy (Leony), 107
Joseph s Jonathan & Lucy, 11
Joseph s John & Mary (Mercy), 139
Joseph B. m Parthena Lord, 162
Joseph s Reuben & Martha, 77
Julia Ann m George F. Langworthy, 167
Julia Ann m Whitman Tibbets, 155
Juliaette m Asahel Clark, 180
Juliaette E. m Edward Tompkins, 174
Juliaette d Samuel & Fanny, 166
Lois d Dan & Hannah, 94
Louisa Ann d Richard & Mary, 145
Luce d Jonathan & Lucy, 11
Luce m Stephen Adset, 59
Lurana d Dan'll & Hannah, 72
Luranah m Joseph Wait, 4
Lurany d Ezra & (Dan'l in original) & Sally, 116
Lydia m Samuell Tilletson, 265
Mercy A. m Samuel Wait, 162
Martha d Allen & Hannah d 1773, 106
Martha d Allen & Hannah b 1774, 106
Martha m James Chadwick, 16
Mary m Alexander Allen, 128
Mary w Samuel died, 16
Mary Ann m John Eldredge, 173
Mary Ann d Samuel & Fanny, 166
Mary Elizabeth d Elihu & Elizabeth, 141
Mary Lay d Robert B. & Fanny Marvin, 139
Mehetable m Nathaniel Wait, 157
Molley d Dan & Hannah, 94
Naby d Reuben & Martha, 77
Nancy Miner d Elihu & Elizabeth, 141
Nathaniel s Allen & Hannah, 106
Phebe d Ezra & Sally, 116
Phebe's children, 16
  Ezra Smith, 16
  Sally Clark, 16
  Susannah Clark, 16
  Fanny Clark, 16
  George Door, 16
  Levy Selden Barthwick, 16

CHADDOCK, cont.
  Polly m Daniel Jacobs, 131
  Polly d John & Mary (Mercy), 139
  Polly d Stephen & Leoamy (Leomy), 107
  Reuben m Martha Miller, 77
  Reuben s Reuben & Martha, 77
  Richard m Hannah Lay, 148
  Richard 2nd m Mary Sill, 145
  Richard s Stephen & Leoamy, 107
  Robert s George & Welthy, 97
  Robert B. m Fanny Marvin Wood, 139
  Russell s Ruben & Martha, 77
  Sam'll m Mary Adset, 16
  Samuel died 1789, 16
  Samuel m Fanny Rogers, 166
  Samuel s Samuel & Fanny, 166
  Samuel died 1833, 166
  Samuel s Stephen & Leoamy (Leomy), 107
  Sarah m Hezekiah Smith, 48
  Sarah Harvey d Richard & Mary, 145
  Selden m Cordelia Otis, 191
  Seth s Stephen & Leoamy, 107
  Seth m Caroline Rowland, 161
  Silas s James & Martha, 16
  Stephen m Fanny Davenport, 196, 202
  Stephen m Leoamy (Leomy) Rogers, 107
  Stephen s Stephen & Leoamy, 107
  Susannah d Nathaniel & Bettey, 73
  Thomas Sr. died 1731, 224
  Thomas s Reuben & Martha, 77
  Ursula died 1848, 214
  Wealthy Ann d Robert B. & Fanny Marvin, 139
  William s Allen & Hannah, 106
  William Augustus s Samuel & Fanny, 166
CHAMBERLAIN, CHAMBERLIN
  Marah (Mary Champion) m Aaron Huntley, 235
  Rebeka m Jonathan Tilletson, 265
  Thomas M. m Harriet Royce, 194
CHAMPION, CHAMPEON, CHAMPEAN, CHAMPENY, CHAMPEN
  Abegull d Henry Jr. & Susanna, 225
  Ales m Jonathan Rogers, 257
  Alse d Henry Jr. & Susanna, 225
  Amon s Chauncy & Mary Ann, 202
  Amon s Reuben & Esther, 131
  Amon died 1870, 216
  Anne d Reuben & Esther, 131
  Betsey d Reuben & Esther, 131
  Bridget d Thomas & Elizabeth, 226
  Caholina Matildea d William & Esther, 126
  Calvin B. m Ann Slate, 186
  Carolina d Reuben & Esther, 130
  Caroline m William Beckwith, 161
  Charles, 207
  Charles s Lynde & Anne, 113
  Charles Frederick s William & Esther, 126
  Charlotte d Stephen & Phebe, 131
  Chauncy s Stephen & Phebe, 131
  Chauncy m Mary Ann Lay, 150, 202
  Clarissa B. d John & Lucy, 204
  Cynthia Maria d William & Esther, 126
  Dan s Ezra & Mary, 76
  Daniel s Lynda & Hepzibah, 113
  Daniel s Roswell & Jaminiah, 128
  Deborah d Stephen & Deborah, 9
  Deborah d Thomas & Hannah, 225

CHAMPION, cont.
  Edward m Mary Dart, 181, 202, 206
  Elisha s Henry & Sarah, 45
  Elisha (Capt.) m Phebe Miller, 105
  Elisha s Elisha & Phebe, 105
  Elizabeth d Thomas & Hanah, 226
  Elizabeth d Thomas & Elizabeth, 226
  Elizabeth d Jasper & Bettey, 96
  Elizabeth m Rowland Rogers, 22
  Emily m Theodore LaMott, 190, 208
  Ester m Daniel Ayer, 218
  Esther d Henry & Sarah, 225
  Esther d Reuben & Esther, 130
  Eunice m Isaac Jones, 135
  Eunice d Jasper & Bettey, 96
  Ezra s Joshua & Mary, 225
  Ezra m Mary Bumpas, 76
  Ezra s Ezra & Mary, 76
  Ezra M. m Elizabeth Jane Richardson, 169, 205
  Fanny d Stephen & Phebe, 131
  Fanny d March 1791, 131*
  Fanny d Stephen & Phebe April 1791, 131
  Fanny d Seabury & Lucy, 138
  Frances d Edward & Mary, 202
  Frederick m Mahala Tinker, 175
  Hanah d Thomas & Hanah, 225
  Hannah d Thomas & Elizabeth, 225
  Hannah d Joshua & Mary, 225
  Hannah m Samuel Clark, 16
  Hannah m Abraham Bishop, 13
  Hannah m Elisha Miller 3rd, 55
  Hannah d Ezra & Mary, 76
  Hannah d Stephen & Phebe, 131
  Hannah m Moses Mather, 130
  Harriot (Harriet) d Elisha & Phebe, 105
  Harriet m George Havens, 145
  Henery s Thomas & Hanah, 225
  Henery Sr. m Deborah Jones, 224
  Henery Sr. died, 224
  Henery born 16 __ s Henry Jr. & Susanna, 224
  Henrey died July 1704, 225
  Henry m Susanna, 224
  Henry m Sarah Peterson, 225
  Henry s Henry & Sarah, 225
  Henry Jr. m Sarah Peck, 45
  Henry s Henry & Sarah, 225*
  Henry s Roswell & Jamimah, 128
  Henry Capt. died 1791, 45*
  Henry Lorenzo s William & Esther, 126
  Hephzibah d Elisha & Phebe, 105
  Horace m Jane Maynard, 182, 198
  Israel s Reuben & Esther, 130
  James Ross s William & Esther, 126
  Jasper m Bettey Chadwick, 96
  Jasper s Joshua & Sarah, 225
  John s Ezra & Mary, 76
  John m Lucy Clark, 176, 204
  John s Roswell & Jamimah, 128
  John s Thomas & Elizabeth, 226
  John M. m Sophia Lay, 149
  Josuah s Henry Jr. & Susanna, 224
  Joshua m Mary Mott, 225
  Joshua s Joshua & Mary, 225
  Joshua m his second wife Sarah Griffing, 225
  Joshua Jr. m Elishabah Beckwith, 26
  Joshua s Ezra & Mary, 76

CHAMPION, cont.
Joshua s Joshua Jr. & Elishabah, 26
Judah d Elisha & Phebey, 105
Jude d Henry & Sarah, 45
Julia Ann m John Clark, 162
Juliatte m Ebenezer Comstock, 162
Kathleen C. d Edward & Mary, 206
Lovice m Elias Brockway, 106
Lovice d Jasper & Bettey, 96
Lucinda d Jasper & Bettey, 96
Lucretia m Samuel Starlin, 54
Lucey d Jasper & Bettey, 96
Lucy m Ezra Roland, 66
Lucy d Thomas & Elizabeth, 226
Lucy A. m Elisha Havens, 169
Lurana d Elisha & Phebe, 105
Lydia d Ezra & Mary, 76
Lydia d Joshua Jr. & Elishabah, 26
Lydia d Stephen & Phebe, 131
Lyman s Charles & Amy, 207
Lynde m Hepzibah Chadwick, 113*
Lynde m Ann Rowland, 113*
Lynde s Lynde & Ann, 113*
Marah d Thomas & Hanah, 225
Martha d Robert M. & Mary Ann, 202
Mary widow m Asael Rowland, 60, 76
Mary d Henry Jr. & Susanna, 225
Mary d Joshua & Mary, 225
Mary wife Joshua died 1730, 225
Mary A. m Enoch S. Lay, 165
Mary L. m Lathrop Slate, 182, 198
Mehatabell d Henry & Sarah, 225
Mehetabil m David Deming, 8
Mehitable m John Marvin, 246
Mercy A. m Samuel Dorr Clark, 189
Miranda d Stephen & Phebe, 131
Nancy Susan d Ezra & Elisabeth I, 205, 215
Nathan s Thomas & Elizabeth, 226
Orren s Seabury & Lucy, 138
Orlando m Nancy Richardson, 179
Parnal d Thomas & Elizabeth, 226
Phebe d Thomas & Elizabeth, 226
Phebe d Elisha & Phebe, 105
Phebe d Joshua & Mary, 225
Phebe twin with Polly d Stephen & Phebe, 131
Polly d Ezra & Mary, 76
Polly (twin with Phebe) d Stephen & Phebe, 131
Rachall d Henry Jr. & Susanna, 225
Rebeckah A. m Edward Bates, 165
Reuben m Esther Chadwick, 131
Reuben s Ezra & Mary, 76
Reuben s Reuben & Esther, 131
Reuben s Stephen & Deborah, 9
Reuben died 1848, 214
Robert m Susan Dart, 193, 209
Robert M. m Mary Ann Murphy, 202, 208
Roswell m Jamimah Mather, 128
Roswell s Roswell & Jamimah, 128
Ruth d Joshua & Sarah, 225
Sally d Stephen & Phebe, 130
Sally m Joseph Lee, 117
Sally m Moses Mather, 130
Samuel s Henry Jr. & Susanna, 225
Samuell s Joshua & Mary, 225
Samuel s Joshua & Sarah, 225
Sands s Jasper & Bettey, 96

CHAMPION, cont.
Sarah m Benjamin Peck, 253
Sarah m Henry Benet, 221
Sarah d Henry & Sarah, 225
Sarah d Horace & Jane, 199
Sarah d Joshua & Sarah, 225
Sarah m Stephen Scofell, 260
Sarah d Thomas & Hanah, 225
Seabury m Lucy Tinker, 138
Sebree s Stephen & Phebe, 131
Stephen m Deborah Leech, 9
Stephen s Ezra & Mary, 76
Stephen m Phebe Moshier, 131
Steven s Henry Jr. & Susanna, 225
Susanna d Henry & Susanna, 224
Susanna d Joshua & Mary, 225
Susannah d Reuben & Esther, 131
Sylvester s Roswell & Jamima, 128
Thankfull d Ezra & Mary, 76
Thomas m Elizabeth Wade, 225
Thomas m Hanah Brockwaye, 225
Thomas s Thomas & Elizabeth, 225
Thomas s Thomas & Hanah, 225
Thomas Sr. died 1705, 226
Thomas Spencer born, 165
Waitey d Jasper & Bettey, 96
William s Jasper & Bettey, 96
William m Esther Ross, 126
William Sands s William & Esther, 126
CHAMPLAIN, CHAMPLIN
Abby m Samuel Warner, 140
Abigail d George & Eunice, 118
Abigail d Silas & Bettey, 36
Bettey d Edward & Elizabeth, 28
Betsey m Tory Maxon, 119
Caleb s Edward & Elizabeth, 29
Caleb m Anna Ely, 106
Christopher s Caleb & Anna, 106
Daniel A. s George & Eunice, 118
Edward m Elizabeth Latham, 28
Edward s Edward & Elizabeth, 29
Eliza m James Dill, 147
Eunice d George & Eunice, 118
Fanny d Edward & Elizabeth, 29
Frances s William & Phebe, 206
George m Eunice Anderson, 117
George s George & Eunice, 117
George s William & Phebe, 206
Harriet d Richard M. & Helena, 154
Harvey Lay s Silas & Bettey, 36
Henry s George & Eunice, 118*
James m Lucinda Fosdick, 189, 203
John s Caleb & Anna, 106
John s Edward & Elizabeth died 1751, 29*
John s Edward & Elizabeth born 1768, 29
John s Nathan & Sarah, 18
John Gardiner s George & Eunice, 118
Julia Ann m John Clark, 162
Lodowick Macketton s William & Polly, 35
Lucinda d James & Lucinda, 203
Lucinda d Nathan & Sarah, 18
Lucinda died Nov. 22, 1848, 214
Lucinda F. died Nov. 30, 1848, 214
Lucretia d Edward & Elizabeth, 27
Lucy d William & Polly, 35
Lurannie m Dan Lee, 35

CHAMPLAIN, cont.
Lurane d William & Polly, 35
Mary Ann m Dan Gilbert, 154
Mary Ann d George & Eunice, 118
Molley d Edward & Elizabeth, 28
Nabbey d Edward & Elizabeth, 29
Nancy m Elisha Fitch, 113
Nathan m Phebe D. Clark, 209
Nathan s George & Eunice, 18, 118
Nathan m Phebe Dow, 193
Phebe m Jared Watrous, 139
Rebeckah d Edward & Elizabeth, 29
Richard Mather s William & Polly, 35
Richard M. m Helena West, 154
Richard M. s Richard & Helena, 154
Sally m Abner Griffing, 24
Sally d Edward & Elizabeth, 28
Sarah d Nathan & Sarah, 18*
Sarah Champlain m James Darrow Jr., 138
Seabury s Edward & Elizabeth, 29
Silas m Betsey Lay, 36
William, 206
William m Polly Mather, 35
William s Silas & Bettey, 36
CHAPMAN, Abby m Elisha Caulkins, 151
Amy m John Cook Smith, 118
Asael s Ebenezer & Elizabeth, 104
Asahel married, 133
Barsheba m Edward Chapman, 104
Bersheba d Ebenezer & Elizabeth, 104
Bersheba d Samuel, 98
Bersheba d Samll & Esther, 98
Betsey m Richard Lee, 184
Caleb s Edward & Barsheba, 104
Christopher B. m Emeline Maynard, 177
Cornelius m Mary Ann Appleby, 179
Ebenezer m Elizabeth Huntley, 103
Edward s Ebenezer & Elizabeth, 104
Ebenezer s Edward & Barsheba, 104
Edward m Molly Huntley, 104
Edward 2nd m Barsheba Chapman, 104
Eliza d Asahel, 133
Elizabeth d Ebenezer & Elizabeth, 104
Eunice d Ebenezer & Elizabeth, 103
Ezekiel s Ebenezer & Elizabeth, 104
Hannah m John Rogers, 173
John s Ebenezer & Elizabeth, 104*
John s Edward & Barsheba, 104
John s Asahel, 133
Lois m Caleb Wood, 118
Mary died 1849, 214
Peter m Eliza Harding, 151
Phebe d Ebenezer & Elizabeth, 104
Plyney d Asahel, 133
Robert s Ebenezer & Elizabeth, 104
Ruth d Ebenezer & Elizabeth, 104
Sarah Ann m Morgan Lewis, 202
Susa d Ebenezer & Elizabeth, 104
Susanna m William Tillotson, 41
CHAPPELL, CHAPEL
Albert m Julia Tillotson, 170
Benjamin Franklin m Nancy Waid, 176
Betsey m Jospeh Tinker, 166
Betsey m Samuel Rogers, 149
Christian m Christopher Brockway, 140
Daniel s Wm. & Abigail, 139

CHAPPELL, cont.
Enoch s Wm. & Abigail, 139
Enoch L. m Lucy Ann Tucker, 144
Ezra m Rachel Bouge, 142
Griswold m Hannah Lesheur, 169
Griswold m Mehetabel Lord, 191, 200
Henry B. m Mary Herrick, 185
Horace m Caroline Banning, 167
Isaac, 202
James m Hannah Maynard, 181
John O., 309
Julia Ann m Ruel Beckwith, 146
Julia Ann d Wm. & Abigail, 139
Levi B. m Sarah Latham, 163
Lois m Peter Mason, 173
Lucretia m Calvin Beckwith, 173
Mary m Edward Moore, 143
Sarah M. m John Rogers, 159
Victoria G. d Horace & Caroline, 167
William s Isaac & Harriet, 202
CHESEBRO, Dudley R. m Jane Tinker, 182
CHURCH, Athena d Edward & Mary, 46
Edward m Mary Clement (d. of Wm.), 46, 226
Edward, 303
Ezra s Edward & Mary, 46
John, 303
Joseph m Elizabeth Bogue, 195
Josiah s Edward & Mary, 46
Loas d Edward & Mary, 46, 226
Mary d Edward & Mary, 46
Phebe m William Bunnel, 171
Susannah d Edward & Mary, 46, 226
CLARK, CLARKE, CLARK
Abigail m Eleser Clark, 226
Abigail w Eleazer died 1750, 226
Abigail m Samuel Ingraham Jr., 20
Abigail d Sylvanus & Elizabeth, 93
Abraham Clark died, 213
Andrew Clark died, 213
Arnold s Daniel & Mary, 126
Arnold s Dudley & Edey, 126
Asahel s Daniel & Mary, 126
Asahel m Juliaette Chadwick, 180
Caroline m Andrew Danolds, 150
Champion s Samuel & Hannah, 16
Charles s Sylvia (nus) & Elizabeth, 93
Dan s Samll & Hannah, 16
Daniel m Mary Baker, 126
Daniel d Danl & Mary, 126
Deborah, 299
Dudley s Danl & Mary, 126
Dudley m Edey Bump, 126
Dudley s Dudley & Edey, 126
Eleaer m Abigail Clark, 226
Eleazer s Nathaniel & Sarah (deWolfe), 226
Eleazer s Sylvanus & Elizabeth, 93
Elijah s Nathan & Phebe, 226
Elijah s Samuel & Hannah, 16
Elizabeth, 300
Elisabeth m Dan Mather, 158
Elizabeth m James Ransom Jr., 137
Elizabeth d Nathaniel & Phebe, 226
Elizabeth m Solomon Sampson, 144
Elizabeth m Sylvanus Higgins, 89
Elizabeth m Watrous Maynard, 140
Elizabeth d William & Hannah, 227

INDEX OF PERSONS

CLARK, cont.
Eunice d Eleazer & Abigail, 226
Eunice m Ezra Peck, 140
Eunice d Sylvanus & Elizabeth, 93
Eunice w Sylvanus died 1776, 92*
Eusebius m Caroline Congdon, 173
Fanny d Phebe (Chadwick), 16
Frances S. m David Manwaring, 168
George D. m Phebe Havens, 144
George D. m Adeline Havens, 183
Gurdon m Mary Maynard, 194
Hannah d William & Hannah. 227
Hannah m William Brockway 2nd., 57
Hannah m Jacob Hall, 16
Henery s Sylvanus & Elizabeth, 93
Henry H. m Almena Loomis, 157
Henry King Peck s Nathaniel & Mahittable, 140
Hope d Nun & Anna, 52
Horace P. m Eleanor Hastings, 196
Isaac s Thomas & Rebeckah, 27, 226
James m Sophia Tooker, 175
Jemima d Eleazer & Abigail, 226
Jemimiah m John Daniels, 105
Joanna m Abner Beckwith, 133
Joel m Olive Tooker, 174
John D. m Jane Tucker, 164
John m Julia Ann Champion, 162
John D m Mary Tefft, 180
John m Mindwell, 227
John s Nathaniell & Sarah, 226
Joseph m Louis Miller, 155
Lester 2nd m Mary Ann Lester, 158
Lot s Thomas & Rebeckah, 27
Louisa m William Harrison, 186
Lucindia d Daniel & Mary, 126
Lucy d William & Hannah, 227
Lucy Ann d Nathaniel & Mehetable, 140
Lucy M. m John Champion, 176, 204
Lucy died 1849, 214
Lusena d Roswell & Parnall, 94
Lydia d Eleazer & Joanna, 26
Lydia m John Anderson, Jr. 39
Margaret m Almon Bacon, 170
Mary d Danel & Mary, 126
Mary d Nathaniel & Phebe, 226
Mary d Roswell & Parnall, 94
Mary m Stephen Prentice, 180
Mary E. m Timothy Wright, 193
Moreley s John, 119
Nun m Anna Jones, 52
Nun s Thomas & Rebeckah, 27
Nancy M. m William Bushnell, 181
Nathl m Mahittable Peck, 140
Nathaniel m Phebe Smith, 226
Nathaniel s Nathaniel & Phebe, 226
Nathaniell m Sarah Lay, 226
Nathaniel s Nathaniell & Sarah, 226
Patty d Dudley & Edey, 126
Peter Peck m Polly Smith, 114
Peter Peck s Roswell & Parnall, 93
Phebe d Danl & Mary, 126
Pheby d Samll & Hannah, 16
Phebe m Simeon Morgan, 152
Polly d Dudley & Edey, 126
Prudence M. m Israel Havens, 195, 211
Ralph B. m Sarah Ann Caulkins, 191

CLARK, cont.
Rebeckah d Thomas & Rebeckah, 27
Reuben s Daniel & Mary, 126
Richard s Dudley & Edey, 126
Richard m Jane Tooker, 174
Roswell m Parnall Peck, 93
Roswell s Roswell & Parnall, 93
Ruth Mary d Nathaniel & Mehetable, 140
Sally m Amos Maxon, 153
Sally d Dudley & Edey, 126
Sally d Phebe (Chadwick), 16
Samuel m Hannah Champion, 16
Samuel s Sam'll & Hannah, 16
Samuel s Nathaniell & Sarah, 226
Samuel Dorr m Mercy Champion, 189
Sarah m Jasper Peck, 253
Sarah m Thomas Hall, 12
Sarah d William & Hannah, 227
Sarah L m Erastus Goodrich, 175
Sarah Lord d Nathaniel & Mehetable, 140
Seth s Eleazer & Abigail, 226
Sheldon s William & Hannah, 227
Silas s Nathaniel & Phebe, 226
Silas m Sarah Elizabeth Ely, 162
Silence d Danl & Mary, 126
Simon s Elezer & Abigail, 226
Susannah d Daniel & Mary, 126
Susannah d Phebe (Chadwick), 16
Susannah d William & Hannah, 227
Sylvanus m Elizabeth Kent, 93
Sylvanus m Eunice Anderson, 92
Thomas, 302
Thomas s Nathaniell & Sarah, 226
Thomas m Rebecka Watrous (Rebeckah) (Watrouse), 27
Thomas s Thomas & Rebeckah, 27
Watrous s Nun & Anna, 52
Watrous s Thomas & Rebeckah, 27
Watson m Sarah Ann Rowley, 155
William m Hannah Peck, 227
William m Jamimah Rogers, 131
William s John & Mindwell, 227
William s Nathaniell & Sarah, 226
William s Roswell & Parnall, 93
Wm. Kent s Sylvanus & Elizabeth, 93
Wm. Sheldon s Nathaniel & Mehetable, 104
CLEMENT, CLEMMENT, CLEMMENTS
John s William, 227
Mary m Edward Church (d of William Clemments Sr.), 226
William s William, 227
CLOSSON, CLOSON
Mary m Alvin Babcock, 156
Oliver m Juliaette Tinker, 165
COATS, Harriet m Edmund Smith, 148
COBB, Ann, 227
Isaac m Fanny Grumley, 174
Jerusha Ann m George Miller, 158
John, 227
Maria m Abel Keeny, 154
Simon, 227
William H. m Ruth Phillips, 178, 308
COGSWELL, Hannah d Westall & Martha, 227
Martha w Westall d 1704, 227*
Sarah d Westall & Martha, 227*
Stephen s Westall & Martha, 227

328 LYME, CONNECTICUT, VITAL RECORDS

COGSWELL, cont.
  Westall m Martha, 227
COLLINS
  Dan s Stephen & Thedy, 136
  David Crocker s Stephen & Thedy, 136
  Jane m Ephraim Douglass, 192, 209
  Jonathan Minor s Stephen & Thedy, 136
  Sally Anderson d Stephen & Thedy, 136
  Sally m Almus Pratt, 158
  Stephen m Thedy Crocker, 136
  Thedy wife Stephen d 1813, 136
  Thomas Mason s Stephen & Thedy, 136
COLTON, COLTEN
  Ann m John Noyes, 175, 198
  Sarah d Thomas, 227
  Capt. Thomas m Sarah Griswold, 227
COMSTOCK, COMSTOCKE
  Abagall w John m Moses Huntley, 237
  Abbegail d John, 227
  Abbigall m William Pike, 255
  Abegail d Wm. & Naomy, 228
  Abigail m Joseph Lord, 243
  Abigail d John & Rebeckah, 228
  Abigail m Jonathan Reed, 53
  Abigail d William & Neomy, 228
  Abigail m Capt. James Ransom, 116
  Abner (Capt.), 303
  Ann d Daniell & Alse, 227
  Ann m John Hale, 178
  Anna m Benjamin Graham, 231
  Charles S., 309
  Christian d John, 227
  Christopher s Samuel & Esther, 103, 113
  Curtise s John & Rebeckah, 228
  Curtiss m Esther Caufield, 79
  Curtiss s Curtiss & Esther, 79
  Daniel died 1725, 227
  Ebenezer m Juliette Champion, 162
  Eleanor d Sam'l & Esther, 113
  Elisha m Hetty Hamilton, 150
  Eliza H. m James Loomis, 154
  Elizabeth d John, 227
  Elizabeth d James & Thankful, 88
  Elizabeth d Samuell & Esther, 103
  Elizabeth S. m Rev. TS Vaill, 183
  Esther m Allen McKnight, 4
  Esther m Benjamin Johnson, 137
  Esther d Curtiss & Esther, 79
  Esther d Sam'l & Esther, 113
  Eunice m Enock Smith, 52
  Eunice m Elijah Selden, 103
  Frederic W. m Dorcas Waterhouse, 181
  Gamwell (Samuel) child John, 228
  Giles s Curtiss & Esther, 79
  Hannah, 150
  Hannah m Abner Beckwith, 117
  Hannah d John, 227
  Hannah R. m David Otis, 162
  Hannah R. d Peter, 150
  Henry J. m Caroline S. Brockway, 182
  Hetta Eliza d Peter, 150
  Hezekiah s Curtiss & Esther, 79
  Indiana m Richard Pearson, 138
  Jabez m Margret Brockway, 153
  Jacob, 301
  James, 302

COMSTOCK, cont.
  James m Thankfull Crosby, 88*
  Joab s James & Thankfull, 30
  John s John, 228*
  John s John, 228*
  John died 1769, 228
  John s Curtiss & Esther, 79
  John s Wm. & Rebeckah Bates, 228
  John s William, 228
  John J. s Peter, 151
  John L. s Sam'll & Esther, 113
  Jonathan s John, 228
  Josephus s Sam'll & Esther, 113
  Laura m Erastus Selden, 168
  Lee m Phobe Miller, 137
  Lee s Samuel & Esther, 113
  Lee m Sarah Caulkins, 151
  Lois W. daughter Peter, 151
  Lucinda d Sam'l & Esther, 113
  Lydia m Lawrence (Lawrrane) Johnson, 75, 78
  Marah d Daniell & Alse, 227
  Mary Ann m James Strictland, 155
  Mary Ann d Peter, 150
  Moses W. s Peter, 150
  Neomey m Consider Tiffany (daughter of William & Naomi), 264
  _____ Oliver, 307
  Peter married Maria Warren, 162
  Peter A. s of Peter, 150
  Phebe d of John & Rebeckah, 228
  Prentice m Lynda Banning, 152
  Prudence m Zachriah Sill, 22
  Rebecka d John & Rebeckah, 228
  Ruth Craskey d James & Thankfull, 88
  Samuel, 302
  Samuel m Esther Lee, 103, 113
  Sam'l m Harriet Minor, 164
  Samuel s Sam'l & Esther, 103
  Savy m John Oliver, 251
  Sarah d Curtiss & Esther, 79
  Sarah m Chapman Warner, 32
  Sarah R. (Raymond) d Peter, 150, 151
  William born 1782, 127
  William s John, 227
  William m Neomy Niles d of Benj., 228
  William s Wm. & Neomy, 228*
  William H. s Peter, 150
COUDELL, CONDOLL, CONDOL
  Huldah m Charles Minor, 176, 203
  Martha B. m George Mason, Jr., 203, 210
CONE
  Andrew Diodate Griswold s Henry & Watestill, 106
  Charles Smith s Henry & Watestill, 106
  Elihu Lyman s Henry & Watestill, 107
  Henry s Henry & Watestill, 106
  Lydia m John Lay, 180
  Lydia Ann m Joseph Luther, 190
  Oliver Bray s Henry & Watestill, 107
  Sarah M. m Henry Robbins, 195, 211
  Silas s Henry & Watestill, 106
  Waitstill died 1850, 216
  William Prince s Henry & Watestill, 106
CONGDON, Caroline m Eusebius Clark, 173
  Edward m Sarah Colt, 194, 210
  Eliza W. m William Howard, 157

INDEX OF PERSONS 329

CONGDON, cont.
 Frances M. m Charles Starkey, 164
 Hannah m Jonathan Brown, 142
 Hannah m Richard Beebe, 165
 John, 301
 Lorenzo m Clarissa Minor, 172
 Wealthy Ann m Adrial Huntley, 173
CONKLIN OR CONKLING
 Betsey m John Sumner, 147
 Nathaniel Capt. m Mehetable Minor, 156
COOK, Cyrus m Mehetable Shipman, 155
 James B. m Lucretia Caulkins, 178
COOLEY
 Abednego (Triplet) w Shadrach & Meshech s Matthew & Jemima, 36
 Absolom s Matthew & Jemiah, 228
 Eunice d Matthew & Jemima, 36
 Jemima d Matthew & Jemima, 36
 Job s Matthew & Jemima, 228
 Job Miller Walker s Matthew & Prudence, 133
 John d 1774, 50*
 John s John & Lydia, 50
 John m Lydia Anderson, 50
 John s Matthew & Jemima, 228
 John How s Matthew & Prudence, 133
 Lydia m Elisha Robbins, 101
 Marcey m Turner Calkins, 86
 Matthew m Jemmiah Rogers, 228
 Matthew s John & Lydia, 50
 Matthew s Matthew & Jemmiah, 228
 Matthew m Prudence Ray, 133
 Matthew Bull s Matthew & Prudence, 133
 Mehetable d John & Lydia, 50
 Mercey d Matthew & Jemiah, 228
 Mesheck s Matthew & Jemima, 36
 Molly Rogers m John Gilbert, 69
 Molly Rogers d Matthew & Jemima, 228
 Paul s Matthew & Jemimah, 36, 228
 Paul s Matthew & Jemima, 228
 Samuel Ingraham Watrous s Matthew & Prudence, 133
 Matthew m Prudence, 133
 Sela d John & Lydia, 50
 Selah m Joseph Walker, 101
 Shadrach s Matthew & Jemima, 36
 Theada d John & Lydia, 50
COOPER, Martha m John Lewis, 33
CORAH, Parnall m Peter Pierson, 117
COSFORD, Hezekiah m Hannah Sanders, 183
COULT, COLT
 Abigail Matson d Wm. & Anne, 119
 Ama (Amy) d Harris & Elizabeth died Oct. 1768, 69
 Ama (Amy) d Harris & Elizabeth born 1771, 69
 Amhurst s John & Mary, 34
 Andrew Gardiner s John & Mary, 34
 Anna w William died, 119
 Anna Maria d William & Anna, 119*
 Arnold s Harris & Elizabeth, 69
 Asenath d Joseph & Desire, 57
 Asenath m Moses Sill, 115
 Benjamin m Elisabeth Denison, 110
 Benjamin s John & Mary, 34
 Benjamin m Merriam Harris d of Thomas, 228
 Benjamin Gardner s Benjamin & Elizabeth, 110
 Charles Bulkley s John & Susannah, 46

COULT, cont.
 Deborah d Joseph & Desire, 56
 Desire m Richard Ely Selden, 8
 Desire d Joseph & Desire, 57
 Dijah s Samuel & Sally, 16
 Elisha s Harris & Elizabeth, 69
 Elizabeth d Harris & Elizabeth, 69
 Ester m Daniel Starling, Jr. 263
 Esther d John & Mary, 34
 Esther m Mather Peck, 90
 George Robert s Benjamin & Elizabeth, 110
 George R. m Catherine Caulkins, 162
 Harris m Elizabeth Turner, 69
 Harris s Harris & Elizabeth, 69
 Israel Bulkley, 46
 Jabez s Joseph & Desire, 57
 John Breed, 46
 John s Benjamin & Merriam, 228
 John s John & Mary (died 1754), 34
 John, Captain died, 34*
 John m Mary Lord, 34*
 John s John & Mary, born 1754, 34, 301
 John m Mary Gardner, 34*
 John m Abigail Matson, 34
 John d 1784, 34
 John m Susannah Bulkley, 46
 John Denison s Benjamin & Elizabeth, 110
 Joseph s Benjamin & Merriam, 228
 Joseph m Desire Pratt, 56
 Joseph Harris s Benjamin & Elizabeth, 110
 Josiah s Joseph & Desire, 56
 Judah s Joseph & Desire, 57
 Lucretia d Harris & Elizabeth, 69
 Martain s Samuell & Abigall, 228
 Martin s Samuell & Sally, 16
 Mary d Benjamin & Merriam, 228
 Mary m Thomas Giddings, 26
 Mary w John died 1759, 34*
 Mary w John died Oct. 1767, 34*
 Mary d Harris & Elizabeth, 69
 Mary Sears d Benjamin & Elisabeth, 110
 Merriam d John & Mary, 34
 Meriam m Joseph Burnham, 18
 Nancy d Benjamin & Elisabeth, 110
 Patthena d Samuel & Abigall, 228
 Peter H. s Harris & Elizabeth, 69
 Sally d Harris & Elizabeth, 69
 Samuel m Abigall Marvin, 228*
 Samuel s Joseph & Desire, 57
 Samuel s Samuel & Abigall, 228
 Samuel m Sally Fowler, 16
 Samuel s Samuel & Sally, 16
 Sarah m Edward Congdon, 194, 210
 Temperance m Abner Lord, 58
 Temperance d Harris & Elizabeth, 69*
 William m Anne Dennison, 119
 William m Mary Marvin, 119
 William s John & Abigail, 34
 William Ely s William & Anne, 119
COURTNEY, Alanson s Neal & Lydia, 112
 Neal m Lydia Mack, 112
COVELL, Edward m Georgianna Parsons, 192, 210
COY, Silas E. m Lorinda Willard, 165
CRANDALL, CRANDA
 Denison m Lucy Moore, 137
 Hannah m Jasper Brockway, 136

CRANE, Emily m John Moore 2nd, 140
CRARY, John W. m Sally Huntley, 175
CRESSE, John m Hannah Perigo, 254
CROWELL, Marriett m James F. Saunders, 184
CROCKER, Eunice m Lt. Elisha Way, 108
Eveline m Norman Daniels, 168
Frances C. m Bartlett Sampson, 188, 209
Hannah B. m Jonathan Martin, 163, 207
Harris m Sabra Manwaring, 167
John s John & Rhoda, 13*
Josiah W. m Elizabeth Tiffany, 184
Mary A. m Justin Beckwith, 164
Rhoda, 13
Sarah m Noah Miller, 96
Thedy m Stephen Collins, 136
CROSBY, John M. m Mary Elizabeth Johnson, 190
Laura R. m Stephen Harlow, 190
Thankful m James Comstock, 88
CULVER, Maria H. m Edgecomb Beckwith, 194
CUMMINGS, John M. died 1850, 216
DAMON, Abby A. m Augustus Morgan, 195, 211
Adeline m Edward Brockway, 172, 209
Amelia m Charles Hayden, 188, 200, 209
Henry N. m Nancy Hayden, 188
J.B., 204
Martha, 204
DANIELS, DANIELL, DANOLDS
Abigail W. m John Mack (See Davis), 245
Andrew m Caroline Clark, 150
Bill s Daniel & Sarah, 26
Caroline w Andrew died, 150
Charles H. m Mary Darrow, 150
Daniel Jr. m Sarah Waite, 26
Eunice w John died, 105*
Jared m Eleanor Bogue, 172
Jemima w John died, 105
John m Eunice Beckwith, 105
John m Esther Waite, 105
John m Huldah_____, 37
John s John & Huldah, 37
John m Jemimiah Clark, 105
John m Nancy Hall, 187
John (Twin with Watrous)s John & Lucretia, 105*
John m Lucretia Watrous,105
John Watrous s John & Esther, 105
Joseph s Daniel & Sarah, 26
Lucretia w John died, 105
Lucretia Watrous d John & Eunice, 105
Mary m John Maynard, 172
Molley d John & Huldah d 1749, 37
Molley d John & Huldah b 1752, 37
Nabby d John & Huldah, 37
Nabby m James Greenfield, 80
Norman m Eveline Crocker, 168
Phebe d John & Hulda, 37
Rebeckah m Wm. Tubbs, 30
Richard B. m Mary Bramble, 180
Roxanna P.M. d Andrew & Caroline, 150
Samuel m Jerusha Miller, 144
Thomas C. m Eliza Dart, 177
Watrous s John & Lucretia, 105*
William m Nancy Havens, 177

DARBY, Elizabeth m Joseph Smith, 98
DARROW, Abi d Ebeneazer & Abi, 229
Ebenezer m Abi Rogers, 228
Elizabeth d Ebeneazer & Abi, 229
Emma d Zadock & Lucy, 123
Frances Champlin d James Jr. & Sarah, 138*
Francis James s James Jr. & Sarah, 138
James Jr. m Sarah Champlin, 138
Lucy m Niles Tooker, 143
Lucy Way d Zadock & Lucy, 123
Mary m Charles Daniels, 150
Mary Lucinda d James Jr. & Sarah, 138
Osmund m Sarah Loomis, 152
Sally Lord d Zadock & Lucy, 123
Sarah d Ebeneazer & Abi, 229
Sarah Maria d James Jr. & Sarah, 138
Zadok s Ebeneazer & Abi, 229
Zadock m Lucy Lord, 123
DART, DAST
Eben m Juliaette Hurlburt, 174
Eliza m Thomas Daniels, 177
Lucretia m John Taggers, 154
Lucretia m Henry Ross, 208
Mary m Edward Champion, 181, 202
Mehetabel m King Miller, 155
Phebe m Samuel Bushnell, 208
Samuel B. m Adaline Hand, 171
Susan A. m Robert Champion, 193, 209
DARTHWICK, Levi Selden s Phebe Chadwick, 16
DATE, David B. m Mary Hughes 2nd, 186
DAVENPORT
Fanny m Stephen Chadwick, 196, 202
DAVIS, DAVISS
Abigail m Ebeneazer Mack, Jr., 244
Abigail (widow) m John Mack, 245
Albert (see Dennis) m Eveline C. Dwyer, 189
Elizabeth m James Tillitson, 19
Elizabeth m Martin Miner, 92
Elizabeth d Wm. & Esther, 26
Freelove m George Roland, 91
Mary m Levi Tillitson, 45
Mary m Consider Tiffany, 39
DAVISON, Eunice M. m William Smith, 174
George W. m Mary Ann Wood, 195
Lydia R. m Samuel Hart, 174
William D. m Abby Manwaring, 161
DAWES, William Jr. m Abby Bogue, 187
DAY, Amasa m Ursula Gates, 174
Amasa m Sarah S. Spencer, 186
Lydia M. m John Morgan, 195
DAYTON, John H. m Frances Nichols, 169
DEAN, Caroline A. m Charles Rogers, 186
Charles H. m Ede Brown, 167
Grace m Shadrach Gillett, 152
DEMING, DEMMING
Asa s David & Mehetabel, 7
David m Mehetabil Champion, 8
David Rev. died, 7
Downing (Pownall) s David & Mehetabel, 7
Elizabeth d David & Mehetabel, 7
Elizabeth m Matthew Marvin, 102
Henry s David & Mehetabel, 7
Jonathan died, 7
Jonathan s David & Mehetabil, 7
Julius s David & Mehetabel, 7
Marcy d David, 5

DEMING, cont.
Prudence d David & Mehetabil, 8
DENISON, Andrew s Robert & Esther, 97
Anna d John & Mary, 71
Anne m William Coult, 119
Candace m Reuben Havens, 137
Charles s Robert & Esther, 97
Elizabeth d John & Mary, 71
Elizabeth m Benjamin Colt, 110
George Washington s John & Mary, 71
James s John, 120
Joanna m Jabez Bogue, 161
John, 120, 229
John s John, 121
John died, 229
John s John & Patience, 229
John Jr. m Mary Sears, 71
John Sears s John & Mary, 71
Joseph s Robert & Esther, 97
Martha Jane d Richard N. & Emeline, 205
Mary wife of John died, 71
Mary m Jared Watrous, 152
Nabby d Robert & Esther, 97
Nancy (twin with Richard) d John, 121
Oliver s John & Mary, 71
Patience d John & Patience, 229
Phebe d John, 120
Phebe d John & Mary, 70
Phebe m Josiah Ely, 57
Richard (twin) s John, 121
Richard N. m Emeline Robbins, 192, 205
Robert (Lex. Alarm), 301
Robert m Esther Wade, 97
Robert s John & Mary, 71
Robert s Robert & Esther, 97
Sam'll s John & Mary, 71
Sam'll s John & Patience (died 1736), 229*
Samuel 2nd s John & Patience, 229
William s John, 121
DESHON, DISHON
Elizabeth m Harris Tinker, 126
Joanna m Silvanus Tinker, 122
DEWOLF, DEWOLFE
Achsah d Jabez & Eunice, 46*
Anna d Josiah & Martha, 10
Anne d Sam'l & Susannah, 125
Azuba d Josiah & Martha, 10
Azuba m Joseph Sill, 49
Benjamin s Edward, 229
Benjamin s Edward & Hannah, 74
Benjamin s Simeon & Parnall, 5
Benjamin s Steven & Hana, 229
Bettey d Simeon & Parnall, 5
Billey s William & Elizabeth, 76
Charles s Edward, 229
Daniel m Azuba Lee, 36
Daniel died 1752, 37
Daniel s Edward & Hannah, 74
Daniel s Josiah & Anna, 229
Daniel s Josiah & Martha, 10
Daniel s Sam'l & Susannah, 125
Daniel s Simon & Sarah, 229
Debra d Steven & Hana, 229
Debrah m Aaron Huntley Jr., 235
Edward Sr., 229
Edward s Steven & his first wife, 230

DEWOLF, cont.
Edward m Hannah Huntley, 74
Edward s Edward & Hannah, 74
Elias s Daniel & Azuba, 37
Elisha s Simon & Lucia, 49
Elizabeth d Josiah & Anna, 229
Elizabeth d William & Elizabeth b-1771, d-1776, 76
Elizabeth d William & Elizabeth born 1781, 76
Ephraim (Twin with Manasseh) s Edward & Hannah, 74
Esther d Josiah & Martha, 10
Eunice d Jabez & Eunice, 46
Eunice wife of Jabez died, 46
Eunice m Nathaniel Mather, 120
Hana d Steven & Hana, 229
Hannah d Josiah & Martha, 10*
Hannah d Sam'l & Susannah, 125
Jabez s Josiah & Anna, 229
Jabez d 1798, 299
Jabez m Eunice Calkins, 46
Jabez s Sam'll & Susannah, 125
Jeremiah s Stephen & Theody, 79
John m Ann_____, 198
John s Jabez & Eunice, 46*
John s Simon & Sarah, 229
John A. m Zylpha A. Johnson, 183
John F., 309
Joseph s Sam'l & Susannah, 125
Josiah m Anna Waterman, 229
Josiah s Josiah & Anna, 229
Josiah 2nd s Josiah & Anna, 229
Josiah Jr. m Martha Ely, 10, 229
Josiah s Sam'l & Susannah, 125
Josiah s Simon & Sarah, 229
Josiah s William & Elizabeth died 1776, 76
Josiah born 1777 s William & Elizabeth, 76
Judith d Josiah & Anna, 229
Lewes s Steven & Hana, 229
Lucy widow of Simon m Abel Beckwith, 65
Luce m John Alger, 56
Lucy d Stephen & Theody, 79
Lydia m James Sullard, 107
Lydia d Stephen & Theody, 79
Manasseh s Edward & Hannah, 74
Marah m Thomas Lees, 241
Margaret d Benjamin m John Banning Jr., 24
Martha d Josiah & Martha, 10
Martha d William & Elizabeth, 76
Martha d Sam'l & Susannah, 125
Phebe m Joseph Mather, 229, 248
Phebe d Sam'l & Susannah, 125
Phebe d Simon & Lucia, 49
Phebe d Simon & Sarah, 229
Phebe d Steven & Hana, 230
Polly d Sam'l & Susannah, 125
Rachell m John Andrus, 218
Sally d Sam'l & Susannah, 125
Sally m Matthew Rowland, 120
Samuel (Lex. Alarm), 301
Samuel s Josiah & Martha, 10
Samuel m Susannah Keeney, 125
Samuel s Sam'l & Susannah, 125
Sarah d Simon & Sarah, 79, 226
Sarah d Simon & Lucia, 49
Sarah d Stephen & Sarah, 229

DEWOLF, cont.
  Sarah wife of Stephen died, 79
  Simeon m Parnall Kirkland, 5
  Simon (Lex. Alarm), 301
  Simon s Edward, 229
  Simon died 1707, 229
  Simon s Josiah & Anna, 229
  Simon m Lucia Calkins, 49
  Simon m Sarah Laye, 229
  Simon s Simon & Sarah, 229
  Simon Sr. died, 229
  Simon died 1750, 49
  Simon s Simon & Lucia, 49
  Stephen (Lex. Alarm), 301
  Stephen m Nabby Beckwith, 122
  Stephen m Sarah Greenfield, 79
  Stephen m Theody Anderson, 79
  Stephen s Stephen & Theody, 79
  Stephen & Julia, 199
  Steven s Steven & Hanna, 229
  Steven died, 229
  Susanna d William & Elizabeth, 76
  Sylvanus s Edward & Hannah, 74
  Theody d Stephen & Theody, 79
  Theody wife of Stephen died, 79
  Thomas E., 309
  William m Elizabeth Roland, 76
  William s Josiah & Martha, 10
  William s Sam'l & Susannah, 125
  Winthrop m Hepsibah Anderson, 161
  Winthrop died, 213
  Winthrop Buck s Stephen & Theody, 79
  Zeporah d William & Elizabeth, 76
DICKENS, Sarah m Samuel Beckwith, 56
DICKERSON, Anna wife of Nath'll, 56*
  Bridget, 278
  Nathaniel m Anne Munsell, 56
  Sam'll s Nath'll & Anne, 56
DICKINSON, Eliza A. m Joseph Martin, 177
  Seth B. m Mariaette Howard, 184
DILL, James m Eliza Champlain, 147
DIMMOCK, Jospeh m Sarah Wing, 192
  Thomas L. died 1850, 215
DIODATE, Elizabeth m Stephen Johnson, 27
DODGE, Anna m Nathan Latimer Jr., 97
  Daniel m Lucy Latimer, 43
  Daniel E. Jr. m Amelia Saunders, 192, 209
  Eusebus m Anne Merchant, 116
  Eusebus s Eusebus & Anne, 116
  Jeremiah s Eusebus & Anne, 116
  John s Eusebus & Anne, 116
  Marcy m Hallam Latimer, 99
  Mary m Sam'll Gilbert, 58
  Nancy d Eusebus & Anne, 116
  Polly d Eusebus & Anne, 116
DOLPH, Azubah m James Wood, 170
DOLY, DOTY, Martin m Eunice Banning, 186
DORR, DOOR, DOW
  Deborah d George Jr. & Molly, 82
  Edmund m Mary Griswould, 230, 303
  Edward, 301
  Edward s Edmund & Mary, 230
  Edward s Matthew & Elizabeth, 61
  Ellenor m Andrew Sill, 98
  Eunice m Samuel Sill, 95
  George s Edmund & Mary, 230

DORR, cont.
  George Jr. m Molly Lovitt, 82
  George[1] s George & Molley died, 82
  George[2] s George & Molley born, 82
  George s Phebe Chadwick, 16
  Helena d Matthew & Elizabeth, 61
  John, 204
  John L. s John & Nancy, 204
  Jonathan s Matthew & Elizabeth, 61
  Joseph s Matthew & Elizabeth, 61
  Joseph s George & Molly, 82
  Lydia m Roswell Beckwith, 79
  Mary d Edmund & Mary, 230
  Mary 2nd m Benjamin Lee Jr., 79
  Mathew s Edmund & Mary, 230
  Matthew m Elizabeth Palmer, 61
  Matthew s Matthew & Elizabeth, 61
  Molly[1] d George & Molley born & died, 82
  Molley[2] d George & Molly born, 82
  Nancy died, 213
  Phebe d Matthew & Elizabeth, 61
  Phebe m Jasper Peck Jr. 69
  Phebe Dow m Nathan Champlain, 193, 301
  Samuel Griswold s Matthew & Elizabeth, 61
  Susan m Calvin King, 189
DOUGLASS, Ephraimh m Jane Collins, 192
  Mary m Marvin Huntley, 110
DOWLEY, DAWLEY, Dr. Dowley, 230
  Sarah widow m George Wade, 267
  William s Dr. & Martha, 230
DOWSETT, DOSETT, Amos died, 141
  Cordelia m Daniel Howard, Jr., 168
  Joseph m Betsey Tillotson, 136, 197
DOWZICK, DOWSICK, DOSETT
  Anne d Gasper & Patience, 42
  David s Gasper & Patience, 42
  Eleonor d Gasper & Patience, 42
  Gasper m Patience Brockway, 42
  Katharine d Gasper & Patience, 42
  Lucy Ann m John Waite, 191
  Lucy Ann m Elderkin Waite, 209
  Marke s Gasper & Patience, 42
  Peter s Gasper & Patience, 42
DUDLEY, Anna m Moses & Anna, 42
  Annah m Sam'll Starlin, 54
  Bushnell s Moses & Anna, 42
  Jemima m Thomas Sill, 52
  John s Moses & Anna, 42
  Mehetable m Sam'll Pearson, 251
  Moses m Anna Bushnell, 42*
  Moses s Moses & Anna, 42
  Rebeckah d Moses & Anna, 42
  William s Moses & Anna, 42
DURANT, DUREN, DURINS
  Elizabeth m George Wade, 267
  Mary m John Waller, 269
  Sarah m Amase Tinker, 266
DURFEY, Esther m Enoch Lord, Jr., 108
  Joseph m Lucy Ann Burnham, 167
DUTTEN, Benjamin s Joseph & Marah, 230
  Joseph, 230
DWYER, Eveline C. m Albert Davis, 189
  Harriet died 1850, 216
  Mariette m Thomas Prentice, 191
EDGECOMB, Asa Park m Mary Bill, 155

INDEX OF PERSONS 333

EDGERTON, EDGORTON, EDGARTON
  Daniel s Jedediah & Esther, 52
  Jedediah m Esther Wallis, 52
  Lucey d Jedediah & Esther, 52
  Polly d Jedediah & Esther, 52
EIDENS, Lucy Ann, 278
EDWARDS, Andrew m Alice Wright, 191
  Bulkeley m Abigail Topliff, 166
ELDREDGE, John m Mary Ann Chadwick, 173
ELMORE, John m Phebe Sterling, 143
ELY, Aaron, 303
  Aaron s Aaron, 303
  Aaron s James & Dorcas, 8
  Aaron died, 8
  Aaron s James & Catharine, 123
  Abby Lee d Eleazer S. & Martha, 175
  Abigail d Seth & Lydia, 62
  Abigail d Esq. Seth, 275
  Abner, 279, 307
  Abner died, 213, 304
  Abner S. m Fanny Griffin, 149
  Abraham s William & Elizabeth, 18
  Abraham P. m Philina Griffin, 165
  Adriel m Sarah Stow, 16, 301, 304
  Ama d Daniel & Ame, 84
  Ame m Ezra Selden, 34
  Ammi s Gurdeon & Parnal, 103
  Ammi m Martha Peck, 72
  (Ammi) Ruhama s William & Hannah, 230
  Andrew s James Dorcas, 8, 301
  Ann d William & Elizabeth, 230
  Anna m Caleb Champlain, 106
  Anna d Daniel, 58
  Anna m Ensign Elihu Ely, 84
  Anna d Elihu & Anna, 84
  Anna m Elisha Ely, 16
  Anna d Ezra & Anna, 49
  Anna d Israel & Eunice, 113
  Anna m Nathaniel Matson, 115
  Anna m Philip Toocker, 58
  Ansel H., 309
  Azubah Lee d Capt. Calleck & Azubah, 108
  Benjamin s Ezra & Anna, 49
  Calvin L., 200
  Calvin s James & Catharine, 123*
  Calvin s Israel & Eunice, 113
  Caroline d Elihu & Anna, 84
  Caroline m Joel Steel, 154
  Cate d Elijah & Catharine, 39
  Cate d James & Catharine, 123
  Charles s Cullick & Sarah, 59
  Charles m Betsey Perkins, 119
  Christopher s Daniel & Ama, 84
  Christopher Capt. (perhaps John Christopher Ely) died, 139, 304
  Clarissa d Gurdon & Parnal, 103
  Cullick Junr. (Capt.) m Azubah Sill, 108
  Cullick (Collick) m Sarah Foot, 59
  Cullick s Cullick & Sarah, 59
  Daniel 2nd wife died, 230
  Daniel, 302
  Daniel Starlin s Ezra & Anna, 49
  Daniel Major, 304
  Daniel s of Daniel, 304
  David s Cullick & Sarah, 59
  David s Josiah & Phebe, 57

ELY, cont.
  David s Richard Jr. & Phebe, 25
  Deborah d William & Hannah, 231
  Deborah m Richard Mather, 1
  Deborah d Seth & Lydia died 1770, 62
  Deborah d Seth & Lydia born 1781, 62
  Deby twin with Margret d Elisha & Anna, 17
  Diadamia m Noyes Palmer, 195, 212
  Dorcas d James & Catharine, 123*
  Dorcas d James & Dorcas, 8
  Ebenezer s Seth & Lydia, 62
  Eleazer S. m Martha Campbell, 175
  Eleazer s Cullick & Sarah, 59
  Eliab s Elisha & Anna, 307
  Eliah s Elisha & Anna, 17
  Elias, 307
  Elias s Elihu & Anna, 84
  Elias m Eliza Nichols, 164
  Elihu s Richard Jr. & Phebe died 1736, 25, 230
  Elihu 2nd s Richard Jr. & Phebe born 1737, 25*, 230*
  Elihu Ensign m Anna Ely, 84
  Elihu s Elihu & Anna, 84
  Elihu died 1815, 84, 304
  Elijah s Samuell & Hannah, 12
  Elijah m Catharine Lee, 39
  Elijah s Elijah & Catharine, 39
  Elisha Surgeon's mate, 304
  Elihu s Richard Jr. & Phebe died, 1736, 230
  Elihu 2nd s Richard Jr. & Phebe born 1739, 230
  Elisha s Daniel & Ama, 84
  Elisha m Anna Ely, 16
  Elisha Olcot s Elisha & Anna, 17
  Elisha O. m Fanny Ely, 123
  Eliza Morgan d Erastus S. & Martha, 176
  Elizabeth m Abraham Perkins, 82
  Elizabeth, m Samuel Selden, 14
  Elizabeth m Capt. Elisha Sheldon, 5
  Elizabeth wife of Richard Ely Sr. Died, 230
  Elizabeth wife Richard Ely Jr. Died, 230
  Elizabeth d Capt. Calleck & Azubah, 109
  Elizabeth d James & Dorcas, 8
  Elizabeth d Richard Jr. & Elizabeth, 230
  Elizabeth d Samuel, 5
  Elizabeth d William & Elizabeth, 18*, 230
  Elizabeth 2nd d William & Elizabeth, 18
  Elizabeth d Zelophd & Elizabeth, 115
  Elizabeth P. m Similius B. Ely, 149
  Enoch s Josiah & Phebe, 57
  Erastus s Gabriel & Eunice, 102
  Erastus S. m Martha Campbell, 175
  Ester d Richard Jr. & Elizabeth, 230
  Esther d Ezra & Sarah, 49
  Esther Jane d John Christopher & Eunice, 139
  Eunice d Cullick & Sarah, 59
  Eunice d Israel & Eunice, 113
  Ezra d Richard Jr. & Elizabeth, 230
  Ezra m Anna Starlin, 49
  Ezra m Sarah Starling, 49
  Faunne d Ammi & Martha died 1755, 72
  Fanne d Ammi & Martha born 1768, 72
  Fanne d Ammi & Martha born 1773, 73
  Fanne d Gabriel & Eunice, 103
  Fanny m Elisha O. Ely, 123
  Gabriel s Ammi & Martha, 72
  Gabriel m Eunice Marvin (Marrimon), 102

LYME, CONNECTICUT, VITAL RECORDS

ELY, cont.
Gad s James & Dorcas, 8
George G. died, 213
Gurdon s Ammi & Martha, 72
Gurdon m Parnal Phelps, 103
Gurdon s Gurdon & Parnal, 103
Hannah wife Wm. died, 231
Hannah d Elijah & Catharine, 39
Hannah d Israel & Eunice, 113
Hannah d Samuell & Hannah, 12
Hannah M. m William Smith, 157
Harriet m William Lord, 133
Henrry, 279
Henry W. s William & Emma, 199
Hepzibah d Elijah & Catharine, 39
Hepzibah d Richard Jr. & Phebe, 25
Hesikiah s William & Hannah, 232
Hiram s Zelophead & Elizabeth, 115
Horace s Adriel & Sarah, 16
Horace m Clarissa Marvin, 162
Horace m Rhoda Tooker, 155
Horation Gates s Ammi & Martha, 73
Irena m Manasah Leach, 31
Israel s Ezra & Anna, 49
Israel m Eunice Noyes, 113
Israel Noyes s Israel & Eunice, 113
Jacob s James & Dorcase, 8
Jacob s William & Hannah, 230
Jacob s Zelophd & Elizabeth, 115
James s William & Hannah, 231
James m Dorcase Andrews, 8
James s James & Dorcase, 8
James Sr., 8
James m Catherine Hayes, 74, 123
James s James & Catharine, 74, 123
James Lawrence s John Christopher & Eunice, 139
Jane Alice m Abiel Stark, Jr., 161
Jerusha m Major William Sterling, 132
John, 307
John s Daniel & Ama, 83
John s James & Catharine, 123
John s James & Dorcas, 8
John s Seth & Lydia, 62
John m Mary Lord, 110
John Christopher m Eunice Noyes, 139
John Noyes s John Christopher & Eunice, 139
John Russell s Zelophead & Elizabeth, 115
Joseph, 302
Joseph s Cullick & Sarah, 59
Joseph Christopher s John Christopher & Eunice, 139
Joseph Elihu s Elihu & Anna, 84
Joseph Marriman s Gabriel & Eunice, 102
Josiah, 301, 304
Josiah s Richard Jr. & Phebe, 25, 230, 301
Josiah m Phebe Denison, 57
Josiah Griswold s Josiah & Phebe, 57
Judah s Israel & Eunice, 113
Julia m William Niles, 148
Leusenda Hannah d Ammi & Martha, 72
Lucia S. d Calleck & Azubah, 108, 109
Lucretia d Daniel & Ama died 1738, 83
Lucretia d Daniel & Ama born 1742, 84
Lucy m Joseph Hayes, 56

ELY, cont.
Lucy Ann m Seth Monroe Brockway, 191, 206, 210
Lydia d Seth & Lydia, 62
Lydia m Matthew Griswold Jr., 105
Lyman s Zelophd & Elizabeth, 115
Mahala d Gurdon & Parnal, 103
Margret twin with Deby d Elisha & Anna, 17
Margaret m Ebenezer Nichols, 156
Marsh, Major, 307
Marsylvia d Elisha & Anna, 16
Marsilva m Samuel Harvey, 135
Martha d Ammi & Martha, 72
Martha d Gurdon & Parnal, 103
Martha m Josiah DeWolf, Jr., 10, 229
Martha d William & Hannah, 231
Mary relict of Richard m Capt. Daniel Starling, 5
Mary m Moses Noyes, 251
Mary d Richard Jr. & Elizabeth, 230
Mary m Benjamin Lee, 239
Mary Ann d William & Hannah, 231
Mary Ann m Richard Person, 3
Mary Ann d Elisha & Anna, 17
Mary Florence d Erastus S. & Martha, 176
Mehetable d Elihu & Anna, 84
Obed B. m Emma Giddings, 170
Oliver s Elihu & Anna, 84
Oru, 200
Parnal d Zelophead & Elizabeth, 115
Phebe d Elihu & Anna, 84
Phebe d Elijah & Catharine, 39
Phebe d James & Catharine, 123
Phebe d Josiah & Phebe, 57
Phebe d Richard Jr. & Phebe, 25
Phebe d Seth & Lydia, 62
Phebe m Israel Matson, 143
Phebe m Lt. Calvin Selden, 109
Phebe A. m Oscar Avery, 181
Phebe H. m Matthew Griswold Jr. 155
Polly d Gabriel & Eunice, 102
Rachel d Gabriel & Eunice, 102
Richard Sr. died, 230
Richard s Elihu & Anna, 84
Richard Jr. m Elizabeth Peck, 230
Richard Jr. m Phebe Hubbard, 25, 230
Richard s Richard & Phebe, 25, 230
Richard s Seth & Lydia died 1771, 62
Richard s Seth & Lydia born 1774 & died, 62
Richard Hayes s James & Catharine, 74, 123
Robert s Richard Jr. & Phebe, 25, 230
Ruhama d James & Dorcase, 8
Ruhammi s William & Hannah, 231
Russel s Capt. Cullick & Azubah, 109
Russell s Cullick & Sarah, 59
Ruth d Gurdon & Parnal, 103
Sam'll s Elijah & Catharine, 39
Samuel s William & Hannah, 231
Samll m Hannah Mash (Mack or Marsh), 5, 12
Samuel s Samll & Hannah, 12
Sarah d Ezra & Sarah, 49
Sarah w Ezra died, 49
Sarah d Cullick & Sarah, 59
Sarah m Elias Minor, 51
Sarah Elizabeth m Silas Clark, 162
Seth s Richard Jr. & Phebe, 25, 230
Seth m Lydia Renold, 62

ELY, cont.
Seth s Seth & Lydia, 62
Seth Jr. m Phebe Marvin, 123
Silame d Gurdon & Parnal, 103
Silas Peck s Gabriel & Eunice, 102
Similius m Maria Anne Stannard, 149
Similius B. m Elizabeth P. Ely, 149
Sophia d Capt. Callick & Azubah, 109
Tabatha d James & Dorcas, 8
Tabitha m Jedediah Peck, 70
Teresa d Gabriel & Eunice, 103
Timothy m Sarah Anne Stark, 178
Walter S. s Calvin & Oru, 200
William, 199
William m Elizabeth Smith, 230
William Jr. m Elizabeth Perkins, 18*
William s William & Elizabeth died, 18*
William 2nd s William & Elizabeth born 1739, 18*
William m Alice Mather, 101
William s Gabriel & Eunice, 102
William m Hannah Thompson, 230
William s James & Catharine, 123
William H. s Eleazer S. & Martha, 175
Zebulon s Ezra & Sarah, 49
Zelophehad s Ammi & Martha, 73
Zelophead m Elizabeth Starling, 115
Ruth 2nd wife of Daniel d Samuel Wells died, 230
EMERSON, EMMERSON
Abigail d Abraham & Deborah, 96
Abraham m Deborah Lord, 96
Abraham s Abrm & Deborah, 96
Abraham m Mary Rathbone, 96
Broadstreet s Abraham & Deborah, 96
Broadstreet m Widow Jemima Sill, 55
Broadstreet s Broadstreet & Jemima, 5
Deborah d Abraham & Deborah, 96
Deborah wife of Abraham died, 96
Dudley s Broadstreet & Jemima, 55
Dudley died 1849, 214
Eliza J. m James Brown, 169
Elizabeth d Abraham & Mary, 96
George C. m Rachal Carter, 177
Joseph s Broadstreet & Jemima (Orig. Name Broadstreet), 55
Joseph s Abraham & Deborah, 96
Judith d Abraham & Deborah, 96
Lewis m Sophia Pilgrim, 168
Lucy m Joseph Tucker, 6
Mary d Abraham & Deborah, 96*
Theophilus s Abraham & Deborah, 96*
EMMONS
Esther (Marvin) formerly wife Thomas Lord died, 90
Wealthy married Russell Babcock, 172
ENES, ENISS, EMISS
Thomas m Marget (Jones Brockway) widow of Walston Brockway, Jr., 231
Thomas s Thomas & Marget, 231
FANNING, Thaddeus m Sarah Greenfield, 173
FELLOWS, Martha m Harvy Roberson, 118
FERLONG, FURLONG
James m Isabella Appleby, 195, 211
FIELD, Almira m Albert Huntley, 154
Lorain m William Huntley, 155

FITCH, Elisha m Nancy Champlin, 113
Freelove m Thomas Strickland, 136
James m Nancy Strickland, 137
Lodowick s Elisha & Nancy, 113
Nancy d Elisha & Nancy, 113
Sally d Elisha & Nancy, 113
FITHIAN, FITKIN, FITTON
Phebe m John Sill, 261
FLYNN, Walter m _____ Bowman, 148
FOOTE, FOOT, Lydia m Thomas Smith Jr., 58
Sarah m Cullick Ely, 59
FORSYTH, Charlotte m Romanta Ives, 156
Elizabeth m David Royce, 160
Mary A. m Griswold Holmes, 166
FOSDICK, Abby m Allen Sisson, 179
Frederick m Lucy Stark, 189
Lucinda m James Champlain, 189, 203
FOWLER, Sally m Samuel Coult, 16
Samuel S. m Emma Marvin, 147
FOX, Amos s Amos & Deborah, 55
Arnold[1] s John & Mary died, 18*
Arnold[2] s John & Mary born, 18
Benjamin s Amos & Deborah, 55
Content m Isaac Tillitson, 117
Danll s John & Mary, 18
Elisha s Amos & Deborah, 55
Ezra B. m Sally Maria Waid, 146
George W. m Emariah Hardin, 165
Hannah d Amos & Deborah, 55
Jane m John Hudson, 53
John, 18*
John s John & Mary, 18
Marcy d Amos & Deborah, 55
Maria m Enoch Waid, 142
Maria A. m Francis Minor, 194
Mary, 18
Mary m Samuel Borden, 222
Phebe m Joshua Rogers, 80
Sarah m Jedediah Brockway, 50
Sarah m Daniel Rogers, 29
Sibbel had a son Samll Saunders, 27
Sylvester W. m Mary Latham, 187
Timothy s Amos & Deborah, 55
William H. m Susan B. Andrews, 183
FREEMAN, Hannah m Rufus Huntley, 119
Isaac s Jordan & Nancy, 69
William s Sophia, 201
FRINK, William, 203
FULLER, George C., 199
Joseph I. m Catharine Kearney, 204, 208
Lucy E. d George C. & Mary Ann, 199
Margaret Jane d Joseph I & Catharine, 204
GALE, Benjamin, 301
GALLUP, Eunice m Seth L. Peck, 210
Gardner Capt. m Phebe Sill, 144
GALUSIAH, Daniel, 231
Jacob s Daniel, 231
Jonas s Daniel, 231
Sarah d Daniel, 231
GARDINER, GARDNER
Benjamin J. m Ethelinda Gee, 152
Emeline F. m Timothy Laplass, 174
Hannah m Calvin Nebo, 161
Mary m John Coult, 34
GASTIN, GUSTIN
Abigail m Nehemiah Rice, 38

GASTIN, cont.
Anna d Samuel Jr. & Mary, 3
Elisha s Samuel Jr. & Mary, 3
Hannah d Samuel Jr. & Mary, 3
John s Samuel Jr. & Mary, 3
Joshua s Samuel Jr. & Mary, 3
Josiah s Samuel Jr. & Mary, 3
Mary d Samuel Jr. & Mary, 3
Samuel Jr. m Mary Tommas, 3
Samuel s Samuel Jr. & Mary, 3*
Thomas s Samuel Jr. & Mary, 3
GATES, GATE, Enos m Mary Ann Payne, 150
Eunice (Euenice) m George Hall, 1, 232
Grace m Dan Gellit, 9
Julia Ann m Ezra Beckwith, 174
Louisa M. m Daniel Shepard, 170
Lydia d Daniel m Solomon Mack, 55
Sarah m Isaac Hall, 11
Ursula m Amasa Day, 174
GEE, Abigail d William & Abigail, 93
Abner s Solomon & Martha, 73
Anson s Zopher & Lura, 121
Betsey m Capt. Nehemiah Smith, 121
Betsey d Wm. & Sally, 114
Betsey m Jesse Jerome, 164
Elinda d William & Sally, 114
Elizabeth d William & Abigail, 93
Esther d Zopher & Esther, 121
Esther wife of Zopher died, 121*
Ethelinda m Benjamin Gardiner Jr., 152
John s Zopher & Esther, 121
Lewmon s Solomon & Martha, 73
Lury d Zopher & Lura, 121
Matthew s William & Sally, 114
Matthew m Polly Rogers, 142
Matthew m Eunice Chadwick, 142
Molley d Solomon & Martha, 73
Polly m Abel Smith, 127
Polly d Wm. & Sally, 114
Ruth m William Mack, 80
Sally d Wm. & Sally, 114
Salmon s Zopher & Esther, 121
Samuel s Zopher & Lura, 121
Sarah d William & Abigail, 93
Sarah m Nathan Tinker, 121
Silas s William & Sally, 114
Solomon Jr. m Martha Bingham, 73
William m Abagail Mack, 93
William s William & Abagail, 93
William Jr. m Sally Tinker, 114
William s William & Sally, 114
Zopher s William & Abigail, 93
Zopher m Esther Beckwith, 121
Zopher m Lura Jones, 121*
GEER, Elihu m Eliza Selden, 192
John, A., 309
GIBS, GILES, GIBBS
Hannah m Dan Mather, 19
Lydia m Ezra Mack, 83
GIDDINGS, Anna d Job & Sarah, 32
Benjamin s Joseph & Unice, 36
Dan s Thomas & Mary, 26
David s Thomas & Mary, 26
Dorcas d Job & Sarah, 32
Dorcas m Ezra Brockway, 50
Emma m Obed B. Ely, 170

GIDDINGS, cont.
George s Job & Sarah, 32
Hannah d Joseph & Unice, 36
James s Joseph & Unice, 36
Job m Sarah Rathbone, 32
Job s Job & Sarah died, 33
John m Susannah Tozer, 32
John s John & Susannah, 32
Jonathan s Joseph & Unice, 36
Joseph m Unice Androse, 36
Loas d John & Susannah, 32
Lydia d Joseph & Unice, 36
Mary d Joseph & Unice, 36
Sarah d Job & Sarah, 32
Solomon s Joseph & Unice, 36
Thomas Jr. m Mary Coult, 26
William s Job & Sarah, 32
Zebulon s Job & Sarah, 33
GIFFORD, Ursula m Lynda McCurdy, 73
GILBERT, GILBART
Ann m Joseph Peck 3rd, 149
Anna d Samll & Mary, 58
Dan m Mary Anne Champlain, 154
Desire d Jonathan & Sarah, 70
Elizabeth d Danill, 231
Elizabeth m Thomas Lee, 47
Elizabeth d Jonathan & Sarah, 70
Eunice d Samll & Mary, 58
Eunice m Rev. David Higgins, 111
Fanny d Samll & Mary, 58
Frances E. m Samuel Mott, 187
Giles, 301
Hannah d Samll & Mary, 58
Henry S., 202
Irene d Samll & Mary, 58
John m Molly Rogers Cooley, 69, 214
John Cooley s John & Molley Rogers, 69
Jonathan s John M. & Sarah Rogers, 70
Jonathan s Jonathan & Sarah, 70
Jonathan m Lous Baker, 71
Lous d Jonathan & Lous, 71
Lydia d Samll & Mary, 58
Marcy d Jonathan & Lous, 71
Mary d Jonathan & Lous, 71
Mathew m Sarah Peak (Peck?), 231
Moley m Ebenezer Bolles, 105
Molley Rogers d John & Molly Rogers, 69
Molley Rogers wife of John died, 69*
Samll m Mary Dodge, 58
Samuel m Almira Maynard, 164
Sarah d Jonathan & Sarah, 70
Sarah wife of Jonathan died, 71
Sarah E. m Edmund Huntley, 189
Susan m Alva West, 169
GILES, Abner s John & Ruth, 96
Hannah (Gibs?) m Dan Mather, 19
Isaac s John & Ruth, 95
John m Ruth Ransom, 95
John[1] s John & Ruth died, 95
John[2] s John & Ruth born, 95
Susannah d John & Ruth, 95, 96
GILLET, GILLETT
Reynold s Shadrack & Elizabeth, 119
Shadrack m Elizabeth Peck, 119
Shadrack s Shadrack & Elizabeth, 119*

INDEX OF PERSONS 337

GILLETT, GELLIT also see GILLES
  Amasa m Lucy Ann Banning, 162
  Benjamin Franklin s Joseph & Mary, 67
  Dan s Jonathan & Phebe, 81
  Dan M., 307
  Dan m Grace Gates, 9
  Dan Marvin s Dan & Grace, 9
  Daniel s Joseph & Mary, 67
  Dudley Peck s James & Elizabeth, 130
  Elisha s Jonathan & Phebe, 81
  Ezra s Jonathan & Phebe, 81
  Ezra m Amy Minor, 109
  Ezra s Ezra & Amy, 109
  Harriet N. m John Reed Brockway, 173
  Huldah d Reynold & Martha, 93
  Irene E. m Timothy H. Peck, 185
  James s Reynold & Martha, 93
  James m Elizabeth Peck, 130
  John Minor s Joseph & Mary, 67
  Jonathan s Ezra & Amy, 109
  Jonathan m Phebe Marvin, 81
  Jona s Jonathan & Phebe, 81
  Jonathan s Reynold & Martha, 93
  Jonathan died 1850, 215
  Joseph s Jonathan & Phebe, 81
  Joseph m Mary Minor, 67
  Joseph s Joseph & Mary, 67
  Joshua s Jonathan & Phebe, 81
  Martin s Jonathan & Phebe, 81
  Martin s Joseph & Mary, 67
  Mehetable (Mihilable) d Joseph & Mary, 67
  Noah Hallock s Joseph & Mary, 67
  Phebe wife of Jonathan died, 81
  Phebe d Joseph & Mary, 67
  Reynold s Jonathan & Phebe, 81
  Reynold m Martha Marvin, 93
  Sally d Ezra & Amy, 109
  Sarah d Jonathan & Phebe, 81
  Sarah m Ezra Hall, 83
  Seth m Catharine Whipp, 192, 210
  Shadrack s Jonathan & Phebe, 81
  Shadrak m Grace Dean, 152
  William W.S. m Huldah Waid, 157
  Zilpha m Moses Marvin, 98
GLADDING, Sarah m Abraham Bishop, 13
GLEASON, Dolly m Rev. Edward Porter, 112
GLOVER, Frances W. m Abigail Brockway, 182
  Orlando R. m Maria Keables, 189, 208
GLOYD, Joel M. m Mary Warner, 196
GOODRICH, Erastus C. m Sarah Clark, 175
GOOLD (SEE UNDER GOULD)
GORTON, Esther Ann d William G. & Eliza R., 159
  John s William G. & Eliza R., 159
  Lacy A. m Simon K. Paine, 165
  Laura Ann m Nelson Gay (or Guy) Loomis, 170
  Loura M. m Allanson Hedden, 171
  Mary m Elisha Smith, 158
  Mary Ann m William A. Smith, 170
  Sarah Mehetable d William G. & Eliza R., 159
  William G. m Eliza R. Warren, 159
GOULD, GOOLD, Alford s James & Mary, 134
  Betsey d Walter, 133
  Betsey d James & Mary, 134
  Charles C. Pinckney s Walter, 133
  David s James & Elizabeth, 35
  Elisha s James & Mary, 134

GOULD, cont.
  Elizabeth d James & Elizabeth, 35
  Ethelinda d Walter, 133
  Gardner s Walter, 133
  Guy s Peter, 67
  Henry Latimer s Walter, 133
  Horace Octavius s Walter, 133
  Hosmer Johnson s Walter, 133
  James, 275
  James Goold m Mary_____, 134
  James s James & Mary, 134
  John s James & Elizabeth, 35
  Joseph s Peter, 67
  Luca d James & Elizabeth, 35
  Lydia d Walter, 133
  Marcy d James & Elizabeth, 35
  Mary, 273
  Mary m Zadock Smith, 63
  Nabby d James & Mary, 134
  Naomi d James & Mary, 134
  Polly d James & Mary, 134
  Sally d James & Mary, 134
  Sally Christopher d Walter, 133
  Sophia d James & Mary, 134
  Walter s James & Elizabeth, 35
  Walter m _____Latimer, 133
  Walter H. s Walter, 133
  William s James & Mary, 134
  Zelinda m Joseph Mather, 115
GRAHAM, GRAYHAM
  Anne wife of Benjamin died, 231
  Anne d Benjamin & Hannah, 231
  Benjamin m Anna Comstock, 231
  Benjamin s Benjamin & Anna, 231
  Benjamin m Hannah Andros, 231
  Clarissa m Aaron E. A. Skinner, 148
  Gurdon m Elizabeth Otis, 161
  James S. m Mary Ingraham, 144
  Martha m William Beckwith, 145
  Mary d Benjamin & Anna, 231
  Martain (Mortain) s Benjamin & Hannah, 231
  Sarah m John Marvin, 246
  Sarah d Benjamin & Anna, 231
  Susannah m Samuell Marvin, 247
GRANT, Jerusha m Daniel Beckwith 3rd, 40
GRAVES, Abigail d Thomas & Mary, 231
  Abigail m John Ageet, 14
  Elizabeth d Thomas & Mary, 231
  Easter d Thomas & Mary, 231
  Ester m Thomas Hudson, 235
  Esther d Mark & Elizabeth, 21
  Liverance d Mark & Elizabeth, 21
  Marke s Thomas & Mary, 231
  Thomas m Mary Hopson, 231
  Thomas s Mark & Elizabeth, 21
GREELEY (SEE GRILLEY)
  Sarah Griswold m Joseph Noyes, 150
GREEN, Jonathan m Sarah Ann Beckwith, 178
  Nathan E. m Mary Ann Beckwith, 170
GREENFIELD, Abby m Asahel Rowland, 158
  Abigail d James & Nabby, 80
  Archibald s Archibald Starr & Sarah, 38
  Charles William s Edward & Ann, 154
  Edward twin with Lucy s James & Nabby, 80
  Edward m Ann Lay, 154
  Edward Lay s James & Nabby, 80*

GREENFIELD, cont.
Elizabeth m Roger Alger Jr., 6
Ezra s James & Nabby, 80
Hannah m Richard Roulin, 259
Hannah d Starr & Sarah, 38
Hannah m Asahel Roland Jr., 115
Harriet Louisa d Edward & Ann, 154
James s Archibald Starr & Sarah, 38
James m Nabby Daniels, 80
James Scott s Edward & Ann, 154
Janett Care d Edward & Ann, 154
Jenett m Horace R. Brockway, 208
John s Starr & Sarah, 38
John s Edward & Ann, 154
Lucy d James & Nabby, 80
Mary d Archibald Starr & Sarah, 38
Mary m Maxamilian (Alexander) Oretel, 173
Polly m Samuel Beckwith, 97
Polly d James & Nabby, 80
Richard s Archibald Starr & Sarah, 38
Richard died, 38
Richard s James & Nabby, 80
Russell Case s Edward & Ann, 154
Sarah d Archibald Starr & Sarah, 38
Sarah m Stephen DeWolf, 79
Sarah d James & Nabby, 80
Sarah A. m Thaddeus Fanning, 173
Sarah Ann d Edward & Ann, 154
Sarah M. m George Avery, 173
Susannah d James & Nabby, 80
GRIFFING, GRIFFIN, GRIFFEN
Abner Lieut., 304
Abner s Jasper & Mary, 74
Abner m Sally Champlin, 24
Abner s Abner & Sally, 24
Allen m Sarah E. Lord, 177
Almira d Jasper & Mahala, 197
Anne d Joshua & Betsey, 125
Catharine Ester Ann d Jasper & Mahala, 197
Catharine widow of Nathan died, 105
Charles s Joshua & Betsey, 125
Christopher s Abner & Sally, 24
Clarissa L. m Richard Parsons, 153
David s Jasper & Eunice, 52
Deborah d Jasper & Mary, 74
Deborah d Abner & Sally, 24
Fanny d Abner & Sally, 24
Fanny m Abner S. Ely, 149
George R. m Annie Johnson, 146
Francis Henry s Jasper & Mahala, 197
Hana d Jasper & Ruth, 231
Harriet m Francis Willcox, 172
Hillard s Jasper & Mahala, 197
Hezekiah s Jasper & Ruth, 232*
James Charles E. s Jasper & Mahala, 197
Jasper, 301, 304
Jasper m Ruth Peck, 231
Jasper m Mahala Terry, 197*
Jasper s Jasper & Ruth, 231
Jasper m Mary Reed, 74
Jasper s Jasper & Eunice, 52
Jasper s Jasper & Mary died 1725, 74
Jasper s Jasper & Mary born 1726, 74
Jasper Jr. m Eunice Rogers, 52
Jasper s Nathan & Catharine, 105
John Griffing Esq. died, 232

GRIFFING, cont.
John s Jasper & Mary died April 1737, 74*
John (Major), 304
John s Abner & Sally, 24
John s Jasper & Mary May 1737, 74*
John m Phebe Taber, 101
John s Nathan & Catharine, 105
Johnson s Joshua & Betsy, 125
Joseph s Jasper & Ruth, 231
Joseph s Jasper Jr., 52
Joseph s Jasper & Eunice, 52
Joseph s Joshua & Betsy, 125
Joshua, 304
Joshua s Jasper & Eunice, 52
Joshua m Betsy Johnson, 125
Laura m Jabez Swan, 147
Lemuel s Jasper & Ruth, 231
Lucy d Nathan & Catharine, 105
Mary m William Lee, 242
Mary d Jasper & Mary, 74
Mary d Nathan & Catharine, 105
Nathan s Jasper & Eunice, 52
Nathan m Catharine Johnson, 105*
Philina m Abraham Ely, 165
Rhoda m Horace Brockway, 166
Ruth d Jasper & Mary, 74*, 231
Ruth d Jasper & Ruth, 74*
Sally d Abner & Sally, 24
Sarah d Jasper & Ruth, 231
Sarah m Joshua Champion, 225
William s Joshua & Betsy, 125
GRILLEY, GRELLEY, see GREELEY
Elizabeth d Hue & Temperance died 1728, 24
Elizabeth d Hue & Temperance born 1736, 24*
Henry s Hue & Temperance, 24
Hue m Temperance Roland, 24
Jehaly s Hue & Temperance, 24
John s Hue & Temperance, 24
Louisa d Hue & Temperance, 24
GRISWOLD, GRISWOULD, GRISOULD
Andrew, 301
Andrew m Eunice Prince, 84
Andrew s Andrew & Eunice, 85
Anna d Thomas & Susannah, 7
Augustus Henry s Roger & Fanny, 131
Candice d George & Elizabeth, 53
Charles C. m Elizabeth Griwold, 146
Charles Chandler s John & Sarah, 95
Charles Chandler s Roger & Fanny, 131
Clerine d John & Hannah, 232*
Clarine 2nd d John & Hannah, 232
Deborah d John & Hannah, 232
Diodate Johnson s John & Sarah, 95
Eliza Woodbridge d Roger & Fanny, 131
Elizabeth m Charles C. Griswold, 146
Elizabeth divorced John Rogers married Peter Pratt, 255
Elizabeth wife of George died, 53
Elizabeth d George & Elizabeth, 53
Elizabeth d George & Hannah, 232
Elizabeth d John & Sarah, 95
Elizabeth d Matthew & Phebe, 232
Elizabeth D. m William Lane, 196
Eunice d George & Elizabeth, 53
Fanny R. m Shubael Bartlett M.D., 181
Florence d Robert, 207

INDEX OF PERSONS 339

GRISWOLD, cont.
Francis Ann d Roger & Fanny, 131
Geog s Matthew & Phebe, 232
George m Hannah Lynde, 232
George s George & Hannah, 232
George Jr. m Elizabeth Lee, 53
George s George & Elizabeth, 53
George s Samll & Mary, 62
Hannan d John & Hannah, 232
Hannah d Capt. Matthew & Ursala, 2
Hannah d Matthew & Ursala died, 2*
Hannah relict John Esq. died, 232
Hannah m Silas Sill, 110
Hannah Lyde d George & Elizabeth, 53
Jane m Jason Lee Jr., 117
Jean d George & Elizabeth, 53
John s Matthew & Phebe, 232
John m Hannah Lee, 232
John s John & Hannah, 232*
John s Capt. Matthew & Ursala, 2
John m Sarah Johnson, 95
John s John & Sarah, 95
Juliette m Roger Griswold, 151
Lous m Sam'l Mather Jr., 78
Lois d Thomas & Susannah, 7
Lovice d Thomas & Susannah, 7
Lovisa m Lee Lay, 85
Lucia m Richard Wait Jr., 74
Lucretia d George & Hannah, 232
Luce d John & Hannah, 232
Lucy d Thomas & Susannah, 7
Maria died, 215
Marian d Roger & Fanny, 132
Marianna d Capt. Matthew & Ursala, 2
Martha d Andrew & Eunice, 84
Martha m Elisha Watrous, 119
Mary d Matthew & Phebe, 232
Mary m Edmund Dorr, 230
Mary m Amos Lay, 14
Mary d Andrew & Eunice, 84
Mary wife of Samuel died, 62
Mary Ann d John & Sarah, 95
Mathew m Phebe Hyde, 232
Mathew s Matthew & Phebe, 232
Mathew s John & Hannah, 232
Mathew died 1715 or 16, 232
Matthew Capt. m Ursala Wolcott, 2*
Matthew s George Jr. & Elizabeth, 53
Matthew s George & Elizabeth, 53
Matthew s Matthew & Ursala,2
Matthew Jr. m Lydia Ely, 105
Matthew Jr. m Phebe H. Ely, 155
Matthew s Roger & Fanny, 131
Nathel Lynde s George & Elizabeth, 53
Phebe d Mathew & Phebe, 232
Phebe died, 232
Phebe d John & Hannah, 232
Phebe d John Griswold Esq. m Rev. Jonathan Parsons, 251
Pheby d Thomas & Susannah, 7
Richard S. m Frances Mather, 178, 215
Richard S. m Louisa Mather, 168
Robert H. 207
Roger s Matthew & Ursala, 2
Roger m Fanny Rogers, 131
Roger Woolcot s Roger & Fanny, 131

GRISWOLD, cont.
Roger W. m Juliette Griswold, 151
Samuell Ens., Died, 232
Samuel m Mary Marvin, 62
Sarah d John & Hannah, 232
Sarah d Matthew & Phebe, 232
Sarah d Thomas & Susannah, 7
Sarah died, 27
Sarah m Thomas Colton (Capt.), 227
Sarah m David Fithen Sill, 88, 108
Matthew Sr. died, 1698, (written in Arnold Index)
Sarah d John & Sarah, 95
Sarah J. m Lorillard Spencer, 188
Susannah wife Thomas died,7
Silvanus s George & Hannah, 232
Sylvanus s Samll & Mary, 62
Sylvanus Rev. m Elizabeth Marvin, 21
Thomas s John & Hannah, 232
Thomas m Susannah Lynde, 7
Thomas died, 7
Thomas s George & Elizabeth, 53
Thomas m Ethelinda Caulkins, 126
Ursula d Capt. Matthew & Ursala died 1744, 2
Ursala d Capt. Matthew & Ursala born 1754, 2
Ursula d George & Elizabeth, 53
Ursula Woolcot d John & Sarah, 95
Ursula Woolcot d John m Richard McCurdy, 73, 118
William s Andrew & Eunice, 84
William s Roger & Fanny, 132
William F. m Sarah Noyes, 161
GROVER, William m Eunice Avery, 187
GRUMLEY, Fanny m Isaac Cobb, 174
Jane L. m Ezra Ingham, 179
Thomas m Eunice Waide, 178
GULLIVER, Amelia m James S. Morris, 179
Frances m Samuel S. Sawyer, 196
Hannah alias Chadwick m Atwell Tucker, Jr., 158
Henrietta m Cornelius Banta, 182, 201
GURLEY, Sarah m Joseph Noyes, 150
GUSTIN see GASTIN
HACKET, Jane, 300
HAGUE see under HOGUE
HAIDEN see under HAYDEN
HAINES, HAYNES, HUMES
Betsey I. m James F. Stephens, 164
Christopher m Maria Bump, 155
Henry (Haynes), 199, 206
James m Mary Hand, 158
James m Harriet Beckwith, 175
James DeGray s Henry & Mary, 199
John Haynes s Henry & Mary, 206, 215
Lydia m Absolam Beckwith, 31
Mary T. m William Hall, 126
Nehemiah m Mary Manwaring, 151
Richard G. s Henry & Mary, 206, 215
Sally C. m George Bump, 146
William (Humes) m Emily Huntley, 167
HALE, John m Ann Comstock, 178
HALL, Abel s Isaac & Sarah, 11
Abel m Caroline Brockway, 81
Abel s Abel & Caroline, 81*
Abel Sr. died, 81
Abigail d Isaac & Sarah, 11
Amasa s Jacob & Hannah, 16

HALL, cont.
Anna d Ezra & Sarah, 83
Caroline d Abel & Caroline, 81
Caroline m Clark Peck, 118
Carolina d William & Sarah, 126
Caroline wife Abel died, 81
Charles H., 309
Daniel s George & Eunice, 2
Daniel m Mehetable Peck, 15
Elisha s George & Euenice (Eunice), 1, 232
Eunice d Isaac & Sarah, 11
Ezra s Isaac & Sarah, 11
Ezra s Jono & Betsy, 127
Ezra s Ezra & Sarah, 83
Ezra m Sarah Gillet, 83
George m Euenice Gate (Eunice Gates), 1, 232
Hannah d Abel & Caroline, 81
Harvey m Sally Mott, 160
Harvey Jr. m Frances A. Tooker, 309
Hepsabe d Isaac & Sarah, 11
Hepzibah d Ezra & Sarah, 83
Isaac m Sarah Gates, 11
Isaac s Abel & Caroline, 81
Isaac died, 11*
Jacob s Isaac & Sarah, 11
Jacob m Hannah Clark, 16
Jesse, 202
John s Thomas & Sarah, 12
Jonathan s Ezra & Sarah, 83
Jonathan m Betsey Lord d Reuben Lord, 127
Jonathan s Jono & Betsy, 127
Josiah s Isaac & Sarah, 11
Lois m Capt. Matthew Peck, 134
Lous d Abel & Caroline, 81
Martha d Jacob & Hannah, 16
Mary d Isaac & Sarah, 11
Mindwell d Thomas & Sarah, 12
Nancy m John Daniels, 187
Nancy Ann m John Tooker, 310
Nathan s Thomas & Sarah, 12
Phebe d Ezra & Sarah, 83
Phebe d George & Eunice, 2
Polly d Abel & Caroline, 81
Reuben L. m Abby W. Lee, 163
Reuben Lord s Jonathan & Betsey, 127
Rufus s George & Eunice died, 2
Rufus 2nd s George & Eunice, 2
Sarah m James Beebe, 172
Sarah d Isaac & Sarah, 11
Sarah relict Isaac died, 11*
Sarah d Jacob & Hannah, 16
Sarah wife William died, 126*
Sarah d Wm. & Mary, 127
Samuel s George & Eunice, 2
Theodore s Jesse & Abbe, 202
Thomas m Nancy Young, 176
Thomas m Sarah Clark, 12
Thomas s Thomas & Sarah, 12
William s Abel & Caroline 81
William m Mary T. Haines, 126
William m Sarah Sill, 126
William s William & Mary, 127
William S., 309
HAMILTON, Hetty R. m Elisha Comstock, 150
John m Hetty Warren, 139
Lois m Joshua Moor (e), 156

HAND, Adaline m Samuel B. Dast, 171
Mary m James Haynes, 158
HARDEN, HARDIN, HARDING
Darius m Irene Scofill, 131
Darius s Darius & Irane, 131
Darius m Sally M. Rogers, 161
Eliza d Darius & Irane, 131
Eliza m Peter Chapman, 151
Emariah C. m George W. Fox, 165
George W. s Darius & Irane, 131
George W. m Eunice C. Brockway, 161
Harriet m Giles Staplins, 180
Irene m Israel Havens, 168
Irane d Darius & Irane, 131
James s Noah & Nancy, 203
Nancy d Darius & Irane, 131
Nancy m Reuben Smith, 161
Noah m Nancy Maria McCreary, 185, 203, 207
Sophronia m Ebenezer Mack, 172
Susan m Adam Manwaring Jr., 151
William s Noah & Maria, 207
HARLIN, Anna m Ezra Ely (see Starlin, Anna), 49
HARLOW, Stephen P. m Laura Crosby, 190
HARRIS, HARRISS, HARIS
Anna m Zerias Beckwith, 92
David s John, 107
Easter d William & Elizabeth 233
Grace m Lawrence Johnson, 44, 78
Ireane d Lt. John, 107*
John Lieut., 107
John s Lt. John, 107
Josiah s Lt. John, 107
Lemuel s Lt. John, 107*
Lois d Lt. John, 107
Lucy m Capt. Joseph Smith, 132
Meriam d Thomas m Benjamin Coult, 228
Polly d Lt. John, 107
Rachill m Mosis Huntly Jr., 233, 237
Sarah d William & Elizabeth, 232
Tabatha d William & Elizabeth, 232
Thankfull d William & Elizabeth, 233
William m Elizabeth Brockway d Wolston Sr., 217, 232
HARRISON, HARISON
Bulah d William & Hepzibah, 71
Charles Capt. 306
Chas W. m Elizabeth A. Sawyer, 148, 309
Charles Major, 307
Dorothy d William & Experience, 25
Elihu s William & Experience, 25
Elisha s William & Hepzibah, 71
Experience wife William died, 25
Henry m Polly Sawyer, 154
John Frederick m Jane Sheldon Brockway, 136
Line d Wm. & Hepzibah, 71
Louisa m William Patten, 179
Nabby m Jason Smith, 47
Polley d Wm. & Hepzibah, 71
Richd Montgomery s Wm. & Hepzibah, 71
Rosetta m Selden M. Hayden, 180
William m Experience Wood, 25
William s William & Experience, 25
William Jr. m Hepzebah Tiffany, 71
William s William & Hepzibah, 71
William B., 308
Wiliam H. m Louisa Clark, 186

INDEX OF PERSONS 341

HARRISON, cont.
    _____first child of William died, 71
HART, Charles E. m Phebe M. Sill, 153
  Elizabeth A. m Rev. Willys Warner, 165
  Elizabeth Ann d John Jr. & Nancy, 144
  John m Margaret Sill, 168, 204
  John Jr. m Nancy Mather, 144
  John Alexander s John Jr. & Nancy, 144
  Samuel m Lydia Davison, 174
  Sylvester M. s John Jr. & Nancy, 144*
HARVEY, HARVE, HARVY
  Abigal d John M_____Reed, 233
  Abigail widow of Thomas m Edw. Stocker, 233
  Abigail d Thomas & Abbegale, 233
  Anna twin with John d John & Elizabeth, 26
  Asahel s Thomas & Grace, 19
  Benjamin s John, 233
  Berthenie d John & Elizabeth, 26
  Betsy d Samuel & Marsilva, 135
  Elisa d Thomas & Grace, 19
  Elisha s John & Elizabeth, 26
  Elizabeth m Hazard Wilcox, 193
  Elizabeth d John & Elizabeth, 26
  Elizabeth d John, 233
  Elizabeth d Thomas & Abbegale died, 233*
  Goodwife w. John Sr. died, 233
  Joana d Thomas & Abbegale, 233
  John, 302
  John Sr. died, 233
  John s Thomas & Abbegale, 233
  John s John, 233
  John twin s John & Elizabeth, 26
  John 2nd m Elizabeth Rathbone, 26
  Joseph s John, 233
  Joshua s John, 233
  Mary died, 233
  Pheby d John & Elizabeth, 26
  Polly Huntley m Ebenezer Mack, 104, 109
  Richard s Thomas & Abbegale, 233
  Samuel s Samuel & Marsilva, 135
  Samuel, 270, 307
  Samuel m Marsilva Ely, 135, 276
  Sarah died, 233
  Sarah d John, 233
  Sylvia, 277
  Thomas m Abbegale Smith d Richard Jr. 233
  Thomas s Thomas & Abbegale, 233
  Thomas m Grace Willey, 19
  Thomas s John & Elizabeth, 26
HASE see under HAYES
HASTINGS, Eleanor A. m Horace Clark, 196
HAVENS, HAVINS
  Adaline m George D. Clark, 183
  Alfred Nelson s Daniel C., 199
  Anna d Nathll & Elizabeth, 233
  Anna Ophelia d Elisha & Lucy, 202
  Anner d Edward & Patience, 73
  Archibald R. m Caroline Hughes, 175
  Calvin m Lydia Maynard, 193
  Candace w Reuben died, 137
  Catharine m Stephen Tucker, 152
  Charles M. m Abby Robbins, 175, 198
  Charles McCurdy s Reuben, 137
  Daniel (Lex. Alarm), 301
  Daniel s Nathaniel & Elizabeth, 234
  Daniel s Edward & Patience, 3

HAVENS, cont.
  Daniel C., 199
  David s Edward & Patience, 3
  David, 300
  David Henry s Reuben & Candace, 137
  Dorcas Ursula d Reuben & Candace, 137
  Edward s Nathanell & Elizabeth, 233
  Edward s Edward & Patience, 3
  Edward m Patience Beebe, 3
  Elisha m Lucy Champion, 169, 202
  Elizabeth d Nathanell & Elizabeth, 234
  Elizabeth B. m John Broadrick, 194
  George s Edward & Patience, 3
  George m Harriot Champion, 145
  Harriet Havens died, 213
  Henry Wolcott s Reuben & Candace, 137
  Israel m Irene Harding, 168
  Israel m Prudence Clark, 195, 211
  Hannah died, 214, 300
  James D. s Charles M & Abby, 198
  Lucy m Silas Tucker, 161
  Lydia d Edward & Patience, 3
  Lydia m John Maynard Jr., 133
  Lydia E. m Stephen Rowland, 164
  Mary Hannah d Reuben & Candace, 137
  Mary J. m William J. Beckwith, 209
  Mary M. m John Anson Baker, 211
  Mary W. m Daniel Brayman, 147
  Nancy m William Daniels, 177
  Nathaniell m Elizabeth Beebe, 233
  Nathaniell s Nathanll & Elizabeth, 233
  Orrin m Martha Merriman, 210
  Peter s Nathanell & Elizabeth, 234
  Phebe m George Clark, 144
  Reuben s Edward & Patience, 3
  Reuben m Candace Dennison, 137
  Sarah d Nathanlel & Elizabeth, 233
  Sarah d Edward & Patience, 3
  Sarah M. m John Quinn, 154
  Silas m _____Griffin, 154
HAYDEN, HAIDEN
  Charles m Amelia Damon, 209, 260
  Ebenezer s John & Marah, 232
  Elizabeth E. m Jedediah Brockway, 192, 210
  Hayden s Charles & Amelia, 200
  Jedediah child John & Marah, 232
  John, 232
  Louisa m Sylvester Wooster, 144
  Nancy K. m Henry Damon, 188, 209
  Nehemiah s John & Marah, 232
  Selden M. m Rosetta Harrison, 180
  Ulysses m Elizabeth Lord, 168
HAYES, HASE, HAYS
  Abigail d Titus & Deborah, 84
  Abner s John & Azubah, 85
  Cathrine d Richd & Patience, 233
  Catherine m James Ely, 74, 123
  Ely s Joseph & Lucy, 56
  John m Azubah Rowland, 85
  John s John & Azubah, 85
  John s Richard & Patience, 233
  Joseph m Lucy Ely, 56
  Joseph s Joseph & Lucy, 56
  Joseph s Richard & Patience, 233
  Lydia s (?) John & Azubah, 85
  Mary m James Smith Jr., 31

HAYES, cont.
  Mehetable m Greenfield Alger, 11
  Patience m Joseph Perkins, 33
  Patience m Joseph Peck, 33
  Philemon s Richd & Patience, 233
  Polly d John & Azubah, 85
  Richd m Patience Mack, 233
  Richd s Richard & Patience, 233
  Richard s Titus & Deborah, 84
  Seth s Richd & Patience, 233
  Silas s Richd & Patience, 233
  Titus s Richd & Patience, 233
  Titus m Deborah Beckwith, 84
  Titus s Titus & Deborah, 84
HAYNES (See under HAINES)
HAZEN, HAZON, HAZER
  Deborah d John & Deborah, 41
  Eunice d John & Deborah, 41
  Hannah d John, 234
  John, 234
  John Jr. m Deborah Peck, 41, 234
  John 3rd s John & Deborah, 41, 234
  Joseph s John & Deborah, 41
  Lydia d John & Deborah, 41
  Marcy (Macy) d John Jr. & Deborah, 41, 234
  Mary d John Jr. & Deborah, 234
  Nathaniel s John & Deborah, 41
  Samuel s John & Deborah, 41
  Thomas s John, 234
HEDDEN, Alanson m Laura Gorton, 171
HERRICK, Mary A. m Henry Chapel, 185
HESS, Henry H. m Mary Tinker, 143
HEWLET
  Comstock m Eliza Banning (Johnson), 181
  Edward m Francisca Mott, 197
HIDE, (See under HYDE)
HIGGINS, Benjamin s Christian & Dorothy, 62
  Benjamin m Jane Peck, 22, 23
  Christian m Dorothy Williams, 62
  Christopher s Christian & Dorothy died 62
  Christopher s Christian & Dorothy born 62
  David Rev. m Eunice Gilbert, 111
  David s Rev. David & Eunice, 111
  Dolly twin d Christian & Dorothy, 63
  Dolly had son Samuel Summers, 136
  Enoch twin s Christian & Dorothy, 63
  Enoch s Benjamen & Jane, 23
  Eunice, 275
  Fanny w William died, 43
  Franna d Benjamen & Jane, 22, 23
  Gurdon Bayley s William & Fanny, 43
  James Gilbert s Rev. David & Eunice, 111
  Jamima twin d Capt. Christian & Dorothy, 63
  Joseph Capt. m Mercy Remick, 5
  Joseph s Christopher (probably Christian) & Dorothy, 62
  Marcy m John Mather, 15
  Marcy Remeck d Silvanus & Elizabeth, 89
  Marcy Remick m Capt. Mechail Huntley, 135
  Polley d William & Fanny, 43
  Rebecca m Richard Wait, 5
  Rebecca d Capt. Joseph & Mary, 5*
  Seth twin s Christian & Dorothy, 63
  Sylvanus m Elizabeth Clark, 89
  Thankful m Daniel Rathbone, 12
  Thankful m Josiah Burnham, 44

HIGGINS, cont.
  William s Christian & Dorothy, 62
  William m Fanny Bayley, 43
HILL, Anna (see MaryAnn) m Seth Lee, 132
  Bettey d Elijah & Mary, 48
  Christopher s Saml & Edith, 84
  Christopher Edward s Edward & Betsy, 134
  Edith w Samuel died, 84
  Edward s Saml & Edith died, 84*
  Edward s Saml & Edith born, 84
  Edward m Betsey Lee, 134
  Eleazer m Sarah Rand, 192
  Elijah m Mary Huntley, 48
  Elijah s Elijah & Mary, 48
  Elizabeth Lee d Edward & Betsey, 134
  Jemima d Elijah & Mary, 48
  Jemimah m Ephraim Sawyer, 87
  Lucia Marvin d Edward & Betsey, 134
  Margaret Jane d Edward & Betsey, 134
  Mary A. m John Bartlet, 162
  Mary Ann d Saml & Edith, 84
  Mary Ann Phebe d Edward & Betsey, 134
  Mehetable d Saml & Edith, 84
  Roxana d Saml & Edith, 84
  Samuel m Edith Bayley, 84
  Sarah d Saml & Edith, 84
  Thomas J. Hitt m Deborah Miller, 156
  William Henry s Edward & Betsey, 134
HILLIARD, Benony m Martha Lord, 234
  Bettey d Benony & Martha, 234
  Bozaleel s Benony & Martha, 234
HINCKLEY, Mary m Theophilus Morgan, 135
HINSDALE, Morris m Martha Waid, 167
HOCKRIDGE, Charles s William & Huldah, 126
  John Dessent s William & Huldah, 126
  William s William & Huldah, 126
  William Dessent s William & Huldah, 126*
  William m Huldah Rogers, 126
HODGE, Mary m Simeon Alger, 23
HOGES, Charles m Ane _____, 234
HOGUE, David m Lucy Wells, 174
HOLDREDGE, HOLDRIDGE
  Sarah L. m Henry Noyes, 184
  _____ m Jonathan Sisson Jr., 136
HOLMES, Griswold m Mary Forsyth, 166
  Joseph m Maria Selden, 182
  Samuel m Wid. Cornelia Buckingham, 184
HOLT, Asa m Polly Smith, 170
  Jane B. m George Vergason, 188
HOLTUM, HALTUM, George died, 263
  John, 234
  Sarah (see under Sarah Spencer), 234
HOPSON, Mary m Thomas Graves, 231
HORTON, Anna m Martin Beckwith, 89
HOWARD, Amanda m Elisha Robbins, 146
  Daniel Jr. m Cordelia Dowsett, 168
  Deborah m Benjamin Brockway, 183
  Electa m Clark Stillman, 157
  Enoch m Joanna Cables, 150
  Mariaette m Seth Dickinson, 184
  Nathan m Cornelia Meigs, 182
  Sally Maria Howard, 279
  William C. m Eliza Congdon, 157
HOWE, Susan M. m Christopher Lee, 170
HOWELL, David m Rhuami Sill, 32*
  Rhuama m Mathew Peck, 90

HUBBARD, Julia Ann m John Babcock, 160
Phebe m Richard Ely Jr., 230
Phebe, 279
HUDSON, Ann m James Bliss, 187
Anna d Stephen & Patience, 89
Benjaman m Mabel Roulen, 234
Benjamin s Nathaniell & Rachall, 235
Benjamin s Benjamin & Mabel, 234
Benjamin m Hannah Terrill, 43
Benjamin Jr. m Bridget Brockway, 32
Brooks s Benjamin & Bridget, 32
Daniel s Benjamin & Hannah, 43
Deborah d Jonathan & Sarah, 234
Elezer s Benjamin & Mabel, 234
Eleazer m Hannah Miller, 89
Eleazer s Eleazer & Hannah, 89
Elias s Eleazer & Hannah, 89
Elias m Lucinda Miller, 124
Elijah s Nathaniell & Lydia, 235
Elisha s Eleazer & Hannah died, 89*
Elisha s Eleazer & Hannah born, 89
Elizabeth d Benjamin & Hannah, 43
Elizabeth d Eleazer & Hannah, 89
Ester d Thomas & Ester, 235
Ester w Thomas died, 235
Hannah, 300
Hannah d Jonathan & Sarah, 234
Hannah d John & Hannah, 234
Hannah d Benjamin & Hannah, 43
Jane d John & Jane, 53
John s Nathaniell & Rachall, 235
John m Hannah Roling, 234
John s John & Hannah, 234
John died, 235
John m Jane Fox, 53
John s John & Jane, 53
Jonathan m Sarah Tinker, 234
Jonathan s Jonathan & Sarah, 234
Joseph s Stephen & Patience, 89
Loas d John & Jane, 53
Lous d Eleazer & Hannah, 89
Louisa d Elias & Lucinda, 124
Loviecy d John & Jane, 53
Lucinda m Andrew Beckwith, 148
Luce d Nathaniell & Lydia, 235
Lucy d John & Jane, 53
Lydia d Nathaniell & Lydia, 235
Lydia m Jonathan Alger, 10
Mabel w Benjamin died, 234, 300
Mabell d Benjn & Hannah, 43
Mary d Eleazer & Hannah, 89
Mary d John & Hannah, 234
Mary d Nathaniell & Rachall, 235
Nancy d Elias & Lucinda, 124
Nathaniell m Rachall (widow, Arter Schofil), 235
Nathaniell s Nathaniell & Rachall, 235
Nathll Jr. m Lydia Tubes (Tubbs), 235
Nathll s Nathaniell & Lydia, 235
Patience w Stephen died, 89
Rachall d John & Hannah, 234
Rachall died, 234
Rachall d John & Hannah born, 234
Rebeckah d Benjamin & Mabel, 234
Rhoda d John & Jane, 53
Richard s John & Hannah, 234, 235
Richd s Nathaniell & Lydia, 235

HUDSON, cont.
Samuel s Benjamin & Mabel, 234
Samll s Benjamin & Bridget, 32
Samuel s Eleazer & Hannah, 89
Samuel m Rhoda Rogers, 123
Sarah d Jonathan & Sarah, 234
Silas s Elias & Lucinda, 124
Stephen s Benjamin & Hannah, 43
Stephen m Patience Bishop, 89
Thomas s Nathaniell & Rachall, 235
Thomas m Ester Graves, 235
HUGHES
Betsey Maria d Capt. John & Jamima, 116
Caroline A. m Archibald Havens, 175
Elizabeth m Charles Manwaring, 165
Frances m James Pilgrim, 186
John G., 199
Nancy m Joseph Beebe, 176, 203
Sarah E. d John G. & Julia, 199
John (Capt) m Jamima Burnham, 116
John Gordon s Capt. John & Jamima, 116
John Gordon m Julia Ann Bell, 149, 199
Joseph Higgins s Capt. John & Jamima, 116
Lucretia M. m Horace Royce, 185
Mary 2nd d John G m David Date, 186
Nancy B. m Joseph Beebe, 176
Polly d John & Jamima, 116
Sarah E. d John G. & Julia, 199
HUMES, HAMES, William m Emily Huntley, 167
HUNGERFORD, China, 276, 277
Francis A. s Richard & Elizabeth, 200
Gurdon m Maria Rowland, 145
Richard A. m Elizabeth Laplass, 188, 200
HUNTLEY, HUNTLY
Aaron m Marah Champion daughter of Henry, 235
Aaron s Aaron & Marah, 235
Aaron Jr. m Debrah DeWolf, 235
Aaron s Aaron Jr. & Debrah, 235
Aaron III m Mary Leech, 235
Aaron Jr. died, 235
Aaron s Samuel & Ruth, 237
Aaron III died, 236
Abel s Jonathan & Sarah Stephens, 33
Abel L. m Lydia Read, 160
Abel Lord s Marvin & Caroline, 110
Abigail d Moses Jr. & Rachill, 237
Abbegail (Bennet) d John & Marah, 221
Abigail d Joseph & Eunice, 32
Abner m Lucretia Rowland, 49
Abner s Abner & Lucretia, 49
Abraham s Joseph & Lydia, 77
Adrial m Wealthy Ann Congdon, 173, 301
Albert m Almira Field, 154
Ama d James & Lucretia, 40
Amos s Daniell & Hannah, 236
Amos m Phebe Mack, 30
Amos s Amos & Phebe, 30
Amos s Elihu & Naomia, 114
Amos the elder died, 30
Asenath d Marvin & Carolina, 110
Azuba d Nathan & Luce, 26
Azubah d Amos & Phebe, 30
Azubah d Jaeber & Azubah, 122*
Azubah m John Munsell, 121
Azubah w William & Sarah, 138

344 LYME, CONNECTICUT, VITAL RECORDS

HUNTLEY, cont.
Barach s Elihu & Naomia, 114
Barnu (Barnabas) s Elihu & Naomia, 114
Benajah s Benajah & Esther, 27
Benjamin s John & Elizabeth, 236
Benjamin m Lydia Beckwith, 236
Benjamin s Samll & Ruth, 237
Beththessell (Bethuel) s Aaron & Mary, 236
Betsey m Selden Rogers, 148
Betsey (Mrs.) m Silas Carter, 167
Betsey d William & Sarah, 138
Calkins s Zenos & Elizabeth, 54
Calvin m Mrs. Betsy Rogers, 160
Carolina d Marvin & Carolina, 110*
Carolina w Marvin died, 110*

Catharine d Stephen & Phebe, 77
Charles s Reu & Eliza, 111
Charles m Nancy Bump, 139
Charlotte d Martin & Mehetabel, 31
Clarry d Martin & Phebe, 31
Curtice s Benjeman & Lydia, 236
Curtiss s John & Loas, 39
Dan s Amos & Phebe, 30
Dan m Lovice Peck, 127
Dan s Zenos & Elizabeth, 54
Daniell s Aaron & Marah (Chamberlain), 235
Daniel m Hannah Brown, 236
Danl s Daniell & Hannah, 236
Daniel died, 236
Daniel m Susannah Beckwith, 13
Daniel s Danll & Sussannah, 13
Daniel s Reynold & Esther, 112
David s Aaron & Marah, 235
David m Mary Tinker, 39, 236
David died, 236
David s Joseph & Eunice, 32
David s Aaron Sr., 236
Deaborah d Aaron Jr. & Debrah, 235
Deborah d Elihu & Naomia, 114
Doran (Duran) s Benjamin & Beththiah, 73
Edmund m Sarah Gilbert, 189
Elihu s David & Mary, 39, 236
Elihu m Naomia Brockway, 114
Elihu s David s Aaron Sr. & Mary, 236
Elijah (Bennet) s John & Marah, 221
Elijah s Jonathan & Sarah Stephens, 33
Elijah Kimball s Richard & Sally, 134
Eliphalet s Jonathan & Sarah Stephens, 33
Elisha s Nathan & Luce, 26
Elisha s Martin & Phebe, 31
Elisha M. m Mary Tinker, 151
Elizabeth d Aaron & Marah, 235
Elizabeth d John & Elizabeth, 236*
Elizabeth d John & Elizabeth b 236*
Elizabeth (Elisheba) d John & Lois, 39
Elizabeth m Ebenezer Chapman, 103
Elizabeth d Dan & Lovice, 127
Elkanah m Anna Bishop, 134
Elkanah s James & Lucretia, 40
Emeline Deliverance d Richard & Sally, 134
Emeline Ursula m Joel Johnson, 155
Emila d Elkanah & Anna, 134
Emily m William Humes, 167
Enoch s James & Lucretia, 40*
Erastus s Martin & Mehetabel, 31

HUNTLEY, cont.
Erastus s William & Sarah, 138
Erastus Calvin s Martin & Phebe, 31
Ester d Aaron Jr. & Debrah, 235
Esther m William Robbins, 8
Esther d Samuel & Ruth, 237
Eunice d Joseph & Eunice, 32
Ezekiel m Ruth Minor, 130
Ezekiel s David, 236
Ezra s Peter & Sarah, 237
Ezra s Jasper & Azubah, 121
Fanny d Reynold & Esther, 112
Frances E. m Emerson Mixter, 188
Gideon s Elihu & Naomia, 114
Giles s Reuben & Lovice, 17
Giles Leonard s Capt. Mechaial & Marcy, 135
Gurdon s Martin & Mehetabel, 31
Hana (Honor) d Aaron Jr. & Debrah, 235
Hannah m Dan Chadwick, 94
Hannah d Danll & Susannah, 13
Hannah m Ebenezer Mack, 20
Hannah m Edward DeWolf, 74
Hannah d Jasper & Azubah, 122
Hannah d John Jr. & Hannah, 9
Hannah d Joseph & Eunice, 32
Hannah d Peter & Sarah, 237
Harriet m John Rogers, Jr. 145
Hariot d Marvin & Carolina, 110
Harry s William & Sarah, 138
Hepsabeth d Samuell & Ruth, 237
Hezekiah s John Jr. & Lydia, 236
Hezekiah s Samuel & Ruth, 237
Honor (Hannah) d Aaron Jr. & Debrah, 235
Hope d Joseph & Lydia, 77
Hulda twin d Amos & Phebe, 30
Ira s James & Lucretia, 40
Isaac s Danll & Susannah died, 13
Isaac s Danll & Susannah born, 13*
Isaiah s Nathan & Luce, 26
Jabez s Moses & Rachall, 4
Jabez m Patience Voan (Vaugn), 4, 20
Jacob s Daniell & Hannah, 236
James s Daniell & Hannah, 236
James m Lucretia Smith, 40*
James s James & Lucretia, 40
James s Elknah & Anna, 134
Jane (Bennet) d John & Marah, 221
Jason s Daniel & Susannah, 13
Jasper s Peter & Sarah, 237
Jasper m Azubah Mack, 121
Jasper s Jasper & Azubah, 122*
Jasper Sr. died, 122
Jeane child Aaron & Marah, 235
Jedediah (Bennet) s John & Marah, 221
Jedediah Brockway s Elihu & Naomia, 114
Jehiel s John & Hannah, 9
Jemima d Aaron Jr. & Debrah, 235
Jemima m Eber Lewis, 10
Jemima d Martin & Mehetabel, 31
Jerusha w Reynold died, 112
John died, 236
John s Aaron & Marah, 235
John m Elizabeth, Pearson, 236
John s John & Elizabeth, 236
John s John, 237
John s Joseph & Lous Beckwith, 39

INDEX OF PERSONS 345

HUNTLEY, cont.
John s Moses & Abagall, 237
John Jr. died, 236
John Jr. m Lydia Robins, 236
John (Bennet) s John & Marah, 221
John M. m Delia Caulkins, 193, 210
John Whittlesey s Richard & Sally, 134
John Jr. m Hannah Person, 9
Jonathan s David & Mary, 33
Jonathan s David s Aaron Sr. & Mary, 236
Jonathan s Jonathan & Sarah Stephens, 33
Jonathan m Sarah Stephens Smith, 33
Jonathan Bishop s Elkanah & Anna, 134
Joseph s John & Elizabeth, 236
Joseph m Eunice Welch, 32
Joseph s Joseph & Eunice, 32
Joseph m Lydia Sawyer, 77
Joseph s Joseph & Lydia, 77
Joseph Douglass s Marvin & Mary, 110
Joseph W. m Mary E. Reed, 169
Joseph Wm. s Capt. Mechail & Marcy Remick, 135
July Ann d Reuben & Lovice, 17
Julia Ann d Adrail & Samuel Saunders Jr., 156
Keturah d Wm. m John Ames, 53
Lemuel s Samuel & Ruth, 237
Lemuel s Samull & Susannah, 75
Lewman (Luman) s Nathan & Luce, 26
Lodowick Mack s Reu & Abigail, 111
Lois d Peter & Sarah, 237
Lois d William & Sarah, 138
Lovice d Amos & Phebe, 30
Lovice d Amos & Reuben Huntley, 17
Lovina d Benjamin & Beththiah, 73
Lovina m Dan Peck, 55
Lucinda d Stephen & Phebe, 77
Lucretia d James & Lucretia, 40
Lucy d John & Elizabeth, 236*
Lucy d Amos & Phebe, 30
Lucy m Gurdon Watrous Jr., 111
Lydia w John Jr. died, 236
Lydia m John Munsell, 61
Lydia d Jonathan & Sarah Stephens, 33
Lydia d Marvin & Carolina, 110
Lydia d Reynol & Jerusha, 111
Marah d Aaron & Marah, 235
Marah m John Benet, 221
Marcy d Johnathan & Sarah, 33
Martha d Joseph & Eunice, 32
Martin s Amos & Phebe, 30
Martin s Jonathan & Sarah, 33
Martin m Mehetabel Sill, 31
Martin m Phebe Mack, 31
Martin s Martin & Phebe, 31
Marvin s James & Lucretia, 40
Marvin m Caroline Lord, 110
Marvin s Marvin & Caroline, 110*
Marvin m Mary Douglass, 110*
Marvin Lord s Marvin & Carolina, 110*
Mary d Abner & Lucretia, 49
Mary m Cyrus Lee, 76
Mary m Elijah Hill, 48
Mary d John & Elizabeth, 236
Mary m Joseph Alger, 217
Mary d Marvin & Mary, 110
Mary d Mosis & Abigall, 237

HUNTLEY, cont.
Mary (Bennett) d John & Marah, 221, 225
Mary O. m Silas Lester, 147
Mary w Peter died, 237*
Matilda d Wm. & Sarah, 139
Matthew s Jonathan & Sarah Stephens, 33
Mechial Capt. m Marcy Remick Higgins, 33
Mehepzibah d Samuel & Ruth, 237
Mehetable d David s Aaron Sr. & Mary, 236
Mehetable d David & Mary, 31, 39, 236
Mehetable d Elihu & Naomia, 114
Mehetable d Martin & Phebe, 31
Mehetable wife Martin died, 31
Mercy G. m Frances B. Lee, 166
Mirichi m Abby Bush, 164
Metilda d William & Sarah, 138
Micarl (Michael) s Ruben & Lovice, 17
Miranda m Abijah Pierson, 153
Molley d Samll & Ruth, 237
Molly m Edward Chapman, 104
Molley d Amos & Phebe, 30
Moses, 4
Mosis m Abigall Comstock, 237
Mosis s Mosis & Abigall, 237
Mosis Jr. m Rachill Haris, 233, 237
Nancy d Elkanah & Anna, 134
Naomy d Aaron III & Mary, 235
Naomy d Johnathan & Sarah Stephens, 33
Nathan s Aaron Jr. & Debrah, 235
Nathan m Luce Smith, 26
Nathan s Nathan & Luce, 26
Nehemiah s Benjah & Esther, 27
Olive d Joseph & Lydia, 77
Patience d Peter & Mary, 237
Peter m Mary Ransom, 237
Peter m 2nd wife Sarah Robbins, 237
Peter twin s Wm. & Sarah, 138
Petter s John & Elizabeth, 236
Phebe d Aaron Jr. & Debrah, 235
Phebe d Amos & Phebe, 30
Phebe m Henry Roland Jr., 84, 97
Phebe d Martin & Phebe, 31
Phebe d Reu & Eliza, 111
Phebe w Stephen died, 77
Phebe (Mrs) m Reuben Huntley, 172
Pheby m Necodemus Miller, 15
Phinehas s James & Lucretia, 40
Polly d Wm. & Sarah, 138
Polly d Martin & Phebe, 31
Polly Alcey d Reuben & Lovice, 17
Rachil, 4
Rena d James & Lucretia, 40
Renald s James & Lucretia, 40*
Reu m Abigail Mack, 111
Reu m Eliza Booge, 111
Reu s Amos & Phebe, 30
Reuben s Aaron & Mary, 236
Reuben s Wid. Mary m Lovice Huntley, 17
Reuben m Phebe Huntley, 172
Reynold died, 112
Reynold m Jerusha Mack, 111
Reynold s Reynold & Jerusha, 111
Reynold m Esther McNight, 112
Richard s Reuben & Lovice, 17
Richard Capt. m Sally Kimball, 134
Richard Harris s Benajah & Esther, 27

HUNTLEY, cont.
Ruel B. m Abby A. Bump, 183
Rufus s Nathan & Luce, 26
Rufus m Hannah Freeman, 119
Russell s Nathan & Luce, 26
Ruth d Aaron Jr. & Debrah, 235
Ruth m Samll Huntley, 237
Ruth d Samll & Ruth, 237
Sabra d John & Lous, 39
Sally d Reu & Abigail, 111
Sally d Elkanah & Anna, 134
Sally m John W. Crary, 175
Sally d Marvin & Carolina, 110
Samuell (Bennet) s John & Marah, 221
Samuell s John & Elizabeth, 236
Samuell m Ruth Huntley, 237
Samuel s Samuel & Ruth, 237
Samll Jr. m Susannah Huntley, 75
Sarah d John & Elizabeth, 236
Sarah, 300
Sarah (Bennett) d John & Marah, 221
Sarah d Peter & Sarah, 237
Sarah w Timothy Mather Jr. died, 249
Sarah d Jasper & Azubah, 121
Sarah d Elihu & Naomia, 114
Sarah m Wm. Huntley, 138
Selden s Martin & Phebe, 31
Seth s Abner & Lucretia, 50
Seth s Elihu & Naomia, 114
Seth s James & Lucretia, 40*
Sila m John Mumsell Jr., 60
Silas s James & Lucretia m Betsey Beebe, 40
Sill s Martin & Mehetabel, 31
Silvanus (see under Sylvanus)
Sollomon s Aaron & Marah, 235
Sollomon m Ruth _____ , 238
Sollomon s Aaron Jr. & Debrah, 235
Sollomon died, 238
Solomon s Samuell & Ruth, 237
Sollomon s Samll & Ruth died, 238*
Sollomon s Samll & Ruth born, 238*
Sophia m Horace B. Manwaring, 164
Sophia d Richard & Sally, 134
Spicer Mack s Reu & Abigail, 111
Stanton s Reynoid & Jerusha, 111
Stephen s Aaron Jr. & Debrah, 235
Stephen s Aaron III & Mary, 235
Stephen m Lydia Brockway, 77
Stephen m Phebe Tubbs, 77
Stephen s Stephen & Lydia, 77
Stephen Mack s Wm & Sarah, 138
Susanah d Joseph & Eunice, 32
Susannah d Daniel & Susannah, 13
Susannah m Samll Huntley, Jr., 75
Silvanus s Aaron & Mary, 236
Silvanus Higgins s Capt. Mechail & Marcy Remmick, 135
Sylvanus H. m Lydia Caulkins, 162
Taber s Reuben & Lovice, 17
Timothy s Aaron Jr. & Debrah, 235
Ursula d Reuben & Lovice, 17
Vashty d John & Lois, 39
William s Abner & Lucretia, 50
William s Ezekiel & Ruth, 130
William died, 138
William S. s John & Lois, 39

HUNTLEY, cont.
Wm. m Lorain Fields, 155
William s Moses Jr. & Rachill, 237
William s Reynold & Jerusha, 111
William m Sarah Huntley, 138
William (twin) s William & Sarah, 138
Zadock s Jonathan & Sarah Stephens, 33
Zeletoes s John Jr. & Hannah, 9
Zenas s Aaron & Mary, 236
Zenas m Elizabeth Peck, 54
Zephaniah s John & Hannah, 9
_____ s Stephen & Phebe, 77
_____ s Marvin & Carolina, 110
Widow m Alanson Bramble, 180
HURLBURT, Juliaette m Eben Dart, 174
Mary Jane R. m Sylvester Slate, 181
Neaome m David Moodey Jewett, 115
HYDE-HIDE, Alexander s Benjamin & Abigail, 7
Alexander s Wm. Rufus & Elizabeth, 87
Alexander m Mary Burnham, 129, 276
Amelia d Benjamin & Abigail, 7
Amelia II d Benjamin & Abigail, 7*
Benjamin m Abigail Lee, 7
Edward G. m Sarah Lord, 188, 208
Elizabeth d Wm. Rufus & Elizabeth, 87
Elizabeth m Ebenezer Rogers, 40
Ira, 201
John s Uriah & Mehetable, 67
Lous (d) Uriah & Mehetable, 67
Marvin s Uriah & Mehetable, 67
Phebe m Mathew Griswould, 232
Uriah m Mehetable Marvin, 67
Wm Rufus m Elizabeth Starlin, 87
Willm Rufus s Wm. Rufus & Elizabeth, 87
William Rufus d, 87*
William R (Lex. Alarm), 301
INGHAM, Ezra m Jane Grumley, 179
INGRAHAM, Abigail twin d Ezra & Betsey, 100
Ann m Thomas Rathburn, 142
Anne d Ezra & Betsey, 100
Asa Saunders s Elisha & Sarah, 147
Betty d Ezra & Betsey, 100
Daniel s Javitt & Marcey, 238
Elizabeth d Javitt & Marcey, 238
Ethelenda m Daniel Anderson, 158
Ethelenda d Ezra & Bettey died, 100
Ethelenda d Ezra & Bettey born, 100*
Ezra m Betsey Robins, 100
Francis m Lucretia Tinker, 95
Giles m Emily Rau (Raud), 197
Harriet m Samuel Ingraham, 155
Javit m Marcey Taylor, 238
Javitt (Jared or Gerard) s Javitt & Marcey, 238
Lucretia w Francis m Samuel Peck, 25
Lucy d Francis & Lucretia, 95
Lucy m David Lay, 122
Lydia m Ezra Robins, 100
Mary m James S. Graham, 144
Mary Jones twin d Elisha & Sarah, 147
Olive d Francis & Lucretia, 95
Parnall m Abner Beckwith, 117
Patience d Javitt & Marcey, 238
Samuel Jr. m Abigail Clark, 20
Samuell twin s Ezra & Betsey, 100
Samuel m Harriet Ingraham, 155
Sarah Taylor twin d Elisha & Sarah, 147

INDEX OF PERSONS 347

IVES, Romanta m Charlotte Forsyth, 156
JACOBS, Daniel m Polly Chadwick, 131
  Erastus s Daniel & Polly, 131
  Mary d Daniel & Polly, 131
  William s Daniel & Polly, 131
JAMES, Albert m Mary Rich, 154
  Mary m Charles Pilgrim, 149
Janner, John Jr. (Tanner) servant to Reynald Marvin, 247
JEROME, Jesse H. m Betsy Gee, 162
  Sarah, 299
  Susan m Abel Smith, 171
JEWETT, JEWITT, JEWIT
  David s Nathan & Deborah, 238
  David s David M & Neaome, 115*
  David M. m Ann Rathbone, 156
  David Moodey (Moody) m Neaome Hurlbut, 115
  Deborah twin d Joseph & Lucretia, 56
  Elizabeth twin d Joseph & Lucretia, 56*
  Francis M. m Charles E. Tiffany, 168
  George Washington s Joseph & Lucretia, 56
  Gibbins s Nathan & Deborah, 238
  Hibbert s Nathan & Deoborah, 238
  John G. s David M. & Neaomy, 115
  John G. m Lois Lay, 129
  John G. m Phebe P. Stark, 142
  Joseph s Nathan & Deborah, 238
  Joseph m Lucretia Rogers, 56
  Joseph s Joseph & Lucretia, 56
  Joseph Capt. died, 56*, 301, 304
  Joshua s Joseph & Lucretia, 56
  Josiah s Joseph & Lucretia, 56
  Laura M. m Victor M Johnson, 152
  Lucretia m Capt. Abner Lee, 30
  Lucretia d Joseph & Lucretia, 56
  Luce d Joseph & Lucretia, 56
  Lucy d Nathan & Deborah, 238
  Mary d Joseph & Lucretia, 56
  Mary d Nathan & Deborah, 238
  Nancy d David M. & Neaome, 115
  Naomi m Charles Tiffany, 148
  Nathan m Deborah Lord, 238
  Nathan s Nathan & Deborah, 238
  Nathan Capt. died, 56, 303
  Nathan Jr. m Lucretia Stark, 171
  Phebe Tabor d David M & Neaome, 115
  Polly m Samuel Perkins, 116
  Sarah Selden m Joseph Higgins Mather, 158
  Zabdiel Rogers s Joseph & Lucretia, 56
JOHNSON, Anna d John & Anna, 70, 146
  Anne d Stephen & Anna, 95
  Annie m George Griffin, 146
  Barack m Mary A. Way, 184, 200
  Benjamin m Esther Comstock, 137
  Benjamin s Reynold & Phebe, 110
  Betsey d Stephen & Anna, 95
  Betsy m Joshua Griffing, 125
  Betsy d Uzal & Mehetable, 133
  Cate d Stepnen & Anna, 95
  Catharine d John & Anna, 70
  Catharine m Nathan Griffing, 105
  Catharine d Rev. Stephen & Elizabeth, 28
  Charles B. s Reynold & Phebe, 110
  Christopher s Lawrence & Lydia, 78
  Daniel s John & Anna, 70

JOHNSON, cont.
  Daniel s Lawrence & Grace, 78
  Daniel m Malinda Austin, 157
  Daniel s Uzal & Mehetable, 120
  David s Uzel & Mehetable, 120
  Diodate s Stephen & Anna, 95
  Diodate s Stephen & Elizabeth, 27*
  Elijah s Reynold & Phebe, 110
  Eliza Banning m Comstock Hewlet, 181
  Elizabeth d John & Anna, 70
  Elizabeth w Rev. Stephen died, 23
  Elizabeth d Rev. Stephen & Elizabeth, 28
  Elizabeth m Stephen Peck, 130
  Elizabeth P. m Levi Bliss, 189
  Fanny d John & Anna, 70
  Grace d Lawrence & Grace, 78
  Hannah w of John, 238
  Hannah m Joseph Minor, 136
  Henry Phelps, 309
  Hulda d Uzel & Mehetable, 120
  Ira s Lawrence & Grace, 78
  James s Reynold & Phebe, 110
  Jon s Uzel & Mehitable, 120
  Joel m Emeline Ursula Huntley, 155
  John, 238
  John s John & Hannah, 238
  John Jr. m Anna Brooks, 70
  John s John & Anna, 70*
  John (Lex. Alarm), 301
  John s Persia & Zilpha, 138
  Joseph Selden s Calvin & Oru, 200
  Lawrence (Lex. Alarm), 301
  Lawrence m Grace Harris, 78
  Lawrence s Lawrence & Grace, 78
  Lawrence m Lydia Comstock, 75
  Lilles Green d Reynold & Phebe, 110
  Lucinda d Reynold & Phebe, 110
  Lydia m John Tibbitts, 148
  Lydia w Lawrence died, 78
  Lydia d Lawrence & Grace, 78
  Mary d Rev. Stephen & Mary, 28
  Mary w Rev. Stephen died, 28
  Mary Ann d Benj. & Esther, 137
  Mary Elizabeth m John M. Crosby, 190
  Mehitable died, 214
  Nathl s Rev. Stephen & Mary, 28
  Nancy d Uzall & Mehetable, 133
  Peria or Persia s Lawrence & Grace, 78
  Persia m Zilpha Bramble, 138
  Phebe d Lawrence & Grace, 78
  Phebe m Ozias H. Bogue, 168
  Phebe d Uzal & Mehetable, 133
  Phebe died, 215
  Polly d Uzal & Mehetable, 133
  Reynolds s John & Anna, 70
  Reynold m Phebe Smith, 110
  Rhoda d Uzal & Mehetable, 120
  Sally d Capt Stephen & Anna, 95
  Sally d Uzal & Mehetable, 133
  Saml s Lawrence & Lydia, 78
  Sarah d Rev. Stephen & Elizabeth, 28
  Sarah m John Griswold, 95
  Sarah P. m Philo Parmelee, 166
  Stepenn m Elizabeth Diodate, 27
  Stephen s Rev. Stephen & Elizabeth, 28
  Stephen Rev. m Mary Blague, 28

JOHNSON, cont.
Stephen Jr. m Anna Lord, 95
Stephen Rev. m Abigail Leveritt, 94
Thomas s Thomas & Mary Ann, 204
Thomas s Uzal & Mehetable, 133
Timothy s Lawrence & Grace, 78
Timothy m Rachal Ransom, 145
Uzal m Mehitable Baker, 120, 133
Victor M. m Laura M. Jewett, 152
William m Emeline J. Bogue, 190
William s John & Anna died, 70*
William s John & Anna born, 70
William s Reynold & Phebe, 110
William s Rev. Stephen & Elizabeth, 28*
William s Rev. Stephen & Elizabeth died, 28*
William H. m Eliza Ann Perkins, 157, 309
Zylpha A. m John A. DeWolf, 183
JONES, Alexander s Isaac & Eunice, 135
Amasa s Asa & Polly, 120
Anna m Nun Clark, 52
Asa m Polly Moor (e), 120
Asa s Asa & Polly, 120
Benjamin a Mulatto m Abigail Menta, 238
Benjamin s Benjamin (a Mulatto) & Abigail, 238
Betsey m William Taylor, 190, 210
Deborah m Henery Champion Sr., 224
Hannah d Asa & Polly, 120
Henry m Phebe S. Marvin, 161
Hester m Jabez Watrous, 86
Isaac m Eunice Champion, 135
Lewis of Saybrook, 224
Margaret d Lewis of Saybrook, 224
Lura m Zolpher Gee, 121
Margaret m Wolston Brockway, 224
Mary m Elisha Wade, 74
Nancy m James Pratt, 153
Polly d Asa & Polly, 120
Marah, 265
JORAM, Elizabeth m Elisha Merrow Jr., 84
JUDD, Delight m Erastus Rogers, 147
KEABLES, Alexander m Roxana Maynard, 160
Maria E. m Orlando R. Glover, 189, 208
KEARNEY, Catharine m Joseph Fuller, 208
KEENY, KEENEY, Abel m Maria Cobb, 154
Chianna m Capt. Manasah Leech, 32, 277
Susannah m Samuel DeWolf, 125
KELLOGG, Joseph m Lydia Utley, 159
Mary m Renold Marvin, 19
Samuel Vine s Josiah & Lydia, 159
KELSEY, James Jr. m Louisa Millard, 151
KENT, Anna m James Chadwick, 14
Elizabeth m Sylvanus Clark, 93
Polly m Lot Peck, 89
KIMBALL, Sally m Capt. Richard Huntley, 134
Silvah d John & Ruhamah, 104
KING, Adeline C. d Leander & Harriet, 198
Calvin m Susan Dorr, 189
Fanny d Joseph & Jane, 59
John m Caroline Saunders, 155
John Lay s Joseph & Jane, 59
Jonathan s Joseph & Jane, 59
Joseph Jr. m Jane Lay, 59
Leander m Harriet E. Moore, 179, 198
KINGSBURY, Mary J. m Lt. S.B. Buckner, 195
Col. Henry W., 310

KIRTLAND
Charles Erastus m Emeline E. Beckwith, 196
John L. m Elizabeth S. Beckwith, 180
Parnall m Simeon DeWolf, 5
LADD, Phebe m Nathaniel Wheeler, 148
LAIGH (see under LEE, LAY)
LAMB, Rebeckah m James Beckwith, 219
LA MOTT, Theodore m Emily Champion, 190, 208
LAMPHEAR, Experience m Joshua Rogers, 44
LANE, William m Jemima Self, 143
William G. m Elizabeth D. Griswold, 196
LANGWORTHY
George F. m Julia Ann Chadwick, 167
LAPLASS
Elizabeth C. m Richard A. Hungerford, 188, 200
Francis, 307
Nancy, 200
Robert H., 200
Robert L. s Robert & Nancy, 200
Timothy A. s Emeline F. Gardiner, 174
LATHAM, Caroline m Chauncey Prentice, 169
Elizabeth m Edward Champlin, 28
Lydia m Elias Barrell, 153
Mary m Sylvester W. Fox, 187
Sarah m Levi B. Chappell, 163
William m Eunice Minor, 143
LATHROP, Andrew m Laura A. Royce, 185
Christopher m Dimmis Truman (perhaps Lothrop), 151
LATIMER, LATERMER, LATTIMER
Abegall d Mr. Lay deceased m Wm Warman, 269
Abigail d Nathan & Jean, 43
Anne d Nathan & Jean, 43
Borredill m Eusebious Bushnell, 92
David s Hallam & Marcy, 99
Edward s Nathan & Jean, 43
Eliza H. m Hanibal Reeve, 141
Frances d Hallam & Marcy, 100
Hallam s Nathan & Jean, 43
Hallam m Marcy Dodge, 99
Jean d Nathan & Jean, 43
Jonathan s Nathan & Anna, 97
Lucy d Nathan & Jean, 43
Lucy m Daniel Dodge, 43
Lucy d Hallam & Marcy, 100
Lydia d Nathan & Jean, 43
Marcy d Hallam & Marcy, 99
Nathan m Jean Lee, 43
Nathan s Nathan & Jean, 43
Nathan Jr. m Anna Dodge, 97
Nicholas Hallam s Hallam & Marcy, 100
Peter s Hallam & Marcy, 100*
Samll s Nathan & Jean, 43
Stephen s Nathan & Jean, 43
_____ m Walter Goold, 133
LAY, LAYE, Abigail m William Warman, 269
Abigail d John Jr. & Sarah, 238
Abigail d John 3rd & Hannah, 6
Abigail d Wm & Betsey, 120
Abner s John 4th & Anna, 62
Adelaide d Oliver J. & Mary A., 164
Alexander s Lee & Lovisa, 85
Amos s John & Sarah, 239
Amos m Mary Griswold, 14
Andrew s John & Rhoda, 65

INDEX OF PERSONS 349

LAY, cont.
Ann m Edward Greenfield, 154
Anna d John & Rhoda, 65
Asa s John & Rhoda, 65
Betsey d Willm & Betsey, 120
Betsey m Silas Bramble, 189
Betsey M. m Ira Tillotson, 168, 198
Bettey d John 3rd & Hannah, 6
Bettey m Silas Champlin, 36
Bridgeham s Joseph & Marcy, 5
Calee d Peter & Hepzibah, 70
Catterne d John Jr. & Sarah, 238
Charles s John & Rhoda, 65
Chorine d John 3rd & Hannah, 6
Clerinea m John Ayer, 93
Daniel s John 4th & Anna, 62
David s John 4th & Anna, 62
David m Lucy Ingraham, 122
Demiss Harriet d Ezra & Lydia, 112*
Edward, 238*
Edward s John Jr. & Sarah, 238*
Edward Jr. m Martha Center, 24
Edway s Joseph & Marcy, 5
Elisha s Edward & Martha, 24
Elisha s John 2nd & Mary, 239
Elisha m Mary Olmsted, 104
Elisha s Elisha & Mary, 104
Elizabeth d John Jr. & Sarah, 238
Elizabeth d John & Sarah, 239
Elizabeth d John 2nd & Mary, 239*
Elizabeth m Elisha Miller, 16
Elizabeth m Richard Smith Jr., 261
Elizabeth d John 2nd & Mary died, 239*
Elizabeth d William & Phebe, 63
Elizabeth d John 2nd (Tavern keeper), 239
Enoch m Hannah Lay, 119
Enoch S. m Mary A. Champion, 165
Eunice d Amos & Mary, 14
Ezra s William & Phebe, 63
Ezra m Lydia Ingraham, 112*
Ezra s Ezra & Lydia, 112*
Fanney d Peter & Hepzibah, 70
Filkin s John 4th & Anna, 62
Francis Ingraham s Ezra & Lydia, 112
Francis J. m Maria Norton, 144
Frederick s Richard & Marcy, 87
Gordius s Lee & Lovisa, 85
Goege Cowles s David & Lucy, 122
Gibbon s Peter & Hepzibah, 70
Hannah d John 4th & Anna, 62
Hannah d John 3rd & Hannah, 6, 239
Hannah died, 6
Hannah m Enoch Lay, 119
Hannah m Richard Chadwick, 148
Hepzibah d Peter & Hepzibah, 70
Hipsabeth d Edward Merah, 238
Horace s Ezra & Lydia, 112*
Hubbell s William & Phebe, 63
Ichabod s John & Ruth, 239
James Benjamin s Lee & Lovisa, 85
Jane m Joseph Marvin, 246
Jane d Edward & Martha, 24*
Jane d Esqr. Lay m Joseph King Jr., 59
Jean d John 3rd & Hannah, 6
Jean d Peter & Hepzibah, 70
Jenet d John & Rhoda, 65

LAY, cont.
Jerusha d John 2nd & Mary, 239
Jerusha d William & Phebe, 63
Johanna d John Jr. & Johanna, 239
John Sr. died, 239
John s John Jr. (Drummer Lay) & Sarah, 238
John Jr. m Johanna Smith, 239
John s John Jr. & Johanna, 239
John s Edward & Merah, 238
John Jnr. drummer, 238
John m Sarah Lee, 239
John s John 2nd (Tavern Keeper), 239
John m Wid. Ruth Robbins, 65
John 2nd m Mary Lewis, 239
John 3rd m Hannah Lee, 6, 239
John s John 3rd & Hannah, 6, 239
John 4th m Anna Sill, 62
John s John 4th & Anna, 62
John 3rd m Rhoda Watrous, 65
John died (father Elisha & grandfather Stephen) 104, 339
John died, 6
John m Lydia Cone, 180
John Olmsted s Elisha & Mary, 104
Joseph s Edward & Merah, 238
Joseph m Marcy Deming, 5
Joseph s Joseph & Marcy, 5
Joseph s Richard & Marcy, 87
Joseph H. m Elizabeth Maxon, 173, 204, 205
Laura d David & Lucy, 122
Laura m Shadrack Sill, 168
Lee (Lex. Alarm), 301
Lee s John 3rd & Hannah, 6
Lee m Lovisa Griswold, 85
Lee s Lee & Lovisa, 85
Lee Capt. died, 86
Lois m John G. Jewitt, 129
Lous d Lee & Lovisa, 85
Lovisa d Lee & Lovisa, 85
Lovisa w Capt. Lee died, 86
Lucia d John & Sarah, 239
Lucia m Stephen Smith, 37
Lucinda d John 4th & Anna, 62
Lucy twin d John 3rd & Hannah, 6
Lucy d Elisha & Mary, 104
Lucy d Richd & Esther, 87
Lucy d David & Lucy, 122
Lucy m William J. Banning, 168
Lydia d John 3rd & Hannah, 6
Lydia m Elihu Southworth, 193
Lydia w Ezra died, 104*
Marah d Edward & Merah, 238
Marcy d Joseph & Marcy, 5
Marcy d Richard & Marcy, 87
Marcy d Richard died, 87*
Marah d John Jr. & Sarah, 238
Margaret Lay (Mrs.) died, 213
Mariette J. d Oliver J. & Mary A., 164
Martha Jean d William & Phebe, 63
Mary d Edward m Joseph Robins, 39
Mary (Mercy) m John Chadwick, 139
Mary w Elisha died, 104*
Mary Ann m Chauncey Champion, 150, 202
Mary Elizabeth d Francis J. & Maria, 144
Mary E. m Dr. Seth Smith, 187
Merah wife Edward Lay, 238

LAY, cont.
Modina d Joseph H. & Elisabeth A., 204
Molley d John 4th & Anna, 62
Nabby d Peter & Hepzibah, 70
Oliver Ingraham s David & Lucy, 122
Oliver J. m Mary Whittlesey, 164
Patty d Willm & Betsey, 120
Peck s Peter & Hepzibah, 70
Peter s John 3rd & Hannah, 6
Peter m Hepzibah Peck, 70
Peter died, 70
Phebe d John Jr. & Sarah, 238
Phebe d John & Sarah, 239
Phebe d Lee & Lovisa, 86
Phebe d Peter & Hepzibah, 70
Phebe d William & Phebe, 63
Phebe w Wm died, 63
Polly d Peter & Hepzibah, 70
Polly d Wm & Betsey, 120
Polly d William & Phebe, 63
Rebeikahe d John Jr. & Sarah, 238
Rebekah m Danell Rayment, 256
Reuben s Joseph & Marcy, 5
Richard s John & Ruth, 239
Richard s John 3rd & Hannah, 6
Richard s Joseph H. & Elisabeth, 205
Richd m Marcy Mather, 87
Richard s Richard & Marcy, 87
Richard m Esther Biggs, 87
Robert s Edward, 238
Robert died, 213
Robert Parsons s Willm & Betsey, 120
Sally m Ezra Chadwick, 116
Samuel s Joseph & Marcy, 5
Sarah d Elisha & Mary, 104
Sarah d John Jr. & Sarah, 238
Sarah m Simon DeWolf, 226, 229
Sarah widow of Simon DeWolf m Nathaniell Clark, 226
Sarah d John & Sarah, 239
Sarah d John 2nd (tavern keeper), 239
Sarah widow m Reynold Marvin Jr., 247
Sarah wife John died, 239*
Sarah m Timothy Mather Jr., 248
Sarah d John 3rd & Hannah, 6
Sarah d William & Phebe, 63
Sarah m Thomas Marvin, 23
Sarah Ann d David & Lucy, 122*
Sarah Ann d Oliver J. & Mary A., 164
Silas twin s John 3rd & Hannah, 6
Sophia M. m John M. Champion, 149
Stephen s Elisha & Mary, 104
Susa d Lee & Lovisa, 85
Thomas Griswold s Lee & Lovisa, 85, 86
William s John 2nd & Mary, 239
William m Phebe Sill, 63
William s William & Phebe, 63
William Jr. m Betsey Parsons, 120
Wm died, 63
Willoughby Lynda s Lee & Lovisa died, 85
Willoughby Lynde s Lee & Lovisa born 85
_____ first daughter Joseph & Marcy, 5
LEACH, LEECH, Christopher, 301
Deborah m Stephen Champion, 9
Deborah d Manasah & Irena, 31
Elijah s Manasah & Irena, 31

LEACH, cont.
Elisha s Manasah & Irena, 31
Elisha Ely s Richd & Hepzh, 130*
Enoch s Manassah & Irena, 31
Hepzibah m Dan Marvin, 141
Irena d Manasah & Irena, 31
Lydia w Ezra, 112
Lydia d Manasah & Irena, 31
Manasah Capt. m Chinanna Keeney, 32
Manasah m Irena Ely, 31, 275
Mary m Aaron Huntley 3rd, 235
Polly d Manasah & Irena, 31
Richard d Manasah & Irena, 31
Richard m Hepzebah Mather, 130
Richard Montgomery s Richard & Hepzebah, 130
LEARNED, Billings P. m Mary A. Noyes, 171
LEE, LEES Abby Frances d John & Anne, 124
Abby W. m Reuben L.Hall, 163
Abby Wells d Seth & Anna, 132
Abel Huntington s John & Anne, 124
Abigail d Mr. Lay deceased m William Warman, 269
Abigail d Stephen & Abigail, 241
Abigail m Benjamin Hide, 7
Abigail w Capt. Stephen died 241*
Abigail d Benjamin & Mary, 240
Abigail m Elisha Ayer, 40
Abigail d Elisha & Abigail, 88
Abigail m Alfred Willes, 115
Abner Jr. married to Deborah, 275
Abner s William & Mary died, 242*
Abner 2nd s William & Mary, 242*
Abner m Elizabeth Lee, 30
Abner s Abner & Elizabeth, 30
Abner Capt., 304
Abner Capt. m Lucretia Jewitt, 30
Albert s Capt. Enoch & Hester, 112
Ama m Zephaniah (Zachariah) Marvin Jr., 23
Amy m Capt Oliver Peck, 123
Andrew s Capt. John & Abigail, 1
Ann wife of Thomas died, 241
Anna d Jason & Abiah, 101
Anna d John & Eunice, 240
Anne d Seth & Betsey, 43
Anson d Ezra & Sarah, 52
Aruna d Ezra & Sarah, 52
Asa S. m Mary Bailey, 174
Azubah d William & Mary, 242
Azubah m Daniel DeWolf, 36
Beeca (Rebecca) d Ezra & Rebecka, 18
Benjamin s Thomas & Marah died, 241*
Benjamin alias Laigh s Thomas, 242
Benjamin s John & Elizabeth, 240
Benjamin s Stephen & Abigail, 241
Benjamin m Mary Ely, 239, 275
Benjamin Jr. m Mary Dorr, 79
Benja s Benjamin & Mary, 79, 239
Betsey d Seth & Betsey, 43
Betsey d Ezra & Sarah, 52
Betsey m Edward Hill, 134
Betsey d Seth & Anne, 132
Betsey Starlin d Lemuel & Sarah, 22
Bettey d Jason & Abiah, 101
Calvin Church s Lemuel & Sarah, 22
Carolina d Capt Enoch Hester, 112
Cate d Elisha & Hepzibah died, 22*

INDEX OF PERSONS 351

LEE, cont.
Catea d Joseph & Mary, 240*
Cate d Elisha & Hepzibah born, 22*
Cate d Seth & Betsey, 43
Catharine m Elijah Ely, 39
Charles s Benjamin Jr. & Mary, 79
Christopher s Martin & Sabra, 47
Christopher s Seth & Anna, 132
Christopher H. m Susan M. Howe, 170
Clarissa d Abner & Elizabeth, 30
Cyrus s William & Mary, 242
Cyrus m Mary Huntley, 76
Dan, 304
Dan s Abner & Elizabeth, 30
Dan m Lurania Champlin, 35
Dan m Nabby Champlin, 35
Daniel s Stephen & Abigail, 241
Danil s Benjamin & Mary, 240
David s Ezra & Sarah, 52
Deborah (Mrs.) wife of Abner Jr., 274, 275
Delia d Capt. Enoch & Hester, 112
Easther (see under Esther)
Edwin s John & Anne, 123
Elias s Stephen & Mehetable, 13
Elias s William & Mary, 242
Elisha (Lex. Alarm), 301
Elisha m Hepzibah Lee, 22*
Elisha s Elisha & Hepzibah, 22*
Elisha died, 22*
Elisha m Abigail Murdock, 88
Elisha s Elisha & Abigail, 88
Elisha s John & Anne, 123
Elisha s Thomas & Elizabeth, 242
Elisha Ann d Seth & Anna, 132
Elizabeth m Abner Lee, 30
Elizabeth wife Aner died, 30
Elizabeth d Abner & Lucretia, 30
Elizabeth d Benjamin & Mary, 240
Elizabeth d Ezra & Deborah, 91
Elizabeth m George Griswold Jr., 53
Elizabeth d John & Elizabeth, 240*
Elizabeth d John & Elizabeth, 240
Elizabeth d John & Lydiah, 240
Elizabeth m Samuell Peck, 253
Elizabeth d Stephen & Abigail, 241
Elizabeth d Thomas & Elizabeth, 242
Elizabeth d Thomas & Elisabeth, 47
Elizabeth d Thomas & Marah, 241
Elizabeth S. m George R. Peck, 150
Enoch s Elisha & Abigail, 88
Enoch Capt. m Hester Calkins, 112
Ester d Thomas & Elizabeth, 241
Easther m Clement Minor, 249
Esther d Benjamin & Mary, 240
Esther m Samuel Comstock, 103, 113
Esther m John Wood, 149
Eunice d Jason & Abiah, 101
Eunice d Thomas & Elizabeth, 242
Eunice m John Lee, 240*
Eunice wife John died, 240*
Eunice d John & Abigail, 1
Eunice m Richard Sill, 64
Ezra s William & Mary, 242
Ezra m Sarah_____, 52
Ezra m Rebecka Southworth, 18
Ezra s Abner & Elizabeth, 30

LEE, cont.
Ezra m Deborah Mather, 91
Fanny d Elisha & Abigail, 88
Frances B. m Mary G. Huntley, 166
Frederick s Stephen & Abigail, 241
George s Benjamin Jr. & Mary, 79
George Dudley s Lemuel & Sarah, 22
George Washington s Elisha & Abigail, 88
Gils s John & Eunice, 240
Han(n)ah d Thomas & Marah, 241
Hannah m John Griswold, 232
Hannah d Stephen & Abigail, 241
Hannah m John Lay 3rd, 239
Harris s Jason & Abiah born, 101
Harris s Jason & Abiah died, 101*
Henry m Julia Miller, 151
Hepzibah m Elisha Lee, 22
Hepsibah m John Sill, 36
Hepzibah d Seth & Betsey, 43
Hepzibah w John Sill, 36
Hester d Joseph & Mary, 240
Hiram s Capt. Enoch & Hester, 112
Irving s Capt. Enoch & Hester, 112
James s Elisha & Abigail, 88
James s Lemuel & Sarah, 22
Jane twin with Thomas d Stephen & Abigail, 241
Jason, 300
Jason s Joseph & Mary, 240
Jason m Abiah Brown, 101
Jason s Jason & Abiah, 101
Jason Jr. m Jane Griswold, 117
Jeane d John & Elizabeth, 240
Jean m Nathan Latimer, 43
Jedediah s Ezra & Sarah, 52
Joanna d John & Elizabeth, 240
John s Thomas & Anne, 241
John alias Laigh s Thomas, 241*
John m Elizabeth Smith, 240
John s John & Elizabeth, 240
John m Lydiah Allen 240
John m Eunice Lee, 240
John s John & Eunice, 240
John Capt. m Abigail Tulley, 1, 240
John Capt. died, 1
John s Stephen & Mehetable, 13*
John s Benjamin & Mary, 240
John s Abner & Elizabeth, 30
John s John & Anne, 123
John m Lydia Allen 240
John Allen s Abner & Elizabeth, 30
John M m Anne Beckwith, 14, 123
John Murdock s Elisha & Abigail, 88
Jonathan s Elisha & Abigail, 88
Joseph s Thomas & Marah, 241
Joseph alias Leigh s Thomas, 242
Joseph died, 242
Joseph s John & Elizabeth, 240
Joseph s Stephen & Abigail, 241*
Joseph m Mary Alin, 240
Joseph s Joseph & Mary, 240
Joseph s Jason & Abiah died, 101
Joseph 2nd s Jason & Abiah died, 101*
Joseph s Benjamin Jr. & Mary, 79
Joseph m Sally Champion, 117
Joseph Woodbridge s Jason & Jane, 117
Julia d John & Anne, 123

LEE, cont.

Lemuel s Joseph & Mary, 240, 241
Lemuel s Benjamin & Mary, 240
Lemuel m Sarah Starlin, 22*
Lemuel s Lemuel & Sarah, 22*
⎯⎯⎯child of Lemuel & Sarah, 22
Lory d Cyrus & Mary, 76
Lucia d Benjamin & Mary, 239
Lucinda d Abner & Elizabeth, 30
Lucinda m Elias Mather, 91
Lucretia d Martin & Sabra, 47
Luci d John & Elizabeth, 240
Luce m Amos Tinker, 265
Luce d Ezra & Deborah, 91*
Lucy d Benjamin Jr. & Mary, 79
Lucy Mather d Ezra & Deborah, 91
Luna d Ezra & Sarah, 52
Lurina d Dan & Lurania, 35
Lurina w Dan died, 35
Lidia d Thomas & Marah, 241
Lydia d Abner & Elizabeth, 30
Lydia d Benjamin Jr. & Mary, 79
Lydia d Cyrus & Mary, 76
Lydia d John & Lydia, 240*
Lydia m Lebbeus Peck, 104
Lydia m Uriah Roland, 2, 258
Lydia d Stephen & Abigail, 241
Lydiah twin with Silas children of Stephen & Abigail, 241*
Lydia d William & Mary, 242
Lydiah w John died, 240*
Marah d Thomas, 241
Margaret Stoughtonbury d Ezra & Deborah, 91
Marshall s Ezra & Sarah, 52
Martain s John & Eunice, 240
Martin s Benjamin & Mary, 240
Martin m Sabra Minor, 47
Martin s Lemuel & Sarah, 22
Mary d John & Elizabeth, 240
Mary d Capt. Enoch & Hester, 112
Mary d Seth & Anna, 132
Mary d Thomas & Elizabeth, 242
Mary A. m Henry Brewer, 175
Mary Ann d Benjamin & Mary, 79, 239, 275
Mary Ann d Benjamin Jr. & Mary, 79
Matthew Griswold s Jason & Jane, 117
Molle d Ezra & Rebecka, 18
Molly d Cyrus & Mary, 76
Nabbe d Ezra & Rebecka, 18
Nabby d Cyrus & Mary, 76
Nabby d Seth & Betsey, 43
Nancy d John & Anne, 123
Orlando E. s John & Anne, 124
Orlando E. m Lydia A. Miller, 165
Parthenia d John & Lydia (h), 240
Phebe d Elisha & Abigail, 88
Phebe d Elisha & Hepzibah, 22
Phebe d Ezra & Deborah, 91
Phebe d John & Elizabeth, 240
Phebe d Thomas & Marah, 241
Polley d Ezra & Deborah b & d, 91
Polley d Jason & Abiah, 101
Polley d Seth & Betsey, 43
Polley m Capt. Thomas Way Jr., 109
Richard s Elisha & Abigail, 88
Richard s Seth & Anna, 132

LEE, cont.

Richard s Seth & Betsey, 43
Richard Theodore s John & Ann, 124
Richard W. m Betsey Chapman, 184
Roxana H. m John D. Welles, 184
Sabra d Martin & Sabra, 47
Sabra m Jedediah Lewis, 115
Sally Marvin d Lemuel & Sarah, 22
Samuel s Jason & Abiah, 101
Samuel s Joseph & Mary, 240
Samuel (Lemuel) s Joseph & Mary died, 241
Samuell s Thomas & Elizabeth, 242
Samuel Holden s Ezra & Deborah, 91
Samuel Sterling s Lemuel & Sarah, 22
Sarah d Thomas & Ann, 241
Sarah d Benjamin Jr. & Mary, 79
Sarah d John & Elizabeth, 240
Sarah m John Lay, 238, 239
Sarah d Joseph & Mary, 240
Sarah d Thomas & Ann, 241
Savelion s John & Anne, 123
Seth s Elijah & Hepzibah, 22
Seth m Bettey Smith, 43
Seth s Seth & Betsey, 43
Seth m Anna Hill, 132
Seth s Seth & Anna, 132
Shubal s Ezra & Sarah, 52
Silas twin with Lydia s Stephen & Abigail, 241*
Silas Champlin s Dan & Luranie, 35
Sollomon s Jason & Abiah, 101
Stephen s Benjamin Jr. & Mary, 79
Stephen s Ezra & Sarah, 52
Stephen Capt. m Abigail Lord, 241
Stephen s Stephen & Abigail, 241
Stephen Capt. m Widow Mary Pickett, 241
Stephen Jr. m Mehitable Marvin 3rd, 13
Steven s Thomas & Marah born, died, 241*
Steven s Thomas & Marah, 241*
Thomas s Thomas & Anne, 241
Thomas alias Laigh s Thomas, 241*
Thomas m Marah DeWolfe, 241
Thomas m Elizabeth ⎯⎯⎯, 242
Thomas Ensign died, 242
Thomas s Thomas & Elizabeth, 242
Thomas Jr. died, 242
Thomas (twin with Jane) s Stephen & Abigail, 241
Thomas m Elizabeth Gilbert, 47
Thomas m Mehetable Peck, 47
William s Thomas & Marah, 241
William alias Leigh s Thomas, 241*
William m Mary Griffing, 242
William s Benjamin & Mary, 239
William s Cyrus & Mary, 76
William Richard Henry s Ezra & Deborah, 91
Zenas s Benjamin Jr. & Mary, 79
LEET, George, 201
Susannah m Abijah Beckwith, 4
LEFFINGWELL, Marvin A. died, 214
LEEVE, Martha, 299
LEONARD, Charity m Ebenezer Staples, 51
LESHEUR, Hannah C. m Griswold Chappell, 169
LESTER, Annis, 279
Alfred m Lucy Peck, 167
Champlin m Sally Miner, 141
Champlin s Champlin & Sally, 141

INDEX OF PERSONS 353

LESTER, cont.
 Charles s Champlin & Sally, 141
 Charles (Chancey) s Champlin & Sally, 141
 Crandle s Timothy & Judeth, 85
 Enoch 2nd m Mary Lester, 165
 Eunice m Elias Smith, 156
 Ezra (Esra) N. m Nancy Otis, 177, 203
 Frances S. m William C. Way, 173, 199, 205
 Giles m Joanna Maynard, 193
 Hannah m George Wade Jr., 17
 Hannah d Timothy & Judeth, 85
 Henry Miner s Champlin & Sally, 141
 Horace Bissell s Champlin & Sally, 141*
 James, 307
 Jeremiah s Timothy & Judeth, 85
 Jesse s Timothy & Judeth, 85
 Joseph Hitchcock s Timothy & Judeth, 85
 Leviah d Timothy & Judith, 85
 Maria d Esra & Nancy, 203
 Martin m Abbey Rowland, 156
 Mary m Enoch Lester, 165
 Mary Ann m Lester Clark 2nd, 158
 Mary Ann d Champlin & Sally, 141
 Mary Anne m Abel Beckwith, 177
 Mary J. m William G. Rowland, 179, 204
 Nathan s Timothy & Judeth, 85
 Parthena d Timothy & Judeth, 85
 Patty d Timothy & Judeth, 85
 Phebe S. m Elihu H. Palmer, 186
 Polly d Timothy & Judeth, 85
 Sally d Champlin & Sally, 141
 Silas m Mary O. Huntley, 147
 Timothy m Judith Rogers, 85
 William s Champlin & Sally, 141
 _____s Champlain & Sarah born, died, 141
LEVERITT, Abigail m Rev. Stephen Johnson, 94
LEWIS, Benjamin s George & Mary, 55*
 Betsey m Stephen White, 170
 Borden s William & Elizabeth, 243
 Clarissa m Hammond Powers, 157
 Cyrus s James & Phebe, 242
 Eber m Jemima Huntley, 10
 Eber s George & Mary, 55
 Elizabeth d William & Elizabeth, 243
 Elizabeth m Thomas Waite, 268
 Ely s William & Elizabeth, 243
 Ester d James & Phebe, 242
 George m Mary Reed, 55
 George Reed s George & Mary, 55
 Hannah d William & Elizabeth, 242
 Hannah m Jonathan Beebe, 12
 James m Phebe Mack, 242
 Jane d William & Elizabeth, 243
 Jean m Jonathan Smith, 8
 Jedediah m Sabra Lee, 115
 Johanna d James & Phebe (Mack), 242
 John Jr. born, 3
 John m Martha Cooper, 33
 John Jr. died, 33
 John s George & Mary, 55
 John Mack s James & Phebe (Mack), 242
 Jonathan G. m Sarah P. Strickland, 139
 Joseph s William & Elizabeth, 242
 Lucy m Daniel Tillitson, 123
 Lydia m Nathan Marvin, 16
 Lydia d Eber & Jemima, 10

LEWIS, cont.
 Martha d John & Martha, 33
 Mary m John Lay 2nd, 239
 Mary d George & Mary, 55
 Morgan m Sarah Ann Chapman, 202
 Nehemiah s James & Phebe (Mack), 242
 Phebe d James & Phebe, 242
 Phebe m Joseph Strickland, 125
 Sarah m Thomas Beckwith, 220
 Seth s James & Phebe (Mack), 242
 Thomas m Mary Moore, 166
 William m Elizabeth Borden, 242
 William s William & Elizabeth, 243
 William s George & Mary, 55
LITTLEFIELD, Lucy E. m John C. Bogue, 176
LOMBARD, Clementine m Edwin Sweitser, 182
 James m Margaret O. Salter, 184, 199, 201
 E. C. s James & Margaret, 201
 William s James & Margaret, 199
LONERGAN
 Atteis (Alles) d Thomas & Fanney, 115
 Polly d Thomas & Fanney, 115
 Thomas m Fanney Bournes, 115
LOOMER, Martha m Jacob Sayer, 259
LOOMIS, LOMIS
 Almena m Henry K. Clark, 157
 Cordelia m Seth Smith, 175
 Ellis m Elisha Palmer, 174
 Emma A. m Orrin F. Smith, 162
 James m Eliza H. Comstock, 154
 Nelson Gay or Guy m Laura Ann Gorton, 170
 Sarah m Osmund Darrow, 152
LOPIRE, LAPIARE
 Eliza Ann m Samuel Woods, 166
LORD, Abigail d Thomas & Mary, 244
 Abigail d Richard m Capt. Stephen Lee, 241
 Abigail d Joseph & Abigail (Comstock) 243
 Abigail m Zachariah Marvin, 247
 Abigail m Daniel Peck, 19
 Abigail d Dan(iell) & Elizabeth, 72
 Abner s Thomas Jr. & Esther, 244
 Abner, 304
 Abner m Temperance Coult, 58
 Abner s Abner & Temperance, 58
 Abner Jr. Capt. m Mary Selden, 109
 Abner s Abner & Mary, 109
 Abner Capt. died, 58, 304
 Abner Col. had servant Sharp Freeman, 67
 Andrew s John Jr. & Sarah, 68
 Ann d Richard & Elizabeth, 243
 Ann d Enoch & Hepzebah, 25
 Anna d John & Hannah, 28
 Anna m Capt. Zebulon Buttler, 65
 Anna m Stephen Johnson Jr., 95
 Anne m John McCurdy, 67
 Anne m James Bill, 177, 203
 Barnabus s David & Elizabeth, 71
 Barnabus Tuthil s Thomas Jr. & Esther, 244
 Benjamin s Joseph & Abigail (Comstock), 243
 Betey d Samll & Katharine, 243
 Betsey d Capt. Abner & Mary, 109
 Betsey d Marvin & Emelia, 91
 Betsey m Jonathan Hall, 127
 Betsey G. d Enoch & Esther, 108
 Carolina m Marvin Huntley, 110
 Caroline m Joseph Selden, 185

LORD, cont.
Catharine m Enoch Noyes, 177
Daniel Capt., 305
Daniell s Thomas & Mary, 244
Danill s Joseph & Abigail (Comstock), 243
Dan (ie) ll m Elizabeth Lord, 71, 274
Danll s Danll & Elizabeth, 71
Daniel (Lex. Alarm), 301
David s Thomas & Mary, 244
David Ely s William & Harriot, 133
Deborah m Nathan Jewitt, 238
Deborah d Theophilus & Deborah, 244
Deborah m Abraham Emmerson, 96
Elijah s Joseph & Abigail, 243
Elizabeth m Ulyssus Hayden, 168
Elizabeth m Danll Lord, 275
Elisabeth d Joseph & Abegail, 243
Elizabeth d Richard & Elizabeth, 243
Elizabeth d Richard & Elizabeth, 243
Elizabeth d Richard & Elizabeth, 243*
Elizabeth d Sylvanus & Huldah died, 58
Elizabeth d Sylvanus & Huldah born, 58
Elizabeth d Theophilus & Deborah, 244
Elizabeth d Thomas & Mary, 244
Elizabeth m Timothy Tiffany, 51
Elizabeth m Barnabas Tutthill, 267
Elisabeth d William J. & Mehitabel, 198
Emelia d Marvin & Amelia, 90
Enoch s Richard & Elizabeth, 243
Enoch m Hepsibah Marvin, 25
Enoch s Enoch & Hepzibah, 25
Enoch Jr. m Esther Durfey, 108
Esther d Daniel & Elizabeth, 72
Esther A. m Richard L. Lord, 171
Esther d Thomas Jr. & Esther, 244
Eunice m David Prigh, 165
Eunice Noyes d Enoch & Esther, 108
Francis s William J. & Mehitabel, 205
George F., 308
George W. m Emily Moore, 175
George W. Lee s Enoch & Esther, 108
Hannah d John Jr. & Sarah, 68
Harriot Ely d William & Harriot, 133
Hephsabeth d Theophilus & Deborah, 244
Hepzibah d Enoch & Hepzibah, 25
Hester Jr. m Nehemiah Marvin, 21
Huldah d Theophilus & Deborah, 244
Jabez s Samuell & Katharine, 243
Jane m Joseph Noyes, 43
Jean d Enoch & Hepzibah, 25
John, 303
John m Hannah Rogers, 28
John s John & Hannah, 28
John Jr. m Sarah Way, 68
John s John Jr. & Sarah, 68
John's Servants, Jana, Curredon & Freedorn, 67
John Mitchell s Richard & Nancy, 109
Joseph s Thomas & Mary, 244
Joseph m Abigail Comstock, 243*
Joseph s Joseph & Abigail, 243*
Joesph died, 243*
Joseph, 305
Joseph m Sarah Wade, 44
Joseph S., 278
Joseph s Enoch & Hepzibah, 25

LORD, cont.
Josephine m Alexander McCurdy, 166
Judah m Mary Beckwith, 186
Linde s Richard & Elizabeth, 243
Linde s Enoch & Hepzibah, 25
Lucia d Samuel & Katharine, 13
Luce d John & Hannah, 28
Lucy d John Jr. & Sarah, 68
Lucy m Zadock Darrow, 122
Lydia d Theophilus & Deborah, 243
Mahitable Burnham d J. Lord, 278
Martha m Benony Hilliard, 234
Martha d Thomas & Mary, 244
Marvin m Emelia Woolcot, 90
Marvin s Marvin & Emelia died, 90
Marvin s Marvin & Emelia born, 91
Mary d Abner & Temperance, 58
Mary m John Coult, 34
Mary m John Ely, 110
Mary m Peter Person, 254
Mary m Charles Tainter, 186
Mary d Thomas Jr. & Esther, 244
Mary d Thomas & Mary, 244
Matilda m Dr. John S. Rogers, 145
Mathew s Thomas Jr. & Esther, 244*
Mehetabel m Griswold Chapell, 191, 210
Mercy d Samll & Katharine, 243
Nabby m Benjamin Mack, 99
Nancy M. d Enoch & Esther, 108
Nathan s Samuell & Katharine, 243
Nicholas s Samuell & Katharine, 243
Parthena m Joseph Chadwick, 162
Peter s Samuell & Katharine, 243, 306
Peter Capt., 307
Phebe d Samuell & Katharine, 243
Phebe m Ralph Tainter, 166
Phebe W. d Enoch & Esther, 108
Polly d Capt. Abner & Mary, 109
Polly Y. d Enoch & Esther, 108
Polly d Marvin & Emelia, 91
Reuben s Elijah & Sally, 130
Reuben s Joseph & Sarah, 44
Reuben Jr. m Sarah Weaver, 166
Renold s Thomas Jr. & Esther, 244*
Reynolds s Danll & Elizabeth, 71
Reynold m _____ Loomis, 128
Richard m Elizabeth Lynd, 243
Richard s Richard & Elizabeth, 243*
Richard's servant Oxford & Temporance had children, Zachry, Luke & Jordan, 243
Richard s Enoch & Hepzebah, 25
Richard s John Jr. & Sarah, 68
Richard died, 25
Richard m Nancy Mitchell, 109
Richard Lynde s Richd & Nancy, 109
Richard L. m Esther Lord, 171
Roger Woolcott s Marvin & Emelia, 90
Sally m Elijah Mather, 129
Sally Read d Enoch & Esther, 108
Samll m Katharine Ransom, 13, 243
Samll s Samll & Katharine, 243
Samuell s Thomas & Mary, 244
Sarah m William Butler, 40, 68
Sarah d John & Hannah, 28
Sarah d John Jr. & Sarah, 68
Sarah d Joseph & Sarah, 44

LORD, cont.
Sarah d Samll & Katharine, 13
Sarah d Theophilus & Deborah, 244
Sarah Ann d Richd & Nancy, 109
Sarah Ann m Charles McCurdy, 146
Sarah Ann m Philip Morgan, 147
Sarah E. m Allen Griffin, 177
Sarah R. m Matthew Marvin, 146
Sarah W. m Edward Hyde, 188
Silas s Danll & Elizabeth, 71, 208
Similius m Lucy Rogers, 153
Sophia d Capt. Abner & Mary, 109
Stephen J. m Sarah McCurdy, 158
Stephen Johnson s Richard & Nancy, 109
Sussanah d Richard & Elizabeth, 243
Sulvens s Joseph & Abigail, 243
Sylvanus m Huldah Brockway, 58*
Sylvanus s Sylvanus & Hulda, 58
Taphenia d Thomas Jr. & Esther, 244
Tempe d Capt. Abner & Mary, 109
Theophilus s Thomas & Mary, 244
Theophilus m Deborah Mack, 243
Thephilus s Samuel & Katharine, 13
Thomas m Mary_____, 244
Thomas s Thomas & Mary, 244*
Thomas Jr. m Esther Marvin, 244
Thomas died, 244
Thomas s Thomas Jr. & Esther, 108, 244
Thomas s Abner & Temperance, 58
Thomas s John Jr. & Sarah, 68
Thomas D. m Caroline Bulkley, 153
Thomas Durfey s Enoch & Esther, 108
Topheas d Marvin & Emelia, 90
Ursula d Marvin & Emelia, 90
William s Jospeh & Sarah, 44
William s Enoch & Hepzibah, 25
William Dr. m Anna Mather, 108
William m Harriot Ely, 133
William J. m Mehetabel Slate, 172, 198, 205
William Marvin s Enoch & Esther, 108
William Mitchell s Richd & Nancy, 109
William Russell s William & Harriot, 133
William (Lex. Alarm), 301
LOVELAND
Samuel m Wid. Susannah Roulin, 244
Samll s Samuel & Susannah, 244
LOVITT, Molley m George Doerr, 82
LUTHER, Ansel, 307
Cornelia m Arnold Buckingham, 169
Frances A. m Charles Brockway, 172
Hannah m Noah Beebe, 91
Harriet N. m Wm. Minor, 176
John, 307, 310
Joseph m Lydia Ann Cone, 190
Laura E. m Aaron Watrous, 156
Levi, 301, 305
Lovica B. m Edward Brockway, 188
Mary m Silvanus Avery, 106
Mary Ann m Ambrose Burdick, 158
Orin, 310
Orin m Catharine Banning, 187
LYNDE or LYND, Elizabeth m Richard Lord, 243
Hannah m George Griswold, 232
Susannah m Thomas Griswold, 7
MCINTOSH, Duncan s Duncan & Rachal, 55
Guy s Duncan & Rachel, 55

MCINTOSH, cont.
Jemima d Duncan & Rachal, 55
Joseph s Duncan & Rachal, 55
Laughlin s Duncan & Rachal, 55, 300
Rachal d Duncan & Rachal, 55
Rhoda d Duncan & Rachal, 55
Timothy s Duncan & Rachal, 55
MACK, MACKE
Abigail d Ebenezer Jr. & Abigail, 244
Abigail m Wm Gee, 93
Abigail d Wm & Ruth, 80
Abigail m Reu Huntley, 111
Abijah s Jonathan & Sarah, 245
Abijah m Eunice Rogers, 88
Ambrous s Abigail, 111
Asenath d Ezra & Lydia, 83
Azuba d Ebenezer & Hannah, 20
Azubah m Jasper Huntley, 121
Benjamin s Nehemiah & Eunice, 99
Benjamin m Nabby Lord, 99
Benjamin s Benjamin & Nabby, 99
Chabris s Ebenezer & Polly, 109
Charles s Ezra & Lydia, 83
Charmis s Ebenezer & Polly, 109
Cornelius s Ebenezer & Polly, 109
Cornelius m Harriet Watrous, 191
David s Nehemiah & Eunice, 99
David m Sarah Rogers, 24
David s David & Sarah, 24
Debbe d Ezra & Lydia, 83
Debrah d John & Sarah, 243
Deborah m Theophilus Lord, 244
Deborah d Ebenezer & Hannah, 20
Deborah m Nathan Woodworth, 54
Delia m John Smith, 162
Delight d William & Ruth, 80
Dorcas d William & Ruth, 80
Dorcas m John Belote, 106
Dorcas d Elijah & Lydia, 128
Dorcas m Orrin Maynerd, 152
Dorithy d John Jr. & Love, 245
Ebenezer s John & Sarah, 244
Ebenezer s John Jr. & Love, 245
Ebenezer m Hannah Huntley, 20
Ebenezer Jr. m Abigail Davis, 244
Ebenezer m Sophronia Harding, 172
Ebenezer s William & Ruth, 80
Ebener m Polly Harvey, 104
Elane d Ezra & Lydia, 83
Elijah s Wm & Ruth, 80
Elijah m Lydia Tillitson, 128
Elisha s Ebenezer & Hannah, 20
Elishabe d Abijah & Eunice, 88
Elizabeth d John Jr. & Love, 245
Elizabeth m Jonathan Reed, 256
Elizabeth d John & Abigail, 245
Elizabeth d Jonathan & Sarah, 245
Elizabeth d Nehemiah & Eunice, 99
Elizabeth d Abijah & Eunice, 88
Ester d John Jr. & Love, 245
Esther d Ebenezer & Polly, 104, 109
Eunice d Nehemiah & Eunice, 99*
Ezra s John Jr. & Love, 245
Ezra m Lydia Gibbs, 83
Ezra s Ezra & Lydia, 83
Hannah d Ebenezer & Hannah, 20

MACK, cont.
Hannah m Levi Bartholomew, 52
Hepzibah d Ebenezer & Hannah, 20
Hezekiah s John Jr. & Love, 245
Hezekiah s Nehemiah & Eunice, 99
Jerush m Reynold Huntley, 111
John m Sarah Bennet, 244
Johana d John & Sarah, 244
John m Wid. Abigail Daniell, 245
John Jr. s John & Abigail, 245
John Jr. m Love Benet, 245
John (Lt.) s John Jr. & Love, 245*
John s Ezra & Lydia, 83
John s Jonathan & Sarah, 245
John s Nehemiah & Eunice, 99
John m Mehetable Smith, 11
Jonathan s Abijah & Eunice, 88
Jonathan m Sarah Benit, 245
Jonathan s Jonathan & Sarah, 245
Jonathan T. m Jane Ransom, 160
Joseph s Abijah & Eunice, 88
Joseph s Jonathan & Sarah, 245
Joshua Tillitson s Elijah & Lydia, 128
Josiah s Jonathan & Sarah, 245
Lidia m Petter Person, 254
Loas m Mathew Rogers, 15
Love wife John died, 245*
Love d Jonathan & Sarah, 245
Lous d Jonathan & Sarah, 245
Lucy m Martin Wade, 66
Lydia d Ebenezer Jr. & Abigail, 244
Lydia d Ezra & Lydia, 83
Lydia m John Wood, 14
Lydia d John Jr. & Love, 245
Lydia d Jonathan & Sarah, 245
Lydia m Neal Courtney, 112
Marah d John & Sarah, 244
Mehetable d Abijah & Eunice, 88
Mehetable d Nehemiah & Eunice, 99*
Molley d Wm & Ruth, 80
Molly had s Daniel Merick Way, 81
Nabbe d Ezra & Lydia, 83
Nehemiah s John Jr. & Love, 245
Nehemiah m Eunice Beckwith, 99
Nehemiah s Nehemiah & Eunice, 99
Patience d John Jr. & Love, 245
Patience m Richard Hase, 233
Phebe d John Jr. & Love, 245
Phebe d Ebenezer & Hannah, 20
Phebe m James Lewis, 242
Phebe m Amos Huntley, 30
Phebe m Martin Huntley, 31
Polley d Ezra & Lydia, 83
Polly d Ebenezer & Polly, 109
Polly m Ezra Minor, 81
Rebecka d John & Sarah, 244
Rebeckah m Cabel Benit Jr., 220*
Salmon (Solomon) s Ebr & Polly, 109
Samuel s Ebenezer & Hannah, 20
Samuel s Jonathan & Sarah, 245
Marah d John & Sarah, 244
Sarah d Abijah & Eunice, 88
Sarah d John Jr. & Love, 245
Sarah d Jonathan & Sarah, 245
Sarah m Joseph Starlin, 263
Silas s Nehemiah & Eunice, 99

MACK, cont.
Solomon s Ebenezer & Hannah, 20
Solomon m Lydia Gates, 55
Sophar (ia) d Ebenezer Jr. & Abigail, 244
Stephen s Ebenezer & Hannah, 20
William m Ruth Gee, 80
William s William & Ruth, 80*
William s Elijah & Lydia, 128
William Warman s Ebenezer Jr. & Abigail, 244
MAIN, Gershom m Eliza Tucker, 169
MANNING, Mary m Rufus Stertevant, 131
MANWARRING, Abby C. m Wm Davison, 161
Abby G. d Giles & Sophia, 146
Adam Jr. m Susan Harding, 151
Benjamin m Freelove Beckwith, 170
Bettey m Joseph Wait, 4
Calvin S. m Nancy Tucker, 149
Charles D. m Elizabeth Hughes, 165
Charles Francis s John J. & Harriet, 157
Daniel m Mary Beebe, 167
David H. m Frances Clark, 168
Esther Ann B. d Giles & Sophia, 146
Frances m Rufus A. Smith, 151
Giles m Sophia Tinker, 146
Giles s Giles & Sophia, 146
Harriet Jane d John J. & Harriet, 157
Horace B. m Sophia Huntley, 164
John Anderson s Giles & Sophia, 146
John J. m Harriet Anderson, 157
Martha Sophia d Giles & Sophia, 146
Mary m Nehemiah Haynes, 151
Matilda m Ira Bush, 163
Ralph Denison s Giles & Sophia, 146
Richard Baxter, 304
Sabra m Harris Crocker, 167
Sarah m Wm Armstrong, 169
Sarah Ellen d John J. & Harriet, 157
William M. s Giles & Sophia, 146
MARRIMON, Eunice m Gabriel Ely, 102
MARTIN, David O. m Roxana Bradburg, 177
George s Jonathan & Hannah, 207
Hannah m Wm Brockway, 160, 170
Hannah, 278
Johnathan R. m Hannah Crocker, 163, 207
Joseph m Eliza Dickinson, 177
William, 310
MARVIN, Abigail d Samuell & Susannah, 247
Abigail m Samuell Coult, 228
Abigail m Marshfield Parsons, 50
Abigail d Elihu & Anne, 59
Abigail d Benj & Phebe, 75
Abigail d Matthew & Elizabeth, 102
Abigail m Capt. Ichabod Smith, 130
Abigail d Thomas & Sarah, 23
Adonijah s John & Mehitable, 246
Adonijah m Diadama Miller, 54
Adonijah died, 54*
Adonijah s John & Sarah, 21
Alexander s Benjamin & Phebe, 75
Ane wife Zachariah Jr., 24
Ann twin d Dea Reynold & Mary, 19
Anna d Nehemiah & Esther, 21
Anna d Elihu & Anne, 59
Asahel s Timothy & Sarah, 90
Azubah d Benjamin & Deborah, 7
Azubah m Marshfield Parker, 146

INDEX OF PERSONS

MARVIN, cont.
Benjamin s John & Sarah, 246
Benjamin m Deborah Mather, 6, 245
Benjamin s Benjamin & Deborah, 6
Benjamin Jr. m Phebe Roland, 75
Benjamin died, 7
Catherine m Abner Brockway, 93
Clarissa d Joseph & Phebe, 51
Clarissa m Horace Ely, 162
Dan s Reynold Jr. & wid. Sarah, 247
Dan m Mehetable Selden, 95
Dan s Dan & Grace, 9
Dan s Dan & Mehetable, 95
Dan Capt. died, 95*, 213
Dan m Hepzibah Leach, 141
Daniell s Renald & Phebe, 246
Daniel s Deacon Zachriah & Abigail, 247*
Daniel s Moses & Zilpha, 98
David s Matthew & Elizabeth, 102
Diadama d Adonijah & Diadama, 54
Diedamy m Azariah Beebe, 103
Elihu s Zechariah & Abigail, 247
Elihu m Anne Beach, 59
Elihu s Elihu & Anne, 59
Elisha, 273
Elisha s Renald & Martha died, 247*
Elisha II s Renald & Martha born 247*
Elisha m Katharine Mather, 245*
Elisha s Elisha & Katherine, 245*
Elisha Capt died, 303
Elizabeth d John & Sarah, 246
Elizabeth d Samuell & Susannah, 247
Elizabeth m John Tucker, 267
Elizabeth d Samuell m Richard Waite, 5, 268
Elizabeth d John & Mehitable, 246
Elizabeth m Jeremiah Minor (Menoir), 47
Elizabeth d Adonijah & Diadama, 54
Elizabeth m Rev. Sylvanus Griswold, 21
Elizabeth m Lee Peck, 94
Elizabeth d Matthew & Elizabeth, 102
Elizabeth wid. Matthew died, 102
Emma S. m Samuel S. Fowler, 14
Easter d Reynald & Phebe, 246
Esther m Thomas Lord, Jr., 244, 90
Easter d John & Mehitable, 246
Esther d Reynold & Mary, 19, 246
Esther m Allen Beckwith, 65
Esther d John & Sarah, 21*
Eunice d Mathew & Mary, 246
Eunice m William Noyes, 81
Eunice d Zachary & Ama, 23
Eunice m Gabriel Ely, 102
Eunice m Smith Watrous, 120
Eve twin d Deacon Renold & Mary, 19
Fanny d Joseph II & Phebe, 5
Frances m Dr. Ambrose Niles, 147
Giles s John & Sarah, 21
Giles s Giles & Sophia, 146
Hannah m Ezra Selden, 34
Henry s Nathan & Lydia, 17
Hepsibeth d Joseph & Jane, 246
Hepzibah Mrs. died, 213
Hepzibah d John & Sarah, 21
Hepsibah m Enoch Lord, 25
Huldah d James & Ruth, 245
James s Renald & Martha, 247

MARVIN, cont.
James m Ruth Mather, 245*
James s James & Ruth, 245*
James died, 95, 246
James Lieut. s James died, 246*
James s Dan & Mehetable, 95
James s Moses & Zilpha, 98
Jemima d John & Sarah, 246
Jemernah m William Peck, 254
Jemima d Joseph & Phebe, 51
Jemima m Dr. Abraham Blatchley, 145
John m Sarah Graham, 246
John s John & Sarah, 21*, 246
John m Mehitable Champen, 246
John s John Mehetable, 246
John m Sarah Brooker, 21
John s John & Sarah died, 21*
John s John & Sarah born, 21
John s Benjamin & Phebe, 75
Jonathan Deming s Matthew & Elizabeth, 102
Joseph s John & Sarah, 246
Joseph m Jane Lay, 246
Joseph s Deacon Zachariah & Abigail died, 247*
Joseph s Elisha & Katharine, 245
Joseph s Matthew & Elizabeth, 102
Joseph II m Phebe Starlin, 51
Joseph s Joseph & Phebe, 51
Joseph, 300, 305
Judith d Reynold & Mary, 19
Judith m Wm Peck, 105
Junius m Adaline C. Raymond, 193, 211
Lebbeas s Nathan & Lydia, 17
Lee s Zachariah & Ama, 23, 24
Loas d John & Sarah, 21
Lucinda d Zachariah & Ama, 24
Lucy d Timothy & Sarah, 90
Lucy[1] d Benjamin & Phebe, 75
Lucy[2] d Benjamin & Phebe, 75
Lucy d Thomas & Sarah, 23
Lurania d Matthew & Elizabeth, 102
Lidia d Reynald & Phebe, 246
Lydia d John & Sarah, 21
Lydia d Reynold Jr. & wid. Sarah, 247
Martha d James & Ruth, 246
Martha d Samuel & Mary, 18
Martha m Reynold Gillet, 93
Martha d Renald & Martha, 247*
Martin s Nathan & Lydia, 17
Mary d Elihu & Anne, 59*
Mary d John & Sarah, 246
Mary d Matthew & Elizabeth, 102
Mary m Samuel Griswold, 62
Mary d Samuell & Susannah (Twin), 247
Mary wid. Deac. Reynold, 19
Mary m William Coult, 119
Mary, 299
Matthew m Elizabeth Demming, 102
Matthew m Mary Beckwith, 246
Mathew s Samuell & Susannah, 247
Matthew m Sarah R. Lord, 146
Mehatabil d John & Sarah, 246
Mehetabel d Benj(ami)n & Deborah, 7
Mehetabel d John & Mehitable, 246
Mehetable d Matthew & Elizabeth, 102
Mehetable m Uriah Hyde, 67
Mehitable 3rd m Stephen Lee Jr., 13

MARVIN, cont.
Meriam d Renald & Martha, 247
Molly d John & Sarah, 21
Moses s James & Ruth, 246
Moses m Zilpha Gill(ett), 98
Nabbe d Benjamin & Phebe, 75
Nathan s Samuell & Susannah, 247
Nathan m Lydia Lewis, 16
Nathan s Nathan & Lydia, 17*
Nehemiah s Samuell & Sussanah, 247
Nehemiah m Hester Lord Jr., 21
Phebe d Benjamin & Phebe, 75
Phebe m Jonathan Gillet, 81
Phebe d Joseph 2d & Phebe, 51
Phebe d Nememiah & Ester, 21
Phebe wife of Renald, 246
Phebe d Renald & Phebe, 246
Phebe d Reynold Jr. & wid. Sarah, 247
Phebe m Seth Ely Jr., 123
Phebe S. m Henry Jones, 161
Phebe, 276
Phebe, 277
Phebe wife of Joseph, 275
Pickett s Elisha & Katharine, 245
Picket s Timothy & Sarah, 90
Reynold s Dan & Mehetable, 95
Re(y)nold dea. had negro Chloe, 19
Re(y)nold had servant John Taner Jr., 247
Renald m Martha Waterman, 246
Re(y)nold m Mary Kellogg, 19
Reynold s Reynold Jr. & wid. Sarah, 247*
Reynold Jr. m Wid. Sarah Lay, 247*
Rhoda m William Mathew, 60
Rosalinda d Matthew & Elizabeth, 102
Ruth d James & Ruth, 245
Sally M. m Stephen Sterling, 150
Samuell m Sussanah Graham, 247*
Samuell s Samuell & Sussanah, 247*
Samuel m Mary Wege, 18*
Samuel s Nathan & Lydia, 17
Sarah wid m Capt. Joseph Sill, 261
Sarah d Dan & Mehetable, 95
Sarah d John & Sarah, 21, 246
Sarah d Renald & Martha, 247
Sarah d Samuel & Mary, 18
Sarah m Sam(ue)l Selden Jr., 82
Sarah d Timothy & Sarah, 90
Selden s Dan & Mehetable, 95
Selden P. m Phebe Reed, 161
Seth s Mathew & Mary, 246
Silas s Deac. Zachariah & Abigail, 248, 301
Susanah d Zachariah & Abigail, 247
Thomas s Samuell & Susannah, 247
Thomas m Sarah Lay, 23*
Thomas s Thomas & Sarah, 23*
Thomas s Deac. Zachariah & Abigail, 247*
Thomas 2nd s Deac. Zachariah & Abigail, 247*
Timothy s Elisha & Katharine 245
Timothy m Sarah Perkins, 90, 248
Timothy s Timothy & Sarah, 90, 248
Uriah s Benjamin & Phebe, 75
William, 307
William s Benjamin Jr. & Phebe, 75
William s Joseph 2nd & Phebe, 51
William E. m Catharine F. Spencer, 190
Zechariah s Samuell & Susannah, 247*

MARVIN, cont.
Zechariah m Abigail Lord, 247*
Zac(h)ariah s Zachariah & Abigail, 247
Zachariah Jr. m Anna Lee, 23
Zachariah s Zachariah & Anna, 24
_____ d John & Sarah, 246
MARSH, Hannah m Sam(ue)ll Ely, 12
MASON
George I. m Martha B. Condall (Condol), 203, 210
John, 203
Peter m Lois Chap(p)el(l), 173
Orris d John & Clorinda, 203
MATHER, Abigail d William & Rhoda, 60
Alice d Sam(ue)l & Alice, 97
Alice wid. Dr. Samuel died, 97
Alice m William Ely, 101
Andrew s Elias & Lucinda, 91
Anne d Joseph & Phebe, 248
Anna d Benj(ami)n & Irena, 42
Anna d Frederick & Elizabeth, 45, 82
Anna d Sam(ue)l & Lous, 78
Anna m Dr. William Lord, 108
Aseph s Timothy Jr. & Sarah, 249
Augustus s Eleazer & Anna, 3
Benjamin & Alice, 274
Benjamin m Abigail Worthington, 43
Benjamin m Irena Person, 42
Benjamin s Joseph & Phebe, 248
Bettey Worthington d Benj(ami)n & Abigail, 43
Catharine d Timothy & Sarah, 248
Charles s Elias & Lucinda, 91
Charles s Silvanus & Caroline, 19
Clarrissa d Elias & Lucinda, 91
Dan m Hannah Gib(b)s, 19
Dan s Jehoiada & Eunice, 81
Dan s John & Marcy, 15
Dan W. m Elizabeth Clark, 158
Dan W. m Mary Ann M. Nash, 181
David s Joseph & Zelinda, 115
Deborah m Benjamin Marvin, 245
Deborah m Ezra Lee, 91
Deborah d Richard & Deborah, 1
Deborah d Samuel & Deborah, 1, 248
Elleazer s Joseph & Phebe, 248
Eleazer m Anna Waterouse, 2
Eleazer s Eleazer & Anna, 3
Eleazer Jr. m Irena Starlin, 53
Eleazer Jr. s Eleazer 2nd & Irena, 53
Elias s Richard & Deborah, 1
Elias m Lucinda Lee, 91*
Elias s Elias & Lucinda, 91*
Elijah m Sally Lord, 129
Elijah s Elijah & Sally, 130
Elijah s John & Hepzibah, 86
Elijah s Stephen & Elizabeth, 99
Elisha s Eleazer & Anna, 3
Elisha Royce s John & Sally, 132
Elisha W. m Mary Ann Smith, 142
Elizabeth m Ebenezer Rogers, 40
Elizabeth d Frederick & Elizabeth, 45, 82
Elizabeth m Richard Peck, 36
Elizabeth d Timothy & Elizabeth, 59*
Elizabeth widow of Timothy died, 59
Elles (Alice) w Dr. Samuel Died, 97
Eunice d Jehoiada & Eunice, 81

INDEX OF PERSONS 359

MATHER, cont.
Eunice d Silvanus & Caroline, 19
Eunice d Timothy Jr. & Sarah, 248
Eunice d William & Rhoda, 60
Ezra m Phebe Wade, 129*
Ezra s Ezra & Phebe, 129*
Ezra s Jehoiada & Eunice, 81
Ezra s Richard & Deborah, 1*
Ezra s Richard & Deborah, 1
Ezra s William & Rhoda, 60
Fanny d Samuel & Lois, 78
Fanny d Silvanus & Caroline, 19
Frances A. m Richard S. Griswold, 178
Francis William s Nathaniel & Eunice, 120
Frederick s Eleazer & Anna died, 2*
Frederick s Eleazer & Anna born, 3
Frederick m Elizabeth Perkins, 45, 82
George, 201, 213
George s Capt. Silvester & Betsey, 111
George s George & Gernah, 201
George E. m Mary J. Bogue, 189, 208
Gibbons s Benj(ami)n & Irena, 42*
Gibbons s Benj(ami)n & Irena, 43
Hannah d John & Marcy, 15
Hannah m John Merrow, 94
Harriet C. m John W. Allen, 159
Henry s Samuel & Lois, 78, 79
Henry s Capt. Silvester & Betsey, 111
Hepzibah d John & Hepzibah, 86
Hepzibah m Richard Leech, 130
Huldah d John & Hepzibah, 86
Irena d Benjamin & Irena, 42
Irena wife Benj(amin), 43
James s Samuel & Lois, 78
James Gould s Joseph & Zelinda, 116
Jamimah d Silvanus & Carolina, 19
Jamimah m Roswell Champion, 128
Jehoiada s Timothy Jr. & Sarah, 248
Jeho(i)ada m Eunice Miller, 81
Jemima d John & Marcy, 15
Jerusha d Joseph & Phebe, 248
Jerusha d John & Marcy, 15*
Jerusha m Daniel Stephenson, 25
Joanna m John Parsons, 27
Joanna d Joseph & Joanna, 66*
Joanna wid. Joseph died, 66*
Joanna d Nathaniel & Eunice, 120*
Joanna d Timothy Jr. & Sarah, 248
John m Marcy Higgins, 15*
John s John & Marcy, 15*
John s Joseph & Phebe, 248
John Jr. m Hebzibah Peck, 86*
John s John & Hepzibah, 86*
John Jr. m Sally Cleveland Royce, 132
John m wid. Ruth Rob(b)ins, 16
John Noyes s Timothy Jr. & Sarah, 248
John Oliver s John & Sally, 132
John Watrous s Dr. Samuel & Sally, 97
Joseph m Anne Boothe, 248*
Joseph Capt. m Joanna Matson, 66*
Joseph s Joseph & Joanna, 66*
Joseph s John & Mary, 15
Joseph m Phebe DeWolfe, 229, 248*
Joseph s Joseph & Phebe, 248*
Joseph s Timothy & Sarah, 248*
Joseph m Zalinda Gould, 115*

MATHER, cont.
Joseph s Joseph & Zalida, 115*
Joseph Higgins s John & Hepzibah, 86
Joseph Higgins m Sarah Selden Jewett, 158
Katharine m Elisha Marvin, 245
Lay m Caroline Wade, 114
Lay s Jehoiada & Eunice, 81
Lewey d Sam(ue)l & Alice, 97
Lois m Nathaniel S(haw) Woodbridge, 118, 119
Lois w Samuel died, 78
Lois G. d (Capt.) Silvester & Betsey, 111
Lous d Sam(ue)l & Alice, 97
Louisa G. m Richard S. Griswold, 168
Lucy m Nathaniel Peck, 11
Lucy d Samuell & Deborah, 248
Lucy d Timothy Jr. & Sarah, 248
Lucy d William & Rhoda, 60
Luther Peck s John & Hepzibah, 86
Lydia d Samuel & Lois, 78
Marcy d John & Mary, 15
Marcy w John Died, 16
Marcy m Richard Lay, 87
Marcy d Samuell & Deborah, 248
Martha d Jehoiada & Eunice, 81
Martha m George Waid, Jr., 116
Mary d William & Rhoda, 60
Mehetable born, 126*
Mehetable d John & Marcy (Mary), 16
Mehetable d Richard & Deborah, 1
Mehetable d Samuell & Deboah, 248
Mehetable m Samuel Holden Parsons 60, 126*
Mehitable d Samuel & Lois, 78
Mehitable m Capt. Thomas Sill, 135
Moses m Hannah Champion, 130*
Moses s Joseph & Joanna, 66
Moses s Joseph & Zelinda, 116
Moses m Sally Champion, 130*
Moses s Timothy & Sarah, 248
Nabby d Benjamin & Abigail, 43
Nabby d Eleazer & Anna, 3
Nabby m Thomas Mathew, 112
Nancy d Capt. Silvester & Betsey, 111
Nancy m John Hart Jr., 141
Nancy Maria d Nathaniel & Eunice, 120
Nathaniel s Joseph & Joanna, 66
Nathaniel m Eunice DeWolf, 120*
Nathaniel s Nathanaiel & Eunice, 120*
Nath(anie)ll Green s Elias & Lucinda, 91
Oliver s Thomas & Nabby, 112
Orlando s Ezra & Phebe, 129*
Peggy d Samuel & Lois, 78
Phebe d Ezra & Phebe, 129
Phebe d Joseph & Phebe, 248
Phebe d Lieut. Jospeh m Andrew Sill, 34
Phebe d Sam(ue)l & Lois, 78
Phebe m Dr. Thomas Minor, 144
Polly m William Champlin, 35
Rebeckah d John & Marcy, 15
Reuben s Timothy Jr. & Sarah, 248
Reuben Lord s Elijah & Sally, 130
Richard Capt. m Eunice Moor(e), 114
Richard m Deborah Ely, 1
Richard s Samuell & Deborah, 248
Richard s Samuel & Lois, 78, 79*
Richard s Capt. Silvester & Betsey, 111
Robert Miller s Ezra & Phebe, 129

MATHER, cont.
Ruth d Timothy & Sarah, 248
Ruth m James Marvin, 245
Ruth w John died, 16
Sally d Moses & Sally, 130*
Sally w Moses died, 130
Sally Ann d Moses & Hannah, 130
Sally M. m Richard Royce, 159
Sally Miranda d Elijah & Sally, 130
Samuel s Azariah & Hannah, 54
Samuell m Debrah Wade, 248
Samuel s Eleazer & Anna, 2
Samuel Dr. m Ellis (Alice) Ransom, 97, 305
Samuell s Joseph & Phebe, 248*
Samuel s Richard & Deborah, 1
Sam(ue)l Jr. m Lous Griswold, 78
Samuel s Sam(ue)l & Lois, 78
Samuel Jr. had negro servant Jack Howard, 68
Sam(ue)l Boerham s Sam(ue)l & Alice, 97
Samuel Dr. m Sally Anderson, 97
Sarah d Timothy Jr. & Sarah, 248
Sarah d Jedoiada & Eunice, 81
Sarah wid. Capt. Timothy died, 67, 248
Sarah m Ezra Miller, 87
Sarah An(n)[1] d Sam(ue)l & Alice (Born, died), 97
Sarah An(n)[2] d Sam(ue)l & Alice born, 97
Sarah Huntley wife Timothy Jr. died, 67
Simon s Joseph & Phebe, 248*
Simon s John & Marcy, 15
Stephen s John & Marcy, 15
Stephen s Richard & Deborah, 1
Stephen m Elizabeth Peck, 99
Selvanus s John & Marcy, 15
Selvester s Richard & Deborah, 1
Silvanus m Caroline Chadwick, 19
Silvester Capt. m Betsey Wait, 58, 111
Sylvester s Elias & Lucinda, 91
Sylvester s Capt. Silvester & Betsey, 111
Thomas s Joseph & Joanna, 66
Thomas s Sam(ue)l & Lois, 78
Thomas m Nabby Mather, 112
Thomas s Tho(ma)s & Nabby, 112
Timothy Jr. m Sarah Lay, 248
Timothy s Timothy Jr. & Sarah, 248
Timothy Capt. m Elizabeth Matson, 59
Timothy Capt. died, 59
Watrous s Eleazer 2nd & Irena, 53
William s Richard & Deborah born, died, 1
William s Richard & Deobrah born, 1*
William m Rhoda Marvin, 60
William s Capt. Silvester & Betsey, 111
Will(ia)m Lee s Elias & Lucinda, 91
MATSON
Aaron s William & Eunice, 91
Abigail d Nath(anie)ll Jr. & Dinah, 68
Abigail m John Coult, 34
Abigail d Nathaniel & Dinah, 68*
Catharine A., 180, 201
David s William & Eunice, 91
David m Lois Sill, 124
David s David & Lois, 124
Dinah d Nathaniel & Dinah, 68*
Dinah w Nathaniel died, 68*
Elizabeth m Capt. Timothy Mather, 59
Ely s William & Eunice, 91
Eunice d David & Lois, 124

MATSON, cont.
Eunice d William & Eunice, 91, 92
Eunice w William died, 92
George s David & Lois, 124
Israel s Nathaniel & Dinah, 68
Israel m Phebe Ely, 143
Joanna m Capt. Joseph Mather, 66
Joanna d Nathaniel & Dinah, 68
Johannah m Samuel Buckingham 3rd, 129
John Sill s David & Lois, 124
Lois d Nathaniel & Dinah, 68
Mary m Joseph Smith Jr., 69
Nathaniel m Anna Ely, 115*
Nathaniel J. m Dinah Newton, 68
Nath(anie)ll s Nath(anie)ll Jr. & Dinah, 68
Nathaniel m Polly Sill, 115*
Polly d David & Lois, 124
Polly wife Nath(anie)l died, 115*
Richard s David & Lois born, died, 124*
Richard s David & Lois born, 124
Ruth m Joseph Sill 2nd, 49
Susannah d Nath(anie)ll Jr. & Dinah, 68
William m Eunice Skinner, 91
William s William & Eunice, 91
William s William & Eunice, 92*
William m Rhoda Newton, 138
William Newton s William & Rhoda, 138
_____ d William & Eunice, 91
MATHEWS, Nathaniel m Betsey Bramble, 159
MAXON-MAXSON, Amos m Sally Clark, 153
Amos C. m Elizabeth Tinker, 144*
Amos C. m Phebe Pierson, 119, 194
Amos Champlin s Tory & Betsey, 119
Amos Champlin s Amos C. & Elizabeth, 144
Betsey d Tory & Betsey, 119
Elizabeth d Amos C. & Elizabeth, 144
Elizabeth A. m Joseph H. Lay, 173, 204, 205
Fabius Beckwith s Amos C. & Elizabeth, 144
John P. s Amos C. & Elizabeth, 144
Nancy d Amos C. & Elizabeth, 144
Nathan s Tory & Betsey, 119
Nathan Tinker s Amos C. & Elizabeth, 144
Phebe Peck twin d Tory & Betsey, 119
Salley Latimer twin d Tory & Betsey, 119
Tory m Betsey Champlin, 119
MAYNARD, MAYNERD
Abby A. m Jason Rogers, 152
Almira m Samuel Gilbert, 164
Betsey m Charles Sleuman (Sloman), 159
Betsey C. m Chas D. Sherman, 134
Charlotte d John Jr. & Lydia, 134
Charlotte m Ezra Maynard Jr., 141
Charlotte, 216
David m Nancy Page, 158
David C. s Richard E. & Almira, 199
Eliza m Joseph Miller, 147
Emeline m Christopher B. Chapman, 177
Ezra s Ezra, 110
Ezra Jr. m Charlotte Maynard, 141
Fanny d John Jr. & Lydia, 134
Gurdon L. m Betsey Ransom, 194
Hannah m James Chapel, 181
Harriot d John Jr. & Lydia, 134
Harriot m Wm Maynard, 189
James Henry s Watrous & Elizabeth, 140
Jane M. m Horace Champion, 182, 199

INDEX OF PERSONS 361

MAYNARD, cont.
  Jerusha d John Jr. & Lydia, 134
  Jerusha m Nathan Sanders, 137
  Joanna m Giles Lester, 193
  John Jr. m Lydia Havens, 133
  John m Mary Daniels, 172
  John s Watrous & Elizabeth, 140
  John Beebe s John Jr. & Lydia, 134
  Lester H. m Mahala Brooks, 173
  Lydia m Calvin Havens, 193
  Lydia d John Jr. & Lydia, 134
  Lydia m Selden Maynerd, 152
  Mary m Harvey Tooker, 161
  Mary E. m Gurdon Clark, 194
  Mary Louisa d Ezra Jr. & Charlotte, 141
  Nancy d John Jr. & Lydia, 134
  Orran s Ezra, 110
  Orrin m Dorcas Mack, 152
  Polly d John Jr. & Lydia, 134
  Richard E., 199
  Roxana m Alexander Keables, 160
  Selden s Ezra, 110
  Selden m Lydia Maynerd, 152
  Watrous m Elizabeth Clark, 140
  Whitman s Ezra, 110
  Wm m Harriet Maynard, 189
M'COY, Alexr, 299*
  Mary m William Bartman, 146
McCRACKIN, James m Elizabeth Smith, 97
  Thomas s James & Elizabeth, 97
  William s James & Elizabeth, 97
McCRARY, MacRARY, McCREARY, McCRERY, McCARY
  Aggness d Wm & Elizabeth, 68
  Chapman s Wm & Elizabeth, 68
  Elijah s Wm & Elizabeth, 68
  Elizabeth, 300
  Elizabeth m John Munsell, Jr., 60
  Elizabeth d Wm & Elizabeth, 68
  John s Wm & Elizabeth, 68
  John m Mary Ann Rowland, 144
  Lurana, 300
  Lucretia, 300
  Nancy Maria m Noah Harding, 185, 203
  Russell s Wm & Elizabeth, 68
  Samuel s Wm & Elizabeth, 68
  Susa d Wm & Elizabeth, 68
  Ulyssus m Lydia Rowth, 164
  William, 274
  William m Elizabeth _____, 68
  William s Wm & Elizabeth, 68
  _____ twin sons Wm & Elizabeth, 68
McCURDY, Alexander L. m Josephine Lord, 166
  Alexander Lynde s Richd & Ursula, 118
  Anne d John & Anne, 67
  Charles J. m Sarah Ann Lord, 146
  Charles Johnson s Richard & Ursula, 118
  Elizabeth d John & Anne, 67
  Jeanet (Jannet) d John & Anne, 67
  John m Anne Lord, 67
  John's negro servants, 67
    Jordan, Ezelphie, Clo, Ceaser, Shambaes
  John s John & Anne, 67
  John Griswold s Richard & Ursula, 118
  Lynde m Mrs. Ursula Griswold, 73
  Lynde s John & Anne, 67

McCURDY, cont.
  Richard s John & Anne, 67
  Richard m Ursula Wolcott Griswold, 118
  Richard Lord s Richard & Ursula, 118
  Robert Henry s Richard & Ursula, 118
  Sarah d John & Anne, 67
  Sarah A. m Stephen J. Lord, 158
  Saryann d Richard & Ursula, 118
  Ursula d Lynde & Ursula, 73
McNIGHT, McKNIGHT
  Allen m Esther Comstock, 4, 301
  Esther m Reynold Huntley, 112
  John s Allen & Esther, 4
MEIGS, Cornelia m Nathan Howard, 182
MELONEY, Harriet m Francis A. Porter, 171
MENTOR, MENTA
  Abigail m Benjamin Jones a mulatto, 238
  Abigail d Robert & Abigail, 7
  Anna d Robert & Abigail, 7
  Elijah Bennett s Robert & Abigail, 7
  Felix s Robert & Abigail, 7
  Gabriel s Robert & Abigail, 7
  Jane d Robert & Abigail, 7
  Mary d Robert & Abigail, 7
  Patience d Robert & Abigail, 7
  Reuben s Robert & Abigail, 7
  Robert m Abigail Bennit, 7*
  Robert m Christian Comstock, 227
  Robert s Robert & Abigail, 7*
  Ruth d Robert & Abigail, 7
MERCHANT, Anne m Eusebus Dodge, 116
MERRICK, Ame m Thomas Way Jr., 108
MERRETT, Ame wife Thomas died, 61
  Amos s Thomas & Ame, 61
  Anson m Betsey Tinker, 153
  Thomas m Ama Avery, 61
MERRIMAN, Martha m Orrin Havens, 211
MERROW, MERRON, Abigail d Elisha & Mary, 47
  Anner d Elisha & Mary, 47
  Cate d Elisha & Mary, 47
  Elisha m Mary Munsell, 47
  Elisha s Elisha & Mary, 47
  Elisha Jr. m Elizabeth Joram, 84, 301
  Elizabeth d Elisha & Mary, 47
  John s Elisha & Mary, 47
  John m Hannah Mather, 94
  John Oliver s John & Hannah, 94
  Molley d Elisha & Mary, 47
  Nathan s Elisha & Mary, 47
  Sarah d Elisha & Mary, 47
MILLARD, Louisa m James Kelsey Jr., 151
MILLER, Alonsa. 201
  Ammasa s Elisha & Lydia, 18
  Anna d John m Elisha Tubbs, 11
  Asa s Wm & Irena, 73
  Ashel m Juliann Brockway, 154
  Bethueal s Nicodemus & Phebe, 15
  Billey s Noah & Mary, 9
  Caroline d George & Sarah, 198
  Cate d Noah & Sarah, 97
  Charles, Capt. 306
  Charles Pinkney or Joseph Miller s Elisha & Lydia, 18
  Deborah H. m Thomas Hill (Hilt), 156
  Deodaymea d Noah & Mary, 9
  Diagama m Adonijah Marvin, 54

MILLER, cont.
Ede A. Miller m Franklin M. Brown, 155
Elias s Noah & Mary, 9
Elias s William & Irena, 73
Eliphalett s Robert, 249
Elisha s Elisha & Lydia, 18*
Elisha m Elizabeth Lay, 16
Elisha s Noah & Mary, 9
Elisha s Robert, 249
Elisha Jr. m Lydia Beckwith Jr., 18*
Elisha Jr. m Caroline Page, 158
Elisha 3rd m Hannah Champion, 55
Elizabeth d Elisha 3rd & Hannah, 55
Elizabeth d Noah & Mary, 9
Elizabeth M. m Samuel Birdseye, 168
Epaphroditus m Catharine Rogers, 173
Esther m Nicodemus & Pheby, 15
Eunice d Ezra & Sarah, 87
Eunice m Jehoada Mather, 81
Eunice d Robert & Martha, 75
Ezra s Elisha & Lydia, 18
Ezra m Sarah Mather, 87
Ezra s Robert & Martha, 75
Ezra W. m Sally Terry, 135
George s Alonso & Harriet, 201
George s Robert & Martha, 75
George m Jerusha Ann Cobb, 158
George m Sarah Way, 176, 198
Hannah m Eleazer Hudson, 89
Hannah m Lemuel Rogers, 77
Hannah d Noah & Mary, 9
Hannah d Robert, 249
Hepzibah (Hephza) d Ezra & Sarah, 87
Hepzibah m John Murdock, 132
Hepzibah d Robert & Martha, 75
Ede A. m Franklin Brown, 155
Jacob m Martha Thompson d William, 249
Jacob s Jacob, 249
Jan m Martin Wade, 66
Jeremiah s Elisha & Lydia, 18
Jerusha m Samuel Daniels, 144
Joanna d Nicodemus & Patience, 15
John s Robert, 249
John s Noah & Sarah, 97
Joseph s Robert & Martha, 75
Joseph died, 75
Joseph s Robert & Martha born, 75
Joseph s Elisha & Lydia, 18
Joseph (Charles Pinkney) s Elisha & Lydia, 18
Joseph m Eliza Maynard, 147
King m Mahitable Dart, 155
Julia m Henry Lee, 151
Julia Ann, 278
Laura A. m Frederick Birdsey, 191
Lemuel s Nicodemus & Pheby, 15
Loas d Noah & Mary, 9
Loas m Latham Smith, 32
Louis s Joseph Clark, 155
Lucia m Maj. Ezra Wait, 114
Lucinda d Robert & Martha, 75
Lucindia d Silas & Loas, 94
Lucindia m Amos Smith, 46
Lucindia m Elias Hudson, 124
Lucy d Ezra & Sarah, 87
Lydia m George H. Armstrong, 149
Lydia Junr. died, 18*

MILLER, cont.
Lydia A. m Orlando Lee, 165
Martha d Jacob, 249
Martha d Ezra & Sarah, 87
Martha d Robert & Martha, 75
Martha m Reuben Chadwick, 77
Mary A. m Adin Tooker, 160
Mary m Benjamin Barter, 161
Mary m Matthew Tinker, 137
Mary d Noah & Mary, 9
Mary m Richard Ransom, 151
Mary d Robert, 249
Mary d William & Irena, 73
Munsell s Silas & Loas, 94*
Munsell s Silas & Loas born, 94
Nancy m David Phelps, 146
Nathan s Jacob, 249
Nathan s Silas & Loas, 94*
Nathan Beebe s Thompson, 81
Nicodemus s Robert, 249
Nicodemus m Patience Bates, 15
Nicodemus 2nd m Phebe Huntley, 15*
Noah s Noah & Mary, 9
Noah m Mary Waller, 9
Noah m Sarah Crocker, 96
Noah s Robert, 249
Noah Jr. m Welthy Brockway, 73
Pathania d Nicodemus & Phebe, 15
Patience wife Nicodemus, 15
Patience d Nicodemus & Phebe, 15
Phebe m Elisha Champion, 104
Phebe d Ezra & Sarah, 87
Phebe M. m Lee Comstock, 137
Phebe d Nicodemus & Phebe, 15
Richard H. m Elizabeth Stebbins, 162
Robert s Jacob, 249
Robert Lt. died, 75
Sally m Ebenezar Morgan, 53
Sarah d Ezra & Sarah, 87
Sarah d Noah & Sarah, 97
Sarah m Joseph Peck, 12
Sarah m Elijah Beckwith, 53
Silas m Loas Smith, 94
Silas s Silas & Loas, 94
Susannah d Elisha 3rd & Hannah, 55
Tomson (Tompson) s Jacob, 249
Valentine A. m Mary Ann Rowland, 178
Welthy d William & Irena, 73
William s Noah & Mary, 9*
William m Irena Brockway, 73
William s Wm & Irena, 73
MINARD, Jesse m Anna Watrous, 78
Mary m Samuel Story, 90
MINOR, MINER, MENOIR
Abby Ann Hayden m Jewett Baker, 185
Abigail m Richard Smith, 37
Abigail d Ebenezer & Bettey, 85
Abigail d Daniel & Ama, 73
Abner s Ezekiel & Margreet, 100
Allen s Stephen & Lydia, 125
Ama d Daniel & Ama, 73
Amy m Ezra Gillett, 109
Anderson s Ezekiel & Margreet, 100
Andrew s Clement & Easther, 249
Anne d William & Anna, 249
Azriah s Ebenezer & Bettey, 85

INDEX OF PERSONS

MINOR, cont.
Benjamin s Elias & Esther, 51
Bettey d Ebenezer & Bettey, 85
Caroline A. m Milton Winslow, 190
Caroline d Charles & Huldah, 203
Charles s Ebenezer & Bettey, 85
Charles s Stephen & Lydia, 126
Charles, 310
Charles m Huldah Condol, 176, 203
Charles H., 310
Charles S. s Charles H. & Betsey F., 204
Christopher s Clement & Esther, 249
Christopher s William & Anna, 249
Clarissa m Lorenzo Congdon, 172
Clarissa m John Way Jr., 178, 203
Clement s William & Anna, 249
Clement m Easther Lee, 249
Daniel, 200
Daniel m Ama Smith, 73
Daniel s Daniel & Ama, 73
Daniel s Stephen & Lydia, 125
Dorcas d Daniel & Ama, 73
Ebenezer s Ebenezer & Bettey, 85
Elias s Ezekiel & Margreet, 100
Elias m Esther Noyes, 51
Elias m Sarah Ely, 51
Elihue s William & Anna, 249
Elisha s Clement & Easther, 249
Elisha m Ruth Robins, 48
Elisha m Fanny Palmer, 189, 209
Elizabeth d Joseph m John Anderson, 20
Elizabeth d Daniel & Ama, 73
Elizabeth d Martin & Elizabeth, 92
Elizabeth d Stephen & Lydia, 125
Elizabeth m David Baker, 184
Esther d Elias & Esther, 51
Esther wife Elias died, 51*
Esther d Joseph & Hannah, 136
Eunice m William Latham, 143
Ezekiel m Margreet Wait, 100
Ezekiel m Margaret Reed widow, 100
Ezekiel died, 100*
Ezra s Ezekiel & Margaret, 100*
Ezra s Ezekiel & Margaret, 100
Ezra m Polly Mack, 81
Fanny d Stephen & Lydia, 125
Fanny m Calvin Spencer, 141
Frances S. m Edmund Smith, 164
Francis M. m Maria Fox, 194
Gilbers s Joseph & Hannah, 137
Grace Turner relict of Joseph, 100
Hannah m Amos Tinker Jr. 31
Hannah d Ebenezer & Bettey, 85
Harriet B. m Samuel Comstock, 164
Hellen m Erastus Bramble Jr., 191
Huldah d Ebenezer & Betty, 85
Huldah d Ebenezer & Betty, 85
Isaac s Elias & Sarah, 51
Jenne d Martin & Elizabeth, 92
Jeremiah m Elizabeth Marvin, 47
Joanna d Martin & Elizabeth, 92
Joel s Clement & Esther, 249
Joel m Mary H. Peck, 177, 198
John s William & Anna, 249
John s Clement & Esther, 249
John s Ezekiel & Margreet, 100

MINOR, cont.
John Mack s Daniel & Ama, 73
Jonathan s Ebenezer & Bettey, 85, 301
Joseph s William & Anna, 38, 249
Joseph Jr. died, 39
Joseph s Elias & Esther, 51*
Joseph died, 100
Joseph m Hannah Johnson, 136
Joseph s Elias & Esther died, 51*
Laura m Enoch Waid, 142
Lous d Martin & Elizabeth, 92
Lorena d Ezekiel & Margreet, 100
Louisa d Joel & Mary, 198
Lurena d Martin & Elizabeth, 92
Lucretia d Clement & Esther, 249
Lucy d Ebenezer & Bettey, 85
Lydia m Joshua Rogers, 44
Lydia d Ebenezer & Bettey, 85
Lydia d Elias & Sarah, 51
Margreet wife of Ezekiel died 100*
Martin s Ezekiel & Margreet, 100
Martin m Elizabeth Davis, 92
Marvin s Martin & Elizabeth, 92
Mary d Daniel & Ama, 73
Mary m Joseph Gillett, 67
Mary F. m Moses Warren, 140
Mehetable d Daniel & Ama, 73
Mehetable m Capt. Nathaniel Conklin, 156
Mercy d Stephen & Lydia, 125
Nancy d Stephen & Lydia, 125
Orlando m Belinda Otis, 158
Parnall m George Bissell, 127
Phebe wife Dr. Thos died, 144
Polly d Stepehn & Lydia, 125
Prentiss s Joseph & Hannah, 136
Rebecca m Pardon Ryon, 114
Ruth m Ezekiel Huntley, 130
Sabra d Clement & Easther, 249
Sabra m Martin Lee, 47
Sally m Champlain Lester, 141
Samuel s Clement & Esther, 249
Samuell s William & Anna, 249
Sarah M., 200
Sarah d Elias & Sarah, 51
Sarah d Ezekiel & Margreet, 100
Sarah d William & Anna, 249
Sarah A. m Gad Baldwin, 187
Sarah E. d Daniel & Sarah, 200
Seldon s Elias & Esther, 51
Seth s Ezekiel & Margreet, 100
Southmayd m Sarah Banning, 167
Stephen born, 125*
Stephen m Lydia Allen, 125*
Stephen s Stephen & Lydia, 126
Stephen s William & Anna, 249
Susanna d William & Anna, 249
Silvester s William & Anna, 249
Thomas s William & Anna, 249
Thomas Dr. m Phebe Mather, 144
William, 249
William s Clement m Sarah Beckwith, 250*
William s Clement, Grandson of Thomas of Stonnington, 250*
William s William & Anna, 249
William s Martin & Elizabeth, 92
William H. m Harriet Luther, 176

MINOR, cont.
  Zenas s Clement & Easther, 249*
  Zenas s Elisha & Ruth, 48
MITCHELL, Annah (widow), 274, 275
  George & his wife Lucy, 274, 275
  George m Parnal Beckwith, 155
  John, 307
  Lydia m John Bogue, 172
  Nancy m Richard Lord, 109
MIXTER, Emerson m Frances Huntley, 188
MOORE or MOOR
  Abel s John & Temperance, 17
  Abigail m Peter Tubbs, 68
  Abigail d John Jr. & Temperance, 17
  Avery s John Jr. & Temperance, 17
  Betsey m Welcome Browning, 172
  Edward m Mary Chappell, 143
  Elias Crane s John 2nd & Emily, 140
  Elisha m Elizabeth Smith, 111*
  Elisha s John Jr. & Temperance, 17
  Elizabeth m Daniel Calkins, 111
  Emily E. m George W. Lord, 175
  Eunice d Elisha & Elizabeth, 111
  Eunice d John Jr. & Temperance, 17
  Eunice m Capt. Richard Mather, 114
  George died, 214
  Grace m Richard Smith, 37
  Harriet E. m Leander King, 179, 198
  John Jr. m Temperance Avery, 17
  John s John Jr. & Temperance, 17
  John 2nd m Emily Crane, 140
  John Alexander s John 2nd & Emily, 140
  Joshua m Lois Hamilton, 156
  Lucy d John Jr. & Temperance, 17
  Lucy m Denison Cranda, 137
  Mary m William Smith, 87
  Mary d John Jr. & Temperance, 17
  Mary m Thomas Lewis, 166
  Polly m Asa Jones, 120
  Richard s John Jr. & Temperance, 17
  Russell s John Jr. & Temperance, 17
  William s John & Temperance, 17
MORGAN, Aeenath, 279
  Alva s Theophilus & Mary, 135
  Asenath m Samuel Talcott, 160
  Augustus m Abby A. Damon, 195, 211
  Carolina d Theophilus & Mary, 135
  Charlotte Meranda d Theophilus & Mary, 135
  Corvill d Theophilus & Mary, 135
  David W. died, 213
  Ebenezer m Sally Miller, 53
  Elisha died, 213
  Henry s Theops & Mary, 135
  James R. m Jan Gray Raymond, 186
  Jennet d Theophilus & Mary, 135
  John R. m Lydia Day, 195
  John Dr., 310
  Julia Ann died, 214
  Lucretia died, 215
  Maria E. m Ichabod Ryon, 170
  Mary d Theops & Mary, 135
  Phebe died, 214
  Phillip m Sarah Ann Lord, 147
  Sidne(y) s Theops & Mary, 135
  Simion m Phebe Clark, 152

MORGAN, cont.
  Theophilus m Mary Hinckley, 135
  Theophilus s Theophilus & Mary, 135
MORLEY, Betsey A., 201, 205
  Caroline, 204
  Charles Jr. s Charles & Betsey, 205
  Charles S., 205
  David, 204
  David s David & Caroline, 204
MORRIS or MORRISON
  Ann m Charles E. Peck, 193, 208
  James S. m Amelia Gulliver, 179
MORSE, Abigail m Hennery Benit Jr., 221
MOSHIER, MOSIER
  Phebe m Stephen Champion, 131
  Stephen, 301
MOSS, MOSE, MOSSE, MOOS
  Jeams m Marah, 250
  Jeams s Jeams & Marah, 250
  Marah d Jeams & Marah, 250
  Mary m Henry Benit, 221
  Sarah d Jeams & Marah, 250
MOTT, Anna d Edward m John Mott, 250
  Azariah s Samuell Jr., 250
  Deborah d Samuell Jr. & Marah, 250
  Ebenezer s Samuell & Marah, 250
  Experience d Samuell Jr. & Marah, 250
  Francisca m Edward Hewlet, 197
  Hannah d Samuell & Marah, 250
  John s Samuell & Marah, 250
  John s Samuell m Annah Mott (2nd), 250
  Lidea d Samuell & Marah, 250
  Marcy d Edward, 250
  Mary d John & Marcy, 250
  Mary d Samuell & Marah, 250
  Mary m Joshuah Champion, 225
  Mary d Samuell Jr., 250
  Nathaniell s Samuell & Marah, 250
  Nathaniell s Samuell Jr., 250
  Sally m Harvey Hall, 160
  Samuel s Samuel & Marah, 250
  Samuel Jr. m _____ Spencer, 250
  Samuell s Samuell Jr., 250*
  Samuell 2nd s Samuell Jr., 250*
  Samuell 3rd s Samuell Jr., 250*
  Samuell m Marah Brockway, 250
  Samuel M. m Frances Gilbert, 187
  Sarah d Samuell Jr., 250
MOWRY, LeRoy m Catharine Noyes, 161
MULFORD, Thomas T. m Phebe Steward, 143
MULHOLLARD, Elizabeth m Henry Spencer, 180
MUMFORD
  Eliza m Nathaniel Shaw Woodbridge, 119
MUNFON, MUNFET, MONFET, MONFELL, MUNFILL, MUNSELL
  Abigail d John, 250
  Anna d Timothy & Elishaba, 90
  Anna d John & Mary, 251
  Anne m Nathaniel Dickerson, 56
  Azubah d John Jr. & Azubah, 121
  Betsey d John Jr. & Azubah, 121
  Bettey d John Jr. & Elizabeth, 60
  Bettey d John Jr. & Elizabeth, 61*
  Bettey w John died, 61*
  Cattaran d John, 250
  James s John, 251

INDEX OF PERSONS 365

MUNFELL, cont.
  James s Timothy & Elishaba, 90
  John s Thomas, 251
  John s John, 250
  John Jr. m Sila Huntley, 60
  John Jr. m Elizabeth McCrary, 60
  John s John Jr. & Elizabeth, 60
  John died, 251
  John Jr. m Azubah Huntley, 121
  John s John & Azubah, 121
  John m Lydia Huntley, 61
  John Andross s Timothy & Elishaba, 90
  Joseph s John, 251
  Joseph s John Jr. & Elizabeth, 61
  Joseph s John Jr. & Azubah, 121
  Lucinda d John Jr. & Elizabeth, 61
  Lucinda m Joseph Tillitson, 118
  Mary d John, 250
  Mary m Elisha Merrow, 47
  Mary d James & Esther, 66
  Mehetable d John Jr. & Azubah, 121
  Polley d John Jr. & Elizabeth, 61
  Sally Ann d Timothy & Elishaba, 90
  Sila d John Jr. & Sila, 60
  Sila wid. John Jr. died, 60*
  Sila d John Jr. & Sila, 60*
  Sila d John Jr. & Elizabeth, 60
  Sherman s John Jr. & Azubah, 121
  Thomas m Deborah Rogers, 251
  Thomas s Thomas & Deborah, 251
  Thomas s John, 251
  Thomas s John Jr. & Elizabeth, 60
  Thomas m Anne Tillitson, 29
  Thomas s Thomas & Anne, 29
  Timothy s John & Mary, 251
  Timothy s Timothy & Elishaba, 90
  William s John Jr. & Sila, 60
  William s John Jr & Elizabeth (perhaps Silla), 61
  William s Thomas & Anne, 29
  William Westcott s Timothy & Elishaba, 90
MURDOCK, Abigail m Elisha Lee, 88
  Ann, 200
  Hannah wid. m Seth Smith, 98
  John m Hepzibah Miller, 132
  John s John & Hepzibah, 132
  Lucy Miller d John & Hepzibah, 132
  Martha d Ann, 200
NASH, Mary Ann M. m Dan Mather, 181
NASON, James S. m Lydia Tibbets, 123
NEBB, Calvin m Hannah Gardner, 161
NELIGAN, Michael s Thomas & Jerusha, 139
  Thomas m Jerusha Boon, 139
  Thomas s Thomas & Jerusha, 139
  William H. s Thomas & Jerusha, 139
NETTLETON, Asahel (Rev), 272
NEWTON or NUTON
  Dinah m Nathaniel Matson Jr., 68
  Hannah m Stephen Beckwith, 23
  Rhoda m William Matson, 138
NICHOLS, Ebenezer m Margaret Ely, 156
  Elija, 279
  Elija m Elias Ely, 164
  Frances J. m John Dayton, 169
  Margaret A. m Frances M. Palmer, 182
NILES, Ambrose Dr. m Frances Mulligan, 147
  Benjamin, 228

NILES, cont.
  Deborah m John Reed, 256
  George E. m Mary Russell, 156
  Neomy d Benj m William Comstock, 228
  Salome m Samuel Brown, 157
  William B. m Julia Ely, 148, 279
NORTON, Maria m Francis Lay, 144
NOWLEY, Sarah Ann m Watson Clark, 155
NOYES, Abigail Leveritt d William & Sarah, 66
  Anna d Moses & Hannah, 29
  Anne Mrs. died, 213
  Calvin s Moses & Hannah, 29
  Catharine d William & Sarah, 66
  Catharine B. m Leroy Mowry, 161
  Catharine Banks d William & Eunice (perhaps Hannah), 143
  Elizabeth m Abraham Avery, 45
  Elizabeth m Jabez Sill, 63
  Elizabeth d Moses & Hannah, 29
  Elten m Daniel Chadwick Jr., 190, 204, 208
  Enoch s Joseph & Jane, 41
  Enock m Catharine Lord, 177
  Esther m Elias Minor, 51
  Esther d Moses & Hannah, 29
  Eunice m Israel Ely, 113
  Eunice d Joseph & Jane died, 44
  Eunice d Joseph & Jane born, 44*
  Eunice d Moses & Hannah, 29
  Hannah d Moses & Hannah, 29
  Helena Decay d William Jr. & Hannah, 143
  Henry B. m Sarah Holdredge, 184
  James s William & Sarah, 66
  Jane Elizabeth d Joseph & Sarah Griswold, 150
  John m Ann Colton, 175, 198
  John Dr. m Anna (Edward Anna) Sill 192, 209
  John s John & Ann, 198
  John Dr. died, 251
  John Dr. died, 82
  John s Dr. Richard & Martha, 138
  John s Wm & Eunice, 81
  Joseph m Jane Lord, 43
  Joseph m Sarah Griswold Gurley, 150
  Joseph s Wm & Eunice, 81
  Martha m Dr. Richard Noyes, 138
  Mary d Moses & Hannah, 29
  Mary A. m Billings Learned, 171
  Mary Ann d William & Hannah, 143
  Mary Gurley d Joseph & Sarah Griswold, 150
  Matthew s Wm & Eunice, 81
  Matthew s Wm & Hannah, 143
  Mindwell d Moses & Hannah, 29
  Moses s Moses, 251
  Moses m Mary Ely, 251
  Moses s Moses & Mary, 251
  Moses Rev. died, 251
  Moses Esq. died, 251
  Moses m Hannah Selden, 29
  Moses s Moses & Hannah, 29, 251
  Richard s Joseph & Jane, 41
  Richard Dr. m Martha Noyes, 138
  Ruth d Moses, 251*
  Ruth d Moses & Mary, 251*
  Ruth 2nd d Moses & Mary, 251
  Sarah B. m William Griswold, 161
  Sarah Banks d William & Hannah, 143
  Stephen Lord s Wm Jr. & Hannah, 143

NOYES, cont.
William m Eunice Marvin, 81
Wm s Wm & Eunice, 66, 81
William Jr. m Sarah Banks, 66
Wm had negro servant Jordon & negro Harry, 69, 70
William had negro servant Biner, 68
William s William & Sarah, 66
William died, 81
William Jr. m Hannah Townsend, 143
William James s William Jr. & Hannah, 143
OLIVER, John m Savy Comstock, 251
OLMSTED (ARMSTEAD),Mary m Elisha Lay, 104
ORETEL, Maxamilian m Mary Greenfield, 173
OSBORN
    Edward Josephus m Fanny Pilgrim, 142, 169
    Lucy m Lothrop Rockwell, 142
OTIS, Anna d Robert & Margret, 35
    Anna d Robert & Polly, 60
    Belinda, 279
    Belinda m Orlando Minor, 159
    Charlotte d Stephen & Lucy, 116
    Cordelia m Selden Chadwick, 191
    Datia (Theodosia) m Guy Beebe, 166
    David P. m Hannah Comstock, 162
    Edward s Stephen & Lucy, 116, 307
    Elizabeth m Gurdon Grayham, 161
    Hayden s Stephen & Lucy, 116
    Heyden, 279
    Israel s Robert & Polly, 60
    Israel m Deborah Maria Babcock, 143
    Lucy Ann m Daniel Rogers, 167
    Lydia d Robert & Polly, 60
    Lydia m Benjamin Albee, 138
    Nancy m Ezra Lester, 177, 203
    Polly d Robert & Polly, 60
    Richard s Robert & Margaret, 35
    Richard s Robert & Polly, 60
    Robert m Margret Sabins, 35
    Robert, 305
    Robert s Robert & Margret, 35
    Robert s Robert & Lydia, 35
    Robert m Polly Smith, 60
    Sally d Robt & Polly, 60
    Sally d Israel, 278
    Selden s Stephen & Lucy (?), 116
    Stephen (Lex. Alarm), 301
    Stephen s Robert & Margret, 35
    Stephen m Lucy Wedger, 116
    Stephen s Stephen & Lucy, 116
    Theadola (Theodosia) d Robert & Polly, 60
PAGE, Caroline m Elisha Miller Jr., 158
    Jonathan m Rachal Waid, 164
    Joseph m Adaline Waid, 166
    Nancy m David Maynard, 158
PAINE, PAYNE, MaryAnn m Enos Gates, 150
    Simon R. m Lacy (Sary) Gorton, 165
PALMER, Elihu H. m Phebe Lester, 186
    Elisha m Ellis Loomis, 174
    Elizabeth m Matthew Dorr, 61
    Fanny m Elisha Minor, 189, 209
    Francis M. m Margaret A. Nichols, 182
    Irene m Henry Rowland, 28
    Noyes W. m Diadamia Ely, 195, 211, 310
PARKER, Ann Maria d Marshfield & Azubah, 146
    Henry Lord s Marshfield & Azubah, 146

PARKER, cont.
    Jane Louisa d Marshfield & Azubah, 146
    John M. m Lucretia Tiffany, 185
    John Brockway s Marshfield & Jane, 206
    John Marvin s Marshfield & Azubah, 146
    Henry Capt., 310
    Marshfield m Azubah Marvin, 146
    Marshfield Sterling s Marshfield & Azubah, 146
    Marshfield Jr. m Jane Amelia Brockway, 190, 206, 210
    Seymour Landon s Marshfield & Azubah, 146
    William Mather s Marshfield & Azubah, 146
PARMELEE, Philo m Sarah Johnson, 166
PARSONS, Abigail d John & Jonna born, 27
    Abigail d John & Lois, 27, 122
    Betsy m William Lay Jr., 120
    Deborah d John & Jonna, 27
    Elizabeth d John & Lois, 123
    Elizabeth m John Huntly, 236
    Enoch s Samll Holden & Mehitable 60, 127
    Ezra s Rev. Jonathan & Phebe, 251*
    George s John & Lois, 122
    Georgeanna L. m Edward Covell, 192, 210
    Joanna w John, 27
    Joanna d John & Lous, 27, 122
    John s Marshfield & Lois, 50
    John m Joanna Mather, 27
    John m Lois Wait, 27, 122
    John s John & Lois, 122
    Jonathan Rev. m Phebe Griswold, 251
    Jonathan s Rev. Jonathan & Phebe, 251
    Loas w Marshfield died, 50
    Lous d John & Joanna, 27
    Lois m Charles Smith, 129
    Luce d Samuel Holden & Mehetable 60, 127
    Lucy d John & Lois, 122
    Lucy Parsons d John & Lois, 123
    Lydia d John & Lois, 122
    Margaret d Samuel Holden & Mehetable, 127
    Margaret Ann d Samuel & Mehetable, 127
    Marshfield s of Rev. Jonathan & Phebe, 251
    Marshfield m Lois Wait, 50
    Marshfield m Abigail Marvin, 50*
    Marshfield m Mrs. Phebe Griffin, 50
    Marshfield s John & Lois, 122
    Mehetable d Samel & Mehetable, 60, 127
    Phebe d Rev. Jonathan & Phebe, 251*
    Phebe died, 251*
    Phebe d Samuel & Mehetable, 127
    Phebe d John & Lois, 27, 122
    Phebe m John Beckwith, 145
    Phebe 2nd m Charles Smith, 129
    Richard W. m Clarissa L. Griffing, 153
    Richard Waite s John & Lois, 122
    Samuel Holden born, 127
    Sam(ue)l Holden s Rev. Jonathan & Phebe, 251
    Samuel Holden m Mehetable Mather, 60, 126
    Samuel Holden s Sam(ue)l & Mehetable, 127
    Samuel Holden, Gen'l-drowned, 127*
    Thomas s Rev. Jonathan & Phebe, 251
    Thomas s Samll & Mehetable, 60, 127
    Thomas born, died, 127*
    Thomas Griswold s John & Lois, 122
    William s Marshfield & Loas, 50*
    William s Samuel Holden & Mehetable, 60
    William s John & Lois, 27, 122

INDEX OF PERSONS

PARSONS, cont.
William Mather s Samuel & Mehetable, 127
―――― s of John & Lois born & died, 122
PATON, Elizabeth m Gurdon Watrous, 124
PATTEN, William m Louisa Harrison, 179
PAYNE (see under PAINEO)
PEARSON, PERSON, PIERSON
Abijah s Peter & Parnial, 117
Allis Pearson (Mrs) m Nathan Avery, 42, 93
Anna d Peter & Parnial, 117
Anna m Luther Reives, 104
Anna d Richd & Mary Ann, 3
Elisha s William & Mehitable, 124
Elizabeth d Richard & Mary Ann, 3
Hannah m John Huntley Jr., 9
Hepsebath m Elijah Peck, 252
Hepsebath d Peter & Mary, 37, 254
Irena m Benjamin Mather, 42
Irene d Peter & Mary, 254
Julany d Peter & Parnial, 117
Lydia d Peter & Lidia, 254
Lydia w Peter died, 254
Martha wid. Peter died, 73
Mary m Abraham Perkins (written in Arnold Index)
Mary d Peter & Mary, 254
Mary d Peter & Parnial, 117
Mary w Peter died, 254*
Mary d Richard & Mary Ann, 3
Mehetable m Josiah Beckwith, 109
Mehetable d Richard & Mary Ann, 3
Mehetable d William & Mehitable, 124
Mehetable wife of Samuel died, 251
Peter m Miss Parnial Corah, 117
Peter m Mary Lord d Richard Lord, 254
Peter m Widow Martha Peck, 254
Peter s Peter & Mary, 254
Peter s Peter & Parniel, 117
Peter s Richard & Mary Ann, 3
Phebe d Peter & Parnial, 117
Phebe d Petter & Lidia, 254
Pheby d Richard & Mary Ann, 3
Rachal d Peter & Parnial, 117
Reeve s William & Mehitable, 124
Richard m Indiana Comstock, 138
Richard m Mary Ann Ely, 3
Richard s Peter & Mary, 254
Richard s Peter & Parnial, 117
Richard s Richard & Mary Ann, 3*
Samuel s Mehetable Dudley, 251
Samuel s Petter & Lidia, 254
Samuel s William & Mehitable, 124
Sarah d Peter & Parnial, 117
Sarah d Richard & Mary Ann, 3
Sarah d William & Mehitable, 124
Tabatha m Jedidiah Peck, 252
Tabitha d Peter & Mary, 254
William Ely s Richard & Mary Ann, 3
PECK, PEECK, PEAK,
Abigail d David & Abigail, 48
Abigail d Mather & Esther, 90
Abijah s Dan(ie)ll & Abigail, 19
Abner s Samuel Jr. & Aless, 254
Abner s Reynold & Deborah, 51
Abner m Caroline Reed, 71
Andrew s Darius & Elizabeth, 102

PECK, cont.
Anna d Elijah & Mehepsebeth, 252
Anna d Reynold & Deborah, 51
Ama d Jedediah & Tabitha, 70
Ame d Jasper & Phebe, 69
Ansel s Dan & Lovina, 55
Asenath d Dan(ie)ll & Jerusha, 89
Azariah s David & Abigail, 48
Azubah d Dan(ie)ll & Abigail, 19
Benjamin s Samuel, 253
Benjamin m Sarah Champion, 253
Benjamin s Benjamin & Sarah, 253
Bettey d Lot & Polley, 89
Betey d Lot & Polley, 90
Bettee d Reynold & Deborah, 51
Caroline M. m Jared W. Watrous, 185
Carter s Samuel Jr. & Aless, 254
Catharine d Lebbeus & Lydia, 104
Catharine d Charles & Ann, 201
Charles s Lot & Polly, 90
Charles s John & Rebeckah, 94
Charles C. s Ezra & Eunice, 140
Charles E. m Ann Morrison (Morris), 193, 201, 208
Charles E. M. s Eleazer C. & Eunice H., 179
Clarissa d Dan(ie)ll & Jerusha, 89
Clark s Jasper & Phebe, 69
Clark m Carolina Hall, 118
Clarry d John & Rebeckah, 94
Cyrus s Benjamin & Sarah, 253
Dan s Benjamin & Sarah, 253*
Dan s Benjamin & Sarah, 253*
Dan m Lovina Huntley, 55
Daniel s Samuel Jr. & Aless, 254
Daniel m Abigail Lord, 19*
Daniel died, 19*
Daniel s Daniel & Abigail, 19, 48
Daniel m Jerush (Yerrington, Yearington), 88
Daniel s David & Abigail, 48
Daniel s Dan(ie)ll & Jerusha, 89
Daniel s Samuell & Aless, 254
Darius s Samuel Jr. & Aless, 254
Darius m Elizabeth Beckwith, 101
Darius s Darius & Elizabeth, 102
David s Joseph & Sarah, 252
David m Abigail Southworth, 48
David s David & Abigail, 48
David s David & Abigail, 48
David Howell s Mather & Rhuehami, 90
David M. died, 213
Deborah m John Hazen Jr., 41, 234
Debrah d Joseph & Sarah, 252
Debrah m Daniel Sperry, 263
Dudley s Jasper & Phebe, 69*
Edward Chapman s Dan & Lovina, 55
Eleazer C. s Ezra & Eunice, 140
Eleazer C. m Eunice H. Warren, 179, 202
Elias s Benjamin & Sarah, 253
Elijah m Hepsebeth Person (Hephzibah) d Peter Pierson, 37, 252
Elijah s Elijah & Hepzibah born, 252
Elijah Jr. s Elijah & Hepzibah died, 37
Elijah died, 37
Elijah s Jedediah & Tabitha born, died, 70
Elijah s Jedediah & Tabitha born, 70
Elisha s Daniel & Jerusha, 88

PECK, cont.

Elisha s Darius & Elizabeth, 102
Elisha s Elijah & Mehipzibah, 252
Elisha s John & Rebeckah, 94
Elisha s Samuel & Aless, 254
Eliza m Silas Wood, 158
Elizabeth d Benjamin & Sarah, 253
Elizabeth d Darius & Elizabeth, 102
Elizabeth d David & Abigail, 48
Elizabeth d Elijah & Mehipzibah, 252
Elizabeth d Elijah & Mehipzibah, 252*
Elizabeth m James Gilet, 130
Elizabeth d Jasper & Phebe, 69
Elizabeth m Joseph Burtt, 83
Elizabeth d Joseph & Sarah, 252
Elizabeth m Richard Ely Jr., 230
Elizabeth m Shadrack Gillet, 119
Elizabeth m Samuel Pratt Or Prate, 255
Elizabeth d Samuel, 253*
Elizabeth d Samuel, 253*
Elizabeth wife Samuel died, 254
Elizabeth m Stephen Mather, 99
Elizabeth w Stephen died, 130*
Elizabeth d William & Jemima, 25
Elizabeth w Deac. William, 253
Elizabeth m Zenos Huntley, 54
Esther d Benjamin & Sarah, 253
Esther m Giles Tiffany, 109
Esther d Mather & Esther, 90
Esther w Mather died, 90
Ezekiel s Dan(ie)ll & Jerusha, 89
Ezra s David & Abigail, 48
Ezra m Eunice Clark, 140
Ezra M. died, 140*
Ezra Miller s Joseph & Sarah, 12
Fanny d Joseph & Sarah, 12
Frankling s William & Judath, 105
George s Reynold & Deborah, 51
George R. m Elizabeth S. Lee, 150
Han child of Joseph Jr., 253
Hananiah s David & Abigail, 48
Hannah m Allen Smith, 127
Hannah wid m Joseph Wait, 5
Hanah d Joseph, 252
Hannah d Reynold & Deborah, 51
Hannah m Silas Robbins, 122
Han(nah) m Thomas Andreuson, 218
Hannah m William Clark, 227
Harriet E. d Eleazer & Eunice H., 179, 202
Hepzibah m Peter Lay, 70
Hepzibah m John Mather Jr., 86
Hepzibah wife Elijah died, 37
Hepzibah d Jedediah & Tabitha, 70
Horace E. s Ezra & Eunice, 140
Hulda (H) d Darius & Elizabeth, 102
Jane m Benjamin Higgins, 23
Jasper s Joseph Jr. 253
Jasper m Sarah Clark, 253
Jasper s Jasper & Sarah, 253
Jasper Jr. m Phebe Dorr, 69
Jasper s Jasper & Phebe, 69
Jasper had servants Ansell & Prince, 67
Jedediah m Tabatha Person, 252
Jedediah s Elijah & Mehipzibah, 252
Jedediah m Tabitha Ely, 70
Jedediah s Jedidiah & Tabitha, 70

PECK, cont.

Jemima wid. William Peck m John Banning Jr., 24
Jerusha d Daniel & Jerusha, 88
Jerusha d Mather & Azubah, 90
Jesse s Mather & Azubah, 90
John Jr. m Rebeckah Smith, 94
John s John & Rebeckah, 94
John Moore s Darius & Elizabeth, 102
John Sean s Reynold & Deborah, 51
Joseph m Sarah _____, 252, 253
Joseph s Joseph & Sarah, born, died, 252*
Joseph s Joseph & Sarah born, 252*
Joseph Juner m Susanna, 253
Joseph (Grandson) Deacon William & Elizabeth, 253
Joseph s Joseph Jr., 253
Joseph s Nathaniel & Lucy, 11
Joseph s David & Abigail, 48
Joseph s Mather & Esther, 90
Joseph m Sarah Miller, 12
Joseph s Joseph & Sarah, 12
Joseph 3rd m Ann Gilbert, 149
Joseph m Patience Hayes, 33
Joshua W. s Eleazer C. & Eunice H., 179, 308
Juda d Jasper & Sarah, 253
Judeth m John Sears, 63
Judith d William & Judith, 106
Larumy d William & Jemima, 25
Lebbeus m Lydia Lee, 104
Lee s Benjamin & Sarah, 253
Lee m Elizabeth Marvin, 94
Lemuel s Dan & Lovina, 55
Lot m Polley Kent, 89
Louisa M. m Benajah P. Bill, 196
Lovice m Dan Huntley, 127
Lucy m Alfred Lester, 167
Lucy m John Sill, 36
Lucy d John & Rebeckah, 94
Lucy d Mather & Esther, 90
Lucy Burnham d Capt. Matthew & Lois, 134
Luisa died, 215
Luther s Elijah & Mehepzibah, 37, 252
Luther s Elijah & Hephzibah, 37
Maria E. d Ezra & Eunice, 140
Maria E. m William W. J. Warren, 178
Martr d Samuel & Martha, 254
Martha m Peter Person, 254
Martha wid Peter Person, 254
Martha m Ammi Ely, 72
Martin s Darius & Elizabeth, 101
Marion or Mary Ann m Fredrick L.C. Brockway, 194, 209
Mary d Elijah & Hepzebeth, 252*
Mary m Martin Tucker, 33
Mary Coult d Mather & Esther, 90
Mary H. m Jack Miner, 177, 198
Mary Haines d Capt. Matthew & Lois, 134
Mather m wid. Esther Coult, 90
Mather s Mather & Esther, 90
Mather m Rhuiami Howell, 90
Mather m Azubah Watrous, 90
Matthew s Jasper & Phebe, 69
Matthew Capt. m Lois Hall, 134
Meheepsebeth d Elijah & Mehepsebeth, 252
Mehetable d Benjamin & Sarah, 253

INDEX OF PERSONS 369

PECK, cont.
Mehetable m Thomas Lee, 47
Mehitable m Daniel Hall, 15
Mahittable m Nath(anie)l Clark, 140
Miriam d Mather & Esther, 90
Mishail s David & Abigail, 48
Nathaniel s Abner & Caroline, 71
Nathll s Jasper & Sarah, 253
Nathaniel s Lot & Polly, 89*
Nathaniel m Lucy Mather, 11
Natn(ane)ll s Rich(ar)d & Elizabeth, 36
Nathaniel s William & Judith, 106
Oliver s Jasper Jr. & Phebe, 69
Oliver Capt. m Amy Lee, 123
Oliver s of Oliver & Amy, 123
Orin M. s Eleazer C. & Eunice H. 179
Orrin Miller s Ezra & Eunice, 140*
Palmer s Jasper & Phebe, 69*
Palmer s Jasper & Phebe, 69
Parnel d Elijah & Mehepsebeth, 252
Parnall m Roswell Clark, 93
Peter s Elijah & Hepsebeth, 252*
Peter s Elijah & Hepsebeth, 252*
Peter s Elijah & Hepsebeth (Hephzibah), 37
Peter s Jedediah & Tabitha, 70
Phebe m Enoch Reed, 82
Phebe d Jasper Jr. & Phebe, 69
Pheby d Joseph & Sarah, 12
Phebe Dorr d Capt. Matthew & Lois, 134
Polly d Dan & Lovina, 55
Polly m David Caulkins, 135
Polly d Jedediah & Tabitha, 70
Polly d Lebbeus & Lydia, 104
Reynold (Lex. Alarm), 301
Re(y)nold s Jasper & Sarah, 253
Reynold m Deborah Beckwith, 51
Reynolds Marvin s William & Judith, 105
Richard m Elizabeth Mather, 36
Richard s Richard & Elizabeth, 36
Richard Sears s Jasper & Phebe, 69
Reheumah d Mather & Azubah, 90
Ruth d Dan(ie)ll & Jerusha, 89
Ruth m Jasper Griffin, 231
Ruth d Joseph & Sarah, 252
Sally m Nathan Boon, 118
Sally d Reynold & Deborah, 51
Samuell Jr. m Aless Way, 254
Samuell s Sam Junr & Aless, 254
Samuell m Elizabeth Lee, 253
Samuel s Joseph & Sarah, 252
Samuell m Lucretia Ingraham wid. of Francis Ingraham, 25
Samuell m Wid Martha Barbor, 254
Samuel s Samuel, 253
Samuel died, 254*
Samuel Giles s David & Abigail, 48
Sarah d Benjamin & Sarah, 253*
Sarah m Henry Champion Jr., 45
Sarah d Joseph, 252
Sarah d Joseph Jr., 253
Sarah m Matthew Gilbert, 231
Sarah Clark d Jasper & Sarah, 253
Sarah E. d Eleazer C. & Eunice, 179
Seth s John & Rebeckah, 94
Seth L. m Eunice Gallup, 210
Seth M. m Sarah Pierson, 149

PECK, cont.
Silas m Elizabeth Calkins, 20
Silas s Dan & Lovina, 55
Simeon s Darius & Elizabeth, 102
Stephen m Elizabeth Johnson, 130
Stephen s John & Rebeckah, 94
Stephen s Lot & Perry, 89
Susanna d Jasper & Sarah, 253
Thomas s Reynold & Deborah, 51
Thomas B. m Hepzibah S. Tooker, 196, 212
Timothy, 307
Timothy s Darius & Elizabeth, 102
Timothy H. m Irene Gillett, 185
Watrous s Reynold & Deborah, 51
William Deac. died, 253
William s David & Abigail, 48
William s Darius & Elizabeth, 102
William s Elijah & Hepzibah, 37
William s Elijah & Mehepsebeth, 252
William m Eliza Wood, 165
William m Jememah Marvin, 254
William s Joseph & Sarah, 12
William m Judith Marvin, 105
William m Mary Caton, 175
William s Samuel, 253
William s William & Jemimah, 25
William s William died, 25
Wm K.C. s Ezra & Eunice, 140
PECKHAM, Gardiner C. m Caroline Rand, 170
Isaac, 202, 206
Richard Wm s Isaac & Frances, 206
Timothy Jr. m Harriet Rand, 162, 171
PENDAL, Mehetable m Moses Trim, 266
PEREGO, PEREGUE, PERREGO
Abegall d Robert & Marah, 254
Anna (Hanna) d Robert & Marah, 254
Elisabeth d Robert & Marah, 254
Hannah m John Creese, 254
Marah wid of Robert m Henery Petterson, 254*
Mary d Robert & Marah, 254
Norman m Ann Tucker, 193
Robert m Marah Perigo, 254
Robert died, 254*
PERKINS, PIRKINS
Abigail[1] d Abraham & Elizabeth, 82*
Abigail[2] d Abraham & Elizabeth, 82*
Abraham m Elizabeth Ely, 82
Abraham s Abraham & Elizabeth, 82
Abraham (Lex. Alarm), 276, 301, 305
Abraham Jr. (Lex. Alarm), 301, 305
Austin F. m Mary M. Way, 165
Benjamin s Abraham & Elizabeth, 82
Betsey m Charles Ely, 119
Danll s Abraham & Elizabeth, 82
Daniel Champion s John & Hester, 80
David m Eunice Rogers, 119
Eliza Ann m William H. Johnson, 157
Elizabeth d Abraham & Elizabeth, 82
Elizabeth w Abraham died, 82
Elizabeth m Frederick Mather, 45, 82
Elizabeth d James & Margaret, 20
Elizabeth d John & Esther, 80
Elizabeth m Samuel Starlin, 54
Elizabeth m William Ely Jr., 18
Esther d John & Esther, 80
Francis s Abraham & Elizabeth, 82

PERKINS, cont.
Hannah d James & Margaret died, 20*
Hannah d James & Margaret, 20
Henry m Mary Shaw Woodbridge, 136
Henry died, 216
Isaac s James & Margaret, 20
James, 273
James Jr. s James & Margaret, 20
James s James & Margaret, 20*
John s James & Margaret, 20
John m Hester Ayer, 80
John Ayer s John & Esther, 80
Joseph s Abraham & Elizabeth, 82
Joseph s Samuel & Polly, 116
Joseph m Patience Hayes, 33
Lucretia d Samuel & Polly, 116
Lucy d James & Margaret, 20
Lucy d John & Esther, 80
Lydia d James & Margaret, 20
Margaret d James & Margaret, 20*
Polly d Saml & Polly died, 116*
Polly d Saml & Polly born, 116
Rogers s Saml & Polly, 116
Ruth d James & Margaret, 20
Ruth d John & Esther, 80
Samuel s Abraham & Elizabeth, 82
Samuel m Polly Jewitt, 116
Samuel s Samuel & Polly, 116
Sarah d Abraham & Elizabeth, 82
Sarah d James & Margaret, 20
Sarah m Timothy Marvin, 90
Sarah D. m John Platt, 191
Sarah Douglass d Henry & Mary Shaw, 136
Seth s James & Margaret, 20
Seth s John & Hester, 80
Sophia d Samuel & Polly, 116
Stephen s James & Margaret, 20
Stephen s John & Esther, 80
Thomas D., 310
William s Abraham & Elizabeth, 82
Ziporah d John & Hester, 80
PETER (perhaps PETERSON), Marah d John, 254
PETERSON or PETTERSON
Henery m Marah Perigo w Robert, 254
Marah d John, 254
Sarah d Henery & Marah, 254
Sarah m Henry Champion, 225
PHELPS, Benjamin s John Clemment, 56
Benjamin m Rachel Waid, 149
Betsey d Nathan & Jerusha, 86
Charles s John m Elizabeth Tiffany, 7, 255*
David m Nancy Miller, 146
David L. m Delia Slate, 192
Elijah, 301
Phanna d Nathan & Jerusha m Seth Huntley, 86
George Washington m Sally Reed, 159
George N. m Abby Warner, 209
Huldah m Simon Bailey, 147
Jerusha d Nathan & Jerusha, 86
John m Dorothy Rathbun, 7, 255
John s John Clemment, 56
John H., 310
Joseph s Nathan & Jerusha, 86
Maro, 310
Molly, 300
Nancy m Horace Way, 185

PHELPS, cont.
Nathan m Jerusha Wade, 86
Parnal m Gurden Ely, 103
Phebe d Nathan & Jerusha, 86
Rebeckah d Nathan & Jerusha, 86
Roswell, 307
Sally m Jesse Stanard, 155
Samuel, 305
Thaddeus (Lex. Alarm), 301
PHILLIPS, Benjamin, 308
Margaret (Mrs.), 278
Ruth m William Cobb, 178
PICKETT, Mary wid m Capt. Stephen Lee, 241
PICKLES (See FIELDS)
Lorain m Wm Huntley, 155
PIER, Hannah d Thomas, 255
Marry d Thomas, 255
Sarah d Thomas, 255
Thomas s Thomas, 255
PIERCE, Hannah died, 214
PIERPONT, Samuel, Rev. died, 255
PIERSON also PEARSON
Abijah m Meranda Huntley, 153
Peter m Betsey Russell, 189, 208
Phebe m Amos Maxon, 194
Sarah m Seth M. Peck, 149
PIKE, Abigal d William died, 255*
Abegail d William & Abbigall, 255*
Abegail m Henry Bennit Jr., 221
Daniell s William & Abbigall, 255
John s William & Abbigall, 255*
William m Abbigall Comstock, 255
William s William & Abbigall, 255
PILGRIM or PILGRAM
Adaline m John Woodstock, 172
Benjamin s Thomas & Dorcas, 127
Charles m Mary James, 149
Fanny m Edward Josephus Osborn, 169
Frances A. m Samuel S. Alison, 165
James m Frances Hughes, 186
Lydia d Thomas & Dorcas, 127
Mahitabel m A.W. Richardson, 182
Sophia m Lewis Emerson, 168
Thomas m Dorcas Ransom, 127
Thomas J. s Thomas & Dorcas, 127
PLATT, John W. m Sarah Perkins, 191
POLLY, Amos s Amos, 115
PORTER, Edward, Rev. m Dolly Gleason, 112
Francis A. m Harriet Meloney, 171
POST, Ezra Jones m Charlotte Rust, 192
Nancy F. m William Brockway, 160
POWERS, Eunice m Gurdon Avery, 117
Hammond m Clarissa Lewis, 157
PRATT, PRAT, Abigail m John Starling, 12, 263
Almos m Sally Collins, 158
David s Samuel, 255
Desire m Joseph Coult, 56
Elisha m Luranna Robbins, 145
Sarah m Isaac Waterous, 269
Henry G. m Caroline Broadway, 174
James m Nancy Jones, 153
Peter m Elizabeth Griswold, 255
Petter died, 255
Prudence d E. Pratt Esq., 279
Prudence m William Brockway Jr., 223
Samuell m Elizabeth Peck, 255

INDEX OF PERSONS 371

PRATT, cont.
Sarah m Isack Watteras, 269
Timothy m Nancy Saunders, 159
PRENTICE, Chauncey m Caroline Latham, 169
Daniel m Lucretia Smith, 151
Stephen m Mary Clark, 180
Thomas F. m Mariette Dwyer, 191
PRIGH, David m Eunice Lord, 165
PRINCE, Eunice m Andre Griswold, 84
PYNE, Caroline C. m Frederick Richardson, 188
QUINBY, David m Roxanna Spencer, 184, 200
David E. Jr. s David & Roxanna, 200
QUINN, John W. m Sarah Havens, 154
RAINER (see under RAYNER)
RAMON, Benjamin s David & Elizabeth, 107*
David Ramon m Elizabeth Tucker, 107
David s David & Elizabeth, 107
Dorcas d David & Elizabeth, 107
Hetty d David & Elizabeth, 107
Joseph s David & Elizabeth, 107
Richard s David & Elizabeth, 107
RAND, Caroline M. m Gardiner Peckham, 170
Harriet m Timothy Peckham Jr., 162, 170
John W. m Harriet Maria Bailey, 183
Sarah A. m Eleazer Hill, 192
RANDALL, Hannah m Richard Brockway 3rd, 10
Hannah m John Stirling, 177, 200
Lydia m Selden Bartherick, 152
RANSOM, Annasa s George & Anna, 77
Amhurst C. s Edward & Anne, 4
Anna d George & Anna, 78
Azubah d George & Anna, 77
Benjamin (twin) s David & Elizabeth, 107*
Betsey N. m Gurdon Maynard, 194
Catharin d Joseph & Jane, 255
Clarrissa d James Jr. & Elizabeth, 137
Clark s James Jr. & Elizabeth, 137
Danll s Matthew & Sarah, 256
Daniel s Richard & Mary, 64
David m Elizabeth Tucker, 107
David s David & Elizabeth, 107
Dorcas d David & Elizabeth, 107
Dorcas m Thomas Pilgrim, 127
Edward m Ann Tooker, 4
Elias s James Jr. & Elizabeth, 137*
Elisha s Matthew & Sarah, 255
Elisha s Richard & Mary, 64
Eliza d Josef & Charlotte, 130
Elizabeth d Edward & Ann, 4
Elizabeth d James Jr. & Elizabeth, 137
Ellis (Alice) m Dr. Samuel Mather, 97
Esther wid. m Matthew Rogers, 15
Francis d James Jr. & Elizabeth, 137
George s Matthew & Sarah, 255
George m Anna Tiffany, 77
George Washington s George & Anna, 78
Hannah d Richard & Mary, 64
Hannah d Edward & Anne, 4
Henry s James Jr. & Elizabeth, 137
Hetty d David & Elizabeth, 107
Horace s James Jr. & Elizabeth, 137
Irena m Stephen Smith 2nd, 65
Irena d George & Anna, 77
Irena d Matthew & Sarah, 255
Isaac s Edward & Anne, 4
James Jr. m Elizabeth Clark, 137

RANSOM, cont.
James Capt. m Abigail Comstock, 116
Jane d Joseph & Jane, 255
Jane m John Starling, 12
Jane D. m Jonathan T. Mack, 160
Joel Benham s Jose & Charlotte, 130
John s Matthew & Sarah, 255
John s Richard & Mary, 64
Jose m Charlotte Benham, 130
Joseph s Joseph & Jane, 255
Joseph (twin) s David & Elizabeth, 107
Katharine m Samll Lord, 243
Katurah d George & Anna, 77
Loas d Richard & Mary, 64
Louisa d Joel & Charlotte, 64
Lucy d Richard & Mary, 64
Lydia d Matthew & Sarah died, 255*
Lydia d Matthew & Sarah born, 255*
Lydia m Joseph Starlin, 64
Lydia d George & Anna, 77
Lydia Clark d James Jr. & Elizabeth, 137
Lynes s Richard & Mary, 64
Mary d Joseph & Jane, 255
Mary m Peter Huntley, 237
Mary d Richard & Mary, 64
Mary Ann m William Banning, 175, 203
Mathew s Joseph & Jane, 255
Matthew m Sarah Way, 255
Matthew s Matthew & Sarah, 256
Matthew died, 256
Mehetable m Gershom Watrous, 98
Nathan Tiffany s George & Anna, 78
Olive d James Jr. & Elizabeth, 137
Orin s James Jr. & Elizabeth, 137
Patience d Richard & Mary, 64
Phebe d Joseph & Jane, 255
Phebe m Duran Wade, 8
Polly d Edward & Anne, 4
Rachal m Timothy Johnson, 145
Richd s Matthew & Sarah, 255
Richard, 307
Richard m Mary Starlin, 64
Richard s Richard & Mary, 64
Richard s David & Elizabeth, 107
Richard m Mary Miller, 151
Ruth m John Giles, 95
Sally m Samuel Russell, 152
Sarah d George & Anna, 78
Sarah d Richard & Mary, 64
Sarah Ann d James Jr. & Elizabeth, 137
Stephen s Joseph & Jane, 255, 301
Vincent s Joel & Charlotte, 130
William S. m Elisabeth Brockway, 211
RASSON, Anna, 22
James, 22
Rachel d James & Anna, 22
RATHBONE, RATHBUN, RATHBURN, WRATHBONE
Ann m David M. Jewett, 156
Benjamin, 310
Daniel m Thankful Higgins, 2
Diadamey d Daniel & Thankful, 2
Dorothy m John Phelps, 7, 255
Ebenezer s Thomas & Mary, 96
Elizabeth m John Harvey 2nd, 26
John s Thomas & Mary, 96

RATHBONE, cont.
  Mary d Daniel & Thankful, 2
  Mary m Abraham Emmerson, 96
  Norris m Luna Swan, 169
  Sarah m Job Giddings, 32
  Sarah d Daniel & Thankful, 2
  Sarah m Jacob Sawyer Jr., 89
  Sybal m Noah Beebe Jr., 120
  Thomas m Mary Wait, 96
  Thomas s Thomas & Mary, 96
  Thomas m Ann Ingraham, 142
  William s Daniel & Thankful, 2
RAU, Emily m Giles Ingraham, 197
RAY, Prudence m Matthew Cooley, 133
RAYMOND, RAYMENT, RAMENT
  Adaline C. m Junius Marvin, 193, 211
  Daniell m Rebekah Laye, 256
  Jane Gray m James R. Morgan, 186
  Martha m Horace Wait, 138
  Mary Ann m William Stark, 167
  Mehetable d Edwd m Moses Warren Jr., 38
  Richard s Daniell & Rebekah, 256
  Sophia died, 214
RAYNER, RAINER
  Diedamia d Josia & Sarah, 256
  Ebenezer s Josia & Sarah, 256
  Elishabe s Josia & Sarah, 220, 256
  John s Josia & Sarah, 256
  Joseph s Josia & Sarah, 256
  Josiah s Josia & Sarah, 256
  Sarah d Josia & Sarah, 256
  Siurll (Sybil) s Josia & Sarah, 256
REED, READ, Abigail d Joseph & Phebe, 129
  Animaaz (Anniaus) s Jonathan & Elizabeth, 257
  Benjamin m Sarah_____, 256
  Benjamin s John & Deborah, 256
  Betsey m William Watrous, 128
  Betsey m Charles D. Williams, 175
  Calvin m Deborah Benjamin, 183
  Caraline d Benjamin & Sarah, 256
  Caroline d Enoch & Phebe, 82
  Caroline m Abner Peck, 71
  Caroline d Joseph & Phebe, 129
  Charles Williams s Joseph & Phebe, 129
  Daniel s Jonathan & Elizabeth, 257
  Elizabeth d John Jr. & Mary, 256
  Elizabeth wife John died, 256
  Elizabeth wife Jonathan died, 256
  Elizabeth d John Jr. & Mary, 256
  Elizabeth d Jonathan & Elizabeth, 257
  Emelia d Joseph & Phebe, 129
  Enoch s Benjamin & Sarah, 256
  Enoch m Phebe Peck, 82
  George, 213
  Henry s Joseph & Phebe, 129, 213
  Hepzibah d Enoch & Phebe, 82
  James, 206
  James s John Jr. & Mary, 256
  John m Debrah Niles, 256
  John s John & Debrah, 256*
  John Jr. m Mary Welch, 256
  John s John Jr. & Mary, 256
  John died, 256
  John s Enoch & Phebe, 82
  John s Joseph & Phebe, 129
  Jonathan s John & Debrah, 256

REED, cont.
  Jonathan m Elizabeth Mack, 256
  Jonathan s Jonathan & Elizabeth, 256
  Jonathan m Widow Elizabeth Smith, 256
  Jonathan m Abigail Comstock, 53
  Jonathan s Jonathan & Abigail, 53
  Joseph s Enoch & Phebe, 82
  Joseph m Phebe Reed, 129
  Laura twin with Nancy d Joseph & Phebe, 129
  Lucy d James & Emaline, 206
  Lydia B. m Abel L. Huntley, 160
  Lynde, Capt. 306
  Marah d John & Debrah, 256
  Margret twin with Mindewell d Benjamin & Sarah, 256
  Margaret m Capt. Thomas Anderson, 38
  Margreet wid. Ahimaz m Ezekiel Miner, 100
  Mary m Jasper Griffing, 74
  Mary m George Lewis, 55
  Mary d Enoch & Phebe, 82
  Mary Ann Phebe m Alpheas Thompson, 118
  Mary E. m Joseph W. Huntley, 169
  Mary or Polly Reed died, 213
  Mary Reed widow of George died, 213
  Mindewell twin with Marg(a)ret d Benjamin & Sarah, 256
  Nancy twin with Laura d Joseph & Phebe, 129
  Nathanyell s Joseph & Deborah, 256
  Nathaniel s Jonathan & Elizabeth, 257
  Pheby d Jonathan & Elizabeth, 257
  Phebe m Selden P. Marvin, 161
  Phebe m Joseph Reed, 129
  Rebeckah d Enoch & Phebe, 82
  Richard died, 213
  Ruth A. m John A. Russ, 171
  Sally d Joseph & Phebe, 129
  Sally m George Washington Phelps, 159
  Sarah d Benjamin & Sarah, 256
  Suse d Jonathan & Elizabeth (Sarah?), 257
REEVES, REEVE, REIVES
  Anne d Luther & Anne, 104
  Benjamin s Luther & Anna, 104
  Benj(ami)n m Patty Sill, 138
  Han(n)ibal m Eliza H. Latimer, 141
  Hannabal s Luther & Anna, 104
  Julia d Benjamin & Patty, 138
  Lucian Bonaparte s Benjamin & Patty, 138
  Luther m Anna Person, 104
  Mehetable m William Ely Pearson, 124
  Polley d Luther & Anna, 104
  Rumsey s Luther & Anna, 104
  Sarah Ann d Benjamin & Patty, 138
  Sarepta d Luther & Anna, 104
REMICK, Mercy m Capt. Joseph Higgins, 5
REYNOLDS, RENOLDS
  Abigail m James Blague, 8
  Ann Maria m Joseph Sanders, 181
  Henry B. L., 203, 206
  John, 310
  John J. m Betsey Wade, 167
  Lydia m Seth Ely, 62
  Nancy Elizabeth d Henry & Temperance, 203
  William H. s Henry B.S. & Temperance, 206
  William, 306
RHODES, Phebe m Gideon Waterhous, 129
  Phebe m Gideon Watrous 2nd, 135

RICE - see - ROYCE
 Adaline m Jonathan Buck, 183
 Elisha s Nehemiah & Abigail, 38
 Jonathan s Nehemiah & Abigail, 38
 Lydia d Nehemiah & Abigail, 38
 Nehemiah m Abigail Gustin, 38
 Ruel s Nehemiah & Abigail, 38
 Ruth m Daniell Beckwith, 219*
 Samuel s Nehemiah & Abigail, 38
RICH, Mary m Albert James, 154
RICHARDSON, A. W. m Mehetabel Pilgrim, 182
 Elizabeth Jane m Ezra M. Champion, 169, 205
 Frederick G. m Caroline C. Pyne, 188
 Nancy S. m Orlando Champion, 179
ROBBINS, ROBINS
 Abby m Charles M. Havens, 175, 198
 Abigail d Elisha & Elizabeth, 101
 Abner s Silas & Hannah, 122
 Alden s Benjamin & Hannah, 64
 Benjamin m Hannah Bradford, 64
 Benjamin s Benjamin & Hannah, 64
 Betsey m Ezra Ingraham, 100
 Bettey d John & Esther, 48
 Birnhall s William & Esther, 8
 Bradford s Benjamin & Hannah, 64
 Daniel s Ezra & Elizabeth, 59
 David s Benjamin & Hannah, 64
 Edward s John & Elizabeth, 257
 Edward died, 257
 Edward s John & Esther, 48
 Edward m Ruth Smith d of John, 257
 Elijah s Joseph & Mary, 39
 Elijah s Benjamin & Hannah, 64
 Elisha s Joseph & Mary, 39
 Ellsha m Elizabeth Tinker, 101
 Elisha s Elisha & Elizabeth, 101
 Elisha s Elisha & Elizabeth born, 101
 Elisha m Lydia Cooley, 101
 Elisha m Amanda Howard, 146
 Elisha Sheffield s Elisha & Elizabeth, 101
 Elizabeth m Thomas Smith, 263
 Elizabeth d Joseph & Mary, 39
 Elizabeth d Elisha & Elizabeth, 101
 Elizabeth wife Elisha died, 101*
 Emeline m Richard Denison, 192, 205
 Emily S. m John Appleby, 178, 201
 Easter d Joseph & Sarah, 257
 Esther d William Jr. & Esther, 8
 Eunice d Joseph & Mary, 39
 Eunice d Elisha & Elizabeth, 101
 Evans s Benjamin & Hannah, 64
 Ezra s Joseph & Mary, 39
 Ezra m Elizabeth Anderson, 58
 Ezra s Ezra & Elizabeth, born, died, 59
 Ezra s Ezra & Elizabeth born, 59
 Hannah d Benjamin & Hannah, 64
 Henry m Sarah M. Cone, 195, 211
 Jeane formerly wife John Tillotson died, 257
 Jean Lay d Ezra & Elizabeth, 58
 Jemima d William & Esther, 8
 Jerusha d Edward & Ruth, 257
 Jerusha m Jesse Beckwith, 40
 John s Benjamin & Hannah, 64
 John s Edward & Ruth, 257
 John m Elizabeth_____, 237
 John m Esther Beckwith, 48

ROBBINS, cont.
 John m Ruth Alger, 257
 John s Silas & Hannah, 122*
 Joseph s Elisha & Lydia, 101
 Joseph s Ezra & Elizabeth, 58
 Joseph m Mary Lay, 39
 Joseph m Sarah (Waterhouse), 257
 Joseph Jr. s Joseph & Sarah, 257
 Joshua s Benjamin & Hannah, 64
 Lucia m Joseph Tubbs, 26
 Lucretia d Nathan & Phebe, 48
 Lucy d Joseph & Sarah, 257
 Lucy d Ezra & Elizabeth, 59
 Lura d Silas & Hannah, 122
 Luranna m Elisha Pratt, 145
 Lidea d Joseph & Sarah, 257
 Lydia d Elisha & Lydia, 101
 Lydia d Nathan & Phebe, 48
 Lydia d William & Esther, 8
 Lydia m John Huntley Jr., 236
 Martha died, 214
 Mary d Elisha & Elizabeth, 101
 Mehetable d Joseph & Sarah, 257
 Nathan s Edward & Ruth, 257
 Nathan m Phebe Beckwith, 47
 Nathan (twin) s Nathan & Phebe, 48*
 Phebe d Ezra & Elizabeth, 59
 Phebe (Twin) d Nathan & Phebe, 48
 Phebe d William Jr. & Esther, 8
 Phebe d Silas & Hannah, 122
 Reuben s William & Esther, 8
 Rufus s Nathan & Phebe, 47
 Rufus died, 48
 Rufus s Silas & Hannah, 122
 Ruth m Edward White, 271
 Ruth d Edward & Ruth, 257
 Ruth m Elisha Minor, 48
 Ruth wid of Edward m John Lay, 2, 39
 Ruth wife of John died, 16, 257
 Ruth d John & Esther, 48
 Ruth (wid) m John Mather, 16
 Ruth d Joseph & Sarah, 257
 Sarah d Benjamin & Hannah, 64
 Sarah d Joseph & Sarah, 257*
 Sarah d Joseph & Sarah, 257
 Sarah m Peter Huntley, 238
 Silas s Nathan & Phebe, 47
 Silas m Hannah Peck, 122
 Susa wife Daniel died, 86
 Theody d Ezra & Elizabeth, 59
 Thomas Anderson s Elisha & Lydia, 101
 William Jr. m Esther Huntley, 8
 William s William & Esther, 8
 William s Elisha & Lydia, 101
 Zenas s Nathan & Phebe, 48
ROBERSON, ROBESON
 Ephandites s Harvy & Martha, 118
 Harvy m Martha Fellows, 118
 Marah d William, 257
 William s Martha, 257*
 William Fellows s Harvy & Martha, 118
ROBERTS, ROBERT
 Ebenezer L. m Clara R. Bacon, 188, 208
ROCKWELL, Lothrop m Lucy Osborn, 142
ROGERS, Abel m Hannah Rogers, 103
 Abel Moore s Abel & Hannah, 103

ROGERS, cont.
Abi m Ebeneazer Darrow, 228
Abijah s Matthew & Loas, 15
Ales d Jonathan & Ales m Jacob Sullard, 257, 264
Alice wid. Jonathan died, 26
Betsey m Calvin Huntley, 160
Bettey d Joseph & Diadamy, 17
Bettey d Ebenezer & Elizabeth, 40
Caleb s Ezekiel & Phebe, 42*
Carolina d Mather & Sally, 134
Caroline M. m Charles E.L. Brockway, 188
Catharine m Epaphrodeitus Miller, 173
Charles W. m Caroline A. Dean, 186
Charlotte A. m Thomas S. Swan, 184
Christopher s Abel & Hannah, 103
Daniel s Daniel & Sarah, 29*
Daniel s Ezekiel & Phebe, 41*
Daniel s Jonathan & Lydia, 61
Daniel s Rowland & Elizabeth, 22
Daniel m Sarah Fox, 29*
Daniel s Susan Thompson alias Rogers, 141*
Daniel G. m Lucy Ann Otis, 166
David[1] s Ezekiel & Phebe, 42
David[2] s Ezekiel & Phebe, 42
David m Betsey Chadwick, 123
David s Susan Thompson alias Rogers, 141
Deborah m Thomas Monsell, 251
Deborah d Roland & Lucretia, 56
Diadama d Joseph & Diadamy, 17
Ebenezer m Elizabeth Mather, 40
Ebenezer s Abel & Hannah, 103
Ebenezer m Elizabeth Hide, 40
Elias s Joshua & Phebe, 80
Elijah s Matthew & Esther, 15
Elijah m Hannah Beckwith, 135
Elisha s Matthew & Esther, 15
Elisha s Rowland & Elizabeth, born, died, 22*
Eliza d Rowland & Elizabeth, 22
Eliza m Gideon M. Rogers, 157
Elizabeth d Abel & Hannah, 103
Elizabeth wife Ebenezer died, 40*
Elizabeth m Ezra Selden, 34, 67
Elizabeth m Silas Wood, 28
Elizabeth wife Rowland died, 150
Erastus m Delight (Judd), 147
Erastus m Anna C. Beebe, 170
Esther d Mather & Sally, 134
Eunice m Abijah Mack, 88
Eunice m David Perkins, 119
Eunice m Jasper Griffing Jr., 52
Eunice d Joshua & Experience, 44
Eunice d Matthew & Loas, 15
Experience wife Joshua died, 44*
Ezekiel s David & Betsey, 123
Ezekiel s Ezekiel & Phebe, 41
Ezekiel s Jonathan & Ales, 257
Ezekiel m Mary Beckwith, 148
Ezekiel m Phebe Bramble, 41
Ezekiel Sr. died, 42
Ezra s Joshua & Phebe, 80
Ezra s Lemuel & Hannah, 77
Fanna d Rowland & Elizabeth, 22
Fanny m Roger Griswold, 131
Fanny m Samuel Chadwick, 167
Jemimah (Jemima) m Matthew Cooley, 228

ROGERS, cont.
Gideon, 305
Gideon s Ebenezer & Elizabeth, 40
Gideon m Lucy Ackley, 64
Gideon 2nd m Eliza Rogers, 157
Gideon Mather s Abel & Hannah, 103
Hannah m Abel Rogers, 103
Hannah d Abel & Hannah, 103
Hannah d Ebenezer & Elizabeth, 40
Hannah d Lt. Joseph & Sarah m John Lord, 28, 146
Hannah d Lemuel & Hannah, 77
Hannah m Nathaniel Roland, 65
Hannah wid. m Robert Sanders, 99
Hannah m Thomas M. Smith, 146
Henry Newell s Ezekiel & Mary, 148
Huldah d Matthew & Loas, 15
Huldah m William Dessent Hockridge, 126
James Ackley s Gideon & Lucy, 64
Jason m Abbey A. Maynard, 152
Jemima d Joshua & Lydia, 44*
Jemima d Jonathan & Lydia, 61
Jemima d Rowland & Elizabeth, 22
Jamimah m William Clark, 131
Jerusha d Jonathan & Ales, 257
John s David & Betsey, 123
John s Ezekiel & Phebe, 42
John s Roland & Lucretia, 56
John Jr. m Harriet Huntley, 145
John m Hannah Chapman, 173
John E. m Sarah M. Chapel, 159
John S. Dr. m Matilda Lord, 145
John Sill s Gideon & Lucy, 64
Jonathan m Ales Champion, 257
Jonathan s Jonathan & Ales, 257
Jonathan died, 257
Jonathan s Joseph & Diadamy, 17
Jonathan m Lydia Watrous, 61
Jonathan Mack s Matthew & Loas, 15
Joseph s Abel & Hannah, 103
Joseph m Diadamy Beckwith, 17
Joseph s Joseph & Diadamy, 17
Joseph s Jonathan & Ales, 257
Joseph Lieut., 28
Joseph died, 17
Joshua m Experience Lamphear, 44
Joshua s Joshua & Experience, 44
Joshua s Ezekiel & Phebe, 42
Joshua m Lydia Minor, 44
Joshua died, 44*
Joshua m Phebe Fox, 80
Joshua s Roland & Elizabeth, 22
Josiah s Joshua & Experience, 44
Josiah Nelson s Ezekiel & Mary, 148
Judeth m Timothy Lester, 85
Lavina d Jonathan & Lydia, 61
Leammy (Leoramy) d Ezekiel & Phebe, 41
Lemuel m Hannah Miller, 77
Lemuel s Lemuel & Hannah, 77
Leoamy m Stephen Chadwick, 107
Lois d Joshua & Experience, 44
Loas d Matthew & Loas, 15
Lois wife of Matthew died, 15*
Lovice d Joseph & Diadamy, 17
Lucina m Diadate G. Wilson, 162
Lucretia (Lucresia) d Jonathan & Ales, 257

INDEX OF PERSONS

ROGERS, cont.
Lucretia m Roland Rogers, 56, 276, 277
Lucretia m Joseph Jewit (t), 56
Lucy m Similius Lord, 153
Lucy died, 215
Lydia d Ezekiel & Phebe, 41
Lydia d Jonathan & Lydia, 61
Lydia d Rowland & Elizabeth, 22
Mary d Joshua & Experience, 44
Mary d Ezekiel & Phebe, 42
Mather m Sally Wickes, 134
Matthew s Joseph & Diadamy, 17
Matthew m Loas Mack, 15
Matthew s Matthew & Loas, 15
Matthew m wid. Esther Ransom, 15
Molley d Jonathan & Lydia, 61
Moses s Roland & Lucretia, 56
Nabba d Jonathan & Lydia, 61
Nathan s Lemuel & Hannah, 77
Niles S., 310
Peter Beckwith s Ezekiel & Mary, 148
Phebe d Ezekiel & Phebe, 41
Polly d Mather & Sally, 134
Polly m Matthew Gee, 142
Rebeca m David Andrews, 153
Rebecca (twin Rowland) d Rowland & Elizabeth, 22*
Rhoda d Joseph & Diadamy, 17
Rhoda d Matthew & Lois, 15
Rhoda m Samuel Hudson, 123
Richard s Ebenezer & Elizabeth, 40
Robert s Lemuel & Hannah, 77
Roland m Elizabeth Rogers, 150
Roland m Lucretia Rogers, 56
Roland s Roland & Lucretia, 56
Roland s Joshua & Lydia, 44
Rowland m Elizabeth Champion, 22
Rowland (twin Rebecca) s Rowland & Elizabeth, 22
Sally d Mather & Sally, 134
Sally M. m Darius Harding, 161
Samuel m Betsey Chap(p)el, 149
Sarah d Daniel & Sarah, 29
Sarah d Ezekiel & Phebe, 41
Sarah d John m Jonathan Gilbert, 70
Sarah d Jonathan & Ales, 257
Sarah d Jonathan & Lydia, 61
Sarah d Lemuel & Hannah died, 77
Sarah d Lemuel & Hannah born, 77
Sarah m David Mack, 24
Sarah m Ezra Rowland, 65
Sarah m Matthew Smith, 263
Sarah m Watrous B. Smith, 153
Selden s Gideon & Lucy, 64
Selden m Betsey Huntley, 148
Seth s Gideon & Lucy, 64
Silvester s Gideon & Lucy, 64
Stephen s Jonathan & Ales, 257
Susan alias Thompson had sons, Daniel & David Rogers, 141
Susannah d Abel & Hannah, 103
Sylvester see Silvester
Ursula d Joshua & Phebe, 80
William s Ezekiel & Phebe, 42*
William Ely s Elijah & Hannah, 135
William Wanton s Jonathan & Lydia, 61

ROLING, Hannah m John Hudson, 234
ROSS, Esther m William Champion, 126
Henry m Lucretia Dart, 208
ROWLAND, ROLAND, ROULIN, ROULING, ROULEN
Abby m Martin Lester, 156
Abby G. m Andrew Ure Jr., 180
Amos s Henry Jr. & Phebe, 97
Anna d Rich'd & Jerusha, 86
Anne m Lynde Champen, 113
Asall s Richard & Rebeckah, 258
Asel m Zipporah Waller, 258
Asael m Anna Walker, 60
Asael m Wid. Mary Champen, 60, 76
Asahel Jr. m Hannah Greenfield, 115
Asahel s Asahel & Hannah, 115
Asahel m Abby Greenfield, 158
Azuba d Uriah & Lydia, 258
Azubah m John Hayes, 85
Benjamin s Richard & Rebeckah, 258
Benjamin m Eunice Wade, 259
Benjamin s George & Freelove, 91
Carolina d Asahel & Hannah, 115
Caroline m Seth Chadwick, 161
Catharine d Rich'd & Jerusha, 86
Dan'll s Richard & Jerusha, 86
Daniel s Uriah & Lydia, 258
Edward s Uriah & Lydia, 258
Edward s Evi, 127
Elizabeth d Asel & Zipporah, 258*
Elizabeth d Asel & Zipporah, 258*
Elizabeth d John & Hannah, 259
Elizabeth d Henery & Temprance, 258
Elizabeth d Henry & Irene, 28
Elizabeth m William DeWolf, 76
Eunice d Benja & Eunice, 259
Eunice d Rich'd & Jerusha, 86
Ezra m Lucy Champion, 66
Ezra m Sarah Rogers, 65
Fanny d Nath'll & Hannah, 65
Francis child of Henery & Temprance, 258*
George (Lex. Alarm), 301
George s Benjamin & Eunice died, 259*
George s Benjamin & Eunice born, 259*
George m Freelove Daviss, 91
George s George & Freelove, 91
George s William G. & Mary Ann, 204
Hannah d Asel & Zipporah, 258
Hannah d John & Hannah died, 259*
Hannah d John & Hannah born, 259*
Hannah m John Hudson, 234
Hannah d Richard & Rebeckah, 258
Hannah relict of Rich'd died, 38
Hannah m William Youngs, 146
Henery m Temprance, 258
Henery s Henery & Temprance, 258
Henery s Asel & Zipporah, 258
Henry m Irene Palmer, 28*
Henry s Henry & Irene, 28*
Henry Jr. m Phebe Huntley, 97
Hepzibah d Asel & Zipporah, 258
Irene d Henry & Irene, 28
Isaac Daviss s George & Freelove, 91
Jesse s Asael & Mary, 60
John m Hannah Anderson, 259
John s Henery & Temprance, 258

ROWLAND, cont.
John[1] s John & Hannah, 259*
John[2] s John & Hannah, 259*
John L. s William G. & Mary Loisa, 204
John Greenfield s Asahel & Hannah, 115
Lucretia m Abner Huntley, 49
Lucy d Asel & Zipporah, 258
Lydia d Uriah & Lydia died, 2
Lydia 2nd d Uriah & Lydia, 2*, 258
Mabell d Richard & Rebeckah, 258
Mabel m Benjamin Hudson, 234
Marah d Richard & Rebeckah, 258
Maria m Gurdon Hungerford, 145
Maria d Matt & Sally, 120
Martha d Ezra & Lucy, 66
Martha d Rich'd & Jerusha, 86
Mary d Asahel & Hannah, 115
Mary d Benja & Eunice, 259
Mary d George & Freelove, 91
Mary A. m Charles Chadwick, 160
Mary Ann m John Macrary, 144
Mary Ann m Valentine Miller, 178
Matthew born, 72
Matthew m Sally DeWolf, 120
Molly d Uriah & Lydia, 258
Nathaniel m Hannah Rogers, 65
Nicalus s John & Hannah, 259
Palmer s Henry Jr. & Phebe, 97
Perthene d Richd & Jerusha, 86
Parthena m Josiah Smith Jr., 37
Pacianes d Henery & Temprance, 258
Pheby d Uriah & Lydia, 2, 258
Phebe m Benjamin Marvin Jr., 75
Rebeckah d Asel & Zipporah, 259
Rebeckah d Benja & Eunice, 259
Rebeckah d Richard & Rebeckah, 258
Rebeckah m John Borden, 222
Richard m Rebecka_____, 258
Richard s Richard & Rebeckah, 258
Richard m Hannah Greenfield, 259
Richd s Benja & Eunice, 259
Richard m Jerush Chadwick, 86
Richard s Richd & Jerusha, 86
Richard s Matthew & Sally, 120
Sally d Nathaniel & Hannah, 65
Sally d Ezra & Sarah, 65
Sally wife Ezra died, 65*
Sary d Henery & Temprance, 258
Sarah d John & Hannah, 259
Shaler s Richard & Jerusha, 86
Silvester s Nathll & Hannah, 65
Stephen L. m Lydia Havens, 164
Susannah d Asel & Zipporah, 258
Susannah widow m Samuel Loveland, 244
Susannah m Zechariah Sill Jr., 62
Temperance d John & Hannah, 259
Temprance d Henery & Temprance, 258
Temprance m Hue Grilley, 24
Thankfull d John & Hannah, 259*
Uriah s Richard & Rebeckah, 258
Uriah m Lydia Lee, 2, 258
William s Uriah & Lydia, 2, 258
William m Eunice Tinker, 53
William s George & Freelove, 91
William G. m Mary Lester, 179, 204

ROWLAND, cont.
William G. m Mary Ann, 204
Zipporah wife Asel died, 259
ROWLEY, Abner, 122
Abner m Anne Wade, 122, 128
Anna d Abner & Anne, 122
Anna wife of Abner died, 122
Joseph s Abner & Anne, 122
Lydia d Abner & Anna, 122, 128
Sarah Ann m Watson Clark, 155
Thomas s Abner & Anne or Anna, 122, 128
ROWTH, Lydia m Ulyssus McCrery, 164
ROYCE (see RICE)
Albert m Frances Fidelia Beckwith, 178
David m Elizabeth Forsyth, 160
David, 308
David G. m Eunice B. Beebe, 153
Emiline m Moses Wright, 177
Harriet D. m Thomas Chamberlain, 194
Horace B. m Lucretia Hughes, 185
Laura A. m Andrew Lathrop, 185
Richard m Eunice Ames, 120
Richard m Sally Mather, 159
Ruel, 308
Sally Cleveland m John Mather Jr., 132
RUBEY
Christopher s Thomas & Phebe Bennet, 59
Rhoda d Thomas & Phebe Bennet, 59
Thomas m Phebe Bennet Sawyer, 59
Thomas s Thomas & Phebe, 59
RUSS, ROSS, John A. m Ruth A. Reed, 171
RUSSELL, Betsey m Peter Pierson, 189, 208
Elizabeth Z. m Elihu Chadwick, 141
Mary m George Niles, 156
Samuel m Sally Ransom, 152
RUST, Charlotte m Ezra Jones Post, 192
RYON, Eliza Caroline d Pardon & Rebecca, 115
Emmeline d Pardon & Rebecca, 115
Fanny Almena d Pardon & Rebecca, 115
Harriot W. d Pardon & Rebecca, 114
Ichabod m Maria Morgan, 170
James s Pardon & Rebecca, 114
Julia m Charles Spencer, 150
Mary m Joseph Brooks, 150
Maryette d Pardon & Rebecca, 114
Mercyann d Pardon & Rebecca, 114
Pardon m Rebecca Minor, 114*
Pardon s Pardon & Rebecca, 114
Rebecca wife of Pardon died, 114*
SABINS, Margret m Robert Otis, 35
SALTER, Margaret O. m James Lombard, 184, 199
SAMPSON
Bartlett P. m Frances Crocker, 188, 209
Solomon m Elizabeth W. Clark, 144
SANDERS, SAUNDERS
Almira d Nathan & Jerusha, 137
Amos s William & Mehitabel, 139
Hannah m Joseph Waid, 133
Hannah d William & Mehetable, 139
Hannah m Hezekiah Cosford, 183
Jean d Robert & Hannah, 99
John, 300
John s Samuell Jr., 259
Joseph m Ann Maria Reynolds, 181
Lydice d Nathan & Jerusha, 137
Nathan m Jerush Maynard, 137

INDEX OF PERSONS 377

SANDERS, cont.
Phebe d Nathan & Jerusha, 137
Robert m Wid. Hannah Rogers, 99
Ruhama d Samuel Jr., 259
Sanford s Simeon & Hannah, 6
Simeon & wife Hannah, 6
W. Palmer s Nathan & Jerusha, 137
SAUNDUS, SANDERS
Albert s Samuel & Phebe, 27
Amelia A. m Daniel E. Dodge Jr., 192, 209
Asa s Elisha & Mary, 147
Asa s Samuel & Phebe, 27
Betsey m Eleazer Spencer, 171, 197
Caroline m John King, 155
Christopher Palmer s Samuel & Phebe, 27
Emily m Ira Watrous, 171
Hannah d Samuel & Phebe, 27
James F. m Marietta Crowell, 184
John (Lex. Alarm), 301
Joshua (Lex. Alarm), 301
Nancy m Timothy Pratt, 159
Nathan s Samuel & Phebe, 27
Phebe[1] d Samuel & Phebe, 27
Phebe[2] d Samuel & Phebe, 27
Samll (so called) s Sibbel Fox, 27
Samuel s Samuel & Phebe, 27
Samuel Jr. m Julia Ann Huntley, 156
Sanford s Simeon & Hannah, 6
Timothy, 300
William s Samuel & Phebe, 27
SAWYER, SAWER, Amy m Silas Bramble, 148
Asa s Jacob & Rose, 89
Betsey d Ephm & Jemimah, 87
Charles, 310
David s Ephm & Jemimah, 87
Desire d Jacob & Sarah, 89
Diadama d Jacob & Sarah, 89
Elias s Jacob & Martha, 260
Elisha M. m Ursula Brainard, 179
Elizabeth A. m Chas Harison, 148
Ephraim m Jemimah Hill, 87
Ephraim twin with Jemimah s Ephraim & Jemimah, 87*
Huldah d Jesse & Sarah, 54
Jacob m Martha Loomer, 259
Jacob m Rose Bennet, 89
Jacob s Jacob & Rose, 89
Jacob Jr. m Sarah Wrathbone, 89
James m Hezediah Bartlet, 259
James s Jacob & Martha, 260
Jemimah (twin with Ephraim) d of Ephriam & Jemimah, 87*
John s Jacob & Rose, 89
John s Ephm & Jemimah, 87
Laura m James Bogue, 161, 205
Lucy (twin with Sarah) d Jacob & Sarah, 89
Lydia m Joseph Huntley, 77
Martin m Eunice A. Tinker, 190, 209
Martha d Jacob & Martha, 260
Matthew s Jacob & Rose, 89
Patty m Henry Harrison, 154
Phebe d Jacob & Rose, 89
Phebe Bennet m Thomas Rubey, 59
Polly d Ephm & Jemimah, 87
Polly m Henry Harrison, 154
Samuel S. m Frances Gulliver 196

SAWYER, cont.
Sarah Ward d James & Hezediah, 259
Sarah m Ithamer Smith, 76
Sarah (twin with Lucy) d Jacob & Sarah, 89
Stephen (Lex. Alarm), 301
Temperance d Ephm & Jemimah, 87
Thankfull d Jacob & Sarah, 89
Zeruiah m David Carpender Smith, 69
SAYER, Jacob m Martha Loomer, 259
James s Jacob & Martha, 260
Martha d Jacob & Martha, 260
Mary m William Sterling, 264
SCOVELL, SCOVEL, SCOVIL, SCOFEL, SCOFFEL, SCOFFELL, SCOFIL, SCOHOFEL, SCHOFELL, SCHOLFELL, SHOFEL
Abigail, 274
Arter m Rachell, 260
Arter s Arter & Rachel (Rachall Hudson 2nd m), 260
Arter died, 260*
Arter m Elizabeth, 260
Arter s James & Elizabeth, 260
Elisabeth d Arter & Elizabeth, 260
Elisabeth d James, 260
Elisabeth m Lemuel Tubbs, 72
Elizabeth m Jeames Tileson, 265
Esther d John & Sarah, 9
Irane m Darius Harden, 131
Irene d James & Elizabeth, 260
Isaac s James & Elizabeth, 260
Jeames s Arter & Rachel, 260*
Jeames s Arter & Elizabeth, 260*
James m_____, 260
John m Sarah Alger, 260
Luce m Benajah Ames, 88
Rachel w Arter, 235
Rhoda d James, 260
Sarah d Stephen & Sarah, 260
Sarah m John Brockway 2nd, 223
Sebbel d James, 260*
Sebbel d James & Elisabeth, 260*
Sibel d James & Elisabeth, 260
Stephen m Sarah Champion, 260
Stephen s Stephen & Sarah, 260
SEARS, Bettey d John & Judith, 63
Elisabeth d John & Elizabeth, 260
Jasper Peck s John & Judith, 63
John m Elizabeth Watrous, 260
John s John & Elizabeth, 260
John m Judith Peck, 63
John died, 63
Mary d John & Elisabeth, 260
Mary m John Denison Jr., 71
Richd s John & Elizabeth, 260
Richard s John & Judith, 63
Seth s John & Elizabeth, 260
SELDEN, Abigail d Ezra & Elizabeth, 34
Ame d Ezra & Ame, 34
Ame wife of Ezra died, 34
Asenath d Richd & Desier, 8
Calvin s Ezra & Elizabeth, 34
Calvin Lt. m Phebe Ely, 109
Charles s Samuel & Elizabeth, 14
Charles s Elijah & Eunice, 103
Deborah d Saml & Elizabeth, 14

SELDEN, cont.
Dorothy d Saml & Elizabeth, 14
Dorothy m Silden Warner, 113
Elijah (Lex. Alarm), 301, 305
Elijah s Samll & Elizabeth, 14
Elijah m Eunice Comstock, 103
Elijah s Elijah & Eunice, 103
Elijah m Hannah Tracy, 103
Elisha s Ezra & Ame, 34
Eliza m Elihu Geer, 192
Elizabeth d Ezra & Elizabeth, 34
Elizabeth wife Ezra died, 34
Elizabeth d Samuel & Elizabeth, 14
Erastus s Ezra & Ame, 34
Erastus m Laura Comstock, 168
Esther d Samll & Elizabeth, 14
Eunice d Elijah & Eunice, 103
Eunice wife of Elijah died, 103
Exra s Calvin & Phebe, 109
Ezra, 273
Ezra Capt., 305
Ezra s Elijah & Eunice, 103
Ezra m Elizabeth Rogers, 34
Ezra s Ezra & Elizabeth, 34
Ezra m Ame Ely, 34
Ezra m Hannah Marvin, 34, 276
George s Saml & Elizabeth, 14
Gurdon s Ezra & Elizabeth, 34
Hannah wife of Ezra, 273, 276
Hannah m Moses Noyes, 29
Jemima d Samll & Elizabeth, 14
John Erastus born, 162
Joseph m Caroline Lord, 185
Joseph Dudley s Saml & Elizabeth, 14
Juliana d Richard Ely & Desier, 8
Henry s Daniel & Maria Spencer, 146
Lois (widow), 274
Lucretia d Ezra & Ame, 34
Lura d Elijah & Eunice, 103
Maria K. m Joseph Holmes, 182
Mary d Saml & Elizabeth, 14
Mary m Capt. Abner Lord Jr., 109
Mehetable m Dan Marvin, 95
Rebeckah d Ezra & Ame, 34
Reynold Marvin s Saml & Sarah, 82
Richard Ely s Samll & Elizabeth, 14
Richard Ely m Desier Coult, 8
Roger s Saml & Elizabeth, 14
Roxana d Lt. Calvin & Phebe, 109
Samuel Capt. died, 13, 303, 305, 306, 308
Samuel m Elizabeth Ely, 14
Samuel s Samuel & Elizabeth, 14
Saml Jr. m Sarah Marvin, 82
Samuel Col. died, 14*, 305
Samuel Rogers s Ezra & Elizabeth, 34
Sarah wife Samuel died, 82
Theophilus Rogers s Ezra & Elizabeth, 34
_____s Elijah & Eunice, 103
SELF, Jemima m William Lane, 143
SELLARD (see SULLARD)
SEWIA, John H. died, 214
SHEFFELIN, Edward L. died, 216
SHELDEN, SHELDON
Asa Jr. m Christiana Waterhouse, 174
Elisha Capt. m Elizabeth Ely, 5
Elisha s Capt. Elisha & Elizabeth, 5

SHELDEN, cont.
Jane m John F. Harrison, 136
Loas d Capt. Elisha & Elizabeth, 5
Mary d Capt. Elisha & Elizabeth died, 5
Mary d Capt. Elisha & Elizabeth born, 5
Samuel s Capt. Elisha & Elizabeth died, 5
Samul s Capt. Elisha & Elizabeth born, 5*
Thomas s Capt. Elisha & Elizabeth died 5*
Thomas s Capt. Elisha & Elizabeth born, 5
SHEPARD, Daniel A. m Louisa Gates, 170
SHIPMAN, Abigail m William Bramble, 117
Abner born, 57*
Abner m Margary Avery, 57
Abner s Abner & Margary, 57
Berwell s Abner & Margary, 57
Betsy d Abner & Margary, 57
Betsey m Charles Beckwith, 157, 198
Charles s Abner & Margary, 57
Christopher s Abner & Margary, 57
Elijah s Abner & Margary, 57
Elisha s Abner & Margary, 57
Hallam s Abner & Margary, 57
Josiah s Abner & Margary, 57
Mehetable A. m Cyrus Cook, 155
Molley m Sylvanus Smith, 83
Nathaniel s Abner & Margary, 57
Parthena d Abner & Margary, 57
Sanford s Abner & Margary, 57
William s Abner & Margary, 57
SILL, Abel s Andrew & Ellenor, 98
Amasa s Jabez & Elizabeth, 63
Amy d Willm & Jemima, 112
Andrew m Phebe Mather, 35
Andrew s Andrew & Phebe, 35
Andrew m Ellenor Dorr, 98
Andrew s Andrew & Ellenor, 98
Anna d John & Phebe, 36
Anna m John Lay 4th, 62
Anna (Edward) m Dr. John Noyes, 192, 209
Azubah d Joseph & Azubah, 49
Azubah wife of Joseph died, 49
Azubah m Capt. Cullick Ely Jr., 108
Bettey d Zechh & Susannah, 62
Bettey d Giles & Lucy, 60
Clarissa d Zechh & Susannah, 62
Clarissa d Wm & Jemima, 113
David s David Fithen & Sarah, 88, 108*
David died, 108*
David F. m Sarah Griswold, 88, 108
David F. Col. died, 108*
David Fitton s John & Phebe, 36
David F. (Lex. Alarm), 301
Elijah s Joseph, 261
Elisha s Joseph, 261
Elisha s Richard & Eunice, 64
Elisha Noyes s Jabez & Elizabeth, 63
Eliza d Pember & Susanah, 128
Elizabeth d Jabez & Elizabeth, 63
Elizabeth d Joseph, 261
Elizabeth d Samuel & Eunice, 95
Enoch s Giles & Lucy, 60
Enoch s John & Hepzibah, 36
Esther d Jabez & Elizabeth, 63
Ezra (Lex. Alarm), 301
Fanny d Samuel & Eunice, 95
Francis d Capt. Thomas & Mehitable, 136

INDEX OF PERSONS 379

SILL, cont.
George Griswold s Silas & Hannah, 110
Giles s Joseph Jr. & Ruth, 49
Gurdon (see under Jurdon)
Hannah d Pember & Susanah, 128
Henry Mather s Capt. Thomas & Mehitable, 135
Hepzibah wife of John died, 36
Hiram s Pember, 128
Horace s Silas & Hannah, 110
Isaac s Thomas & Jemima, 52
Isaac (Lex. Alarm), 301, 305
Isaac Watts m Mercy Wilcox Beckwith, 136
Jabez (twin with Richard) s Joseph, 261
Jabez m Elizabeth Noyes, 63
Jabez s Jabez & Elizabeth, 63
Jemima d Thomas & Jemima, 52
Jemima widow m Broadstreet Emmerson, 55
Jemima m William Starlin, 61
Jerusha d Wm & Jemima, 112
John died, 36
John s Joseph, 261
John m Phebe Fitkin (Fitton, Fithian), 36, 261
John s John & Phebe, 36
John m Hepzibah Lee, 36
John s David Fithen & Sarah, 88, 108*
John 3rd m Lucy Peck, 36
John Comstock s Zachariah & Prudence, 22
John Griswold s Capt. Thomas & Mehetable, 135
Jonathan Palmer s Andrew & Ellenor, 98
Joseph Capt. m Widow Sarah Marvin, 261
Joseph s Joseph & Sarah, 261
Joseph s Joseph, 261
Joseph s John & Phebe, 36
Joseph ?nd m Ruth Matson, 49
Joseph m Azubah DeWolf, 49
Joseph Capt. died, 261
Joseph died, 49, 261
Joseph Lee s Joseph & Azubah, 49
Jurdon Goold s Giles & Lucy, 60
Lois d David Fithen & Sarah, 88, 108
Lois m David Matson, 124
Luce d Joseph, 261
Lucia d Joseph Jr. & Ruth, 49
Lucy d Wm & Jemima, 113
Margaret d Capt. Thomas & Mehetable, 135
Margaret m John Hart, 168, 204
Mary d Jabez & Elizabeth, 63
Mary d John & Phebe, 36
Mary d Capt. Thomas & Mehetable, 136
Mary m Richard Chadwick 2nd, 145
Mehetabel d Thomas & Jemima, 52
Mehetabel m Martin Huntley, 31
Micha (Lex. Alarm), 301, 305
Mica s Thomas & Jemima, 52
Moses s Jabez & Elizabeth, 63
Moses m Asenath Coult, 115
Nancy d Capt. Thomas & Mehetable, 135
Naomi d Jabez & Elizabeth, 63
Nathaniel s Giles & Lucy, 60
Nathaniel s Joseph Jr. & Ruth, 49*
Patty m Benjn Reeve, 138
Phebe d Andrew & Ellenor, 98
Phebe d John & Phebe, 36
Phebe wife of John died, 36
Phebe d Joseph, 261

SILL, cont.
Phebe wife of Joseph died, 261
Phebe d Joseph & Azubah, 49
Phebe m Capt. Gardner Gallup, 144
Phebe m William Lay, 63
Phebe m Dudley Sterling, 120
Phebe M. m Charles E. Hart, 153
Phebe Mather d Capt. Thomas & Mehetable, 135
Polly d David Fithen & Sarah, 88, 108*
Polly m Nathaniel Matson, 115
Polly d Silas & Hannah, 110
Polly Matson d Wm & Jemima, 112
Richard m Eunice Lee, 64
Richard (twin with Jabez) s Joseph, 261
Richard s John & Hepzibah, 36
Richard s Silas & Hannah, 110*
Richard s Zechh & Susannah, 62
Ruhama d Joseph Jr. & Ruth, 49
Rhumi m David Howell, 32
Ruth d Joseph Jr. & Ruth, 49
Ruth wife Joseph Jr. died, 49
Sally d Silas & Hannah, 110
Samuel, 308
Samuel s Andrew & Phebe, 35
Samuel m Eunice Dorr, 95
Samuel s Thomas & Jemima, 52
Samuel Dudley s Samuel & Eunice, 95
Sarah wife of David F. died, 108*
Sarah m William Hall, 126
Sarah d Joseph, 261
Sarah d John & Phebe, 36
Sarah d Silas & Hannah, 110*
Sarah G. m Alfred Wells, 168
Sarah Griswold d Capt. Thomas & Mehetable, 135
Shadrac, 279
Shadrack s Jabez & Elizabeth, 63
Shadrack s Samuel & Eunice, 95
Shadrack m Laura Lay, 168
Silas s John & Phebe, 36
Silas m Hannah Griswold, 110
Susannah d Zech & Susannah, 62
Thomas s Joseph, 261
Thomas m Jemima Dudley, 52
Thomas s Thomas & Jemima, 52
Thomas s David Fithen & Sarah, 88, 108
Thomas Capt. m Mehetable Mather, 135
Uriah s Andrew & Phebe, 35
Ursula d Samuel & Eunice, 95
Wanda, 276
William s Joseph & Ruth, 49
William m Jemima Starling, 112
William Travis s Wm & Jemima, 112
Ursula died, 214
Zachariah s Joseph & Sarah, 261
Zachariah s Zechh & Susannah, 62
Zachariah m Prudence Comstock, 22
Zechariah Jr. m Susannah Rowland, 62
_____ s Andrew & Phebe, 35
SISSON, Allen M. m Abby Fosdick, 179
Elizabeth d Jonathan Jr., 136
Jonathan Capt., 306
Jonathan Jr. m _____ Holdridge, 136
Jonathan m Hope Spencer, 149
Mary d Jonathan Jr., 136

SISSON, cont.
Nathan H. s Jonathan Jr., 136
Oliver, 308
SKINNER, SKINER
Aaron E.A. m Clarissa Graham, 148
Abigall d Abraham & Abbigale, 261
Abigale s Abraham & Abbigale, 261
Abraham m Abigale, 261
Abraham s Abraham & Abbigale, 261
Eunice m William Matson, 91
Richard s Abraham & Abbigale, 261
SLATE, Ann R. m Calvin Champion, 186
Delia m John Tooker Jr., 183
Delia M. m David Phelps, 192
Ellen d George & Elisabeth, 201
Esther m Chauncey Bliss, 166
George R., 201
John T., 310
Lathop E. Jr. m Mary Champion, 182, 198
Mary A. m Henry Bramble, 187
Mehetable S. m William J. Lord, 172, 198, 205
Phebe d Lathrop E. Jr. & Mary C., 198
Sylvester W. m Mary Jane Hurlburt, 181
SLUMAN, SLEUMAN, SLEUMON, SLOMAN
Alice M died, 214
Betsey Maria d Charles & Betsey, 159
Betsey Maynard w Charles died, 159
Catharine Ann d Charles & Betsey, 159
Charles m Betsey Maynard, 159
Charles Alexander s Charles & Betsey, 159
Charles D. died, 159
Charles Henry s Charles & Betsey, 159
Evelyn Maria d Charles & Betsey, 159
John Andrew s Charles & Betsey, 159
Joseph Albert s Charles & Betsey, 159
Joseph Ely s Charles & Betsey, 159
Mary Eliza d Charles & Betsey, 159
Niles Alexander s Charles & Betsey, 159
William Eagles s Charles & Betsey, 159, 310
_____ s Charles & Betsey, 159
SMITH
Abby Carolina d Capt. Joseph & Lucy, 133
Abel m Polly Gee, 127
Abel m Susan Jerome, 171
Abbegale m Thomas Harvey, 233, 264
Abegall d Richard Jr. & Elizabeth, 233, 261
Abigail d Ichd. & Abigail, 130
Abigail d Joseph & Mary, 69
Abigail w Josiah Jr. died, 34
Abigail d Nathan & Elizabeth, 42
Abigail d Josiah & Parthena, 37
Abigail d Nehemiah & Betsey, 121
Abigail d Richard & Abigail, 37*
Abigail w Richard died, 37
Abigail d Richard & Grace, 37
Abigail Marvin d Capt. Icabod & Abigail, 130
Alias s Stephen & Irene, 65
Alis d Thomas & Elizabeth, 263*
Allen m Hannah Peck, 127*
Alls d Henery & Marah, 262
Almira d Capt. Joseph & Lucy, 132
Almira m Ely Tiffany, 156
Alvin was born, 153
Ama d Josiah & Anna, 35
Ama m Daniel Miner, 73
Ama d Sylvanus & Molly, 83

SMITH, cont.
Ambrose s Josiah & Anna, 35*
Ambrous s Joseph & Elizabeth, 99
Ame w John C. Smith died, 118
Amon s Elijah & Elizabeth, 262
Amos s Richard & Grace, 37
Amos m Lucinda Miller, 46
Amos s Amos & Lucinda, 46
Andrew s Elijah & Elizabeth, 262
Andrew m Hester Beckwith, 85
Anna d Richard & Abigail, 37
Asa s Richard & Grace, 37
Azariah s Wm & Marcy, 87*
Azubah m Elihu Wade, 66
Azubah d Josiah & Anna, 35
Azubah d Joseph & Rhoda, 9
Beckah d Stephen & Lucia, 38
Benjamin s Joseph, 263
Betsey m Daniel Ayers, 31
Betsey d Joseph & Elizabeth, 98
Betsey m Capt. John Burnham, 113
Betsy d Nehemiah & Betsy, 121
Bettey d Richard & Abigail, 37
Bettey m Seth Lee, 43
Bettey d Zadock & Mary, 63
Briant s Matthew & Sarah, 263
Carlos Adolphus s Capt. Joseph & Lucy, 132
Catee d Latham & Loas, 32
Charles s Nehemiah & Betsey, 121
Charles m Lois Parsons, 129
Charles m Phebe Parsons 2nd, 129
Charles E. m Mary E. Brockway, 169
Charles Henry s Charles & Phebe, 129
Charles Henry s Elisha & Mary, 158
Clarinda Frink d Gilbert s. & Maria, 141
Clarissa d Stephen & Lucia, 38
Clement s Richard & Grace, 37
Dan s William & Mary, 87
Daniel m Elizabeth Smith, 262*
Daniel born, died, 261*
Daniel s John (Cook) & Ame, 118
David s David Carpender & Zeruiah, 69
David M. s Abel Southworth (Written in Arnold Index)
David Carpenter s Thomas & Elizabeth, 263
David Carpender m Zeruiah Sawyer, 69
Deborah d Joseph, 263
Deborah d Allan & Hannah, 127
Deborah died, 214
Dudley s Thomas & Lydia, 58
Edmund s Elisha & Mary, 158
Edmund m Harriet Coats, 148
Edmund W. m Frances S. Miner, 164
Edward s Thomas & Elizabeth, 263
Edwin m Mary E. Tubbs, 155
Elias s Hepekiah & Sarah, 49
Elias s Stephen & Irena, 65
Eliaz m Eunice Lester, 156
Elihu m MaryAnn Appleby, 193, 205, 211
Elihu s Elihu & Mary Ann, 205
Elijah m Elizabeth Beckwith, 262
Elijah s Elijah & Elizabeth, 262
Elijah s Andrew & Hester, 85
Elisha s Jason & Nabby, 47
Elisha s Joseph, 263
Elisha m Azubah Tinker, 76

INDEX OF PERSONS 381

SMITH, cont.
Elisha s Latham & Loas, 32
Elisha m Mary Gorton, 158
Elisha s Elisha & Mary, 158
Elisha H. was born, 153
Elisha H. m Maria Brockway, 170
Elishaba d Hezekiah & Sarah, 49
Eliza d Seth & Hannah, 98*
Eliza Ann d Dr. John L. & Fanny, 141
Elizabeth m William Ely, 230
Elizabeth d Ithamer & Sarah, 76
Elizabeth d John & Marah, 262
Elizabeth d Josiah & Ama, 34
Elizabeth m John Lee, 240
Elizabeth m James McCrackin, 97
Elizabeth m Elisha Moore, 111
Elizabeth d Nathan & Elizabeth, 42
Elizabeth d Richard Jr. & Elizabeth, 261
Elizabeth w Richard Jr. died, 261
Elizabeth (wid) m Jonathan Reed, 256
Elizabeth m Daniel Smith, 262
Elizabeth w Sylvanus died, 84
Elizabeth d Sylvanus & Molly, 83
Elizabeth d Thomas & Elizabeth, 263
Ellen Maria d Gilbert S. & Maria, 141
Emelia d Capt. Joseph & Lucy, 132
Enoch (Lex. Alarm), 301
Enoch s Elijah & Elizabeth, 262
Enoch m Eunice Comstock, 52
Ephraim s Thomas & Lydia, 58
Erastus s Joseph & Elizabeth, 98
Erastus s Nehemiah & Betsey, 121
Esther d Allen & Hannah, 98
Esther m Jesse Beckwith Jr., 75
Esther d Jonathan & Jean, 8
Esther d Josiah & Parthena, 37
Esther d Nathan & Elizabeth, 42
Esther d Thomas & Lydia, 58
Eunice m Capt. Joseph Burnham, 118*, 130
Eunice d David Carpender & Zeruiah, 69
Eunice m Joseph Smith, 118*
Eunice d Josiah & Parthena, 37
Eunice died, 118*
Eunice Burnham d Charles & Lois, 129
Ezra s Sylvanus & Molley, 83
Ezra s Amos & Lucinda, 46
Ezra s Phebe Chadwick, 16
Fanny d Zadock & Mary, 63
Fitch C. m Lois C. Watrous, 195, 211
Frances d Charles & Lois, 129
Frances Elizabeth d Elisha & Mary, 158
Francis s Zadock & Mary, 63
Gilbert T. m Maria Smith, 118, 141
Gilbert Tenant s Joseph & Eunice, 118
Grace d Richard & Grace. 37
Henery m Marah, 261
Henery Sr. died, 262
Henery s David Carpender & Zeruiah, 69
Henery s Thomas & Elizabeth, 263
Henry Bela s Nathaniel & Lucinda, 47
Hezekiah m Sarah Chadwick, 48
Hibbard s Nathaniel & Lucinda, 47
Ichabode s Hezekiah & Sarah, 48
Ichabod s Nathaniel & Lucinda, 47
Ishabod Capt. m Abigail Marvin, 130
Ithamer s James & Elizabeth, 262

SMITH, cont.
Ithamer s Thomas & Lydia, 58
Ithamer m Sarah Sawyer, 76
Jabez s Ithamer & Sarah, 76
James m Elizabeth Way, 262
James s James & Elizabeth, 262
James Jr. m Mary Hayes, 31
James s Nehemiah & Betsey, 121
James Rogers (twin Sarah Stephens) Mathew & Sarah, 263
James s Zadock & Mary, 63
Jane d Mathew & Sarah, 263
Jean d Zadock & Mary, 63
Jane Ewens d Thomas & Elizabeth, 263
Jason s Elijah & Elizabeth, 47
Jason m Nabby Harrison, 47
Jasper s Elijah & Elizabeth, 262
Jeames s Henery & Marah, 262
Jemima m Samuell Tinker Jr., 266
Jemima d John & Marah, 262
Jerusha d James & Elizabeth, 262
Jesse s Joseph, 263
Jessee s David Carpender & Zeruiah, 69
Johanna d Henery & Marah, 262
Johanna m John Lay Junr., 239
John m Marah _____, 262
John s John (Cook) & Amey, 118
John s Joseph, 263
John m Delia Mack, 162
John Cook s Josiah & Ama, 35
John Cook m Amy Chapman, 118
John Gorton s Elisha & Mary, 158
John L. Dr. m Fanny Strickland, 141
John Lay s Seth & Hannah, 98
John M., 153
Jonathan m Jean Lewis, 8
Joseph m Elizabeth Darby, 98
Joseph 2nd Capt. m Lucy Harris, 132
Joseph s John & Marah, 262
Joseph s Joseph, 263
Joseph s Joseph & Elizabeth, 99
Joseph s Joseph & Mary, 69
Joseph s Josiah & Ama, 35
Joseph s Josiah & Rhoda, 8*
Joseph s Josiah & Rhoda, 8
Joseph Jr. m Mary Matson, 69
Joseph m Eunice Smith, 118
Joseph died, 118
Joseph Denison s Joseph & Eunice, 118
Josiah m Rhoda _____, 8
Josiah s Josiah & Rhoda, 9
Josiah Jr. m Abigail Tinker, 34
Josiah s Josiah Jr. & Abigail, 34
Josiah Jr. m 2nd wife Ama Tinker, 34
Josiah s Josiah Jr. & Ama, 34
Josiah Jr. m Parthena Roland, 37
Josiah s John & Marah, 262
Julia d Charles & Lois, 129
Latham m Loas Miller, 32
Lee s Latham & Loas, 32
Leonard Whiting s Capt. Joseph & Lucy, 133
Lita d Ithamer & Sarah, 76
Livingston H. m Abbey M. Wait, 168
Livingston H. m Louisa S. Wait, 168
Livingston Harris s Capt. Joseph & Lucy, 132
Loas d Hezekiah & Sarah, 49

SMITH, cont.

Lois w Charles died, 129
Lous m Silas Miller, 94
Lucinda d Elisha & Azubah, 76
Lucinda d Nathaniel & Lucinda, 47
Lucretia d Allen & Hannah, 127
Lucretia d Josiah & Rhoda, 9
Lucretia m James Huntley, 40
Lucretia m Daniel Prentice, 151
Luce m Nathan Huntley, 26
Luce d Ithamer & Sarah, 76
Luce d Jonathan & Jean, 8
Luce d Richard & Grace, 37
Lucy d John (Cook) & Amey, 118
Lucy d Sylvanus & Molley, 83
Lucy m Nathan Tinker, 121
Lucy m John Tubbs, 151
Lydia m Jerimiah Brown, 29
Lydia d Hezekiah & Sarah, 49
Lydia d Josiah & Rhoda, 9
Lydia d Richard & Abigail, 37
Lydia w Stephen Jr. died, 65*
Lydia d Stephen & Irena, 65
Lydia d Thomas & Lydia, 58
Lydia m Gershom Watteras, 269
Marah d Henery & Marah, 262
Marah d John & Marah m Isaac Tubbs, 262
Margaret d Joseph, 263
Margaret d Zadock & Mary, 63
Maria m Gilbert T. Smith, 141
Martha d John & Marah, 262
Mary m Lay Ayer, 168
Mary d Charles & Lois, 129
Mary m Charles W. Waite, 142
Mary d Zadock & Mary, 63
Mary Ann d Thomas & Azubah, 128
Mary Ann m Elisha W. Mather, 142
Mary Gorton d Elisha & Mary, 158
Matthew m Sarah Rogers, 263
Matthew s Matthew & Sarah, 263
Mehetable m John Mack, 11
Molly d Elijah & Elizabeth, 262
Nabby d Nathaniel & Lucinda, 47
Nancy d Nathaniel & Lucinda, 47
Nancy H. m Isaac Stanton, 153
Nathan, 308
Nathan m Hannah Stark, 150
Nathan m Elizabeth Starlin, 42
Nathaniel s Allen & Hannah, 127
Nathaniel m Lucinda Armsby, 47
Nathaniel s Nathaniel & Lucinda, 47
Nathaniel s Hezekiah & Sarah, 49
Nathaniel s James & Elizabeth, 262
Nehemiah Capt. m Betsey Gee, 121
Nelson Hamilton s Joseph & Lucy, 132
Noah s Thomas 3rd & Lydia, 35
Olive d Richard & Grace, 37
Oliver Comstock s Enock & Eunice, 52
Orrin F. m Emma A. Loomis, 162
Parnal s James & Elizabeth, 262
Parnal d James Jr. & Mary, 31
Peter s Jonathan & Jean, 8
Phebe m Jonathan Brockway, 72
Phebe d Elisha & Azubah, 76
Phebe d Josiah & Rhoda, 9
Phebe m Reynold Johnson, 110

SMITH, cont.

Phebe d Richard Jr. m Nathaniel Clark, 226
Phinehas s Hezekiah & Sarah, 48
Polly m Peter Peck Clark, 114
Polly m Asa Holt, 170
Polly m Robert Otis, 60
Polly d Sylvanus & Molly, 83
Polley d Joseph & Elizabeth, 99
Preserved m Jonathan Avery, 94
Quaries s John & Marah, 262
Rachal d Mathew & Sarah, 263
Rachal d Thomas & Lydia, 58
Rane d Hezekiah & Sarah, 49
Rebecca m Henry Boon, 275
Rebeckah m John Peck Jr., 94
Reuben s John (Cook) & Ame, 118
Reuben m Nancy Harding, 161
Rhoda d Josiah & Ama, 35*
Rhoda d Josiah & Rhoda, 9
Rhoda d Thomas & Lydia, 58
Rhode m Phinehas Watrouse, 29
Rhodey d Josiah & Parthena, 37
Richard Jr. m Elizabeth Lay, 261
Richard s Richard Jr. & Elizabeth, 261
Richard s Daniel & Elizabeth, 262
Richard Sr. died, 6
Richard m Abigail Miner, 37
Richard s Richard & Abigail, 37
Richard m Grace Moore, 37
Richard Ransom s Stephen & Irena, 65
Rufus s Josiah & Ama, 35*
Rufus A. m Frances Manwaring, 151
Russell s Richard & Grace, 37
Ruth m Edward Robbins, 257
Ruth d John & Marah, 262
Ruth d Nathaniel & Lucinda, 47
Samuel s John & Marah, 262
Sarah d Henery & Marah, 262
Sarah d Jonathan & Jean, 8
Sarah d Nathaniel & Lucinda, 47
Sarah d Thomas & Elizabeth, 263
Sarah d Thomas & Lydia, 58
Sarah Stevens (twin James Rogers) d Mathew & Sarah, 263
Sarah Stephens m Jonathan Huntley, 33
Sarah died, 213
Sears Peck s Allen & Hannah, 127
Seth 1st s Dr. John L. & Fanny, 141
Seth 2nd s Dr. John L. & Fanny, 141
Seth s Josiah & Ama, 35
Seth m Cordelia Loomis, 175
Seth m Hannah Murdock, 98
Seth s Stephen & Lucia, 37
Seth Dr. m May E. Lay, 187
Simeon s Itharmer & Sarah, 76
Simon s James & Elizabeth, 262
Sophronia d Capt. Joseph & Lucy, 132
Stephen s Hezekiah & Sarah, 48
Stephen m Lucia Lay, 37
Stephen s Thomas & Lydia, 58
Stephen Jr. m Lydia Alger, 65
Stephen 2nd m Irena Ransom, 65
Stephen Sawyer s David Carpender & Zeruiah, 69
Sukey d Nehemiah & Betsey, 121
Susanna d Richard Jr. & Elizabeth, 261

INDEX OF PERSONS 383

SMITH, cont.
Susannah m Gershom Bardner, 14
Sylvanus m Molley Shipman, 83
Sylvanus s Sylvanus & Molley, 83
Sylvanus m Elizabeth Wait, 84
Theode d Ithamer & Sarah, 76
Theodora d James & Elizabeth, 266
Thomas s Mathew & Sarah, 263
Thomas m Elizabeth Robins, 263
Thomas Jr. m Lydia Foot, 58
Thomas s Thomas & Lydia, 58
Thomas m Azubah Wade, 128
Thomas M. m Hannah Rogers, 146
Thomas Merrett s Thomas & Azubah, 128
Tinker s Josiah & Anna, 35*
Tinker s Josiah & Parthena, 37
Tubel see Azubah d Josiah & Rhoda, 9
Union d of Wm & Mary, 87
Union m Richard Sparrow, 121
Uriah s Stephen & Irena, 65
Watrous B. m Sarah Rogers, 153
William m Hannah M. Ely, 157
William s Josiah & Rhoda, 9
William m Mary Moore, 87
William s Zadock & Mary, 63
William A. m Mary Ann Gorton, 170
William Angus s Elisha & Mary, 158
William D. m Eunice M. Davison, 174
William Lay s Seth & Hannah, 98
William Moore s William & Mary, 87
William Parsons s Charles & Lois, 129
Zadock m Mary Goold, 63
Zadock s Zadock & Mary, 63
Zeruiah d Thomas & Lydia, 58
Zeruiah d David Carpender & Zeruiah, 69
Zillah d Daniel & Elizabeth, 262
Zillah m John Terril Jr., 23
———— s Dr. John & Fanny, 140
————, two children of Capt. Ichabod, 130
SOBUCK, Joseph A. m Sally Warhead, 158
SOUTHWORTH
Abigail (twin Amos) d Samuel, 262
Abigail m David Peck, 48
Amos (twin Abigail) s Samuel, 262*
Constant s Joseph, 262
Elihu B. m Lydia Lay, 193
Elizabeth d Joseph, 262
Joseph, 262
Mary d Samuel, 262
Rebecka m Ezra Lee, 18
Samuel, 262
Samuell s Samuell, 262
SPARROW
Mary H. m George Hazard Chadwick, 160
Mary Howland d Richard & Union, 121
Richard m Union Smith, 121
SPENCER, Amelia D. m Benjamin H. Catlin, 169
Austin m Charlotte C. Spencer, 156, 308
Betsey died, 213
Calvin m Mehetable Brainard, 113
Calvin s Calvin & Mehetable, 114
Calvin m Fanny Miner, 141
Catharine F. m William E. Marvin, 190
Charles s Calvin & Mehetable, 114
Charles m Julia Ryon, 150
Charlotte C. m Austin Spencer, 156

SPENCER, cont.
Daniel Washington s Daniel & Maria, 147
Eleazer m Betsey Saunders, 171, 197
Elijah s Calvin & Mehetable, 114
Hannah Maria d Daniel & Maria, 147
Houghton m Amilia Sarah Strutt, 141
Henry m Elizabeth Mulhollard, 180
Henry Selden s Daniel & Maria, 147
Hovy d Calvin & Mehetable, 113
Hope m Jonathan Sisson, 149
Ichabod Lieut. (Lex. Alarm), 306
Jedediah s Calvin & Mehetable, 114
Jedidah m Ladock D. Beckwith, 149
John Harvey s Daniel & Maria, 147
John Ward s Houghton & Amilia Sarah, 141
Lorillard m Sarah J. Griswold, 188
Nancy d Calvin & Mehetable, 113
Oliver died, 214
Penelope m Lyde L. Tinker, 139
Polly m Stephen D. Sellard, 129
William, 308
Roxanna m David Quinbly, 184
Sarah S. m Amasa Day, 186
———— m Samuel Mott Jr., 250
Sarah wife of John Haltum died, 234, 263
SPERRY, SPERY, Danell m Deborah Peck, 263
STACK-see STARK
Lucretia m Nathan Jewett Jr., 171
STAMMERS, Mary m William Stanner, 152
STANNARD, Jesse m Sally Phelps, 155
Maria Ann m Similius Ely, 149
STANNER, William m Mary Stammers, 152
STANTON, Isaac m Nancy H. Smith, 153
STAPLES, Asa s Ebenezer & Charity, 51
Ebenezer m Charity Leonard, 51
Lucy d Ebenezer & Charity, 51
Parthena d Ebenezer & Charity, 51
STAPLINS, Giles m Harriet Harding, 180
STARK (see also STACK)
Abiel, 308
Abial Jr. m Jane Alice Ely, 161, 200
Christopher, 308
Hannah m Nathan Smith, 150
Jane A., 200
Lucretia m Nathan Jewett Jr., 171
Lucy m Frederick Fosdick, 189
Mary Jane d Abial & Jane, 200
Phebe m John G. Jewett, 142
Sarah Anne m Timothy Ely, 178
William H. m Mary Ann Raymond, 167
STARKEY, Charles F. m Frances Congdon, 164
Sybil m Joel Beckwith, 160
STARLING, STARLIN, see STERLING
Abigail d Capt. Daniel & Mary, 6
Abigail d Jacob & Edey died, 71
Abigail d Jacob & Edey, 71
Abigail d John & Abigail, 12
Abigail wife of John died, 12*
Abigail[1] d John & Jane died, 12*
Abigail[2] d John & Jane, 12
Allias d Jacob & Edey, 71
Annah wife of Samll died, 54*
Anne twin with Esther d Danil Jr. & Ester, 263
Anna m Ezra Ely, 49
Ansell s William & Jemima, 61
Clarissa d William & Jemima, 61

STARLING, cont.
Daniel s Danll & Demiss, 32
Daniel Capt. m Mary Ely relict, 5
Daniel s Capt. Danll & Mary, 6
Daniel Jr. m Ester Coult, 263
Daniel s John & Jane, 12
Daniel Capt. m Wid. Mary Beckwith, 6*
Daniel Capt. died, 6
Deborah d Jacob & Edey, 71
Dudley[1] s Wm & Jemima, 61, 120
Dudley[2] s Wm & Jemima, 61
Edey d Jacob & Edey, 71*
Easter d Daniel & Ester died, 263
Elijah s Joseph & Lydia, 65
Elisha s William & Jemima, 61
Elizabeth d Capt. Daniel & Mary, 6
Elizabeth m Zelophead Ely, 115
Elizabeth m Wm Rufus Hyde, 87
Elizabeth d John & Abigail, 12
Elizabeth m Nathan Smith, 42
Elizabeth w Samll died, 54*
Elizabeth Ann d Stephen & Elizabeth, 41
Elizabeth Marvin d Jacob & Edey, 71
Erastus s William & Jemima, 61
Easter twin with Ann d Daniel Jr. & Ester, 263
Esther, 276, 277
Esther d John & Jane, 12
Esther d Stephen & Elizabeth, 41
Hannah d Joseph & Lydia, 64
Hannah d Joseph & Sarah, 264
Hannah d Samll & Annah, 54
Hepzibah d Jacob & Edey, 71
Irena m Eleazer Mather Jr., 53
Irene d Samuel & Elizabeth, 54
Isaac s Stephen & Elizabeth, 41
Jacob s John & Jane, 12
Jacob m Edey Tucker, 71
James s Danll & Demiss, 32
James s Samll & Elizabeth, 54
Jane d John & Jane, 12
Jemima d Wm & Jemima, 61, 276
Jemima m William Sill, 112
John s Capt. Daniel & Mary, 6
John m Abigail Pratt, 12*, 263*
John m Jane Ransom, 12*
John s John & Jane, 12
John s Stephen & Polly, 125
Joseph s Capt. Daniel & Mary, 6, 301
Joseph m Sarah Mack, 263
Joseph s Joseph & Sarah, 264
Joseph died, 264
Joseph m Lydia Ransom, 64
Joseph s Joseph & Lydia, 64
Joseph s William & Jemima, 61
Lena d Samuel & Elizabeth, 54
Lizze d Samll & Elizabeth, 54
Lord s Samll & Annah, 54
Lucia d John & Jane, 12
Lucy d Samll & Elizabeth, 54
Lydia d Joseph & Lydia, 64
Lydia d Joseph & Sarah, 264
Marian d John & Jane, 12
Marshfield s Stephen & Elizabeth, 41
Mary d Danll & Demiss, 32
Mary d Joseph & Sarah, 264
Mary wife Capt. Daniel died, 6

STARLING, cont.
Mary d John & Jane, 12
Mary m Richard Ransom, 64
Meeah (Micah) s William & Jemima, 61
Nathan s John & Jane, 12
Phebe d Joseph & Sarah, 264
Phebe d William & Jemima, 61
Phebe m Joseph Marvin 2nd, 51
Rachal d Daniel & Demiss, 32
Ruth Perkins d Samll & Elizabeth, 54
Samuel m Lucretia Champion, 54
Samuel m Elizabeth Perkins, 54
Samll m Anna Dudley, 54
Samuell s Joseph & Sarah, 264
Samll s Samuel & Elizabeth, 54
Sarah m Ezra Ely, 49
Sarah d Danll & Demiss, 32
Sarah d Joseph & Lydia, 64
Sarah d Joseph & Sarah, 264
Sarah wife of Joseph died, 264
Sarah m Lemuel Lee, 22
Sarah d Samuel & Elizabeth, 54
Seth s Joseph & Lydia, 64
Simon s John & Jane, 12
Stephen s John & Jane, 12
Stephen m Elizabeth Tucker, 41
Stephen s Stephen & Elizabeth, 41*
Stephen m Polly Brown, 124
Thomas Sill s Wm & Jemima, 61
William died, 263, 264
William s Daniel J. & Ester, 263
William s Joseph & Sarah, 264
William m Jemima Sill, 61
William s William & Jemima, 61
_____ child of Stephen & Polly, 124
_____ first child & d of Joseph & Sarah died, 264
William m Mrs. Mary Sayer, 264
STOTEN, Sarah m Roger Alger Jr., 218
STEBBINS, Elizabeth m Richard H. Miller, 162
STEEL, Joel m Caroline Ely, 154
STEPHENS, James F. m Betsey Haynes, 164
STEPHENSON, Daniel m Jerusha Mather, 25
Daniel s Daniel & Jerusha, 25*
STERLING (see STARLING)
Dudley m Phebe Sill, 120
Florence A., 200
Georgiana m Henry Steward, 114
Jerusha Lay d William & Jerusha, 132
John m Hannah Randall, 177, 200
Joseph, 65
Maria Ely, 179
Phebe m John Elmore, 143
Robert Ely s Wm & Jerusha, 132
Stephen Jr. m Sally Marvin, 150
Thomas Sill s Wm & Jerusha, 132
William Maj. m Jerusha Ely, 132
William Erastus s Wm & Jerusha, 132
STURTEVANT, Anna d Rufus & Mary, 131
George Foster s Rufus & Mary, 131
Harnot d Rufus & Mary, 131
Josiah s Rufus & Mary, 131
Mary d Rufus & Mary, 131
Rufus m Mary Manning, 131

INDEX OF PERSONS 385

STEWARD, Calvin M. s Daniel & Sarah, 152
  Daniel m Sarah Tinker, 152
  Henry m Georgiana Sterling, 164
  Lucy Ann m Ezra Brockway, 154
  Phebe m Thomas Mulford, 143
STILL, Eliza d Pember W. & Susannah, 128
  Hannah d Pember W. & Susannah, 128
  Hiram s Pember W. & Susannah, 128
STILLMAN, Clark G. m Electa Howard, 157
STOCKER, Edward s Edward & Marah, 264
  Edward m Wid Abigail Harvy, 233
  Experience d Edward & Marah, 264
  John s Edward & Marah, 264, 300
  Marah wife of Edward died, 264
  Martha 2nd wife of Edward died, 264
  Mary d Edward & Martha, 264
  William s Edward & Martha, 264
STONE, William m Mary Ann Swan, 196
STORY, STOREY, Samuel m Mary Minard, 90
  William s Saml & Mary, 90
STOW, Sarah m Adriel Ely, 16
STRUTT, Amilia Sarah m Houghton Spencer, 141
STRICKLAND, STRICTLAND
  Charles William s Joseph & Phebe, 125
  Eliza d Joseph & Phebe, 125
  Fanny d Joseph & Phebe, 125
  Fanny m Dr. John L. Smith, 141
  James L. m Mary Ann Comstock, 155
  James Lewis s Joseph & Phebe, 125
  Joseph m Phebe Lewis, 125
  Mariette d Joseph & Phebe, 125
  Nancy d Joseph & Phebe, 125
  Nancy m James Fitch, 137
  Polly m Stephen Tinker, 129
  Ruel R. m Harriet Tinker, 147
  Sarah P. m Jonathan G. Lewis, 139
  Thomas W. m Freelove Fitch, 136
STRONG, Elihu m Christiana Beckwith, 159
  William m Mary Ann Swan, 212
SULLARD, SELLARD
  Calvin Spencer s Stephen D. & Polly, 129
  Ellis d James & Lydia, 107
  James m Lydia DeWolf, 107
  Lucy d James & Lydia, 107
  Stephen DeWolf s James & Lydia, 107
  Stephen D. m Polly Spencer, 129
SUMMERS, Samuel s Dolly Higgins, 136
SUMNER, John H. m Betsey Conkling, 147
SWAN, Frederick L. m Laura A. Tiffany, 185
  Jabez m Laura Griffin, 147
  Johnathan, 203
  Luna L. m Norris Rathbun, 168
  Mary Ann m William Stone, 196
  Mary Ann m William Strong, 211
  Thomas S. m Charlotte A. Rogers, 184
SWANEY, George Bigelow s John & Abigail, 120
SWEITSER, Edwin m Clementine Lombard, 182
TABOR, Phebe m John Griffing, 101
TAGGERS, John H. m Lucretia Dart, 154
TAINTER, Charles M. m Mary Lord, 186
  Ralph m Phebe Lord, 166
TALCOTT, Samuel m Asenath Morgan, 160
TALLMAN, Deliverance m Isaac Willy Jr., 271
TAYLOR, George m Polly Wood, 139
  John s George & Polly, 139
  Joseph s George & Polly, 139

TAYLOR, cont.
  Marcy m Javitt Ingraham, 238
  Niles m Eliza Bailey, 173
  Phebe d George & Polly, 139
  William s George & Polly, 139
  William m Betsey Jones, 190, 210
TEFFT, Mary m John D. Clark, 180
TERRILL, TERRIL, Anna m Simeon Beebe, 33
  Elizabeth d John & Zillah, 23
  Gardiner s John & Zillah, 23
  Hannah m Benjamin Hudson, 43
  John Jr. m Zillah Smith, 23
  John s John & Zillah, 23
  Joseph s John & Zillah, 23
  Susannah d John & Zillah, 23
  Zilla d John & Zillah, 23
TERRY, Ann E. d James & Catharine, 201
  James P. m Catharine Matson, 180, 201
  Mahala m Jasper Griffing, 197
  Sally m Ezra Miller, 135
THOMAS, TOMMAS
  George m Matilda Banning, 176
  Mary m Samuel Gastin Jr., 3
  Rebecca m Samuel Waller, 22
THOMPSON, THOMSON, TOMSONE
  Alpheas m Mary Ann Phebe Reed, 118
  Erastus s Alpheas & Phebe, 119
  Fanny d Alpheas & Phebe, 118
  George s John & Susannah, 124
  Hannah d Deacon William m William Ely, 230
  Isaac s Alpheas & Phebe, 118
  Jeane d William & Silla, 266*
  John m Susannah Willson, 124
  Lyna d Alpheas & Phebe, 118
  Martha d William & Philadelphia, 249
  Martha m Jacob Miller, 249
  Mary Ann d John & Susannah, 124
  Maryan Phebe w William Alpheas died, 119*
  Philadelphia (Fidalelfia) d William & Silla (Delfa), 266
  Rachell d William & Silla, 266
  Susan alias Rogers had son Daniel Rogers, 141
  Susan alias Rogers had son David, 141
  William m Silla (Delfa) Tileson, 266
TIBBETS, TIBBETTS, TIBBITTS
  John m Lydia Johnson, 148
  Lydia m James Nason, 123
  Whitman m Julia Ann Chaddock, 155
TIFFANY, Anna m George Ransom, 77
  Charles m Naomi Jewett, 143
  Charles E. m Francis M. Jewett, 168
  Consider m Neomey Comstock, 264
  Consider s Consider & Neomey, 264
  Consider m Mary Davis, 223
  Ebenezer, 275
  Elizabeth d Lt. Nathan, 255
  Elizabeth m Charles Phelps, 255
  Elizabeth m Richard Brockway, 223
  Elizabeth A. m Josiah Crocker, 184
  Ely m Almira Smith, 156
  Giles m Esther Peck, 109
  Hepzibah m William Harrison, 71
  Humphrey s Consider & Neomey, 264
  Laura A. m Frederick Swan, 185
  Lucretia M. m John M. Parker, 185
  Luther s Consider & Neomey, 264

TIFFANY, cont.
Molly, 300
Nabbe Lord d Timothy & Elizabeth, 51
Neomey d Consider & Neomey m Ezekiel Huntley, 264
Neomey wife of Consider died, 264
Samll s Consider & Neomey, 264
Timothy s Consider & Mary, 39
Timothy m Elizabeth Lord, 51
Titus s Consider & Mary, 39
TILLOTSON, TILLITSON, TILLSON, TILLETSON, TILESON, TILLOTSON
Abigail d James & Elizabeth, 19
Abigail d Nathl & Elizabeth, 92
Ame d Wm & Susanna, 41
Anna d Wm & Susannah, 41
Anne m Thomas Munsill, 29
Azubah d William & Susanna, 41
Bella s William & Susannah, 41
Bettey d Nathl & Elizabeth, 92
Betsy m Joseph Dowsett, 131, 197
Charlotte d Nathl & Elizabeth, 92
Chauncey s Isaac & Content, 117
Damarius d Wm & Susannah, 41
Daniel s Simeon & Martha, 45
Danll s James & Elizabeth, 19
Daniel m Lucy Lewis, 123
David s Jonathan & Marah, 265
David s David, 264
David s Levi & Mary, 45
Deborah d David, 265
Deborah d Levi & Mary, 45
Delfa (or Silla), 266
Delight d Levi & Mary, 45
Eleazer s Samuell & Lydia, 265
Eleazer s Levi & Mary, 45
Eleazer s Simeon & Martha, 45
Elijah s Simeon & Martha (Mary), 45
Elizabeth d James & Elizabeth, 19
Elizabeth m Nathaniel Tillitson, 92
Elizabeth d Daniel & Lucy, 123
Ephriam s Daniel & Lucy, 123
Eunis d David, 265
Eunice[1] d James & Elizabeth died, 19*
Eunice[2] d James & Elizabeth born, 19*
Eunice d Nathl & Elizabeth, 92
Ezra s Levi & Mary, 45
George Dr., 305
George s William & Susanna, 41
George Franklin m Laura Caulkins, 194
Ira m Betsey Lay, 168, 198
Isaac s Wm & Susannah, 41
Isaac m Content Fox, 117
Isaac s Isaac & Content, 117
Isaiah s Levi & Mary, 45
Jacob s David, 265*
Jeames m Elizabeth Scovil, 265
Jeames died, 265*
Jeames d Jonathan & Marah, 265
James s David, 264
James m Elizabeth Davis, 19*
James s James & Elizabeth, 19*
James s Daniel & Lucy, 123
Jemima d James & Elizabeth, 19
Johannah d Jeames & Elizabeth, 265
Johannah married John Lewis, 265

TILLOTSON, cont.
Joel s Joseph & Lucinda, 118
John s Jonathan & Marah, 265*
John m Jeane _____, 257
Jonathan Jr. m Rebeka Chamberlin, 265
Jonathan Sr. died, 265*
Jonathan, 265
Jonathan s David, 265
Jonathan s James & Elizabeth, 19
Jonathan s Nath'l & Elizabeth, 92
Joseph s Joseph & Lucinda, 118
Joseph m Lucinda Munsell, 118
Joseph s Nath'l & Elizabeth, 92
Joseph s Samuell & Lydia, 265
Julia E. m Albert Chappell, 170
Levi m Mary Davis, 45
Levi s Levi & Mary, 45
Levi (Twin Simeon) s David, 264
Lina d Wm & Susannah, 41
Lois d Simeon & Martha, 45
Lucy d Simeon & Martha, 45
Lydia d Nath'l & Elizabeth, 92
Lydia m Elijah Mack, 128
Mary d Jonathan & Marah, 265
Mary d David, 265
Mary d Simeon & Martha, 45
Morehouse s Wm & Susannah, 41
Nathan s Samuell & Lydia, 265
Nathan s Nath'l & Elizabeth, 92
Nathaniell s Samuell & Lydia, 265
Nathaniel m Elizabeth Tillitson, 92
Nathaniel s Nath'l & Elizabeth, 92*
Phebe d Levi & Mary, 45
Rane d Levi & Mary, 45
Reuben s Isaac & Content, 117
Rhoda d Levi & Mary, 45
Richard s Wm & Susannah, 41*
Salome d James & Elizabeth, 19
Salome d Daniel & Lucy, 123
Samuell s Jonathan & Marah, 265
Samuell m Lydia Chadwick, 265
Samuell s Samuell & Lydia, 265
Sarah M. d Ira & Betsey, 198
Sila m Russell Bogue, 163
Silla (Delfa) m William Tomson, 266
Simeon twin Levi s David, 264
Simeon m Martha Welch, 45
Simeon s Simeon & Martha, 45
Susa d William & Susannah, 41
Susanna wife William died, 41*
Temperance d Jonathan & Marah, 265
Temperance m John Alger, 217*
Temperance d Samuell & Lydia, 265
Temperance d Simeon & Martha, 45
Thomas s of Simeon & Martha, 45
William, 308
William s of David 265
William m Susanna Chapman, 41
William H. died, 214
TINKER, Abigail m Josiah Smith Jr., 34
Abigail d Samuell Jr. & Jemimah, 266
Allen s Nathan & Mehetable, 99
Allen m _____, 136
Ama m Josiah Smith Jr., 34
Amos s Amos & Luce, 265
Amos m Luce Lee, 265

INDEX OF PERSONS

TINKER, cont.
Amos m Sarah Duren, 266
Amos Jr. m Hannah Minor, 31
Amos m _____ Tucker, 132
Anna d Nathan & Mehetable, 99
Anna d Nathan & Lucy, 121*
Arribilla d Stephen & Lovina, 46
Azubah d Amos & Hannah, 31
Azuba m Elisha Smith, 76
Benjamin s Amos & Luce, 265
Betsey m Anson Merrett, 153
Bettey d Amos & Luce, 266
Catharine C. d Silvanus & Joanna, 122
Charles[1] s Nathan & Lucy died, 121*
Charles[2] s Nathan & Lucy d, 121*
Charles s Allen, 136
Charles m Mahala Beckwith, 145
Dan m (Czrina) Austen, 164
Daniel s Allen, 136
Eliza Ann S. d Matthew & Mary, 137
Eliza B. d Silvanus & Joanna, 122
Eliza D. m Gershom Main, 169
Elizabeth m Amos C. Maxson, 144
Elizabeth m Elisha Robbins, 101
Elizabeth d Harris & Elizabeth, 126
Elizabeth d Lynde & Penelope, 139
Elizabeth d Nathan & Mehetable, 99
Elizabeth B. m William Brockway, 176
Emily d Stephen & Polly, 129
Eunice d Amos & Luce, 265
Eunice m William Rowland, 53
Eunice A. m Martin Sawyer, 190, 209
Evelin B. m Roswell W. Tinker, 193
Fanny C. d Silvanus & Joanna, 122
Fanny C. m M. Jab Tubbs, 157
Frederick Augustus s Lynde & Penelope, 139
George s Lynde & Penelope, 139
Harriot d Harris & Elizabeth, 126
Harriot m Ruel Strickland 147
Harris m Elizabeth Deshon, 126
Harris s Harris & Elizabeth, 126
Harris s Stephen & Lovina, 46
Henry Mather s Amos, 132
Jane d Amos & Hannah, 31
Jane R. m Dudley Cheseboro, 182
Johlel s Amos & Lucy, 266
Joanna d Silvanus & Joanna, 122
John s Amase & Sarah, 266
Jonathan s Nathan & Mehetable, 99
Joseph s Amos & Luce, 265
Joseph s Amos & Hannah, 31
Joseph m Betsey Chapel, 166
Joseph Deshon s Harris & Elizabeth, 126
Julia d Lynde & Penelope, 140
Juliaette m Oliver Closon, 165
Lebbeus Peck s Martin & Mary, 33
Lucretia m Frances Ingraham, 95
Lucretia m Samuel Peck, 25
Luce d Amos & Luce, 265
Luce m Seabury Champion, 138
Luce m William Braddick, 196
Lucy Smith d Silvanus & Joanna, 122
Lurena d Nathan & Mehetable, 99
Luraney d Nathan & Lucy, 121
Lydia d Amos & Luce, 265
Lydia d Capt. Wm II & Elizabeth, 114

TINKER, cont.
Lyndia d Stephen & Polly, 129
Lynde L. s Amos, 132
Lynde L. m Penelope Spencer, 139
Lynde L. born, 140
Lynde L. s Lynde L. & Penelope, 140
Mahala m Frederick Champion, 175
Marah d Amase & Sarah, 266
Maria d Stephen & Polly, 129
Maria d Lynde L. & Penelope, 139
Martain s Amos & Luce, 265
Martin m Mary Peck, 33
Mary d Samuell Jr. & Jemimah, 266
Mary m David Huntley, 39, 236
Mary d Nathan & Mehetable, 99
Mary d Lynde L. & Penelope, 140
Mary m Elisha Huntley, 151
Mary m Henry H. Hess, 143
Mary M. d Wm & Nancy, 204
Mary Ann d Allen, 136
Maryette m Nathan Burdick, 173
Matthew m Mary Miller, 137
Matthew s William & ELizabeth, 114
Nancy m William B. Tooker, 144
Nancy m Calvin Manwaring, 149
Nathan m Mehetable Beckwith, 99
Nathan m Lucy Smith, 121*
Nathan s Nathan & Mehetable, 99
Nathan died, 99*
Nathan m Sarah Gee, 121
Nathan s Nathan & Sarah, 121
Nehemiah D. m Roxana Beckwith, 181
Partheny d Amos & Luce, 265
Phebe d Martin & Mary, 33
Phinehas m Amos & Luce, 265
Polly d Amos, 132
Polly d Silvanus & Joanna, 122
Rachal d Amos, 132, 299
Reuben C. m Almira Waid, 172
Roswell W. m Evelin Tinker, 193
Sabra d Capt. Wm & Elizabeth, 114
Sally m William Gee Jr., 114
Sally d Silvanus & Joanna, 122
Sally d Nathan & Lucy, 121
Sally d Amos, 132
Salmon s Nathan & Sarah (d), 121*
Samuell Jr. m Jemimah Smith, 266
Sam'll s Samuell Jr. & Jemimah, 266
Sarah d Amase & Sarah, 266
Sarah m Daniel Steward, 152
Sarah d John, 234
Sarah w Nathan died, 121*
Sarah m Silas Brown, 128
Seth s Samuell Jr. & Jemimah, 266
Silas s Amos & Hannah, 31
Silranus s Amos & Luce, 265
Silvanus m Joanna Dishon, 122
Sophia d Esther Beckwith, 65
Sophia m Giles Manwaring, 146
Stephen m Lovina Wade, 46
Stephen m Polly Strickland, 129
Stephen s Stephen & Polly, 129
Tamor d Samuell & Jemimah, 266
Teressa d Harris & Elizabeth, 126
William II Capt. m Elizabeth Turner, 114
William s Amos, 132

TINKER, cont.
William, 204
William III s Matthew & Mary, 137
William m Eleanor Jane Bill, 172
TOMPKINS, Edward m Juiaette Chadwick, 174
TOOKER, TOOCHER, TUCKER
  Adin m Mary A. Miller, 160
  Anna m Edward Ransom, 4
  Chester, 310
  Dorkis d Noah, 266
  Frances A. m Harvey Hall Jr., 309
  Harvey m Mary Maynard, 161
  Hepzibah S. m Thomas B. Peck, 196, 211
  Jane E. m Richard Clark, 174
  John Jr. m Delia Slate, 183
  John m Nancy Ann Hall, 310
  Mary wife of Niles H., 278
  Niles H. m Lucy Darrow, 143
  Niles H. m Mary, 278
  Olive m Joel Clark, 174
  Philip m Anna Ely, 58
  Rhoda m Horrace W. Ely, 155
  Samuel W. s William B. & Nancy, 144
  Sophia m James Clark, 175
  Tabor d Noah, 266
  William B. m Nancy Tinker, 144
TOPLIFF, Abigail m Bulkeley Edwards, 166
TOWNSEND, Hannah m William Noyes Jr., 143
TOZER, Elishame child Thomas & Deborah, 266
  Susannah m John Giddings, 32
  Thomas m Deborah Bates, 266, 300
TRACY, Hannah m Elijah Selden, 103
TRIBBLE, Caroline d John & Caroline, 205
  John, 205
  Mary L. m Amasa S. Buckingham, 196, 212
TRIM, Moses m Mahitable Pendal, 266
TRUMAN, Dimmis m Christopher Lathrop (Lathrope), 151
TUBBS, TUBS, TUBES
  Abigail d Peter & Abigail, 69
  Abigail d John & Eliza, 132
  Abisha s Joseph & Lucia, 26
  Abner s Isaac & Martha, 266
  Ahimaz s Elisha & Anna, 11
  Alpheas s Isaac & Martha, 266
  Amos s Elisha & Anna, 11
  Ame (Ann) d Joseph & Lucia, 26
  Clement s William & Rebeckah, 30
  Dan s Joseph & Lucia, 26
  Elisha s Isaac & Martha, 266
  Elisha m Anna Miller, 11
  Eliza d John & Eliza, 132
  Elizabeth d Lemuel & Elizabeth, 72
  Elizabeth w John died, 132
  Elizabeth m Simeon Wood, 79
  Ezeckell s Isaac & Martha, 266
  Frederick s Joseph & Lucia, 26
  Hannah d John & Elizabeth, 132
  Hepzibah d Joseph & Lucia, 26
  Isaac s Isaac & Martha, 266
  Isaac m Martha Smith, 262
  Isaac died, 266*
  Isaac s Isaac & Sarah, 90
  Isaac s Lemuel & Elizabeth, 72
  Israel s William & Rebeckah, 30
  Israel s Lemuel & Elizabeth, 72

TUBBS, cont.
  Jemima d John & Eliza, 132
  Job s John & Eliza, 132
  M. Job m Fanny Tinker, 157
  John m Elizabeth Bush, 132
  John m Lucy Smith, 151
  John s Peter & Abigail, 68
  John G. s John & Eliza, 132
  John Miller s Elisha & Anna, 11
  Jonathan s William & Rebeckah, 30
  Joseph s Isaac & Martha, 266
  Joseph m Lucia Robins, 26
  Judith d William & Rebeckah, 30
  Leana (e) d Lemuel & Elizabeth, 72
  Lemuel s William & Rebeckah, 30
  Lemuel m Elizabeth Scovel, 72
  Lucia d Joseph & Lucia, 26
  Lucy d Joseph & Lucy, 26
  Lydia m Natha'll Hudson Jr., 235
  Lydia d Joseph & Lucia, 26
  Lydia d Lemuel & Elizabeth, 72
  Lydia d Peter & Sarah, 267
  Lydia d William & Rebeckah, 30
  Martha, 299
  Martha d Isaac & Martha, 266
  Mary d Isaac & Martha, 266
  Mary d Peter & Abigail, 69
  Mary E. m Edwin Smith, 155
  Peter, 300
  Peter m Abigail Moore, 68
  Peter m Sarah Brockway, 267
  Phebe m Stephen Huntley, 77
  Rebeckah d William & Rebeckah, 30
  Richard s Peter & Sarah, 267*
  Samuell s Samuell & Elizabeth, 267
  Sarah d Peter & Sarah, 267, 299
  William m Rebeckah Daniels, 30
  William s William & Rebeckah, 30
  Zephaniah s Joseph & Lucia, 26
  Zephaniah s Isaac & Martha, 266
TUCKER (TOOKER)
  Ann m Norman Perrego, 193
  Atwell s Stephen & Elizabeth, 100
  Atwell Jr. m Hannah Chadwick, 158
  Atwell m Lucy Waid, 158
  Catharine m William H. Bauta, 187
  Catharine M. m Simeon Whipp, 147
  Clarice B. m George Appleby, 119
  Eed (Edey) d John & Elizabeth, 267
  Edey m Jacob Starlin, 71
  Elizabeth d John & Elizabeth, 267
  Elizabeth m Stephen Starlin, 41
  Elizabeth m David Ransom, 107
  Esther d Stephen & Elizabeth, 100
  George m Lucy Way, 194, 206, 211
  Hannah d John & Elizabeth, 267
  Banta B. m Frederick Bouta, 181
  James s Stephen & Elizabeth, 100, 300
  Jane E. m John D. Clark, 164
  Job (Lex. Alarm), 301
  John m Elizabeth Marvin, 267
  John s John & Elizabeth, 267
  Joseph m Lucy Emerson, 6
  Joshua died, 267
  Lucy Ann m Enoch Chappell, 144
  Martin m Mrs. Mary Peck, 33

INDEX OF PERSONS

TUCKER, cont.
 Sarah m George Wade, 267
 Silas m Lucy Havens, 161
 Stephen m Elizabeth Wade, 100
 Stephen s Stephen & Elizabeth, 100*
 Stephen m Catharine Havens, 152
 William m Mary Ann Banta, 182
 _____ m Amos Tinker, 132
TULLY, TULLEY
 Abigail (widow) m Capt. John Lee, 1, 240
TURNER, Elizabeth m Harris Coult, 69
 Elizabeth m Capt. Wm Tucker II, 114
TUTTLE (TUTHILL)
 Abia Relict Barnabus died, 54
 Barnabas m Elizabeth Lord, 267
 Barabas died, 54
TWIST, Thomas Jr. m Harriet Beckwith, 169
TYLER, Daniel C. (Rev.), 272
URE, Andrew Jr. m Abby Rowland, 180
UTLEY, Lydia m Josiah Kellogg, 159
VAILL, T.S. Rev. m Elizabeth S. Comstock, 183
VAUGN, VAUN, Patience m Jabez Huntley, 4*
VERGASON, George C. m Jane Holt, 188
VERNON, Edward, 201
 Francis, 201
 Willis s Edward & Francis, 201
WADE, WAID, WAIDE
 Adaline m Joseph Page, 166
 Almira d Geo & Martha, 116
 Almira m Reuben Tinker, 172
 Ann born, 267
 Anna d Durin & Phebe, 8
 Anna d Mortin & Lucy, 66
 Anna m Abner Rowley, 122, 128
 Asenath d George & Sarah, 267
 Azubah d Elihu & Azubah, 66
 Azubah m Thomas Smith, 128
 Betsey m John J. Reynolds, 167
 Carolina d Elihu & Azubah, 66
 Caroline m Lay Mather, 114
 Dan s Elihu & Azubah, 66
 Dan s George & Martha, 116
 Deborah m Samuel Mather, 243
 Durant born, 267*
 Duran m Phebe Ransom, 8
 Elether d Martin & Lucy, 66
 Elihu s Gorge & Sarah, 267
 Elihu m Azubah Smith, 66
 Elisha (Lex. Alarm), 301
 Elisha s George & Sarah, 261
 Elisha m Mary Jones, 74
 Elizabeth d George & Elizabeth, 267
 Elizabeth d George & Hannah, 17
 Elisabeth w George died, 267
 Elizabeth w John died, 267, 268
 Elizabeth d Martin & Lucy, 66
 Elizabeth m Stephen Tucker, 100
 Elizabeth m Thomas Champion, 225
 Enoch m Laura Minor, 142
 Enoch m Maria Fox, 142
 Esther m Robert Denison, 97
 Eunice m Benjamin Roulin, 259
 Eunice d Geo. & Martha, 116
 Eunice d George & Elizabeth, 267
 Eunice B. m Thomas Grumley, 178
 Ezekiel m Lydia Way, 130

WADE, cont.
 Fanny d Elisha & Mary, 74
 George (Gorge) m Elizabeth Durant, 267
 George s George & Elizabeth, 267
 George m Martha Mather, 116
 George m Sarah Tucker, 267
 George m Wid. Dowey (Dowley, Dawley), 267
 George Jr. m Hannah Lester, 17
 George died, 267
 George s Elihu & Azubah, 66
 George s Martin & Lucy, 66
 Hannah d George & Elizabeth, 267
 Hannah m Samuel Bennet, 10, 222
 Harriot d George & Martha, 116
 Huldah m William W.S. Gillett, 157
 James s Ezekiel & Lydia, 130
 Jerusha d Joseph & Esther, 32
 Jerusha m Nathan Phelps, 86
 John S. died, 268
 John Juner, 267
 John s Duran & Phebe, 8
 Jonathan born, 268
 Joseph m Hannah Sanders, 133
 Joseph s George & Elizabeth, 267
 Joseph m Esther Chadwick, 32
 Joseph s Elihu & Azubah, 66
 Joseph (twin) s Martin & Lucy, 66
 Loas d Joseph & Esther, 32
 Lovina d Elisha & Mary, 74
 Lovina m Stephen Tucker, 46
 Lucy born, 268
 Lucy, 300
 Lucy m Greenfield Alger, 11
 Lucey[1] d Martin & Lucy born, died, 66
 Lucey[2] d Martin & Lucy born, 66
 Lucy w Martin died, 66
 Lucy m Atwell Tucker, 158
 Lydia d Martin & Lucy, 66
 Maria m George Appleby, 171
 Martha Ann d Geo. & Martha, 116
 Martha d George & Elizabeth, 267
 Martha A. m Morris Hinsdale, 167
 Martin (Lex. Alarm), 301
 Martin s George & Hannah (Anna), 17
 Martin m Lucy Mack, 66
 Martin twin son Martin & Lucy, 66
 Martin died, 66
 Martin m Jan Miller, 66
 Mary d George & Elizabeth, 267*
 Mary died, 267*
 Mary d George & Sarah, 267
 Nancy m Benjamin Franklin Chapel
  (Chappell), 176
 Pheby d Duran & Phebe, 8
 Phebe m Ezra Mather, 129
 Polly d Elisha & Mary, 74
 Polly m Richard Wait Jr., 115
 Rachel m Benjamin Phelps, 149
 Rachal m Jonathan Page, 164
 Sally d Elisha & Mary, 74
 Sally Maria m Ezra Fox, 148
 Sarah d Ezekiel & Lydia, 130
 Sarah w George died, 267
 Sarah d George & Sarah, 267
 Sarah m Joseph Lord, 44
 Stephen born, 268

LYME, CONNECTICUT, VITAL RECORDS

WADE, cont.
Thomas s Duran & Phebe, 8
Thomas s Martin & Lucy, 66*
Wade s George & Martha, 116
William s Martin & Lucy, 66
——— s Elihu & Azubah, 66
WAIT, WAITE, WAIGHT
Abby Eliza m George Miller Avery, 159
Abby M. m Livingstone H. Smith, 168
Alexander s Samuel & Mercy (Mary), 206
Betsey m Capt. Sylvester Mather, 58, 111
Bettey w Joseph died, 4*
Bettey d Joseph & Bettey, 4
Carlos Adolphos s Major Ezra & Lucia, 114
Charles W. m Mary Smith, 142
Charlottey d Joseph & Luraney, 4
Cloe d Thomas & Elizabeth, 268
Cloe m Alexander Bushnell, 65
Daniel s Richard & Elizabeth, 5, 268
Daniel s Richard & Lucia, 75
David s Rich'd & Lucia, 75
David m Sophia Eliza Wood, 133
Diodate s Joseph & Hannah, 5
Elderkin m Lucy Dowsick, 209
Elisabeth d Thomas & Mary, 268
Elisabeth d Thomas & Elizabeth, 268
Elisabeth d Rich'd & Elizabeth, 5, 268
Elisabeth w Richard died, 5, 268, 269
Elisabeth m Sylvanus Smith, 84
Elizabeth d Richard & Lucia, 74
Elisabeth d Lowen & Jeruiah, 67
Eliz Hale d David & Sophia Eliza, 133
Emile d Capt. Thos & Hannah, 112
Emily Maria d David & Sophia Eliza, 133
Esther m John Daniels, 105
Esther d Lowen & Zeruiah, 67
Esther d Thomas & Elizabeth, 268
Ezra s Richard & Rebecca, 5
Ezra Major m Lucia Miller (Major), 114
Ezra Smith s Ezra & Lucia, 114*
Fanney d Joseph & Bettey, 4
George R. died, 214
Hannah d Joseph & Bettey, 4
Horace m Matha Raymond, 138
James s Rich'd & Lucia, 74
Johannah d Thomas & Elizabeth, 268
John, 202
John s Rich'd & Elizabeth, 5, 268
John s Thomas & Mary, 268
John E. m Lucy Ann Dowsick, 191
Joseph s Thomas & Mary, 268
Joseph m Betsey Manwaring, 4
Joseph m Wid. Hannah Peck, 5
Joseph s Joseph & Bettey, 4
Joseph m Luranah Chadwick, 4*
Lee s Thomas & Elizabeth, 268
Loas m Marshfield Parson, 50
Lois d Richard & Lucia, 74
Lois m John Parsons, 27, 122
Lois d Capt. Thomas & Hannah, 112
Louisa m Livingston H. Smith, 168
Lous d Richard & Elizabeth, 5, 268
Lowen m Zeruiah Calkins, 67
Lucia wid (Maj) Ezra died, 114*
Lucy d Lt. Richard & Lucia, 74
Lucy w Richard died (Lucia), 75

WAIT, cont.
Luranah d Joseph & Luranah, 4
Luraney w Joseph died, 4
Lynde s Lt. Richard & Lucia, 74
Margreet m Ezekiel Minor, 100
Maria d Capt. Thomas G. & Hannah, 112
Martin s Lowen & Zeruiah, 67
Marvin s Richard & Elizabeth, 5, 268
Mary d Thomas & Mary, 268
Mary w Thomas died, 268
Mary d Thomas & Elizabeth, 268
Mary m Thomas Rathbone, 96
Mary Lay d David & Sophia Eliza, 133
Mercy A. m Silas C. Beebe, 160
Morrison R. m Amelia C. Warner, 176
Nancy m Daniel Chadwick, 142
Nathaniel M. m Mehetable Chadwick, 142, 157, 213
Phebe d Richard & Elizabeth, 5, 268
Phebe d Lowen & Zeruiah, 67
Phebe[1] d Richard & Lucia died, 75
Phebe[2] d Richard & Lucia born, 75*
Phebe[3] d Richard & Lucia born, 75
Rebecca w Richard died, 5
Remmick s Richard & Rebecca, 5
Richard s Thomas & Mary, 268
Richard m Elizabeth Marvin, 5, 268
Richard s Richard & Elizabeth, 5, 268
Richard m Rebecca Higgins, 5
Richard Jr. m Lucia Griswold, 74
Richard s Lt. Richard & Lucia, 74
Richard Jr. m Polly Wade, 115
Richard s Capt. Thomas & Hannah, 112
Richard m Mary Wood, 75
Richard s David & Sophia b, d, 133
Richard s David & Sophia b, 133
Samuel A. m Marcy (Mercy) A. Chadwick, 162, 206
Sarah[1] d Thomas & Mary born, 268
Sarah[2] d Thomas & Mary born, 268
Sarah d Richard & Elizabeth, 5, 268
Sarah d Lowen & Zeruiah, 67
Sarah m Daniel Daniels Jr., 26
Sarah d Joseph & Bettey, 4
Seth Henry s John Jr. & Mary Ann, 165, 214
Stephen s Lowen & Zeruiah, 67
Susannah d Richard & Lucia, 74
Tabitha d Thomas & Elizabeth, 269
Tabitha m Gideon Watrous, 26
Thomas m Mary, 268
Thomas s Thomas & Mary, 268
Thomas died, 268
Thomas m Elizabeth Lewis, 268
Thomas s Thomas & Elizabeth, 268
Thomas s Lowen & Zeruiah, 67
Thomas G. Capt. m Hannah Calkins, 112
Thomas Griswold s Thomas & Hannah, 112
Thomas Griswold s Richard & Lucia, 74
William m Rebecca Avery, 131
——— Triplets s Richard & Lucia, 75
——— s Richard & Lucia, 75
WALKER, Amos s Joseph & Selah, 101
Anna m Asa(h)el Roland, 60
James s Joseph & Selah, 101
John Cooley s Joseph & Selah, 101

WALKER, cont.
Joseph m Selah Cooley, 101
Walter s Joseph & Selah, 101
WALLER, Edey m Noah Beebe, 31
Elisabeth (d Richard & Elizabeth Brockway)
    died Wife Samuel Waller, 223*
Elisabeth d Samuel & Rebecca, 23
John m Mary Durins, 269
John s John & Mary, 269
Mary m Noah Miller, 9
Mary d Samuel decd & Rebecca, 23
Samuel m Elisabeth Brockway, 269
Samuel m Rebecca Thomas, 22
Samuel died, 23
Zeruiah d Samuel & Rebecca, 22
Zipporah m Asel Rouling, 258
WALLIS, Esther m Jedediah Edgerton, 52
WARHEAD, Sally m Joseph Sobuck, 158
WARMAN, Abbigal d William & Abegall, 269
    William m Abigail Lay, 269*
WARNER, Abby m George N. Phelps, 209
Amelia m Morrison Waite, 176
Andrew s Selden & Dorothy, 113
Caroline m Walter Wilkie, 171
Chapman m Sarah Comstock, 32
David W., 310
Ebenezer, 308
Elizabeth d Chapman & Sarah, 32
John Lieut., 306
Joseph s Selden & Dorothy, 113
Mary d Samuel M. Joel M. Gloyd, 196
Matthew Griswold s Selden & Dorothy, 113
Richard s Selden & Dorothy, 113
Ulysses S., 310
Samuel m Abby Champlain, 140, 308
Selden m Dorothy Selden, 113
Selden, 306
Selden s Selden & Dorothy, 113
William Henry s Selden & Dorothy, 113
Willys m Elizabeth Hart, 165
WARREN, Caleb s Moses & Mehetable, 38
Caleb s Joshua & Harriet, 140
Edward Raymond s Moses & Mehetable, 38
Eliza d Moses & Mehetable, 38
Eliza R. m William Gorton, 159
Eliza W. m Ebenezer Bacon, 172
Ellen d Joshua & Harriet, 140
Eunice m Eleazer Peck, 179
Eunice Harriet d Joshua & Harriet, 140
Hetty d Moses & Mehetable, 38
Hetty m John Hamilton, 139
Jane d Joshua & Harriet, 140
Jennie d Walter & Maria, 178
John s Joshua & Harriet, 140
Josuha s Moses & Mehetable, 38
Josuha m Harriet Way, 140
Joshua R. 2nd s William & Maria, 178, 206
Lois d Moses & Mehetable, 38
Maria d Moses & Mehetable, 38
Maria m Peter Comstock, 162
Maria E. twin with William W. J. Jr. d of William
    W. J. & Maria, 178*
Mehetable W. wid. of Moses, 38
Mahitable d Joshua & Harriet, 140
Moses s Moses & Mehetable, 38
Moses Jr. m Mehetable Raymond, 38

WARREN, cont.
Moses Harris m Mary F. Miner, 38, 140
Robert s Moses & Mehetable, 38
Sally d Moses & Mehetable, 38
Sarah Mehitable d Joshua & Harriet, 140
Thomas Jefferson s Joshua & Harriet, 140
Walter S. s William W. J. & Maria, 178
William W. J. m Maria Peck, 178, 206
William W. J. Jr. twin with Maria E. s William
    W.J. & Maria, 178
William Watts Jones s Joshua & Harriet, 140
WATERMAN, Anna m Josiah DeWolfe, 229
Martha m Renold Marvin, 246
WATROUS, WATEROUSE, WATTERUS,
    WATTERAS, WATTROUSE, WATERHOUS
Aaron m Laura Luther, 156
Abner s Isaac Jr. & Sarah, 270
Allen s Gideon & Martha, 78
Allen s Gurdon & Lucy, 111
Amos Huntley s Gurdon & Lucy, 111
Andrew s Isaac & Elizabeth, 269
Andrew m Dinah Westcot, 3
Andrew s Phinehas & Rhoda, 30
Anna d Gideon & Martha, 78*
Anna m Eleazer Mather, 2
Anna d Andrew & Dinah, 4
Anne d Isaac & Elizabeth, 269
Asa s Gideon & Martha, 78
Asa s Gurdon & Elizabeth, 124*
Azubah d Phinehas & Rhoda, 30
Azubah m Mather Peck, 90
Benjamin s Gurdon & Elizabeth, 124
Bettey d Andrew & Dinah, 4
Billey s Gideon & Martha, 78
Christiana m Asa Sheldon, 174
Christopher s Gearshom & Mehetable, 98
Dan Huntley s Gurdon & Lucy, 111
Daniel s Gurdon & Theody, 124
Daniel s Gurdon & Lucy, 111
Dorcas m Frederic Comstock, 181
Edward Allen s Andrew & Dinah, 4
Eleazer s Elijah, 120
Elias s Jabez & Hester, 86
Elijah m _____, 120
Elisha s Jabez & Hester, 86
Elisha m Martha Griswold, 119
Elizabeth d Isack & Sarah, 269
Elizabeth d Isaac & Elizabeth, 269
Elizabeth m John Sears, 260
Elizabeth d Gurdon & Elizabeth, 124
Erastus s Gurdon & Lucy, 111
Eunice s Smith & Eunice, 120
Fanne d Gideon & Tabitha, 27
George Payton s Gideon 2nd & Phebe, 135
Gershom, 269*
Gershom s Isack & Sarah, 269*
Gershom m Lydia Smith, 269
Gershom s Phinehas & Rhoda, 30
Gearshom m Mehetable Ransom, 98
Gideon m Martha Beckwith, 78
Gideon s Gideon & Martha, 78
Gideon m Tabitha Wait, 26
Gideon s Gurdon & Elizabeth, 124
Gideon s Gideon & Tabitha, 27
Gideon m Phebe Rhodes, 129, 135
Gilbert s Gurdon & Elizabeth, 124

WATROUS, cont.
Gurdon s Gideon & Martha, 78
Gurdon m Theody Beckwith, 124
Gurden s Gurdon & Theody, 124
Gurden 2nd m Elizabeth Paton, 124
Gurden Jr. m Lucy Huntley, 111
Hannah d Isaac & Elizabeth, 269
Harriet m Cornelius Mack, 191
Harry s William & Betsey, 128
Huldah d Gurdon & Theody, 124
Ira m Emily Saunders, 171
Irena d Gideon & Martha, 78
Isa(a)ck m Sarah Pratt, 269
Isa(a)ck s Isack & Sarah, 269
Isaac s Isaac, 270
Jabez s Isack & Sarah, 269
Jabez m Sarah Richards, 9
Jabez s Jabez & Sarah, 9
Jabez m Hester Jones, 86
Jacob s Gideon & Martha, 78*
Jane d Isaac & Elizabeth, 269
Jared s Gideon & Tabitha, 27
Jared m Phebe Champlain, 139
Jared m Mary Denison, 152
Jared W. m Caroline Peck, 185
Jedidiah s Samuell & Frances, 270
Jerusha d Jabez & Sarah, 9
Jerusha m Stephen Beckwith, 23
John s Jabez & Sarah, 9
John Rhodes s Gideon 2nd & Phebe, 135
Joshua M. s Elijah, 120
Lee Marvin s Smith & Eunice, 120
Lois C. m Fitch C. Smith, 195, 211
Lucretia d Phinehas & Rhoda, 29
Lucretia m John Daniels, 105
Lucy m Benjamin Beckwith, 132
Lydia d Isack & Sarah, 269
Lydia m Jonathan Rogers, 61
Mary Ann d Andrew & Dinah, 4
Mehetable d Gearshom & Mehetable, 98
Naomi d Andrew & Dinah, 4
Naomy d Gideon & Martha, 78
Oliver s Gideon & Martha, 78
Oliver s Gurdon & Lucy, 111
Parnal d Gershom & Lydia, 269
Patience d Gershom & Lydia, 269
Patience d Temperance, 23
Patience d Phinehas & Rhoda, 29
Phinious s Gershom & Lydia, 269
Phinehas m Rhoda Smith, 29
Phineas s Gearshom & Mehetable, 98
Phineas s Phineas & Rhoda, 30
Polly (Polley) d Gearshom & Mehetable, 98
Polly d Gurdon & Elizabeth, 124
Rebeca d Isack & Sarah, 269
Rebeckah d Isaac & Elizabeth, 226, 269
Rebeckah m Thomas Clark, 27
Rebeckah d Andrew & Dinah, 4
Rhoda d Phinehas & Rhoda, 30
Rhoda d Gurdon & Theody, 124
Rhoda m John Lay, 65
Richard s Isaac & Elizabeth, 269
Richard s Gurdon & Lucy, 111
Richard N. m Ann Jenette Austin, 171
Richard s Gideon & Martha, 78
Ruth d Isack & Sarah (twin), 269

WATROUS, cont.
Ruth twin with Sarah d Jabez & Sarah, 9
Samuell m Frances Brounson, 270
Samuell s Gideon & Tabitha, 27
Samuell s Isack & Sarah, 269
Samuell s Isa(a)ck, 270
Samuell s William & Sarah, 13
Sarah d Isack & Sarah, 269
Sarah m Joseph Robins, 257
Sarah twin with Ruth d Jabez & Sarah, 9
Sylvanus s Gideon & Martha, 78
Silvanus s Gurdon & Elizabeth, 124
Smith s Phinehas & Rhoda, 30
Smith m Eunice Marvin, 120
Susan M. m Dudley Wells, 187
Temperance, 23
Temperance d Isaac & Elizabeth, 269
Temperance d Andrew & Dinah, 4
Theody d Gurdon & Theody, 124
Theody died, 124*
Urrin child of Elijah, 120
William m Sarah Bartlett, 13
William s Gurdon & Elizabeth, 124
William m Betsey Reed, 128
Zeraiah born, died, 1
Zeruiah d Jabez & Sarah, 9
_____ s Gershom & Mehetable, 98
WAY, Abigail A. d William C. & Frances S, 205
Aless d George, 270
Aless m Samuel Peck, 254, 270
Ame d Thomas & Ame, 108
Ame d Elisha & Eunice, 108
Daniel Merick s Daniel Shaw Way & Molly Mack, 81
Daniel Shaw s Thomas & Ame, 108
Delight d Thomas, 270
Delight d Thomas & Ame, 108
Elisha s Thomas & Ame, 108*
Elisha m Eunice Crocker, 108*
Elizabeth d George, 270
Elizabeth m James Smith, 262
Elizabeth d Thomas, 270
Elizabeth d Elisha & Eunice, 108
Elliph d George, 270
Esther d Elisha & Eunice, 108
Eunice d Thomas, 270
Eunice d Thomas & Ame, 108
Eunice d Elisha & Eunice, 108
George, 270
Gererges, 270
Grace d Thomas & Ame, 108*
Hanna(h) d George, 270
Harriet m Joshua Warren, 140
Henry C., 310
Horace m Nancy Phelps, 185, 310
Ireney d George, 270
Irene m Jonathan Alger, 9, 217
Jane w Thomas died, 270
Jane Elizabeth d Thomas & Ame, 108
Jane d John & Clarissa, 203
John s George, 270
John s Thomas & Ame, 108*
John Jr. m Clarissa Minor, 179
Joseph s Thomas, 270
Lous d Thomas, 270
Lucy m George Tucker, 194, 211

INDEX OF PERSONS 393

WAY, cont.
  Lydia d George born, died, 270*
  Lydia 2nd d George born, 270*
  Lydia m Ezekiel Wade, 130
  Marten s Thomas, 270
  Mary m Barack Johnson, 184, 200
  Mary M. m Austin Perkins, 165
  Mehetable d George, 270
  Merrick s Thomas & Ame, 108*
  Sarah m Matthew Ransom, 256
  Sarah Ann d Wm C. & Frances, 199
  Sarah m John Lord Jr., 68
  Sarah m George Miller, 176, 198
  Thomas s George, 270*
  Thomas m Jane _____, 270
  Thomas s Thomas, 270*
  Thomas Jr. m Ame Merrick (Lex. Alarm), 108, 301
  Thomas s Thomas & Ame, 108
  Thomas Jr. m Polly Lee, 109
  Thomas J. m Mary Bump, 199, 205
  William C. m Frances Lester, 173
WEAVER, Sarah m Reuben Lord, 166
WEDGER, Lucy m Stephen Otis, 116
WEBB, James s Josiah & Margaret, 270
  John s Josiah & Margaret, 270
  Josiah died, 270
  Margaret, 270
  Nathan s Josiah & Margaret, 270
  Thomas s Josiah & Margaret, 270
WEEKS, Jethro s Jonathan, 270
  Jonathan, 270
  Jonathan s Jonathan, 270
WEGE, Mary m Samuel Marvin, 18
WELCH, Eunice m Joseph Huntley, 32
  Martha m Simeon Tillitson, 45
  Mary m John Reed Jr., 256
WELLS, WELLES, Alfred L. m Sarah Sill, 168
  Dudley m Susan Waterhouse, 187
  John B. m Roxana Lee, 184
  Lucy G. m David Hogue, 174
  Ruth d Samuel, 230
  Ruth d Daniel Elys, 230
WEST, Alva m Susan Gilbert, 169
  Helena m Richard M. Champlin, 154
  Samuel West died, 214
WESTCOT, Dinah m Andrew Waterouse, 3
WHEELER, Nathaniel m Phebe Ladd, 148
WHIPP, Catharine m Seth Gillett, 192, 210
  Simeon m Catharine Tucker, 147
WHITE, Benjamin, 300
  Edward m Ruth Rob(b)ins, 271
  Stephen m Betsey Lewis, 170
WHITTLESEY, Mary m Oliver J. Lay, 164
WICKES, Sally m Matthew Rogers, 134
WILCOX, WILLCOX
  Francis m Harriet Griffing, 172
  Hazard m Polly Wright, 152, 308
  Hazard B. m Elizabeth Harvey, 193
WILDER, WILDEN, John s Jonas & Eunice, 33
WILKIE, Walter Rev. m Caroline Warner, 171
WILLARD, Lorinda m Silas E. Coy, 165
WILLEY, WILLY, Abel s Isaac & Rose, 271
  Abigail d Isaac Jr. & Deliverance, 271
  Abraham W. m Catharine S. Brockway, 178, 205

WILLEY, cont.
  Bezella s Isaac Jr. & Deliverance, 271
  Deborah d Isaac & Rose, 271
  Deliverance d Isaac Jr. & Deliverance, 271
  Derias child of Isaac Jr. & Deliverance, 271
  Grace m Thomas Harvey, 19
  Hanna(h) d Isaac & Rose, 270
  Isaac m Rose Ben(n)it, 270
  Isaac s Isaac & Rose, 270
  Isaac Jr. m Deliverance Tallman, 271
  James Monroe s A.W. & Catharines, 205
  John s Isaac & Rose, 270
  Merriam d Isaac & Rose, 271
  Nathaniel s Isaac Jr. & Deliverance, 271
  Rachal d Isaac & Rose, 270
  Sarah d Isaac & Rose, 270
  Zachary s Isaac & Rose, 271
WILLIAMS, Charles D. m Betsey Reed, 175
  Dorothy m Christian Higgins, 62
WILLS, Alfred m Abigail Lee, 115
WILSON, WILLSON
  David s George & Susannah, 105
  Diodate m Lucinda Rogers, 162
  Ruel s George & Susannah, 105
  Susannah d George & Susannah, 105
  Susannah m John Thompson, 124
  William s George & Susannah, 105
  William m Elizabeth M. Chadwick, 154
WING, Sarah m Joseph Dimmock, 192
WINSLOW, Milton S. m Caroline A. Minor, 190
WOLCOTT, WOOLCOT
  Emelia m Marvin Lord, 90
  Ursala m Capt. Matthew Griswold, 2
WOOD, WOODS
  Benjamin s Silas & Elizabeth, 28
  Betsey d Silas & Elizabeth, 28
  Betsey, 276, 277
  Betsey m John Bates, 180
  Caleb m Dorothy Bacon, 87
  Caleb m Lois Chapman, 118
  Caroline d Simeon & Elizabeth, 79
  David Jr., 23
  Dorothy (Dorrilly) m John Ames, 53
  Eleazer s Simeon & Elizabeth, 79
  Eliza m William Peck, 165
  Elizabeth d Simeon & Elizabeth, 79
  Elizabeth wife Silas died, 28
  Experience m William Harrison, 25
  Fanny d Silas & Elizabeth, 28
  Fanny Marvin m Robert Chadwick, 139
  Hannah d David Jr. & Mary, 23
  James m Azubah Dolph, 170
  John, 306, 310
  John m Lydia Mack, 14
  John m Esther Lee, 149
  Lydia d John & Lydia, 15
  Lydia d Simeon & Elizabeth, 79
  Mary m Richar(d) Wait, 75
  Mary Ann m George Davison, 195, 212
  Nathaniel M., 310
  Polly d Silas & Elizabeth, 28
  Polly m George Taylor, 139
  Rachal d John & Lydia, 14, 15
  Russell s Silas & Elizabeth, 28
  Samuel m Elisa Ann Lopire, 166
  Silas s David Jr. & Mary, 23

WOOD, cont.
  Silas m Elizabeth Rogers, 28
  Silas m Eliza Peck, 158
  Simeon s John & Lydia, 14
  Simeon m Elizabeth Tubbs, 79
  Sophia Eliza m David Wait, 133
  Susannah, 276, 277
  Susannah d David Jr. & Mary, 23
  William s John & Lydia, 15
  William s Simeon & Elizabeth, 79
  William s Silas & Elizabeth, 28
WOODBRIDGE
  Eliza w Nathaniel Shaw died, 119
  Lucretia M d Nathaniel Shaw & Eliza, 119
  Mary Shaw m Henry Perkins, 136
  Nathaniel S. s Nathaniel & Lois, 119
  Nathaniel Shaw m Eliza Mumford, 119
  Nathaniel Shaw m Lois Mather, 118, 119
  Nathaniel Shaw Sr. died, 119
  Polly S. d Nathaniel Shaw & Eliza, 119
WOODSTOCK, John C. m Adaline Pilgrim, 172
WOODWORTH
  Asenthy d Nathan & Deborah, 54
  Huldah d Nathan & Deborah, 54
  Isaac died, 52
  Isaac s Nathan & Deborah, 54
  Lucy d Nathan & Deborah, 54
  Nathan m Deborah Mack, 54*
  Nathan s Nathan & Deborah, 54*
  Nathan died, 54
  Nathan s Nathan & Deborah, 54
  Ruel s Nathan & Deborah, 54
  Wealthy d Nathan & Deborah, 54
WOOSTER, Sylvester m Louisa Hayden, 144
  Sylvester Jr. s Sylvester & Louisa C., 144*
WORTHINGTON
  Abigail m Benjamin Mather, 43
WRIGHT, Allanson m Emily Banning, 157
  Alice m A(n)drew Edwards, 191
  Meriam m Joseph Armistead, 57
  Moses m Emeline Royce, 177
  Phineas, 299
  Polly m Hazard Wilcox, 152
  Timothy m Mary E. Clark, 193
YERRINGTON, Jerusha m Daniel Peck, 88
YOUNG, YOUNGS
  Benjamin H. married Lucy _____, 149
  Esther (alias Perkins), 275
  Herman m Clarissa Brooks, 149
  John M. s Benjamin H. & Lucy, 149, 171
  Nancy M. m Thomas Hall, 176
  William m Hannah Rowland, 146

NO SURNAME
  Calsar, 299
  Elizabeth Lay m Richard Smith Jr. (?Lay), 261
  Elizabeth m Richard Ely (Smith)
  Esther (Marvin) widow Thomas Lord m
    Jonathan Emmons, 90, 244
  Marah m Henery Petterson (widow of Robert
    Perigo), 254
  Cloe, Negro Servant Dea. Reynold Marvin, 19
  Biner, Negro d of Nancy Servant of Willm
    Noyes, 64
  Jack Howard son of Janny servant of Samuel
    Mather jr., 68
  Pornham, 300
  Janner, John, 247
  York, 299

INDEX OF CHURCH RECORDS 395

indicates name appears more than once on page.

ACKLEY, Deborah, 290
ALLABY, _____, 298
  Maby, 298
ALLEN, Alexander, 290
ALWELL, Joseph, 289
AMES, Eunice, 290
ANDERSON, Ansyl, 289
  Laura, 278, 283
  Laura 2nd, 280, 283
  Mary, 290, 298
  Polly, 275
  Rebeckah, 278
  Thomas, 278, 297
AUGER, Elijah Greenfield, 288
AVERY, Mary Agusta, 287
  Phebe A., 282, 283, 287
BABCOCK, Delia, 278, 285, 292
  Saloma, 282
BACON, Broadstreet, 295
BANNING, Benjamin, 276, 277, 290, 295, 296
  Caroline, 279, 283
  Clarissa, 290
  Ebenezer, 275, 293
  Lucy Ann, 292
  Marvin, 290
  Sarah, 275
  _____, 294
BAKER, Della, 283
  Nathaniel, 292
BATES, Ammaniah, 289
BAXTER, Obiaiah, 290
BECKET, _____, 298
BECKWITH, Bezahel, 290
  Dyer, 289
  Edgecomb, 281, 282
  Elisha, 289
  Frederick, 278, 291
  George, Rev. 272, 273, 294
  George, Jr., 275
  George, 291
  Jesse, 293*
  Mary L., 280, 282
  Patience, 275
  Sally, 296, 297
  Sarah, 273, 281, 282, 294
  Thomas, 290
BEEBE, David, 273, 293
  Gidn, 293
  Grace, 288
  Lucy, 289
  Phebe, 289
  Rhoda, 289
  Sarah, 293
  Theodsdia, 280, 282
BIDWELL, Martha, 289
BILL, Hiram Lodowich, 289
  Julia Ann, 292
  Mary, 292
BINGHAM, Malinda, 289
BLACKS, Eunice Crosly, 291
BLATCHLEY, Abraham, 291
BOAGUE, James, 288
BOOGUE, Rebecka, 293
BOON, Ketura, 289

BOONE, Rebecka, 275, 276, 297
BRADBURY, Betsey, 279, 281
BRADFORD, Esther, 273, 293
BRAINARD, Deborah, 273, 295
BRAMBLE, Abigail, 291
  Betsey, 278, 285, 292
  Silas, 292
BRINK, Emily, 282
BRISTOL, Eli, 291
BRODS, David, 297
BROOKS, Lonsil, 293
BROCKWAY, Abner, 275
  Benjamin, 274, 297
  Betsey, 276, 277, 281, 283
  Bettey, 297
  Caroline L., 291
  Catharine, 275
  Celia, 287
  David, 284, 290
  Desiah (Desire), 275, 297
  Dorcas, 290
  Dorothy, 275
  Ebenezer, 285, 287, 296
  Ebenezer, Unham, 285
  Elihu, 290
  Elijah, 296
  Eliphant, 275, 294
  Elisabeth B, 283
  Eliza Dunham, 285, 292
  Elizabeth, 281, 282, 285
  Elizabeth L., 279
  Elizabeth Spencer, 287
  Ezra, 273
  Ezra Junr., 291
  Frederic Lord Cordin, 285
  Gamahel, 274
  Grabiel, 273
  Hannah, 283, 287*, 294
  Harriel Lizabeth, 287
  Horace, 280, 283
  Horace, Austin, 285, 287
  Israell Dunham, 287
  James, 295
  Jane Amelia, 285
  Jeddiah, 279, 283, 285, 296
  Joel, 293
  John, 296
  John Cotton Mather, 279, 283, 285, 291
  John Griffin, 285
  Laura Ann, 285
  Leonora, 291
  Lois, 273, 288
  Louis, 293
  Lucina, 291
  Maria meline, 286
  Mary, 275, 276, 277, 283
  Mary Adalaide, 287
  Mary C., 278, 282, 287
  Mary Emeline, 285
  Mary Sophia, 285
  Nancy, 286
  Nancy F., 276, 277, 284, 291
  Phebe, 278, 283, 284, 285
  Polly, 289, 290, 291

BROCKWAY, cont.
Rhoda, 283
Rhoda B., 287
Richard, 275, 298
Richard William, 286
Samuel Anderson, 284
Samuel Clark, 288
Samuel M., 286, 287
Sarah, 276, 277, 281
Susan, 276, 291
Temperance, 286
Thankful, 274
Ulysses Hiram, 285
William, 273, 286, 287*, 292, 294
William Mosely, 287
Zebulon, 293
Zebulon Jr., 291
BROWN, Betsey, 280, 283
Charles Nathan, 284
David, 291
Franklin, 292
Hannah Eliott, 286
Henry, 294, 295
Lurania, 277, 283
Nathaniel M., 292
Saloma, 286
Silas, 276, 277, 283, 284, 298
Susanna, 276
BUCKLEY, Caroline, 278, 284, 292
BUSHNELL, Mahetable, 284
Hannah B., 278, 281
Harvey Rev., 272
BURR, Enoch Fitch Rev., 272
BUTLER, Betsy, 289
Isaac, 296
John, 294
Mabel, 294
Molly, 277, 284
Rhoda, 279, 285
Sarah, 273, 274
William, 273
⎯⎯⎯, 297
BULL, William Clark, 291
BUMP, Allan, 296
Betsey H., 297
Elisabeth M., 276, 277
John, 294
Penelope, 278, 294
Rebeckah, 276, 277, 283
William, 297
BURNHAM, Jemmima, 288
Joseph, 290, 294
Miriam, 294
CHADWICK, Elisabeth M., 292
Mary, 290
Silas, 290
CHAMPLIN, Betsey (Lee), 276
Edward Junr., 289
CHAPMAN, Joseph, 295
CHAPPELL, Mehitable, 282
CLARK, Ebenezer, 289
Elizabeth Wood, 284
Molly, 296
Peter Peck, 289
CLARKE, David, 289
Lucenda, 289

CLARKE, cont.
Uriah, 298
Waterous, 291
COLT, Amy, 288
Aseenith, 298
David, 296
Dean Joseph, 293
Desire, 273, 274
Elisabeth, 275
Hannah, 274
Harris, 273, 294
Samuel, 295
Sarah, 295
Tempe, 293
COMSTOCK, Hezakiah, 291
Laura, 279, 286
Phebe, 277, 297
Rodney, 284, 296
Samuel, 289
Sarah Smith, 284, 296
William, 298
CONE, Jonah, Jr., 290
Sylvester, 297
CONKLIN, (Nathaniel) Capt., 292
CORWIN, Clarissa, 290
DAMAN, Damon Adaline, 284
Addison Ezra, 284
Nathan, 283, 284, 291
DANIELS, Samuel, 291
DARROW, ⎯⎯⎯, 298
DATE, Datte David, 280, 282
Deborah, 291
DAVID, Jupiter (Jube), 290
DEAN, Olive, 278, 285
⎯⎯⎯, 294
DENISON, Nancy, 275
Richard N., 281, 282
Patience, 279
DESHON, Henry, 291
Moses, 290
DICKINSON, Bridget, 278, 283
Richard, 278
DINAH, (Negro), 296
DISON, ⎯⎯⎯, 291
DODETT, Clarissa, 298
DRGON, Dennis, 288
EDGECOMB, Asa Park, 292
ELMORE, John Jr., 290
ELY, Abby, 280
Abigail, 275, 277, 281, 291, 296
Abigail Deborah, 284
Abner S., 275, 279, 283, 284, 285, 286, 292, 297
Adriel, 274, 275, 283, 298
Amma, 295
Amy, 291
Ann, 274
Anna, 273, 276
Annah, 273
Ansel Rodney, 284
Arabella, 279
Bridget, 277, 290
Calvin, 293, 294
Calvin Lee, 284
Calvin Lynds, 284
Caroline, 275, 277, 291
Charles, 289

ELY, cont.
  Christopher, 275, 277, 293, 296
  Clarissa, 283
  Cullick, 274
  Cullick, Jr., 288, 294
  Dan, 296
  Daniel Noyes, 286
  David, 280
  David J., 281
  David Josiah, 285
  Dorcas, 294, 297, 298
  Ebenezer, 284, 297
  Eleazer, 291, 297
  Eliab, 291
  Elias Esq., 292
  Elias Peck, 285, 279
  Elihu, 275, 276, 296, 298
  Elijah, 275, 276, 296, 298
  Elisha, 281
  Elisha Olcott, 298
  Elizabeth, 282
  Elizabeth Colt, 284
  Elizabeth P., 281, 282
  Elizah, 284
  Eloases, 296
  Emma, 298
  Enoch Denison, 280, 282, 285
  Essi, 298
  Esther, 273, 293
  Eunice, 274, 278, 281, 286
  Ezra, 273
  Ezra, Capt., 294
  Fanny, 277, 286
  Frances, 283, 285, 286
  Frances Elizabeth, 285
  Gabdiel Rogers, 278
  George, 280, 281, 283
  Gordon, 293
  Gurdon, 296, 297
  Hannah, 297
  Hannah A., 281
  Hannah Marilla, 278, 285, 292
  Henry, 294
  Henry Adriel, 279, 285
  Hepsibah, 290
  Horace, 278, 283, 284, 285, 286, 298
  Horace 2nd, 279, 286
  Isabella, 295
  James, 273, 294, 298
  John, 276, 277, 284*, 286, 288, 296
  John C., 278, 281, 296
  John Griswold, 284
  John James, 286
  Jonathon, 284
  Josiah, 273, 276, 277, 298
  Josiah Griffin, 286
  Josiah Griswold, 289
  Katharine, 296
  Katty, 293
  Kesiah, 275
  Lewerett Huntington, 283
  Lucreatia, 275
  Lucy, 276, 277, 283, 284
  Lucy Ann, 286
  Lydia, 273, 288
  Mahetable, 276, 277, 282

ELY, cont.
  Maria, 285
  Martha, 274, 291, 297
  Mary, 279, 282, 283
  Mary Ann, 278, 283
  Mary E., 282, 283
  Mary Emilene, 285
  Miranda, 279, 283, 286
  Nimma, 274
  Patience, 277
  Perkins, 279, 286
  Phebe, 275, 277, 278, 284, 288, 289, 291
  Phebe Agusta, 285
  Pheby Comstock, 276
  Phebe H., 292
  Phebe Hubbard, 284
  Philura, 287
  Polly, 275
  Rebekah, 273, 295
  Rhoda, 279, 283, 287
  Rhode Catharine, 286
  Richard, 282, 294
  Richard Edwin, 285
  Richard Hayes, 275
  Rossiana, 284
  Ruhama, 273, 293
  Russell, 293
  Sally, 275, 277, 278, 285, 294
  Samuel, 290
  Sarah, 280, 298
  Sarah Aurelia, 285
  Sarah Catherine, 287
  Sarah Elizabeth, 285
  Seimilius B., 281, 282
  Selden Marvin, 284
  Seth, 277, 284, 297
  Seth Elisha, 284
  Seth Jr., 279, 281, 290
  Wells, 294
  William, 297
  William Horace, 285, 286
  William James, 284
  Zebdial Rogers, 285
  Zebulon Styles, 285
  E(ID)ENS, Lucy Ann, 278
  ELDRIDGE, Laura, 282
  EMERSON, _____, 272
    Abraham, 295, 297
    Joseph, 290
    Polly, 289
    Stephen, 294
  EMMONS, Dyer, 289
    Elisha, 289
    Jonathan, 293
  EVANS, Richard, 291
  EWENS, Lucy Ann, 285
  FOX, Amos, 288
    Polly, 288
    Sybbel, 293
  FRANKLIN, Esther, 278, 283, 285
  FRAZIER, Roxanna J., 281
  FREEMAN, Mindy (Negro), 290
  FULLER, Matthias, 289
  GALLOP, Gardner, Capt., 291
    Phebe, 283
  GATES, James, 290

GIBBS, Elizabeth, 273, 274
GILLET, Amassa H., 292
    Dan, 295
    Grace, 295
    Sophia, 290
GILLUM, Nathan, 289
GOOLD, Elihu, 289
    Elizabeth, 273
    James, 275
    Lavinia, 290
    Zelinda, 289
GOULD, James, 296
GRAHAM, James S., 291
GREENE, Eliza P., 288
GRIDLEY, Theodore, 291
GRIFFIN, Abner, 293
    Allen, 285, 287*, 296
    Allen Josiah, 287
    Allen W., 278, 280, 282, 283, 285, 296
    Benjamin, 298
    Caroline Lord, 287
    Deborah, 289
    Eliza Morgan, 287
    Elizabeth, 291
    Ellen More, 287
    Ellen Sophia, 287
    Fanny, 292
    Francis, 280, 283, 287
    George, 287
    George R., 291
    Harriet, 287
    Harriet Newel, 285
    Henry, 285
    Jane J., 283
    John, 293
    Josh, 293
    Lydia, 294
    Mary, 283, 287*
    Mary Eliza, 287
    Phebe, 278, 280, 282, 283*, 285, 289
    Phebe Ellen, 285
    Philura, 280, 286
    Rhoda, 278
    Rhoda Beckwith, 285
    Sally, 289
    Sarah, 283, 287*
    Samuel, 293
GRISWOLD, Matthew, 292
    Matthew Jnur., 288
    Samuel, Rev., 272
HATT, Joseph S., 279
HARRIS, Renah, 293
HARRISON, Charles Jr., 279, 286
    Charles, Capt., 297
    Charles F., 281
    China, 290
    Elihu, 273, 297
    Horace, 284
    Jane J., 280
    Jane Jemmima, 286
    Jane Shelden, 276, 277, 283
    Jemima, 279
    John A., 285
    John F., 276, 277
    Louisa, 279, 286

HARRISON, cont.
    Richard Rush, 286
    Seth, 290
HARVEY-HARVY-HERVY, Deborah Ely, 284
    Hannah, 293
    James, 289
    Joseph, 275, 293, 295
    Joshua, 296
    Josiah, 273
    Lucratia Minere, 283
    Marsilva, 276, 277
    Samuel, 276, 277
    Vashti, 288
HATHWAY, _____ (Mrs.), 294
HAWES, Josiah, Rev., 272
    Mary, 277, 281
    Mary Ann R., 279, 281
    William Burrit, 284
    Prince Beach, 284
HAYS, Phiney, 288
HAYS, Abigail, 275
    Abner, 288
    Elisabeth, 275, 277
    Richard, 293
HAYSE, Richard, 273
HIGGINS, David, Rev., 272
    Eunice, 275
HILL, Thomas M., 292
    _____ (a child), 298
HITHING, Robert Ely, 295
HOWARD, Sally Maria, 279
HUBBARD, Phebe, 279
HUDSON, widow, 298
HUGHES, John, 288
    John Gordon, 292
    Mary, 280, 282
HALLOCK, Ezra, 288
HUNGERFORD, Alonzo Cushman, 284
    Amos, 283, 290
    Amos Franklin, 284
    Ann Maria, 284
    China, 276, 277, 283
    Emme Elizabeth, 284
    Horrace Harrison, 284
    Justin Worthington, 284
HUNTINGTON, Betty Kimberly, 276
    David, Rev., 272
    Elizabeth, 282
    Leveritt F., 291
    Louisa, 277, 283
    Nancy, 276, 277, 282
    Phebe (Marvin), 277
HUNTLY-HUNTLEY, Barney, 298
    David, 289
    Lanson, 291
    _____ Marlow, N.H., 290
    Lydia, 288
    Seth, 296
HURLBERT, Naomi, 288
HYDE-HIDE, Mercy, 276, 277
    Sarah W., 282
INDIAN, Aaron, 290
INGRAHAM, Mary, 291
JACK, Eliza, 279
    Morrison, 291
    Roselina, 280

INDEX OF CHURCH RECORDS 399

JEWETT-JEWET, David, 294
  David M., 292, 293, 294
  David Moody, 288
  Laura M., 292
  Lucretia, 288
  Moody, 297
  Nancy, 293
  ———, 298
JOHNSON, Annis, 291
  ——— Rev., 296
  Victor M, 292
  William, 292
JONES, Henry, 280, 282, 283, 287, 292
  Henry Marvin, 287
  Phebe Catherine, 287
  Phebe S., 280, 282, 287
  Phebe L., 283
JONSTON, Katty, 288
KING, Parmenius, 289
LAY, ——— widow, 297
LATIMER, David, 295
  Irene (Ely), 275, 277
  Marshfield, Capt., 297
LEACH, Richard, 290
LEANORD, Elias (Negro), 290
LEE, Abner, 289
  Ann (Mary Ann), 275
  Betsey, 276
  Deborah, 274, 275
  Joseph, 295
  Mary, 275, 277
  Lemuel, 277
  Lucy, 288
  Samuel, 275
  Sarah, 274, 290
LESTER, Annis, 279, 283, 286
  James, 279, 283, 286
  Jededidah, 284
  Lucy, 283
  Martin, 292
  Marshfield Parker, 284
LONNARGAN, Thomas, 288
LORD, Abner, 273, 274, 275, 293
  Agustus, 285, 297
  Almira, 279
  Andrew, 297
  Anne, 290
  Ann Selden, 286
  Azubah, 280, 287
  Benjamin, 274, 297
  Benjamin Jr., 297
  Betsey, 276
  Catharine, 273, 288, 295
  Christopher, 297
  Cornelia, 286
  Daniel, 279, 285, 294
  Elisabeth, 275, 286
  Elisabeth Agusta, 287
  Elisabeth Mather, 286
  Elisabeth T., 275, 278, 282
  Elisha, 297
  Erastus, 279
  Erastus Abel, 285, 287
  Erastus A. Junr., 280, 282, 283, 291
  Frederick Agustus, 287
  Hannah, 274, 278

LORD, cont.
  Hannah W., 281, 287*
  Harriet A., 280, 282
  James J., 281, 286
  John A., 286
  John B. B., 283
  John S., 278, 279, 285
  Judah, 280, 282, 286
  Lois, 290
  Lucy, 277
  Mary, 279, 282, 286, 288
  Marvin, 295
  Mehitable Burnham, 278
  Phebe C., 280, 282, 283
  Phebe H., 280, 286
  Peter, 279, 286
  Rebecca, 280, 286
  Reuben, 276, 277, 280, 282, 284, 285, 291
  Reuben, Jr., 284
  Reuben 2nd, 286
  Reynold, 298
  Sally, 290
  Samuel H., 280, 284
  Samuel M., 282
  Sarah, 279, 293
  Sarah Ann, 292
  Sarah E., 280, 284
  Sarah W., 280, 282
  Similius, 292
  Solomon, 289
  Temperance, 273, 274
  Theophilus, 291, 296
  Thomas, 273, 274
  Thomas D., 292
  Ursula, 277, 284
  William, 279, 286
LUTHER, Benjamin, 293
MACK, Abigail, 289
  Aseeniah, 290
  Elizabeth (Betty), 290
  Ezra, 273
  Fanny, 290
  John, 290
MANWARING, Mary, 278
MARSH, Holmes, 289
MARTIN, Hannah, 278, 282
  Lucy, 280, 283
  Mary, 278, 283
MARVIN, Abijah, Perkins, 284
  Adaline, 278, 282
  Ajahel Mather, 284
  Asabel, 284, 296
  Asahel, 290
  Azubah, 276, 277, 283, 291
  Azubah Hervy, 284
  Betty alias Elisabeth, 275
  Catharine, 273, 295
  Clarrissa, 276, 277
  Dan, 288
  Dan Junr., 291
  Elisabeth, 274, 280, 283, 288
  Elisha, 273, 296
  Elisha Tomas, 284
  Ellen Clarissa, 285
  Emily, 278
  Esther, 273

MARVIN, cont.
  Frances, 292
  Francis Griffin, 287
  George Griffin, 284
  Huldah, 289
  Jemima, 276, 291
  Jim, Capt., 294
  Joseph, 275, 276
  Junius, 284
  Mary, 275
  Phebe, 275, 276*, 290, 291, 297
  Phebe S., 292
  Phebe Sill, 284
  Sally, 289
  Sally M., 292
  Sally Maria, 284
  Sarah, 273, 294
  Selden, 294
  Sophia, 278, 283, 284*, 285, 287
  Timothy, 275, 289
  Timothy Dwight, 284
  William, 278, 282, 284*, 285, 287
  William Joseph, 286
MATHER, Alice, 274, 275
  Eleazer, 274, 275, 295
  Elijah, 290
  Fanny, 290
  Hepsibah, 290
  Huldah, 288
  Irene, 274, 275
  Jansha (Jershua), 288
  Joseph, 289
  Lois, 289
  Lucinda, 290
  Lucy, 275
  Nabby, 288
  Richard, 293
  Samuel, 274, 275
  Samuel Dr., 298
  Sarah Ann, 288
  Thomas, 288
MATHEWS, MATHEWS, Betsey, 283
  Nathaniel, 292
MATSON, David, 290
  Israel, 291
  Lewis, 291
MAYNARD, John, 295
  Mary, 292
MacKENTOSH, _____, 295
McCOY, Alexander, 294
McCRERY, McCARY, Emily, 279, 283, 285
  Lurania, 276, 277, 285
  Mary Ann, 280, 293
  Samuel, 273, 288, 293, 296
  William, 293
MENTOR, Chrisrina, 289
MICHEL, John, 294
  Sarah, 294
MILLARD, Julia Ann, 282, 283
MILLAR, Caleb, 277
MILLER, Betty, 294
  Clarissa, 280, 282, 287
  Deborah, 279, 283, 292
  Ede, 292
  Elisha, 280, 282, 287, 294
  Elizabeth Marvin, 285

MILLER, cont.
  Gilbert, 287
  Griffin, 285
  Hepsibah Lucy, 285
  Jerush, 291
  James Monroe, 287
  Julia Ann, 278
  Laura Ann, 285
  Mary A, 292
  Mary Abba, 287
  Mary Allice, 285
  Nathan Beebe, 294
  Sarah Maria, 287
  Silas, 288
  Thompson (Tempson), 274
  Valentine, 285, 295
  Valentine Ansel, 285
MINARD, Asa, 290
MINER, Daniel, Elder, 295
  Mehitabel, 292
  Orlando, 292
  William, 298
MITCHEL, Alfred Rev., 291
  Annah, 274, 275
  Annas, 297
  George, 296
  John, 296
  Lucy, 274
  Sarah, 293
MOORE, Abel, 280
  James D. Rev., 272
MORGAN, Aseenath, 279, 292
  Bethey, 285
  Betsey, 279, 283
  Mary, 280, 283
MOSIER, Phebe, 291
MOTT, Rebecca, 293
MUMFORD, _____, 293
  Catharine, 290
MURDOCK, Charles E. Rev., 272
  Lucy H., 278, 281
MUSSEL, Betsey, 285
  William Wallace, 285
NETTLETON, Asahel Rev., 272
NICHOLS, Bethiah Clay, 285
  Caroline Brainard, 285
  Eliza, 279, 292
  Henry, 285
  Henry Brainard, 285
  Margaret Ann, 285
  Prudence, 285*, 278, 281
  Prudence Brainard, 285
NILES, Ambrose, 275, 277, 293, 296
  Ambrose Ely, 286
  Ambrose Dr., 292
  Ambrose, Capt., 294, 295
  Ambrose Jr., 276, 288
  Benjamin, 294, 296
  Enoch Marvin, 287
  Mary, 276, 277, 291
  Julia, 279, 286, 287*
  Julia Ann, 286
  Mary Emily, 287
  Polly, 290
  William B., 279, 282, 283, 286, 287*

OTIS, Belinda, 279, 292
　Charles, 288
　Heyden, 279
　John, 289
　Mary, 297
　Robert, 295
　Sally, 278, 284
　Stephen, 289
PALMER, _____, 298
PARKER, A. H. _____, 287*
　Azubah, 278, 283, 285, 286
　Henry Lord, 287
　Jane Louisa, 287
　John Marvin, 285
　Marshfield, 277, 283, 289, 291
　Marshfield S., 285, 286
　Marshfield Sterling, 285, 287*
　William Mather, 286
PATTEN, Louisa, 282, 283
PAYSON, Elizabeth, 287
　Edward Phillips, 287
　Phillip, 272
　Phillips, Rev., 287
PECK, _____, 297, 298
　Alice, 290, 297, 298
　Esther, 288
　Lucy, 289
　Mather, 288
　Samuel, 295
PEMBLETON, Anne, 289
　Hannah, 289
PERKINS, Abraham, 284
　Abram Ely, 276, 280, 281
　Bertha, 289
　Betsey, 289*
　Eliza Ann, 283, 292
　Ely, 284
　Esther, 273, 274, 275, 289
　Hannah Baker, 284
　James, 273, 293
　John, 273, 274
　Jonathan, 296
　Joseph, 289
　Mary, 281, 288
　Phebe, 289
　Seth Baker, 284, 296
PERRY, Catherine, 279
PHELPS, John, 288
PHILLIPS, Margaret, 278, 282, 283
PILGRIM, Charles, 296
PORRY, Rufus, 295
POST, Asa D., 291
　Joseph, 293
　Nancy, 292
　Ziporah, 293
PRATT, Betsey, 290
　_____ Capt., 295
　Charles Agustus Brewster, 284
　Ezra, 284, 277*
　Ezra Huntington, 284
　Fanny, 277
　Frances, 277
　Jane Wood, 285
　Prudence, 279
PRENTIS, Samuel, 283

RANSOM, Olive, 291
　Stephen, 274, 294
RATHBORNE-RATHBUM-RATHBORN
　Ann, 292
　Daniel, 292
　Huldah, 272, 274
　Samuel, 294
RAWSON, Thos. H. Doct., 289
RAYMOND, Jane G., 280, 282
　Mary, 280, 282
　Thaddeus H., 281, 282
REEVES, Agnes, 272
　John, 296
REYNOLDS, Phebe, 275
RICE, Polly, 289
RICHARDS, George, 276
ROB, William Capt., 288
ROBBINS, Luranie, 291
ROBINSON, _____, 297
ROGERS
　Ebenr, 295
　Ezra, 290
　Gideon, 296
　John, 294
　Lucretia, 276, 277, 296
　Lucy, 292
　William, 289
ROWLAND, Abbe C., 292
ROYCE, Amanda, 291
　Azuba, 291
　Joseph L., 280, 283
RUE, Richard, 290
SAMPSON, _____, 298
SASETON, Emily, 285
　James Taylor, 285
　Noah C. Revd., 285
SAUNDERS, Ephriam, 295
SAWYER-SERVY, Amy, 292
　Ephriam Jr., 293
SCOVIL, Abigail, 272, 294
　Lucy, 290
SELDEN, Calvin, 288, 297
　_____, 284
　Elizabeth, 291
　Erastus, 287, 294, 295
　Ezra, 273
　Hannah, 273, 289
　Laura, 287
　Laura C., 282, 283
　Lois, 274, 288
　Lucy, 280
　Lucy Elizabeth, 287
　Phebe C., 281, 282
　Roxanna, 291
SHIPMAN, Christopher, 290
SILL, Amy, 295
　Azubah, 277, 288, 289, 290
　Betsey, 289
　Emiline, 278, 285
　Eunice, 294, 297
　Fanny, 297
　George Worthington, 280, 281, 284
　Giles, 274
　Hannah Beckwith, 284
　Isaac, 276, 277, 296
　Issac W., 284

SILL, cont.
    Jerusha, 291
    Lois, 290
    Lucy, 274
    Mahetabel, 296
    Moses, 289
    Phebe, 276, 277, 290, 291
    Sally, 289
    Samuel, 273, 294, 295
    Shadrac, 279, 281
    Ursula, 277, 282, 283
    Wanda, 276
    William, 288, 294
SMITH, _____, 298
    Ann Maria, 281, 282, 286
    Betsey, 290
    Elihu, 290, 295
    Eunice, 290
    Hannah, 283, 286
    Lucinda, 291
    Martin, 289
    Matson, 288
    Polly, 289
    Sally, 289
    William, 279, 282, 283, 286*, 292
    William Jr., 295
SOUTHWORTH, Sally, 281
    Ichabod Lieut., 297
    Israel, 291
SPENCER, Joseph, 291
STARK, James Fitch, 294
    James, 294
STEELE, Joel, 291
STEPHENSON, Daniel, 288
STERLING-STARLING-STARLIN-STERLIN
    Annah, 294
    Betty, 288
    Dudley, 290
    Eliza, 284
    Ellis, 291
    Erastus, 276, 277, 284
    Esther, 276, 277, 283, 298
    Frances Cornelia, 284
    Georgianna, 292
    Hannah Ellen, 284
    Harriot Alma, 284
    Jacob, 297
    Jane, 279, 283
    Jemima, 273, 288, 296
    Jerusha, 277, 278
    John, 273, 279, 283, 286
    Marcus Aurchus Dudley, 284
    Maria Ely, 279
    Phebe, 276, 277, 284, 291
    Phebe H., 298
    Phebe Sill, 284
    Ruth, 289
    Samuel, 273, 286, 294, 297
    Sarah, 281, 282
    Stephen Junr., 292
    William, 273, 296, 298
STEWARD, Henry, 281, 282, 292
STORY-STOREY, Lucy, 290
    Rachel, 289
    William, 289

STOUTENBURGH, John J., 289
SULLARD, Allan, 295
SUPIO, Solomon Jr., 289
SWANY, Lanny, 288
SWEETLAND, Elizabeth, 288
TAINTOR-TAINFOR, Mary, 282
    Phebe H., 281
TALCOTT, Samuel, 292
TATSON, Taffena, 290
TAYLOR, Fanny, 297
    George, 297
TERLIN, John S., 292
THOMPSON, Isaac, 290
    Rachel, 278, 285
TIFFANY, Ebenezer, 275, 294, 295
    Giles, 288
    Humphry, 293
    Lucretia, 275
    Nathan, 290
    Rhuamama, 294
    Sila, 289
TILLINGHAST, Pardon, 288
TINKER, Mary, 276
TOOKER, Adin, 292
    Harvey, 292, 298
    Hepzibah S., 280, 282
    Julia, 291
    Mary, 282, 283
    Vashtte, 279
TRUBEE, Almira, 282
TUBBS, Lucinda, 288
TUCKER, John, 297
    Timothy, 288
TYLER, Daniel C. Revd., 272
WADE-WAID, Hannah, 274
    Pember, 290
    Polly, 289, 290
    Sally, 288
WARNER, Carloss, 297
    Caroline, 279
    George, 297
    Selden, 296
    Selden S., 291
WAIT, Richard Junr., 289
WARWICK, _____ Negro, 293
WATROUS, Azuba, 288
    John R., 291
WAY, Thomas, 289
WELCH, Daniel, 288
WIDGER, Lucy, 289
WILKEY, Caroline, 283
WILKINSON, John Hart, 290
WILLEY, Allen, 290
WILLIAMS, Bethuel, 280, 282, 291
    Betsey, 291
    Clarissa, 286
    Martha, 280, 282
WILSON, William, 292
WOLFE, _____, 298

WOOD, Betsey B., 277, 283
　——, 295
　Betty Rogers, 277, 284
　Chas. Henry, 287
　David, 297
　Elizabeth, 290
　Eliza Ann, 281, 282, 287
　Eunice Ann, 287
　Jerushua, 290
　Nathaniel M., 281, 282
　Russel, 296, 297
　Silas, 287, 290, 297
　Silas B., 282
　Silas Bates, 287
　Susannah, 276, 277, 283, 284
　Wm. Thomas, 287

WOODBRIDGE, Lois, 291
　Lucretia, 291
　Nathaniel Shaw Esq., 289, 294
WOODWARD, Polly, 288
WRIGHT, Joshua, 293
　Lebbeus, 289
　Phineas, 289
　Sarah, 288, 289
YOUNG alias PERKINS
　Esther, 274
　Thomas, 289

www.ingramcontent.com/pod-product-compliance
Lightning Source LLC
Chambersburg PA
CBHW050831230426
43667CB00012B/1961